EARTHA
World TRAVELOG™

DeLorme has made reasonable efforts to ensure that the travel information provided is as accurate as possible.
We cannot, however, exclude the possibility of errors or omissions in sources or of changes in actual conditions,
so we do not assume responsibility for any loss, injury or inconvenience to any person using this publication.
When making travel plans, you should verify and supplement information in this publication, including
transportation facilities and schedules, banking facilities, sightseeing and event suggestions, and political or
other travel conditions with your travel agent, local authorities or consular officials, as appropriate.

The Eartha globe, located in Yarmouth, Maine

Photograph © Jeffrey Stevenson

Since the 1976 publication of the *Maine Atlas and Gazetteer*™, DeLorme has grown from a kitchen table operation to one of the most trusted names in mapping technology. The latest achievement in the company's 24-year mapmaking journey is Eartha™, a one-of-a-kind, 42-foot revolving and rotating globe housed in the company's corporate headquarters in Yarmouth, Maine. Eartha represents a combination of cutting edge technology and traditional cartography driven by the concept that the new millennium will see a world that seems bigger, yet is actually smaller than ever before. This concept focuses on the possibility of a more heightened global awareness, through not only the relationships between elements of ecology, travel, communication, politics and culture, but also the relationship between paper, digital and online forms of media. Contentment with one's own backyard is being eclipsed by a desire to explore the world more extensively and adventurously than ever before. This unique atlas, *Eartha World Travelog*™, attempts to capture both the accessibility and the grand scope of our magnificent planet by combining enhanced satellite imagery with practical travel information and interesting facts about places in the world.

Eartha World Travelog covers 192 countries and their territories and possessions, arranged by continent. The maps showcased in this book are the result of years of research and database development by the DeLorme technical and mapmaking staff. This database is at the core of the highly detailed and beautiful views of the Earth, complete with the lush greens of the forests and dusty browns of the deserts, shown within these pages. We have chosen varying degrees of scale to ensure that even the tiniest islands of the South Pacific are as easy to view as the vast Northwest Territories of Canada. Over 15,000 placenames and geographical features are listed in a comprehensive 22-page index located in the back of the book, keyed to the latitude/longitude coordinates referenced on the maps. The atlas also highlights over 120 urban centers, islands and territories.

Augmenting the maps are thousands of useful and interesting gazetteer and chart listings. Taking into account current travel trends, we have focused on unique, off-the-beaten-track points of interest and geophysical features, historic sites, regional traditions, customs and cuisine, and entertaining side trip and outdoor adventure suggestions. This travelog features descriptions of everything from a beach in New Zealand where you can dig your own hot tub, to China's unearthed, life-sized terra cotta warriors, to the only underwater national monument in the United States (US Virgin Islands).

Whether using *Eartha World Travelog* for travel planning or recreational purposes, readers can acclimate themselves to different parts of the world by means of useful travel charts. Our transportation charts include airline, train, bus and ferry information, as well as general travel advisories for each region. Our money charts offer information on currency, availability of ATMs, and acceptance of credit cards and traveler's checks. Other charts include country overviews, with population, area, languages and yearly tourism statistics; climate charts, complete with the average temperatures and precipitation for a particular region's centrally located city as well as a general description of a region's seasonal climate; and highlighted regional fare and activities. In addition, we have provided a time zone map and a mileage chart for reference.

All the elements of *Eartha World Travelog* combine to offer an enticing vision of the world that will stimulate the wanderlust in us all. The beautiful topographic map images will give readers an instant feel for what kind of adventure to plan, the charts will provide helpful information for navigating the trip, and the gazetteer entries will fill out a diverse wish list of exciting places to see and adventurous side trips to take.

Legend

—— Country Maps ——

========	Primary Route
————	Secondary Route
————	Tertiary Route
————	Minor Connector
··············	Unimproved Connector
+++++++	Passenger Railroad
– – – –	Passenger Ferry
– – – – –	Passenger/Auto Ferry
☐	National Route
⬖	Interstate (US only)
⬡	Route (US only)
✪	National Capital
★	Administrative Division Capital
•	City or Town
New Haven	Locality
========	National Boundary
————	State/Provincial Boundary
♣	National Park
▲	Summit
▼	Island
✈ BOS	Major Airport with IATA Code
▨	Dry Lake

—— City Maps ——

========	Interstate (US only)
————	Highway (US, Canada or Mexico)
————	Major Connector
————	City Street
+++++++	Railroad
+++■+++	Railroad Station
– – – –	Passenger Ferry
◼ TUNNEL ◼	Tunnel
——◆——	Monorail
▦▦▦▦	City Wall
✈ LOGAN	Major Airport
■	Point of Interest
▬	Park or Recreation Site

Table of Contents

Abbreviations

AB .... Alberta
AC .... Acre
ACT .... Australian Capital Territory
Afg .... Afghanistan
Ags .... Aguascalientes
AK .... Alaska
AL .... Alabama
AL .... Alagoas
Alb .... Albania
Alg .... Algeria
AM .... Amazonas
AMEX .... American Express
And .... Andorra
Ang .... Angola
Angu .... Anguilla
Ant .... Antarctica
Ant & Bar .... Antigua and Barbuda
AP .... Amapa
AR .... Arkansas
Arg .... Argentina
Arm .... Armenia
Aruba .... Aruba
AS .... American Samoa
Ash & Car Is .... Ashmore and Cartier Islands
Aus .... Austria
Austl .... Australia
AVE .... Avenue
AZ .... Arizona
Azer .... Azerbaijan
B da Ind .... Bassas da India
BA .... Bahia
Bah .... Bahamas
Bahr .... Bahrain
Baker I .... Baker Island
Barb .... Barbados
BC .... British Columbia
BC .... Baja California
BCS .... Baja California Sur
Bela .... Belarus
Belg .... Belgium
Ben .... Benin
Ber .... Bermuda
Bhu .... Bhutan
BIOT .... British Indian Ocean Territory
BLVD .... Boulevard (English)
Blz .... Belize
Bngl .... Bangladesh
Bol .... Bolivia
Bos & Herz .... Bosnia and Herzegovina
Bots .... Botswana
BOUL .... Boulevard (French)
Braz .... Brazil
Bru .... Brunei Darussalam
Bulg .... Bulgaria
Burk .... Burkina Faso
Buru .... Burundi
BVI .... British Virgin Islands
CA .... California
Cam .... Cameroon
Camb .... Cambodia
Camp .... Campeche
Can .... Canada
CAR .... Central African Republic
Cay Is .... Cayman Islands
CE .... Ceara
Cem .... Cemetery
Chad .... Chad
Chih .... Chihuahua
Chile .... Chile
China .... China
Chis .... Chiapas
Chr I .... Christmas Island
CO .... Colorado
Coah .... Coahuila de Zaragoza
Cocos Is .... Cocos (Keeling) Islands
Col .... Colima
Col .... Colombia
Com .... Comoros
Con .... Congo
Cook Is .... Cook Islands
Cor Sea Is .... Coral Sea Islands
Côte d'Ivoire .... Côte d'Ivoire
CR .... Costa Rica
Cro .... Croatia
CT .... Connecticut
Cuba .... Cuba
CV .... Cape Verde
Cyp .... Cyprus
Czech .... Czech Republic
DC .... District of Columbia
DC .... Diners Club
DE .... Delaware
Den .... Denmark
DF .... Distrito Federal
Dgo .... Durango
Disp .... Disputed
Djib .... Djibouti
Dom .... Dominica
Dom Rep .... Dominican Republic
DRC .... The Democratic Republic of the Congo
E Tim .... East Timor
Ecu .... Ecuador
Egypt .... Egypt
El Sal .... El Salvador
Eq Gui .... Equatorial Guinea
Eritrea .... Eritrea
ES .... Espirito Santo
Est .... Estonia
Eth .... Ethiopia
Eur I .... Europa Island
EXPY .... Expressway
Falk Is .... Falkland Islands (Malvinas)
Far Is .... Faroe Islands
Fiji .... Fiji
Fin .... Finland
FL .... Florida
Fr .... France
Fr Gu .... French Guiana
Fr Poly .... French Polynesia
FSM .... Federated States of Micronesia
FST .... French Southern Territories
Ft .... Fort
FWY .... Freeway
FYRM .... The Former Yugoslav Republic of Macedonia
GA .... Georgia
Gabon .... Gabon
Gam .... Gambia
Gaza .... Gaza Strip
Geo .... Georgia
Ger .... Germany
Gha .... Ghana
Gib .... Gibraltar
Glor Is .... Glorioso Islands
GO .... Goiás
Grc .... Greece
Gren .... Grenada
Grld .... Greenland

Gro .... Guerrero
Grsy .... Guernsey
Gto .... Guanajuato
Guad .... Guadeloupe
Guam .... Guam
Guat .... Guatemala
Gui .... Guinea
Gui-Bis .... Guinea-Bissau
Guy .... Guyana
Haiti .... Haiti
Hgo .... Hidalgo
HI .... Hawaii
Hist .... Historic
Hon .... Honduras
How I .... Howland Island
Hrd I & McD Is .... Heard Island and McDonald Islands
Hun .... Hungary
HWY .... Highway
I .... Island
IA .... Iowa
Ice .... Iceland
ID .... Idaho
IL .... Illinois
IN .... Indiana
Ind .... India
Indo .... Indonesia
IOM .... Isle of Man
Iran .... Iran
Iraq .... Iraq
Ire .... Ireland
Is .... Islands
Isr .... Israel
It .... Italy
Jal .... Jalisco
Jam .... Jamaica
Jap .... Japan
Jar I .... Jarvis Island
JN I .... Juan de Nova Island
Jnst At .... Johnston Atoll
Jor .... Jordan
JR .... Jiron (Spanish)
Jrsy .... Jersey
Kaz .... Kazakhstan
Ken .... Kenya
King Rf .... Kingman Reef
Kir .... Kiribati
KS .... Kansas
Kuw .... Kuwait
KY .... Kentucky
Kyr .... Kyrgyzstan
LA .... Louisiana
Laos .... Laos
Lat .... Latvia
Leb .... Lebanon
Les .... Lesotho
Libr .... Liberia
Libya .... Libya
Liech .... Liechtenstein
Lith .... Lithuania
Lux .... Luxembourg
MA .... Maranhão
MA .... Massachusetts
Madag .... Madagascar
Malay .... Malaysia
Mald .... Maldives
Mali .... Mali
Malta .... Malta
Malw .... Malawi
Mar Is .... Marshall Islands
Mart .... Martinique
May .... Mayotte
MB .... Manitoba
MC .... MasterCard
Mco .... Monaco
MD .... Maryland
ME .... Maine
Mem .... Memorial
Mex .... Mexico
MG .... Minas Gerais
MI .... Michigan
Mich .... Michoacán de Campo
Midway Is .... Midway Islands
MN .... Minnesota
MO .... Missouri
Mol .... Moldova
Mong .... Mongolia
Monts .... Montserrat
Mor .... Morocco
Mor .... Morelos
Moz .... Mozambique
Mrta .... Mauritania
Mrts .... Mauritius
MS .... Mississippi
MS .... Mato Grosso do Sul
MT .... Mato Grosso
Mt .... Mount
MT .... Montana
Mtn(s) .... Mountain(s)
Myanmar .... Myanmar
N Kor .... North Korea
Nam .... Namibia
Nat .... National
Nauru .... Nauru
Nav I .... Navassa Island
Nay .... Nayarit
NB .... New Brunswick
NC .... North Carolina
ND .... North Dakota
NE .... Nebraska
Nepal .... Nepal
Neth .... Netherlands
Neth Ant .... Netherlands Antilles
New Cal .... New Caledonia
NF .... Newfoundland
Nga .... Nigeria
NH .... New Hampshire
NHP .... National Historic Park
Nic .... Nicaragua
Niger .... Niger
Niue .... Niue
NJ .... New Jersey
NL .... Nuevo León
NM .... New Mexico
NM Is .... Northern Mariana Islands
NO .... Number
Nor .... Norway
Nor I .... Norfolk Island
NP .... National Park
NS .... Nova Scotia
NSW .... New South Wales
NT .... Northern Territory
NT .... Northwest Territories
NU .... Nunavut
NV .... Nevada
NWR .... National Wildlife Refuge
NY .... New York
NZ .... New Zealand
Oax .... Oaxaca
OH .... Ohio
OK .... Oklahoma
Oman .... Oman

ON .... Ontario
OR .... Oregon
PA .... Pennsylvania
PA .... Pará
Pak .... Pakistan
Pal .... Palau
Pal At .... Palmyra Atoll
Pan .... Panama
Para .... Paraguay
Para Is .... Paracel Islands
PB .... Paraiba
PE .... Pernambuco
PE .... Prince Edward Island
Peru .... Peru
Phil .... Philippines
PI .... Piaui
Pit .... Pitcairn
PKWY .... Parkway
PNG .... Papua New Guinea
Pol .... Poland
Port .... Portugal
PR .... Puerto Rico
PR .... Paraná
Pue .... Puebla
Qatar .... Qatar
QC .... Québec
Qld .... Queensland
QR .... Quintana Roo
Qro .... Querétaro de Arteaga
R .... River
RD .... Road
Rec .... Recreation
REP .... Republica
Réun .... Réunion
RI .... Rhode Island
RJ .... Rio de Janeiro
RN .... Rio Grande do Norte
RO .... Rondônia
Rom .... Romania
RR .... Roraima
RS .... Rio Grande do Sul
Rus Fed .... Russian Federation
Rwn .... Rwanda
S Afr .... South Africa
S Kor .... South Korea
S Mar .... San Marino
SA .... South Australia
Samoa .... Samoa
Sau Ar .... Saudi Arabia
SC .... South Carolina
SC .... Santa Catarina
SD .... South Dakota
SE .... Sergipe
Sen .... Senegal
Sey .... Seychelles
SG & SS Is .... South Georgia and the South Sandwich Islands
Sin .... Sinaloa
Sing .... Singapore
SK .... Saskatchewan
SL .... Sierra Leone
Slov .... Slovenia
SLP .... San Luis Potosí
Slvk .... Slovakia
Sol Is .... Solomon Islands
Som .... Somalia
Son .... Sonora
SP .... Sao Paulo
Sp .... Spain
Sprt Is .... Spratly Islands
Sri L .... Sri Lanka
ST .... Street
St H .... St Helena
St KN .... St Kitts and Nevis
St L .... St Lucia
St PM .... St Pierre and Miquelon
St VG .... St Vincent and the Grenadines
St(e) .... Saint(e)
STP .... Sao Tome and Principe
Sud .... Sudan
Sur .... Suriname
Sval .... Svalbard
Swaz .... Swaziland
Swe .... Sweden
Switz .... Switzerland
Syria .... Syria
T & T .... Trinidad and Tobago
Tab .... Tabasco
Taiwan .... Taiwan
Taj .... Tajikistan
Tamps .... Tamaulipas
Tanz .... Tanzania
Tas .... Tasmania
TC Is .... Turks and Caicos Islands
Thai .... Thailand
Tlax .... Tlaxcala
TN .... Tennessee
TO .... Tocantins
Togo .... Togo
Tok .... Tokelau
Ton .... Tonga
Tro .... Tromelin
Tun .... Tunisia
Turk .... Turkey
Turkm .... Turkmenistan
Tuv .... Tuvalu
TX .... Texas
UAE .... United Arab Emirates
Ug .... Uganda
UK .... United Kingdom
Ukr .... Ukraine
Univ .... University
Ur .... Uraguay
US .... United States
USVI .... US Virgin Islands
UT .... Utah
Uzb .... Uzbekistan
VA .... Virginia
Van .... Vanuatu
VC .... Holy See (Vatican City)
Ven .... Venezuela
Ver .... Veracruz-Llave
Vic .... Victoria
Viet .... Viet Nam
VT .... Vermont
W Bank .... West Bank
W Sah .... Western Sahara
WA .... Western Australia
WA .... Washington
Wake I .... Wake Island
WF .... Wallis and Futuna
WI .... Wisconsin
WV .... West Virginia
WY .... Wyoming
Yem .... Yemen
YT .... Yukon Territory
Yuc .... Yucatán
Yugo .... Yugoslavia
Zac .... Zacatecas
Zam .... Zambia
Zimb .... Zimbabwe

Foreign Terms

Adrar .... mountain
'Ain, Aïn .... spring, well
Alpe .... mountain
Alto .... high
Anse .... bay, inlet
Archipiélago .... archipelago
Arcipelago .... archipelago
Arquipélago .... archipelago
Arroyo .... brook, creek, stream
Bab .... strait
Bahía .... bay
Bahr .... river, sea
Baía .... bay
Baie .... bay
Bi'r .... spring, well
Boca .... estuary, mouth
Bogaz, Bogazi .... strait
Bol'shaya, Bol'shoy .... big
Bucht .... bay
Buhayrat .... lagoon, lake
Cabo .... cape
Campo .... plain
Cay, Cayo .... islet
Cerro .... hill
Chaîne .... mountain range
Ciudad .... city, town
Cordillera .... mountain range
Costa .... coast
Dao .... island
Do .... island(s), rock(s)
Dome .... ice dome
Erg .... desert
Foz .... estuary, mouth
Golf, Golfe, Golfo .... gulf
Gran, Grande .... great
Hu .... lake
Île .... island
Ilha .... island
Îlot .... islet
Isla .... island
Isola .... island
Jabal, Jebel .... mountain
Jaza'ir, Jazirat, Jazireh .... island
Jezero, Jezioro .... lake
Jima .... island
Kangri .... mountain
Kepulauan .... archipelago
Kólpos .... gulf
Kuh, Kuhha .... mountain
Kum .... desert
Kyun .... island
Lac .... lake
Lago .... lake
Lagoa .... lagoon
Laguna .... lagoon, lake
Lagune .... lagoon
Mauna .... mountain
Misaki .... cape
Mong .... city, town
Mont .... mountain
Monte .... mountain
Nevado .... snow-covered mountain
Nosy .... island
Nur .... lake
Nuruu .... mountain range
Nuur .... lake
Ostrov, Ostrvo .... island
Otok .... island
Ozero .... lake
Parbat .... mountain
Pico .... peak
Pik .... peak
Poluostrov .... peninsula
Presa .... reservoir
Puerto .... port
Pulau .... island
Puu .... mountain
Puy .... peak
Qolleh .... peak
Represa .... reservoir
Rio, Río .... river
Sammyaku .... mountain range
San .... saint
Sanmaek .... mountain range
Santa .... saint
Santo .... saint
São .... saint
Selat .... strait
Serra .... mountain range
Shan .... mountain, mountain range
Sierra .... mountain range
Sint .... saint
Tassili .... upland
Teluk .... bay
Volcan, Volcán .... volcano
Wan .... bay
Zemlya .... land

Arctic
Circle

Tropic of
Cancer

Equator

Tropic of
Capricorn

Antarctic
Circle

Prime
Meridian

© DeLorme

AREA
Total: 197 million square miles (510 million sq km)
Land: 58 million square miles (149 million sq km)
Water: 139 million square miles (361 million sq km)
Equatorial Circumference: 24,902 miles (40,075 km)
Polar Circumference: 24,860 miles (40,007 km)

POPULATION
Total: 6 Billion
The five most populated countries in the world are China (1,209 million), India (945 million), United States (266 million), Indonesia (197 million) and Brazil (162 million). There is room to breathe in Canada, the second-largest country in the world, ranking 33rd in population (30 million). Russia is the largest in land mass and ranks 6th in population (149 million).

LANGUAGES
The most common languages in the world are of Indo-European base, which includes English, Russian, Spanish, French, German, Iranian and Indian. Basque, Gaelic and several Indian dialects are some of the least common.

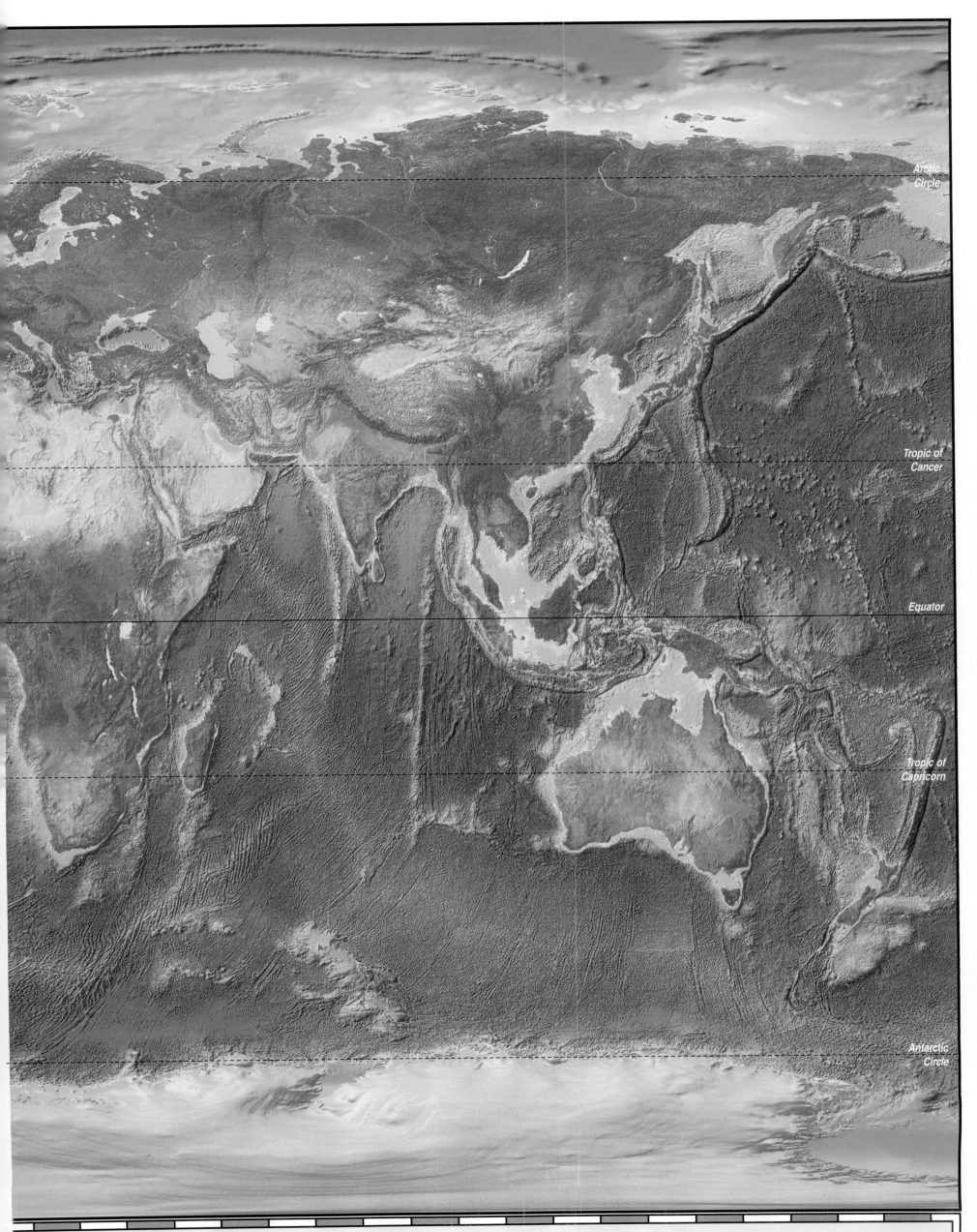

Arctic Circle

Tropic of Cancer

Equator

Tropic of Capricorn

Antarctic Circle

CLIMATE
One of the wettest places on Earth is Mt Waialeale in Hawaii with an annual rainfall of approximately 455 inches (1,153 cm). The driest place in the world, the Atacama Desert near Copiapó, Chile, has gone years without any rainfall at all. The hottest place on the planet is in Libya, where a temperature of 136°Farenheit (58°Celsius) was once recorded. Parts of Antarctica have reached -129°Farenheit (-90°Celsius), the coldest temperature ever recorded on earth.

HIGHS AND LOWS
The highest point on Earth is Mt Everest at 29,035 feet (8,850 m).
The lowest is the Dead Sea at 1,300 feet below sea level (400 m).
The highest waterfall in the world is Angel Falls in Venezuela at 3,212 feet (979 m).

TRANSPORTATION
Airports: More passengers travel through Chicago's O'Hare International Airport than any other in the world; it also claims the highest number of airplanes landing and taking off every year.
Railways: 746,000 miles (1,201,000 km)
Ships: There are at least 25,500 ships weighing over 1,000 tons (907 metric tons) each in the world.

EUROPE

Countries

Territories and Featured Lands

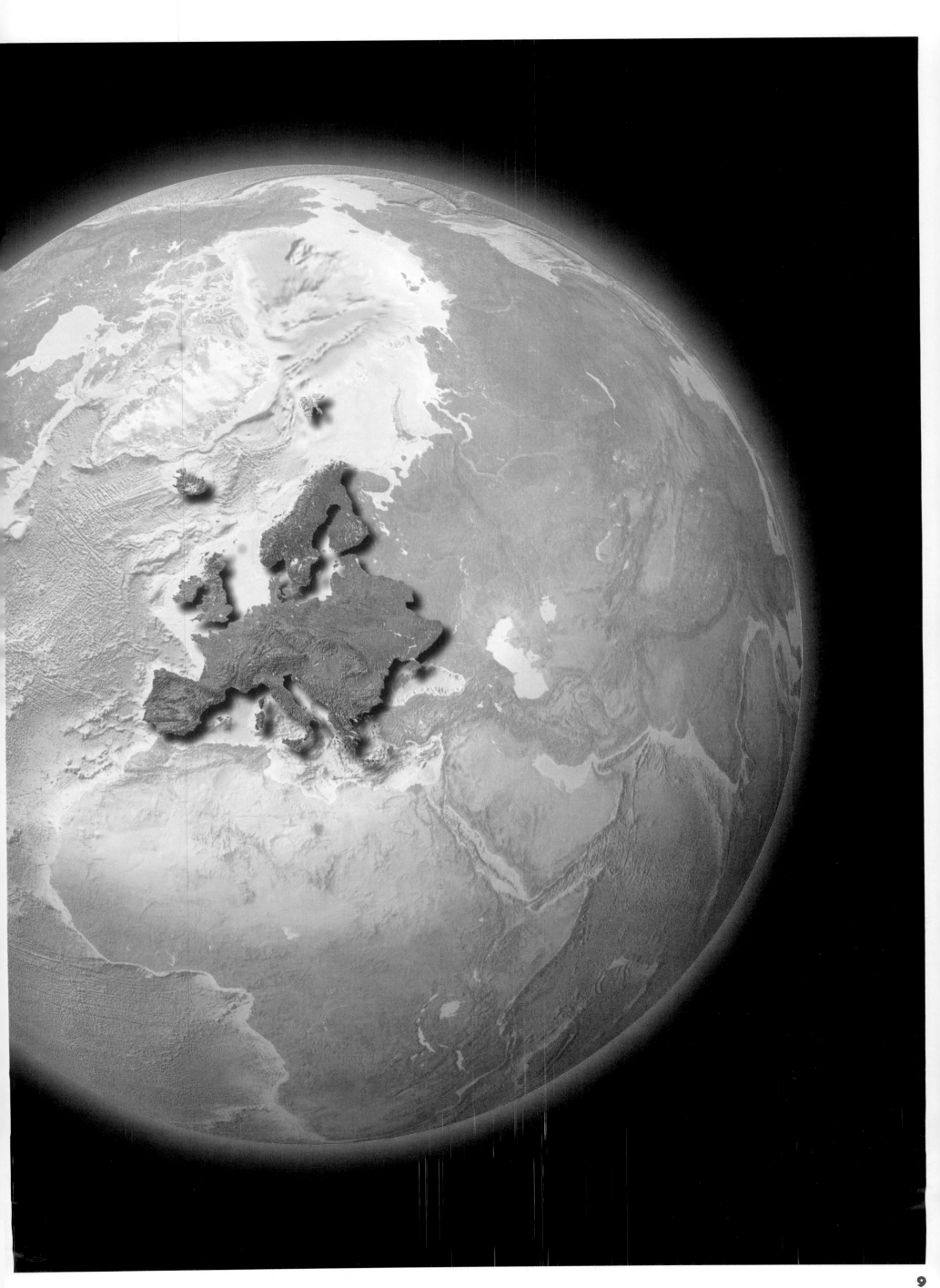

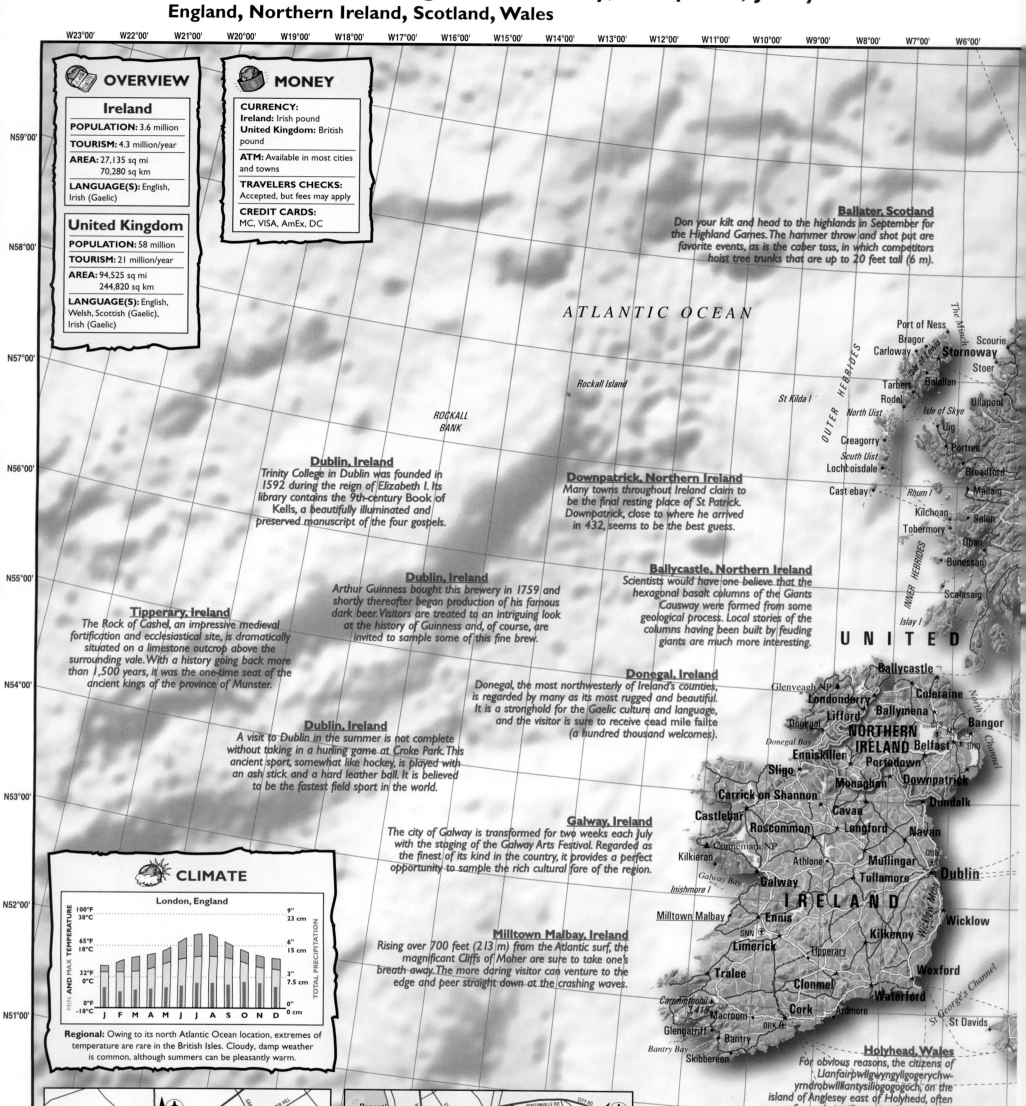

OVERVIEW

Ireland

POPULATION: 3.6 million

TOURISM: 4.3 million/year

AREA: 27,135 sq mi
70,280 sq km

LANGUAGE(S): English,
Irish (Gaelic)

United Kingdom

POPULATION: 58 million

TOURISM: 21 million/year

AREA: 94,525 sq mi
244,820 sq km

LANGUAGE(S): English,
Welsh, Scottish (Gaelic),
Irish (Gaelic)

MONEY

CURRENCY:
Ireland: Irish pound
United Kingdom: British
pound

ATM: Available in most cities
and towns

TRAVELERS CHECKS:
Accepted, but fees may apply

CREDIT CARDS:
MC, VISA, AmEx, DC

ATLANTIC OCEAN

ROCKALL
BANK

Rockall Island

Ballater, Scotland
Don your kilt and head to the highlands in September for
the Highland Games. The hammer throw and shot put are
favorite events, as is the caber toss, in which competitors
hoist tree trunks that are up to 20 feet tall (6 m).

Dublin, Ireland
Trinity College in Dublin was founded in
1592 during the reign of Elizabeth I. Its
library contains the 9th-century Book of
Kells, a beautifully illuminated and
preserved manuscript of the four gospels.

Downpatrick, Northern Ireland
Many towns throughout Ireland claim to
be the final resting place of St Patrick.
Downpatrick, close to where he arrived
in 432, seems to be the best guess.

Dublin, Ireland
Arthur Guinness bought this brewery in 1759 and
shortly thereafter began production of his famous
dark beer. Visitors are treated to an intriguing look
at the history of Guinness and, of course, are
invited to sample some of this fine brew.

Ballycastle, Northern Ireland
Scientists would have one believe that the
hexagonal basalt columns of the Giants
Causeway were formed from some
geological process. Local stories of the
columns having been built by feuding
giants are much more interesting.

Tipperary, Ireland
The Rock of Cashel, an impressive medieval
fortification and ecclesiastical site, is dramatically
situated on a limestone outcrop above the
surrounding vale. With a history going back more
than 1,500 years, it was the one-time seat of the
ancient kings of the province of Munster.

Donegal, Ireland
Donegal, the most northwesterly of Ireland's counties,
is regarded by many as its most rugged and beautiful.
It is a stronghold for the Gaelic culture and language,
and the visitor is sure to receive cead mile failte
(a hundred thousand welcomes).

Dublin, Ireland
A visit to Dublin in the summer is not complete
without taking in a hurling game at Croke Park. This
ancient sport, somewhat like hockey, is played with
an ash stick and a hard leather ball. It is believed
to be the fastest field sport in the world.

Galway, Ireland
The city of Galway is transformed for two weeks each July
with the staging of the Galway Arts Festival. Regarded as
the finest of its kind in the country, it provides a perfect
opportunity to sample the rich cultural fare of the region.

CLIMATE

London, England

100°F 38°C	9" 23 cm
65°F 18°C	6" 15 cm
32°F 0°C	3" 7.5 cm
0°F -18°C	0" 0 cm

J F M A M J J A S O N D

MIN AND MAX TEMPERATURE / TOTAL PRECIPITATION

Regional: Owing to its north Atlantic Ocean location, extremes of
temperature are rare in the British Isles. Cloudy, damp weather
is common, although summers can be pleasantly warm.

Milltown Malbay, Ireland
Rising over 700 feet (213 m) from the Atlantic surf, the
magnificent Cliffs of Moher are sure to take one's
breath away. The more daring visitor can venture to the
edge and peer straight down at the crashing waves.

Port of Ness
Bragor
Carloway
Stornoway
Stoer
St Kilda I
Tarbert
Rodel
Balallan
Ullapool
North Uist
Uig
Isle of Skye
Portree
Creagorry
South Uist
Lochboisdale
Broadford
Cast ebay
Rhum I
Mallaig
Kilchoan
Salen
Tobermory
Oban
Bunessan
Scalasaig
Islay I

UNITED

Ballycastle
Glenveagh NP
Coleraine
Londonderry
Ballymena
Lifford
Donegal
Bangor
NORTHERN
Enniskillen
Belfast
Donegal Bay
IRELAND
Portadown
Sligo
Monaghan
Downpatrick
Carrick on Shannon
Cavan
Dundalk
Castlebar
Roscommon
Longford
Navan
Connemara NP
Mullingar
Kilkieran
Athlone
Tullamore
Dublin
Galway Bay
Galway
IRELAND
Inishmore I
Milltown Malbay
Ennis
Wicklow
SNN
Limerick
Tipperary
Kilkenny
Tralee
Clonmel
Wexford
Carrantoohil
Macroom
Waterford
3,415
Ardmore
St George's Channel
Glengarriff
Cork
St Davids
Bantry
Bantry Bay
Skibbereen

Holyhead, Wales
For obvious reasons, the citizens of
Llanfairpwllgwyngyllgogerychw-
yrndrobwllllantysiliogogogoch, on the
island of Anglesey east of Holyhead, often
refer to their village simply as Llanfair.

**CELTIC
SEA**

Cork, Ireland
Blarney Castle was built in 1446 by the MacCarthy
Clan. The Blarney Stone, a gift from Robert the
Bruce of Scotland, is located in the ruined keep of
the castle. For centuries, kissing the stone has been
said to result in the gift of eloquence.

Truro
Camborne
Helston
Isles of Scilly
Hugh Town
Lizard

Caernarfon, Wales
An anomaly of architecture, the Italianate-style
village of Portmeirion (just south of Caernarfon)
represents the work and fantasy of Sir Clough
Williams–Ellis. Ignoring the weather, one might
imagine oneself to be on the Italian Riviera.

DUBLIN

DUBLIN
Connelly Station
Custom House
GPO
Four Courts
Liffey
Tara St Station
Guinness Brewery
Dublin Castle
Trinity College
Pearse Station
Leinster House
Merrion Square
St Stephen's Green

LONDON

Regent's Park
STANSTED
Tussaud's Wax Museum
BBC Broadcasting
British Museum and Library
St Paul's Cathedral
Piccadilly Circus
Hyde Park
Green Park
St James Park
Blackfriars Bridge
Thames
Queen Victoria Memorial
Westminster Hall
International Rail Terminal Waterloo
HEATHROW
Buckingham Palace
Houses of Parliament
Lambeth Palace
Imperial War Museum
GATWICK

Plymouth, England
The town of Plymouth is steeped in British naval
tradition. It was here that Sir Francis Drake
insisted on finishing his game of bowls before
engaging the approaching Spanish Armada.

© DeLorme

Scale 1:4,000,000 at map center

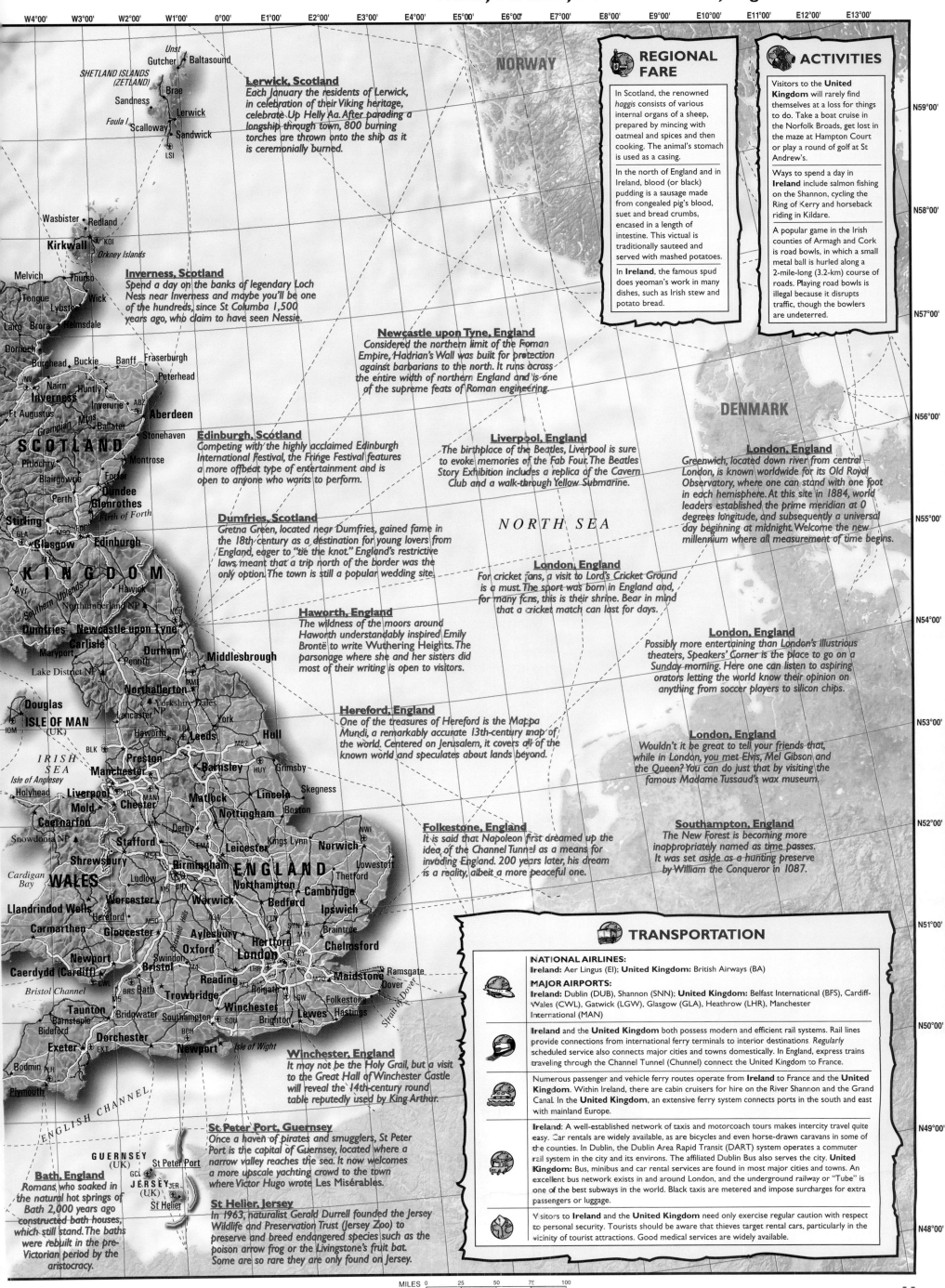

REGIONAL FARE

In Scotland, the renowned *haggis* consists of various internal organs of a sheep, prepared by mincing with oatmeal and spices and then cooking. The animal's stomach is used as a casing.

In the north of England and in Ireland, blood (or black) pudding is a sausage made from congealed pig's blood, suet and bread crumbs, encased in a length of intestine. This victual is traditionally sauteed and served with mashed potatoes.

In **Ireland**, the famous spud does yeoman's work in many dishes, such as Irish stew and potato bread.

ACTIVITIES

Visitors to the **United Kingdom** will rarely find themselves at a loss for things to do. Take a boat cruise in the Norfolk Broads, get lost in the maze at Hampton Court or play a round of golf at St Andrew's.

Ways to spend a day in **Ireland** include salmon fishing on the Shannon, cycling the Ring of Kerry and horseback riding in Kildare.

A popular game in the Irish counties of Armagh and Cork is road bowls, in which a small metal ball is hurled along a 2-mile-long (3.2-km) course of roads. Playing road bowls is illegal because it disrupts traffic, though the bowlers are undeterred.

Lerwick, Scotland
Each January the residents of Lerwick, in celebration of their Viking heritage, celebrate Up Helly Aa. After parading a longship through town, 800 burning torches are thrown onto the ship as it is ceremonially burned.

Inverness, Scotland
Spend a day on the banks of legendary Loch Ness near Inverness and maybe you'll be one of the hundreds, since St Columba 1,500 years ago, who claim to have seen Nessie.

Newcastle upon Tyne, England
Considered the northern limit of the Roman Empire, Hadrian's Wall was built for protection against barbarians to the north. It runs across the entire width of northern England and is one of the supreme feats of Roman engineering.

Edinburgh, Scotland
Competing with the highly acclaimed Edinburgh International Festival, the Fringe Festival features a more offbeat type of entertainment and is open to anyone who wants to perform.

Liverpool, England
The birthplace of the Beatles, Liverpool is sure to evoke memories of the Fab Four. The Beatles Story Exhibition includes a replica of the Cavern Club and a walk-through Yellow Submarine.

London, England
Greenwich, located down river from central London, is known worldwide for its Old Royal Observatory, where one can stand with one foot in each hemisphere. At this site in 1884, world leaders established the prime meridian at 0 degrees longitude, and subsequently a universal day beginning at midnight. Welcome the new millennium where all measurement of time begins.

Dumfries, Scotland
Gretna Green, located near Dumfries, gained fame in the 18th century as a destination for young lovers from England, eager to "tie the knot." England's restrictive laws meant that a trip north of the border was the only option. The town is still a popular wedding site.

London, England
For cricket fans, a visit to Lord's Cricket Ground is a must. The sport was born in England and, for many fans, this is their shrine. Bear in mind that a cricket match can last for days.

Haworth, England
The wildness of the moors around Haworth understandably inspired Emily Brontë to write Wuthering Heights. The parsonage where she and her sisters did most of their writing is open to visitors.

London, England
Possibly more entertaining than London's illustrious theaters, Speakers' Corner is the place to go on a Sunday morning. Here one can listen to aspiring orators letting the world know their opinion on anything from soccer players to silicon chips.

Hereford, England
One of the treasures of Hereford is the Mappa Mundi, a remarkably accurate 13th-century map of the world. Centered on Jerusalem, it covers all of the known world and speculates about lands beyond.

London, England
Wouldn't it be great to tell your friends that, while in London, you met Elvis, Mel Gibson and the Queen? You can do just that by visiting the famous Madame Tussaud's wax museum.

Folkestone, England
It is said that Napoleon first dreamed up the idea of the Channel Tunnel as a means for invading England. 200 years later, his dream is a reality, albeit a more peaceful one.

Southampton, England
The New Forest is becoming more inappropriately named as time passes. It was set aside as a hunting preserve by William the Conqueror in 1087.

Winchester, England
It may not be the Holy Grail, but a visit to the Great Hall of Winchester Castle will reveal the 14th-century round table reputedly used by King Arthur.

St Peter Port, Guernsey
Once a haven for pirates and smugglers, St Peter Port is the capital of Guernsey, located where a narrow valley reaches the sea. It now welcomes a more upscale yachting crowd to the town where Victor Hugo wrote Les Misérables.

St Helier, Jersey
In 1963, naturalist Gerald Durrell founded the Jersey Wildlife and Preservation Trust (Jersey Zoo) to preserve and breed endangered species such as the poison arrow frog or the Livingstone's fruit bat. Some are so rare they are only found on Jersey.

Bath, England
Romans who soaked in the natural hot springs of Bath 2,000 years ago constructed bath houses, which still stand. The baths were rebuilt in the pre-Victorian period by the aristocracy.

TRANSPORTATION

NATIONAL AIRLINES:
Ireland: Aer Lingus (EI); United Kingdom: British Airways (BA)

MAJOR AIRPORTS:
Ireland: Dublin (DUB), Shannon (SNN); United Kingdom: Belfast International (BFS), Cardiff-Wales (CWL), Gatwick (LGW), Glasgow (GLA), Heathrow (LHR), Manchester International (MAN)

Ireland and the United Kingdom both possess modern and efficient rail systems. Rail lines provide connections from international ferry terminals to interior destinations. Regularly scheduled service also connects major cities and towns domestically. In England, express trains traveling through the Channel Tunnel (Chunnel) connect the United Kingdom to France.

Numerous passenger and vehicle ferry routes operate from Ireland to France and the United Kingdom. Within Ireland, there are cabin cruisers for hire on the River Shannon and the Grand Canal. In the United Kingdom, an extensive ferry system connects ports in the south and east with mainland Europe.

Ireland: A well-established network of taxis and motorcoach tours makes intercity travel quite easy. Car rentals are widely available, as are bicycles and even horse-drawn caravans in some of the counties. In Dublin, the Dublin Area Rapid Transit (DART) system operates a commuter rail system in the city and its environs. The affiliated Dublin Bus also serves the city. United Kingdom: Bus, minibus and car rental services are found in most major cities and towns. An excellent bus network exists in and around London, and the underground railway or "Tube" is one of the best subways in the world. Black taxis are metered and impose surcharges for extra passengers or luggage.

Visitors to Ireland and the United Kingdom need only exercise regular caution with respect to personal security. Tourists should be aware that thieves target rental cars, particularly in the vicinity of tourist attractions. Good medical services are widely available.

NORWAY

DENMARK

NORTH SEA

SHETLAND ISLANDS (ZETLAND)

SCOTLAND

KINGDOM

ENGLAND

WALES

IRISH SEA

Cardigan Bay

Bristol Channel

ENGLISH CHANNEL

Strait of Dover

GUERNSEY (UK)

JERSEY (UK)

MILES 0 25 50 75 100
KILOMETERS 0 25 50 75 100 125 150

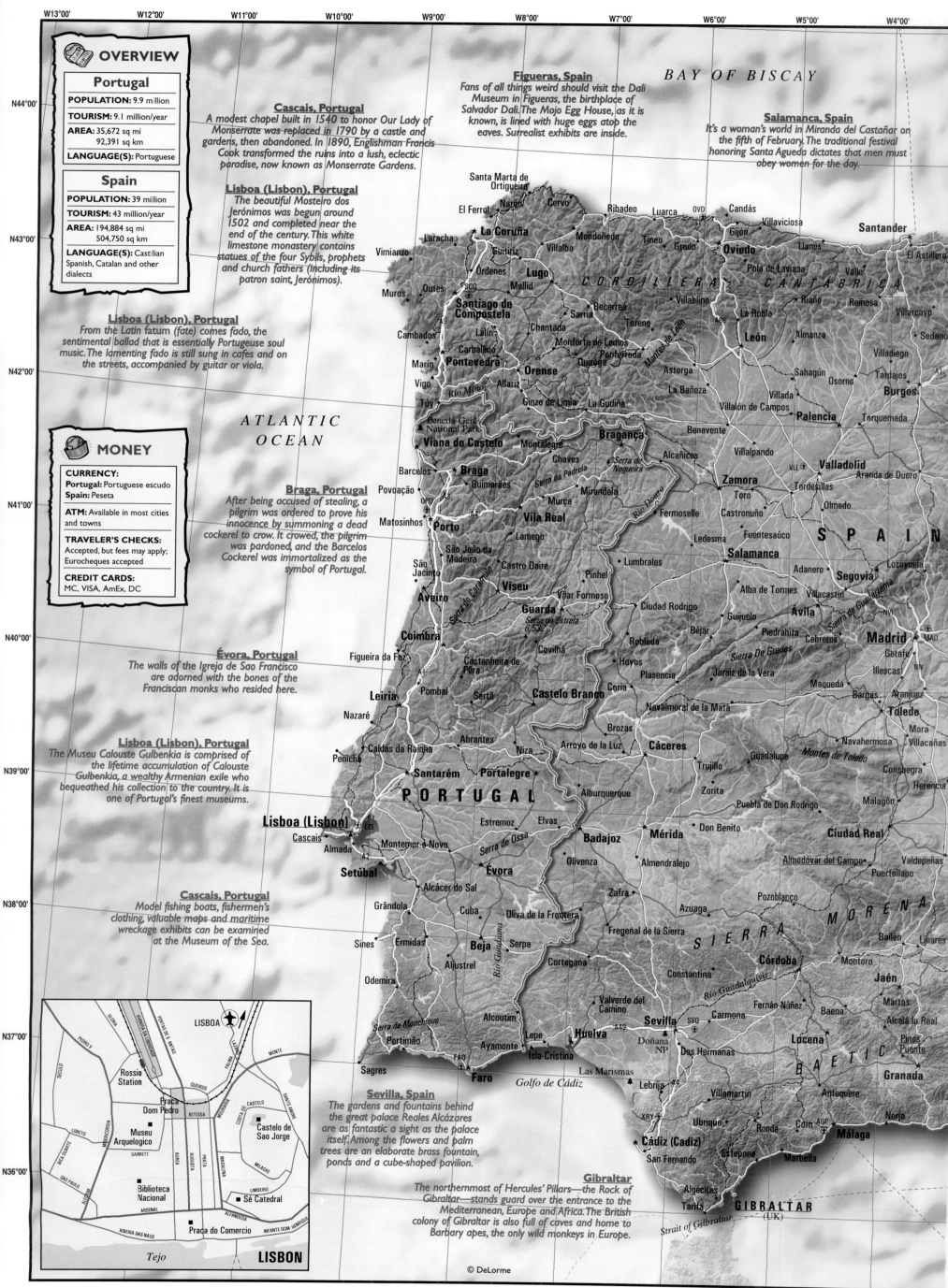

OVERVIEW

Portugal
POPULATION: 9.9 million
TOURISM: 9.1 million/year
AREA: 35,672 sq mi
92,391 sq km
LANGUAGE(S): Portuguese

Spain
POPULATION: 39 million
TOURISM: 43 million/year
AREA: 194,884 sq mi
504,750 sq km
LANGUAGE(S): Castilian
Spanish, Catalan and other
dialects

MONEY

CURRENCY:
Portugal: Portuguese escudo
Spain: Peseta

ATM: Available in most cities
and towns

TRAVELER'S CHECKS:
Accepted, but fees may apply;
Eurocheques accepted

CREDIT CARDS:
MC, VISA, AmEx, DC

Cascais, Portugal
A modest chapel built in 1540 to honor Our Lady of Monserrate was replaced in 1790 by a castle and gardens, then abandoned. In 1890, Englishman Francis Cook transformed the ruins into a lush, eclectic paradise, now known as Monserrate Gardens.

Lisboa (Lisbon), Portugal
The beautiful Mosteiro dos Jerónimos was begun around 1502 and completed near the end of the century. This white limestone monastery contains statues of the four Sybils, prophets and church fathers (including its patron saint, Jerónimos).

Lisboa (Lisbon), Portugal
From the Latin fatum (fate) comes fado, the sentimental ballad that is essentially Portugeuese soul music. The lamenting fado is still sung in cafes and on the streets, accompanied by guitar or viola.

Braga, Portugal
After being accused of stealing, a pilgrim was ordered to prove his innocence by summoning a dead cockerel to crow. It crowed, the pilgrim was pardoned, and the Barcelos Cockerel was immortalized as the symbol of Portugal.

Évora, Portugal
The walls of the Igreja de Sao Francisco are adorned with the bones of the Franciscan monks who resided here.

Lisboa (Lisbon), Portugal
The Museu Calouste Gulbenkia is comprised of the lifetime accumulation of Calouste Gulbenkia, a wealthy Armenian exile who bequeathed his collection to the country. It is one of Portugal's finest museums.

Cascais, Portugal
Model fishing boats, fishermen's clothing, valuable maps and maritime wreckage exhibits can be examined at the Museum of the Sea.

Figueras, Spain
Fans of all things weird should visit the Dali Museum in Figueras, the birthplace of Salvador Dali. The Mojo Egg House, as it is known, is lined with huge eggs atop the eaves. Surrealist exhibits are inside.

Salamanca, Spain
It's a woman's world in Miranda del Castañar on the fifth of February. The traditional festival honoring Santa Agueda dictates that men must obey women for the day.

Sevilla, Spain
The gardens and fountains behind the great palace Reales Alcázares are as fantastic a sight as the palace itself. Among the flowers and palm trees are an elaborate brass fountain, ponds and a cube-shaped pavilion.

Gibraltar
The northernmost of Hercules' Pillars—the Rock of Gibraltar—stands guard over the entrance to the Mediterranean, Europe and Africa. The British colony of Gibraltar is also full of caves and home to Barbary apes, the only wild monkeys in Europe.

BAY OF BISCAY

ATLANTIC OCEAN

PORTUGAL

S P A I N

© DeLorme

LISBON

Scale 1:3,000,000 at map center

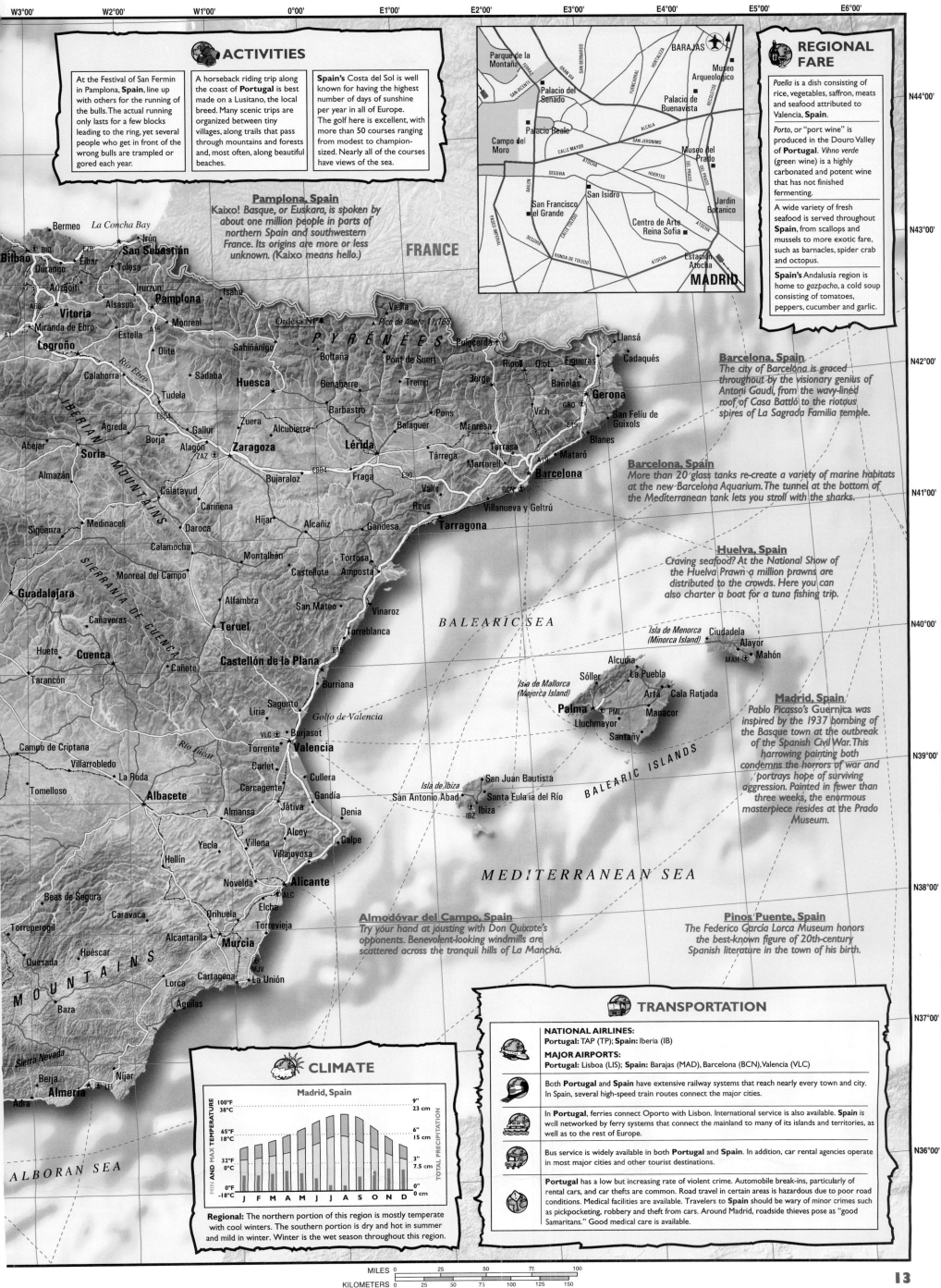

ACTIVITIES

At the Festival of San Fermin in Pamplona, **Spain**, line up with others for the running of the bulls. The actual running only lasts for a few blocks leading to the ring, yet several people who get in front of the wrong bulls are trampled or gored each year.

A horseback riding trip along the coast of **Portugal** is best made on a Lusitano, the local breed. Many scenic trips are organized between tiny villages, along trails that pass through mountains and forests and, most often, along beautiful beaches.

Spain's Costa del Sol is well known for having the highest number of days of sunshine per year in all of Europe. The golf here is excellent, with more than 50 courses ranging from modest to championship-sized. Nearly all of the courses have views of the sea.

REGIONAL FARE

Paella is a dish consisting of rice, vegetables, saffron, meats and seafood attributed to Valencia, **Spain**.

Porto, or "port wine" is produced in the Douro Valley of **Portugal**. *Vinho verde* (green wine) is a highly carbonated and potent wine that has not finished fermenting.

A wide variety of fresh seafood is served throughout **Spain**, from scallops and mussels to more exotic fare, such as barnacles, spider crab and octopus.

Spain's Andalusía region is home to *gazpacho*, a cold soup consisting of tomatoes, peppers, cucumber and garlic.

Pamplona, Spain
Kaixo! Basque, or Euskara, is spoken by about one million people in parts of northern Spain and southwestern France. Its origins are more or less unknown. (Kaixo means hello.)

Barcelona, Spain
The city of Barcelona is graced throughout by the visionary genius of Antoni Gaudí, from the wavy-lined roof of Casa Battló to the riotous spires of La Sagrada Familia temple.

Barcelona, Spain
More than 20 glass tanks re-create a variety of marine habitats at the new Barcelona Aquarium. The tunnel at the bottom of the Mediterranean tank lets you stroll with the sharks.

Huelva, Spain
Craving seafood? At the National Show of the Huelva Prawn a million prawns are distributed to the crowds. Here you can also charter a boat for a tuna fishing trip.

Madrid, Spain
Pablo Picasso's Guernica was inspired by the 1937 bombing of the Basque town at the outbreak of the Spanish Civil War. This harrowing painting both condemns the horrors of war and portrays hope of surviving aggression. Painted in fewer than three weeks, the enormous masterpiece resides at the Prado Museum.

Almodóvar del Campo, Spain
Try your hand at jousting with Don Quixote's opponents. Benevolent-looking windmills are scattered across the tranquil hills of La Mancha.

Pinos Puente, Spain
The Federico García Lorca Museum honors the best-known figure of 20th-century Spanish literature in the town of his birth.

CLIMATE

Madrid, Spain

Regional: The northern portion of this region is mostly temperate with cool winters. The southern portion is dry and hot in summer and mild in winter. Winter is the wet season throughout this region.

TRANSPORTATION

NATIONAL AIRLINES:
Portugal: TAP (TP); **Spain:** Iberia (IB)
MAJOR AIRPORTS:
Portugal: Lisboa (LIS); **Spain:** Barajas (MAD), Barcelona (BCN), Valencia (VLC)

Both **Portugal** and **Spain** have extensive railway systems that reach nearly every town and city. In Spain, several high-speed train routes connect the major cities.

In **Portugal**, ferries connect Oporto with Lisbon. International service is also available. **Spain** is well networked by ferry systems that connect the mainland to many of its islands and territories, as well as to the rest of Europe.

Bus service is widely available in both **Portugal** and **Spain**. In addition, car rental agencies operate in most major cities and other tourist destinations.

Portugal has a low but increasing rate of violent crime. Automobile break-ins, particularly of rental cars, and car thefts are common. Road travel in certain areas is hazardous due to poor road conditions. Medical facilities are available. Travelers to **Spain** should be wary of minor crimes such as pickpocketing, robbery and theft from cars. Around Madrid, roadside thieves pose as "good Samaritans." Good medical care is available.

MILES 0   25   50   75   100
KILOMETERS 0   25   50   75   100   125   150

OVERVIEW

Andorra
POPULATION: 64,000
TOURISM: 6 million/year
AREA: 174 sq mi
450 sq km
LANGUAGE(S): Catalan (official), French, Castilian

France
POPULATION: 59 million
TOURISM: 61 million/year
AREA: 209,664 sq mi
543,030 sq km
LANGUAGE(S): French

Liechtenstein
POPULATION: 32,000
TOURISM: 62,000/year
AREA: 62 sq mi
161 sq km
LANGUAGE(S): German (official), Alemannic dialect

Monaco
POPULATION: 32,000
TOURISM: 217,000/year
AREA: 0.7 sq mi
1.9 sq km
LANGUAGE(S): French (official), English, Italian

Switzerland
POPULATION: 7.2 million
TOURISM: 12 million/year
AREA: 15,942 sq mi
41,290 sq km
LANGUAGE(S): German, French, Italian

MONEY

CURRENCY:
Andorra: French franc, Spanish peseta
France, Monaco: French franc
Liechtenstein: Swiss franc
Switzerland: Swiss franc
ATM: Widely available in cities and towns; 24-hour service
TRAVELER'S CHECKS: Generally accepted, but fees may apply
CREDIT CARDS: MC, VISA, AmEx
France, Switzerland: DC also accepted

Paris, France
One either loves or hates the glass pyramid outside the Louvre in Paris. Designed and constructed in 1989 by I.M. Pei, it dominates the museum's entrance and provides a striking contrast to the 16th-century facade behind.

St-Malo, France
The unique architectural creation known as Mont St-Michel has been a major religious and strategic site for over 1,000 years. Surrounded by the sea at high tide and linked to the mainland at low, visitors may be stranded until the next low tide. Not a bad place to be stranded, though.

Le Mans, France
Every summer the roads south of Le Mans are closed for 24 hours and become the site of the world's oldest car race. Originally a way for manufacturers to prove the durability of their cars, today it tests the endurance of both machine and driver.

Vannes, France
One of the most important prehistoric sites in the world, Carnac has over 3,000 standing stones, or menhirs, dating back as far as 5000 B.C. Why they were put in place is unclear, although some answers may be found at the Archeoscope study center.

Vichy, France
The mineral springs in the elegant town of Vichy have been attracting health seekers since Roman times. Napoleon III was a frequent visitor. Today, water from its alkaline springs is bottled and shipped all over the world.

Andorra la Vella, Andorra
The House of the Valleys is a 16th-century building that houses Andorra's government. It was sold to the General Council in 1702, and councilors lived here while assembly was in session. It features a number of important murals thought to be based on Flemish tapestries.

Grasse, France
The charming medieval town of Grasse, in the foothills of the Alps, is a major center of the perfume industry. Factories such as the one founded by Jean de Galimard in 1747 use natural ingredients of the area for their scents.

© DeLorme

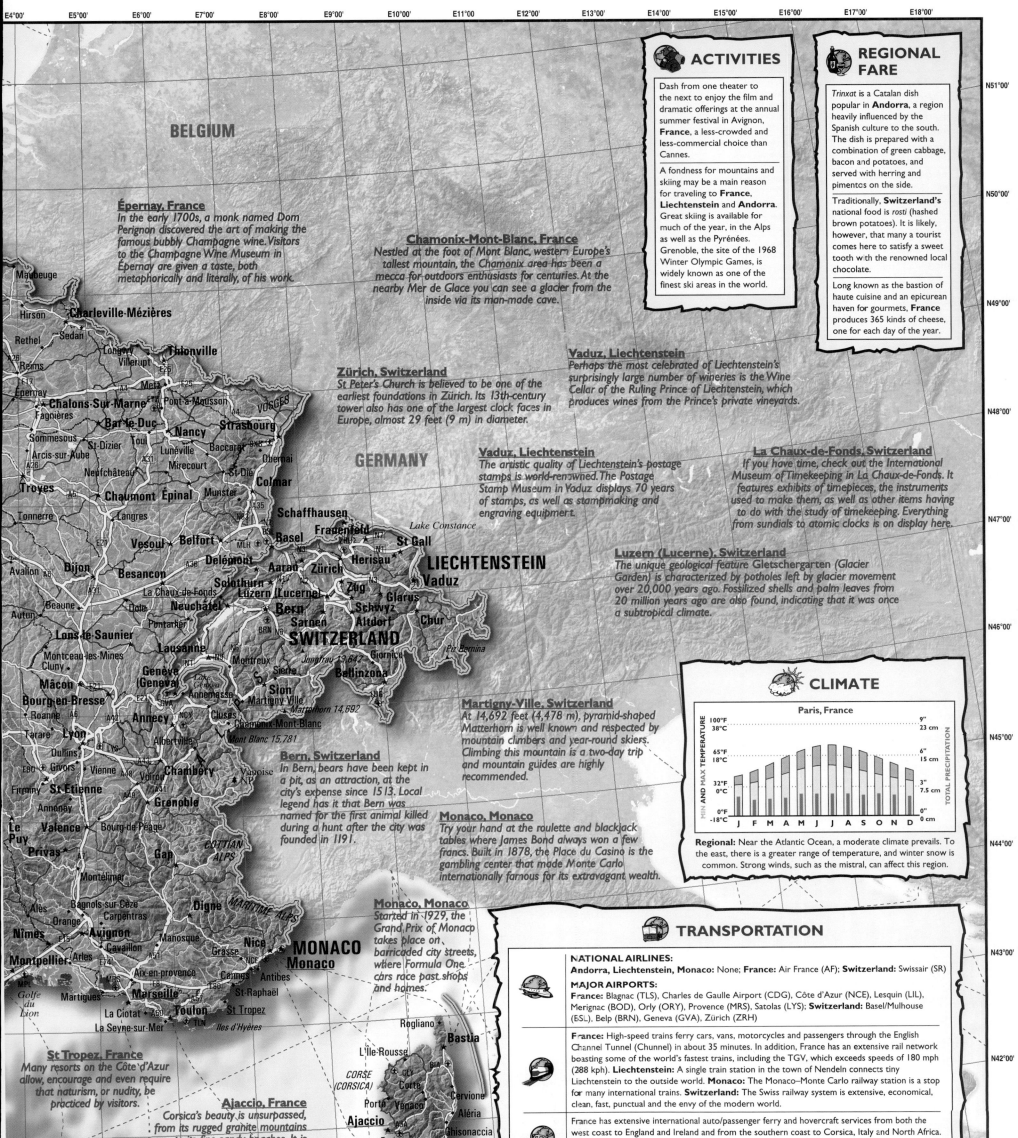

ACTIVITIES

Dash from one theater to the next to enjoy the film and dramatic offerings at the annual summer festival in Avignon, **France**, a less-crowded and less-commercial choice than Cannes.

A fondness for mountains and skiing may be a main reason for traveling to **France, Liechtenstein and Andorra**. Great skiing is available for much of the year, in the Alps as well as the Pyrénées. Grenoble, the site of the 1968 Winter Olympic Games, is widely known as one of the finest ski areas in the world.

REGIONAL FARE

Trinxat is a Catalan dish popular in **Andorra**, a region heavily influenced by the Spanish culture to the south. The dish is prepared with a combination of green cabbage, bacon and potatoes, and served with herring and pimentos on the side.

Traditionally, **Switzerland's** national food is rosti (hashed brown potatoes). It is likely, however, that many a tourist comes here to satisfy a sweet tooth with the renowned local chocolate.

Long known as the bastion of haute cuisine and an epicurean haven for gourmets, **France** produces 365 kinds of cheese, one for each day of the year.

Épernay, France
In the early 1700s, a monk named Dom Perignon discovered the art of making the famous bubbly Champagne wine. Visitors to the Champagne Wine Museum in Épernay are given a taste, both metaphorically and literally, of his work.

Chamonix-Mont-Blanc, France
Nestled at the foot of Mont Blanc, western Europe's tallest mountain, the Chamonix area has been a mecca for outdoors enthusiasts for centuries. At the nearby Mer de Glace you can see a glacier from the inside via its man-made cave.

Zürich, Switzerland
St Peter's Church is believed to be one of the earliest foundations in Zürich. Its 13th-century tower also has one of the largest clock faces in Europe, almost 29 feet (9 m) in diameter.

Vaduz, Liechtenstein
Perhaps the most celebrated of Liechtenstein's surprisingly large number of wineries is the Wine Cellar of the Ruling Prince of Liechtenstein, which produces wines from the Prince's private vineyards.

Vaduz, Liechtenstein
The artistic quality of Liechtenstein's postage stamps is world-renowned. The Postage Stamp Museum in Vaduz displays 70 years of stamps, as well as stampmaking and engraving equipment.

La Chaux-de-Fonds, Switzerland
If you have time, check out the International Museum of Timekeeping in La Chaux-de-Fonds. It features exhibits of timepieces, the instruments used to make them, as well as other items having to do with the study of timekeeping. Everything from sundials to atomic clocks is on display here.

Luzern (Lucerne), Switzerland
The unique geological feature Gletschergarten (Glacier Garden) is characterized by potholes left by glacier movement over 20,000 years ago. Fossilized shells and palm leaves from 20 million years ago are also found, indicating that it was once a subtropical climate.

Martigny-Ville, Switzerland
At 14,692 feet (4,478 m), pyramid-shaped Matterhorn is well known and respected by mountain climbers and year-round skiers. Climbing this mountain is a two-day trip and mountain guides are highly recommended.

Bern, Switzerland
In Bern, bears have been kept in a pit, as an attraction, at the city's expense since 1513. Local legend has it that Bern was named for the first animal killed during a hunt after the city was founded in 1191.

Monaco, Monaco
Try your hand at the roulette and blackjack tables where James Bond always won a few francs. Built in 1878, the Place du Casino is the gambling center that made Monte Carlo internationally famous for its extravagant wealth.

Monaco, Monaco
Started in 1929, the Grand Prix of Monaco takes place on barricaded city streets, where Formula One cars race past shops and homes.

St Tropez, France
Many resorts on the Côte d'Azur allow, encourage and even require that naturism, or nudity, be practiced by visitors.

Ajaccio, France
Corsica's beauty is unsurpassed, from its rugged granite mountains to its fine sandy beaches. It is separated from the mainland not only by water, but also by a distinct culture.

Arles, France
In late May the town of Saintes Maries de la Mer, south of Arles, plays host to the Gypsy Festival. This colorful celebration with singing and dancing honors Sarah, Patron Saint of Gypsies.

Marseille, France
Uncovered after the Port of Marseille was destroyed during WWII, the artifacts exhibited in the Museum of Roman Docks attest to the ancient activity of this port. Pieces on display date back to the 6th century B.C.

CLIMATE

Paris, France

100°F 38°C		9" 23 cm
65°F 18°C		6" 15 cm
32°F 0°C		3" 7.5 cm
0°F -18°C	J F M A M J J A S O N D	0" 0 cm

MIN AND MAX TEMPERATURE — TOTAL PRECIPITATION

Regional: Near the Atlantic Ocean, a moderate climate prevails. To the east, there is a greater range of temperature, and winter snow is common. Strong winds, such as the mistral, can affect this region.

TRANSPORTATION

NATIONAL AIRLINES:
Andorra, Liechtenstein, Monaco: None; **France:** Air France (AF); **Switzerland:** Swissair (SR)

MAJOR AIRPORTS:
France: Blagnac (TLS), Charles de Gaulle Airport (CDG), Côte d'Azur (NCE), Lesquin (LIL), Merignac (BOD), Orly (ORY), Provence (MRS), Satolas (LYS); **Switzerland:** Basel/Mulhouse (ESL), Belp (BRN), Geneva (GVA), Zürich (ZRH)

France: High-speed trains ferry cars, vans, motorcycles and passengers through the English Channel Tunnel (Chunnel) in about 35 minutes. In addition, France has an extensive rail network boasting some of the world's fastest trains, including the TGV, which exceeds speeds of 180 mph (288 kph). **Liechtenstein:** A single train station in the town of Nendeln connects tiny Liechtenstein to the outside world. **Monaco:** The Monaco–Monte Carlo railway station is a stop for many international trains. **Switzerland:** The Swiss railway system is extensive, economical, clean, fast, punctual and the envy of the modern world.

France has extensive international auto/passenger ferry and hovercraft services from both the west coast to England and Ireland and from the southern coast to Corsica, Italy and North Africa. Within France, riverboat cruises on the vast network of navigable canals and rivers provide a popular, alternative way to explore its cities and countryside.

Andorra: All surface access to Andorra is over roads. Residents of France and Spain, in addition to tourists, often manage day trips to Andorra to take advantage of duty-free goods and cheap gasoline. Long waits at customs upon departure are not unusual. **France:** Because France is so well served by trains, long distance bus service is limited. Rental cars are widely available, but should be booked and paid for in advance to ensure fair pricing. **Liechtenstein:** There is scheduled bus service to Liechtenstein from railroad stations at Sargans and Buchs in Switzerland. **Monaco:** The A8 autoroute, which connects with the whole of European motorway system, serves the principality by means of easy-access roads from France and Italy. Buses, taxis and rental cars are also widely available. **Switzerland:** The popular Swiss Pass allows travelers to purchase unlimited travel during a fixed period on virtually any form of Swiss surface transportation, including trains, buses and lake steamers.

Few concerns, save petty theft, affect travelers. In Switzerland, drivers should exercise caution on mountainous, winding roads. Good medical care is widely available.

MILES 0 25 50 75 100
KILOMETERS 0 25 50 75 100 125 150

EUROPE Holy See (Vatican City), Italy, Malta, San Marino

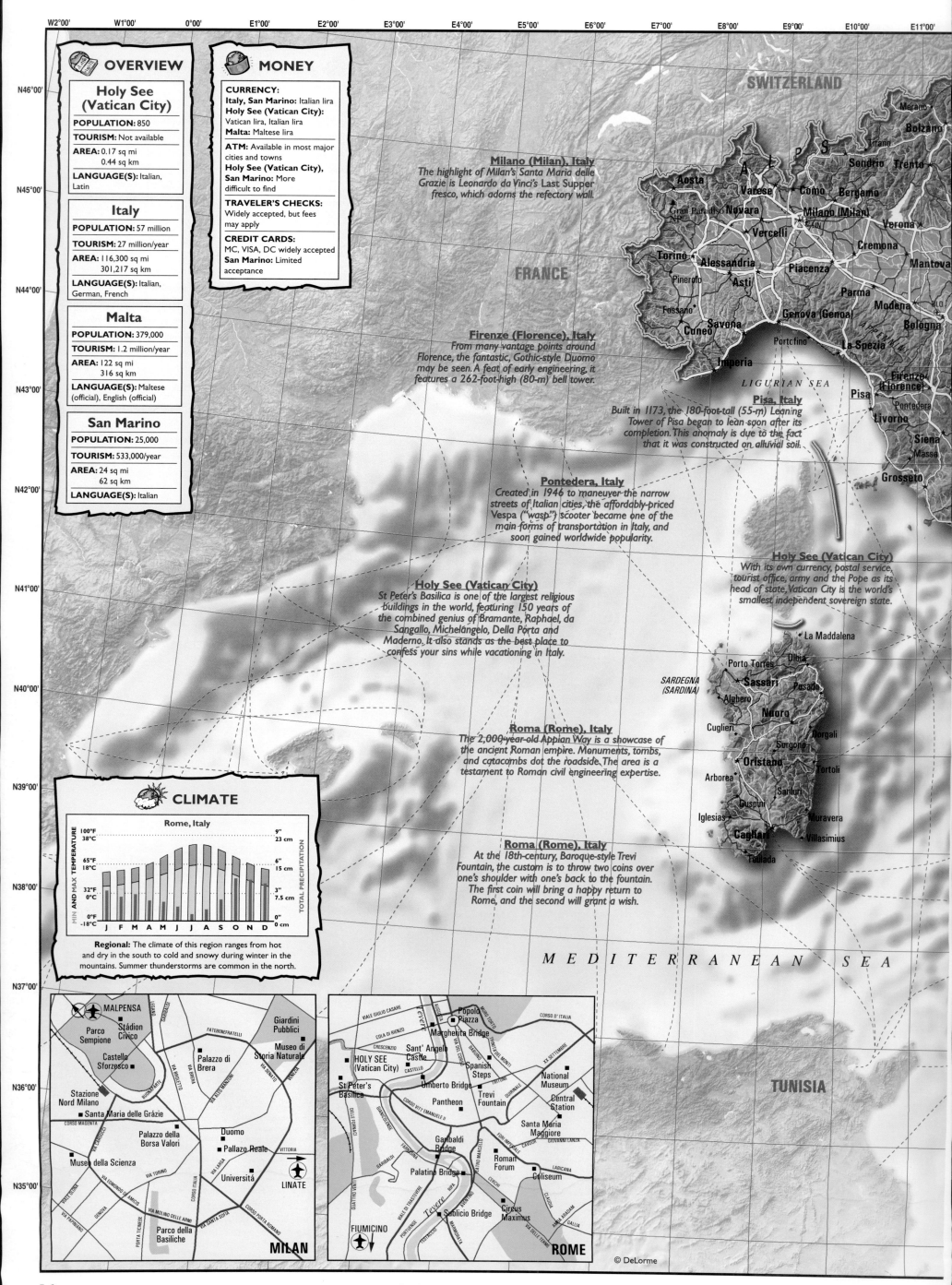

OVERVIEW

Holy See (Vatican City)
POPULATION: 850
TOURISM: Not available
AREA: 0.17 sq mi
0.44 sq km
LANGUAGE(S): Italian, Latin

Italy
POPULATION: 57 million
TOURISM: 27 million/year
AREA: 116,300 sq mi
301,217 sq km
LANGUAGE(S): Italian, German, French

Malta
POPULATION: 379,000
TOURISM: 1.2 million/year
AREA: 122 sq mi
316 sq km
LANGUAGE(S): Maltese (official), English (official)

San Marino
POPULATION: 25,000
TOURISM: 533,000/year
AREA: 24 sq mi
62 sq km
LANGUAGE(S): Italian

MONEY

CURRENCY:
Italy, San Marino: Italian lira
Holy See (Vatican City): Vatican lira, Italian lira
Malta: Maltese lira

ATM: Available in most major cities and towns
Holy See (Vatican City), San Marino: More difficult to find

TRAVELER'S CHECKS: Widely accepted, but fees may apply

CREDIT CARDS: MC, VISA, DC widely accepted
San Marino: Limited acceptance

CLIMATE

Rome, Italy

Regional: The climate of this region ranges from hot and dry in the south to cold and snowy during winter in the mountains. Summer thunderstorms are common in the north.

W2°00' W1°00' 0°00' E1°00' E2°00' E3°00' E4°00' E5°00' E6°00' E7°00' E8°00' E9°00' E10°00' E11°00'
N46°00' N45°00' N44°00' N43°00' N42°00' N41°00' N40°00' N39°00' N38°00' N37°00' N36°00' N35°00'
SWITZERLAND
FRANCE
TUNISIA
LIGURIAN SEA
MEDITERRANEAN SEA
SARDEGNA (SARDINA)
Milano (Milan), Italy
The highlight of Milan's Santa Maria delle Grazie is Leonardo da Vinci's Last Supper fresco, which adorns the refectory wall.
Firenze (Florence), Italy
From many vantage points around Florence, the fantastic, Gothic-style Duomo may be seen. A feat of early engineering, it features a 262-foot-high (80-m) bell tower.
Pisa, Italy
Built in 1173, the 180-foot-tall (55-m) Leaning Tower of Pisa began to lean soon after its completion. This anomaly is due to the fact that it was constructed on alluvial soil.
Pontedera, Italy
Created in 1946 to maneuver the narrow streets of Italian cities, the affordably-priced Vespa ("wasp") scooter became one of the main forms of transportation in Italy, and soon gained worldwide popularity.
Holy See (Vatican City)
With its own currency, postal service, tourist office, army and the Pope as its head of state, Vatican City is the world's smallest independent sovereign state.
Holy See (Vatican City)
St Peter's Basilica is one of the largest religious buildings in the world, featuring 150 years of the combined genius of Bramante, Raphael, da Sangallo, Michelangelo, Della Porta and Maderno. It also stands as the best place to confess your sins while vacationing in Italy.
Roma (Rome), Italy
The 2,000-year-old Appian Way is a showcase of the ancient Roman empire. Monuments, tombs, and catacombs dot the roadside. The area is a testament to Roman civil engineering expertise.
Roma (Rome), Italy
At the 18th-century, Baroque-style Trevi Fountain, the custom is to throw two coins over one's shoulder with one's back to the fountain. The first coin will bring a happy return to Rome, and the second will grant a wish.
Merano Bolzano Tirano Sondrio Trento Aosta Varese Como Bergamo Gran Paradiso NP Novara Milano (Milan) Verona Vercelli Cremona Torino Alessandria Piacenza Mantova Pinerolo Asti Parma Modena Fossano Genova (Genoa) Bologna Cuneo Savona Portofino La Spezia Imperia Firenze (Florence) Pisa Pontedera Livorno Siena Massa Grosseto
La Maddalena Porto Torres Olbia Sassari Posada Alghero Nuoro Cuglieri Dorgali Sorgono Oristano Tortoli Arborea Sanluri Guspini Iglesias Muravera Cagliari Villasimius Teulada
MALPENSA Parco Sempione Stadion Civico Castello Sforzesco Giardini Pubblici Palazzo di Brera Museo di Storia Naturale Stazione Nord Milano Santa Maria delle Grázie Palazzo della Borsa Valori Duomo Palazzo Reale Museo della Scienza Università LINATE Parco della Basiliche MILAN
CORSO MAGENTA VIA TORINO CORSO ITALIA VIA MOLINO DELLE ARMI CORSO PORTA ROMANO VIA SANTA SOFIA CORSO DI PORTA TICINESE VITTORIA VIA SENATO VENEZIA VIA MANZONI VIA BRERA
Popolo Piazza Margherita Bridge HOLY SEE (Vatican City) Sant' Angelo Castle Spanish Steps St Peter's Basilica Umberto Bridge National Museum Pantheon Trevi Fountain Central Station Santa Maria Maggiore Garibaldi Bridge Roman Forum Palatino Bridge Coliseum Circus Maximus Sublicio Bridge FIUMICINO ROME Tevere
VIALE GIULIO CESARE COLA DI RIENZO CRESCENZIO CORSO D' ITALIA XX SETTEMBRE CORSO VITTORIO EMANUELE II VIA DEL CORSO TRITONE QUIRINALE CAVOUR FORI IMPERIALI LABICANA GIOVANNI LANZA CERCHI AVENTINO
© DeLorme

Scale 1:4,000,000 at map center

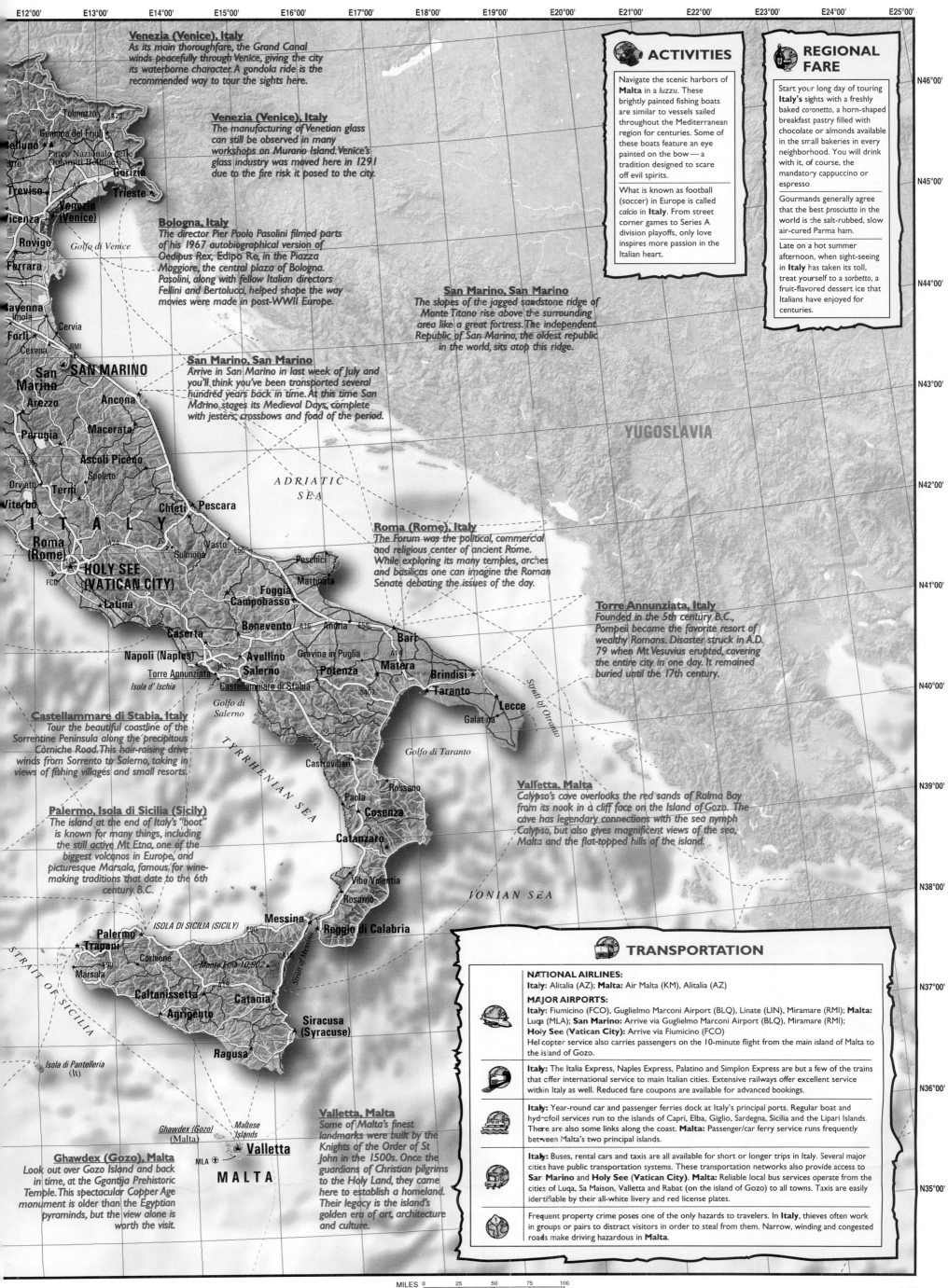

Venezia (Venice), Italy
As its main thoroughfare, the Grand Canal winds peacefully through Venice, giving the city its waterborne character. A gondola ride is the recommended way to tour the sights here.

Venezia (Venice), Italy
The manufacturing of Venetian glass can still be observed in many workshops on Murano Island. Venice's glass industry was moved here in 1291 due to the fire risk it posed to the city.

Bologna, Italy
The director Pier Paolo Pasolini filmed parts of his 1967 autobiographical version of Oedipus Rex, Edipo Re, in the Piazza Maggiore, the central plaza of Bologna. Pasolini, along with fellow Italian directors Fellini and Bertolucci, helped shape the way movies were made in post-WWII Europe.

San Marino, San Marino
The slopes of the jagged sandstone ridge of Monte Titano rise above the surrounding area like a great fortress. The independent Republic of San Marino, the oldest republic in the world, sits atop this ridge.

San Marino, San Marino
Arrive in San Marino in last week of July and you'll think you've been transported several hundred years back in time. At this time San Marino stages its Medieval Days, complete with jesters, crossbows and food of the period.

Roma (Rome), Italy
The Forum was the political, commercial and religious center of ancient Rome. While exploring its many temples, arches and basilicas one can imagine the Roman Senate debating the issues of the day.

Torre Annunziata, Italy
Founded in the 5th century B.C., Pompeii became the favorite resort of wealthy Romans. Disaster struck in A.D. 79 when Mt Vesuvius erupted, covering the entire city in one day. It remained buried until the 17th century.

Castellammare di Stabia, Italy
Tour the beautiful coastline of the Sorrentine Peninsula along the precipitous Corniche Road. This hair-raising drive winds from Sorrento to Salerno, taking in views of fishing villages and small resorts.

Palermo, Isola di Sicilia (Sicily)
The island at the end of Italy's "boot" is known for many things, including the still active Mt Etna, one of the biggest volcanos in Europe, and picturesque Marsala, famous for wine-making traditions that date to the 6th century B.C.

Valletta, Malta
Calypso's cave overlooks the red sands of Ramla Bay from its nook in a cliff face on the Island of Gozo. The cave has legendary connections with the sea nymph Calypso, but also gives magnificent views of the sea, Malta and the flat-topped hills of the island.

Ghawdex (Gozo), Malta
Look out over Gozo Island and back in time, at the Ggantija Prehistoric Temple. This spectacular Copper Age monument is older than the Egyptian pyraminds, but the view alone is worth the visit.

Valletta, Malta
Some of Malta's finest landmarks were built by the Knights of the Order of St John in the 1500s. Once the guardians of Christian pilgrims to the Holy Land, they came here to establish a homeland. Their legacy is the island's golden era of art, architecture and culture.

ACTIVITIES

Navigate the scenic harbors of **Malta** in a *luzzu*. These brightly painted fishing boats are similar to vessels sailed throughout the Mediterranean region for centuries. Some of these boats feature an eye painted on the bow—a tradition designed to scare off evil spirits.

What is known as football (soccer) in Europe is called *calcio* in **Italy**. From street corner games to Series A division playoffs, only love inspires more passion in the Italian heart.

REGIONAL FARE

Start your long day of touring **Italy's** sights with a freshly baked *cornetto*, a horn-shaped breakfast pastry filled with chocolate or almonds available in the small bakeries in every neighborhood. You will drink with it, of course, the mandatory cappuccino or espresso.

Gourmands generally agree that the best *prosciutto* in the world is the salt-rubbed, slow air-cured Parma ham.

Late on a hot summer afternoon, when sight-seeing in **Italy** has taken its toll, treat yourself to a *sorbetto*, a fruit-flavored dessert ice that Italians have enjoyed for centuries.

TRANSPORTATION

NATIONAL AIRLINES:
Italy: Alitalia (AZ); **Malta:** Air Malta (KM), Alitalia (AZ)

MAJOR AIRPORTS:
Italy: Fiumicino (FCO), Guglielmo Marconi Airport (BLQ), Linate (LIN), Miramare (RMI); **Malta:** Luqa (MLA); **San Marino:** Arrive via Guglielmo Marconi Airport (BLQ), Miramare (RMI); **Holy See (Vatican City):** Arrive via Fiumicino (FCO)
Helicopter service also carries passengers on the 10-minute flight from the main island of Malta to the island of Gozo.

Italy: The Italia Express, Naples Express, Palatino and Simplon Express are but a few of the trains that offer international service to main Italian cities. Extensive railways offer excellent service within Italy as well. Reduced fare coupons are available for advanced bookings.

Italy: Year-round car and passenger ferries dock at Italy's principal ports. Regular boat and hydrofoil services run to the islands of Capri, Elba, Giglio, Sardegna, Sicilia and the Lipari Islands. There are also some links along the coast. **Malta:** Passenger/car ferry service runs frequently between Malta's two principal islands.

Italy: Buses, rental cars and taxis are all available for short or longer trips in Italy. Several major cities have public transportation systems. These transportation networks also provide access to **San Marino** and **Holy See (Vatican City)**. **Malta:** Reliable local bus services operate from the cities of Luqa, Sa Maison, Valletta and Rabat (on the island of Gozo) to all towns. Taxis are easily identifiable by their all-white livery and red license plates.

Frequent property crime poses one of the only hazards to travelers. In **Italy**, thieves often work in groups or pairs to distract visitors in order to steal from them. Narrow, winding and congested roads make driving hazardous in **Malta**.

MILES 0 25 50 75 100
KILOMETERS 0 25 50 75 100 125 150

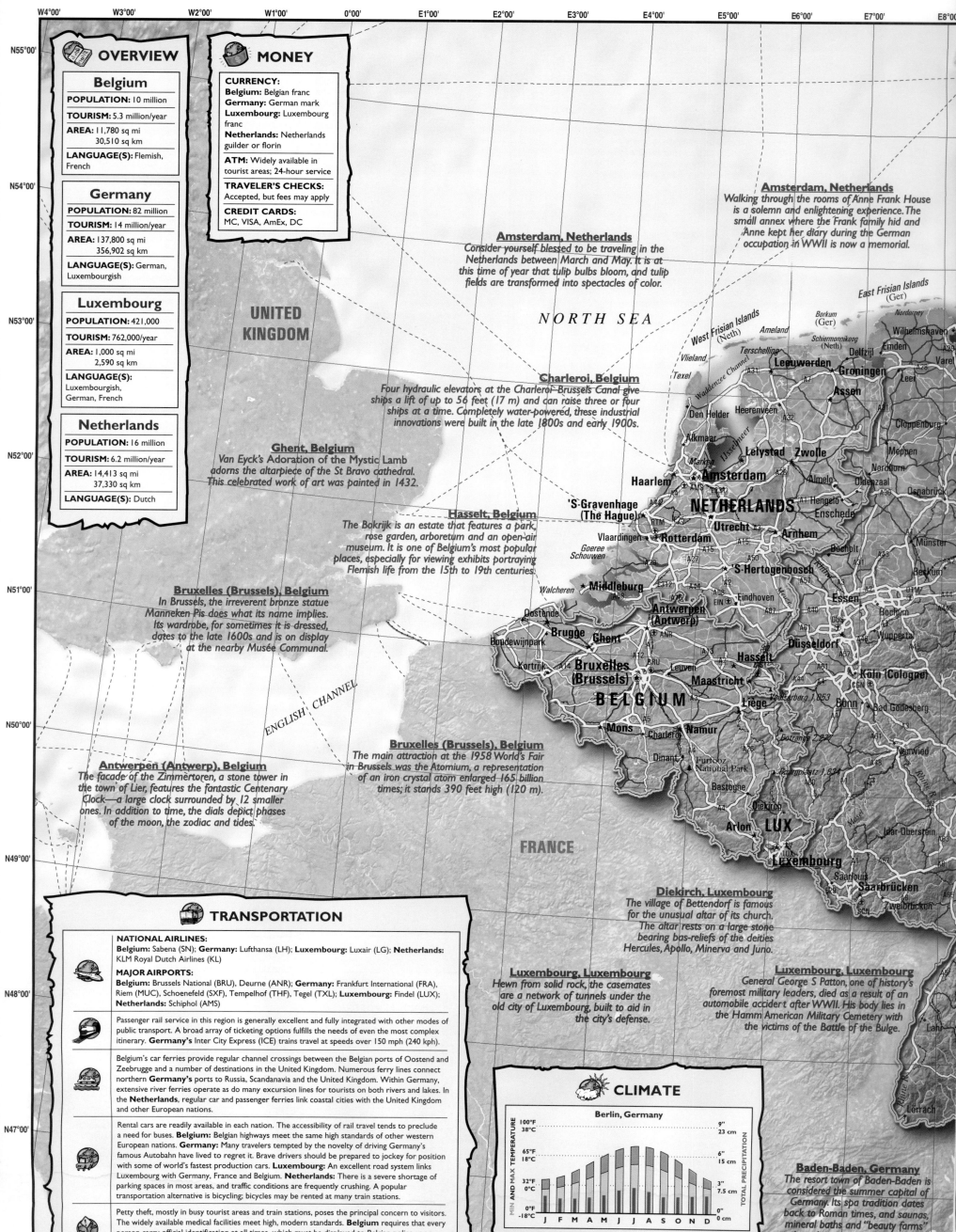

OVERVIEW

Belgium
POPULATION: 10 million
TOURISM: 5.3 million/year
AREA: 11,780 sq mi
30,510 sq km
LANGUAGE(S): Flemish, French

Germany
POPULATION: 82 million
TOURISM: 14 million/year
AREA: 137,800 sq mi
356,902 sq km
LANGUAGE(S): German, Luxembourgish

Luxembourg
POPULATION: 421,000
TOURISM: 762,000/year
AREA: 1,000 sq mi
2,590 sq km
LANGUAGE(S): Luxembourgish, German, French

Netherlands
POPULATION: 16 million
TOURISM: 6.2 million/year
AREA: 14,413 sq mi
37,330 sq km
LANGUAGE(S): Dutch

MONEY

CURRENCY:
Belgium: Belgian franc
Germany: German mark
Luxembourg: Luxembourg franc
Netherlands: Netherlands guilder or florin
ATM: Widely available in tourist areas; 24-hour service
TRAVELER'S CHECKS: Accepted, but fees may apply
CREDIT CARDS: MC, VISA, AmEx, DC

Amsterdam, Netherlands
Consider yourself blessed to be traveling in the Netherlands between March and May. It is at this time of year that tulip bulbs bloom, and tulip fields are transformed into spectacles of color.

Amsterdam, Netherlands
Walking through the rooms of Anne Frank House is a solemn and enlightening experience. The small annex where the Frank family hid and Anne kept her diary during the German occupation in WWII is now a memorial.

Charleroi, Belgium
Four hydraulic elevators at the Charleroi-Brussels Canal give ships a lift of up to 56 feet (17 m) and can raise three or four ships at a time. Completely water-powered, these industrial innovations were built in the late 1800s and early 1900s.

Ghent, Belgium
Van Eyck's Adoration of the Mystic Lamb adorns the altarpiece of the St Bravo cathedral. This celebrated work of art was painted in 1432.

Hasselt, Belgium
The Bokrijk is an estate that features a park, rose garden, arboretum and an open-air museum. It is one of Belgium's most popular places, especially for viewing exhibits portraying Flemish life from the 15th to 19th centuries.

Bruxelles (Brussels), Belgium
In Brussels, the irreverent bronze statue Manneken Pis does what its name implies. Its wardrobe, for sometimes it is dressed, dates to the late 1600s and is on display at the nearby Musée Communal.

Bruxelles (Brussels), Belgium
The main attraction at the 1958 World's Fair in Brussels was the Atomium, a representation of an iron crystal atom enlarged 165 billion times; it stands 390 feet high (120 m).

Antwerpen (Antwerp), Belgium
The facade of the Zimmertoren, a stone tower in the town of Lier, features the fantastic Centenary Clock—a large clock surrounded by 12 smaller ones. In addition to time, the dials depict phases of the moon, the zodiac and tides.

Diekirch, Luxembourg
The village of Bettendorf is famous for the unusual altar of its church. The altar rests on a large stone bearing bas-reliefs of the deities Hercules, Apollo, Minerva and Juno.

Luxembourg, Luxembourg
Hewn from solid rock, the casemates are a network of tunnels under the old city of Luxembourg, built to aid in the city's defense.

Luxembourg, Luxembourg
General George S Patton, one of history's foremost military leaders, died as a result of an automobile accident after WWII. His body lies in the Hamm American Military Cemetery with the victims of the Battle of the Bulge.

Baden-Baden, Germany
The resort town of Baden-Baden is considered the summer capital of Germany. Its spa tradition dates back to Roman times, and saunas, mineral baths and "beauty farms" have been popular ever since.

TRANSPORTATION

NATIONAL AIRLINES:
Belgium: Sabena (SN); **Germany:** Lufthansa (LH); **Luxembourg:** Luxair (LG); **Netherlands:** KLM Royal Dutch Airlines (KL)

MAJOR AIRPORTS:
Belgium: Brussels National (BRU), Deurne (ANR); **Germany:** Frankfurt International (FRA), Riem (MUC), Schoenefeld (SXF), Tempelhof (THF), Tegel (TXL); **Luxembourg:** Findel (LUX); **Netherlands:** Schiphol (AMS)

Passenger rail service in this region is generally excellent and fully integrated with other modes of public transport. A broad array of ticketing options fulfills the needs of even the most complex itinerary. **Germany's** Inter City Express (ICE) trains travel at speeds over 150 mph (240 kph).

Belgium's car ferries provide regular channel crossings between the Belgian ports of Oostend and Zeebrugge and a number of destinations in the United Kingdom. Numerous ferry lines connect northern **Germany's** ports to Russia, Scandanavia and the United Kingdom. Within Germany, extensive river ferries operate as do many excursion lines for tourists on both rivers and lakes. In the **Netherlands**, regular car and passenger ferries link coastal cities with the United Kingdom and other European nations.

Rental cars are readily available in each nation. The accessibility of rail travel tends to preclude a need for buses. **Belgium:** Belgian highways meet the same high standards of other western European nations. **Germany:** Many travelers tempted by the novelty of driving Germany's famous Autobahn have lived to regret it. Brave drivers should be prepared to jockey for position with some of world's fastest production cars. **Luxembourg:** An excellent road system links Luxembourg with Germany, France and Belgium. **Netherlands:** There is a severe shortage of parking spaces in most areas, and traffic conditions are frequently crushing. A popular transportation alternative is bicycling; bicycles may be rented at many train stations.

Petty theft, mostly in busy tourist areas and train stations, poses the principal concern to visitors. The widely available medical facilities meet high, modern standards. **Belgium** requires that every person carry official identification at all times, which must be displayed to Belgian police upon request.

CLIMATE

Berlin, Germany

100°F 38°C		9" 23 cm
65°F 18°C		6" 15 cm
32°F 0°C		3" 7.5 cm
0°F -18°C		0" 0 cm

J F M A M J J A S O N D

MIN AND MAX TEMPERATURE — TOTAL PRECIPITATION

Regional: Because of its proximity to the Atlantic Ocean, this region has a fairly moderate climate with few extremes, especially towards the northern coast. In winter, heavy snow falls in the south.

Map labels: NORTH SEA, UNITED KINGDOM, ENGLISH CHANNEL, FRANCE, NETHERLANDS, BELGIUM, LUX, North Sea, East Frisian Islands (Ger), West Frisian Islands (Neth), Leeuwarden, Groningen, Assen, Amsterdam, Haarlem, Den Helder, Alkmaar, Lelystad, Zwolle, 'S-Gravenhage (The Hague), Utrecht, Arnhem, Rotterdam, Eindhoven, 'S-Hertogenbosch, Enschede, Münster, Essen, Antwerpen (Antwerp), Brugge, Ghent, Bruxelles (Brussels), Hasselt, Maastricht, Liège, Düsseldorf, Köln (Cologne), Bonn, Mons, Charleroi, Namur, Dinant, Bastogne, Diekirch, Arlon, Luxembourg, Saarbrücken

© DeLorme

Bonn, Germany
Beethovenhaus was the birthplace of Ludwig van Beethoven (1770 to 1827). Since 1889, the 16th-century house has been a museum of artifacts and objects relating to the composer's life, including his piano and ear-horns.

Berlin, Germany
You no longer have to show your passport at Checkpoint Charlie, the West's guardpost and watchtower over the Berlin Wall. The actual post and tower are gone, but the museum recalls its heyday and several memorable escapes from communism.

Dachau, Germany
Dachau, the first concentration camp the Nazis built in Germany, held Jews, Christian priests, gypsies and other "enemies" of the regime during WWII. Tours of the camp and a nearby memorial are open to the public.

München (Munich), Germany
Oktoberfest (which actually starts in September) is attended by over five million beer-lovers every year in Munich. Try one of the many varieties of beer, in at least 12 different beer tents.

Stuttgart, Germany
An engine factory started by Gottlieb Daimler and Wilhelm Maybach in the late 1800s later merged with Karl Benz's factory to become Daimler-Benz, the makers of Mercedes-Benz automobiles. These two companies were among the first to make automobiles.

Füssen, Germany
Built by King Ludwig II of Bavaria, Neuschwanstein is a storybook castle set on a rock outcropping in the Bavarian Alps. Tours are given, though it is a hike up 170 stairs to get there. Ludwig, who became known as "Mad King Ludwig," never completed its construction.

REGIONAL FARE

Eat an acronym for a snack! *Banketletters* are delicious, flaky, almond-filled pastries shaped into letters by confectioners throughout the **Netherlands**.

Quenelles (calf liver dumplings) are often served with boiled potatoes and sauerkraut in **Luxembourg**. A local favorite to accompany the meal is black currant wine, straight from the Château de Beaufort vineyards.

Perhaps no region of the world enjoys its beer more than Bavaria in southern **Germany**. Any town of substance has its own brewery, and the casual *Biergartens* (beer gardens) make the perfect spot to relax with friends over a liter of the local brew.

ACTIVITIES

Wadlopen is the rather strenuous practice of taking long, low-tide walks along the drying banks and mud flats of the Wadden Sea across to outlying islands. The best place for *wadlopen*, also known as horizontal mountaineering, is around Holwerd or Wierum in the **Netherlands**.

Taking a night-time boat ride along Amsterdam's canals is a great way to see the sights. The arched bridges are lined with lights, creating a festive effect as boats glide alongside busy streets.

Tour the land of cuckoo clocks. Tiny villages, mountain meadows and trails through the *Schwarzwald* (Black Forest) await visitors to one of **Germany's** most scenic areas.

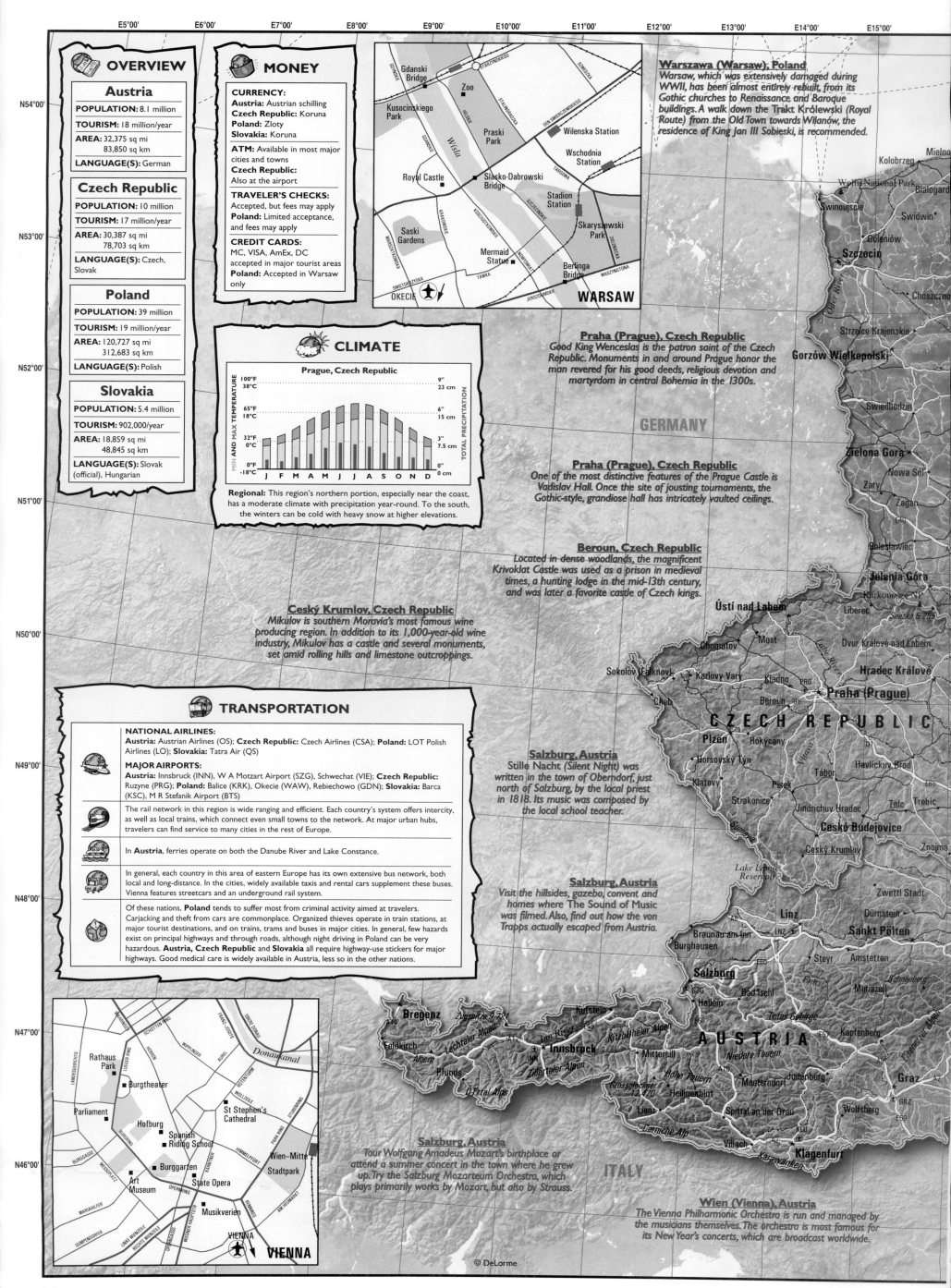

OVERVIEW

Austria
POPULATION: 8.1 million
TOURISM: 18 million/year
AREA: 32,375 sq mi
83,850 sq km
LANGUAGE(S): German

Czech Republic
POPULATION: 10 million
TOURISM: 17 million/year
AREA: 30,387 sq mi
78,703 sq km
LANGUAGE(S): Czech, Slovak

Poland
POPULATION: 39 million
TOURISM: 19 million/year
AREA: 120,727 sq mi
312,683 sq km
LANGUAGE(S): Polish

Slovakia
POPULATION: 5.4 million
TOURISM: 902,000/year
AREA: 18,859 sq mi
48,845 sq km
LANGUAGE(S): Slovak (official), Hungarian

MONEY

CURRENCY:
Austria: Austrian schilling
Czech Republic: Koruna
Poland: Zloty
Slovakia: Koruna

ATM: Available in most major cities and towns
Czech Republic: Also at the airport

TRAVELER'S CHECKS: Accepted, but fees may apply
Poland: Limited acceptance, and fees may apply

CREDIT CARDS: MC, VISA, AmEx, DC accepted in major tourist areas
Poland: Accepted in Warsaw only

CLIMATE

Prague, Czech Republic

Regional: This region's northern portion, especially near the coast, has a moderate climate with precipitation year-round. To the south, the winters can be cold with heavy snow at higher elevations.

TRANSPORTATION

NATIONAL AIRLINES:
Austria: Austrian Airlines (OS); **Czech Republic:** Czech Airlines (CSA); **Poland:** LOT Polish Airlines (LO); **Slovakia:** Tatra Air (QS)

MAJOR AIRPORTS:
Austria: Innsbruck (INN), W A Motzart Airport (SZG), Schwechat (VIE); **Czech Republic:** Ruzyne (PRG); **Poland:** Balice (KRK), Okecie (WAW), Rebiechowo (GDN); **Slovakia:** Barca (KSC), M R Stefanik Airport (BTS)

The rail network in this region is wide ranging and efficient. Each country's system offers intercity, as well as local trains, which connect even small towns to the network. At major urban hubs, travelers can find service to many cities in the rest of Europe.

In **Austria**, ferries operate on both the Danube River and Lake Constance.

In general, each country in this area of eastern Europe has its own extensive bus network, both local and long-distance. In the cities, widely available taxis and rental cars supplement these buses. Vienna features streetcars and an underground rail system.

Of these nations, **Poland** tends to suffer most from criminal activity aimed at travelers. Carjacking and theft from cars are commonplace. Organized thieves operate in train stations, at major tourist destinations, and on trains, trams and buses in major cities. In general, few hazards exist on principal highways and through roads, although night driving in Poland can be very hazardous. **Austria, Czech Republic** and **Slovakia** all require highway-use stickers for major highways. Good medical care is widely available in Austria, less so in the other nations.

WARSAW

Gdanski Bridge · Zoo · Kusocinskiego Park · Praski Park · Wilenska Station · Royal Castle · Slasko-Dabrowski Bridge · Wschodnia Station · Saski Gardens · Stadion Station · Mermaid Statue · Skaryszewski Park · Berlinga Bridge · OKECIE

Warszawa (Warsaw), Poland
Warsaw, which was extensively damaged during WWII, has been almost entirely rebuilt, from its Gothic churches to Renaissance and Baroque buildings. A walk down the Trakt Królewski (Royal Route) from the Old Town towards Wilanów, the residence of King Jan III Sobieski, is recommended.

Praha (Prague), Czech Republic
Good King Wenceslas is the patron saint of the Czech Republic. Monuments in and around Prague honor the man revered for his good deeds, religious devotion and martyrdom in central Bohemia in the 1300s.

Praha (Prague), Czech Republic
One of the most distinctive features of the Prague Castle is Vadislav Hall. Once the site of jousting tournaments, the Gothic-style, grandiose hall has intricately vaulted ceilings.

Beroun, Czech Republic
Located in dense woodlands, the magnificent Krivoklat Castle was used as a prison in medieval times, a hunting lodge in the mid-13th century, and was later a favorite castle of Czech kings.

Cesky Krumlov, Czech Republic
Mikulov is southern Moravia's most famous wine producing region. In addition to its 1,000-year-old wine industry, Mikulov has a castle and several monuments, set amid rolling hills and limestone outcroppings.

Salzburg, Austria
Stille Nacht (Silent Night) was written in the town of Oberndorf, just north of Salzburg, by the local priest in 1818. Its music was composed by the local school teacher.

Salzburg, Austria
Visit the hillsides, gazebo, convent and homes where The Sound of Music was filmed. Also, find out how the von Trapps actually escaped from Austria.

Salzburg, Austria
Tour Wolfgang Amadeus Mozart's birthplace or attend a summer concert in the town where he grew up. Try the Salzburg Mozarteum Orchestra, which plays primarily works by Mozart, but also by Strauss.

Wien (Vienna), Austria
The Vienna Philharmonic Orchestra is run and managed by the musicians themselves. The orchestra is most famous for its New Year's concerts, which are broadcast worldwide.

VIENNA

Rathaus Park · Burgtheater · Parliament · Hofburg · Spanish Riding School · Burggarten · Art Museum · State Opera · Musikverien · St Stephen's Cathedral · Wien-Mitte · Stadtpark · Donaukanal

© DeLorme

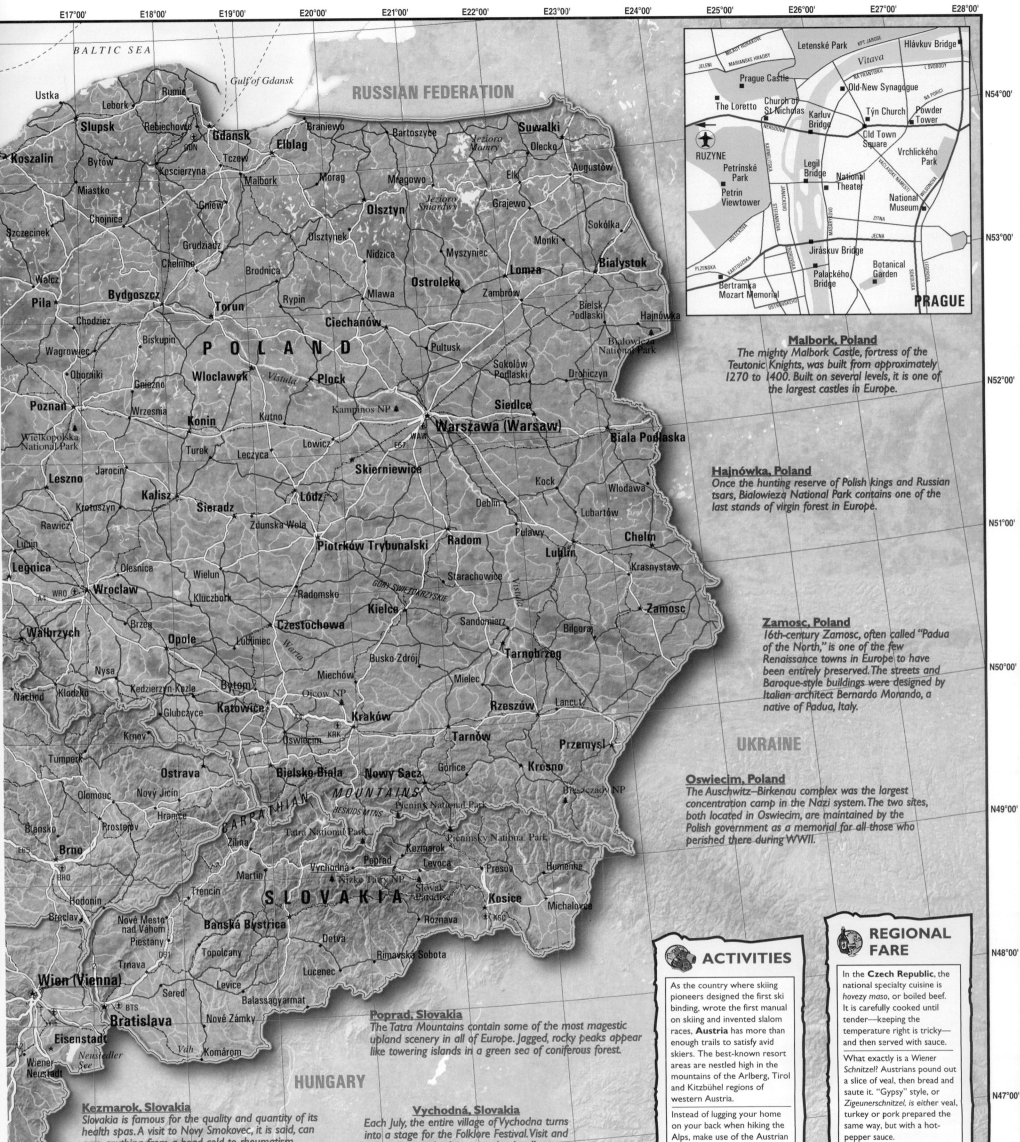

Malbork, Poland
The mighty Malbork Castle, fortress of the Teutonic Knights, was built from approximately 1270 to 1400. Built on several levels, it is one of the largest castles in Europe.

Hajnówka, Poland
Once the hunting reserve of Polish kings and Russian tsars, Bialowieza National Park contains one of the last stands of virgin forest in Europe.

Zamosc, Poland
16th-century Zamosc, often called "Padua of the North," is one of the few Renaissance towns in Europe to have been entirely preserved. The streets and Baroque-style buildings were designed by Italian architect Bernardo Morando, a native of Padua, Italy.

Oswiecim, Poland
The Auschwitz–Birkenau complex was the largest concentration camp in the Nazi system. The two sites, both located in Oswiecim, are maintained by the Polish government as a memorial for all those who perished there during WWII.

Poprad, Slovakia
The Tatra Mountains contain some of the most magestic upland scenery in all of Europe. Jagged, rocky peaks appear like towering islands in a green sea of coniferous forest.

Kezmarok, Slovakia
Slovakia is famous for the quality and quantity of its health spas. A visit to Novy Smokovec, it is said, can cure anything from a head cold to rheumatism.

Vychodná, Slovakia
Each July, the entire village of Vychodna turns into a stage for the Folklore Festival. Visit and you will hear the fujara, or shepherd's pipe, being played; it is one of over 140 instruments used in Slovak folk music.

Wien (Vienna), Austria
Known as "dancing" horses, the Royal Lipizzan Stallions are revered for their ability to dance gracefully on their hind legs. They perform at the Spanish Riding School in Vienna and are bred near Graz in southern Austria.

Levoca, Slovakia
Once one of the largest castles in Europe, Spissky Hrad (Spis Castle) withstood countless attacks between the 11th and 18th centuries. Ironically, it was eventually destroyed by fire. The spectacular ruins that remain date to the 13th century.

ACTIVITIES
As the country where skiing pioneers designed the first ski binding, wrote the first manual on skiing and invented slalom races, **Austria** has more than enough trails to satisfy avid skiers. The best-known resort areas are nestled high in the mountains of the Arlberg, Tirol and Kitzbühel regions of western Austria.

Instead of lugging your home on your back when hiking the Alps, make use of the Austrian hut system. Small cabins are positioned three to four hours apart on many hiking trails. Their presence may add a measure of safety to outings in a potentially harsh mountain climate.

Skiing and hiking are also popular in the spectacular Tatra mountains in **Slovakia**, along the northern border with Poland. For a more leisurely trip into the countryside, visitors can take cruises along the Danube River.

REGIONAL FARE
In the **Czech Republic**, the national specialty cuisine is *hovezy maso*, or boiled beef. It is carefully cooked until tender—keeping the temperature right is tricky—and then served with sauce.

What exactly is a *Wiener Schnitzel?* Austrians pound out a slice of veal, then bread and saute it. "Gypsy" style, or *Zigeunerschnitzel*, is either veal, turkey or pork prepared the same way, but with a hot-pepper sauce.

Slovaks may offer visitors *slanina*, home-smoked bacon and *slivovica*, a very strong plum liquor.

Vodka is a popular beverage in **Poland**, due in part to the many local distilleries. It should be served very cold.

Traditional Polish food is generally delicious and hearty—and highly caloric. Try the native mushroom soup and *pierogis* (dumplings filled with meat, cheese or mushrooms).

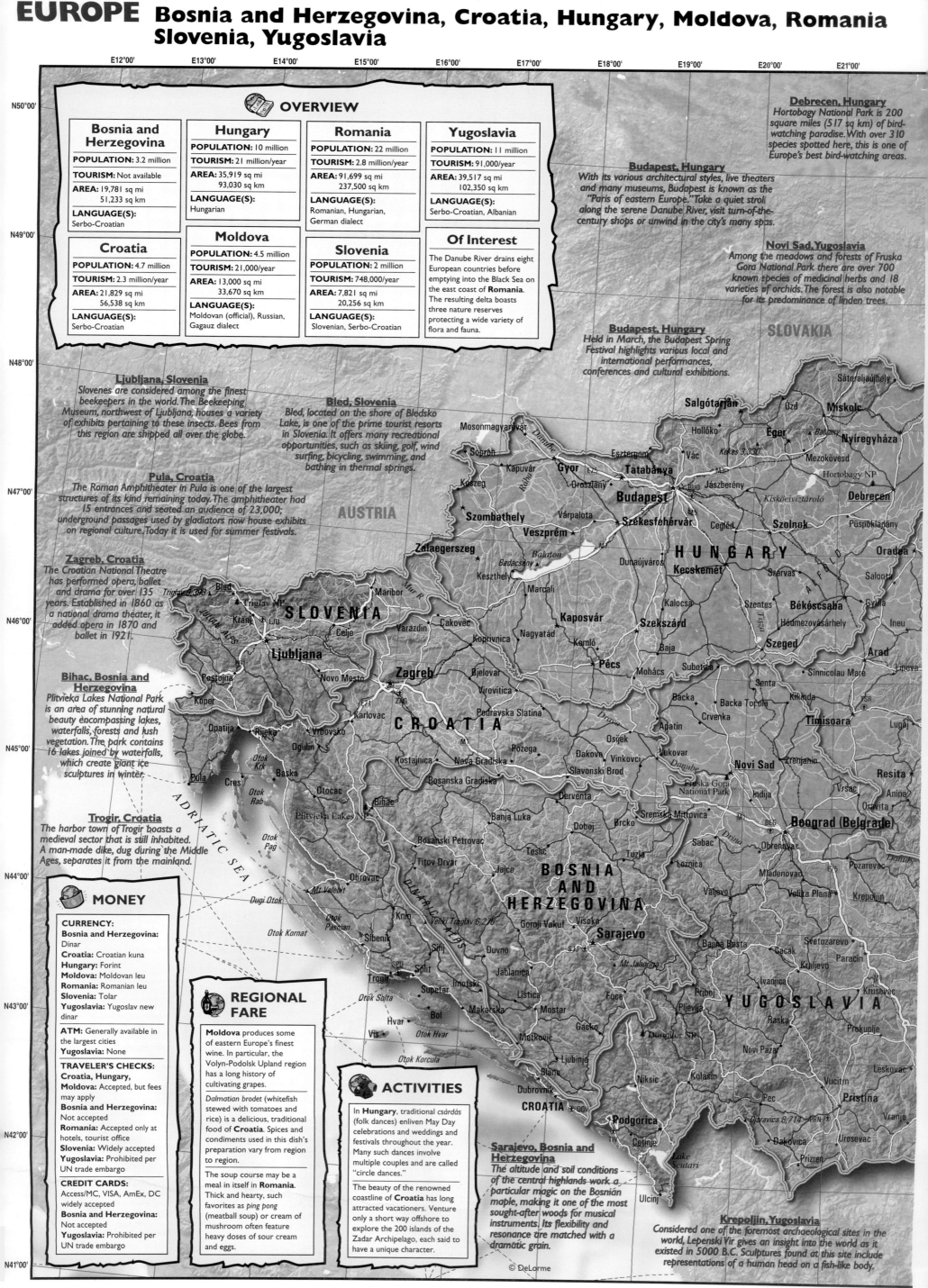

OVERVIEW

Bosnia and Herzegovina
POPULATION: 3.2 million
TOURISM: Not available
AREA: 19,781 sq mi
51,233 sq km
LANGUAGE(S): Serbo-Croatian

Croatia
POPULATION: 4.7 million
TOURISM: 2.3 million/year
AREA: 21,829 sq mi
56,538 sq km
LANGUAGE(S): Serbo-Croatian

Hungary
POPULATION: 10 million
TOURISM: 21 million/year
AREA: 35,919 sq mi
93,030 sq km
LANGUAGE(S): Hungarian

Moldova
POPULATION: 4.5 million
TOURISM: 21,000/year
AREA: 13,000 sq mi
33,670 sq km
LANGUAGE(S): Moldovan (official), Russian, Gagauz dialect

Romania
POPULATION: 22 million
TOURISM: 2.8 million/year
AREA: 91,699 sq mi
237,500 sq km
LANGUAGE(S): Romanian, Hungarian, German dialect

Slovenia
POPULATION: 2 million
TOURISM: 748,000/year
AREA: 7,821 sq mi
20,256 sq km
LANGUAGE(S): Slovenian, Serbo-Croatian

Yugoslavia
POPULATION: 11 million
TOURISM: 91,000/year
AREA: 39,517 sq mi
102,350 sq km
LANGUAGE(S): Serbo-Croatian, Albanian

Of Interest
The Danube River drains eight European countries before emptying into the Black Sea on the east coast of **Romania**. The resulting delta boasts three nature reserves protecting a wide variety of flora and fauna.

Debrecen, Hungary
Hortobagy National Park is 200 square miles (517 sq km) of bird-watching paradise. With over 310 species spotted here, this is one of Europe's best bird-watching areas.

Budapest, Hungary
With its various architectural styles, live theaters and many museums, Budapest is known as the "Paris of eastern Europe." Take a quiet stroll along the serene Danube River, visit turn-of-the-century shops or unwind in the city's many spas.

Novi Sad, Yugoslavia
Among the meadows and forests of Fruska Gora National Park there are over 700 known species of medicinal herbs and 18 varieties of orchids. The forest is also notable for its predominance of linden trees.

Budapest, Hungary
Held in March, the Budapest Spring Festival highlights various local and international performances, conferences and cultural exhibitions.

Ljubljana, Slovenia
Slovenes are considered among the finest beekeepers in the world. The Beekeeping Museum, northwest of Ljubljana, houses a variety of exhibits pertaining to these insects. Bees from this region are shipped all over the globe.

Bled, Slovenia
Bled, located on the shore of Bledsko Lake, is one of the prime tourist resorts in Slovenia. It offers many recreational opportunities, such as skiing, golf, wind surfing, bicycling, swimming, and bathing in thermal springs.

Pula, Croatia
The Roman Amphitheater in Pula is one of the largest structures of its kind remaining today. The amphitheater had 15 entrances and seated an audience of 23,000; underground passages used by gladiators now house exhibits on regional culture. Today it is used for summer festivals.

Zagreb, Croatia
The Croatian National Theatre has performed opera, ballet and drama for over 135 years. Established in 1860 as a national drama theater, it added opera in 1870 and ballet in 1921.

Bihac, Bosnia and Herzegovina
Plitvicka Lakes National Park is an area of stunning natural beauty encompassing lakes, waterfalls, forests and lush vegetation. The park contains 16 lakes joined by waterfalls, which create giant ice sculptures in winter.

Trogir, Croatia
The harbor town of Trogir boasts a medieval sector that is still inhabited. A man-made dike, dug during the Middle Ages, separates it from the mainland.

MONEY

CURRENCY:
Bosnia and Herzegovina: Dinar
Croatia: Croatian kuna
Hungary: Forint
Moldova: Moldovan leu
Romania: Romanian leu
Slovenia: Tolar
Yugoslavia: Yugoslav new dinar

ATM: Generally available in the largest cities
Yugoslavia: None

TRAVELER'S CHECKS:
Croatia, Hungary, Moldova: Accepted, but fees may apply
Bosnia and Herzegovina: Not accepted
Romania: Accepted only at hotels, tourist office
Slovenia: Widely accepted
Yugoslavia: Prohibited per UN trade embargo

CREDIT CARDS:
Access/MC, VISA, AmEx, DC widely accepted
Bosnia and Herzegovina: Not accepted
Yugoslavia: Prohibited per UN trade embargo

REGIONAL FARE

Moldova produces some of eastern Europe's finest wine. In particular, the Volyn-Podolsk Upland region has a long history of cultivating grapes.

Dalmatian brodet (whitefish stewed with tomatoes and rice) is a delicious, traditional food of **Croatia**. Spices and condiments used in this dish's preparation vary from region to region.

The soup course may be a meal in itself in **Romania**. Thick and hearty, such favorites as ping pong (meatball soup) or cream of mushroom often feature heavy doses of sour cream and eggs.

ACTIVITIES

In **Hungary**, traditional csárdás (folk dances) enliven May Day celebrations and weddings and festivals throughout the year. Many such dances involve multiple couples and are called "circle dances."

The beauty of the renowned coastline of **Croatia** has long attracted vacationers. Venture only a short way offshore to explore the 200 islands of the Zadar Archipelago, each said to have a unique character.

Sarajevo, Bosnia and Herzegovina
The altitude and soil conditions of the central highlands work a particular magic on the Bosnian maple, making it one of the most sought-after woods for musical instruments. Its flexibility and resonance are matched with a dramatic grain.

Krepoljin, Yugoslavia
Considered one of the foremost archaeological sites in the world, Lepenski Vir gives an insight into the world as it existed in 5000 B.C. Sculptures found at this site include representations of a human head on a fish-like body.

© DeLorme

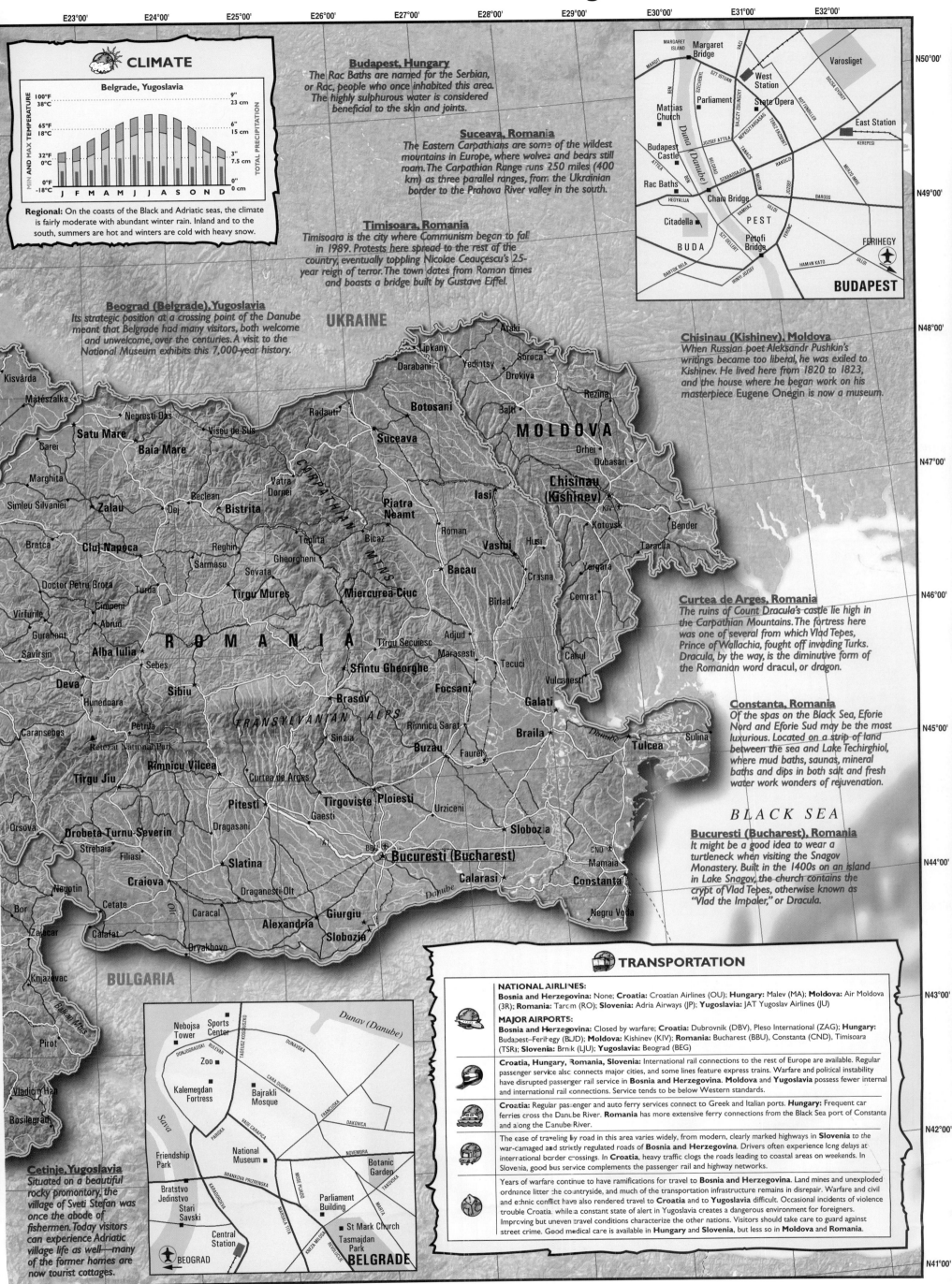

E23°00' E24°00' E25°00' E26°00' E27°00' E28°00' E29°00' E30°00' E31°00' E32°00'

CLIMATE

Belgrade, Yugoslavia

100°F 38°C — 9" 23 cm
65°F 18°C — 6" 15 cm
32°F 0°C — 3" 7.5 cm
0°F -18°C — 0" 0 cm

J F M A M J J A S O N D

MIN AND MAX TEMPERATURE

TOTAL PRECIPITATION

Regional: On the coasts of the Black and Adriatic seas, the climate is fairly moderate with abundant winter rain. Inland and to the south, summers are hot and winters are cold with heavy snow.

Budapest, Hungary
The Rac Baths are named for the Serbian, or Rac, people who once inhabited this area. The highly sulphurous water is considered beneficial to the skin and joints.

Suceava, Romania
The Eastern Carpathians are some of the wildest mountains in Europe, where wolves and bears still roam. The Carpathian Range runs 250 miles (400 km) as three parallel ranges, from the Ukrainian border to the Prahova River valley in the south.

Timisoara, Romania
Timisoara is the city where Communism began to fall in 1989. Protests here spread to the rest of the country, eventually toppling Nicolae Ceauşescu's 25-year reign of terror. The town dates from Roman times and boasts a bridge built by Gustave Eiffel.

Beograd (Belgrade), Yugoslavia
Its strategic position at a crossing point of the Danube meant that Belgrade had many visitors, both welcome and unwelcome, over the centuries. A visit to the National Museum exhibits this 7,000-year history.

Chisinau (Kishinev), Moldova
When Russian poet Aleksandr Pushkin's writings became too liberal, he was exiled to Kishinev. He lived here from 1820 to 1823, and the house where he began work on his masterpiece Eugene Onegin is now a museum.

Curtea de Arges, Romania
The ruins of Count Dracula's castle lie high in the Carpathian Mountains. The fortress here was one of several from which Vlad Tepes, Prince of Wallachia, fought off invading Turks. Dracula, by the way, is the diminutive form of the Romanian word dracul, or dragon.

Constanta, Romania
Of the spas on the Black Sea, Eforie Nord and Eforie Sud may be the most luxurious. Located on a strip of land between the sea and Lake Techirghiol, where mud baths, saunas, mineral baths and dips in both salt and fresh water work wonders of rejuvenation.

BLACK SEA

Bucuresti (Bucharest), Romania
It might be a good idea to wear a turtleneck when visiting the Snagov Monastery. Built in the 1400s on an island in Lake Snagov, the church contains the crypt of Vlad Tepes, otherwise known as "Vlad the Impaler," or Dracula.

BUDAPEST map labels: Margaret Island, Margaret Bridge, Varosliget, West Station, Parliament, State Opera, Mattias Church, Duna Danube, East Station, Budapest Castle, Rac Baths, Chain Bridge, Citadella, PEST, Petofi Bridge, BUDA, FERIHEGY, KEREPESI

UKRAINE

MOLDOVA — Ataki, Lipkany, Darabani, Yedintsy, Soroca, Drokiya, Rezina, Balti, Botosani, Radauti, Suceava, Orhei, Dubasari, Chisinau (Kishinev), Iasi, Roman, Kotovsk, Bender, Vaslui, Husi, Taraclia, Yargara, Crasna, Comrat, Cahul

MOLDOVA: Kisvárda, Mátészalka, Negresti-Oas, Viseu de Sus, Satu Mare, Baia Mare, Carei, Marghita, Simleu Silvaniei, Zalau, Dej, Beclean, Bistrita, Vatra Dornei, Piatra Neamt, Bacau, Bratca, Cluj-Napoca, Reghin, Teplita, Bicaz, Sarmasu, Gheorgheni, Doctor Petru Broza, Turda, Tirgu Mures, Miercurea-Ciuc, Sovata, Virfurile, Cimpeni, Abrud, Alba Iulia, Adjud, Tirgu Secuiesc, Marasesti, Tecuci, Gurahont, Sebes, Sfintu Gheorghe, Savirsin, Deva, Sibiu, Brasov, Focsani, Galati, Hunedoara, TRANSYLVANIAN ALPS, Rimnicu Sarat, Braila, Petrila, Sinaia, Buzau, Faurei, Tulcea, Sulina, Retezat National Park, Caransebes, Rimnicu Vilcea, Tirgu Jiu, Curtea de Arges, Tirgoviste, Ploiesti, Urziceni, Slobozia, Orsova, Drobeta-Turnu-Severin, Dragasani, Pitesti, Gaesti, Mamaia, Strehaia, Filiasi, Slatina, Bucuresti (Bucharest), Constanta, Negotin, Slatina, Draganesti-Olt, Calarasi, Bor, Cetate, Craiova, Caracal, Giurgiu, Negru Voda, Zajecar, Calafat, Alexandria, Slobozia, Oryakhovo

ROMANIA

CARPATHIAN MTNS

BULGARIA

Knjazevac, Pirot, Balkan Mtns, Vladicin Han, Bosilegrad

Cetinje, Yugoslavia
Situated on a beautiful rocky promontory, the village of Sveti Stefan was once the abode of fishermen. Today visitors can experience Adriatic village life as well—many of the former homes are now tourist cottages.

BELGRADE map: Dunav (Danube), Nebojsa Tower, Sports Center, Zoo, Kalemegdan Fortress, Bajrakli Mosque, Sava, Friendship Park, National Museum, Botanic Garden, Bratstvo Jedinstvo Stari Savski, Parliament Building, Central Station, St Mark Church, Tasmajdan Park, BEOGRAD

TRANSPORTATION

NATIONAL AIRLINES:
Bosnia and Herzegovina: None; **Croatia:** Croatian Airlines (OU); **Hungary:** Malev (MA); **Moldova:** Air Moldova (3R); **Romania:** Tarom (RO); **Slovenia:** Adria Airways (JP); **Yugoslavia:** JAT Yugoslav Airlines (JU)

MAJOR AIRPORTS:
Bosnia and Herzegovina: Closed by warfare; **Croatia:** Dubrovnik (DBV), Pleso International (ZAG); **Hungary:** Budapest–Ferihegy (BUD); **Moldova:** Kishinev (KIV); **Romania:** Bucharest (BBU), Constanta (CND), Timisoara (TSR); **Slovenia:** Brnik (LJU); **Yugoslavia:** Beograd (BEG)

Croatia, Hungary, Romania, Slovenia: International rail connections to the rest of Europe are available. Regular passenger service also connects major cities, and some lines feature express trains. Warfare and political instability have disrupted passenger rail service in **Bosnia and Herzegovina. Moldova** and **Yugoslavia** possess fewer internal and international rail connections. Service tends to be below Western standards.

Croatia: Regular passenger and auto ferry services connect to Greek and Italian ports. **Hungary:** Frequent car ferries cross the Danube River. **Romania** has more extensive ferry connections from the Black Sea port of Constanta and along the Danube River.

The ease of traveling by road in this area varies widely, from modern, clearly marked highways in **Slovenia** to the war-damaged and strictly regulated roads of **Bosnia and Herzegovina.** Drivers often experience long delays at international border crossings. In **Croatia,** heavy traffic clogs the roads leading to coastal areas on weekends. In Slovenia, good bus service complements the passenger rail and highway networks.

Years of warfare continue to have ramifications for travel to **Bosnia and Herzegovina.** Land mines and unexploded ordnance litter the countryside, and much of the transportation infrastructure remains in disrepair. Warfare and civil and ethnic conflict have also rendered travel to **Croatia** and to **Yugoslavia** difficult. Occasional incidents of violence trouble Croatia, while a constant state of alert in Yugoslavia creates a dangerous environment for foreigners. Improving but uneven travel conditions characterize the other nations. Visitors should take care to guard against street crime. Good medical care is available in **Hungary** and **Slovenia,** but less so in **Moldova** and **Romania.**

N50°00'
N49°00'
N48°00'
N47°00'
N46°00'
N45°00'
N44°00'
N43°00'
N42°00'
N41°00'

MILES 0 25 50 75 100
KILOMETERS 0 25 50 75 100 125 150

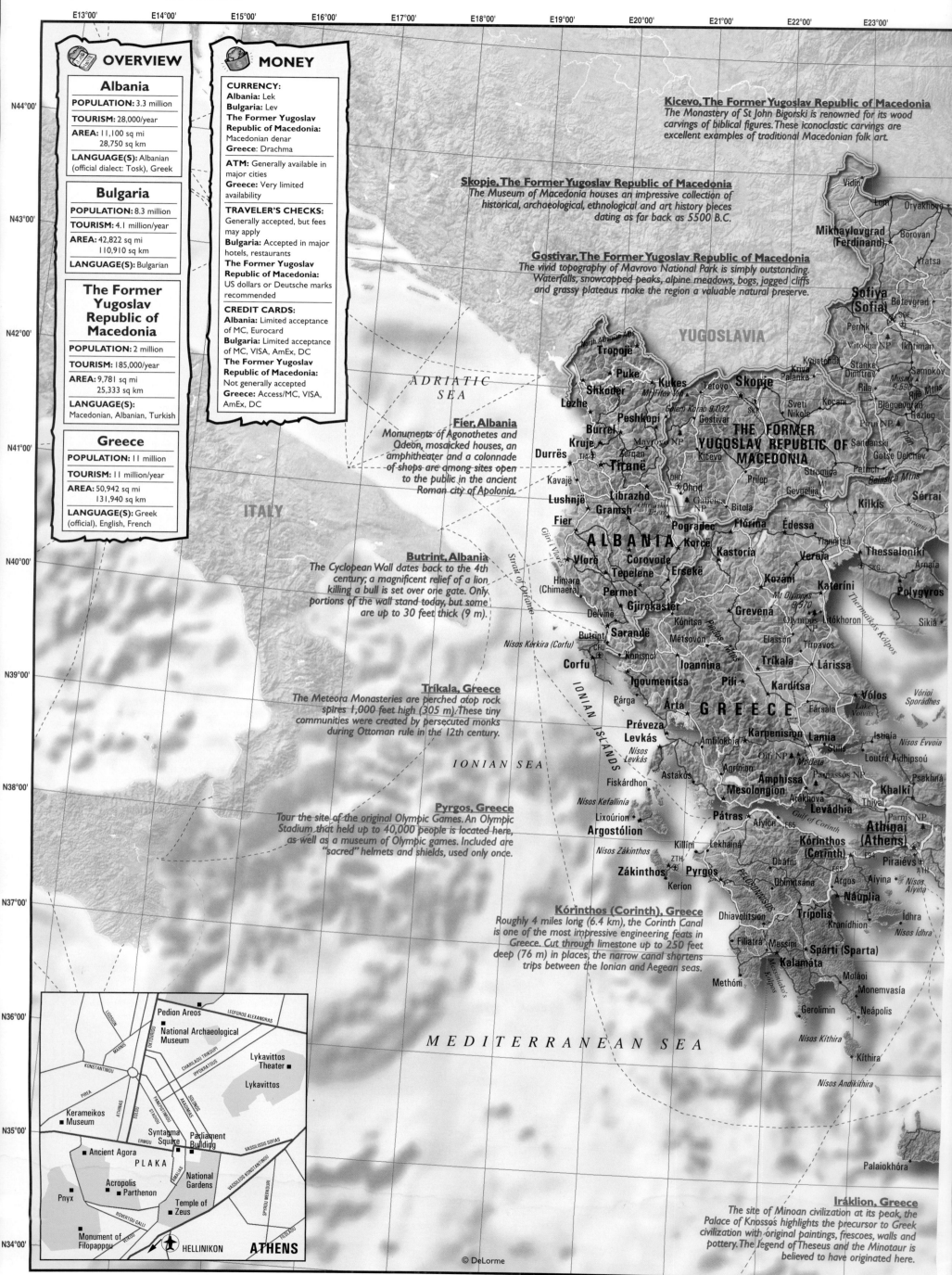

OVERVIEW

Albania
POPULATION: 3.3 million
TOURISM: 28,000/year
AREA: 11,100 sq mi
28,750 sq km
LANGUAGE(S): Albanian
(official dialect: Tosk), Greek

Bulgaria
POPULATION: 8.3 million
TOURISM: 4.1 million/year
AREA: 42,822 sq mi
110,910 sq km
LANGUAGE(S): Bulgarian

The Former Yugoslav Republic of Macedonia
POPULATION: 2 million
TOURISM: 185,000/year
AREA: 9,781 sq mi
25,333 sq km
LANGUAGE(S): Macedonian, Albanian, Turkish

Greece
POPULATION: 11 million
TOURISM: 11 million/year
AREA: 50,942 sq mi
131,940 sq km
LANGUAGE(S): Greek (official), English, French

MONEY

CURRENCY:
Albania: Lek
Bulgaria: Lev
The Former Yugoslav Republic of Macedonia: Macedonian denar
Greece: Drachma

ATM: Generally available in major cities
Greece: Very limited availability

TRAVELER'S CHECKS: Generally accepted, but fees may apply
Bulgaria: Accepted in major hotels, restaurants
The Former Yugoslav Republic of Macedonia: US dollars or Deutsche marks recommended

CREDIT CARDS:
Albania: Limited acceptance of MC, Eurocard
Bulgaria: Limited acceptance of MC, VISA, AmEx, DC
The Former Yugoslav Republic of Macedonia: Not generally accepted
Greece: Access/MC, VISA, AmEx, DC

Kicevo, The Former Yugoslav Republic of Macedonia
The Monastery of St John Bigorski is renowned for its wood carvings of biblical figures. These iconoclastic carvings are excellent examples of traditional Macedonian folk art.

Skopje, The Former Yugoslav Republic of Macedonia
The Museum of Macedonia houses an impressive collection of historical, archaeological, ethnological and art history pieces dating as far back as 5500 B.C.

Gostivar, The Former Yugoslav Republic of Macedonia
The vivid topography of Mavrovo National Park is simply outstanding. Waterfalls, snowcapped peaks, alpine meadows, bogs, jagged cliffs and grassy plateaus make the region a valuable natural preserve.

Fier, Albania
Monuments of Agonothetes and Odeon, mosaicked houses, an amphitheater and a colonnade of shops are among sites open to the public in the ancient Roman city of Apolonia.

Butrint, Albania
The Cyclopean Wall dates back to the 4th century; a magnificent relief of a lion killing a bull is set over one gate. Only portions of the wall stand today, but some are up to 30 feet thick (9 m).

Trikala, Greece
The Meteora Monasteries are perched atop rock spires 1,000 feet high (305 m). These tiny communities were created by persecuted monks during Ottoman rule in the 12th century.

Pyrgos, Greece
Tour the site of the original Olympic Games. An Olympic Stadium that held up to 40,000 people is located here, as well as a museum of Olympic games. Included are "sacred" helmets and shields, used only once.

Kórinthos (Corinth), Greece
Roughly 4 miles long (6.4 km), the Corinth Canal is one of the most impressive engineering feats in Greece. Cut through limestone up to 250 feet deep (76 m) in places, the narrow canal shortens trips between the Ionian and Aegean seas.

Iráklion, Greece
The site of Minoan civilization at its peak, the Palace of Knossos highlights the precursor to Greek civilization with original paintings, frescoes, walls and pottery. The legend of Theseus and the Minotaur is believed to have originated here.

ADRIATIC SEA

ITALY

IONIAN SEA

MEDITERRANEAN SEA

YUGOSLAVIA

THE FORMER YUGOSLAV REPUBLIC OF MACEDONIA

ALBANIA

GREECE

IONIAN ISLANDS

Strait of Otranto

ATHENS

Pedion Areos
National Archaeological Museum
Lykavittos Theater
Lykavittos
Kerameikos Museum
Syntagma Square
Parliament Building
Ancient Agora
PLAKA
Acropolis
Parthenon
Pnyx
National Gardens
Temple of Zeus
Monument of Filopappou
HELLINIKON

© DeLorme

Scale 1:3,500,000 at map center

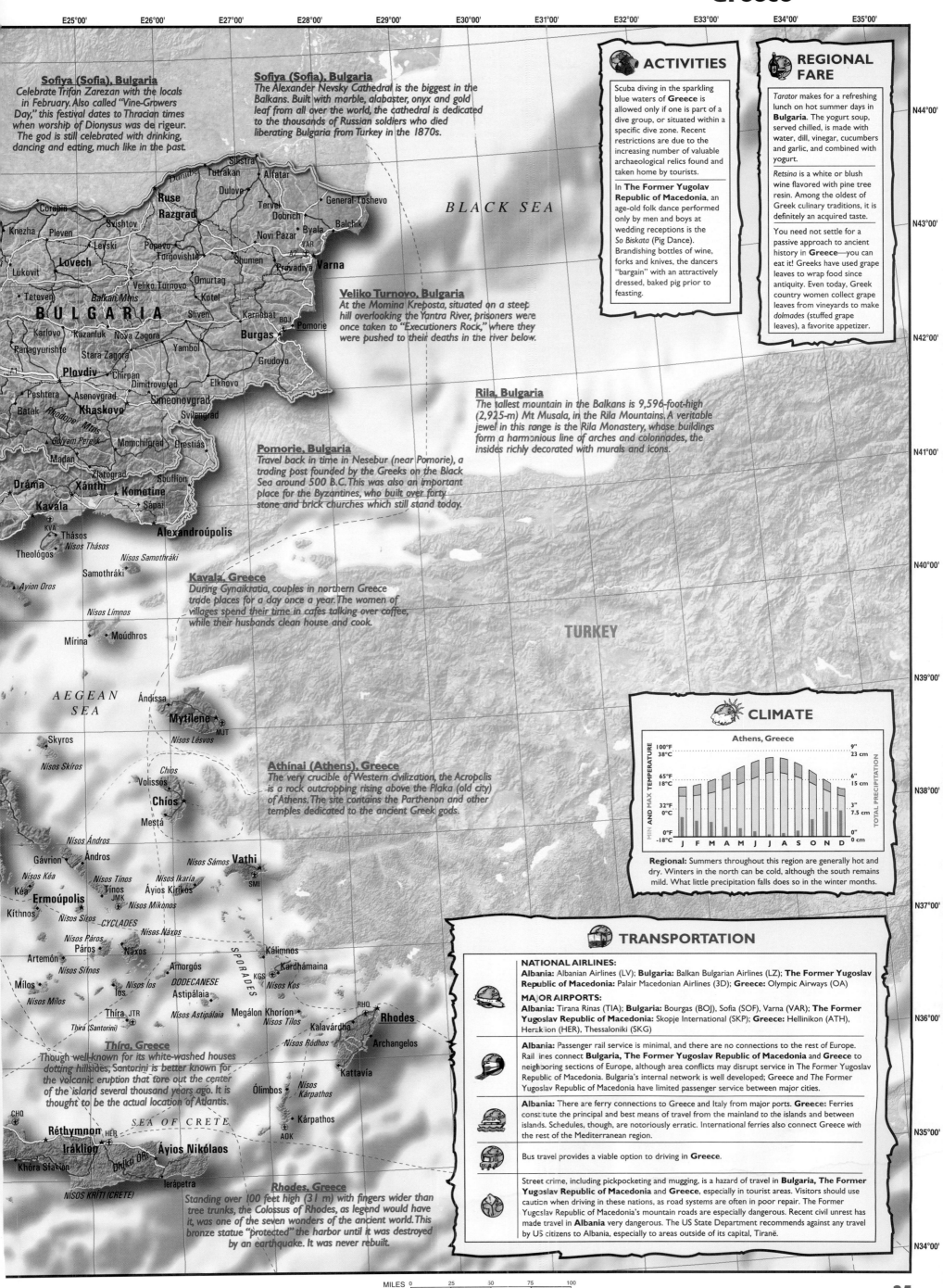

Sofiya (Sofia), Bulgaria
Celebrate Trifon Zarezan with the locals in February. Also called "Vine-Growers Day," this festival dates to Thracian times when worship of Dionysus was de rigeur. The god is still celebrated with drinking, dancing and eating, much like in the past.

Sofiya (Sofia), Bulgaria
The Alexander Nevsky Cathedral is the biggest in the Balkans. Built with marble, alabaster, onyx and gold leaf from all over the world, the cathedral is dedicated to the thousands of Russian soldiers who died liberating Bulgaria from Turkey in the 1870s.

Veliko Turnovo, Bulgaria
At the Momina Kreposta, situated on a steep hill overlooking the Yantra River, prisoners were once taken to "Executioners Rock," where they were pushed to their deaths in the river below.

Rila, Bulgaria
The tallest mountain in the Balkans is 9,596-foot-high (2,925-m) Mt Musala, in the Rila Mountains. A veritable jewel in this range is the Rila Monastery, whose buildings form a harmonious line of arches and colonnades, the insides richly decorated with murals and icons.

Pomorie, Bulgaria
Travel back in time in Nesebur (near Pomorie), a trading post founded by the Greeks on the Black Sea around 500 B.C. This was also an important place for the Byzantines, who built over forty stone and brick churches which still stand today.

Kavala, Greece
During Gynaikratia, couples in northern Greece trade places for a day once a year. The women of villages spend their time in cafes talking over coffee, while their husbands clean house and cook.

Athínai (Athens), Greece
The very crucible of Western civilization, the Acropolis is a rock outcropping rising above the Plaka (old city) of Athens. The site contains the Parthenon and other temples dedicated to the ancient Greek gods.

Thíra, Greece
Though well-known for its white-washed houses dotting hillsides, Santorini is better known for the volcanic eruption that tore out the center of the island several thousand years ago. It is thought to be the actual location of Atlantis.

Rhodes, Greece
Standing over 100 feet high (31 m) with fingers wider than tree trunks, the Colossus of Rhodes, as legend would have it, was one of the seven wonders of the ancient world. This bronze statue "protected" the harbor until it was destroyed by an earthquake. It was never rebuilt.

ACTIVITIES

Scuba diving in the sparkling blue waters of **Greece** is allowed only if one is part of a dive group, or situated within a specific dive zone. Recent restrictions are due to the increasing number of valuable archaeological relics found and taken home by tourists.

In **The Former Yugoslav Republic of Macedonia**, an age-old folk dance performed only by men and boys at wedding receptions is the So Biskata (Pig Dance). Brandishing bottles of wine, forks and knives, the dancers "bargain" with an attractively dressed, baked pig prior to feasting.

REGIONAL FARE

Tarator makes for a refreshing lunch on hot summer days in **Bulgaria**. The yogurt soup, served chilled, is made with water, dill, vinegar, cucumbers and garlic, and combined with yogurt.

Retsina is a white or blush wine flavored with pine tree resin. Among the oldest of Greek culinary traditions, it is definitely an acquired taste.

You need not settle for a passive approach to ancient history in **Greece**—you can eat it! Greeks have used grape leaves to wrap food since antiquity. Even today, Greek country women collect grape leaves from vineyards to make dolmades (stuffed grape leaves), a favorite appetizer.

CLIMATE

Athens, Greece

Regional: Summers throughout this region are generally hot and dry. Winters in the north can be cold, although the south remains mild. What little precipitation falls does so in the winter months.

TRANSPORTATION

NATIONAL AIRLINES:
Albania: Albanian Airlines (LV); **Bulgaria:** Balkan Bulgarian Airlines (LZ); **The Former Yugoslav Republic of Macedonia:** Palair Macedonian Airlines (3D); **Greece:** Olympic Airways (OA)

MAJOR AIRPORTS:
Albania: Tirana Rinas (TIA); **Bulgaria:** Bourgas (BOJ), Sofia (SOF), Varna (VAR); **The Former Yugoslav Republic of Macedonia:** Skopje International (SKP); **Greece:** Hellinikon (ATH), Heraklion (HER), Thessaloniki (SKG)

Albania: Passenger rail service is minimal, and there are no connections to the rest of Europe. Rail lines connect **Bulgaria, The Former Yugoslav Republic of Macedonia** and **Greece** to neighboring sections of Europe, although area conflicts may disrupt service in The Former Yugoslav Republic of Macedonia. Bulgaria's internal network is well developed; Greece and The Former Yugoslav Republic of Macedonia have limited passenger service between major cities.

Albania: There are ferry connections to Greece and Italy from major ports. **Greece:** Ferries constitute the principal and best means of travel from the mainland to the islands and between islands. Schedules, though, are notoriously erratic. International ferries also connect Greece with the rest of the Mediterranean region.

Bus travel provides a viable option to driving in **Greece**.

Street crime, including pickpocketing and mugging, is a hazard of travel in **Bulgaria, The Former Yugoslav Republic of Macedonia** and **Greece**, especially in tourist areas. Visitors should use caution when driving in these nations, as road systems are often in poor repair. The Former Yugoslav Republic of Macedonia's mountain roads are especially dangerous. Recent civil unrest has made travel in **Albania** very dangerous. The US State Department recommends against any travel by US citizens to Albania, especially to areas outside of its capital, Tiranë.

EUROPE Belarus, Estonia, Latvia, Lithuania, Ukraine

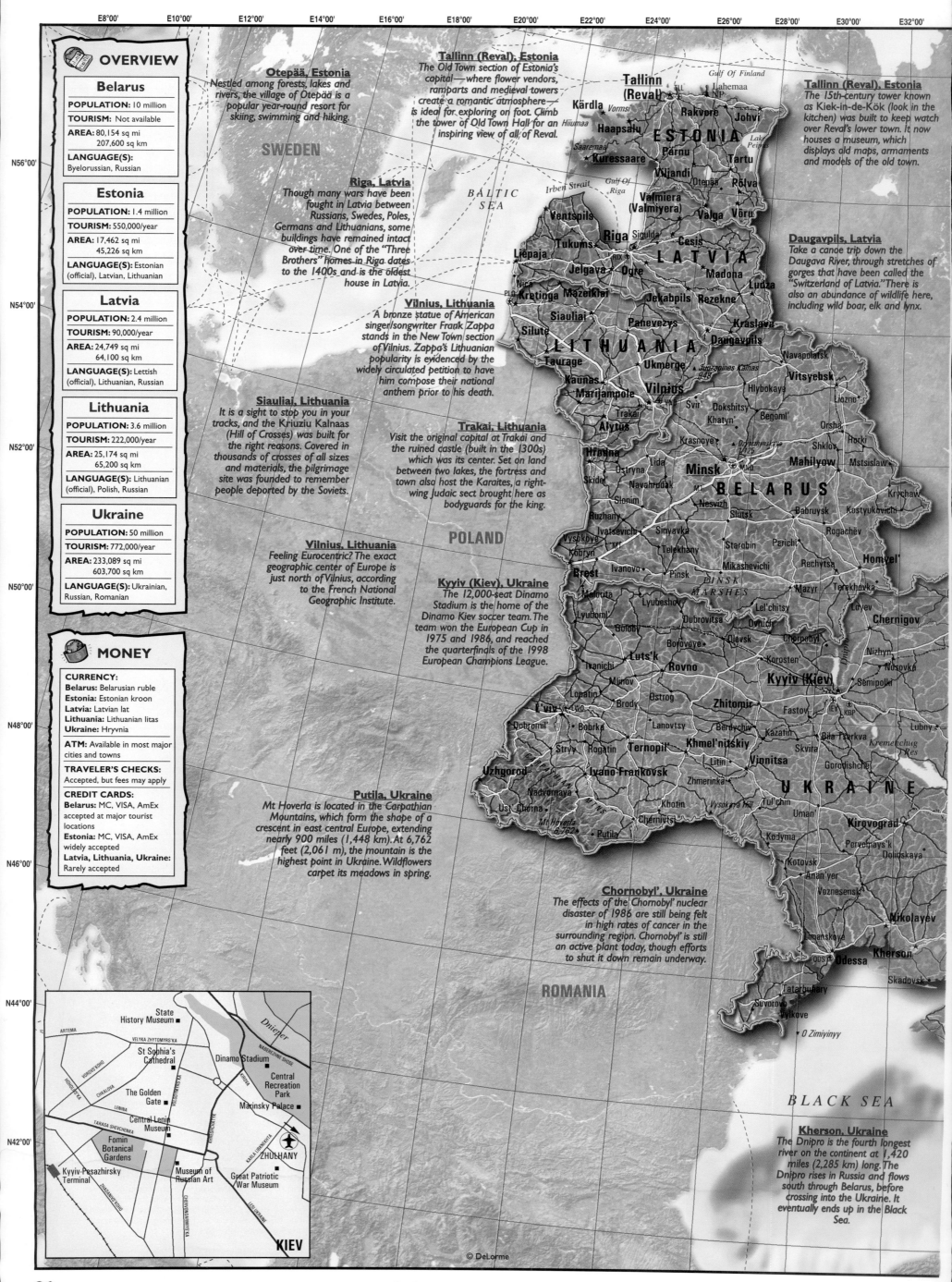

OVERVIEW

Belarus
POPULATION: 10 million
TOURISM: Not available
AREA: 80,154 sq mi
203,600 sq km
LANGUAGE(S):
Byelorussian, Russian

Estonia
POPULATION: 1.4 million
TOURISM: 550,000/year
AREA: 17,462 sq mi
45,226 sq km
LANGUAGE(S): Estonian
(official), Latvian, Lithuanian

Latvia
POPULATION: 2.4 million
TOURISM: 90,000/year
AREA: 24,749 sq mi
64,100 sq km
LANGUAGE(S): Lettish
(official), Lithuanian, Russian

Lithuania
POPULATION: 3.6 million
TOURISM: 222,000/year
AREA: 25,174 sq mi
65,200 sq km
LANGUAGE(S): Lithuanian
(official), Polish, Russian

Ukraine
POPULATION: 50 million
TOURISM: 772,000/year
AREA: 233,089 sq mi
603,700 sq km
LANGUAGE(S): Ukrainian,
Russian, Romanian

MONEY

CURRENCY:
Belarus: Belarusian ruble
Estonia: Estonian kroon
Latvia: Latvian lat
Lithuania: Lithuanian litas
Ukraine: Hryvnia

ATM: Available in most major
cities and towns

TRAVELER'S CHECKS:
Accepted, but fees may apply

CREDIT CARDS:
Belarus: MC, VISA, AmEx
accepted at major tourist
locations
Estonia: MC, VISA, AmEx
widely accepted
Latvia, Lithuania, Ukraine:
Rarely accepted

Otepää, Estonia
Nestled among forests, lakes and
rivers, the village of Otepää is a
popular year-round resort for
skiing, swimming and hiking.

Tallinn (Reval), Estonia
The Old Town section of Estonia's
capital—where flower vendors,
ramparts and medieval towers
create a romantic atmosphere—
is ideal for exploring on foot. Climb
the tower of Old Town Hall for an
inspiring view of all of Reval.

Tallinn (Reval), Estonia
The 15th-century tower known
as Kiek-in-de-Kök (look in the
kitchen) was built to keep watch
over Reval's lower town. It now
houses a museum, which
displays old maps, armaments
and models of the old town.

Riga, Latvia
Though many wars have been
fought in Latvia between
Russians, Swedes, Poles,
Germans and Lithuanians, some
buildings have remained intact
over time. One of the "Three
Brothers" homes in Riga dates
to the 1400s and is the oldest
house in Latvia.

Vilnius, Lithuania
A bronze statue of American
singer/songwriter Frank Zappa
stands in the New Town section
of Vilnius. Zappa's Lithuanian
popularity is evidenced by the
widely circulated petition to have
him compose their national
anthem prior to his death.

Daugavpils, Latvia
Take a canoe trip down the
Daugava River, through stretches of
gorges that have been called the
"Switzerland of Latvia." There is
also an abundance of wildlife here,
including wild boar, elk and lynx.

Siauliai, Lithuania
It is a sight to stop you in your
tracks, and the Kriuziu Kalnaas
(Hill of Crosses) was built for
the right reasons. Covered in
thousands of crosses of all sizes
and materials, the pilgrimage
site was founded to remember
people deported by the Soviets.

Trakai, Lithuania
Visit the original capital at Trakai and
the ruined castle (built in the 1300s)
which was its center. Set on land
between two lakes, the fortress and
town also host the Karaites, a right-
wing Judaic sect brought here as
bodyguards for the king.

Vilnius, Lithuania
Feeling Eurocentric? The exact
geographic center of Europe is
just north of Vilnius, according
to the French National
Geographic Institute.

Kyiv (Kiev), Ukraine
The 12,000-seat Dinamo
Stadium is the home of the
Dinamo Kiev soccer team. The
team won the European Cup in
1975 and 1986, and reached
the quarterfinals of the 1998
European Champions League.

Putila, Ukraine
Mt Hoverla is located in the Carpathian
Mountains, which form the shape of a
crescent in east central Europe, extending
nearly 900 miles (1,448 km). At 6,762
feet (2,061 m), the mountain is the
highest point in Ukraine. Wildflowers
carpet its meadows in spring.

Chornobyl', Ukraine
The effects of the Chornobyl' nuclear
disaster of 1986 are still being felt
in high rates of cancer in the
surrounding region. Chornobyl' is still
an active plant today, though efforts
to shut it down remain underway.

Kherson, Ukraine
The Dnipro is the fourth longest
river on the continent at 1,420
miles (2,285 km) long. The
Dnipro rises in Russia and flows
south through Belarus, before
crossing into the Ukraine. It
eventually ends up in the Black
Sea.

SWEDEN

BALTIC SEA

POLAND

ROMANIA

BLACK SEA

ESTONIA
LATVIA
LITHUANIA
BELARUS
UKRAINE

KIEV

© DeLorme

Scale 1:6,000,000 at map center

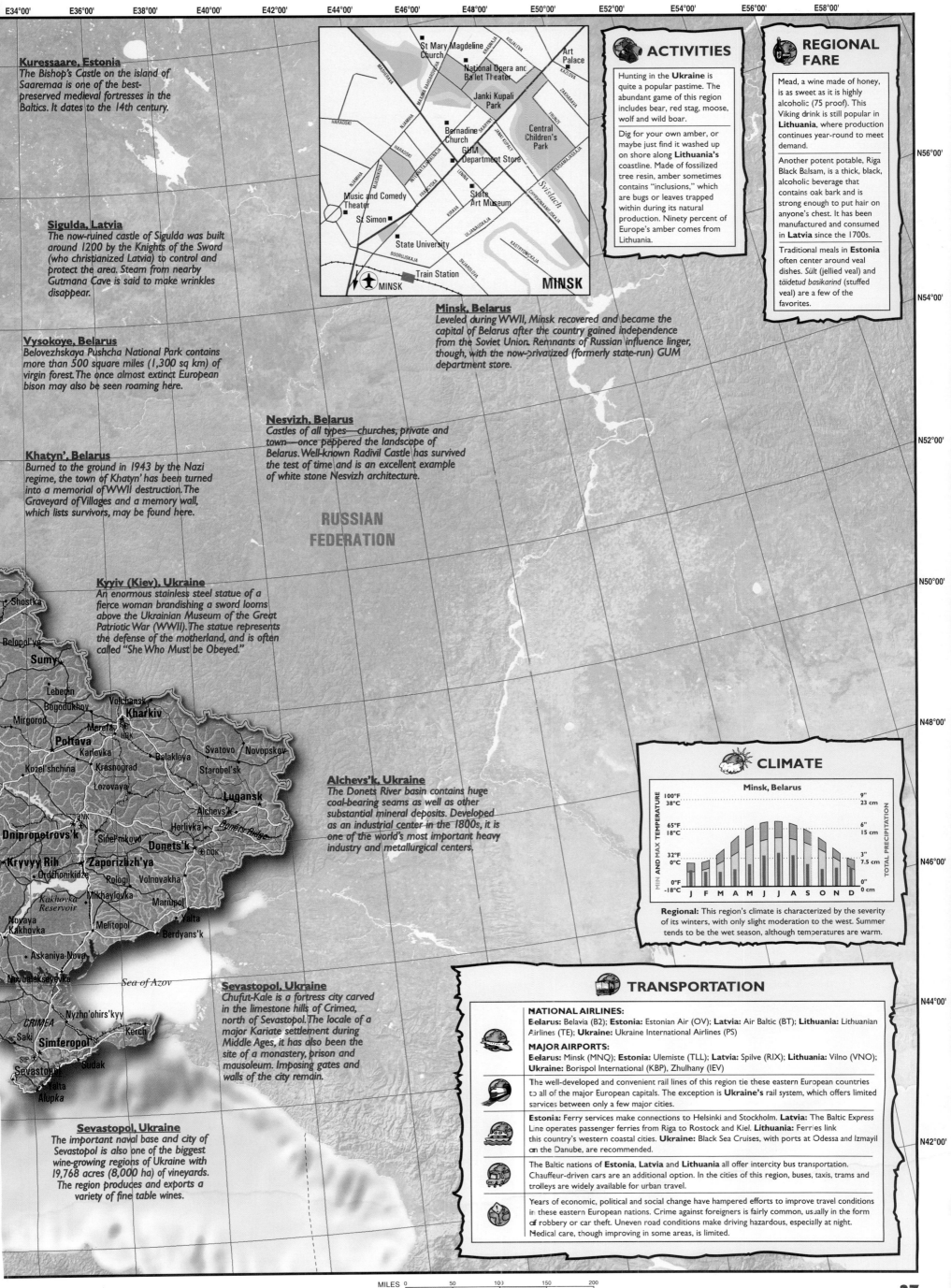

Kuressaare, Estonia
The Bishop's Castle on the island of Saaremaa is one of the best-preserved medieval fortresses in the Baltics. It dates to the 14th century.

Sigulda, Latvia
The now-ruined castle of Sigulda was built around 1200 by the Knights of the Sword (who christianized Latvia) to control and protect the area. Steam from nearby Gutmana Cave is said to make wrinkles disappear.

Vysokoye, Belarus
Belovezhskaya Pushcha National Park contains more than 500 square miles (1,300 sq km) of virgin forest. The once almost extinct European bison may also be seen roaming here.

Khatyn', Belarus
Burned to the ground in 1943 by the Nazi regime, the town of Khatyn' has been turned into a memorial of WWII destruction. The Graveyard of Villages and a memory wall, which lists survivors, may be found here.

Kyyiv (Kiev), Ukraine
An enormous stainless steel statue of a fierce woman brandishing a sword looms above the Ukrainian Museum of the Great Patriotic War (WWII). The statue represents the defense of the motherland, and is often called "She Who Must be Obeyed."

Alchevs'k, Ukraine
The Donets River basin contains huge coal-bearing seams as well as other substantial mineral deposits. Developed as an industrial center in the 1800s, it is one of the world's most important heavy industry and metallurgical centers.

Sevastopol, Ukraine
Chufut-Kale is a fortress city carved in the limestone hills of Crimea, north of Sevastopol. The locale of a major Kariate settlement during Middle Ages, it has also been the site of a monastery, prison and mausoleum. Imposing gates and walls of the city remain.

Sevastopol, Ukraine
The important naval base and city of Sevastopol is also one of the biggest wine-growing regions of Ukraine with 19,768 acres (8,000 ha) of vineyards. The region produces and exports a variety of fine table wines.

Minsk, Belarus
Leveled during WWII, Minsk recovered and became the capital of Belarus after the country gained independence from the Soviet Union. Remnants of Russian influence linger, though, with the now-privatized (formerly state-run) GUM department store.

Nesvizh, Belarus
Castles of all types—churches, private and town—once peppered the landscape of Belarus. Well-known Radivil Castle has survived the test of time and is an excellent example of white stone Nesvizh architecture.

RUSSIAN FEDERATION

MINSK

St Mary Magdeline Church • National Opera and Ballet Theater • Janki Kupali Park • Art Palace • Bernadine Church • GUM Department Store • Central Children's Park • Music and Comedy Theater • St Simon • State Art Museum • State University • Train Station • MINSK

ACTIVITIES
Hunting in the **Ukraine** is quite a popular pastime. The abundant game of this region includes bear, red stag, moose, wolf and wild boar.

Dig for your own amber, or maybe just find it washed up on shore along **Lithuania's** coastline. Made of fossilized tree resin, amber sometimes contains "inclusions," which are bugs or leaves trapped within during its natural production. Ninety percent of Europe's amber comes from Lithuania.

REGIONAL FARE
Mead, a wine made of honey, is as sweet as it is highly alcoholic (75 proof). This Viking drink is still popular in **Lithuania**, where production continues year-round to meet demand.

Another potent potable, Riga Black Balsam, is a thick, black, alcoholic beverage that contains oak bark and is strong enough to put hair on anyone's chest. It has been manufactured and consumed in **Latvia** since the 1700s.

Traditional meals in **Estonia** often center around veal dishes. *Sült* (jellied veal) and *täidetud basikarind* (stuffed veal) are a few of the favorites.

CLIMATE
Minsk, Belarus

Regional: This region's climate is characterized by the severity of its winters, with only slight moderation to the west. Summer tends to be the wet season, although temperatures are warm.

TRANSPORTATION
NATIONAL AIRLINES:
Belarus: Belavia (B2); **Estonia:** Estonian Air (OV); **Latvia:** Air Baltic (BT); **Lithuania:** Lithuanian Airlines (TE); **Ukraine:** Ukraine International Airlines (PS)

MAJOR AIRPORTS:
Belarus: Minsk (MNQ); **Estonia:** Ulemiste (TLL); **Latvia:** Spilve (RIX); **Lithuania:** Vilno (VNO); **Ukraine:** Borispol International (KBP), Zhulhany (IEV)

The well-developed and convenient rail lines of this region tie these eastern European countries to all of the major European capitals. The exception is **Ukraine's** rail system, which offers limited services between only a few major cities.

Estonia: Ferry services make connections to Helsinki and Stockholm. **Latvia:** The Baltic Express Line operates passenger ferries from Riga to Rostock and Kiel. **Lithuania:** Ferries link this country's western coastal cities. **Ukraine:** Black Sea Cruises, with ports at Odessa and Izmayil on the Danube, are recommended.

The Baltic nations of **Estonia, Latvia** and **Lithuania** all offer intercity bus transportation. Chauffeur-driven cars are an additional option. In the cities of this region, buses, taxis, trams and trolleys are widely available for urban travel.

Years of economic, political and social change have hampered efforts to improve travel conditions in these eastern European nations. Crime against foreigners is fairly common, usually in the form of robbery or car theft. Uneven road conditions make driving hazardous, especially at night. Medical care, though improving in some areas, is limited.

MILES 0 50 100 150 200
KILOMETERS 0 50 100 150 200 250 300

27

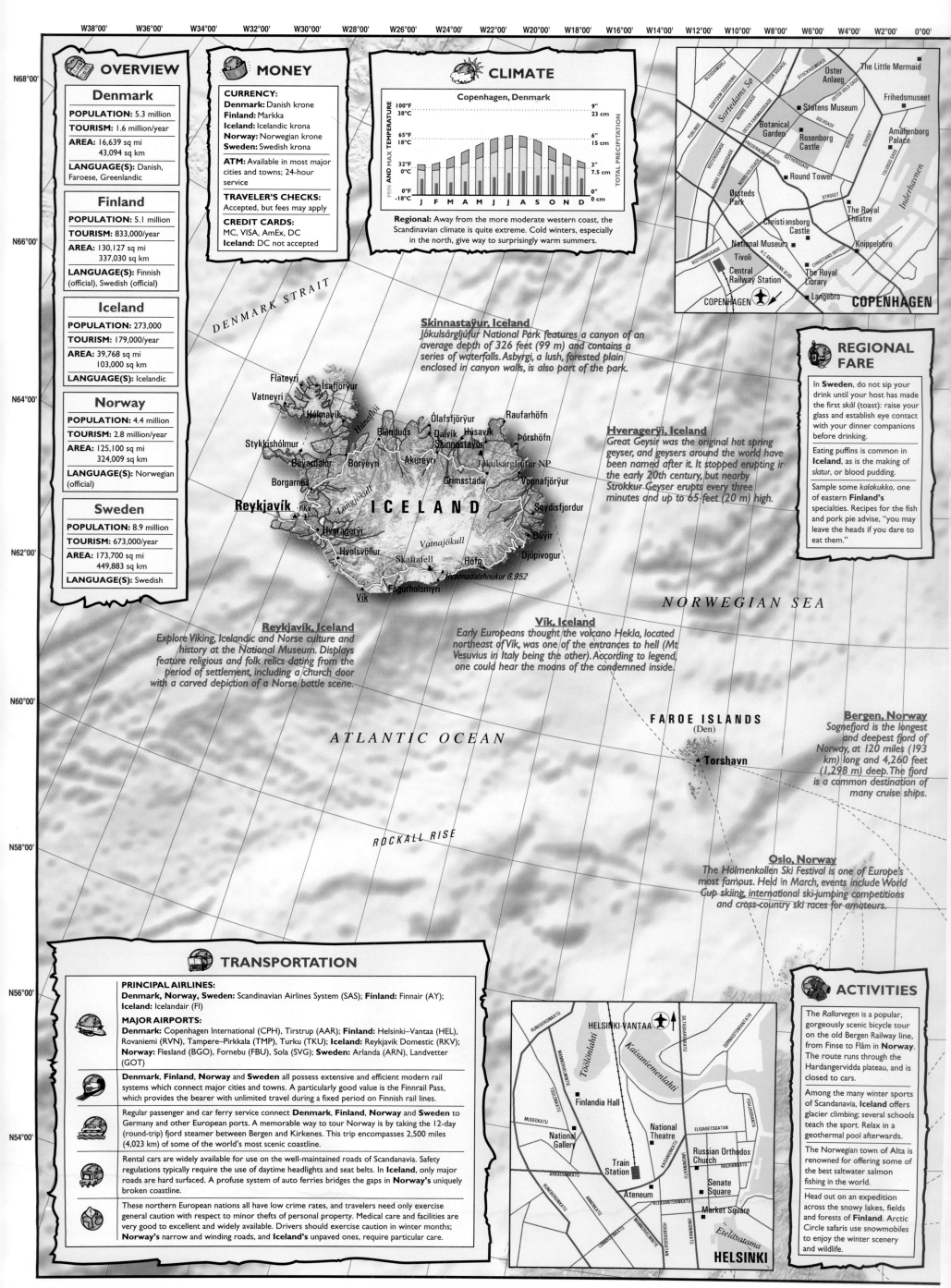

W38°00' W36°00' W34°00' W32°00' W30°00' W28°00' W26°00' W24°00' W22°00' W20°00' W18°00' W16°00' W14°00' W12°00' W10°00' W8°00' W6°00' W4°00' W2°00' 0°00'

OVERVIEW

Denmark
POPULATION: 5.3 million
TOURISM: 1.6 million/year
AREA: 16,639 sq mi
43,094 sq km
LANGUAGE(S): Danish, Faroese, Greenlandic

Finland
POPULATION: 5.1 million
TOURISM: 833,000/year
AREA: 130,127 sq mi
337,030 sq km
LANGUAGE(S): Finnish (official), Swedish (official)

Iceland
POPULATION: 273,000
TOURISM: 179,000/year
AREA: 39,768 sq mi
103,000 sq km
LANGUAGE(S): Icelandic

Norway
POPULATION: 4.4 million
TOURISM: 2.8 million/year
AREA: 125,100 sq mi
324,009 sq km
LANGUAGE(S): Norwegian (official)

Sweden
POPULATION: 8.9 million
TOURISM: 673,000/year
AREA: 173,700 sq mi
449,883 sq km
LANGUAGE(S): Swedish

MONEY

CURRENCY:
Denmark: Danish krone
Finland: Markka
Iceland: Icelandic krona
Norway: Norwegian krone
Sweden: Swedish krona

ATM: Available in most major cities and towns; 24-hour service

TRAVELER'S CHECKS: Accepted, but fees may apply

CREDIT CARDS:
MC, VISA, AmEx, DC
Iceland: DC not accepted

CLIMATE

Copenhagen, Denmark

Regional: Away from the more moderate western coast, the Scandinavian climate is quite extreme. Cold winters, especially in the north, give way to surprisingly warm summers.

COPENHAGEN

REGIONAL FARE

In **Sweden**, do not sip your drink until your host has made the first *skål* (toast): raise your glass and establish eye contact with your dinner companions before drinking.

Eating puffins is common in **Iceland**, as is the making of *slatur*, or blood pudding.

Sample some *kalakukko*, one of eastern **Finland's** specialties. Recipes for the fish and pork pie advise, "you may leave the heads if you dare to eat them."

DENMARK STRAIT

Skinnastaÿur, Iceland
Jökulsárgljúfur National Park features a canyon of an average depth of 326 feet (99 m) and contains a series of waterfalls. Asbyrgi, a lush, forested plain enclosed in canyon walls, is also part of the park.

Hveragerÿi, Iceland
Great Geysir was the original hot spring geyser, and geysers around the world have been named after it. It stopped erupting in the early 20th century, but nearby Strokkur Geyser erupts every three minutes and up to 65 feet (20 m) high.

Flateyri
Ísafjörÿur
Vatneyri
Hólmavík
Ólafsfjörÿur
Raufarhöfn
Blönduós
Dalvík
Húsavík
Þórshöfn
Stykkishólmur
Skinnastaÿur
Akureyri
Búÿardalur
Borÿeyri
Jökulsárgljúfur NP
Borgarnes
Grimsstaðir
Vopnafjörÿur

Reykjavík
RKV
ICELAND
Langjökull
Seydisfjordur

Hveragerÿi
Búÿir
Hvolsvöllur
Vatnajökull
Skaftafell
Djúpivogur
Höfn

Hvannadalshnúkur 6,952

Vík
Fagurhólsmyri

Reykjavík, Iceland
Explore Viking, Icelandic and Norse culture and history at the National Museum. Displays feature religious and folk relics dating from the period of settlement, including a church door with a carved depiction of a Norse battle scene.

Vík, Iceland
Early Europeans thought the volcano Hekla, located northeast of Vík, was one of the entrances to hell (Mt Vesuvius in Italy being the other). According to legend, one could hear the moans of the condemned inside.

NORWEGIAN SEA

ATLANTIC OCEAN

FAROE ISLANDS
(Den)
★Torshavn

Bergen, Norway
Sognefjord is the longest and deepest fjord of Norway, at 120 miles (193 km) long and 4,260 feet (1,298 m) deep. The fjord is a common destination of many cruise ships.

ROCKALL RISE

Oslo, Norway
The Holmenkollen Ski Festival is one of Europe's most famous. Held in March, events include World Cup skiing, international ski-jumping competitions and cross-country ski races for amateurs.

TRANSPORTATION

PRINCIPAL AIRLINES:
Denmark, Norway, Sweden: Scandinavian Airlines System (SAS); **Finland:** Finnair (AY); **Iceland:** Icelandair (FI)

MAJOR AIRPORTS:
Denmark: Copenhagen International (CPH), Tirstrup (AAR); **Finland:** Helsinki–Vantaa (HEL), Rovaniemi (RVN), Tampere–Pirkkala (TMP), Turku (TKU); **Iceland:** Reykjavik Domestic (RKV); **Norway:** Flesland (BGO), Fornebu (FBU), Sola (SVG); **Sweden:** Arlanda (ARN), Landvetter (GOT)

Denmark, Finland, Norway and **Sweden** all possess extensive and efficient modern rail systems which connect major cities and towns. A particularly good value is the Finnrail Pass, which provides the bearer with unlimited travel during a fixed period on Finnish rail lines.

Regular passenger and car ferry service connect **Denmark, Finland, Norway** and **Sweden** to Germany and other European ports. A memorable way to tour Norway is by taking the 12-day (round-trip) fjord steamer between Bergen and Kirkenes. This trip encompasses 2,500 miles (4,023 km) of some of the world's most scenic coastline.

Rental cars are widely available for use on the well-maintained roads of Scandanavia. Safety regulations typically require the use of daytime headlights and seat belts. In Iceland, only major roads are hard surfaced. A profuse system of auto ferries bridges the gaps in **Norway's** uniquely broken coastline.

These northern European nations all have low crime rates, and travelers need only exercise general caution with respect to minor thefts of personal property. Medical care and facilities are very good to excellent and widely available. Drivers should exercise caution in winter months; **Norway's** narrow and winding roads, and **Iceland's** unpaved ones, require particular care.

HELSINKI-VANTAA

HELSINKI

ACTIVITIES

The *Rallarvegen* is a popular, gorgeously scenic bicycle tour on the old Bergen Railway line, from Finse to Flåm in **Norway**. The route runs through the Hardangervidda plateau, and is closed to cars.

Among the many winter sports of Scandinavia, **Iceland** offers glacier climbing; several schools teach the sport. Relax in a geothermal pool afterwards.

The Norwegian town of Alta is renowned for offering some of the best saltwater salmon fishing in the world.

Head out on an expedition across the snowy lakes, fields and forests of **Finland**. Arctic Circle safaris use snowmobiles to enjoy the winter scenery and wildlife.

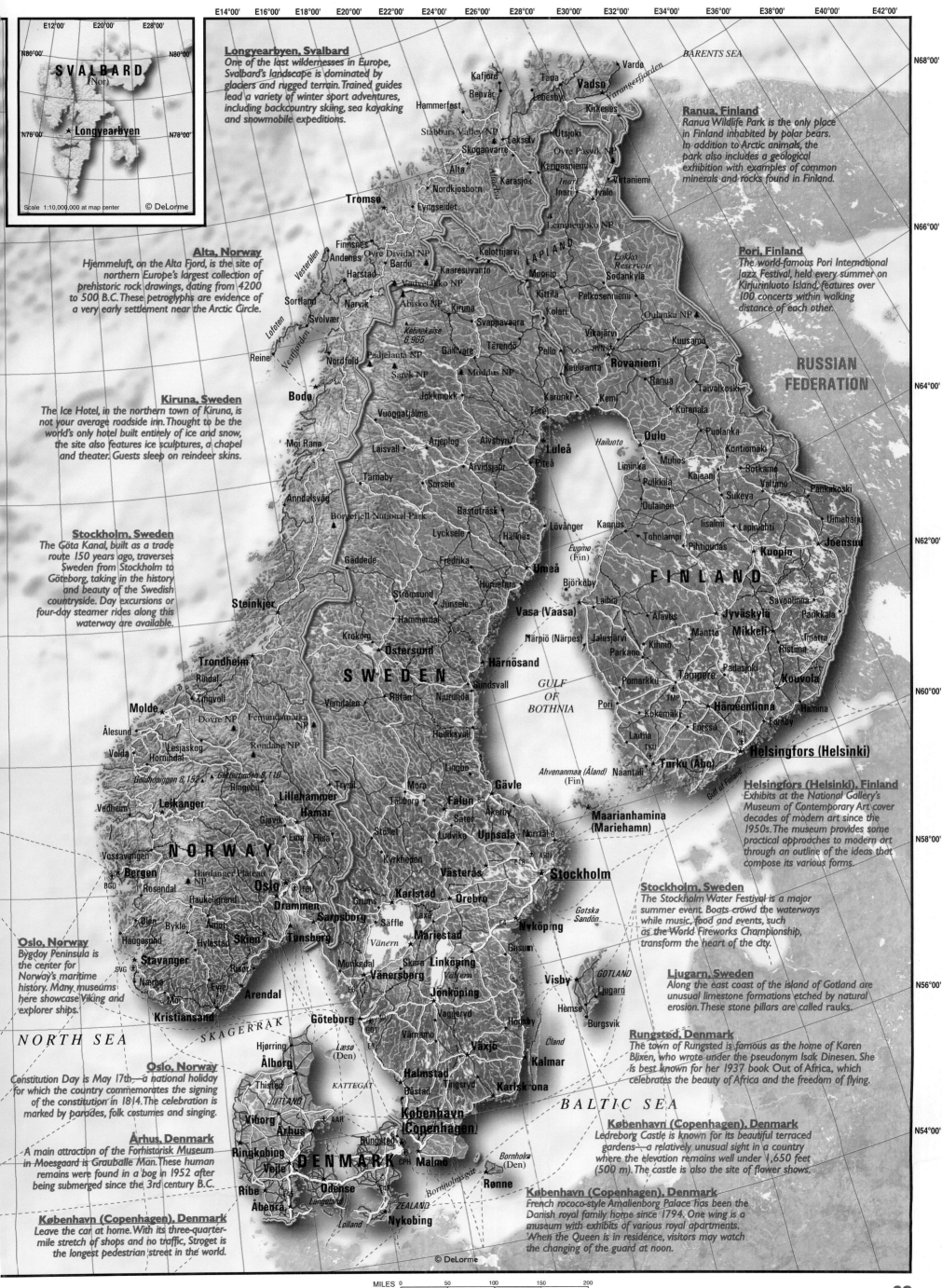

SVALBARD (Nor)

★ Longyearbyen

Scale 1:10,000,000 at map center   © DeLorme

Longyearbyen, Svalbard
One of the last wildernesses in Europe, Svalbard's landscape is dominated by glaciers and rugged terrain. Trained guides lead a variety of winter sport adventures, including backcountry skiing, sea kayaking and snowmobile expeditions.

Ranua, Finland
Ranua Wildlife Park is the only place in Finland inhabited by polar bears. In addition to Arctic animals, the park also includes a geological exhibition with examples of common minerals and rocks found in Finland.

Alta, Norway
Hjemmeluft, on the Alta Fjord, is the site of northern Europe's largest collection of prehistoric rock drawings, dating from 4200 to 500 B.C. These petroglyphs are evidence of a very early settlement near the Arctic Circle.

Pori, Finland
The world-famous Pori International Jazz Festival, held every summer on Kirjurinluoto Island, features over 100 concerts within walking distance of each other.

Kiruna, Sweden
The Ice Hotel, in the northern town of Kiruna, is not your average roadside inn. Thought to be the world's only hotel built entirely of ice and snow, the site also features ice sculptures, a chapel and theater. Guests sleep on reindeer skins.

Stockholm, Sweden
The Göta Kanal, built as a trade route 150 years ago, traverses Sweden from Stockholm to Göteborg, taking in the history and beauty of the Swedish countryside. Day excursions or four-day steamer rides along this waterway are available.

Helsingfors (Helsinki), Finland
Exhibits at the National Gallery's Museum of Contemporary Art cover decades of modern art since the 1950s. The museum provides some practical approaches to modern art through an outline of the ideas that compose its various forms.

Stockholm, Sweden
The Stockholm Water Festival is a major summer event. Boats crowd the waterways while music, food and events, such as the World Fireworks Championship, transform the heart of the city.

Oslo, Norway
Bygdøy Peninsula is the center for Norway's maritime history. Many museums here showcase Viking and explorer ships.

Ljugarn, Sweden
Along the east coast of the island of Gotland are unusual limestone formations etched by natural erosion. These stone pillars are called rauks.

Oslo, Norway
Constitution Day is May 17th, a national holiday for which the country commemorates the signing of the constitution in 1814. The celebration is marked by parades, folk costumes and singing.

Rungsted, Denmark
The town of Rungsted is famous as the home of Karen Blixen, who wrote under the pseudonym Isak Dinesen. She is best known for her 1937 book Out of Africa, which celebrates the beauty of Africa and the freedom of flying.

Århus, Denmark
A main attraction of the Forhistorisk Museum in Moesgaard is Grauballe Man. These human remains were found in a bog in 1952 after being submerged since the 3rd century B.C.

København (Copenhagen), Denmark
Ledreborg Castle is known for its beautiful terraced gardens — a relatively unusual sight in a country where the elevation remains well under 1,650 feet (500 m). The castle is also the site of flower shows.

København (Copenhagen), Denmark
Leave the car at home. With its three-quarter-mile stretch of shops and no traffic, Strøget is the longest pedestrian street in the world.

København (Copenhagen), Denmark
French rococo-style Amalienborg Palace has been the Danish royal family home since 1794. One wing is a museum with exhibits of various royal apartments. When the Queen is in residence, visitors may watch the changing of the guard at noon.

MILES   0   50   100   150   200
KILOMETERS   0   50   100   150   200   250   300

© DeLorme

Countries

Territories and Featured Lands

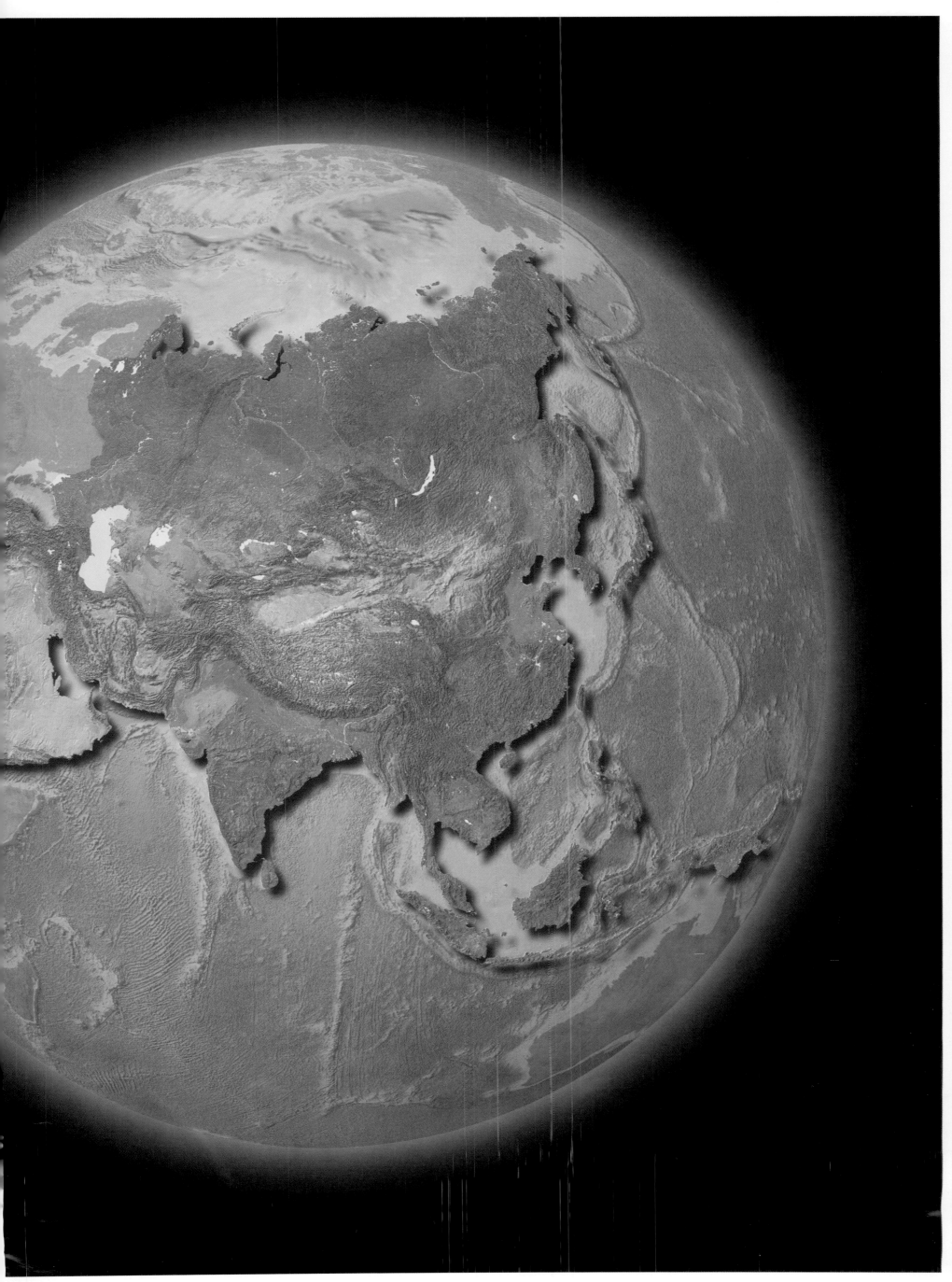

OVERVIEW

Russian Federation

POPULATION: 147 million

TOURISM: 4.6 million/year

AREA: 6,592,797 sq mi
17,075,352 sq km

LANGUAGE(S): Russian

MONEY

CURRENCY: Russian ruble

ATM: Available in major cities

TRAVELER'S CHECKS: Accepted, but fees may apply

CREDIT CARDS: VISA, AmEx; DC in Moscow, St Petersburg

Moskva (Moscow), Russia

For the kid in all of us, a trip to the Moscow circus is a must. Keep an eye out for the trained hedgehog performance.

Teberda, Russia

The Teberdinsky Nature Reserve extends over a broad area to the crestline of the main Caucasus Mountains ridge. The reserve is popular with hikers and contains many challenging walks among mountain ridges, glaciers and waterfalls.

Novosibirsk, Russia

The Novosibirsk Ballet and Opera Theater is one of the largest such organizations in Russia. Though the city itself is known for drab buildings and the presence of industry, the theater has a huge ballet school and often entertains scientists from nearby Akademgorodok (Academic Town).

ACTIVITIES

The world's longest continuous rail line, the Trans-Siberian Express, crosses 6,000 miles (9,600 km) of scenic Asian Russia to connect European Russia with the Pacific Ocean. Passengers board in Moscow and journey for seven days to the terminus in Vladivostok.

Siberia is certainly not exile for outdoors enthusiasts. The possibilities for adventure include the chance to view bears and moose in wildlife preserves, to trek along the slopes of active volcanoes or to ride a dog sled in a local race.

It would take every river of the world a year to fill the vast Lake Baykal. Boat tours in the summer, sleigh rides across the winter ice or railway trips along the shore introduce visitors to the deepest lake in the world. The Russian government has made an effort in recent years to preserve Lake Baykal by declaring the entire lake and its surroundings a national park.

REGIONAL FARE

A cold-weather climate makes for a hearty, calorie-packed cuisine. Traditional Siberian *pelmeni* (dumplings) and stews provide hungry natives and visitors with the fuel necessary to combat the 10 months of winter.

The clear, blue waters of Lake Baykal are home to *omul*, a tasty whitefish that is a relative of salmon. Restaurants in Irkutsk, near the lake's southern end, serve omul either smoked or broiled. Some natives of the region freeze the fish, salt it and enjoy it raw.

Vanavara, Russia

On June 30th, 1908, a meteorite exploded above the central Siberian area of Tunguska, wiping out more than 772 square miles (2,000 sq km) of land and knocking over up to 60 million trees. Because of the remoteness of the area, 14 years passed before it was investigated. Still, the force of the blast was said to have been up to 2,000 times that of the Hiroshima atom bomb.

NOVOSIBIRSK

Circus
Central Market
Train Station
Stadium
Museum of Local Studies
Central Park
Red Torch Theatre
Opera and Ballet Theater
Museum of Local Studies Exhibition Hall
TOLMACHEVO

© DeLorme

Scale 1:18,500,000 at map center

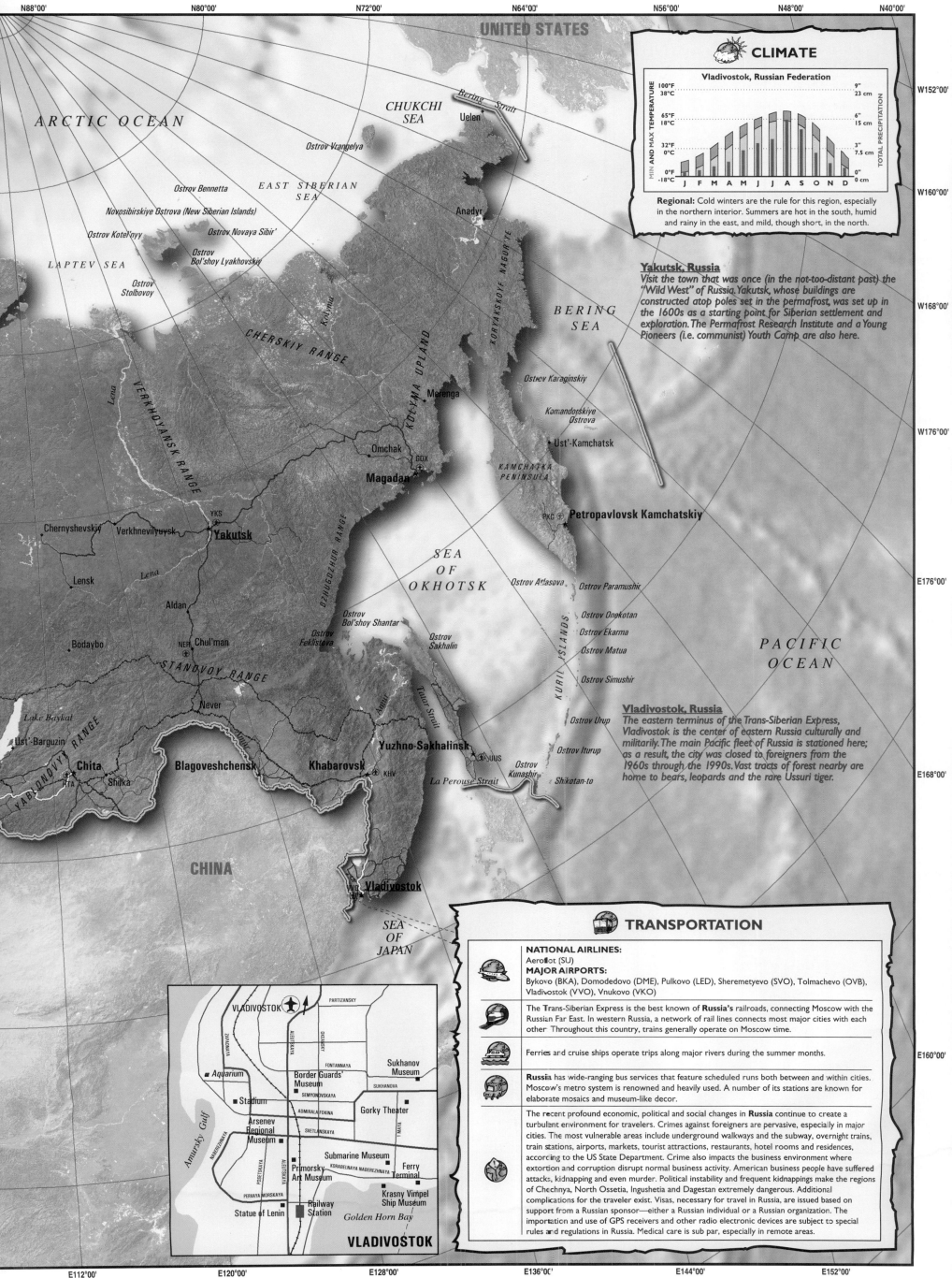

CLIMATE

Vladivostok, Russian Federation

Regional: Cold winters are the rule for this region, especially in the northern interior. Summers are hot in the south, humid and rainy in the east, and mild, though short, in the north.

Yakutsk, Russia
Visit the town that was once (in the not-too-distant past) the "Wild West" of Russia. Yakutsk, whose buildings are constructed atop poles set in the permafrost, was set up in the 1600s as a starting point for Siberian settlement and exploration. The Permafrost Research Institute and a Young Pioneers (i.e. communist) Youth Camp are also here.

Vladivostok, Russia
The eastern terminus of the Trans-Siberian Express, Vladivostok is the center of eastern Russia culturally and militarily. The main Pacific fleet of Russia is stationed here; as a result, the city was closed to foreigners from the 1960s through the 1990s. Vast tracts of forest nearby are home to bears, leopards and the rare Ussuri tiger.

TRANSPORTATION

NATIONAL AIRLINES:
Aeroflot (SU)
MAJOR AIRPORTS:
Bykovo (BKA), Domodedovo (DME), Pulkovo (LED), Sheremetyevo (SVO), Tolmachevo (OVB), Vladivostok (VVO), Vnukovo (VKO)

The Trans-Siberian Express is the best known of **Russia's** railroads, connecting Moscow with the Russian Far East. In western Russia, a network of rail lines connects most major cities with each other. Throughout this country, trains generally operate on Moscow time.

Ferries and cruise ships operate trips along major rivers during the summer months.

Russia has wide-ranging bus services that feature scheduled runs both between and within cities. Moscow's metro system is renowned and heavily used. A number of its stations are known for elaborate mosaics and museum-like decor.

The recent profound economic, political and social changes in **Russia** continue to create a turbulent environment for travelers. Crimes against foreigners are pervasive, especially in major cities. The most vulnerable areas include underground walkways and the subway, overnight trains, train stations, airports, markets, tourist attractions, restaurants, hotel rooms and residences, according to the US State Department. Crime also impacts the business environment where extortion and corruption disrupt normal business activity. American business people have suffered attacks, kidnapping and even murder. Political instability and frequent kidnappings make the regions of Chechnya, North Ossetia, Ingushetia and Dagestan extremely dangerous. Additional complications for the traveler exist. Visas, necessary for travel in Russia, are issued based on support from a Russian sponsor—either a Russian individual or a Russian organization. The importation and use of GPS receivers and other radio electronic devices are subject to special rules and regulations in Russia. Medical care is sub par, especially in remote areas.

MILES
KILOMETERS

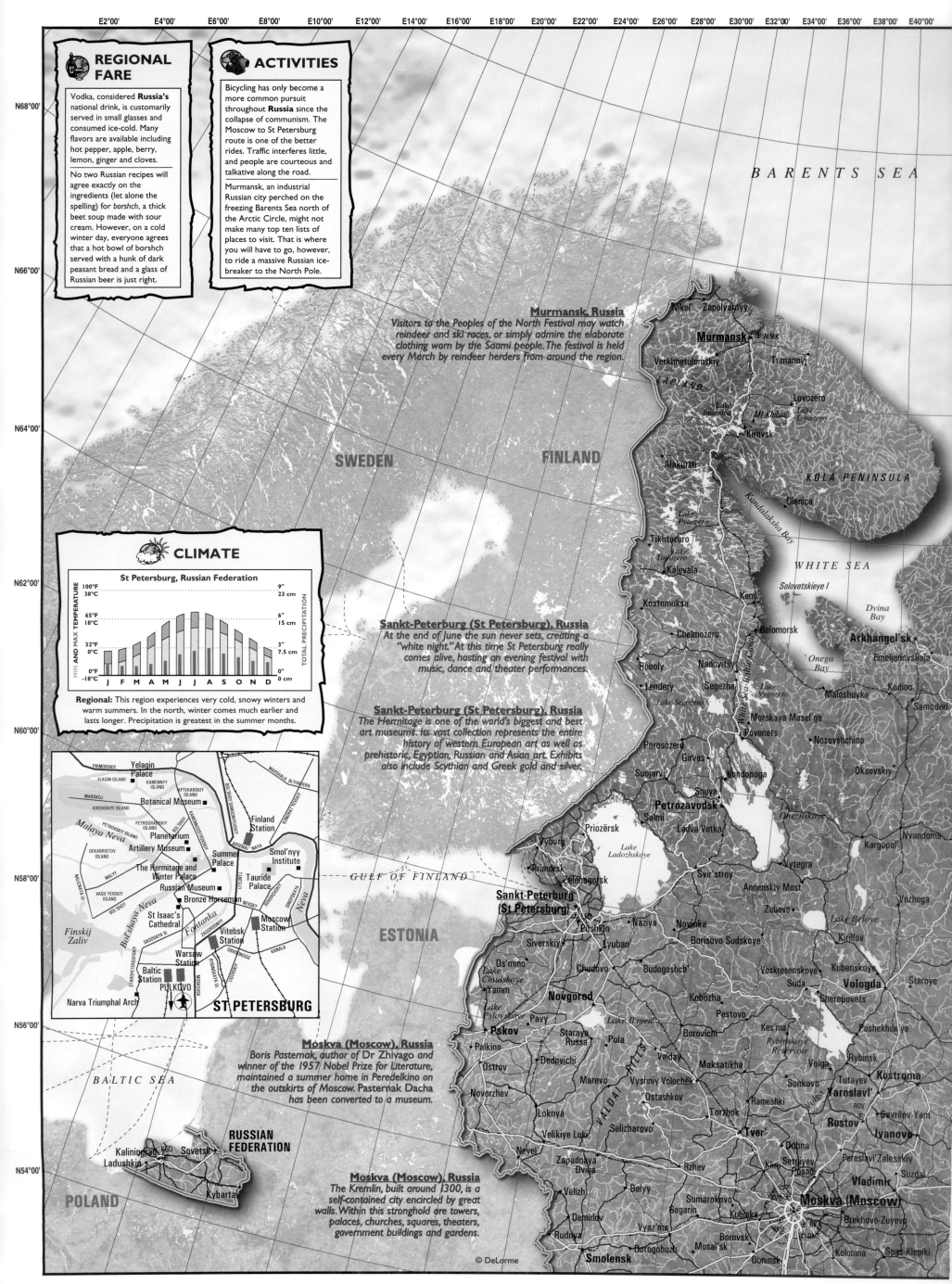

REGIONAL FARE

Vodka, considered **Russia's** national drink, is customarily served in small glasses and consumed ice-cold. Many flavors are available including hot pepper, apple, berry, lemon, ginger and cloves.

No two Russian recipes will agree exactly on the ingredients (let alone the spelling) for borshch, a thick beet soup made with sour cream. However, on a cold winter day, everyone agrees that a hot bowl of borshch served with a hunk of dark peasant bread and a glass of Russian beer is just right.

ACTIVITIES

Bicycling has only become a more common pursuit throughout **Russia** since the collapse of communism. The Moscow to St Petersburg route is one of the better rides. Traffic interferes little, and people are courteous and talkative along the road.

Murmansk, an industrial Russian city perched on the freezing Barents Sea north of the Arctic Circle, might not make many top ten lists of places to visit. That is where you will have to go, however, to ride a massive Russian ice-breaker to the North Pole.

CLIMATE

St Petersburg, Russian Federation

Regional: This region experiences very cold, snowy winters and warm summers. In the north, winter comes much earlier and lasts longer. Precipitation is greatest in the summer months.

Murmansk, Russia
Visitors to the Peoples of the North Festival may watch reindeer and ski races, or simply admire the elaborate clothing worn by the Saami people. The festival is held every March by reindeer herders from around the region.

Sankt-Peterburg (St Petersburg), Russia
At the end of June the sun never sets, creating a "white night." At this time St Petersburg really comes alive, hosting an evening festival with music, dance and theater performances.

Sankt-Peterburg (St Petersburg), Russia
The Hermitage is one of the world's biggest and best art museums. Its vast collection represents the entire history of western European art as well as prehistoric, Egyptian, Russian and Asian art. Exhibits also include Scythian and Greek gold and silver.

Moskva (Moscow), Russia
Boris Pasternak, author of Dr Zhivago and winner of the 1957 Nobel Prize for Literature, maintained a summer home in Peredelkino on the outskirts of Moscow. Pasternak Dacha has been converted to a museum.

Moskva (Moscow), Russia
The Kremlin, built around 1300, is a self-contained city encircled by great walls. Within this stronghold are towers, palaces, churches, squares, theaters, government buildings and gardens.

ST PETERSBURG

© DeLorme

Scale 1:6,000,000 at map center

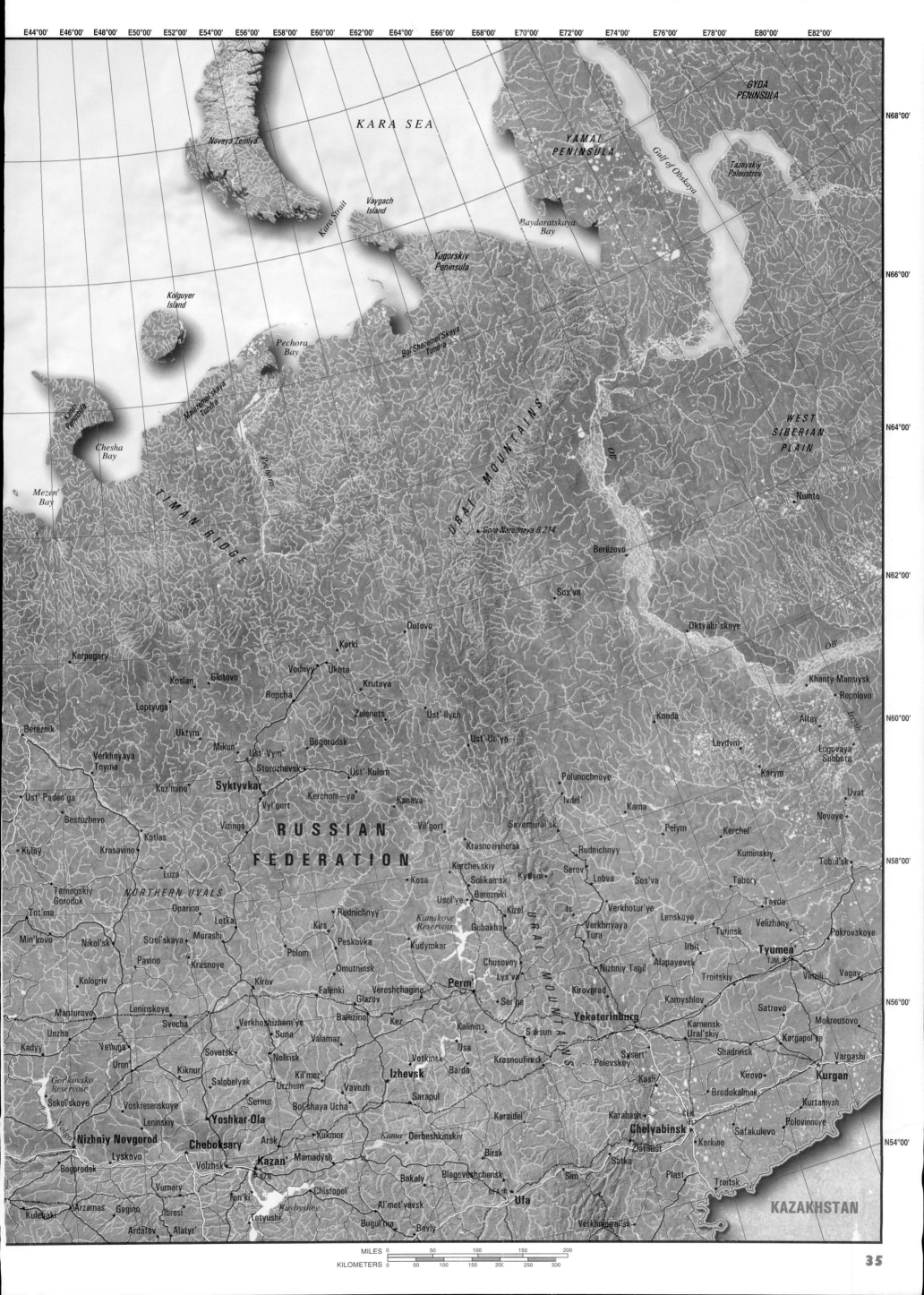

E44°00' E46°00' E48°00' E50°00' E52°00' E54°00' E56°00' E58°00' E60°00' E62°00' E64°00' E66°00' E68°00' E70°00' E72°00' E74°00' E76°00' E78°00' E80°00' E82°00'

N68°00'

GYDA PENINSULA

KARA SEA

YAMAL PENINSULA

Novaya Zemlya

Gulf of Obskaya

N66°00'

Vaygach Island

Kara Strait

Tazovskiy Poloustrov

Yugorskiy Peninsula

Kolguyev Island

Baydaratskaya Bay

Pechora Bay

Bol'shezemel'Skaya Tundra

N64°00'

WEST SIBERIAN PLAIN

Kanin Peninsula

Malozemel'skaya Tundra

Chesha Bay

TIMAN RIDGE

Pechora

URAL MOUNTAINS

OB'

Numto

Mezen' Bay

Gora Narodnaya 6,214

N62°00'

Berëzovo

Sos'va

Oktyabr'skoye

OB'

Dutovo

Karpogory

Kerki

Khanty-Mansiysk
Repolovo

Koslan
Gidovo

Vodnyy Ukhta
Krutaya

Konda

Altay

Irtysh

Loptyuga

Ropcha

Zelenets

Ust'-Ilych

N60°00'

Levdym

Lugovaya Subbota

Bereznik

Uktym

Ust'-Ui'ya

Ust'-Vym'

Mikun

Bogorodsk

Karym

Verkhnyaya Toyma

Storozhevsk

Ust'-Kulom

Polunochnoye

Kez'mino'

Syktyvkar

Kerchom—ya'

Kanava

Ivdel'

Kama

Uvat

Ust'-Paden'ga

Vyl'gort

RUSSIAN

Vil'gort

Severural'sk

Pelym

Kerchel'

Novoye

Bestuzhevo

Vizinga

FEDERATION

Krasnovishersk

Rudnichnyy

Kuminskiy

Kotlas

Kerchevskiy

Kulay

Krasavino

Kosa

Kosa

Solikamsk

Kytym

Serov

Lobva

Sos'va

Tobol'sk

N58°00'

Luza

Usol'ye

Berezniki

Kizel

Is

Verkhotur'ye

Tabory

Tarnogskiy Gorodok

NORTHERN UVALS

Oparino

Rudnichnyy

Kumskoye Reservoir

Gubakha

Verkhnyaya Tura

Lenskoye

Velizhany

Tavda

Tot'ma

Letka

Kirs

Peskovka

Kudymkar

Chusovoy

Nizhniy Tagil

Irbit

Turinsk

Pokrovskoye

Min'kovo

Nikol'sk

Strel'skaya

Murashi

Polom

Omutninsk

Lys'va

Kirovgrad

Alapayevsk

Tyumen'

TJM

Pavino

Krasnoye

Kirov

Ser'ga

Troitskiy

Vinali

Vagay

Kologriv

Falënki

Vereshchagino

Perm

Yekaterinburg

Kamyshlov

N56°00'

Manturovo

Leninskoye

Svecha

Verkhoshizhem'ye

Glazov

Balëzino

Kez

Kalinino

Suksun

Kamensk-Ural'skiy

Satrovo

Mokrousovo

Unzha

Kadyy

Vetluga

Uren

Suna

Valamaz

Osa

Krasnoufim'sk

Sysert'
Polevskoy

Shadrinsk

Kargapol'ye

Vargashi

Kiknur

Sovetsk

Nolinsk

Votkinsk

Barda

Kasli

Kirovo

Kurgan

Gor'kovsko Reservoir

Salobelyak

Kil'mez'

Urzhum

Vavozh

Izhevsk

Sarapul

Karaidel

Karabash

Brodokalmak

Kurtamysh

Sokol'skoye

Voskresenskoye

Sernur

Bol'shaya Ucha

Kama

Derbeshkinskiy

Birsk

Chelyabinsk

Zlatoust

Korkino

Safakulevo

Polovinnoye

Leninskiy

Yoshkar-Ola

Arsk

Kukmor

N54°00'

Volga

Nizhniy Novgorod

Cheboksary

Volzhsk

Kazan'

KZN

Mamadysh

Blagoveshchensk

Sim

Satka

Troitsk

Bogrodsk

Ken'ki

Chistopol'

Al'met'yevsk

Ufa

UFA

Kuybyshev

Bakaly

Arzamas

Gagino

Ibresi

Tetyushi

Bugul'ma

Verkhneural'sk

Kulebaki

Alatyr'

Ardatov

Bavly

KAZAKHSTAN

MILES 0   50   100   150   200
KILOMETERS 0   50   100   150   200   250   300

Klin, Russia
The famous composer Peter Ilyich Tchaikovsky spent the last eight years of his life in a house in Klin, which was purchased and turned into a museum by his brother. Tchaikovsky wrote Pathetique, The Nutcracker and Sleeping Beauty here.

BELARUS

Moskva (Moscow), Russia
Established in 1776 at the Petrovsky Theater, the Bolsoi Ballet and Opera was taken over by the Bolshoi Theater in 1825. Tchaikovsky's ballet Swan Lake premiered here in 1877, and was not well received.

Moskva (Moscow), Russia
Krasnaya Ploshchad (Red Square) lies in the center of Moscow, flanked by the Kremlin and the beautiful St Basil's Cathedral. This enormous square was once a market, and has always been a congregating place for the Russian people.

UKRAINE

Sochi, Russia
The country's biggest resort, Sochi was founded in 1896. Subtropical trees, beaches, prevalent sun and several curative mineral springs make this area a popular destination.

RUSSIAN FEDERATION

REGIONAL FARE

Russia's neighbors and its own many ethnic groups have strongly influenced this country's cuisine. In the southern portion of the country, *perogy* is a common snack that originated in the Ukraine. A small pocket of dough with a cheese and potato filling is either baked or fried to a golden brown color and served hot.

Prior to lunch, but especially before dinner, Russians enjoy *zakuski* (appetizers)—often smoked fish, pickled vegetables or salads.

Fortunate visitors to Russia will have the chance to sample its best known *zakuski*, caviar. The roe of sturgeon fish found in the Caspian Sea, Russian caviar comes in three varieties: *beluga*, *osetra* and *sevruga*, with beluga being the finest. Caviar is best eaten chilled on bland crackers or toast in order to fully appreciate its intricate flavors.

ACTIVITIES

If reading Tolstoy is too daunting, then plan a cruise on **Russia's** Volga River to learn more about the complex Russian people. Some of the nation's oldest and most beautiful cities, many of which were established along medieval-era trade routes, are located along Europe's longest river at 2,300 miles (3,700 km).

An easy item to add to a Russian travel itinerary is an evening out at one of Moscow's numerous theaters. The Bolshoi Theater, the Maly Theater and the Moscow Arts Theater (MKhAT) are the big three. Many other innovative and well-known companies perform nightly at theaters around the city.

Yessentuki, Russia
Yessentuki is a small spa in the Caucasian foothills that is famous for its therapeutic mud bath treatments and bottled mineral spring waters.

BLACK SEA

GEORGIA

AZERBAIJAN

© DeLorme

Scale 1:6,000,000 at map center

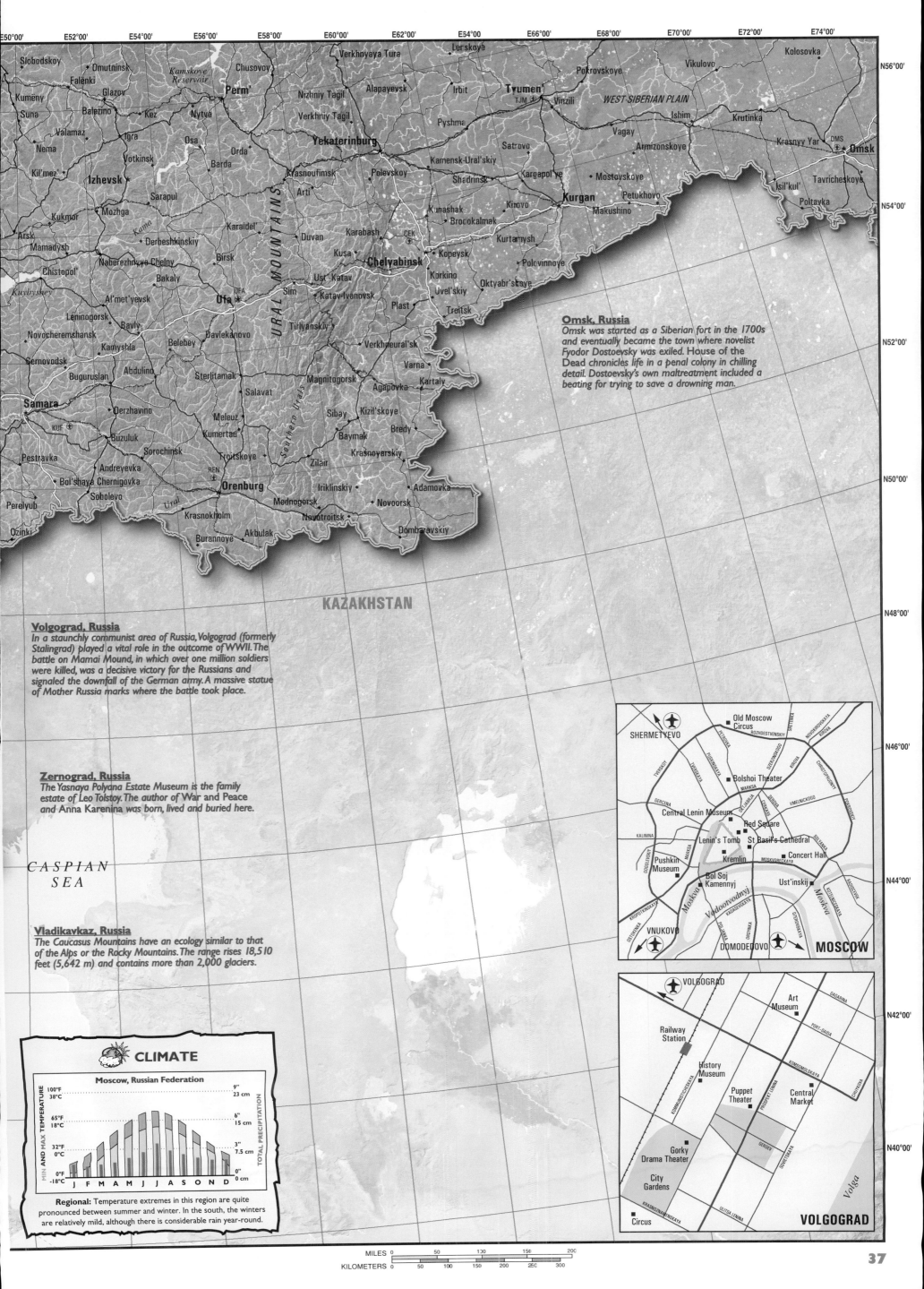

Omsk, Russia
Omsk was started as a Siberian fort in the 1700s and eventually became the town where novelist Fyodor Dostoevsky was exiled. House of the Dead chronicles life in a penal colony in chilling detail. Dostoevsky's own maltreatment included a beating for trying to save a drowning man.

Volgograd, Russia
In a staunchly communist area of Russia, Volgograd (formerly Stalingrad) played a vital role in the outcome of WWII. The battle on Mamai Mound, in which over one million soldiers were killed, was a decisive victory for the Russians and signaled the downfall of the German army. A massive statue of Mother Russia marks where the battle took place.

Zernograd, Russia
The Yasnaya Polyana Estate Museum is the family estate of Leo Tolstoy. The author of War and Peace and Anna Karenina was born, lived and buried here.

Vladikavkaz, Russia
The Caucasus Mountains have an ecology similar to that of the Alps or the Rocky Mountains. The range rises 18,510 feet (5,642 m) and contains more than 2,000 glaciers.

CASPIAN SEA

KAZAKHSTAN

WEST-SIBERIAN PLAIN

URAL MOUNTAINS

Southern Urals

CLIMATE

Moscow, Russian Federation

MIN AND MAX TEMPERATURE — TOTAL PRECIPITATION

100°F 38°C / 9" 23 cm
65°F 18°C / 6" 15 cm
32°F 0°C / 3" 7.5 cm
0°F -18°C / 0" 0 cm

J F M A M J J A S O N D

Regional: Temperature extremes in this region are quite pronounced between summer and winter. In the south, the winters are relatively mild, although there is considerable rain year-round.

MOSCOW

SHERMETYEVO · VNUKOVO · DOMODEDOVO

Old Moscow Circus · Bolshoi Theater · Central Lenin Museum · Red Square · Lenin's Tomb · St Basil's Cathedral · Concert Hall · Pushkin Museum · Kremlin · Bol Soj Kamennyj · Ust'inskij

VOLGOGRAD

Art Museum · Railway Station · History Museum · Puppet Theater · Central Market · Gorky Drama Theater · City Gardens · Circus

MILES 0 50 100 150 200
KILOMETERS 0 50 100 150 200 250 300

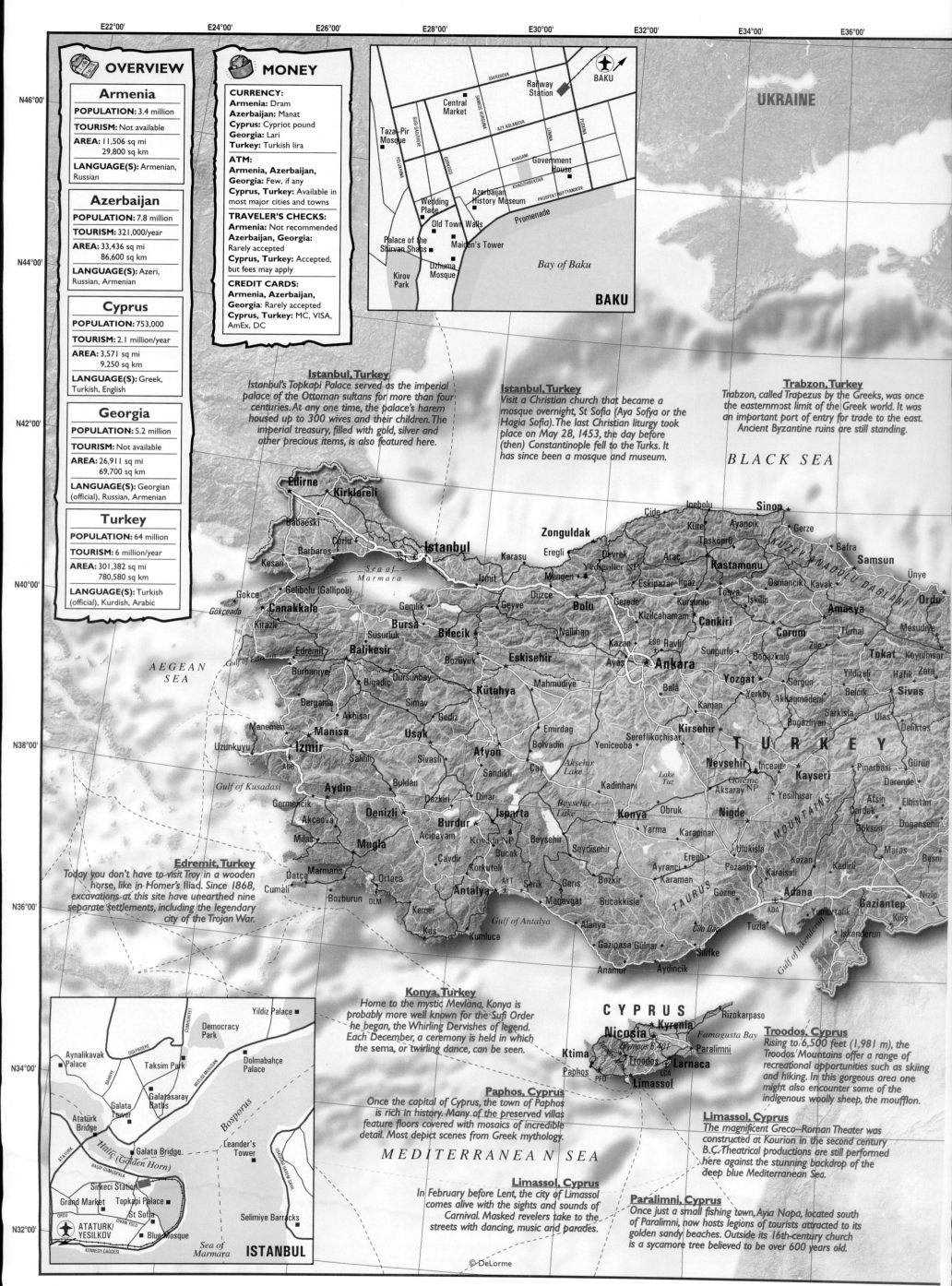

OVERVIEW

Armenia
POPULATION: 3.4 million
TOURISM: Not available
AREA: 11,506 sq mi
29,800 sq km
LANGUAGE(S): Armenian, Russian

Azerbaijan
POPULATION: 7.8 million
TOURISM: 321,000/year
AREA: 33,436 sq mi
86,600 sq km
LANGUAGE(S): Azeri, Russian, Armenian

Cyprus
POPULATION: 753,000
TOURISM: 2.1 million/year
AREA: 3,571 sq mi
9,250 sq km
LANGUAGE(S): Greek, Turkish, English

Georgia
POPULATION: 5.2 million
TOURISM: Not available
AREA: 26,911 sq mi
69,700 sq km
LANGUAGE(S): Georgian (official), Russian, Armenian

Turkey
POPULATION: 64 million
TOURISM: 6 million/year
AREA: 301,382 sq mi
780,580 sq km
LANGUAGE(S): Turkish (official), Kurdish, Arabic

MONEY

CURRENCY:
Armenia: Dram
Azerbaijan: Manat
Cyprus: Cypriot pound
Georgia: Lari
Turkey: Turkish lira

ATM:
Armenia, Azerbaijan, Georgia: Few, if any
Cyprus, Turkey: Available in most major cities and towns

TRAVELER'S CHECKS:
Armenia: Not recommended
Azerbaijan, Georgia: Rarely accepted
Cyprus, Turkey: Accepted, but fees may apply

CREDIT CARDS:
Armenia, Azerbaijan, Georgia: Rarely accepted
Cyprus, Turkey: MC, VISA, AmEx, DC

BAKU

Istanbul, Turkey
Istanbul's Topkapi Palace served as the imperial palace of the Ottoman sultans for more than four centuries. At any one time, the palace's harem housed up to 300 wives and their children. The imperial treasury, filled with gold, silver and other precious items, is also featured here.

Istanbul, Turkey
Visit a Christian church that became a mosque overnight, St Sofia (Aya Sofya or the Hagia Sofia). The last Christian liturgy took place on May 28, 1453, the day before (then) Constantinople fell to the Turks. It has since been a mosque and museum.

Trabzon, Turkey
Trabzon, called Trapezus by the Greeks, was once the easternmost limit of the Greek world. It was an important port of entry for trade to the east. Ancient Byzantine ruins are still standing.

Edremit, Turkey
Today you don't have to visit Troy in a wooden horse, like in Homer's Iliad. Since 1868, excavations at this site have unearthed nine separate settlements, including the legendary city of the Trojan War.

Konya, Turkey
Home to the mystic Mevlana, Konya is probably more well known for the Sufi Order he began, the Whirling Dervishes of legend. Each December, a ceremony is held in which the sema, or twirling dance, can be seen.

Paphos, Cyprus
Once the capital of Cyprus, the town of Paphos is rich in history. Many of the preserved villas feature floors covered with mosaics of incredible detail. Most depict scenes from Greek mythology.

Limassol, Cyprus
In February before Lent, the city of Limassol comes alive with the sights and sounds of Carnival. Masked revelers take to the streets with dancing, music and parades.

Troodos, Cyprus
Rising to 6,500 feet (1,981 m), the Troodos Mountains offer a range of recreational opportunities such as skiing and hiking. In this gorgeous area one might also encounter some of the indigenous woolly sheep, the moufflon.

Limassol, Cyprus
The magnificent Greco-Roman Theater was constructed at Kourion in the second century B.C. Theatrical productions are still performed here against the stunning backdrop of the deep blue Mediterranean Sea.

Paralimni, Cyprus
Once just a small fishing town, Ayia Napa, located south of Paralimni, now hosts legions of tourists attracted to its golden sandy beaches. Outside its 16th-century church is a sycamore tree believed to be over 600 years old.

ISTANBUL

© DeLorme

Scale 1:5,000,000 at map center

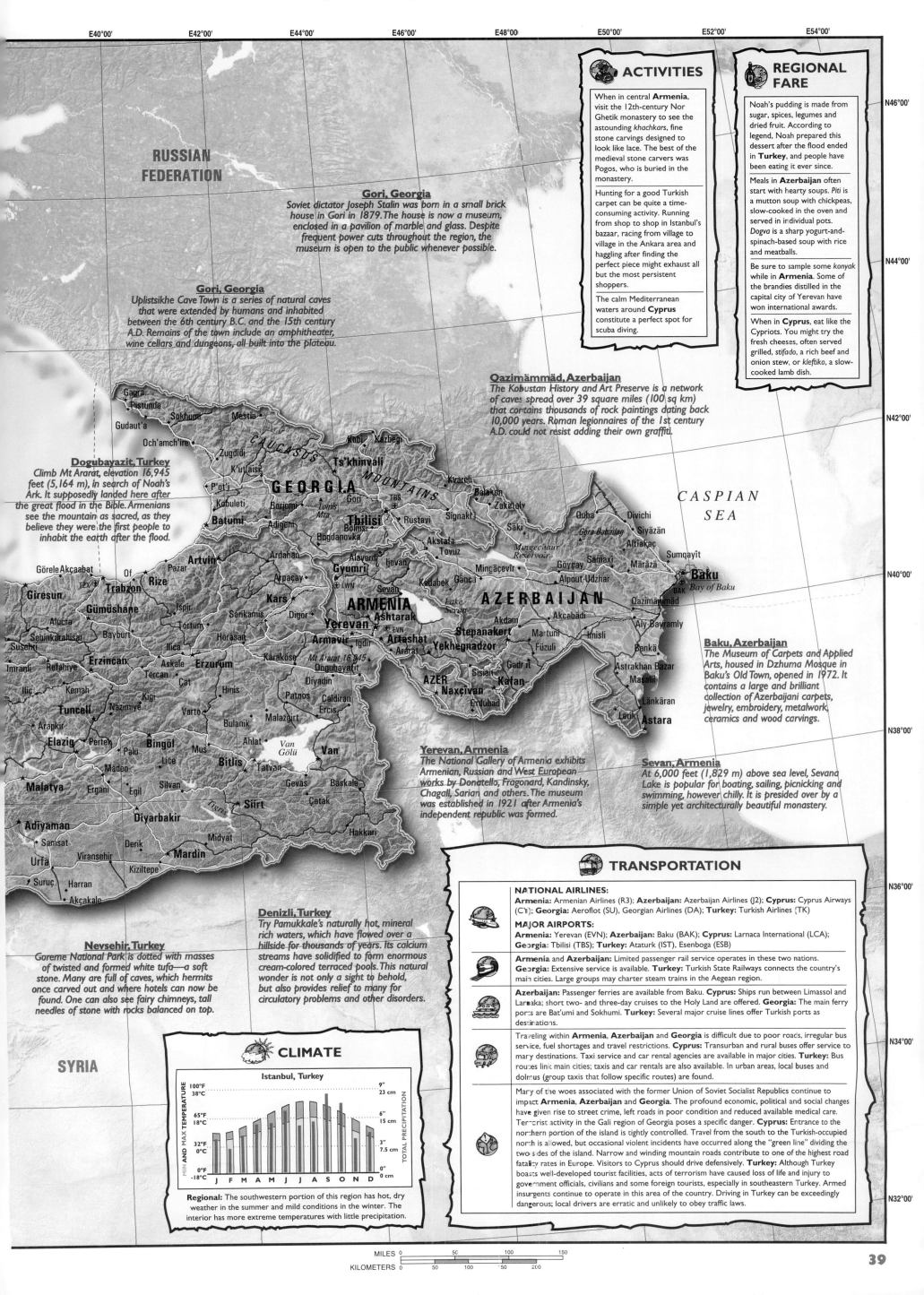

ACTIVITIES

When in central **Armenia**, visit the 12th-century Nor Ghetik monastery to see the astounding *khachkars*, fine stone carvings designed to look like lace. The best of the medieval stone carvers was Pogos, who is buried in the monastery.

Hunting for a good Turkish carpet can be quite a time-consuming activity. Running from shop to shop in Istanbul's bazaar, racing from village to village in the Ankara area and haggling after finding the perfect piece might exhaust all but the most persistent shoppers.

The calm Mediterranean waters around **Cyprus** constitute a perfect spot for scuba diving.

REGIONAL FARE

Noah's pudding is made from sugar, spices, legumes and dried fruit. According to legend, Noah prepared this dessert after the flood ended in **Turkey**, and people have been eating it ever since.

Meals in **Azerbaijan** often start with hearty soups. *Piti* is a mutton soup with chickpeas, slow-cooked in the oven and served in individual pots. *Dogva* is a sharp yogurt-and-spinach-based soup with rice and meatballs.

Be sure to sample some *konyak* while in **Armenia**. Some of the brandies distilled in the capital city of Yerevan have won international awards.

When in **Cyprus**, eat like the Cypriots. You might try the fresh cheeses, often served grilled, *stifado*, a rich beef and onion stew, or *kleftiko*, a slow-cooked lamb dish.

Gori, Georgia

Soviet dictator Joseph Stalin was born in a small brick house in Gori in 1879. The house is now a museum, enclosed in a pavilion of marble and glass. Despite frequent power cuts throughout the region, the museum is open to the public whenever possible.

Gori, Georgia

Uplistsikhe Cave Town is a series of natural caves that were extended by humans and inhabited between the 6th century B.C. and the 15th century A.D. Remains of the town include an amphitheater, wine cellars and dungeons, all built into the plateau.

Qazimämmäd, Azerbaijan

The Kobustan History and Art Preserve is a network of caves spread over 39 square miles (100 sq km) that contains thousands of rock paintings dating back 10,000 years. Roman legionnaires of the 1st century A.D. could not resist adding their own graffiti.

Dogubayazit, Turkey

Climb Mt Ararat, elevation 16,945 feet (5,164 m), in search of Noah's Ark. It supposedly landed here after the great flood in the Bible. Armenians see the mountain as sacred, as they believe they were the first people to inhabit the earth after the flood.

Baku, Azerbaijan

The Museum of Carpets and Applied Arts, housed in Dzhuma Mosque in Baku's Old Town, opened in 1972. It contains a large and brilliant collection of Azerbaijani carpets, jewelry, embroidery, metalwork, ceramics and wood carvings.

Yerevan, Armenia

The National Gallery of Armenia exhibits Armenian, Russian and West European works by Donatello, Fragonard, Kandinsky, Chagall, Sarian and others. The museum was established in 1921 after Armenia's independent republic was formed.

Sevan, Armenia

At 6,000 feet (1,829 m) above sea level, Sevana Lake is popular for boating, sailing, picnicking and swimming, however chilly. It is presided over by a simple yet architecturally beautiful monastery.

Denizli, Turkey

Try Pamukkale's naturally hot, mineral rich waters, which have flowed over a hillside for thousands of years. Its calcium streams have solidified to form enormous cream-colored terraced pools. This natural wonder is not only a sight to behold, but also provides relief to many for circulatory problems and other disorders.

Nevsehir, Turkey

Goreme National Park is dotted with masses of twisted and formed white tufa—a soft stone. Many are full of caves, which hermits once carved out and where hotels can now be found. One can also see fairy chimneys, tall needles of stone with rocks balanced on top.

CLIMATE

Istanbul, Turkey

Regional: The southwestern portion of this region has hot, dry weather in the summer and mild conditions in the winter. The interior has more extreme temperatures with little precipitation.

TRANSPORTATION

NATIONAL AIRLINES:
Armenia: Armenian Airlines (R3); **Azerbaijan:** Azerbaijan Airlines (J2); **Cyprus:** Cyprus Airways (CY); **Georgia:** Aeroflot (SU), Georgian Airlines (DA); **Turkey:** Turkish Airlines (TK)

MAJOR AIRPORTS:
Armenia: Yerevan (EVN); **Azerbaijan:** Baku (BAK); **Cyprus:** Larnaca International (LCA); **Georgia:** Tbilisi (TBS); **Turkey:** Ataturk (IST), Esenboga (ESB)

Armenia and Azerbaijan: Limited passenger rail service operates in these two nations. **Georgia:** Extensive service is available. **Turkey:** Turkish State Railways connects the country's main cities. Large groups may charter steam trains in the Aegean region.

Azerbaijan: Passenger ferries are available from Baku. **Cyprus:** Ships run between Limassol and Larnaka; short two- and three-day cruises to the Holy Land are offered. **Georgia:** The main ferry ports are Bat'umi and Sokhumi. **Turkey:** Several major cruise lines offer Turkish ports as destinations.

Traveling within **Armenia**, **Azerbaijan** and **Georgia** is difficult due to poor roads, irregular bus service, fuel shortages and travel restrictions. **Cyprus:** Transurban and rural buses offer service to many destinations. Taxi service and car rental agencies are available in major cities. **Turkey:** Bus routes link main cities; taxis and car rentals are also available. In urban areas, local buses and dolmus (group taxis that follow specific routes) are found.

Many of the woes associated with the former Union of Soviet Socialist Republics continue to impact **Armenia**, **Azerbaijan** and **Georgia**. The profound economic, political and social changes have given rise to street crime, acts of terrorism, left roads in poor condition and reduced available medical care. Terrorist activity in the Gali region of Georgia poses a specific danger. **Cyprus:** Entrance to the northern portion of the island is tightly controlled. Travel from the south to the Turkish-occupied north is allowed, but occasional violent incidents have occurred along the "green line" dividing the two sides of the island. Narrow and winding mountain roads contribute to one of the highest road fatality rates in Europe. Visitors to Cyprus should drive defensively. **Turkey:** Although Turkey boasts well-developed tourist facilities, acts of terrorism have caused loss of life and injury to government officials, civilians and some foreign tourists, especially in southeastern Turkey. Armed insurgents continue to operate in this area of the country. Driving in Turkey can be exceedingly dangerous; local drivers are erratic and unlikely to obey traffic laws.

MILES 0 50 100 150
KILOMETERS 0 50 100 150 200

OVERVIEW

Israel
POPULATION: 5.5 million
TOURISM: 1.8 million/year
AREA: 8,019 sq mi
20,770 sq km
LANGUAGE(S): Hebrew (official), English, Arabic

Jordan
POPULATION: 4.3 million
TOURISM: 844,000/year
AREA: 34,445 sq mi
89,213 sq km
LANGUAGE(S): Arabic (official), English

Lebanon
POPULATION: 3.4 million
TOURISM: 335,000/year
AREA: 4,016 sq mi
10,401 sq km
LANGUAGE(S): Arabic (official), French (official), Armenian

Syria
POPULATION: 16 million
TOURISM: 718,000/year
AREA: 71,500 sq mi
185,185 sq km
LANGUAGE(S): Arabic (official), Kurdish, Armenian

MONEY

CURRENCY:
Israel: New Israeli shekel
Jordan: Jordanian dinar
Lebanon: Lebanese pound
Syria: Syrian pound
ATM: Generally available in major cities
Syria: Few, if any
TRAVELER'S CHECKS: Generally accepted, but fees may apply
Lebanon, Syria: More limited acceptance
CREDIT CARDS:
Israel: MC, VISA, AmEx, DC
Jordan: VISA, AmEx widely accepted; MC, DC more limited
Lebanon: Limited acceptance of MC, VISA, DC
Syria: AmEx, DC widely accepted

Tadmur, Syria
Palmyra's most famous ruler was the warrior Queen Zenobia, who fought against the Roman Empire and captured Syria, Egypt, Arabia and Anatolia, but fell short of taking Rome in 271. The city's fantastic ruins are even more renowned today.

Tarabulus (Tripoli), Lebanon
The "Cedars of the Lord" have grown in the mountains of Lebanon since time immemorial. Though only individual groves remain of the trees that were used to build King Solomon's Temple, they are still fragrant and impressively large.

Al Labwah, Lebanon
Though the Shiite Muslim guerrilla group Hezbollah may reside in the area, they aren't the first to do so. Once called Heliopolis, or City of the Sun, by the Egyptians, the city was also run by Romans, who left several major temples here, some still standing.

Sur (Tyre), Lebanon
Walk through the ruins of a city built around 3,000 B.C. Tyre has been in the possession of Egyptians, Phoenicians, Romans, Greeks, Assyrians and now the Lebanese, all of whom have left their cultural mark upon the site. Over 100,000 people live in Tyre today.

Bayrut (Beirut), Lebanon
Often called the "Paris of the Middle East," Beirut suffered severely during the Lebanese civil wars. Today the city is in the process of active reconstruction, and a trip to a museum or local beach is an option for visitors.

Jerusalem, Israel
A memorial and education center, Yad Vashem serves as a remembrance of the six million Jews who died in the Holocaust. The center features ashes collected from concentration camps, and a memorial to those who risked their lives to save Jews.

Tel Aviv-Yafo, Israel
Tel Aviv-Yafo was founded in 1909 as the first all-Jewish city in the 20th century, and it is now the cultural, industrial and financial center of Israel. Its beach on the Mediterranean Sea and the Yemenite Quarter of the city are two main points of interest.

Jerusalem, Israel
Three worlds of religion meet in Israel's capital, Jerusalem. This city serves as a spiritual and historic center for Judaism, Christianity and Islam. With its 3,000-year-old history, it is a living museum.

En-Gedi, Israel
In need of relaxation or rejuvenation? Visit the lowest point on Earth: the Dead Sea. At about 1,300 feet (400 m) below sea level, the Dead Sea has such a high salinity that one can float on the water. According to legend, the sea also possesses healing powers.

Elat, Israel
The International Birdwatching Centre is an excellent spot to view some of the millions of birds that migrate across the southern tip of Israel and the Red Sea each year. Guided walking and auto tours are also offered.

Ramm, Jordan
Situated in a region popular with mountain climbers, Mt Ramm is Jordan's highest peak, at 5,788 feet (1,764 km).

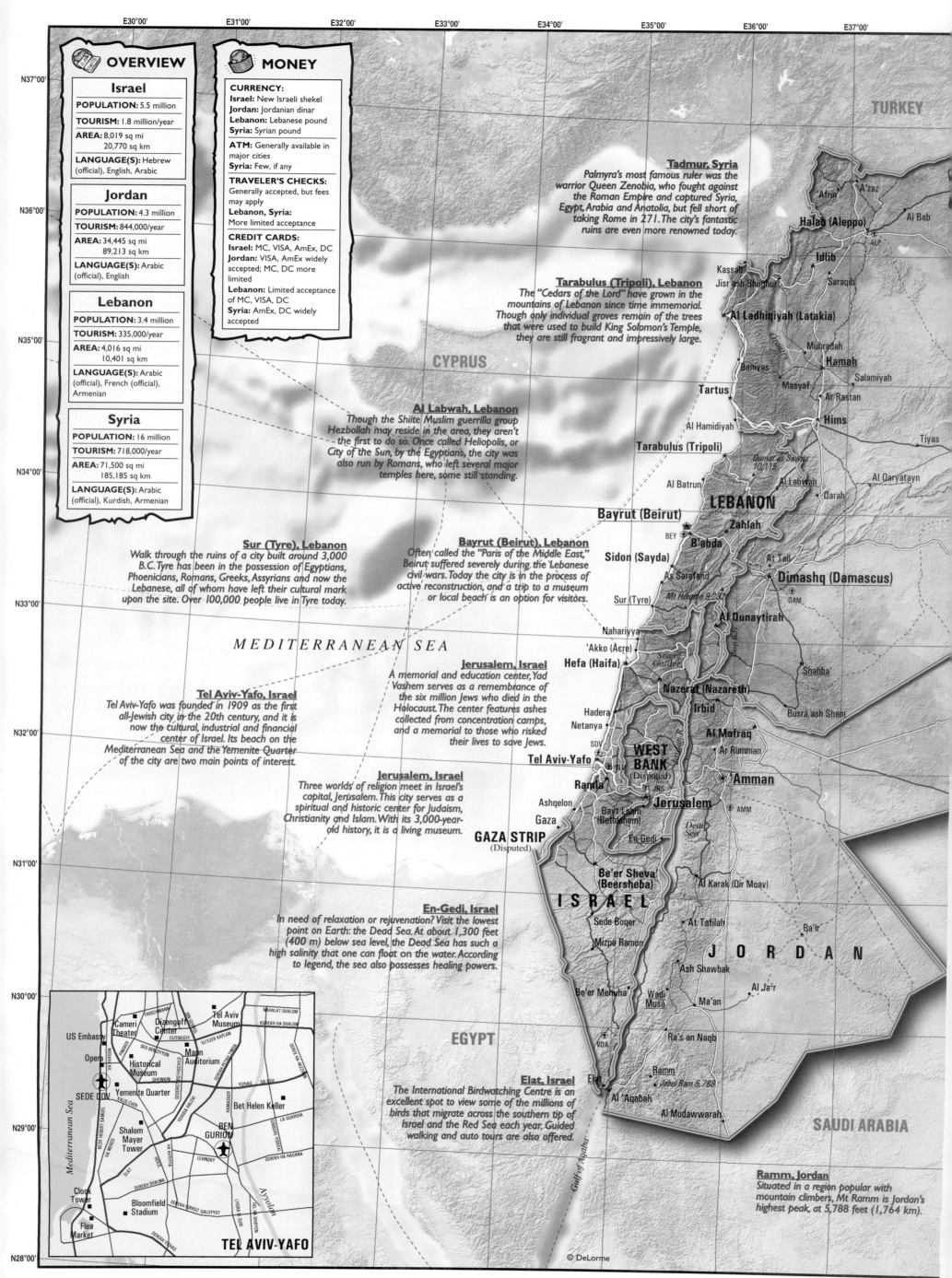

© DeLorme

Scale 1:3,000,000 at map center

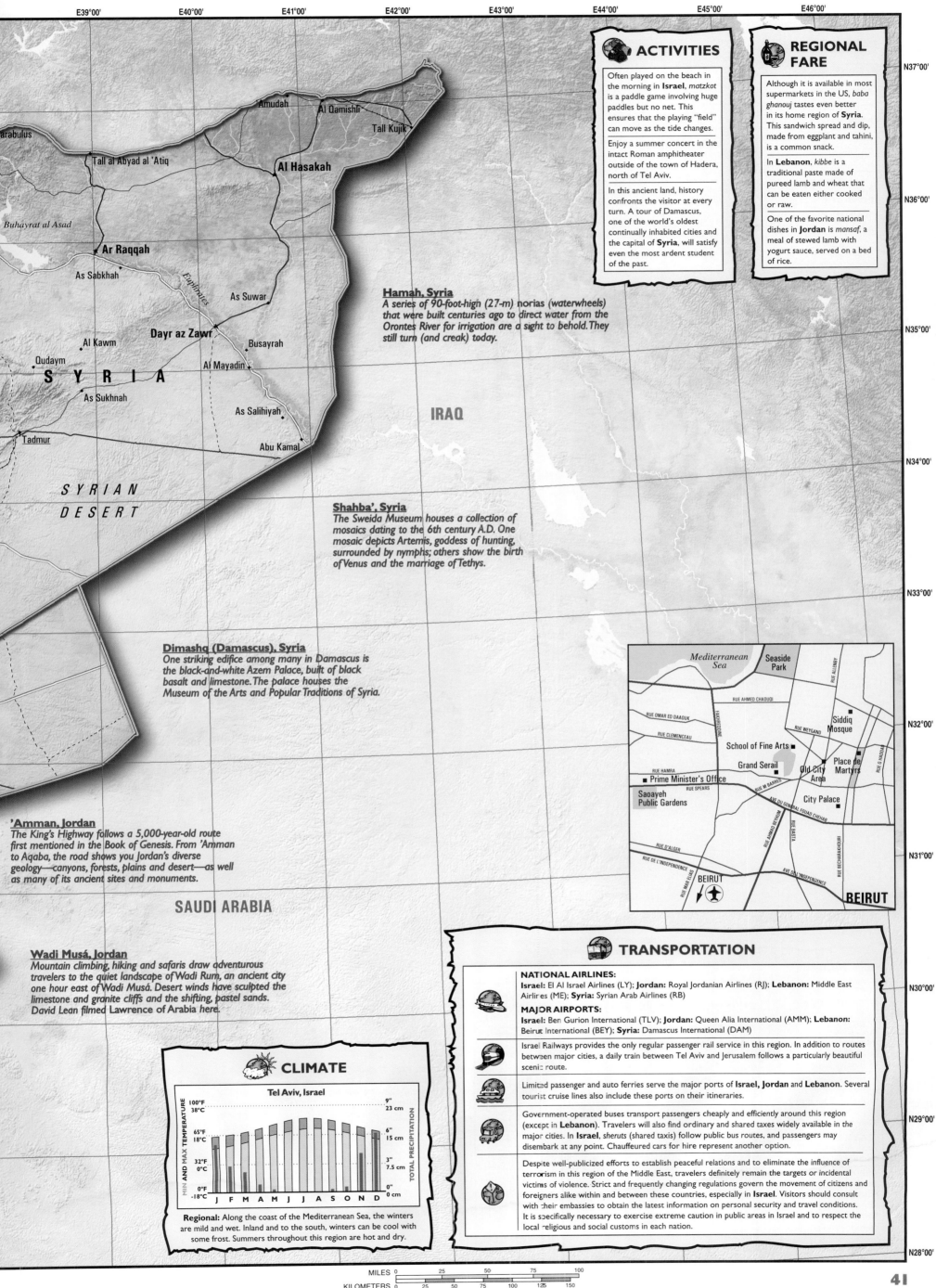

Jarabulus

Tall al Abyad al 'Atiq

Amudah

Al Qamishli

Tall Kujik

Al Hasakah

Buhayrat al Asad

Ar Raqqah

As Sabkhah

Euphrates

As Suwar

Qudaym

Al Kawm

Dayr az Zawr

Busayrah

Al Mayadin

As Sukhnah

As Salihiyah

Tadmur

Abu Kamal

S Y R I A

S Y R I A N   D E S E R T

IRAQ

SAUDI ARABIA

ACTIVITIES

Often played on the beach in the morning in **Israel**, *matzkot* is a paddle game involving huge paddles but no net. This ensures that the playing "field" can move as the tide changes.

Enjoy a summer concert in the intact Roman amphitheater outside of the town of Hadera, north of Tel Aviv.

In this ancient land, history confronts the visitor at every turn. A tour of Damascus, one of the world's oldest continually inhabited cities and the capital of **Syria**, will satisfy even the most ardent student of the past.

REGIONAL FARE

Although it is available in most supermarkets in the US, *baba ghanouj* tastes even better in its home region of **Syria**. This sandwich spread and dip, made from eggplant and tahini, is a common snack.

In **Lebanon**, *kibbe* is a traditional paste made of pureed lamb and wheat that can be eaten either cooked or raw.

One of the favorite national dishes in **Jordan** is *mansaf*, a meal of stewed lamb with yogurt sauce, served on a bed of rice.

Hamah, Syria
A series of 90-foot-high (27-m) *norias* (waterwheels) that were built centuries ago to direct water from the Orontes River for irrigation are a sight to behold. They still turn (and creak) today.

Shahba', Syria
The Sweida Museum houses a collection of mosaics dating to the 6th century A.D. One mosaic depicts Artemis, goddess of hunting, surrounded by nymphs; others show the birth of Venus and the marriage of Tethys.

Dimashq (Damascus), Syria
One striking edifice among many in Damascus is the black-and-white Azem Palace, built of black basalt and limestone. The palace houses the Museum of the Arts and Popular Traditions of Syria.

'Amman, Jordan
The King's Highway follows a 5,000-year-old route first mentioned in the Book of Genesis. From 'Amman to Aqaba, the road shows you Jordan's diverse geology—canyons, forests, plains and desert—as well as many of its ancient sites and monuments.

Wadi Musá, Jordan
Mountain climbing, hiking and safaris draw adventurous travelers to the quiet landscape of Wadi Rum, an ancient city one hour east of Wadi Musá. Desert winds have sculpted the limestone and granite cliffs and the shifting, pastel sands. David Lean filmed *Lawrence of Arabia* here.

BEIRUT

Mediterranean Sea

Seaside Park

RUE ALLENBY

RUE AHMED CHAOUQI

RUE OMAR ED DAAOUK

FAKHREDDINE

RUE WEYGAND

Siddiq Mosque

RUE CLEMENCEAU

School of Fine Arts

RUE HAMRA

Grand Serail

Place de Martyrs

Old City Area

RUE G HADDAD

Prime Minister's Office

RUE M BARRES

RUE SPEARS

RUE AHMAD BEYHUM

RUE BASTA

Saoayeh Public Gardens

AVE DU GENERAL FOUAD CHEHAB

City Palace

RUE D'ALGER

RUE DE L'INDEPENDENCE

AVE DE L'INDEPENDENCE

RUE BECHARAKHOURI

RUE MAR ELIAS

BEIRUT

CLIMATE

Tel Aviv, Israel

	MIN AND MAX TEMPERATURE	TOTAL PRECIPITATION

100°F / 38°C — 9" / 23 cm
65°F / 18°C — 6" / 15 cm
32°F / 0°C — 3" / 7.5 cm
0°F / -18°C — 0" / 0 cm

J F M A M J J A S O N D

Regional: Along the coast of the Mediterranean Sea, the winters are mild and wet. Inland and to the south, winters can be cool with some frost. Summers throughout this region are hot and dry.

TRANSPORTATION

NATIONAL AIRLINES:
Israel: El Al Israel Airlines (LY); **Jordan:** Royal Jordanian Airlines (RJ); **Lebanon:** Middle East Airlines (ME); **Syria:** Syrian Arab Airlines (RB)

MAJOR AIRPORTS:
Israel: Ben Gurion International (TLV); **Jordan:** Queen Alia International (AMM); **Lebanon:** Beirut International (BEY); **Syria:** Damascus International (DAM)

Israel Railways provides the only regular passenger rail service in this region. In addition to routes between major cities, a daily train between Tel Aviv and Jerusalem follows a particularly beautiful scenic route.

Limited passenger and auto ferries serve the major ports of **Israel, Jordan** and **Lebanon**. Several tourist cruise lines also include these ports on their itineraries.

Government-operated buses transport passengers cheaply and efficiently around this region (except in **Lebanon**). Travelers will also find ordinary and shared taxes widely available in the major cities. In **Israel**, *sheruts* (shared taxis) follow public bus routes, and passengers may disembark at any point. Chauffeured cars for hire represent another option.

Despite well-publicized efforts to establish peaceful relations and to eliminate the influence of terrorism in this region of the Middle East, travelers definitely remain the targets or incidental victims of violence. Strict and frequently changing regulations govern the movement of citizens and foreigners alike within and between these countries, especially in **Israel**. Visitors should consult with their embassies to obtain the latest information on personal security and travel conditions. It is specifically necessary to exercise extreme caution in public areas in **Israel** and to respect the local religious and social customs in each nation.

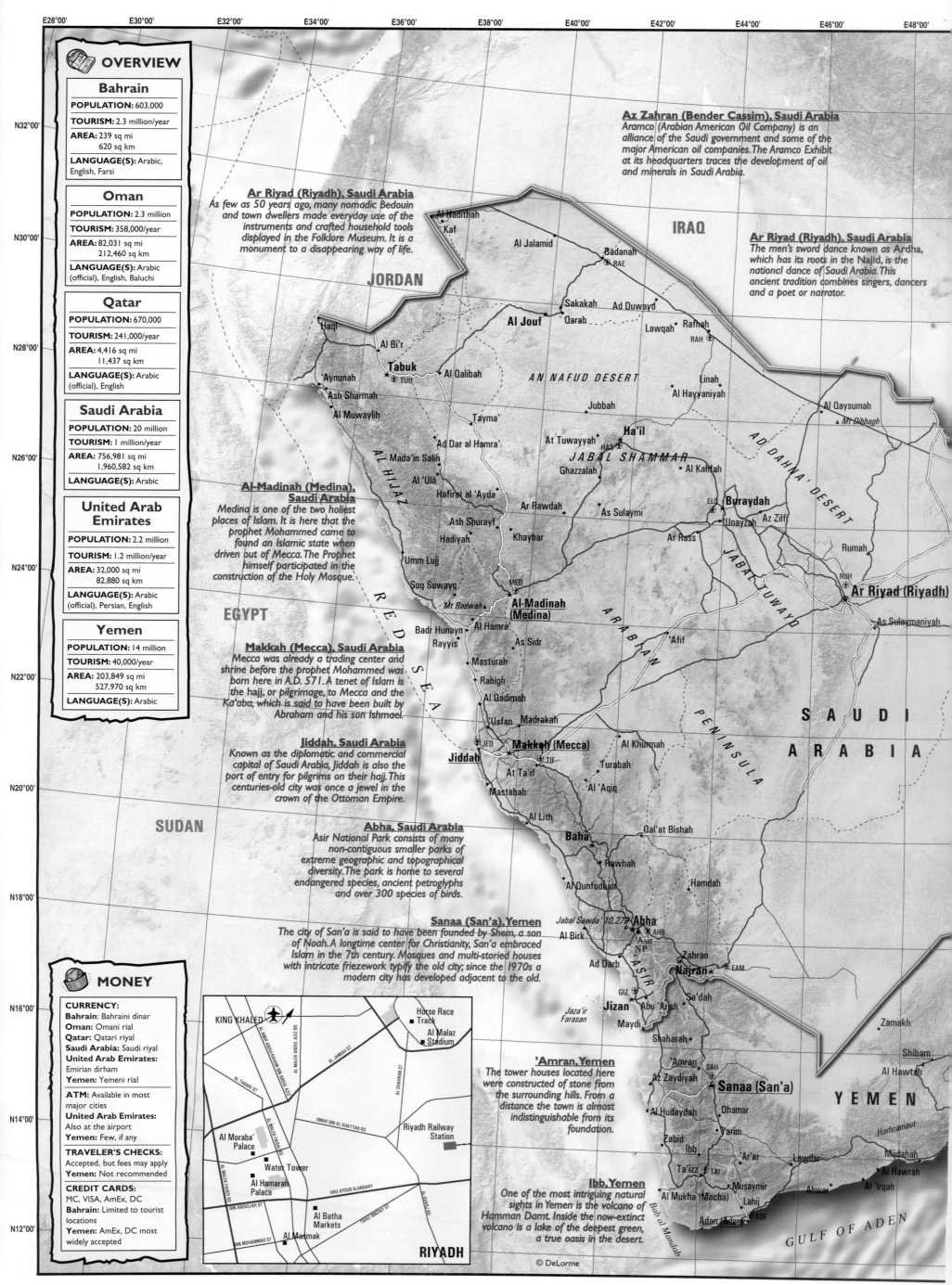

OVERVIEW

Bahrain
POPULATION: 603,000
TOURISM: 2.3 million/year
AREA: 239 sq mi
620 sq km
LANGUAGE(S): Arabic, English, Farsi

Oman
POPULATION: 2.3 million
TOURISM: 358,000/year
AREA: 82,031 sq mi
212,460 sq km
LANGUAGE(S): Arabic (official), English, Baluchi

Qatar
POPULATION: 670,000
TOURISM: 241,000/year
AREA: 4,416 sq mi
11,437 sq km
LANGUAGE(S): Arabic (official), English

Saudi Arabia
POPULATION: 20 million
TOURISM: 1 million/year
AREA: 756,981 sq mi
1,960,582 sq km
LANGUAGE(S): Arabic

United Arab Emirates
POPULATION: 2.2 million
TOURISM: 1.2 million/year
AREA: 32,000 sq mi
82,880 sq km
LANGUAGE(S): Arabic (official), Persian, English

Yemen
POPULATION: 14 million
TOURISM: 40,000/year
AREA: 203,849 sq mi
527,970 sq km
LANGUAGE(S): Arabic

MONEY

CURRENCY:
Bahrain: Bahraini dinar
Oman: Omani rial
Qatar: Qatari riyal
Saudi Arabia: Saudi riyal
United Arab Emirates: Emirian dirham
Yemen: Yemeni rial

ATM: Available in most major cities
United Arab Emirates: Also at the airport
Yemen: Few, if any

TRAVELER'S CHECKS: Accepted, but fees may apply
Yemen: Not recommended

CREDIT CARDS:
MC, VISA, AmEx, DC
Bahrain: Limited to tourist locations
Yemen: AmEx, DC most widely accepted

Az Zahran (Bender Cassim), Saudi Arabia
Aramco (Arabian American Oil Company) is an alliance of the Saudi government and some of the major American oil companies. The Aramco Exhibit at its headquarters traces the development of oil and minerals in Saudi Arabia.

Ar Riyad (Riyadh), Saudi Arabia
The men's sword dance known as Ardha, which has its roots in the Najid, is the national dance of Saudi Arabia. This ancient tradition combines singers, dancers and a poet or narrator.

Ar Riyad (Riyadh), Saudi Arabia
As few as 50 years ago, many nomadic Bedouin and town dwellers made everyday use of the instruments and crafted household tools displayed in the Folklore Museum. It is a monument to a disappearing way of life.

Al-Madinah (Medina), Saudi Arabia
Medina is one of the two holiest places of Islam. It is here that the prophet Mohammed came to found an Islamic state when driven out of Mecca. The Prophet himself participated in the construction of the Holy Mosque.

Makkah (Mecca), Saudi Arabia
Mecca was already a trading center and shrine before the prophet Mohammed was born here in A.D. 571. A tenet of Islam is the hajj, or pilgrimage, to Mecca and the Ka'aba, which is said to have been built by Abraham and his son Ishmael.

Jiddah, Saudi Arabia
Known as the diplomatic and commercial capital of Saudi Arabia, Jiddah is also the port of entry for pilgrims on their hajj. This centuries-old city was once a jewel in the crown of the Ottoman Empire.

Abha, Saudi Arabia
Asir National Park consists of many non-contiguous smaller parks of extreme geographic and topographical diversity. The park is home to several endangered species, ancient petroglyphs and over 300 species of birds.

Sanaa (San'a), Yemen
The city of San'a is said to have been founded by Shem, a son of Noah. A longtime center for Christianity, San'a embraced Islam in the 7th century. Mosques and multi-storied houses with intricate friezework typify the old city; since the 1970s a modern city has developed adjacent to the old.

'Amran, Yemen
The tower houses located here were constructed of stone from the surrounding hills. From a distance the town is almost indistinguishable from its foundation.

Ibb, Yemen
One of the most intriguing natural sights in Yemen is the volcano of Hamman Damt. Inside the now-extinct volcano is a lake of the deepest green, a true oasis in the desert.

© DeLorme

RIYADH (inset map)
KING KHALED · Horse Race Track · Al Malaz Stadium · Al Moraba' Palace · Water Tower · Al Hamarah Palace · Al Batha Markets · Al Masmak · Riyadh Railway Station

Scale 1:7,500,000 at map center

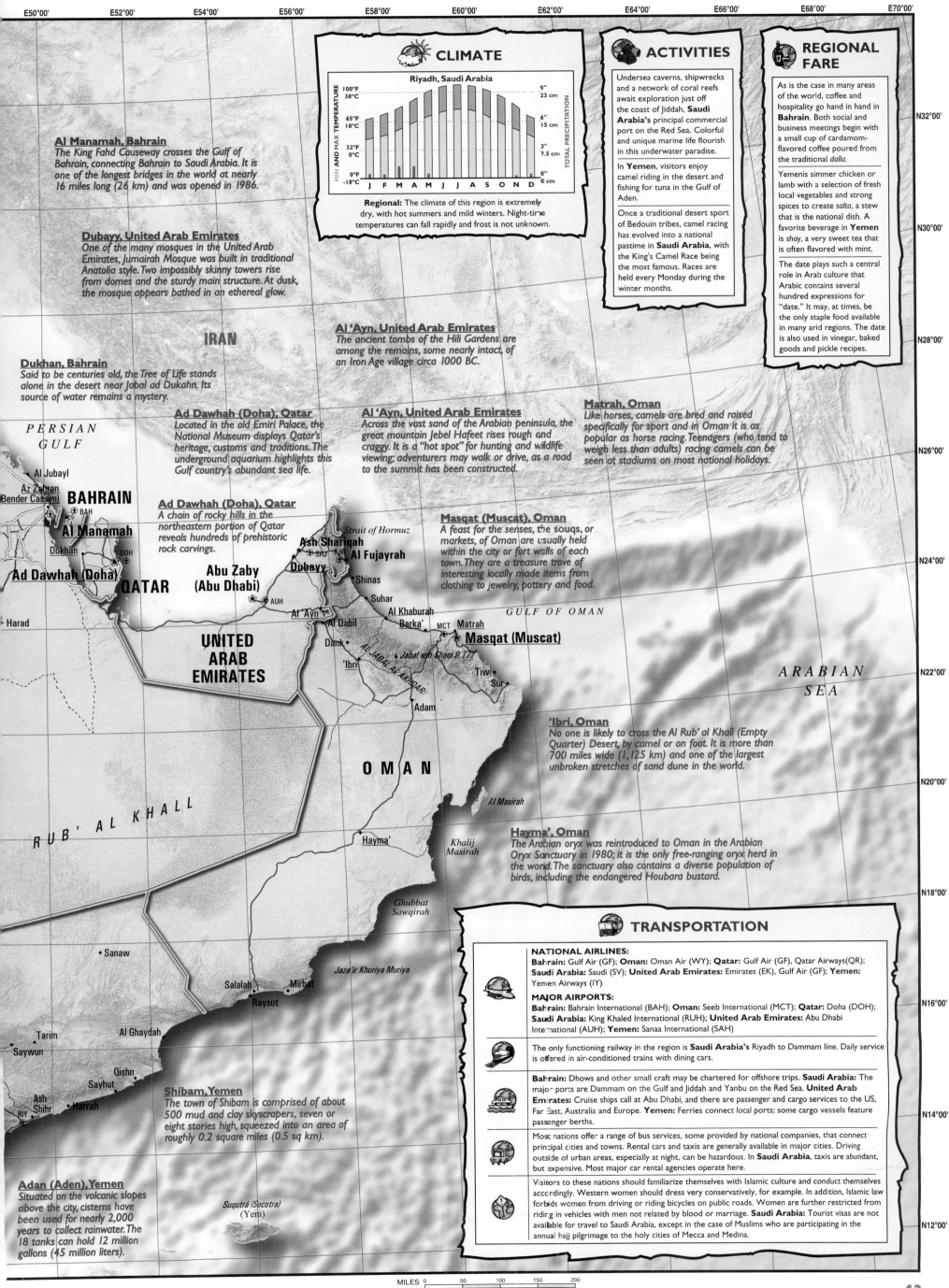

CLIMATE

Riyadh, Saudi Arabia

MIN AND MAX TEMPERATURE
100°F 38°C
65°F 18°C
32°F 0°C
0°F -18°C

TOTAL PRECIPITATION
9" 23 cm
6" 15 cm
3" 7.5 cm
0" 0 cm

J F M A M J J A S O N D

Regional: The climate of this region is extremely dry, with hot summers and mild winters. Night-time temperatures can fall rapidly and frost is not unknown.

ACTIVITIES

Undersea caverns, shipwrecks and a network of coral reefs await exploration just off the coast of Jiddah, **Saudi Arabia's** principal commercial port on the Red Sea. Colorful and unique marine life flourish in this underwater paradise.

In **Yemen**, visitors enjoy camel riding in the desert and fishing for tuna in the Gulf of Aden.

Once a traditional desert sport of Bedouin tribes, camel racing has evolved into a national pastime in **Saudi Arabia**, with the King's Camel Race being the most famous. Races are held every Monday during the winter months.

REGIONAL FARE

As is the case in many areas of the world, coffee and hospitality go hand in hand in **Bahrain**. Both social and business meetings begin with a small cup of cardamom-flavored coffee poured from the traditional *dalla*.

Yemenis simmer chicken or lamb with a selection of fresh local vegetables and strong spices to create *salta*, a stew that is the national dish. A favorite beverage in **Yemen** is *shay*, a very sweet tea that is often flavored with mint.

The date plays such a central role in Arab culture that Arabic contains several hundred expressions for "date." It may, at times, be the only staple food available in many arid regions. The date is also used in vinegar, baked goods and pickle recipes.

Al Manamah, Bahrain
The King Fahd Causeway crosses the Gulf of Bahrain, connecting Bahrain to Saudi Arabia. It is one of the longest bridges in the world at nearly 16 miles long (26 km) and was opened in 1986.

Dubayy, United Arab Emirates
One of the many mosques in the United Arab Emirates, Jumairah Mosque was built in traditional Anatolia style. Two impossibly skinny towers rise from domes and the sturdy main structure. At dusk, the mosque appears bathed in an ethereal glow.

Al 'Ayn, United Arab Emirates
The ancient tombs of the Hili Gardens are among the remains, some nearly intact, of an Iron Age village circa 1000 BC.

Dukhan, Bahrain
Said to be centuries old, the Tree of Life stands alone in the desert near Jabal ad Dukahn. Its source of water remains a mystery.

Ad Dawhah (Doha), Qatar
Located in the old Emiri Palace, the National Museum displays Qatar's heritage, customs and traditions. The underground aquarium highlights this Gulf country's abundant sea life.

Al 'Ayn, United Arab Emirates
Across the vast sand of the Arabian peninsula, the great mountain Jebel Hafeet rises rough and craggy. It is a "hot spot" for hunting and wildlife viewing; adventurers may walk or drive, as a road to the summit has been constructed.

Matrah, Oman
Like horses, camels are bred and raised specifically for sport and in Oman it is as popular as horse racing. Teenagers (who tend to weigh less than adults) racing camels can be seen at stadiums on most national holidays.

Ad Dawhah (Doha), Qatar
A chain of rocky hills in the northeastern portion of Qatar reveals hundreds of prehistoric rock carvings.

Masqat (Muscat), Oman
A feast for the senses, the souqs, or markets, of Oman are usually held within the city or fort walls of each town. They are a treasure trove of interesting locally made items from clothing to jewelry, pottery and food.

'Ibri, Oman
No one is likely to cross the Al Rub' al Khall (Empty Quarter) Desert by camel or on foot. It is more than 700 miles wide (1,125 km) and one of the largest unbroken stretches of sand dune in the world.

Hayma', Oman
The Arabian oryx was reintroduced to Oman in the Arabian Oryx Sanctuary in 1980; it is the only free-ranging oryx herd in the world. The sanctuary also contains a diverse population of birds, including the endangered Houbara bustard.

Shibam, Yemen
The town of Shibam is comprised of about 500 mud and clay skyscrapers, seven or eight stories high, squeezed into an area of roughly 0.2 square miles (0.5 sq km).

Adan (Aden), Yemen
Situated on the volcanic slopes above the city, cisterns have been used for nearly 2,000 years to collect rainwater. The 18 tanks can hold 12 million gallons (45 million liters).

Map labels
IRAN
PERSIAN GULF
Al Jubayl
Az Zahran (Bender Cassim)
BAHRAIN
BAH
Al Manamah
Dukhan
DOH
Ad Dawhah (Doha)
QATAR
Harad
Ash Shariqah SHJ
FJR Al Fujayrah
Dubayy
Abu Zaby (Abu Dhabi)
AUH
Shinas
Suhar
Al Khaburah
Barka'
Al 'Ayn
Al Qabil
Dank
'Ibri
AL JABAL AL AKHDAR
Jabal ash Sham 9,777
Strait of Hormuz
MCT Matrah
Masqat (Muscat)
GULF OF OMAN
Tiwi
Sur
UNITED ARAB EMIRATES
Adam
OMAN
RUB' AL KHALL
Hayma'
Al Masirah
Khalij Masirah
ARABIAN SEA
Ghubbat Sawqirah
Sanaw
Jaza'ir Khuriya Muriya
Salalah
Mirbat
Raysut
Tarim
Al Ghaydah
Saywun
Qishn
Sayhut
Ash Shihr
Riy
Harrah
Suqutrá (Socotra) (Yem)

TRANSPORTATION

NATIONAL AIRLINES:
Bahrain: Gulf Air (GF); **Oman:** Oman Air (WY); **Qatar:** Gulf Air (GF), Qatar Airways(QR); **Saudi Arabia:** Saudi (SV); **United Arab Emirates:** Emirates (EK), Gulf Air (GF); **Yemen:** Yemen Airways (IY)

MAJOR AIRPORTS:
Bahrain: Bahrain International (BAH); **Oman:** Seeb International (MCT); **Qatar:** Doha (DOH); **Saudi Arabia:** King Khaled International (RUH); **United Arab Emirates:** Abu Dhabi International (AUH); **Yemen:** Sanaa International (SAH)

The only functioning railway in the region is **Saudi Arabia's** Riyadh to Dammam line. Daily service is offered in air-conditioned trains with dining cars.

Bahrain: Dhows and other small craft may be chartered for offshore trips. **Saudi Arabia:** The major ports are Dammam on the Gulf and Jiddah and Yanbu on the Red Sea. **United Arab Emirates:** Cruise ships call at Abu Dhabi, and there are passenger and cargo services to the US, Far East, Australia and Europe. **Yemen:** Ferries connect local ports; some cargo vessels feature passenger berths.

Most nations offer a range of bus services, some provided by national companies, that connect principal cities and towns. Rental cars and taxis are generally available in major cities. Driving outside of urban areas, especially at night, can be hazardous. In **Saudi Arabia**, taxis are abundant, but expensive. Most major car rental agencies operate here.

Visitors to these nations should familiarize themselves with Islamic culture and conduct themselves accordingly. Western women should dress very conservatively, for example. In addition, Islamic law forbids women from driving or riding bicycles on public roads. Women are further restricted from riding in vehicles with men not related by blood or marriage. **Saudi Arabia:** Tourist visas are not available for travel to Saudi Arabia, except in the case of Muslims who are participating in the annual hajj pilgrimage to the holy cities of Mecca and Medina.

MILES 0 50 100 150 200
KILOMETERS 0 50 100 150 200 250 300

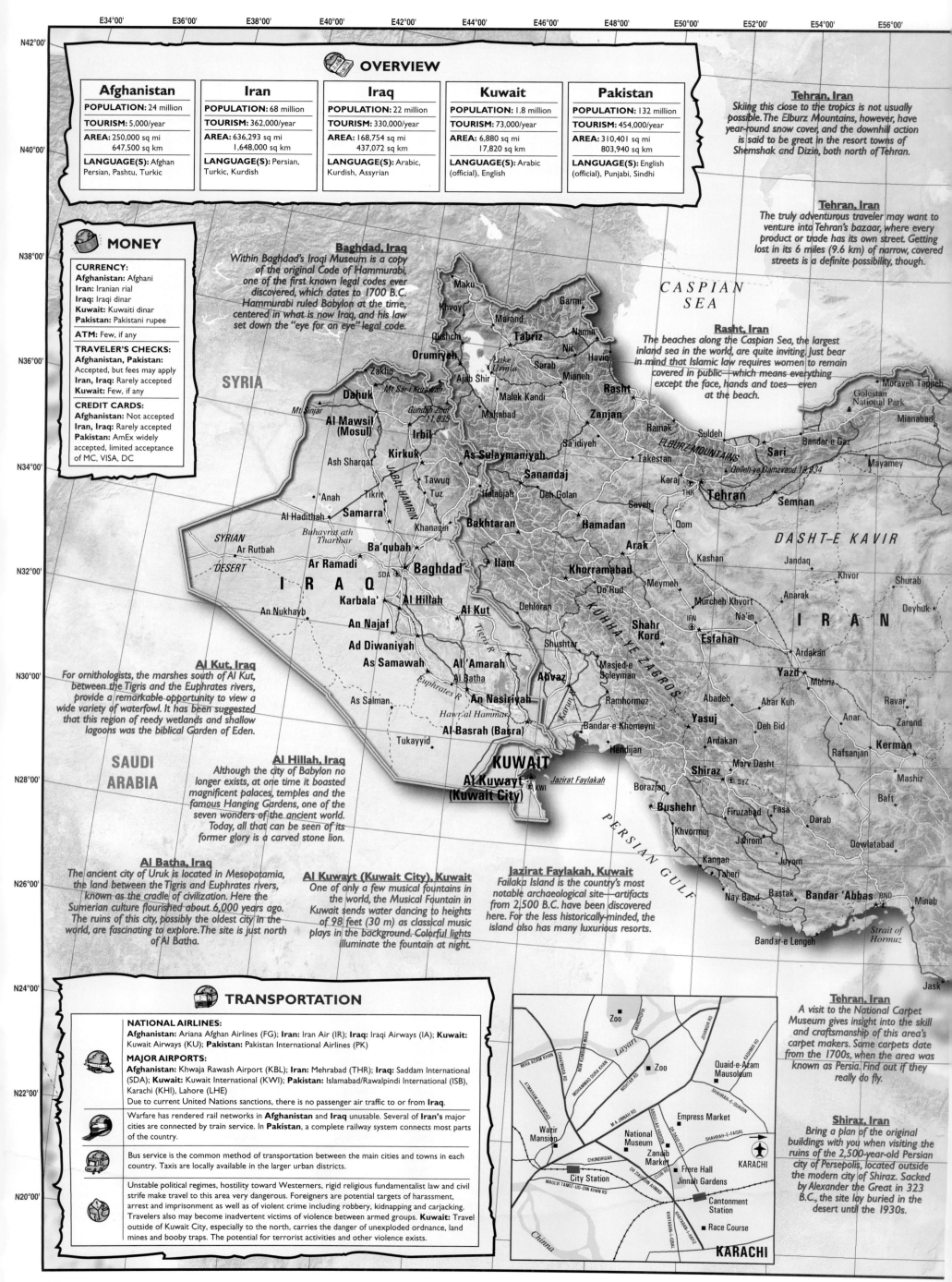

OVERVIEW

Afghanistan
POPULATION: 24 million
TOURISM: 5,000/year
AREA: 250,000 sq mi
647,500 sq km
LANGUAGE(S): Afghan Persian, Pashtu, Turkic

Iran
POPULATION: 68 million
TOURISM: 362,000/year
AREA: 636,293 sq mi
1,648,000 sq km
LANGUAGE(S): Persian, Turkic, Kurdish

Iraq
POPULATION: 22 million
TOURISM: 330,000/year
AREA: 168,754 sq mi
437,072 sq km
LANGUAGE(S): Arabic, Kurdish, Assyrian

Kuwait
POPULATION: 1.8 million
TOURISM: 73,000/year
AREA: 6,880 sq mi
17,820 sq km
LANGUAGE(S): Arabic (official), English

Pakistan
POPULATION: 132 million
TOURISM: 454,000/year
AREA: 310,401 sq mi
803,940 sq km
LANGUAGE(S): English (official), Punjabi, Sindhi

MONEY

CURRENCY:
Afghanistan: Afghani
Iran: Iranian rial
Iraq: Iraqi dinar
Kuwait: Kuwaiti dinar
Pakistan: Pakistani rupee
ATM: Few, if any
TRAVELER'S CHECKS:
Afghanistan, Pakistan: Accepted, but fees may apply
Iran, Iraq: Rarely accepted
Kuwait: Few, if any
CREDIT CARDS:
Afghanistan: Not accepted
Iran, Iraq: Rarely accepted
Pakistan: AmEx widely accepted, limited acceptance of MC, VISA, DC

Baghdad, Iraq
Within Baghdad's Iraqi Museum is a copy of the original Code of Hammurabi, one of the first known legal codes ever discovered, which dates to 1700 B.C. Hammurabi ruled Babylon at the time, centered in what is now Iraq, and his law set down the "eye for an eye" legal code.

Tehran, Iran
Skiing this close to the tropics is not usually possible. The Elburz Mountains, however, have year-round snow cover, and the downhill action is said to be great in the resort towns of Shemshak and Dizin, both north of Tehran.

Tehran, Iran
The truly adventurous traveler may want to venture into Tehran's bazaar, where every product or trade has its own street. Getting lost in its 6 miles (9.6 km) of narrow, covered streets is a definite possibility, though.

Rasht, Iran
The beaches along the Caspian Sea, the largest inland sea in the world, are quite inviting. Just bear in mind that Islamic law requires women to remain covered in public—which means everything except the face, hands and toes—even at the beach.

Al Kut, Iraq
For ornithologists, the marshes south of Al Kut, between the Tigris and the Euphrates rivers, provide a remarkable opportunity to view a wide variety of waterfowl. It has been suggested that this region of reedy wetlands and shallow lagoons may be the biblical Garden of Eden.

Al Hillah, Iraq
Although the city of Babylon no longer exists, at one time it boasted magnificent palaces, temples and the famous Hanging Gardens, one of the seven wonders of the ancient world. Today, all that can be seen of its former glory is a carved stone lion.

Al Batha, Iraq
The ancient city of Uruk is located in Mesopotamia, the land between the Tigris and Euphrates rivers, known as the cradle of civilization. Here the Sumerian culture flourished about 6,000 years ago. The ruins of this city, possibly the oldest city in the world, are fascinating to explore. The site is just north of Al Batha.

Al Kuwayt (Kuwait City), Kuwait
One of only a few musical fountains in the world, the Musical Fountain in Kuwait sends water dancing to heights of 98 feet (30 m) as classical music plays at night. Colorful lights illuminate the fountain at night.

Jazirat Faylakah, Kuwait
Failaka Island is the country's most notable archaeological site—artifacts from 2,500 B.C. have been discovered here. For the less historically-minded, the island also has many luxurious resorts.

Tehran, Iran
A visit to the National Carpet Museum gives insight into the skill and craftsmanship of this area's carpet makers. Some carpets date from the 1700s, when the area was known as Persia. Find out if they really do fly.

Shiraz, Iran
Bring a plan of the original buildings with you when visiting the ruins of the 2,500-year-old Persian city of Persepolis, located outside the modern city of Shiraz. Sacked by Alexander the Great in 323 B.C., the site lay buried in the desert until the 1930s.

TRANSPORTATION

NATIONAL AIRLINES:
Afghanistan: Ariana Afghan Airlines (FG); **Iran:** Iran Air (IR); **Iraq:** Iraqi Airways (IA); **Kuwait:** Kuwait Airways (KU); **Pakistan:** Pakistan International Airlines (PK)
MAJOR AIRPORTS:
Afghanistan: Khwaja Rawash Airport (KBL); **Iran:** Mehrabad (THR); **Iraq:** Saddam International (SDA); **Kuwait:** Kuwait International (KWI); **Pakistan:** Islamabad/Rawalpindi International (ISB), Karachi (KHI), Lahore (LHE)
Due to current United Nations sanctions, there is no passenger air traffic to or from **Iraq**.

Warfare has rendered rail networks in **Afghanistan** and **Iraq** unusable. Several of **Iran's** major cities are connected by train service. In **Pakistan**, a complete railway system connects most parts of the country.

Bus service is the common method of transportation between the main cities and towns in each country. Taxis are locally available in the larger urban districts.

Unstable political regimes, hostility toward Westerners, rigid religious fundamentalist law and civil strife make travel to this area very dangerous. Foreigners are potential targets of harassment, arrest and imprisonment as well as of violent crime including robbery, kidnapping and carjacking. Travelers also may become inadvertent victims of violence between armed groups. **Kuwait:** Travel outside of Kuwait City, especially to the north, carries the danger of unexploded ordnance, land mines and booby traps. The potential for terrorist activities and other violence exists.

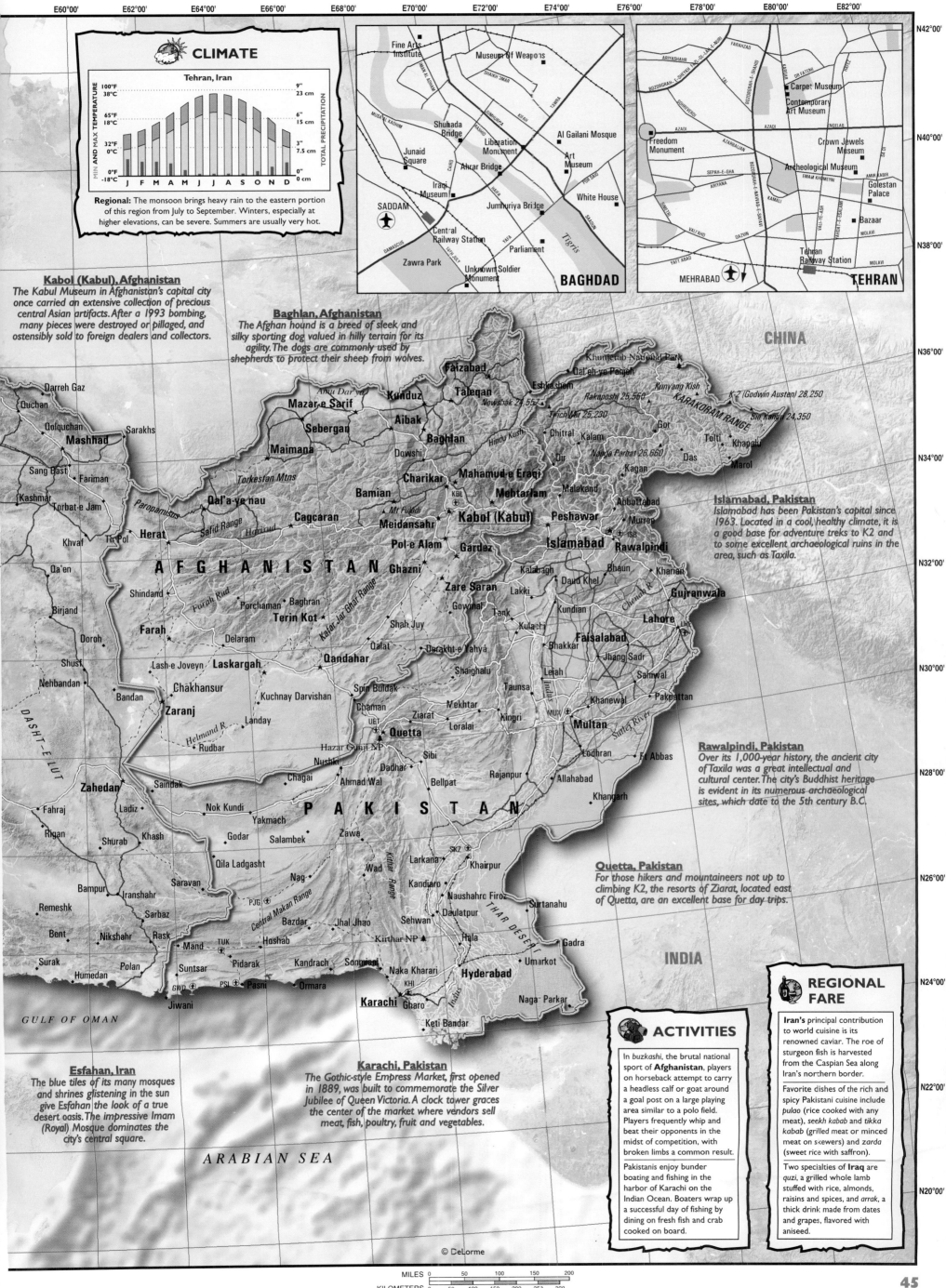

CLIMATE

Tehran, Iran

Regional: The monsoon brings heavy rain to the eastern portion of this region from July to September. Winters, especially at higher elevations, can be severe. Summers are usually very hot.

BAGHDAD

TEHRAN

Kabol (Kabul), Afghanistan
The Kabul Museum in Afghanistan's capital city once carried an extensive collection of precious central Asian artifacts. After a 1993 bombing, many pieces were destroyed or pillaged, and ostensibly sold to foreign dealers and collectors.

Baghlan, Afghanistan
The Afghan hound is a breed of sleek and silky sporting dog valued in hilly terrain for its agility. The dogs are commonly used by shepherds to protect their sheep from wolves.

Islamabad, Pakistan
Islamabad has been Pakistan's capital since 1963. Located in a cool, healthy climate, it is a good base for adventure treks to K2 and to some excellent archaeological ruins in the area, such as Taxila.

Rawalpindi, Pakistan
Over its 1,000-year history, the ancient city of Taxila was a great intellectual and cultural center. The city's Buddhist heritage is evident in its numerous archaeological sites, which date to the 5th century B.C.

Quetta, Pakistan
For those hikers and mountaineers not up to climbing K2, the resorts of Ziarat, located east of Quetta, are an excellent base for day trips.

Esfahan, Iran
The blue tiles of its many mosques and shrines glistening in the sun give Esfahan the look of a true desert oasis. The impressive Imam (Royal) Mosque dominates the city's central square.

Karachi, Pakistan
The Gothic-style Empress Market, first opened in 1889, was built to commemorate the Silver Jubilee of Queen Victoria. A clock tower graces the center of the market where vendors sell meat, fish, poultry, fruit and vegetables.

ACTIVITIES

In buzkashi, the brutal national sport of **Afghanistan**, players on horseback attempt to carry a headless calf or goat around a goal post on a large playing area similar to a polo field. Players frequently whip and beat their opponents in the midst of competition, with broken limbs a common result.

Pakistanis enjoy bunder boating and fishing in the harbor of Karachi on the Indian Ocean. Boaters wrap up a successful day of fishing by dining on fresh fish and crab cooked on board.

REGIONAL FARE

Iran's principal contribution to world cuisine is its renowned caviar. The roe of sturgeon fish is harvested from the Caspian Sea along Iran's northern border.

Favorite dishes of the rich and spicy Pakistani cuisine include pulao (rice cooked with any meat), seekh kabab and tikka kabab (grilled meat or minced meat on skewers) and zarda (sweet rice with saffron).

Two specialties of **Iraq** are quzi, a grilled whole lamb stuffed with rice, almonds, raisins and spices, and arrak, a thick drink made from dates and grapes, flavored with aniseed.

© DeLorme

MILES
KILOMETERS

OVERVIEW

Kazakhstan
POPULATION: 17 million
TOURISM: Not available
AREA: 1,049,150 sq mi
2,717,300 sq km
LANGUAGE(S): Russian (official), Kazakh (official)

Kyrgyzstan
POPULATION: 4.5 million
TOURISM: 11,000/year
AREA: 76,641 sq mi
198,500 sq km
LANGUAGE(S): Kirghiz (official), Russian (official)

Tajikistan
POPULATION: 6 million
TOURISM: Not available
AREA: 55,251 sq mi
143,100 sq km
LANGUAGE(S): Tajik (official), Russian

Turkmenistan
POPULATION: 4.2 million
TOURISM: Not available
AREA: 188,456 sq mi
488,100 sq km
LANGUAGE(S): Turkmen, Russian, Uzbek

Uzbekistan
POPULATION: 23 million
TOURISM: Not available
AREA: 172,741 sq mi
447,400 sq km
LANGUAGE(S): Uzbek, Russian, Tajik

MONEY

CURRENCY:
Kazakhstan: Kazakhstani tenge
Kyrgyzstan: Kyrgyzstani som
Tajikistan: Tajikistani ruble
Turkmenistan: Tukmen manat
Uzbekistan: Uzbekistani som

ATM: Few, if any

TRAVELER'S CHECKS:
Rarely accepted, if at all
Kazakhstan: AmEx checks recommended

CREDIT CARDS:
Kazakhstan, Tajikistan: VISA, DC
Kyrgyzstan, Uzbekistan: Accepted at tourist locations
Turkmenistan: Accepted only at new hotels

Kazalinsk, Kazakhstan
The Baykonur Space Center was the launch site for Soviet space shots. When they first began, the Soviets identified the launch site as Baykonur, 186 miles away (300 km), in an effort to maintain secrecy. Today, Russia leases it from Kazakhstan.

Muynoq, Uzbekistan
The former port city of Muynoq once thrived on fishing the Aral Sea. The sea, drying up progressively, has been transformed into a salt-pan desert, and the town is now full of rusting boats. The dying Aral Sea is one of the worst environmental disasters of our times.

Krasnovodsk, Turkmenistan
The world's largest inland lake, the Caspian Sea, forms Turkmenistan's northwest border. Turkmenistan and other bordering nations are currently dealing with flooding and water-shortage problems caused by the fluctuation of the sea's water level, as well as disputes over fishing it.

Ashgabat (Ashkhabad), Turkmenistan
Five specific designs for carpets are found in Turkmenistan and are all reflected in the design of the country's flag. These carpet designs are so popular that several factories have opened to produce them commercially.

Gyzylarbat, Turkmenistan
Climb down through caves to Bakharden, a hot mineral lake south of Gyzylarbat which lies almost 200 feet (61 m) beneath the Kopet Mountains. Locals claim that the water has healing powers and that Alexander the Great swam here.

Farghona, Uzbekistan
Tour a cotton- or silk-producing factory in the Fergana Valley, one of the oldest centers of civilization. Since this area has traditionally been heavily irrigated, agronomists have created hybrid plants that thrive in the changing landscape and can continue to supply the industry.

Samarkand, Uzbekistan
Evoking images from its days as a major Silk Road oasis, the city of Samarkand is renowned for its monumental cobalt domes and intricate tile work. The spirit of trade continues: at the colorful town bazaar, all goods imaginable are sold.

ALMA-ATA

TASHKENT

© DeLorme

Scale 1:7,500,000 at map center

Almaty (Alma-Ata), Kazakhstan
A large modern museum, the State Museum of Art has a comprehensive collection of Kazakh applied art—carpets, jewelry and wood carving—and some nice Russian and European pieces.

CLIMATE

Alma-Ata, Kazakhstan

Regional: Seasonal extremes of temperature characterize the climate of this region. The hot summers are bearable because of low humidity. Winters are cold, but tend to be dry and sunny.

REGIONAL FARE

When unexpected guests arrive for dinner in **Tajikistan**, fry up some leftover mutton, mix it with rice and onions, and presto: *plov*. This typical central Asia dish is often served with *lipioshka*, a typical round bread of the area.

On a more formal occasion, Kazakhs often treat favored guests to a whole sheep's head stewed in fragrant broth. The guest then shares the meal with those present in a ritual of respect.

Moshkichiri and *moshhurda* fill you up during the long, cold central Asian winter. Both are forms of meat and mung bean gruel, served piping hot.

The shish-ke-bob, called *shashlyk* in **Turkmenistan**, traditionally includes lamb or goat meat, onions, tomatoes and cucumbers.

One more lamb recipe of this region is *beshbarmak* (which means five fingers), a favorite dish in **Kyrgyzstan**. The cook serves cubed mutton brisket over homemade noodles and tops it with crispy onion rings.

ACTIVITIES

Only serious adventurers journey through the Pamir Mountains that cover the eastern half of **Tajikistan**. This trekking route, considered one of the more spectacular and dangerous in the world, winds through some of this region's most remote mountains.

Rugged mountains also dominate the land of **Kazakhstan**. Trekking is a popular activity, if not a lifestyle necessity, here as well. The long winters make for good skiing and heli-skiing.

Karakol, Kyrgyzstan
Sandwiched into the high mountains of Kyrgyzstan, Lake Issyk-Kul is one of the largest and most beautiful alpine lakes in the world. The lake has a high mineral content, making it unsuitable for drinking or irrigation but great for the health resorts that line its shores.

Karakol, Kyrgyzstan
Once cited as being "the Iliad of steppe tribes," the Manas is actually a much longer orally presented epic. It chronicles the main events in the history of the Kyrgyz people from the 6th to the 18th centuries.

Tashkent, Uzbekistan
As recently as the 19th century, infidels to Islam were brought before the Emir of Bukharan and thrown into a "bug pit" to fester for days or weeks amongst rodents and insects until their fate was decided—usually at the tip of the executioner's sword.

Murghob, Tajikistan
The sprawling Pamir Mountains anchor the center of Asia. Climbers and hunters from the former USSR have enjoyed adventures here for years; the area is now opening to foreigners as well. Kommunizma Peak is its highest point, at 24,590 feet (7,495 m).

Dushanbe, Tajikistan
The Tajik cultural and political capital of Dunshanbe was built with a low skyline in order to withstand earthquakes. The daily outdoor market is a social (if not commercial) lifeblood for this city, its nation newly emerged from civil war.

TRANSPORTATION

NATIONAL AIRLINES:
Kazakhstan: Kazakhstan Airlines (9Y); **Kyrgyzstan:** Kyrgyzstan Airlines (K2); **Tajikistan:** Tajikistan International Airlines (W5); **Turkmenistan:** Turkmenistan Airlines (T5); **Uzbekistan:** Uzbekistan Airlines (HY)

MAJOR AIRPORTS:
Kazakhstan: Alma-Ata (ALA), Chimkent (CIT); **Kyrgyzstan:** Bishkek (FRU); **Tajikistan:** Dushanbe (DYU); **Turkmenistan:** Ashgabat (ASB); **Uzbekistan:** Tashkent (TAS)
Air service in central Asia tends to be unreliable. Difficult schedules, sudden cancellations and overloading typify operations.

Rail lines connect these central Asian nations with each other and with Russia, but train travel is irregular, arduous and not on par with Western standards. In **Tajikistan**, travelers should avoid international train travel as the US State Department warns that criminals operate on board.

Although buses are dependent on road conditions and fuel supplies, they travel to many major cities and towns. Driving in cities can be risky; doing so outside of urban areas is perilous at best. Deteriorating and narrow roads, checkpoints manned by armed police and soldiers, and delays caused by livestock and large agricultural vehicles in the road contribute to the poor motoring conditions.

Tajikistan: Travel to Tajikistan should be avoided. The kidnapping of Westerners in November 1997 resulted in the death of one of the hostages. Ongoing civil strife generates occasional armed conflicts in Dushanbe and outlying areas. The unstable political and economic environment has also fostered increasingly bold criminal activities, including armed robberies. Despite some improvements, security conditions remain unsettled, and foreigners should take strict security precautions. Profound economic and political change have continued to make **Kazakhstan** and **Kyrgyzstan** less than hospitable. The nations lack adequate tourist facilities and do not have many of the goods and services taken for granted in other countries. In Kazakstan, police officers should be avoided on the street as there have been incidents of fake policemen robbing tourists.

Turkmenistan, Uzbekistan: Common street crime and limited medical care are the principal concerns of visitors. In Uzbekistan, Islamic custom dictates that women dress conservatively.

MILES 0 50 100 150 200
KILOMETERS 0 50 100 150 200 250 300

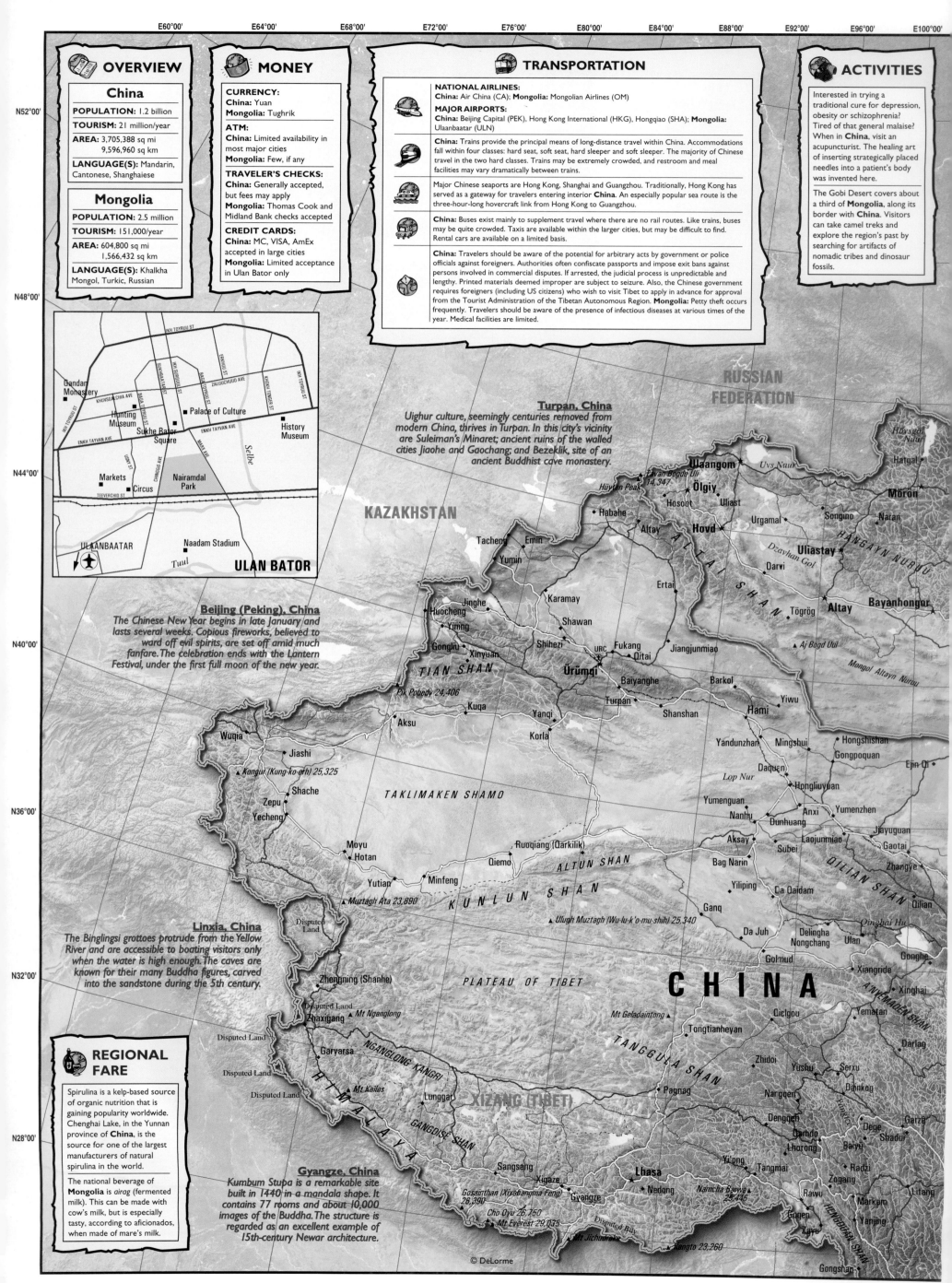

OVERVIEW

China
POPULATION: 1.2 billion
TOURISM: 21 million/year
AREA: 3,705,388 sq mi
9,596,960 sq km
LANGUAGE(S): Mandarin, Cantonese, Shanghaiese

Mongolia
POPULATION: 2.5 million
TOURISM: 151,000/year
AREA: 604,800 sq mi
1,566,432 sq km
LANGUAGE(S): Khalkha Mongol, Turkic, Russian

MONEY

CURRENCY:
China: Yuan
Mongolia: Tughrik

ATM:
China: Limited availability in most major cities
Mongolia: Few, if any

TRAVELER'S CHECKS:
China: Generally accepted, but fees may apply
Mongolia: Thomas Cook and Midland Bank checks accepted

CREDIT CARDS:
China: MC, VISA, AmEx accepted in large cities
Mongolia: Limited acceptance in Ulan Bator only

TRANSPORTATION

NATIONAL AIRLINES:
China: Air China (CA); **Mongolia:** Mongolian Airlines (OM)
MAJOR AIRPORTS:
China: Beijing Capital (PEK), Hong Kong International (HKG), Hongqiao (SHA); **Mongolia:** Ulaanbaatar (ULN)

China: Trains provide the principal means of long-distance travel within China. Accommodations fall within four classes: hard seat, soft seat, hard sleeper and soft sleeper. The majority of Chinese travel in the two hard classes. Trains may be extremely crowded, and restroom and meal facilities may vary dramatically between trains.

Major Chinese seaports are Hong Kong, Shanghai and Guangzhou. Traditionally, Hong Kong has served as a gateway for travelers entering interior **China**. An especially popular sea route is the three-hour-long hovercraft link from Hong Kong to Guangzhou.

China: Buses exist mainly to supplement travel where there are no rail routes. Like trains, buses may be quite crowded. Taxis are available within the larger cities, but may be difficult to find. Rental cars are available on a limited basis.

China: Travelers should be aware of the potential for arbitrary acts by government or police officials against foreigners. Authorities often confiscate passports and impose exit bans against persons involved in commercial disputes. If arrested, the judicial process is unpredictable and lengthy. Printed materials deemed improper are subject to seizure. Also, the Chinese government requires foreigners (including US citizens) who wish to visit Tibet to apply in advance for approval from the Tourist Administration of the Tibetan Autonomous Region. **Mongolia:** Petty theft occurs frequently. Travelers should be aware of the presence of infectious diseases at various times of the year. Medical facilities are limited.

ACTIVITIES

Interested in trying a traditional cure for depression, obesity or schizophrenia? Tired of that general malaise? When in **China**, visit an acupuncturist. The healing art of inserting strategically placed needles into a patient's body was invented here.

The Gobi Desert covers about a third of **Mongolia**, along its border with **China**. Visitors can take camel treks and explore the region's past by searching for artifacts of nomadic tribes and dinosaur fossils.

ULAN BATOR
(inset map labels)
Gandan Monastery
Hunting Museum
Palace of Culture
Sukhe Bator Square
History Museum
Markets
Circus
Nairamdal Park
ULAANBAATAR
Naadam Stadium
Tuul
IKH TOYRUU ST
SUKHBAATAR ST
KHUVSGALÇHIA AVE
BAGA TOYRUU ST
ENKHTAYVAN AVE
ZALUUÇHUUD AVE
KHUKH TIMGER ST
IKH TOYRUU ST
PEACE AVE
ENKH TAYVAN AVE
MARX AVE
CHINGGIS AVE
Selbe
TEEVERÇHID ST

Turpan, China
Uighur culture, seemingly centuries removed from modern China, thrives in Turpan. In this city's vicinity are Suleiman's Minaret; ancient ruins of the walled cities Jiaohe and Gaochang; and Bezeklik, site of an ancient Buddhist cave monastery.

Beijing (Peking), China
The Chinese New Year begins in late January and lasts several weeks. Copious fireworks, believed to ward off evil spirits, are set off amid much fanfare. The celebration ends with the Lantern Festival, under the first full moon of the new year.

Linxia, China
The Binglingsi grottoes protrude from the Yellow River and are accessible to boating visitors only when the water is high enough. The caves are known for their many Buddha figures, carved into the sandstone during the 5th century.

REGIONAL FARE

Spirulina is a kelp-based source of organic nutrition that is gaining popularity worldwide. Chenghai Lake, in the Yunnan province of **China**, is the source for one of the largest manufacturers of natural spirulina in the world.

The national beverage of **Mongolia** is airag (fermented milk). This can be made with cow's milk, but is especially tasty, according to aficionados, when made of mare's milk.

Gyangze, China
Kumbum Stupa is a remarkable site built in 1440 in a mandala shape. It contains 77 rooms and about 10,000 images of the Buddha. The structure is regarded as an excellent example of 15th-century Newar architecture.

RUSSIAN FEDERATION
KAZAKHSTAN
CHINA
XIZANG (TIBET)
PLATEAU OF TIBET
TIAN SHAN
TAKLIMAKEN SHAMO
KUNLUN SHAN
ALTUN SHAN
QILIAN SHAN
ALTAI SHAN
HANGAYN NURUU
Mongol Altayn Nuruu
HIMALAYA
GANGDISE SHAN
NGANGLONG KANGRI
TANGGULA SHAN
ANYEMAQEN SHAN
HENGDUAN SHAN

Hövsgöl Nuur
Uvs Nuur
Dzavhan Gol

Waangom
Ölgiy
Hatgal
Möron
Naran
Songino
Urgamal
Hovd
Uliast
Uliastay
Darvi
Törög
Altay
Bayanhongor
Aj Bogd Uil
Habahe
Hosoot
Tacheng
Emin
Yumin
Jinghe
Karamay
Shawan
Ertai
Huocheng
Yining
Shihezi
Gongliu
Xinyuan
Fukang
Qitai
Jiangjunmiao
URC Ürümqi
Baiyanghe
Barkol
Yiwu
Pik Pobedy 24,406
Kuqa
Yanqi
Turpan
Shanshan
Hami
Aksu
Korla
Yandunzhan
Mingshui
Hongshishan
Gongpoquan
Ejin Qi
Daquan
Lop Nur
Wuqia
Jiashi
Kangur (Kung-ko-erh) 25,325
Shache
Zepu
Yecheng
Hongliuyuan
Yumenguan
Anxi
Yumenzhen
Nanhu
Dunhuang
Jiayuguan
Moyu
Hotan
Ruoqiang (Qarklik)
Aksay
Laojunmiao
Gaotai
Yutian
Minfeng
Qiemo
Bag Narin
Subei
Zhangye
Muztagh Ata 23,890
Yiliping
Da Qaidam
Qilian
Ulugh Muztagh (Wu-lu-k'o-mu-shih) 25,340
Ganq
Da Juh
Delingha
Nongchang
Ulan
Gonghe
Golmud
Xiangride
Qinghai Hu
Zhengning (Shanhe)
Mt Geladaintong
Ciclgou
Xinghai
Tongtianheyan
Yematan
Disputed Land
Zhaxigang
Mt Nganglong
Disputed Land
Garyarsa
Zhidoi
Yushu
Serxu
Darlag
Disputed Land
Lunggar
Mt Kailas
Nargqen
Dengqen
Dainkog
Disputed Land
Sangsang
Xigaze
Gyangze
Nedong
Lhasa
Yi'ong
Tangmai
Qamdo
Garzê
Dege
Baiyu
Sbadui
Gosainthan (Xixabangma Feng) 26,390
Cho Oyu 26,750
Mt Everest 29,035
Namcha Barwa 25,445
Lhorong
Zogang
Markam
Yanjing
Litang
Rawu
Mt Jichudrake
Gangto 23,260
Pagnag
Zayu
Gngon
Gongshan

Pk Pobedy 24,406
Tavan Bogdu Uli 14,347
Hüytun Peak
Mt Namjagbarwa

© DeLorme

Scale 1:11,000,000 at map center

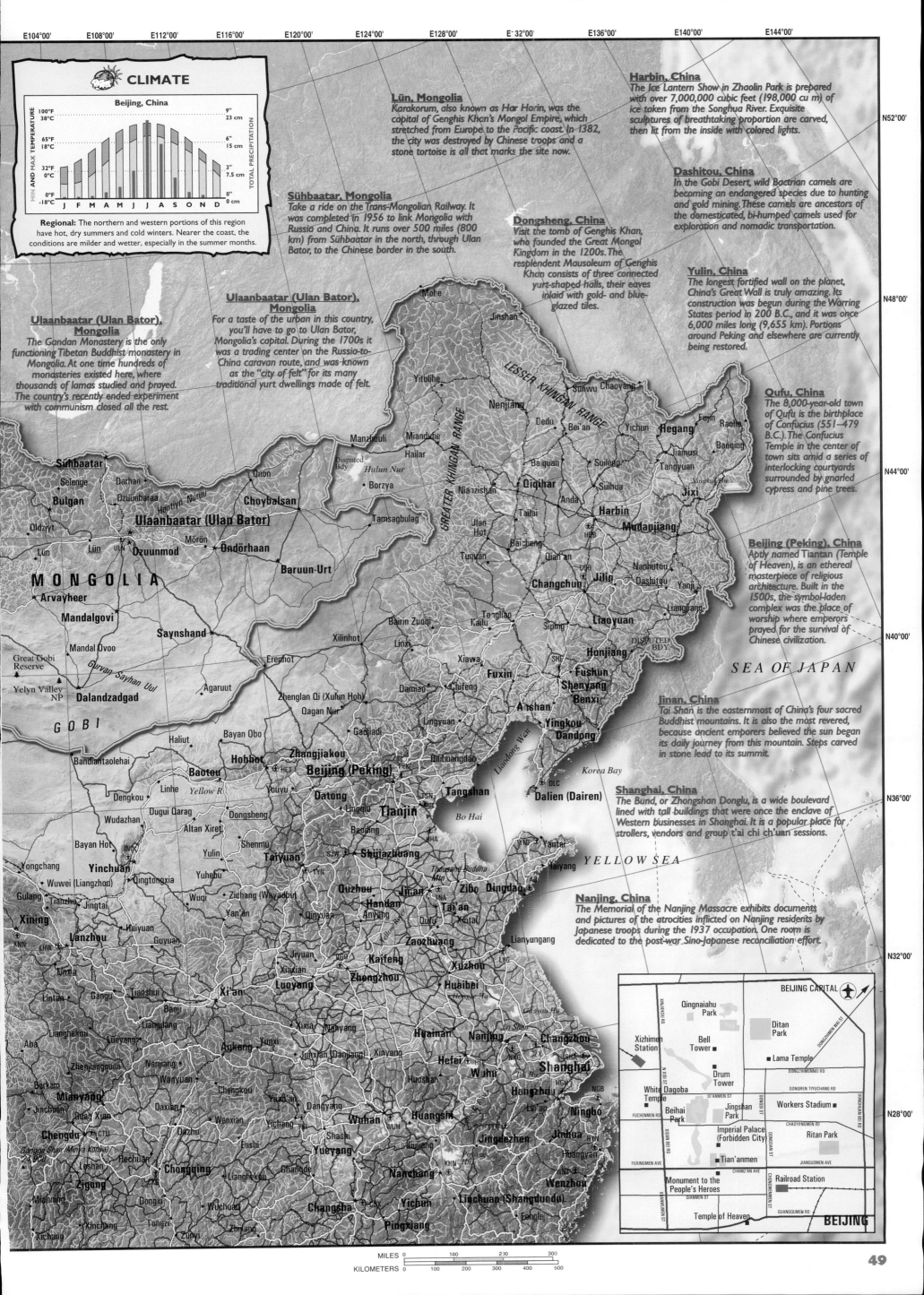

CLIMATE

Beijing, China

Regional: The northern and western portions of this region have hot, dry summers and cold winters. Nearer the coast, the conditions are milder and wetter, especially in the summer months.

Lün, Mongolia
Karakorum, also known as Har Horin, was the capital of Genghis Khan's Mongol Empire, which stretched from Europe to the Pacific coast. In 1382, the city was destroyed by Chinese troops and a stone tortoise is all that marks the site now.

Sühbaatar, Mongolia
Take a ride on the Trans-Mongolian Railway. It was completed in 1956 to link Mongolia with Russia and China. It runs over 500 miles (800 km) from Sühbaatar in the north, through Ulan Bator, to the Chinese border in the south.

Ulaanbaatar (Ulan Bator), Mongolia
The Gandan Monastery is the only functioning Tibetan Buddhist monastery in Mongolia. At one time hundreds of monasteries existed here, where thousands of lamas studied and prayed. The country's recently ended experiment with communism closed all the rest.

Ulaanbaatar (Ulan Bator), Mongolia
For a taste of the urban in this country, you'll have to go to Ulan Bator, Mongolia's capital. During the 1700s it was a trading center on the Russia-to-China caravan route, and was known as the "city of felt" for its many traditional yurt dwellings made of felt.

Dongsheng, China
Visit the tomb of Genghis Khan, who founded the Great Mongol Kingdom in the 1200s. The resplendent Mausoleum of Genghis Khan consists of three connected yurt-shaped halls, their eaves inlaid with gold- and blue-glazed tiles.

Harbin, China
The Ice Lantern Show in Zhaolin Park is prepared with over 7,000,000 cubic feet (198,000 cu m) of ice taken from the Songhua River. Exquisite sculptures of breathtaking proportion are carved, then lit from the inside with colored lights.

Dashitou, China
In the Gobi Desert, wild Bactrian camels are becoming an endangered species due to hunting and gold mining. These camels are ancestors of the domesticated, bi-humped camels used for exploration and nomadic transportation.

Yulin, China
The longest fortified wall on the planet, China's Great Wall is truly amazing. Its construction was begun during the Warring States period in 200 B.C., and it was once 6,000 miles long (9,655 km). Portions around Peking and elsewhere are currently being restored.

Qufu, China
The 8,000-year-old town of Qufu is the birthplace of Confucius (551–479 B.C.). The Confucius Temple in the center of town sits amid a series of interlocking courtyards surrounded by gnarled cypress and pine trees.

Beijing (Peking), China
Aptly named Tiantan (Temple of Heaven), is an ethereal masterpiece of religious architecture. Built in the 1500s, the symbol-laden complex was the place of worship where emperors prayed for the survival of Chinese civilization.

Jinan, China
Tai Shan is the easternmost of China's four sacred Buddhist mountains. It is also the most revered, because ancient emperors believed the sun began its daily journey from this mountain. Steps carved in stone lead to its summit.

Shanghai, China
The Bund, or Zhongshan Donglu, is a wide boulevard lined with tall buildings that were once the enclave of Western businesses in Shanghai. It is a popular place for strollers, vendors and group t'ai chi ch'uan sessions.

Nanjing, China
The Memorial of the Nanjing Massacre exhibits documents and pictures of the atrocities inflicted on Nanjing residents by Japanese troops during the 1937 occupation. One room is dedicated to the post-war Sino-Japanese reconciliation effort.

49

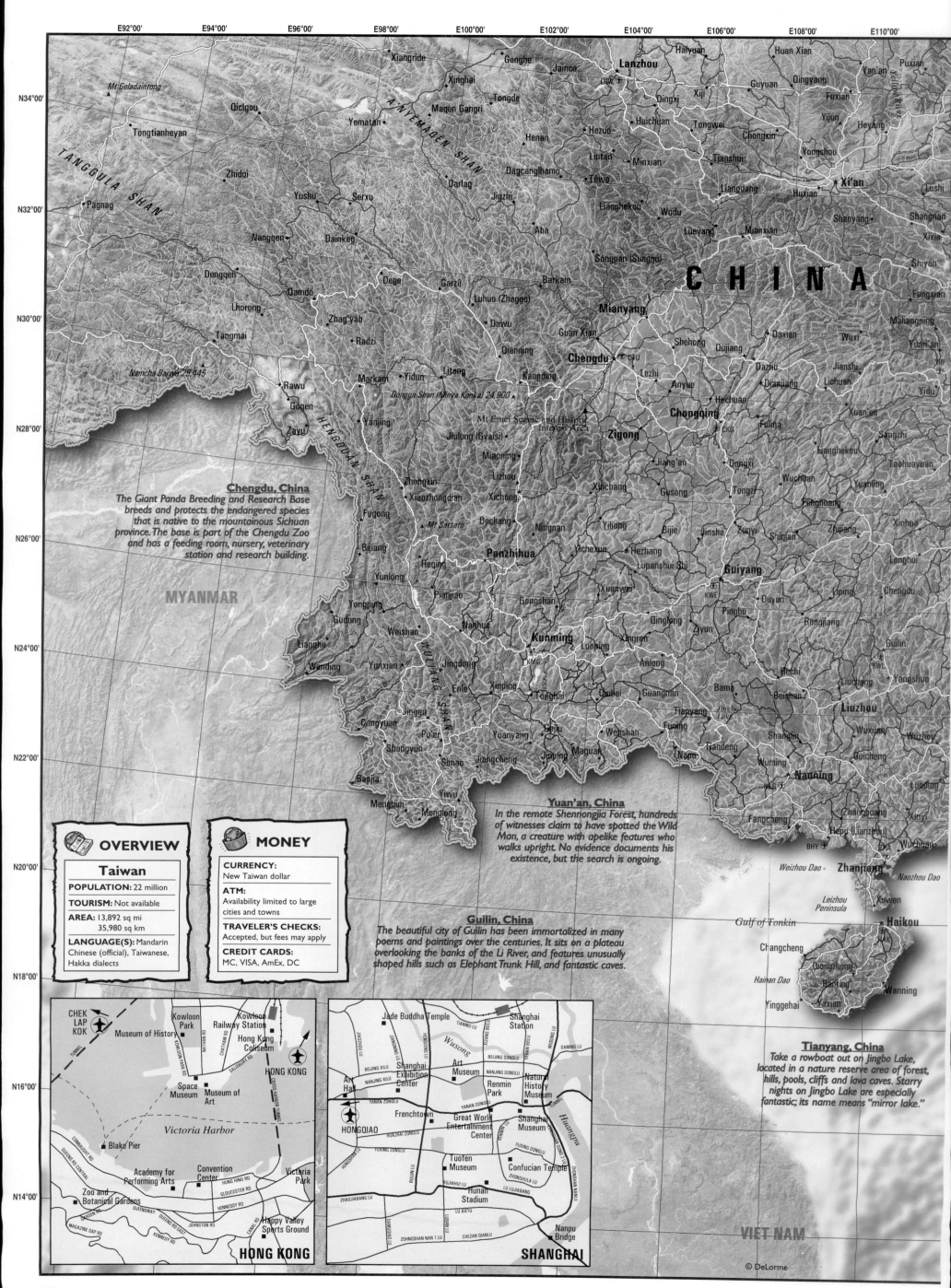

Chengdu, China
The Giant Panda Breeding and Research Base breeds and protects the endangered species that is native to the mountainous Sichuan province. The base is part of the Chengdu Zoo and has a feeding room, nursery, veterinary station and research building.

Yuan'an, China
In the remote Shennongjia Forest, hundreds of witnesses claim to have spotted the Wild Man, a creature with apelike features who walks upright. No evidence documents his existence, but the search is ongoing.

Guilin, China
The beautiful city of Guilin has been immortalized in many poems and paintings over the centuries. It sits on a plateau overlooking the banks of the Li River, and features unusually shaped hills such as Elephant Trunk Hill, and fantastic caves.

Tianyang, China
Take a rowboat out on Jingbo Lake, located in a nature reserve area of forest, hills, pools, cliffs and lava caves. Starry nights on Jingbo Lake are especially fantastic; its name means "mirror lake."

OVERVIEW

Taiwan

POPULATION: 22 million

TOURISM: Not available

AREA: 13,892 sq mi 35,980 sq km

LANGUAGE(S): Mandarin Chinese (official), Taiwanese, Hakka dialects

MONEY

CURRENCY:
New Taiwan dollar

ATM:
Availability limited to large cities and towns

TRAVELER'S CHECKS:
Accepted, but fees may apply

CREDIT CARDS:
MC, VISA, AmEx, DC

Scale 1:7,500,000 at map center

© DeLorme

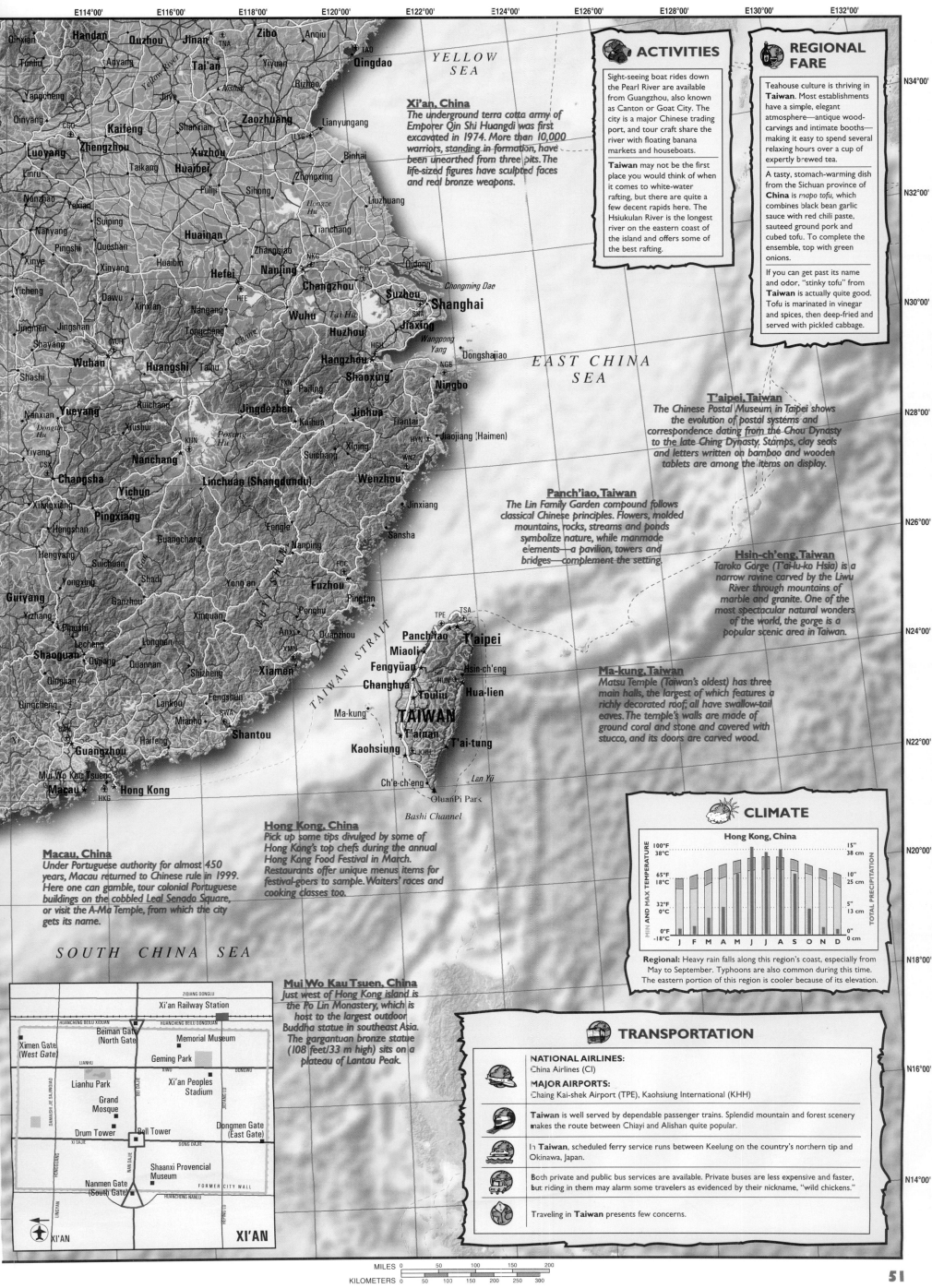

YELLOW SEA

Xi'an, China
The underground terra cotta army of Emperor Qin Shi Huangdi was first excavated in 1974. More than 10,000 warriors, standing in formation, have been unearthed from three pits. The life-sized figures have sculpted faces and real bronze weapons.

EAST CHINA SEA

TAIWAN STRAIT

TAIWAN

SOUTH CHINA SEA

Bashi Channel

ACTIVITIES

Sight-seeing boat rides down the Pearl River are available from Guangzhou, also known as Canton or Goat City. The city is a major Chinese trading port, and tour craft share the river with floating banana markets and houseboats.

Taiwan may not be the first place you would think of when it comes to white-water rafting, but there are quite a few decent rapids here. The Hsiukulan River is the longest river on the eastern coast of the island and offers some of the best rafting.

REGIONAL FARE

Teahouse culture is thriving in **Taiwan**. Most establishments have a simple, elegant atmosphere—antique wood-carvings and intimate booths—making it easy to spend several relaxing hours over a cup of expertly brewed tea.

A tasty, stomach-warming dish from the Sichuan province of **China** is mapo tofu, which combines black bean garlic sauce with red chili paste, sauteed ground pork and cubed tofu. To complete the ensemble, top with green onions.

If you can get past its name and odor, "stinky tofu" from **Taiwan** is actually quite good. Tofu is marinated in vinegar and spices, then deep-fried and served with pickled cabbage.

T'aipei, Taiwan
The Chinese Postal Museum in Taipei shows the evolution of postal systems and correspondence dating from the Chou Dynasty to the late Ching Dynasty. Stamps, clay seals and letters written on bamboo and wooden tablets are among the items on display.

Panch'iao, Taiwan
The Lin Family Garden compound follows classical Chinese principles. Flowers, molded mountains, rocks, streams and ponds symbolize nature, while manmade elements—a pavilion, towers and bridges—complement the setting.

Hsin-ch'eng, Taiwan
Taroko Gorge (T'ai-lu-ko Hsia) is a narrow ravine carved by the Liwu River through mountains of marble and granite. One of the most spectacular natural wonders of the world, the gorge is a popular scenic area in Taiwan.

Ma-kung, Taiwan
Matsu Temple (Taiwan's oldest) has three main halls, the largest of which features a richly decorated roof; all have swallow-tail eaves. The temple's walls are made of ground coral and stone and covered with stucco, and its doors are carved wood.

Hong Kong, China
Pick up some tips divulged by some of Hong Kong's top chefs during the annual Hong Kong Food Festival in March. Restaurants offer unique menus items for festival-goers to sample. Waiters' races and cooking classes too.

Macau, China
Under Portuguese authority for almost 450 years, Macau returned to Chinese rule in 1999. Here one can gamble, tour colonial Portuguese buildings on the cobbled Leal Senado Square, or visit the A-Ma Temple, from which the city gets its name.

CLIMATE

Hong Kong, China

MIN AND MAX TEMPERATURE: 100°F 38°C / 65°F 18°C / 32°F 0°C / 0°F -18°C

TOTAL PRECIPITATION: 15" 38 cm / 10" 25 cm / 5" 13 cm / 0" 0 cm

J F M A M J J A S O N D

Regional: Heavy rain falls along this region's coast, especially from May to September. Typhoons are also common during this time. The eastern portion of this region is cooler because of its elevation.

Mui Wo Kau Tsuen, China
Just west of Hong Kong island is the Po Lin Monastery, which is host to the largest outdoor Buddha statue in southeast Asia. The gargantuan bronze statue (108 feet/33 m high) sits on a plateau of Lantau Peak.

XI'AN (inset map)

ZIQIANG DONGLU
Xi'an Railway Station
HUANCHENG BEILU XIDUAN · HUANCHENG BEILU DONGDUAN
Beiman Gate (North Gate)
Memorial Museum
Ximen Gate (West Gate)
LIANHU
Geming Park
LIANHU
DONGWU
Lianhu Park
Xi'an Peoples Stadium
BEI DAJIE
XI DAJIE · JIEFANG LU · DONG DAJIE
Grand Mosque
Dongmen Gate (East Gate)
Drum Tower
Bell Tower
DAMAISHI JIE SILIANJIAO
NAN DAJIE
DONG DAJIE
Shaanxi Provincial Museum
Nanmen Gate (South Gate)
FORMER CITY WALL
HUANCHENG NANLU
XI'AN

TRANSPORTATION

NATIONAL AIRLINES:
China Airlines (CI)

MAJOR AIRPORTS:
Chaing Kai-shek Airport (TPE), Kaohsiung International (KHH)

Taiwan is well served by dependable passenger trains. Splendid mountain and forest scenery makes the route between Chiayi and Alishan quite popular.

In **Taiwan**, scheduled ferry service runs between Keelung on the country's northern tip and Okinawa, Japan.

Both private and public bus services are available. Private buses are less expensive and faster, but riding in them may alarm some travelers as evidenced by their nickname, "wild chickens."

Traveling in **Taiwan** presents few concerns.

MILES 0 50 100 150 200
KILOMETERS 0 50 100 150 200 250 300

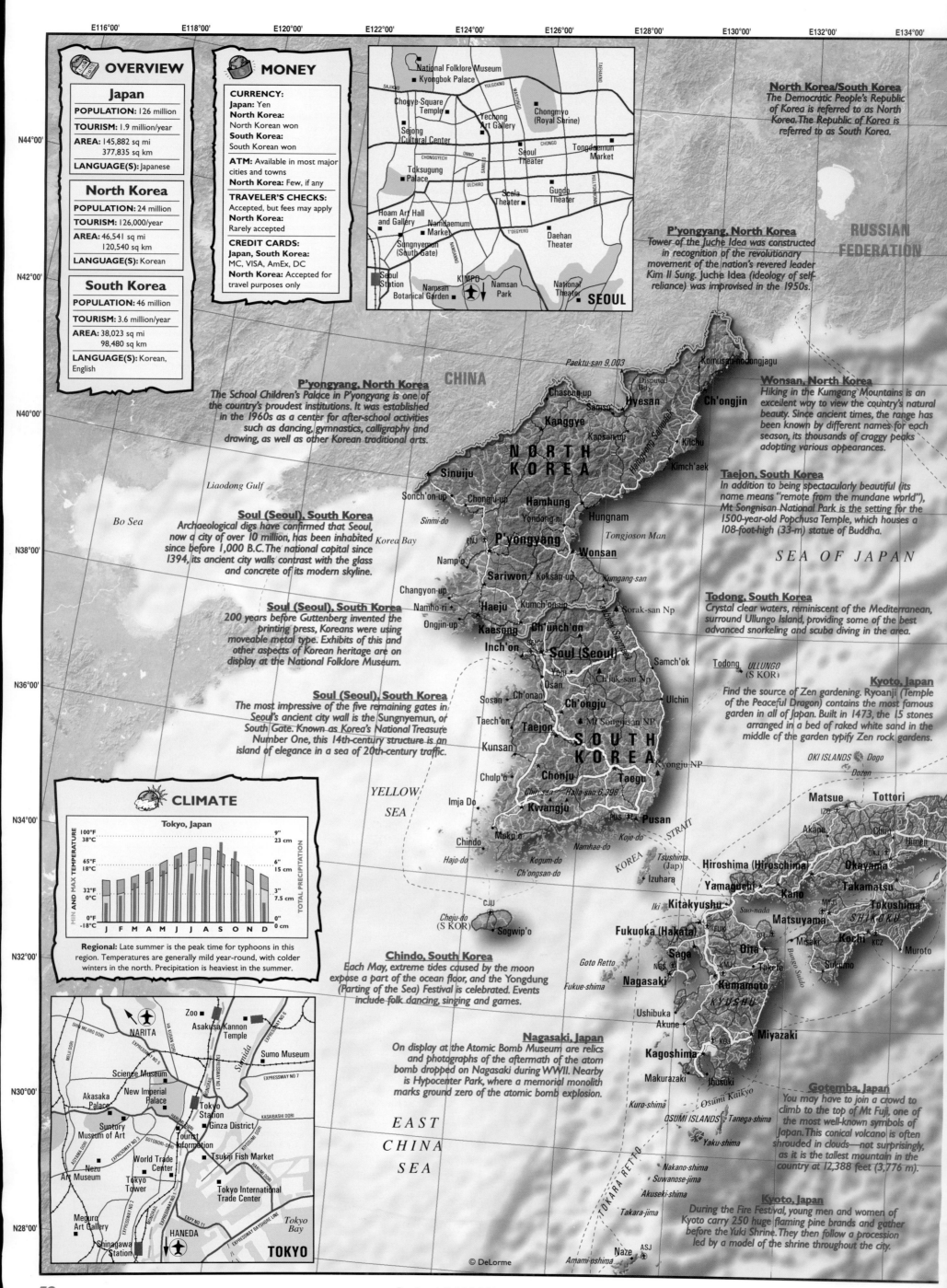

OVERVIEW

Japan
POPULATION: 126 million
TOURISM: 1.9 million/year
AREA: 145,882 sq mi
377,835 sq km
LANGUAGE(S): Japanese

North Korea
POPULATION: 24 million
TOURISM: 126,000/year
AREA: 46,541 sq mi
120,540 sq km
LANGUAGE(S): Korean

South Korea
POPULATION: 46 million
TOURISM: 3.6 million/year
AREA: 38,023 sq mi
98,480 sq km
LANGUAGE(S): Korean,
English

MONEY

CURRENCY:
Japan: Yen
North Korea:
North Korean won
South Korea:
South Korean won

ATM: Available in most major
cities and towns
North Korea: Few, if any

TRAVELER'S CHECKS:
Accepted, but fees may apply
North Korea:
Rarely accepted

CREDIT CARDS:
Japan, South Korea:
MC, VISA, AmEx, DC
North Korea: Accepted for
travel purposes only

North Korea/South Korea
The Democratic People's Republic of Korea is referred to as North Korea. The Republic of Korea is referred to as South Korea.

P'yongyang, North Korea
Tower of the Juche Idea was constructed in recognition of the revolutionary movement of the nation's revered leader Kim Il Sung. Juche Idea (ideology of self-reliance) was improvised in the 1950s.

P'yongyang, North Korea
The School Children's Palace in P'yongyang is one of the country's proudest institutions. It was established in the 1960s as a center for after-school activities such as dancing, gymnastics, calligraphy and drawing, as well as other Korean traditional arts.

Soul (Seoul), South Korea
Archaeological digs have confirmed that Seoul, now a city of over 10 million, has been inhabited since before 1,000 B.C. The national capital since 1394, its ancient city walls contrast with the glass and concrete of its modern skyline.

Soul (Seoul), South Korea
200 years before Guttenberg invented the printing press, Koreans were using moveable metal type. Exhibits of this and other aspects of Korean heritage are on display at the National Folklore Museum.

Soul (Seoul), South Korea
The most impressive of the five remaining gates in Seoul's ancient city wall is the Sungnyemun, or South Gate. Known as Korea's National Treasure Number One, this 14th-century structure is an island of elegance in a sea of 20th-century traffic.

Wonsan, North Korea
Hiking in the Kumgang Mountains is an excellent way to view the country's natural beauty. Since ancient times, the range has been known by different names for each season, its thousands of craggy peaks adopting various appearances.

Taejon, South Korea
In addition to being spectacularly beautiful (its name means "remote from the mundane world"), Mt Songnisan National Park is the setting for the 1500-year-old Popchusa Temple, which houses a 108-foot-high (33-m) statue of Buddha.

Todong, South Korea
Crystal clear waters, reminiscent of the Mediterranean, surround Ullungo Island, providing some of the best advanced snorkeling and scuba diving in the area.

Kyoto, Japan
Find the source of Zen gardening. Ryoanji (Temple of the Peaceful Dragon) contains the most famous garden in all of Japan. Built in 1473, the 15 stones arranged in a bed of raked white sand in the middle of the garden typify Zen rock gardens.

CLIMATE

Tokyo, Japan

Regional: Late summer is the peak time for typhoons in this region. Temperatures are generally mild year-round, with colder winters in the north. Precipitation is heaviest in the summer.

Chindo, South Korea
Each May, extreme tides caused by the moon expose a part of the ocean floor, and the Yongdung (Parting of the Sea) Festival is celebrated. Events include folk dancing, singing and games.

Nagasaki, Japan
On display at the Atomic Bomb Museum are relics and photographs of the aftermath of the atom bomb dropped on Nagasaki during WWII. Nearby is Hypocenter Park, where a memorial monolith marks ground zero of the atomic bomb explosion.

Gotemba, Japan
You may have to join a crowd to climb to the top of Mt Fuji, one of the most well-known symbols of Japan. This conical volcano is often shrouded in clouds—not surprisingly, as it is the tallest mountain in the country at 12,388 feet (3,776 m).

Kyoto, Japan
During the Fire Festival, young men and women of Kyoto carry 250 huge flaming pine brands and gather before the Yuki Shrine. They then follow a procession led by a model of the shrine throughout the city.

© DeLorme

Scale 1:6,000,000 at map center

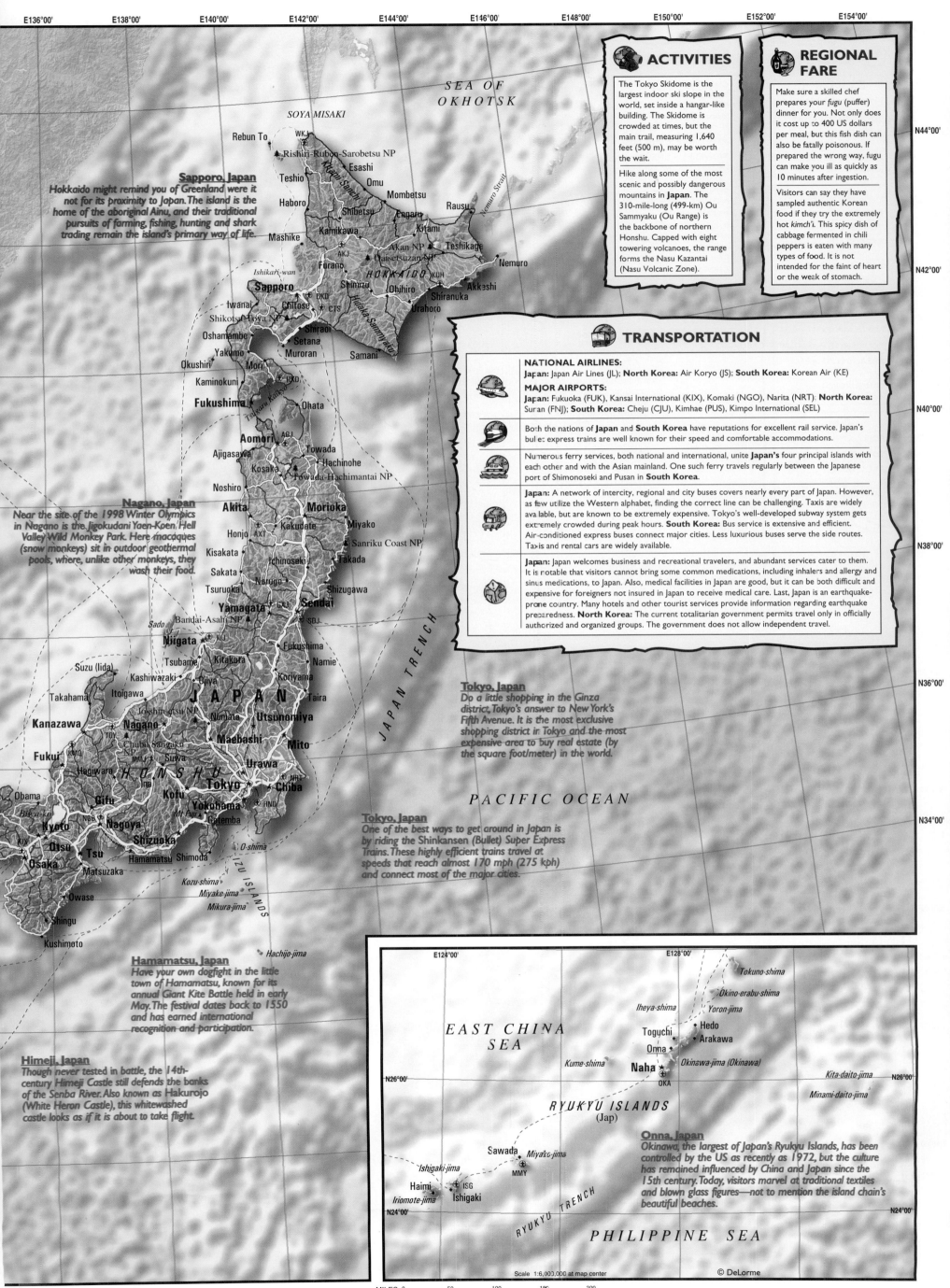

SEA OF OKHOTSK

Sapporo, Japan
Hokkaido might remind you of Greenland were it not for its proximity to Japan. The island is the home of the aboriginal Ainu, and their traditional pursuits of farming, fishing, hunting and shark trading remain the island's primary way of life.

Nagano, Japan
Near the site of the 1998 Winter Olympics in Nagano is the Jigokudani Yaen-Koen, Hell Valley Wild Monkey Park. Here macaques (snow monkeys) sit in outdoor geothermal pools, where, unlike other monkeys, they wash their food.

Hamamatsu, Japan
Have your own dogfight in the little town of Hamamatsu, known for its annual Giant Kite Battle held in early May. The festival dates back to 1550 and has earned international recognition and participation.

Himeji, Japan
Though never tested in battle, the 14th-century Himeji Castle still defends the banks of the Senba River. Also known as Hakurojo (White Heron Castle), this whitewashed castle looks as if it is about to take flight.

Tokyo, Japan
Do a little shopping in the Ginza district, Tokyo's answer to New York's Fifth Avenue. It is the most exclusive shopping district in Tokyo and the most expensive area to buy real estate (by the square foot/meter) in the world.

Tokyo, Japan
One of the best ways to get around in Japan is by riding the Shinkansen (Bullet) Super Express Trains. These highly efficient trains travel at speeds that reach almost 170 mph (275 kph) and connect most of the major cities.

PACIFIC OCEAN

ACTIVITIES

The Tokyo Skidome is the largest indoor ski slope in the world, set inside a hangar-like building. The Skidome is crowded at times, but the main trail, measuring 1,640 feet (500 m), may be worth the wait.

Hike along some of the most scenic and possibly dangerous mountains in **Japan**. The 310-mile-long (499-km) Ou Sammyaku (Ou Range) is the backbone of northern Honshu. Capped with eight towering volcanoes, the range forms the Nasu Kazantai (Nasu Volcanic Zone).

REGIONAL FARE

Make sure a skilled chef prepares your fugu (puffer) dinner for you. Not only does it cost up to 400 US dollars per meal, but this fish dish can also be fatally poisonous. If prepared the wrong way, fugu can make you ill as quickly as 10 minutes after ingestion.

Visitors can say they have sampled authentic Korean food if they try the extremely hot kimch'i. This spicy dish of cabbage fermented in chili peppers is eaten with many types of food. It is not intended for the faint of heart or the weak of stomach.

TRANSPORTATION

NATIONAL AIRLINES:
Japan: Japan Air Lines (JL); **North Korea:** Air Koryo (JS); **South Korea:** Korean Air (KE)
MAJOR AIRPORTS:
Japan: Fukuoka (FUK), Kansai International (KIX), Komaki (NGO), Narita (NRT); **North Korea:** Suran (FNJ); **South Korea:** Cheju (CJU), Kimhae (PUS), Kimpo International (SEL)

Both the nations of **Japan** and **South Korea** have reputations for excellent rail service. Japan's bullet express trains are well known for their speed and comfortable accommodations.

Numerous ferry services, both national and international, unite **Japan's** four principal islands with each other and with the Asian mainland. One such ferry travels regularly between the Japanese port of Shimonoseki and Pusan in **South Korea.**

Japan: A network of intercity, regional and city buses covers nearly every part of Japan. However, as few utilize the Western alphabet, finding the correct line can be challenging. Taxis are widely available, but are known to be extremely expensive. Tokyo's well-developed subway system gets extremely crowded during peak hours. **South Korea:** Bus service is extensive and efficient. Air-conditioned express buses connect major cities. Less luxurious buses serve the side routes. Taxis and rental cars are widely available.

Japan: Japan welcomes business and recreational travelers, and abundant services cater to them. It is notable that visitors cannot bring some common medications, including inhalers and allergy and sinus medications, to Japan. Also, medical facilities in Japan are good, but it can be both difficult and expensive for foreigners not insured in Japan to receive medical care. Last, Japan is an earthquake-prone country. Many hotels and other tourist services provide information regarding earthquake preparedness. **North Korea:** The current totalitarian government permits travel only in officially authorized and organized groups. The government does not allow independent travel.

EAST CHINA SEA

RYUKYU ISLANDS (Jap)

Onna, Japan
Okinawa, the largest of Japan's Ryukyu Islands, has been controlled by the US as recently as 1972, but the culture has remained influenced by China and Japan since the 15th century. Today, visitors marvel at traditional textiles and blown glass figures—not to mention the island chain's beautiful beaches.

PHILIPPINE SEA

Scale 1:6,900,000 at map center

© DeLorme

MILES 0 50 100 150 200
KILOMETERS 0 50 100 150 200 250 300

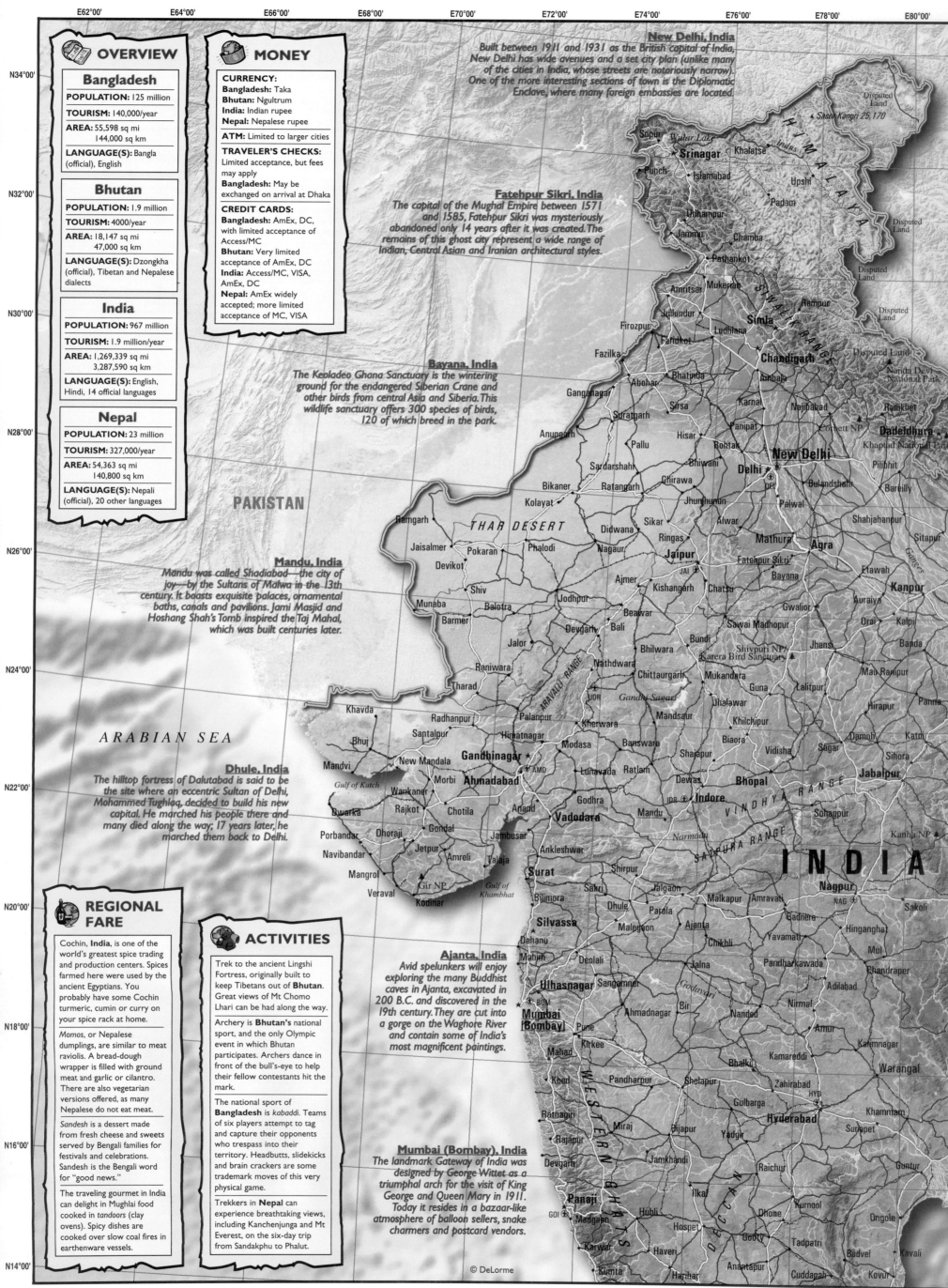

OVERVIEW

Bangladesh
POPULATION: 125 million
TOURISM: 140,000/year
AREA: 55,598 sq mi
144,000 sq km
LANGUAGE(S): Bangla (official), English

Bhutan
POPULATION: 1.9 million
TOURISM: 4000/year
AREA: 18,147 sq mi
47,000 sq km
LANGUAGE(S): Dzongkha (official), Tibetan and Nepalese dialects

India
POPULATION: 967 million
TOURISM: 1.9 million/year
AREA: 1,269,339 sq mi
3,287,590 sq km
LANGUAGE(S): English, Hindi, 14 official languages

Nepal
POPULATION: 23 million
TOURISM: 327,000/year
AREA: 54,363 sq mi
140,800 sq km
LANGUAGE(S): Nepali (official), 20 other languages

MONEY

CURRENCY:
Bangladesh: Taka
Bhutan: Ngultrum
India: Indian rupee
Nepal: Nepalese rupee

ATM: Limited to larger cities

TRAVELER'S CHECKS:
Limited acceptance, but fees may apply
Bangladesh: May be exchanged on arrival at Dhaka

CREDIT CARDS:
Bangladesh: AmEx, DC, with limited acceptance of Access/MC
Bhutan: Very limited acceptance of AmEx, DC
India: Access/MC, VISA, AmEx, DC
Nepal: AmEx widely accepted; more limited acceptance of MC, VISA

New Delhi, India
Built between 1911 and 1931 as the British capital of India, New Delhi has wide avenues and a set city plan (unlike many of the cities in India, whose streets are notoriously narrow). One of the more interesting sections of town is the Diplomatic Enclave, where many foreign embassies are located.

Fatehpur Sikri, India
The capital of the Mughal Empire between 1571 and 1585, Fatehpur Sikri was mysteriously abandoned only 14 years after it was created. The remains of this ghost city represent a wide range of Indian, Central Asian and Iranian architectural styles.

Bayana, India
The Keoladeo Ghana Sanctuary is the wintering ground for the endangered Siberian Crane and other birds from central Asia and Siberia. This wildlife sanctuary offers 300 species of birds, 120 of which breed in the park.

Mandu, India
Mandu was called Shadiabad—the city of joy—by the Sultans of Malwa in the 13th century. It boasts exquisite palaces, ornamental baths, canals and pavilions. Jami Masjid and Hoshang Shah's Tomb inspired the Taj Mahal, which was built centuries later.

Dhule, India
The hilltop fortress of Dalutabad is said to be the site where an eccentric Sultan of Delhi, Mohammed Tughlaq, decided to build his new capital. He marched his people there and many died along the way; 17 years later, he marched them back to Delhi.

REGIONAL FARE

Cochin, **India**, is one of the world's greatest spice trading and production centers. Spices farmed here were used by the ancient Egyptians. You probably have some Cochin turmeric, cumin or curry on your spice rack at home.

Momos, or Nepalese dumplings, are similar to meat raviolis. A bread-dough wrapper is filled with ground meat and garlic or cilantro. There are also vegetarian versions offered, as many Nepalese do not eat meat.

Sandesh is a dessert made from fresh cheese and sweets served by Bengali families for festivals and celebrations. Sandesh is the Bengali word for "good news."

The traveling gourmet in India can delight in Mughlai food cooked in *tandoors* (clay ovens). Spicy dishes are cooked over slow coal fires in earthenware vessels.

ACTIVITIES

Trek to the ancient Lingshi Fortress, originally built to keep Tibetans out of **Bhutan**. Great views of Mt Chomo Lhari can be had along the way.

Archery is **Bhutan's** national sport, and the only Olympic event in which Bhutan participates. Archers dance in front of the bull's-eye to help their fellow contestants hit the mark.

The national sport of **Bangladesh** is *kabaddi*. Teams of six players attempt to tag and capture their opponents who trespass into their territory. Headbutts, slidekicks and brain crackers are some trademark moves of this very physical game.

Trekkers in **Nepal** can experience breathtaking views, including Kanchenjunga and Mt Everest, on the six-day trip from Sandakphu to Phalut.

Ajanta, India
Avid spelunkers will enjoy exploring the many Buddhist caves in Ajanta, excavated in 200 B.C. and discovered in the 19th century. They are cut into a gorge on the Waghore River and contain some of India's most magnificent paintings.

Mumbai (Bombay), India
The landmark Gateway of India was designed by George Wittet as a triumphal arch for the visit of King George and Queen Mary in 1911. Today it resides in a bazaar-like atmosphere of balloon sellers, snake charmers and postcard vendors.

© DeLorme

Scale 1:7,000,000 at map center

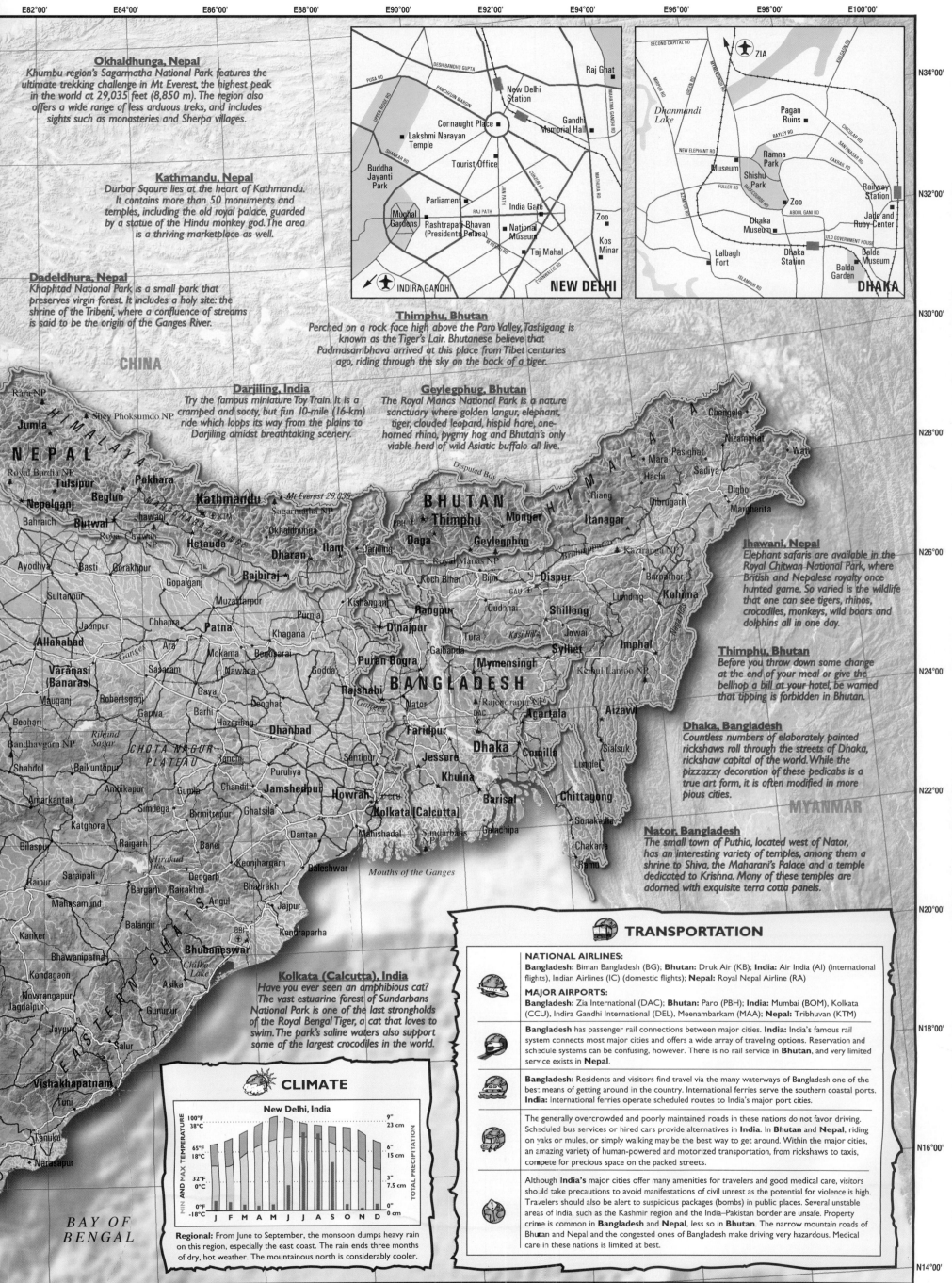

Okhaldhunga, Nepal
Khumbu region's Sagarmatha National Park features the ultimate trekking challenge in Mt Everest, the highest peak in the world at 29,035 feet (8,850 m). The region also offers a wide range of less arduous treks, and includes sights such as monasteries and Sherpa villages.

Kathmandu, Nepal
Durbar Sqaure lies at the heart of Kathmandu. It contains more than 50 monuments and temples, including the old royal palace, guarded by a statue of the Hindu monkey god. The area is a thriving marketplace as well.

Dadeldhura, Nepal
Khaptad National Park is a small park that preserves virgin forest. It includes a holy site: the shrine of the Tribeni, where a confluence of streams is said to be the origin of the Ganges River.

Thimphu, Bhutan
Perched on a rock face high above the Paro Valley, Tashigang is known as the Tiger's Lair. Bhutanese believe that Padmasambhava arrived at this place from Tibet centuries ago, riding through the sky on the back of a tiger.

Darjiling, India
Try the famous miniature Toy Train. It is a cramped and sooty, but fun 10-mile (16-km) ride which loops its way from the plains to Darjiling amidst breathtaking scenery.

Geylegphug, Bhutan
The Royal Mancs National Park is a nature sanctuary where golden langur, elephant, tiger, clouded leopard, hispid hare, one-horned rhino, pygmy hog and Bhutan's only viable herd of wild Asiatic buffalo all live.

Jhawani, Nepal
Elephant safaris are available in the Royal Chitwan National Park, where British and Nepalese royalty once hunted game. So varied is the wildlife that one can see tigers, rhinos, crocodiles, monkeys, wild boars and dolphins all in one day.

Thimphu, Bhutan
Before you throw down some change at the end of your meal or give the bellhop a bill at your hotel, be warned that tipping is forbidden in Bhutan.

Dhaka, Bangladesh
Countless numbers of elaborately painted rickshaws roll through the streets of Dhaka, rickshaw capital of the world. While the pizzazzy decoration of these pedicabs is a true art form, it is often modified in more pious cities.

Nator, Bangladesh
The small town of Puthia, located west of Nator, has an interesting variety of temples, among them a shrine to Shiva, the Maharani's Palace and a temple dedicated to Krishna. Many of these temples are adorned with exquisite terra cotta panels.

Kolkata (Calcutta), India
Have you ever seen an amphibious cat? The vast estuarine forest of Sundarbans National Park is one of the last strongholds of the Royal Bengal Tiger, a cat that loves to swim. The park's saline waters also support some of the largest crocodiles in the world.

NEW DELHI

DHAKA

TRANSPORTATION

NATIONAL AIRLINES:
Bangladesh: Biman Bangladesh (BG); **Bhutan:** Druk Air (KB); **India:** Air India (AI) (international flights), Indian Airlines (IC) (domestic flights); **Nepal:** Royal Nepal Airline (RA)

MAJOR AIRPORTS:
Bangladesh: Zia International (DAC); **Bhutan:** Paro (PBH); **India:** Mumbai (BOM), Kolkata (CCU), Indira Gandhi International (DEL), Meenambarkam (MAA); **Nepal:** Tribhuvan (KTM)

Bangladesh has passenger rail connections between major cities. **India:** India's famous rail system connects most major cities and offers a wide array of traveling options. Reservation and schedule systems can be confusing, however. There is no rail service in **Bhutan**, and very limited service is in **Nepal**.

Bangladesh: Residents and visitors find travel via the many waterways of Bangladesh one of the best means of getting around in the country. International ferries serve the southern coastal ports. India: International ferries operate scheduled routes to India's major port cities.

The generally overcrowded and poorly maintained roads in these nations do not favor driving. Scheduled bus services or hired cars provide alternatives in **India**. In **Bhutan** and **Nepal**, riding on yaks or mules, or simply walking may be the best way to get around. Within the major cities, an amazing variety of human-powered and motorized transportation, from rickshaws to taxis, compete for precious space on the packed streets.

Although **India's** major cities offer many amenities for travelers and good medical care, visitors should take precautions to avoid manifestations of civil unrest as the potential for violence is high. Travelers should also be alert to suspicious packages (bombs) in public places. Several unstable areas of India, such as the Kashmir region and the India–Pakistan border are unsafe. Property crime is common in **Bangladesh** and **Nepal**, less so in **Bhutan**. The narrow mountain roads of Bhutan and Nepal and the congested ones of Bangladesh make driving very hazardous. Medical care in these nations is limited at best.

CLIMATE

New Delhi, India

Regional: From June to September, the monsoon dumps heavy rain on this region, especially the east coast. The rain ends three months of dry, hot weather. The mountainous north is considerably cooler.

MILES 0 50 100 150 200
KILOMETERS 0 50 100 150 200 250 300

Cambodia, India (South), Laos, Maldives, Myanmar, Sri Lanka, Thailand, Viet Nam

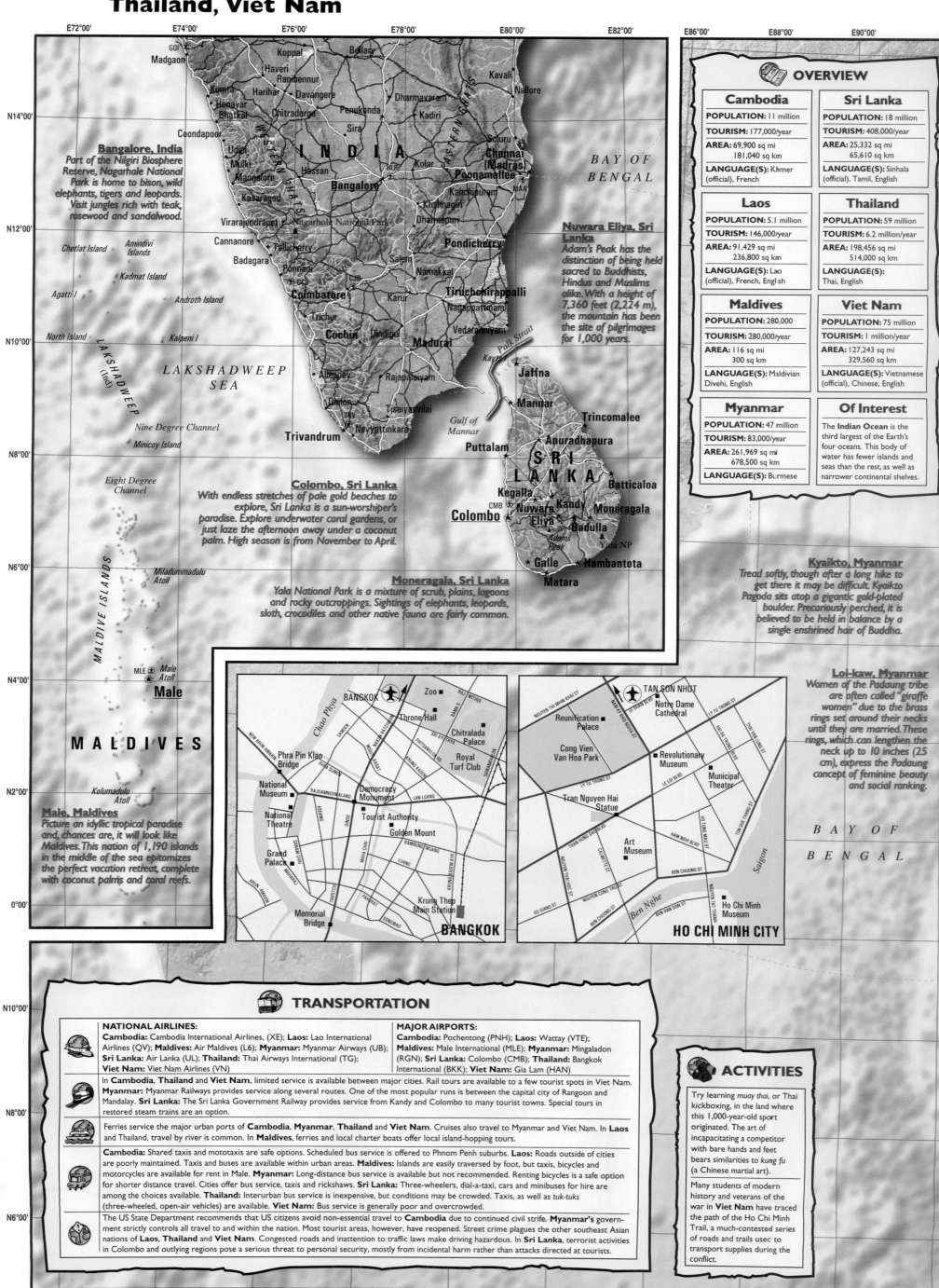

Bangalore, India
Part of the Nilgiri Biosphere Reserve, Nagarhole National Park is home to bison, wild elephants, tigers and leopards. Visit jungles rich with teak, rosewood and sandalwood.

Nuwara Eliya, Sri Lanka
Adam's Peak has the distinction of being held sacred to Buddhists, Hindus and Muslims alike. With a height of 7,360 feet (2,224 m), the mountain has been the site of pilgrimages for 1,000 years.

Colombo, Sri Lanka
With endless stretches of pale gold beaches to explore, Sri Lanka is a sun-worshiper's paradise. Explore underwater coral gardens, or just laze the afternoon away under a coconut palm. High season is from November to April.

Moneragala, Sri Lanka
Yala National Park is a mixture of scrub, plains, lagoons and rocky outcroppings. Sightings of elephants, leopards, sloth, crocodiles and other native fauna are fairly common.

Male, Maldives
Picture an idyllic tropical paradise and, chances are, it will look like Maldives. This nation of 1,190 islands in the middle of the sea epitomizes the perfect vacation retreat, complete with coconut palms and coral reefs.

OVERVIEW

Cambodia
POPULATION: 11 million
TOURISM: 177,000/year
AREA: 69,900 sq mi
181,040 sq km
LANGUAGE(S): Khmer (official), French

Sri Lanka
POPULATION: 18 million
TOURISM: 408,000/year
AREA: 25,332 sq mi
65,610 sq km
LANGUAGE(S): Sinhala (official), Tamil, English

Laos
POPULATION: 5.1 million
TOURISM: 146,000/year
AREA: 91,429 sq mi
236,800 sq km
LANGUAGE(S): Lao (official), French, English

Thailand
POPULATION: 59 million
TOURISM: 6.2 million/year
AREA: 198,456 sq mi
514,000 sq km
LANGUAGE(S): Thai, English

Maldives
POPULATION: 280,000
TOURISM: 280,000/year
AREA: 116 sq mi
300 sq km
LANGUAGE(S): Maldivian Divehi, English

Viet Nam
POPULATION: 75 million
TOURISM: 1 million/year
AREA: 127,243 sq mi
329,560 sq km
LANGUAGE(S): Vietnamese (official), Chinese, English

Myanmar
POPULATION: 47 million
TOURISM: 83,000/year
AREA: 261,969 sq mi
678,500 sq km
LANGUAGE(S): Burmese

Of Interest
The **Indian Ocean** is the third largest of the Earth's four oceans. This body of water has fewer islands and seas than the rest, as well as narrower continental shelves.

Kyaikto, Myanmar
Tread softly, though after a long hike to get there it may be difficult. Kyaikto Pagoda sits atop a gigantic gold-plated boulder. Precariously perched, it is believed to be held in balance by a single enshrined hair of Buddha.

Loi-kaw, Myanmar
Women of the Padaung tribe are often called "giraffe women" due to the brass rings set around their necks until they are married. These rings, which can lengthen the neck up to 10 inches (25 cm), express the Padaung concept of feminine beauty and social ranking.

TRANSPORTATION

NATIONAL AIRLINES:
Cambodia: Cambodia International Airlines, (XE); **Laos:** Lao International Airlines (QV); **Maldives:** Air Maldives (L6); **Myanmar:** Myanmar Airways (UB); **Sri Lanka:** Air Lanka (UL); **Thailand:** Thai Airways International (TG); **Viet Nam:** Viet Nam Airlines (VN)

MAJOR AIRPORTS:
Cambodia: Pochentong (PNH); **Laos:** Wattay (VTE); **Maldives:** Male International (MLE); **Myanmar:** Mingaladon (RGN); **Sri Lanka:** Colombo (CMB); **Thailand:** Bangkok International (BKK); **Viet Nam:** Gia Lam (HAN)

In **Cambodia, Thailand** and **Viet Nam**, limited service is available between major cities. Rail tours are available to a few tourist spots in Viet Nam. **Myanmar:** Myanmar Railways provides service along several routes. One of the most popular runs is between the capital city of Rangoon and Mandalay. **Sri Lanka:** The Sri Lanka Government Railway provides service from Kandy and Colombo to many tourist towns. Special tours in restored steam trains are an option.

Ferries service the major urban ports of **Cambodia, Myanmar, Thailand** and **Viet Nam**. Cruises also travel to Myanmar and Viet Nam. In **Laos** and Thailand, travel by river is common. In **Maldives**, ferries and local charter boats offer local island-hopping tours.

Cambodia: Shared taxis and mototaxis are safe options. Scheduled bus service is offered to Phnom Penh suburbs. **Laos:** Roads outside of cities are poorly maintained. Taxis and buses are available within urban areas. **Maldives:** Islands are easily traversed by foot, but taxis, bicycles and motorcycles are available for rent in Male. **Myanmar:** Long-distance bus service is available but not recommended. Renting bicycles is a safe option for shorter distance travel. Cities offer bus service, taxis and rickshaws. **Sri Lanka:** Three-wheelers, dial-a-taxi, cars and minibuses for hire are among the choices available. **Thailand:** Interurban bus service is inexpensive, but conditions may be crowded. Taxis, as well as tuk-tuks (three-wheeled, open-air vehicles) are available. **Viet Nam:** Bus service is generally poor and overcrowded.

The US State Department recommends that US citizens avoid non-essential travel to **Cambodia** due to continued civil strife. **Myanmar's** government strictly controls all travel to and within the nation. Most tourist areas, however, have reopened. Street crime plagues the other southeast Asian nations of **Laos, Thailand** and **Viet Nam**. Congested roads and inattention to traffic laws make driving hazardous. In **Sri Lanka**, terrorist activities in Colombo and outlying regions pose a serious threat to personal security, mostly from incidental harm rather than attacks directed at tourists.

ACTIVITIES

Try learning muay thai, or Thai kickboxing, in the land where this 1,000-year-old sport originated. The art of incapacitating a competitor with bare hands and feet bears similarities to kung fu (a Chinese martial art).

Many students of modern history and veterans of the war in **Viet Nam** have traced the path of the Ho Chi Minh Trail, a much-contested series of roads and trails used to transport supplies during the conflict.

Scale 1:8,000,000 at map center

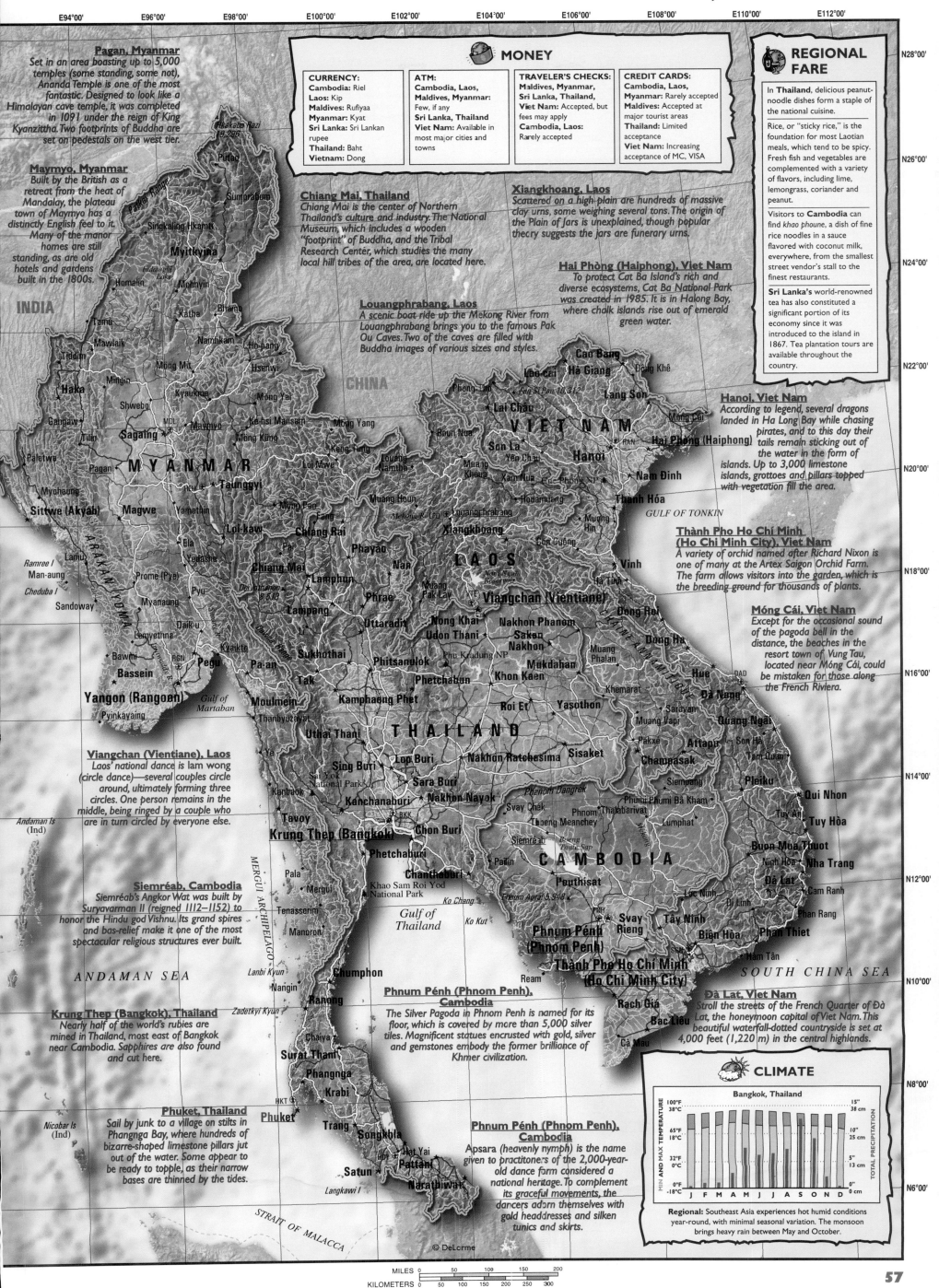

Pagan, Myanmar
Set in an area boasting up to 5,000 temples (some standing, some not), Ananda Temple is one of the most fantastic. Designed to look like a Himalayan cave temple, it was completed in 1091 under the reign of King Kyanzittha. Two footprints of Buddha are set on pedestals on the west tier.

Maymyo, Myanmar
Built by the British as a retreat from the heat of Mandalay, the plateau town of Maymyo has a distinctly English feel to it. Many of the manor homes are still standing, as are old hotels and gardens built in the 1800s.

MONEY

CURRENCY:
Cambodia: Riel
Laos: Kip
Maldives: Rufiyaa
Myanmar: Kyat
Sri Lanka: Sri Lankan rupee
Thailand: Baht
Vietnam: Dong

ATM:
Cambodia, Laos, Maldives, Myanmar: Few, if any
Sri Lanka, Thailand Viet Nam: Available in most major cities and towns

TRAVELER'S CHECKS:
Maldives, Myanmar, Sri Lanka, Thailand, Viet Nam: Accepted, but fees may apply
Cambodia, Laos: Rarely accepted

CREDIT CARDS:
Cambodia, Laos, Myanmar: Rarely accepted
Maldives: Accepted at major tourist areas
Thailand: Limited acceptance
Viet Nam: Increasing acceptance of MC, VISA

REGIONAL FARE

In **Thailand**, delicious peanut-noodle dishes form a staple of the national cuisine.

Rice, or "sticky rice," is the foundation for most Laotian meals, which tend to be spicy. Fresh fish and vegetables are complemented with a variety of flavors, including lime, lemongrass, coriander and peanut.

Visitors to **Cambodia** can find *khao phoune*, a dish of fine rice noodles in a sauce flavored with coconut milk, everywhere, from the smallest street vendor's stall to the finest restaurants.

Sri Lanka's world-renowned tea has also constituted a significant portion of its economy since it was introduced to the island in 1867. Tea plantation tours are available throughout the country.

Chiang Mai, Thailand
Chiang Mai is the center of Northern Thailand's culture and industry. The National Museum, which includes a wooden "footprint" of Buddha, and the Tribal Research Center, which studies the many local hill tribes of the area, are located here.

Louangphrabang, Laos
A scenic boat ride up the Mekong River from Louangphrabang brings you to the famous Pak Ou Caves. Two of the caves are filled with Buddha images of various sizes and styles.

Xiangkhoang, Laos
Scattered on a high plain are hundreds of massive clay urns, some weighing several tons. The origin of the Plain of Jars is unexplained, though popular theory suggests the jars are funerary urns.

Hai Phòng (Haiphong), Viet Nam
To protect Cat Ba Island's rich and diverse ecosystems, Cat Ba National Park was created in 1985. It is in Halong Bay, where chalk islands rise out of emerald green water.

Hanoi, Viet Nam
According to legend, several dragons landed in Ha Long Bay while chasing pirates, and to this day their tails remain sticking out of the water in the form of islands. Up to 3,000 limestone islands, grottoes and pillars topped with vegetation fill the area.

Thành Pho Ho Chí Minh (Ho Chi Minh City), Viet Nam
A variety of orchid named after Richard Nixon is one of many at the Artex Saigon Orchid Farm. The farm allows visitors into the garden, which is the breeding ground for thousands of plants.

Móng Cái, Viet Nam
Except for the occasional sound of the pagoda bell in the distance, the beaches in the resort town of Vung Tau, located near Móng Cái, could be mistaken for those along the French Riviera.

Viangchan (Vientiane), Laos
Laos' national dance is lam wong (circle dance)—several couples circle around, ultimately forming three circles. One person remains in the middle, being ringed by a couple who are in turn circled by everyone else.

Siemréab, Cambodia
Siemréab's Angkor Wat was built by Suryavarman II (reigned 1112–1152) to honor the Hindu god Vishnu. Its grand spires and bas-relief make it one of the most spectacular religious structures ever built.

Krung Thep (Bangkok), Thailand
Nearly half of the world's rubies are mined in Thailand, most east of Bangkok near Cambodia. Sapphires are also found and cut here.

Phnum Pénh (Phnom Penh), Cambodia
The Silver Pagoda in Phnom Penh is named for its floor, which is covered by more than 5,000 silver tiles. Magnificent statues encrusted with gold, silver and gemstones embody the former brilliance of Khmer civilization.

Phnum Pénh (Phnom Penh), Cambodia
Apsara (heavenly nymph) is the name given to practitioners of the 2,000-year-old dance form considered a national heritage. To complement its graceful movements, the dancers adorn themselves with gold headdresses and silken tunics and skirts.

Phuket, Thailand
Sail by junk to a village on stilts in Phangnga Bay, where hundreds of bizarre-shaped limestone pillars jut out of the water. Some appear to be ready to topple, as their narrow bases are thinned by the tides.

Đà Lat, Viet Nam
Stroll the streets of the French Quarter of Đà Lat, the honeymoon capital of Viet Nam. This beautiful waterfall-dotted countryside is set at 4,000 feet (1,220 m) in the central highlands.

CLIMATE

Bangkok, Thailand

Regional: Southeast Asia experiences hot humid conditions year-round, with minimal seasonal variation. The monsoon brings heavy rain between May and October.

© DeLorme

MILES 0 50 100 150 200
KILOMETERS 0 50 100 150 200 250 300

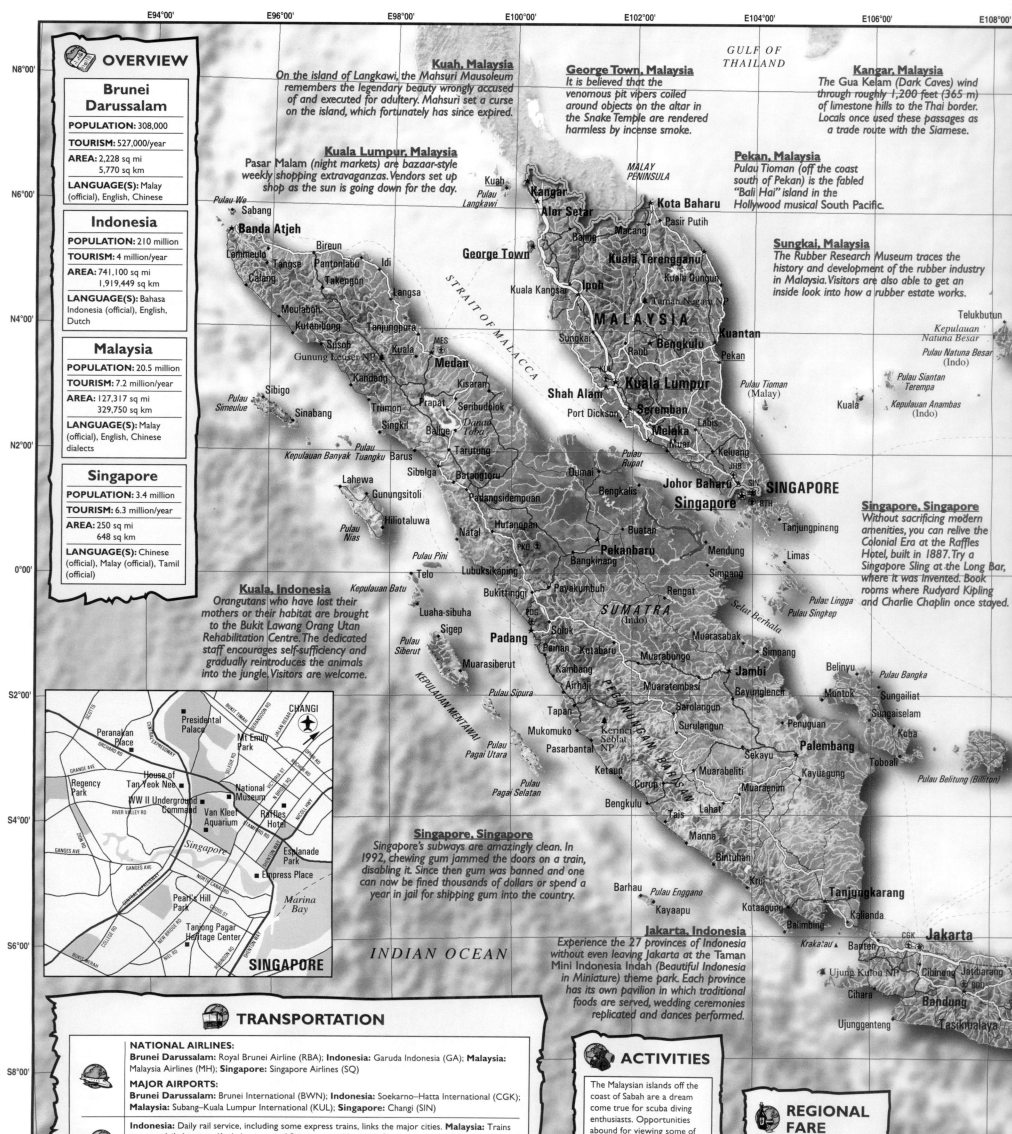

OVERVIEW

Brunei Darussalam

POPULATION: 308,000

TOURISM: 527,000/year

AREA: 2,228 sq mi
5,770 sq km

LANGUAGE(S): Malay (official), English, Chinese

Indonesia

POPULATION: 210 million

TOURISM: 4 million/year

AREA: 741,100 sq mi
1,919,449 sq km

LANGUAGE(S): Bahasa Indonesia (official), English, Dutch

Malaysia

POPULATION: 20.5 million

TOURISM: 7.2 million/year

AREA: 127,317 sq mi
329,750 sq km

LANGUAGE(S): Malay (official), English, Chinese dialects

Singapore

POPULATION: 3.4 million

TOURISM: 6.3 million/year

AREA: 250 sq mi
648 sq km

LANGUAGE(S): Chinese (official), Malay (official), Tamil (official)

Kuah, Malaysia
On the island of Langkawi, the Mahsuri Mausoleum remembers the legendary beauty wrongly accused of and executed for adultery. Mahsuri set a curse on the island, which fortunately has since expired.

Kuala Lumpur, Malaysia
Pasar Malam (night markets) are bazaar-style weekly shopping extravaganzas. Vendors set up shop as the sun is going down for the day.

George Town, Malaysia
It is believed that the venomous pit vipers coiled around objects on the altar in the Snake Temple are rendered harmless by incense smoke.

Kangar, Malaysia
The Gua Kelam (Dark Caves) wind through roughly 1,200 feet (365 m) of limestone hills to the Thai border. Locals once used these passages as a trade route with the Siamese.

Pekan, Malaysia
Pulau Tioman (off the coast south of Pekan) is the fabled "Bali Hai" island in the Hollywood musical South Pacific.

Sungkai, Malaysia
The Rubber Research Museum traces the history and development of the rubber industry in Malaysia. Visitors are also able to get an inside look into how a rubber estate works.

Kuala, Indonesia
Orangutans who have lost their mothers or their habitat are brought to the Bukit Lawang Orang Utan Rehabilitation Centre. The dedicated staff encourages self-sufficiency and gradually reintroduces the animals into the jungle. Visitors are welcome.

Singapore, Singapore
Without sacrificing modern amenities, you can relive the Colonial Era at the Raffles Hotel, built in 1887. Try a Singapore Sling at the Long Bar, where it was invented. Book rooms where Rudyard Kipling and Charlie Chaplin once stayed.

Singapore, Singapore
Singapore's subways are amazingly clean. In 1992, chewing gum jammed the doors on a train, disabling it. Since then gum was banned and one can now be fined thousands of dollars or spend a year in jail for shipping gum into the country.

Jakarta, Indonesia
Experience the 27 provinces of Indonesia without even leaving Jakarta at the Taman Mini Indonesia Indah (Beautiful Indonesia in Miniature) theme park. Each province has its own pavilion in which traditional foods are served, wedding ceremonies replicated and dances performed.

TRANSPORTATION

NATIONAL AIRLINES:
Brunei Darussalam: Royal Brunei Airline (RBA); **Indonesia:** Garuda Indonesia (GA); **Malaysia:** Malaysia Airlines (MH); **Singapore:** Singapore Airlines (SQ)

MAJOR AIRPORTS:
Brunei Darussalam: Brunei International (BWN); **Indonesia:** Soekarno–Hatta International (CGK); **Malaysia:** Subang–Kuala Lumpur International (KUL); **Singapore:** Changi (SIN)

Indonesia: Daily rail service, including some express trains, links the major cities. **Malaysia:** Trains operate daily between Kuala Lumpur and Singapore, and between Butterworth and Bangkok, Thailand. The Malayan Railway Pass gives unlimited travel on all trains through Peninsular Malaysia and Singapore except express trains.

Regular national and international ferry lines serve the port cities of these nations. Passengers have a wide variety of choices with respect to schedule and type of service. Residents and visitors rely on water taxis for shorter trips; charter boats also serve special needs.

In **Indonesia**, **Malaysia** and **Singapore**, regular bus service operates between major cities. Within the cities themselves, travelers can find taxis readily, although local customs regarding fares and additional fees may exist. Rental cars are another option, but extra documentation may be required.

Recent economic and political uncertainty has made for a highly unstable environment for travel in **Indonesia**. Political tension, military interventions and public demonstrations have resulted in violence which may or may not persist. The draconian legal systems of **Brunei Darussalam** and **Singapore** serve as a deterrent to crime, but tourists occasionally suffer petty theft. Visitors themselves should take care to adhere to local laws, as what might be considered minor offenses elsewhere may result in harsh penalties here. In **Malaysia**, visitors should be aware of credit card fraud and of frequently unhealthy air conditions caused by fires burning in Indonesia.

ACTIVITIES

The Malaysian islands off the coast of Sabah are a dream come true for scuba diving enthusiasts. Opportunities abound for viewing some of this region's most exotic sea creatures.

One of **Malaysia's** most popular sports is sepak takraw. Participants keep a small rattan ball aloft by using any part of any appendage except the hands.

Singapore's warm, wet climate supports an amazing abundance of plant life. The displays of thousands of tropical and subtropical plants at the Botanic Gardens, including over 500,000 specimens in the Herbarium, are astounding.

REGIONAL FARE

Rice, the staple of Indonesian cuisine, is the perfect complement to the fresh vegetables and seafood that typically accompany it. In **Malaysia**, chiles, coriander and garlic are often added to rice to enhance the flavor and to turn up the heat.

Brunei Durassalam's cuisine reflects the cultural diversity of the country. Satay is a popular meal of marinated beef or chicken barbecued on a skewer. Another favorite local dish, nasi lemak, is rice cooked with coconut milk.

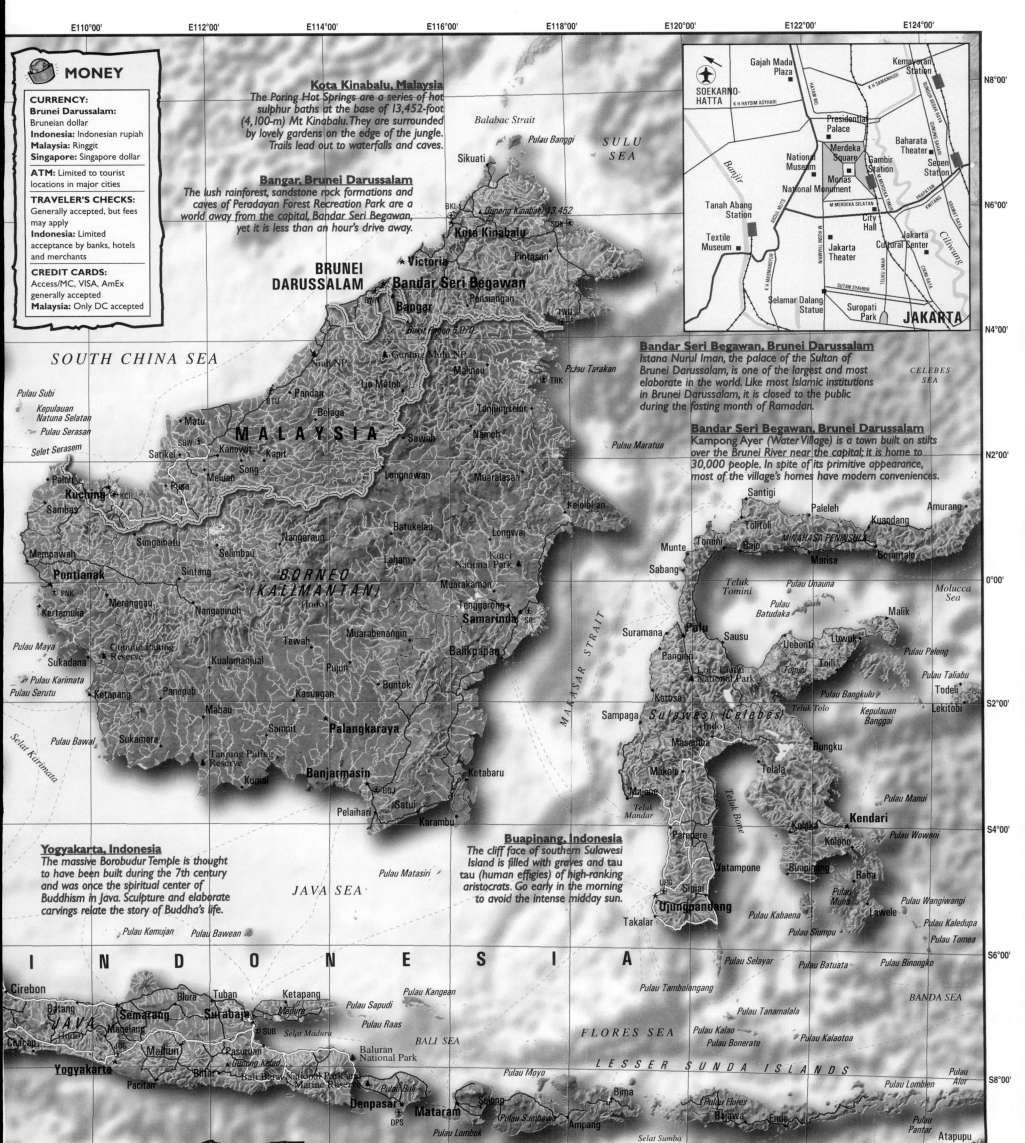

MONEY

CURRENCY:
Brunei Darussalam: Bruneian dollar
Indonesia: Indonesian rupiah
Malaysia: Ringgit
Singapore: Singapore dollar

ATM: Limited to tourist locations in major cities

TRAVELER'S CHECKS: Generally accepted, but fees may apply
Indonesia: Limited acceptance by banks, hotels and merchants

CREDIT CARDS:
Access/MC, VISA, AmEx generally accepted
Malaysia: Only DC accepted

Kota Kinabalu, Malaysia
The Poring Hot Springs are a series of hot sulphur baths at the base of 13,452-foot (4,100-m) Mt Kinabalu. They are surrounded by lovely gardens on the edge of the jungle. Trails lead out to waterfalls and caves.

Bangar, Brunei Darussalam
The lush rainforest, sandstone rock formations and caves of Peradayan Forest Recreation Park are a world away from the capital, Bandar Seri Begawan, yet it is less than an hour's drive away.

Bandar Seri Begawan, Brunei Darussalam
Istana Nurul Iman, the palace of the Sultan of Brunei Darussalam, is one of the largest and most elaborate in the world. Like most Islamic institutions in Brunei Darussalam, it is closed to the public during the fasting month of Ramadan.

Bandar Seri Begawan, Brunei Darussalam
Kampong Ayer (Water Village) is a town built on stilts over the Brunei River near the capital; it is home to 30,000 people. In spite of its primitive appearance, most of the village's homes have modern conveniences.

Yogyakarta, Indonesia
The massive Borobudur Temple is thought to have been built during the 7th century and was once the spiritual center of Buddhism in Java. Sculpture and elaborate carvings relate the story of Buddha's life.

Buapinang, Indonesia
The cliff face of southern Sulawesi Island is filled with graves and tau tau (human effigies) of high-ranking aristocrats. Go early in the morning to avoid the intense midday sun.

Selong, Indonesia
Traditional handicrafts are plentiful on Lombok Island. Pottery, textiles and woodcarving are distinguished by their variety and clean, traditional lines. Villages such as Penunjak specialize in pottery and Sukarare in cloth weaving.

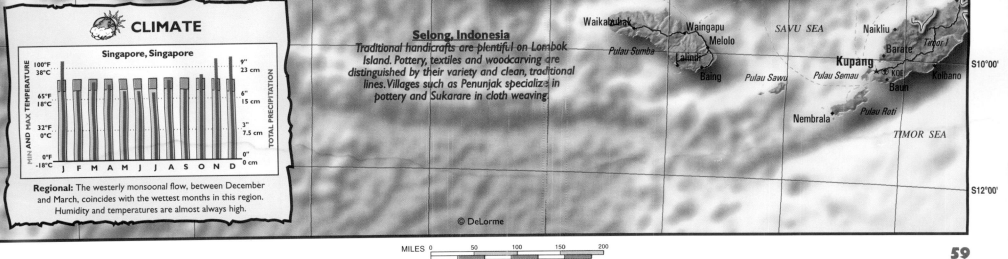

CLIMATE

Singapore, Singapore

Regional: The westerly monsoonal flow, between December and March, coincides with the wettest months in this region. Humidity and temperatures are almost always high.

© DeLorme

MILES
KILOMETERS

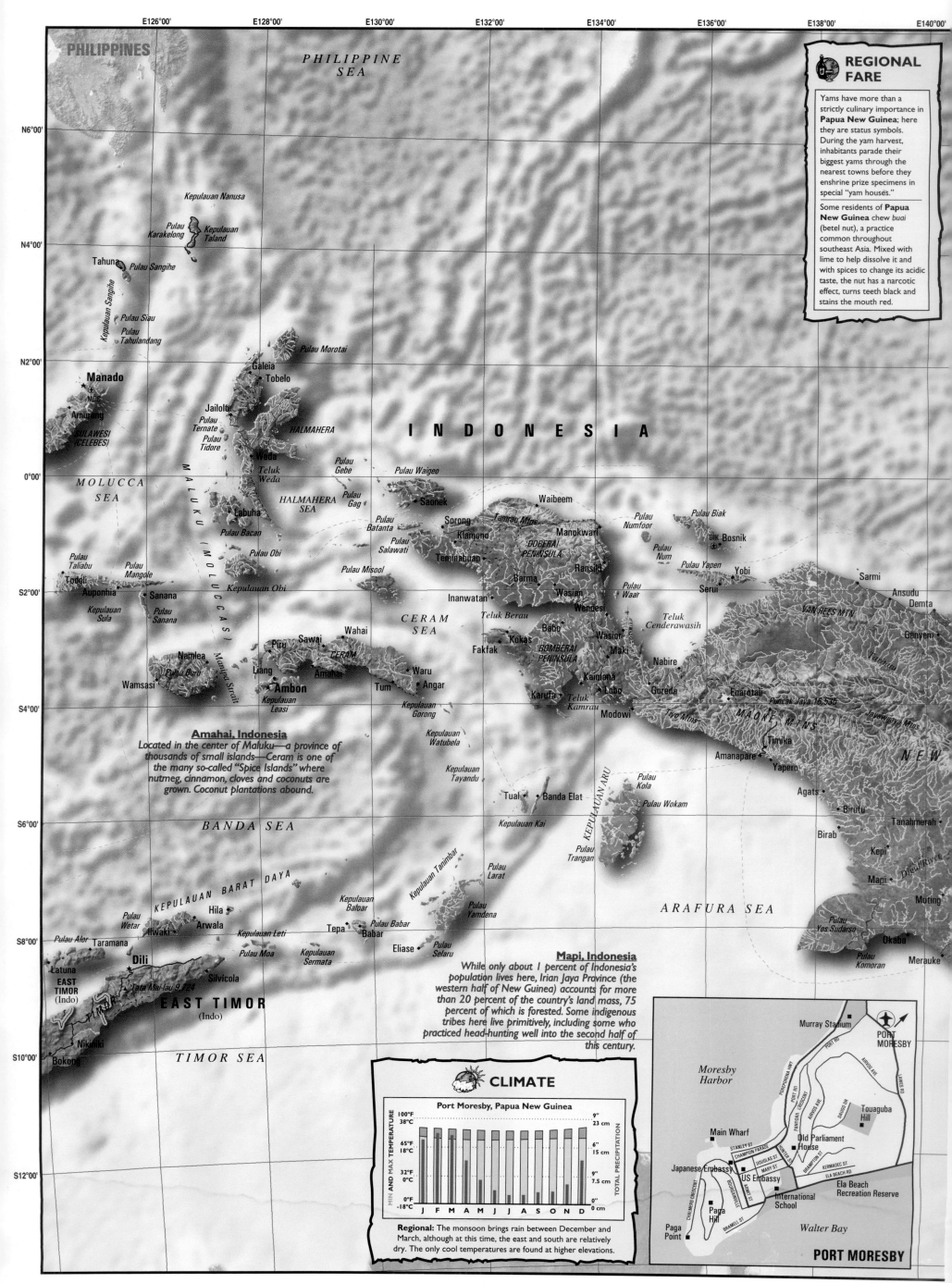

PHILIPPINES

PHILIPPINE SEA

REGIONAL FARE

Yams have more than a strictly culinary importance in **Papua New Guinea**; here they are status symbols. During the yam harvest, inhabitants parade their biggest yams through the nearest towns before they enshrine prize specimens in special "yam houses."

Some residents of **Papua New Guinea** chew *buai* (betel nut), a practice common throughout southeast Asia. Mixed with lime to help dissolve it and with spices to change its acidic taste, the nut has a narcotic effect, turns teeth black and stains the mouth red.

Kepulauan Nanusa

Pulau Karakelong   Kepulauan Talaud

Tahuna   Pulau Sangihe

Pulau Siau

Pulau Tahulandang

Kepulauan Sangihe

Manado

Amurang

SULAWESI (CELEBES)

MOLUCCA SEA

Pulau Morotai

Galeia   Tobelo

Jailolo

Pulau Ternate   HALMAHERA

Pulau Tidore

Weda

Teluk Weda

Pulau Gebe

HALMAHERA SEA   Pulau Gag

Labuha   Pulau Batanta

Pulau Bacan

Pulau Obi

Pulau Waigeo

Saonek

Sorong   Tanau Mtns

Klamono

Pulau Salawati   DOBERAI PENINSULA

Teminabuan

Barma

Pulau Talaibu

Pulau Mangole

Todeli   Auponhia

Sanana   Kepulauan Obi

Pulau Sanana

Kepulauan Sula

Namlea   Wahai

Piru   Sawai

Pulau Buru   Liang   CERAM

Wamsasi   Amahai

Manipa Strait   **Ambon**

Kepulauan Leasi

Pulau Misool

CERAM SEA

Waru

Tum   Angar

Kepulauan Gorong

Kepulauan Watubela

Kepulauan Tayandu

I N D O N E S I A

Waibeem

Manokwari

Pulau Numfoor   Pulau Biak

BIK   Bosnik

Pulau Num   Pulau Yapen

Ransiki   Yobi

Pulau Waar   Serui

Wasian   Sarmi

Wendesi   Teluk Cenderawasih

Babo   Ansudu

Kokas   Wasior   Demta

Fakfak   BOMBERAI PENINSULA   Maki

Karufa   Nabire   VAN REES MTN

Teluk Kamrau   Lobo   Gureda

Modowi   Enarotali

Two Mtns   Puncak Jaya 16,535

MAOKE MTNS

Timika   Jayawijaya Mtns

Amanapare   N E W

Yapero

Agats   Birutu

Tanahmerah

Birab

Kepi

Mapi

Muting

Pulau Yos Sudarso

Okaba

Merauke

Pulau Komoran

Amahai, Indonesia
Located in the center of Maluku—a province of thousands of small islands—Ceram is one of the many so-called "Spice Islands" where nutmeg, cinnamon, cloves and coconuts are grown. Coconut plantations abound.

BANDA SEA

Pulau Kola

Tual   Banda Elat

Pulau Wokam

Kepulauan Kai

Pulau Trangam

Pulau Larat

Kepulauan Tanimbar   *ARAFURA SEA*

Pulau Yamdena

KEPULAUAN BARAT DAYA

Hila

Pulau Wetar   Ilwaki   Arwala

Taramana   Kepulauan Leti   Tepa   Pulau Babar

Pulau Alor   Babar

Dili   Pulau Moa   Kepulauan Sermata   Eliase   Pulau Selaru

Latuna   EAST TIMOR (Indo)

Tata Mai-lau 9,724

Silvicola

EAST TIMOR
(Indo)

Nikiniki

Bokong   *TIMOR SEA*

Mapi, Indonesia
While only about 1 percent of Indonesia's population lives here, Irian Jaya Province (the western half of New Guinea) accounts for more than 20 percent of the country's land mass, 75 percent of which is forested. Some indigenous tribes here live primitively, including some who practiced head-hunting well into the second half of this century.

CLIMATE

Port Moresby, Papua New Guinea

	9" 23 cm
MIN AND MAX TEMPERATURE	6" 15 cm
	3" 7.5 cm
	0 cm

100°F 38°C
65°F 18°C
32°F 0°C
0°F -18°C

J F M A M J J A S O N D

TOTAL PRECIPITATION

Regional: The monsoon brings rain between December and March, although at this time, the east and south are relatively dry. The only cool temperatures are found at higher elevations.

Murray Stadium   **PORT MORESBY**

Moresby Harbor

Main Wharf   Old Parliament House

Japanese Embassy   US Embassy

International School   Ela Beach Recreation Reserve

Paga Hill

Paga Point   *Walter Bay*

PORT MORESBY

Touaguba Hill

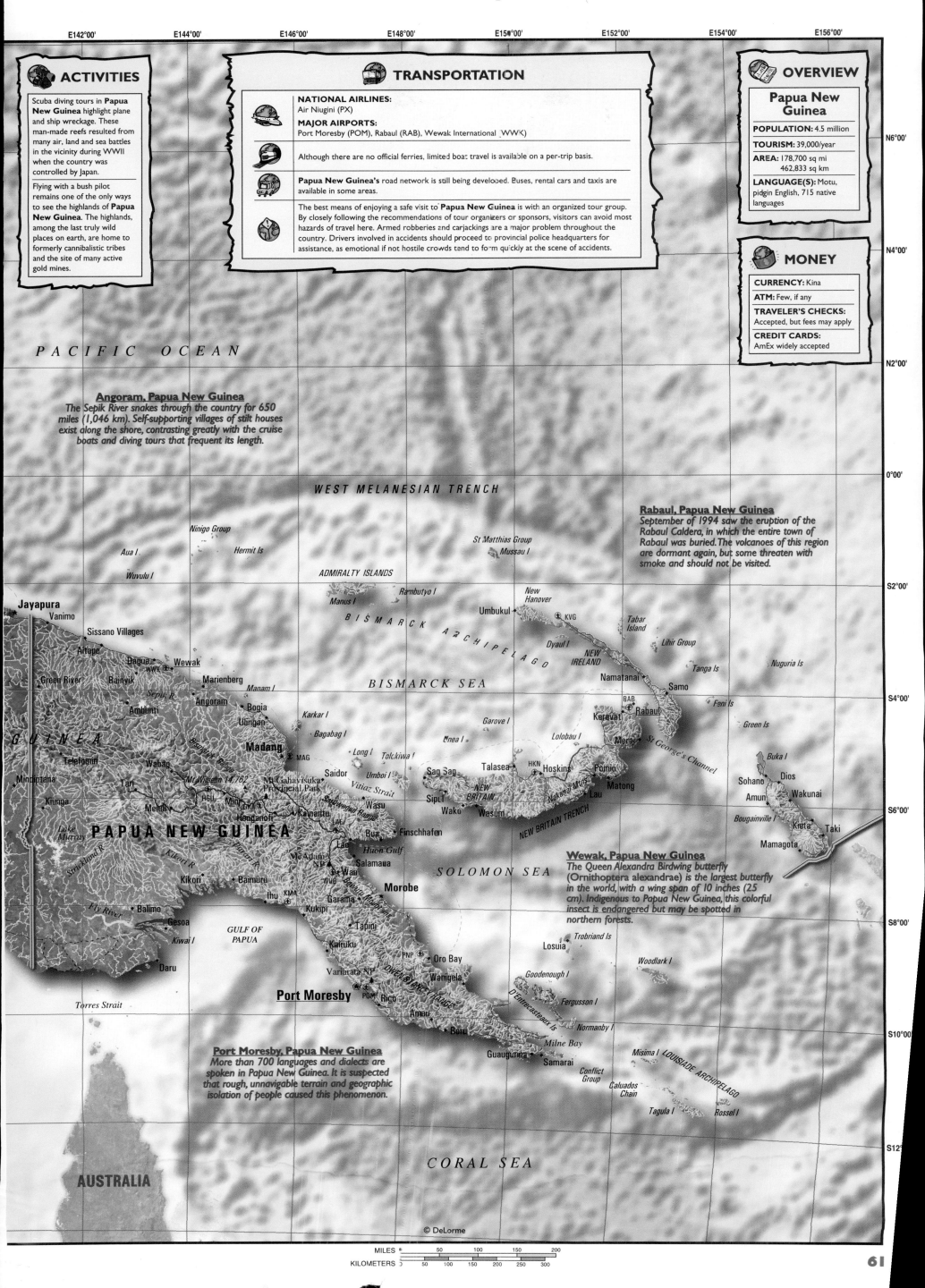

ACTIVITIES

Scuba diving tours in **Papua New Guinea** highlight plane and ship wreckage. These man-made reefs resulted from many air, land and sea battles in the vicinity during WWII when the country was controlled by Japan.

Flying with a bush pilot remains one of the only ways to see the highlands of **Papua New Guinea**. The highlands, among the last truly wild places on earth, are home to formerly cannibalistic tribes and the site of many active gold mines.

TRANSPORTATION

NATIONAL AIRLINES:
Air Niugini (PX)

MAJOR AIRPORTS:
Port Moresby (POM), Rabaul (RAB), Wewak International (WWK)

Although there are no official ferries, limited boat travel is available on a per-trip basis.

Papua New Guinea's road network is still being developed. Buses, rental cars and taxis are available in some areas.

The best means of enjoying a safe visit to **Papua New Guinea** is with an organized tour group. By closely following the recommendations of tour organizers or sponsors, visitors can avoid most hazards of travel here. Armed robberies and carjackings are a major problem throughout the country. Drivers involved in accidents should proceed to provincial police headquarters for assistance, as emotional if not hostile crowds tend to form quickly at the scene of accidents.

OVERVIEW

Papua New Guinea

POPULATION: 4.5 million

TOURISM: 39,000/year

AREA: 178,700 sq mi
462,833 sq km

LANGUAGE(S): Motu, pidgin English, 715 native languages

MONEY

CURRENCY: Kina

ATM: Few, if any

TRAVELER'S CHECKS: Accepted, but fees may apply

CREDIT CARDS: AmEx widely accepted

PACIFIC OCEAN

Angoram, Papua New Guinea
The Sepik River snakes through the country for 650 miles (1,046 km). Self-supporting villages of stilt houses exist along the shore, contrasting greatly with the cruise boats and diving tours that frequent its length.

WEST MELANESIAN TRENCH

Rabaul, Papua New Guinea
September of 1994 saw the eruption of the Rabaul Caldera, in which the entire town of Rabaul was buried. The volcanoes of this region are dormant again, but some threaten with smoke and should not be visited.

Ninigo Group

Aua I. *Hermit Is*

Wuvulu I

St Matthias Group
Mussau I

ADMIRALTY ISLANDS

Rambutyo I New Hanover

Jayapura *Manus I* Umbukul • KVG *Tabar Island*
Vanimo

Sissano Villages *Dyaul I* *Lihir Group*
BISMARCK ARCHIPELAGO **NEW IRELAND**
Aitape Namatanai *Tanga Is* *Nuguria Is*
Dagua Wewak *BISMARCK SEA* Samo
Green River Rainyik WWK *Manam I*
Marienberg RAB *Feni Is*
Amunti Angoram Bogia *Karkar I* Keravat Rabaul *Green Is*
Telefomin Ulingan *Bagabag I* *Garove I* *Lolobau I* *St George's Channel* *Buka I*
Madang *Lnea I* Merai Sohano Dios
Wabag MAG *Long I* *Tolokiwa I* Talasea HKN Hoskins Pomio Amun Wakunai
Mt Wilhelm 14,762 Saidor *Umboi I* Sag Sag Matong Lau
Minj Mt Gahavisuka *Vitiaz Strait* **NEW BRITAIN** *Bougainville I* Kreta Taki
Mendi Provincial Park Wasu Sipu Wako Wasum *NEW BRITAIN TRENCH* Mamagota
PAPUA NEW GUINEA Kainantu
Bua • Finschhafen
Lake Murray Lae Huon Gulf
McAdam NP Salamaua *SOLOMON SEA*
Kikori Baimuru Wau
Ihu Garama **Morobe**
Kukipi

Fly River Balimo *GULF OF PAPUA*
Gesoa Tapini
Kiwai I Kairuku
Daru PNP Oro Bay

Wewak, Papua New Guinea
The Queen Alexandra Birdwing butterfly (Ornithoptera alexandrae) is the largest butterfly in the world, with a wing span of 10 inches (25 cm). Indigenous to Papua New Guinea, this colorful insect is endangered but may be spotted in northern forests.

Trobriand Is
Losuia *Woodlark I*
Varirata NP Wamgela Goodenough I
Port Moresby Rigo D'Entrecasteaux Is Fergusson I
Amau Normanby I
Bori Milne Bay
Guagurina Samarai *Misima I* *LOUISIADE ARCHIPELAGO*
Conflict Group
Torres Strait Caluados Chain
Tagula I Rossel I

Port Moresby, Papua New Guinea
More than 700 languages and dialects are spoken in Papua New Guinea. It is suspected that rough, unnavigable terrain and geographic isolation of people caused this phenomenon.

AUSTRALIA

CORAL SEA

© DeLorme

MILES 50 100 150 200
KILOMETERS 0 50 100 150 200 250 300

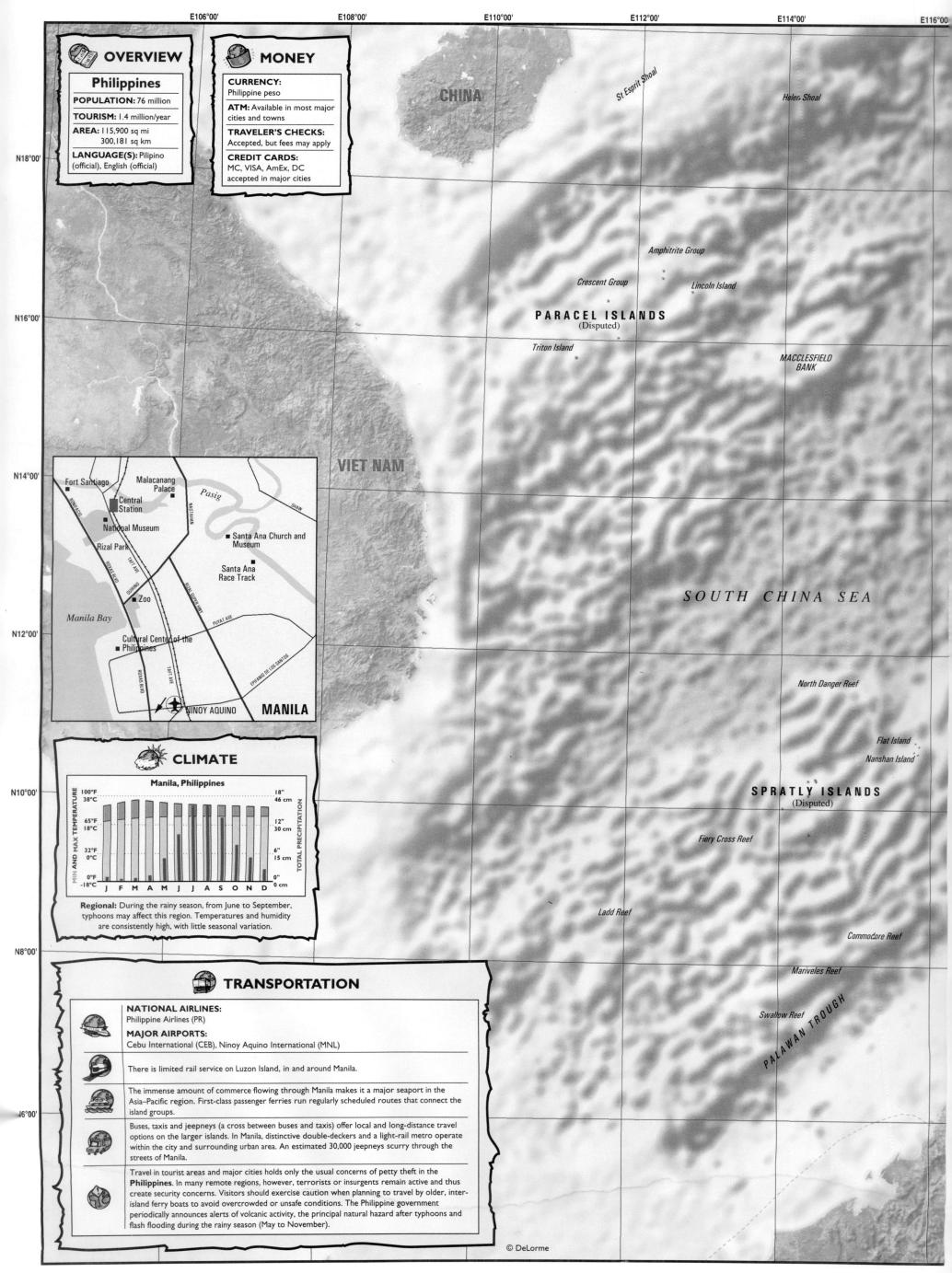

OVERVIEW

Philippines

POPULATION: 76 million

TOURISM: 1.4 million/year

AREA: 115,900 sq mi
300,181 sq km

LANGUAGE(S): Pilipino (official), English (official)

MONEY

CURRENCY:
Philippine peso

ATM: Available in most major cities and towns

TRAVELER'S CHECKS: Accepted, but fees may apply

CREDIT CARDS:
MC, VISA, AmEx, DC accepted in major cities

CHINA

St Esprit Shoal

Helen Shoal

Amphitrite Group

Crescent Group

Lincoln Island

PARACEL ISLANDS
(Disputed)

Triton Island

MACCLESFIELD BANK

VIET NAM

SOUTH CHINA SEA

North Danger Reef

Flat Island

Nanshan Island

SPRATLY ISLANDS
(Disputed)

Fiery Cross Reef

Ladd Reef

Commodore Reef

Mariveles Reef

Swallow Reef

PALAWAN TROUGH

MANILA map:
Fort Santiago — Malacanang Palace — Central Station — National Museum — Rizal Park — Pasig — Santa Ana Church and Museum — Santa Ana Race Track — Zoo — Manila Bay — Cultural Center of the Philippines — NINOY AQUINO — **MANILA**

CLIMATE

Manila, Philippines

MIN AND MAX TEMPERATURE: 100°F 38°C / 65°F 18°C / 32°F 0°C / 0°F -18°C

TOTAL PRECIPITATION: 18" 46 cm / 12" 30 cm / 6" 15 cm / 0" 0 cm

J F M A M J J A S O N D

Regional: During the rainy season, from June to September, typhoons may affect this region. Temperatures and humidity are consistently high, with little seasonal variation.

TRANSPORTATION

NATIONAL AIRLINES:
Philippine Airlines (PR)

MAJOR AIRPORTS:
Cebu International (CEB), Ninoy Aquino International (MNL)

There is limited rail service on Luzon Island, in and around Manila.

The immense amount of commerce flowing through Manila makes it a major seaport in the Asia–Pacific region. First-class passenger ferries run regularly scheduled routes that connect the island groups.

Buses, taxis and jeepneys (a cross between buses and taxis) offer local and long-distance travel options on the larger islands. In Manila, distinctive double-deckers and a light-rail metro operate within the city and surrounding urban area. An estimated 30,000 jeepneys scurry through the streets of Manila.

Travel in tourist areas and major cities holds only the usual concerns of petty theft in the **Philippines**. In many remote regions, however, terrorists or insurgents remain active and thus create security concerns. Visitors should exercise caution when planning to travel by older, inter-island ferry boats to avoid overcrowded or unsafe conditions. The Philippine government periodically announces alerts of volcanic activity, the principal natural hazard after typhoons and flash flooding during the rainy season (May to November).

© DeLorme

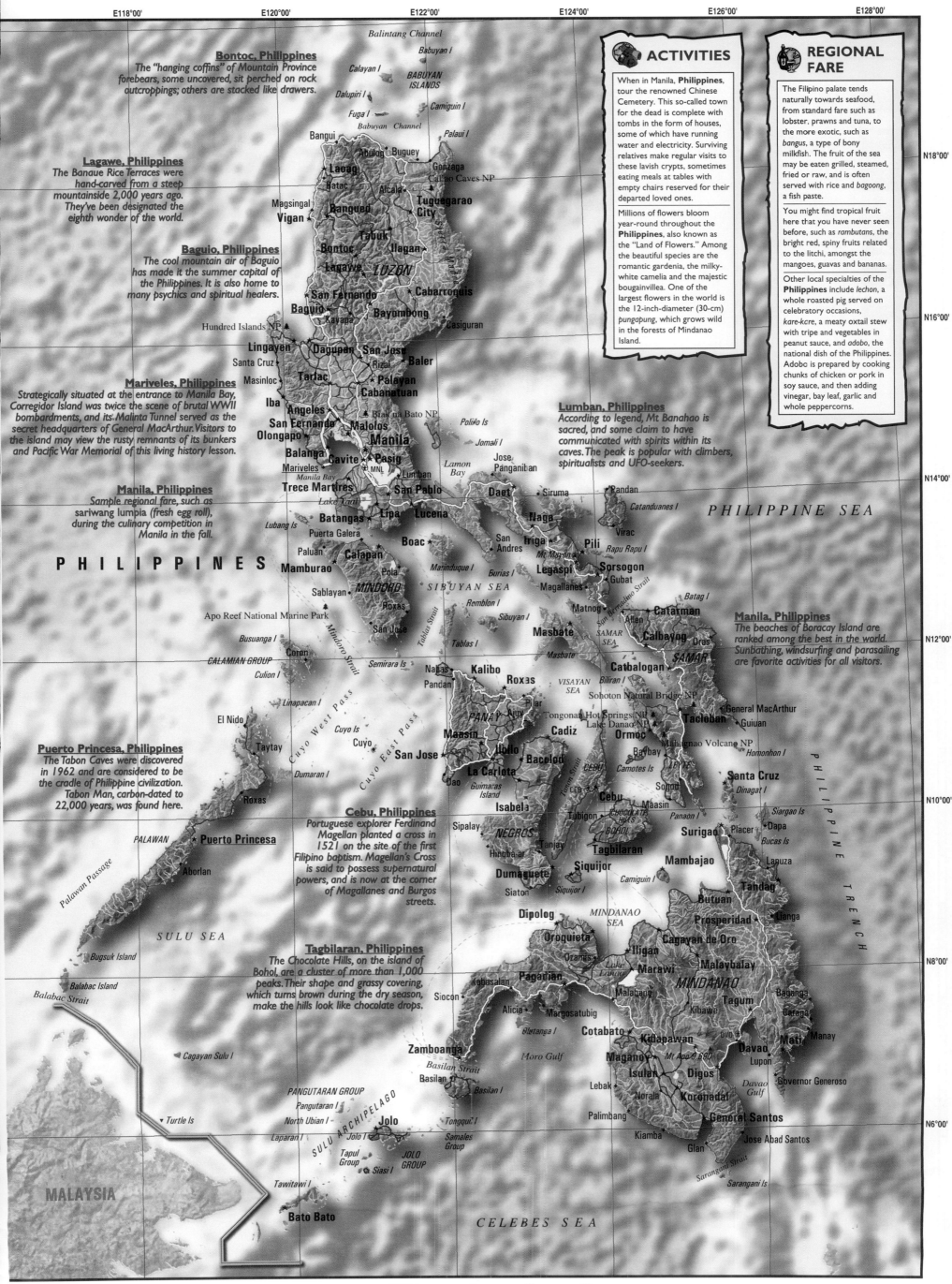

Bontoc, Philippines
The "hanging coffins" of Mountain Province forebears, some uncovered, sit perched on rock outcroppings; others are stacked like drawers.

Lagawe, Philippines
The Banaue Rice Terraces were hand-carved from a steep mountainside 2,000 years ago. They've been designated the eighth wonder of the world.

Baguio, Philippines
The cool mountain air of Baguio has made it the summer capital of the Philippines. It is also home to many psychics and spiritual healers.

Mariveles, Philippines
Strategically situated at the entrance to Manila Bay, Corregidor Island was twice the scene of brutal WWII bombardments, and its Malinta Tunnel served as the secret headquarters of General MacArthur. Visitors to the island may view the rusty remnants of its bunkers and Pacific War Memorial of this living history lesson.

Manila, Philippines
Sample regional fare, such as sariwang lumpia (fresh egg roll), during the culinary competition in Manila in the fall.

Puerto Princesa, Philippines
The Tabon Caves were discovered in 1962 and are considered to be the cradle of Philippine civilization. Tabon Man, carbon-dated to 22,000 years, was found here.

Cebu, Philippines
Portuguese explorer Ferdinand Magellan planted a cross in 1521 on the site of the first Filipino baptism. Magellan's Cross is said to possess supernatural powers, and is now at the corner of Magallanes and Burgos streets.

Tagbilaran, Philippines
The Chocolate Hills, on the island of Bohol, are a cluster of more than 1,000 peaks. Their shape and grassy covering, which turns brown during the dry season, make the hills look like chocolate drops.

Lumban, Philippines
According to legend, Mt Banahao is sacred, and some claim to have communicated with spirits within its caves. The peak is popular with climbers, spiritualists and UFO-seekers.

Manila, Philippines
The beaches of Boracay Island are ranked among the best in the world. Sunbathing, windsurfing and parasailing are favorite activities for all visitors.

ACTIVITIES

When in Manila, **Philippines**, tour the renowned Chinese Cemetery. This so-called town for the dead is complete with tombs in the form of houses, some of which have running water and electricity. Surviving relatives make regular visits to these lavish crypts, sometimes eating meals at tables with empty chairs reserved for their departed loved ones.

Millions of flowers bloom year-round throughout the **Philippines**, also known as the "Land of Flowers." Among the beautiful species are the romantic gardenia, the milky-white camelia and the majestic bougainvillea. One of the largest flowers in the world is the 12-inch-diameter (30-cm) pungapung, which grows wild in the forests of Mindanao Island.

REGIONAL FARE

The Filipino palate tends naturally towards seafood, from standard fare such as lobster, prawns and tuna, to the more exotic, such as bangus, a type of bony milkfish. The fruit of the sea may be eaten grilled, steamed, fried or raw, and is often served with rice and bagoong, a fish paste.

You might find tropical fruit here that you have never seen before, such as rambutans, the bright red, spiny fruits related to the litchi, amongst the mangoes, guavas and bananas.

Other local specialties of the **Philippines** include lechon, a whole roasted pig served on celebratory occasions, kare-kcre, a meaty oxtail stew with tripe and vegetables in peanut sauce, and adobo, the national dish of the Philippines. Adobc is prepared by cooking chunks of chicken or pork in soy sauce, and then adding vinegar, bay leaf, garlic and whole peppercorns.

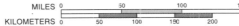

MILES
KILOMETERS

OCEANIA

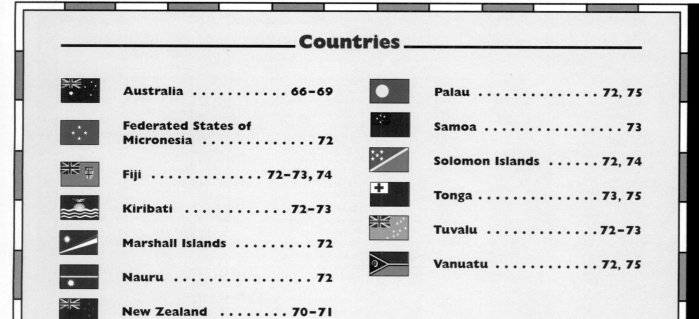

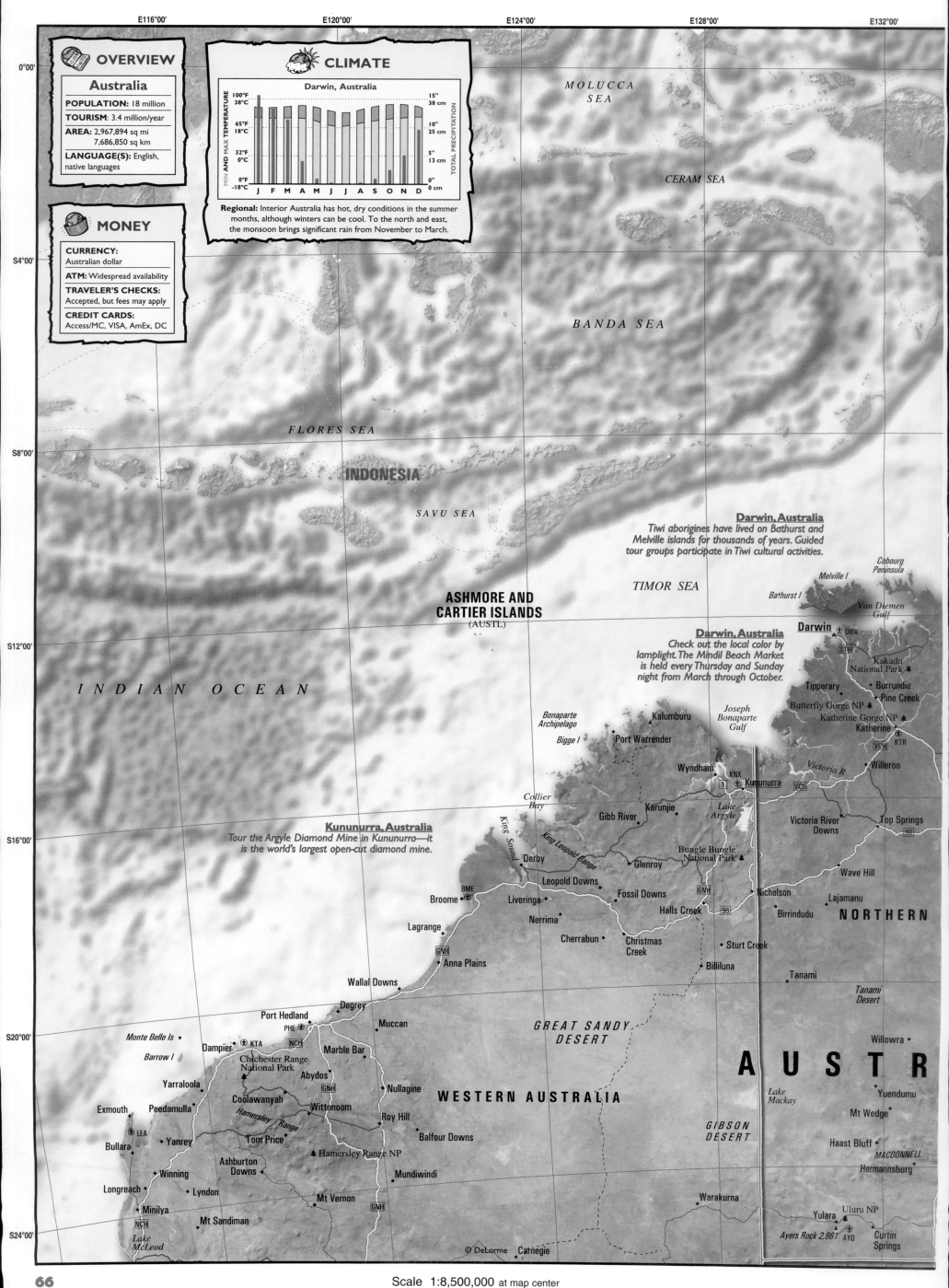

0°00'
S4°00'
S8°00'
S12°00'
S16°00'
S20°00'
S24°00'

OVERVIEW

Australia

POPULATION: 18 million

TOURISM: 3.4 million/year

AREA: 2,967,894 sq mi
7,686,850 sq km

LANGUAGE(S): English, native languages

CLIMATE

Darwin, Australia

MIN AND MAX TEMPERATURE
100°F 38°C
65°F 18°C
32°F 0°C
0°F -18°C

TOTAL PRECIPITATION
15" 38 cm
10" 25 cm
5" 13 cm
0" 0 cm

J F M A M J J A S O N D

Regional: Interior Australia has hot, dry conditions in the summer months, although winters can be cool. To the north and east, the monsoon brings significant rain from November to March.

MONEY

CURRENCY:
Australian dollar

ATM: Widespread availability

TRAVELER'S CHECKS:
Accepted, but fees may apply

CREDIT CARDS:
Access/MC, VISA, AmEx, DC

MOLUCCA SEA

CERAM SEA

BANDA SEA

FLORES SEA

INDONESIA

SAVU SEA

Darwin, Australia
Tiwi aborigines have lived on Bathurst and Melville islands for thousands of years. Guided tour groups participate in Tiwi cultural activities.

TIMOR SEA

Cobourg Peninsula
Melville I
Bathurst I
Van Diemen Gulf

ASHMORE AND CARTIER ISLANDS
(AUSTL)

Darwin, Australia
Check out the local color by lamplight. The Mindil Beach Market is held every Thursday and Sunday night from March through October.

Darwin ✈ DRW
STH
Kakadu National Park ▲

INDIAN OCEAN

Bonaparte Archipelago
Bigge I
Port Warrender
Kalumburu
Joseph Bonaparte Gulf
Wyndham
KNX Kununurra
Tipperary
Burrundie
Pine Creek
Butterfly Gorge NP ▲
Katherine Gorge NP ▲
Katherine
VCH KTR
Victoria R
Willeroo

Collier Bay
Gibb River
Karunjie
Lake Argyle
VCH

Kununurra, Australia
Tour the Argyle Diamond Mine in Kununurra—it is the world's largest open-cut diamond mine.

King Sound
King Leopold Range
Derby
Glenroy
Bungle Bungle National Park ▲
Victoria River Downs
Top Springs
95

Leopold Downs
Fossil Downs
GNH
Nicholson
Wave Hill

BME
Broome ✈
Liveringa
Halls Creek
96
Birrindudu
Lajamanu

Nerrima
Cherrabun
Christmas Creek
Sturt Creek

NORTHERN

Lagrange

Billiluna
Tanami

GNH
Anna Plains

Tanami Desert

Wallal Downs

Degrey
Muccan

GREAT SANDY DESERT

Willowra

Port Hedland
PHE
Monte Bello Is
Dampier ✈ KTA
NCH
Marble Bar
Lake Mackay
Yuendumu

Barrow I
Chichester Range National Park
Abydos
Nullagine
WESTERN AUSTRALIA
Mt Wedge

Yarraloola
GNH
Wittenoom
Roy Hill
A U S T R

Exmouth
Peedamulla
Coolawanyah
Hamersley Range
Roy Hill
GIBSON DESERT

Bullara
✈ LEA
Yanrey
Tom Price
Balfour Downs
Haast Bluff
MACDONNELL

Winning
Ashburton Downs
Mt Vernon
Mundiwindi
Hermannsburg

Longreach
Lyndon
Hamersley Range NP ▲

Minilya
NCH
Mt Sandiman
GNH
Warakurna
Yulara
Uluru NP

Lake McLeod
Carnegie
Ayers Rock 2,861 ▲ AYQ
Curtin Springs

© DeLorme

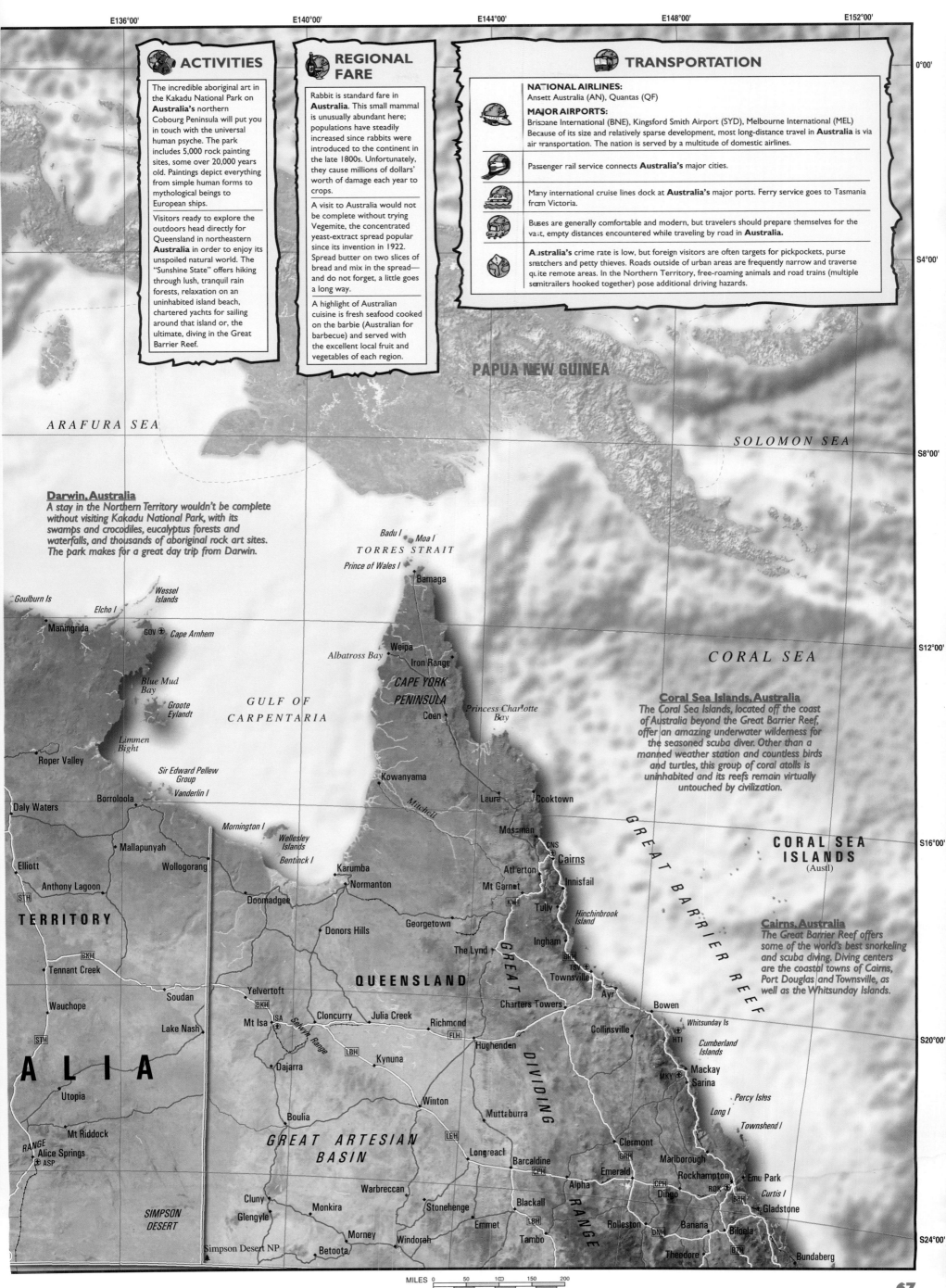

ACTIVITIES

The incredible aboriginal art in the Kakadu National Park on **Australia's** northern Cobourg Peninsula will put you in touch with the universal human psyche. The park includes 5,000 rock painting sites, some over 20,000 years old. Paintings depict everything from simple human forms to mythological beings to European ships.

Visitors ready to explore the outdoors head directly for Queensland in northeastern **Australia** in order to enjoy its unspoiled natural world. The "Sunshine State" offers hiking through lush, tranquil rain forests, relaxation on an uninhabited island beach, chartered yachts for sailing around that island or, the ultimate, diving in the Great Barrier Reef.

REGIONAL FARE

Rabbit is standard fare in **Australia**. This small mammal is unusually abundant here; populations have steadily increased since rabbits were introduced to the continent in the late 1800s. Unfortunately, they cause millions of dollars' worth of damage each year to crops.

A visit to Australia would not be complete without trying Vegemite, the concentrated yeast-extract spread popular since its invention in 1922. Spread butter on two slices of bread and mix in the spread—and do not forget, a little goes a long way.

A highlight of Australian cuisine is fresh seafood cooked on the barbie (Australian for barbecue) and served with the excellent local fruit and vegetables of each region.

TRANSPORTATION

NATIONAL AIRLINES:
Ansett Australia (AN), Quantas (QF)

MAJOR AIRPORTS:
Brisbane International (BNE), Kingsford Smith Airport (SYD), Melbourne International (MEL) Because of its size and relatively sparse development, most long-distance travel in **Australia** is via air transportation. The nation is served by a multitude of domestic airlines.

Passenger rail service connects **Australia's** major cities.

Many international cruise lines dock at **Australia's** major ports. Ferry service goes to Tasmania from Victoria.

Buses are generally comfortable and modern, but travelers should prepare themselves for the vast, empty distances encountered while traveling by road in **Australia.**

Australia's crime rate is low, but foreign visitors are often targets for pickpockets, purse snatchers and petty thieves. Roads outside of urban areas are frequently narrow and traverse quite remote areas. In the Northern Territory, free-roaming animals and road trains (multiple semitrailers hooked together) pose additional driving hazards.

Darwin, Australia
A stay in the Northern Territory wouldn't be complete without visiting Kakadu National Park, with its swamps and crocodiles, eucalyptus forests and waterfalls, and thousands of aboriginal rock art sites. The park makes for a great day trip from Darwin.

Coral Sea Islands, Australia
The Coral Sea Islands, located off the coast of Australia beyond the Great Barrier Reef, offer an amazing underwater wilderness for the seasoned scuba diver. Other than a manned weather station and countless birds and turtles, this group of coral atolls is uninhabited and its reefs remain virtually untouched by civilization.

Cairns, Australia
The Great Barrier Reef offers some of the world's best snorkeling and scuba diving. Diving centers are the coastal towns of Cairns, Port Douglas and Townsville, as well as the Whitsunday Islands.

MILES 0 50 100 150 200
KILOMETERS 0 50 100 150 200 250 300

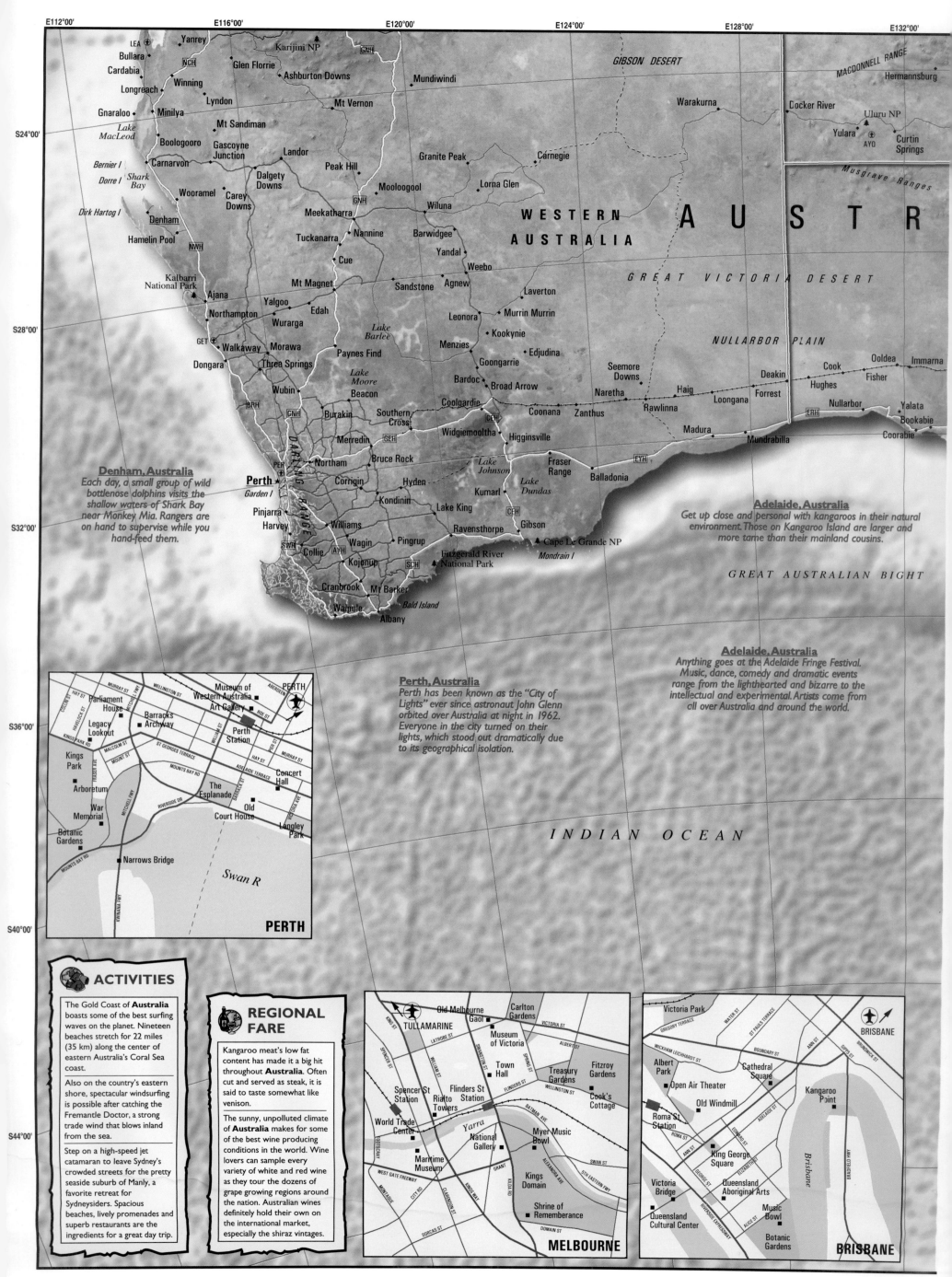

E112°00' E116°00' E120°00' E124°00' E128°00' E132°00'

S24°00'
S28°00'
S32°00'
S36°00'
S40°00'
S44°00'

GIBSON DESERT

MACDONNELL RANGE

WESTERN AUSTRALIA

AUSTR

GREAT VICTORIA DESERT

NULLARBOR PLAIN

Musgrave Ranges

GREAT AUSTRALIAN BIGHT

INDIAN OCEAN

Denham, Australia
Each day, a small group of wild bottlenose dolphins visits the shallow waters of Shark Bay near Monkey Mia. Rangers are on hand to supervise while you hand-feed them.

Perth, Australia
Perth has been known as the "City of Lights" ever since astronaut John Glenn orbited over Australia at night in 1962. Everyone in the city turned on their lights, which stood out dramatically due to its geographical isolation.

Adelaide, Australia
Get up close and personal with kangaroos in their natural environment. Those on Kangaroo Island are larger and more tame than their mainland cousins.

Adelaide, Australia
Anything goes at the Adelaide Fringe Festival. Music, dance, comedy and dramatic events range from the lighthearted and bizarre to the intellectual and experimental. Artists come from all over Australia and around the world.

PERTH
Museum of Western Australia · Art Gallery · PERTH · Parliament House · Barracks · Archway · Legacy Lookout · Perth Station · Kings Park · Arboretum · The Esplanade · Concert Hall · War Memorial · Old Court House · Langley Park · Botanic Gardens · Narrows Bridge · Swan R · MURRAY ST · MITCHELL FWY · WELLINGTON ST · HAY ST · ROE ST · ABERDEEN ST · WILLIAM ST · ST GEORGES TERRACE · HAY ST · MURRAY ST · ADELAIDE TERRACE · RIVERSIDE DR · MOUNTS BAY RD · KWINANA FWY

ACTIVITIES
The Gold Coast of **Australia** boasts some of the best surfing waves on the planet. Nineteen beaches stretch for 22 miles (35 km) along the center of eastern Australia's Coral Sea coast.

Also on the country's eastern shore, spectacular windsurfing is possible after catching the Fremantle Doctor, a strong trade wind that blows inland from the sea.

Step on a high-speed jet catamaran to leave Sydney's crowded streets for the pretty seaside suburb of Manly, a favorite retreat for Sydneysiders. Spacious beaches, lively promenades and superb restaurants are the ingredients for a great day trip.

REGIONAL FARE
Kangaroo meat's low fat content has made it a big hit throughout **Australia**. Often cut and served as steak, it is said to taste somewhat like venison.

The sunny, unpolluted climate of **Australia** makes for some of the best wine producing conditions in the world. Wine lovers can sample every variety of white and red wine as they tour the dozens of grape growing regions around the nation. Australian wines definitely hold their own on the international market, especially the shiraz vintages.

MELBOURNE
Old Melbourne Gaol · Carlton Gardens · TULLAMARINE · Museum of Victoria · Town Hall · Treasury Gardens · Fitzroy Gardens · Cook's Cottage · Spencer St Station · Flinders St Station · Rialto Towers · World Trade Center · Myer Music Bowl · Yarra · National Gallery · Maritime Museum · Kings Domain · Shrine of Remembrance

BRISBANE
Victoria Park · BRISBANE · Albert Park · Open Air Theater · Cathedral Square · Old Windmill · Kangaroo Point · Roma St Station · King George Square · Victoria Bridge · Queensland Aboriginal Arts · Music Bowl · Queensland Cultural Center · Botanic Gardens · Brisbane

Scale 1:8,500,000 at map center

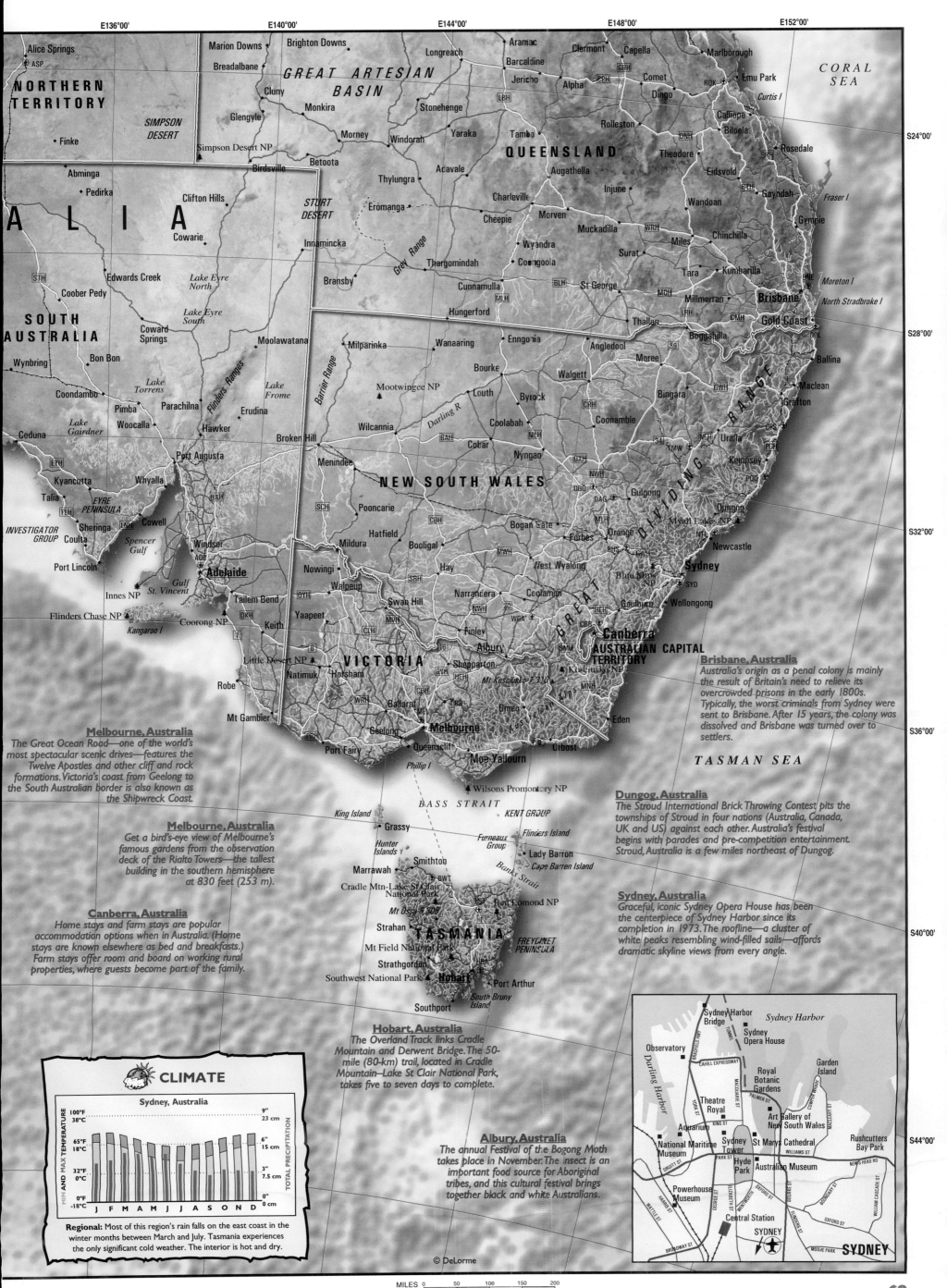

Melbourne, Australia
The Great Ocean Road—one of the world's most spectacular scenic drives—features the Twelve Apostles and other cliff and rock formations. Victoria's coast from Geelong to the South Australian border is also known as the Shipwreck Coast.

Melbourne, Australia
Get a bird's-eye view of Melbourne's famous gardens from the observation deck of the Rialto Towers—the tallest building in the southern hemisphere at 830 feet (253 m).

Canberra, Australia
Home stays and farm stays are popular accommodation options when in Australia. (Home stays are known elsewhere as bed and breakfasts.) Farm stays offer room and board on working rural properties, where guests become part of the family.

Hobart, Australia
The Overland Track links Cradle Mountain and Derwent Bridge. The 50-mile (80-km) trail, located in Cradle Mountain–Lake St Clair National Park, takes five to seven days to complete.

Albury, Australia
The annual Festival of the Bogong Moth takes place in November. The insect is an important food source for Aboriginal tribes, and this cultural festival brings together black and white Australians.

Brisbane, Australia
Australia's origin as a penal colony is mainly the result of Britain's need to relieve its overcrowded prisons in the early 1800s. Typically, the worst criminals from Sydney were sent to Brisbane. After 15 years, the colony was dissolved and Brisbane was turned over to settlers.

Dungog, Australia
The Stroud International Brick Throwing Contest pits the townships of Stroud in four nations (Australia, Canada, UK and US) against each other. Australia's festival begins with parades and pre-competition entertainment. Stroud, Australia is a few miles northeast of Dungog.

Sydney, Australia
Graceful, iconic Sydney Opera House has been the centerpiece of Sydney Harbor since its completion in 1973. The roofline—a cluster of white peaks resembling wind-filled sails—affords dramatic skyline views from every angle.

CLIMATE

Sydney, Australia

Regional: Most of this region's rain falls on the east coast in the winter months between March and July. Tasmania experiences the only significant cold weather. The interior is hot and dry.

© DeLorme

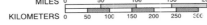

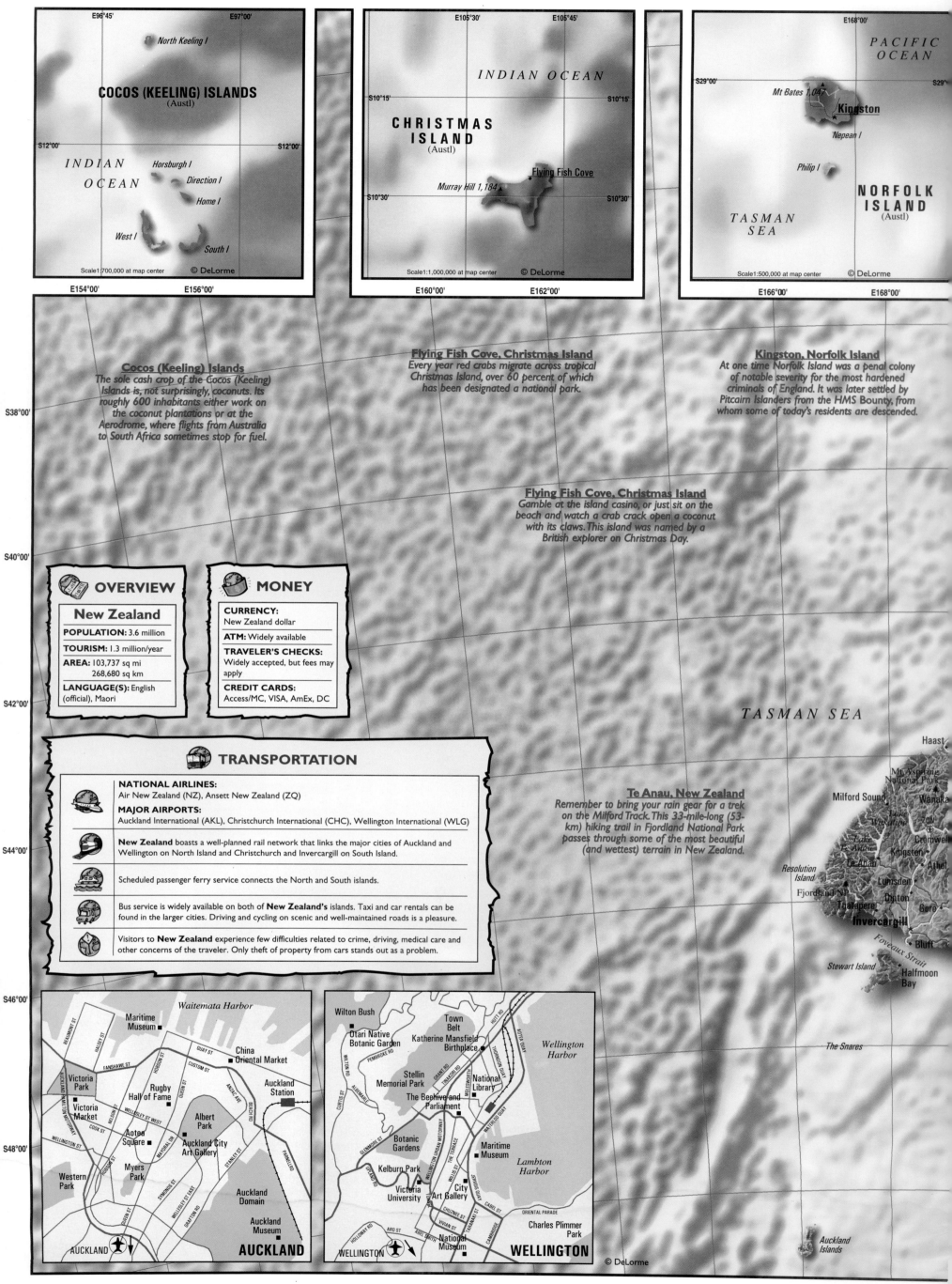

COCOS (KEELING) ISLANDS
(Austl)

North Keeling I

INDIAN
OCEAN

Horsburgh I
Direction I
Home I
West I   South I

Scale 1:700,000 at map center   © DeLorme

**CHRISTMAS
ISLAND**
(Austl)

INDIAN OCEAN

Flying Fish Cove
Murray Hill 1,184

Scale 1:1,000,000 at map center   © DeLorme

PACIFIC
OCEAN

Mt Bates 1,047
Kingston
Nepean I

Philip I

**NORFOLK
ISLAND**
(Austl)

TASMAN
SEA

Scale 1:500,000 at map center   © DeLorme

Cocos (Keeling) Islands
The sole cash crop of the Cocos (Keeling) Islands is, not surprisingly, coconuts. Its roughly 600 inhabitants either work on the coconut plantations or at the Aerodrome, where flights from Australia to South Africa sometimes stop for fuel.

Flying Fish Cove, Christmas Island
Every year red crabs migrate across tropical Christmas Island, over 60 percent of which has been designated a national park.

Kingston, Norfolk Island
At one time Norfolk Island was a penal colony of notable severity for the most hardened criminals of England. It was later settled by Pitcairn Islanders from the HMS Bounty, from whom some of today's residents are descended.

Flying Fish Cove, Christmas Island
Gamble at the island casino, or just sit on the beach and watch a crab crack open a coconut with its claws. This island was named by a British explorer on Christmas Day.

OVERVIEW

New Zealand

POPULATION: 3.6 million

TOURISM: 1.3 million/year

AREA: 103,737 sq mi
268,680 sq km

LANGUAGE(S): English (official), Maori

MONEY

CURRENCY:
New Zealand dollar

ATM: Widely available

TRAVELER'S CHECKS:
Widely accepted, but fees may apply

CREDIT CARDS:
Access/MC, VISA, AmEx, DC

TASMAN SEA

TRANSPORTATION

NATIONAL AIRLINES:
Air New Zealand (NZ), Ansett New Zealand (ZQ)

MAJOR AIRPORTS:
Auckland International (AKL), Christchurch International (CHC), Wellington International (WLG)

New Zealand boasts a well-planned rail network that links the major cities of Auckland and Wellington on North Island and Christchurch and Invercargill on South Island.

Scheduled passenger ferry service connects the North and South islands.

Bus service is widely available on both of **New Zealand's** islands. Taxi and car rentals can be found in the larger cities. Driving and cycling on scenic and well-maintained roads is a pleasure.

Visitors to **New Zealand** experience few difficulties related to crime, driving, medical care and other concerns of the traveler. Only theft of property from cars stands out as a problem.

Te Anau, New Zealand
Remember to bring your rain gear for a trek on the Milford Track. This 33-mile-long (53-km) hiking trail in Fjordland National Park passes through some of the most beautiful (and wettest) terrain in New Zealand.

Haast
Mt Aspiring
National Park
Milford Sound   Wanaka
Cromwell
Te Anau   Kingston
Resolution
Island   Lumsden   Clinton
Fjordland NP   Thalapere   Gore
Invercargill
Bluff
Foveaux Strait
Stewart Island   Halfmoon
Bay

The Snares

AUCKLAND

Waitemata Harbor
Maritime Museum
China Oriental Market
Victoria Park
Rugby Hall of Fame
Auckland Station
Victoria Market
Albert Park
Aotea Square
Auckland City Art Gallery
Myers Park
Western Park
Auckland Domain
Auckland Museum
AUCKLAND

WELLINGTON

Wilton Bush
Otari Native Botanic Garden
Town Belt
Katherine Mansfield Birthplace
Wellington Harbor
Stellin Memorial Park
National Library
The Beehive and Parliament
Botanic Gardens
Kelburn Park
Maritime Museum
Lambton Harbor
Victoria University
City Art Gallery
Charles Plimmer Park
National Museum
WELLINGTON

Oriental Parade

© DeLorme

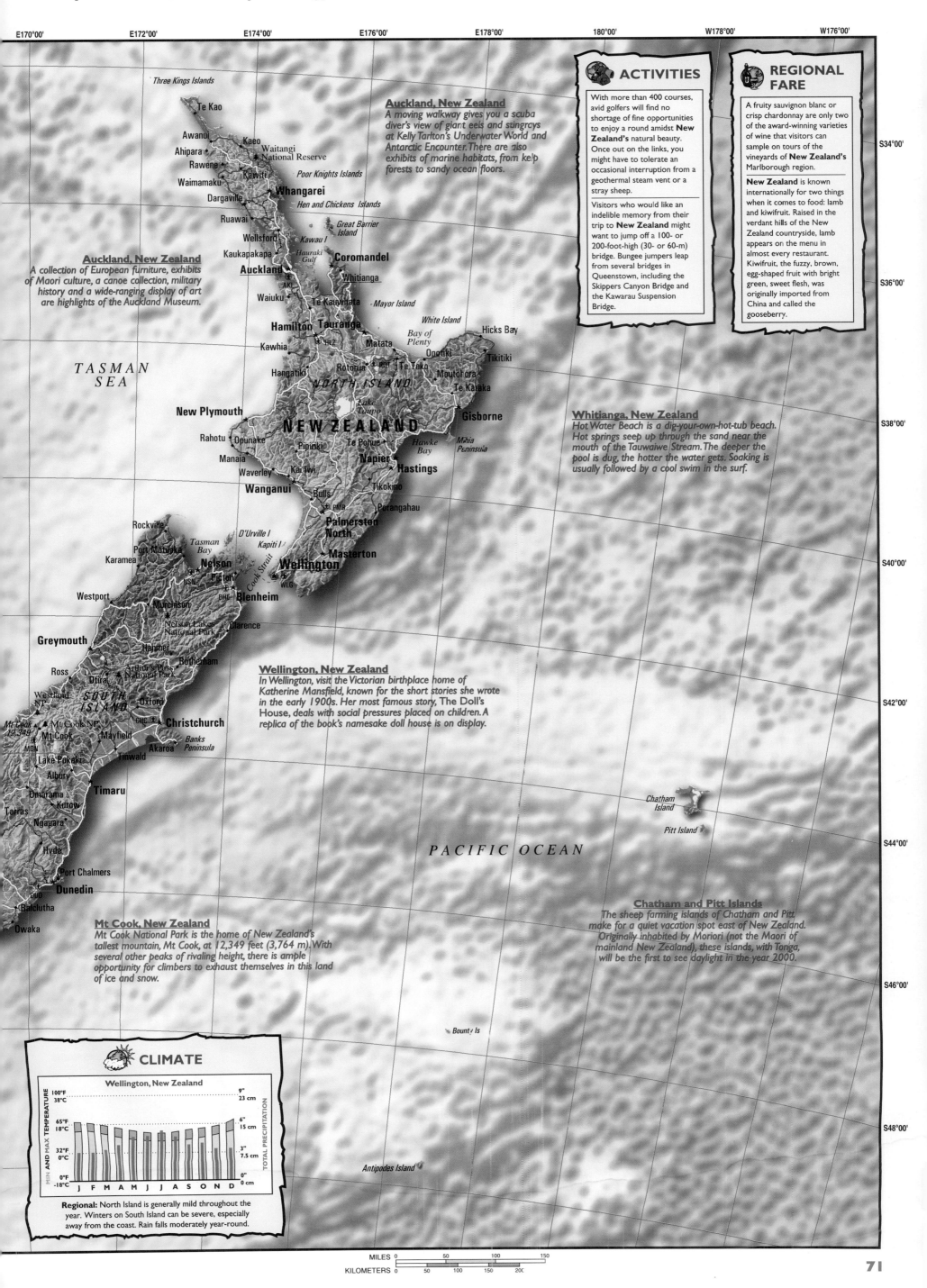

Auckland, New Zealand
A moving walkway gives you a scuba diver's view of giant eels and stingrays at Kelly Tarlton's Underwater World and Antarctic Encounter. There are also exhibits of marine habitats, from kelp forests to sandy ocean floors.

Auckland, New Zealand
A collection of European furniture, exhibits of Maori culture, a canoe collection, military history and a wide-ranging display of art are highlights of the Auckland Museum.

ACTIVITIES
With more than 400 courses, avid golfers will find no shortage of fine opportunities to enjoy a round amidst **New Zealand's** natural beauty. Once out on the links, you might have to tolerate an occasional interruption from a geothermal steam vent or a stray sheep.

Visitors who would like an indelible memory from their trip to **New Zealand** might want to jump off a 100- or 200-foot-high (30- or 60-m) bridge. Bungee jumpers leap from several bridges in Queenstown, including the Skippers Canyon Bridge and the Kawarau Suspension Bridge.

REGIONAL FARE
A fruity sauvignon blanc or crisp chardonnay are only two of the award-winning varieties of wine that visitors can sample on tours of the vineyards of **New Zealand's** Marlborough region.

New Zealand is known internationally for two things when it comes to food: lamb and kiwifruit. Raised in the verdant hills of the New Zealand countryside, lamb appears on the menu in almost every restaurant. Kiwifruit, the fuzzy, brown, egg-shaped fruit with bright green, sweet flesh, was originally imported from China and called the gooseberry.

Whitianga, New Zealand
Hot Water Beach is a dig-your-own-hot-tub beach. Hot springs seep up through the sand near the mouth of the Tauwaiwe Stream. The deeper the pool is dug, the hotter the water gets. Soaking is usually followed by a cool swim in the surf.

Wellington, New Zealand
In Wellington, visit the Victorian birthplace home of Katherine Mansfield, known for the short stories she wrote in the early 1900s. Her most famous story, The Doll's House, deals with social pressures placed on children. A replica of the book's namesake doll house is on display.

Chatham and Pitt Islands
The sheep farming islands of Chatham and Pitt make for a quiet vacation spot east of New Zealand. Originally inhabited by Moriori (not the Maori of mainland New Zealand), these islands, with Tonga, will be the first to see daylight in the year 2000.

Mt Cook, New Zealand
Mt Cook National Park is the home of New Zealand's tallest mountain, Mt Cook, at 12,349 feet (3,764 m). With several other peaks of rivaling height, there is ample opportunity for climbers to exhaust themselves in this land of ice and snow.

CLIMATE

Wellington, New Zealand

Regional: North Island is generally mild throughout the year. Winters on South Island can be severe, especially away from the coast. Rain falls moderately year-round.

MILES 0 50 100 150

KILOMETERS 0 50 100 150 200

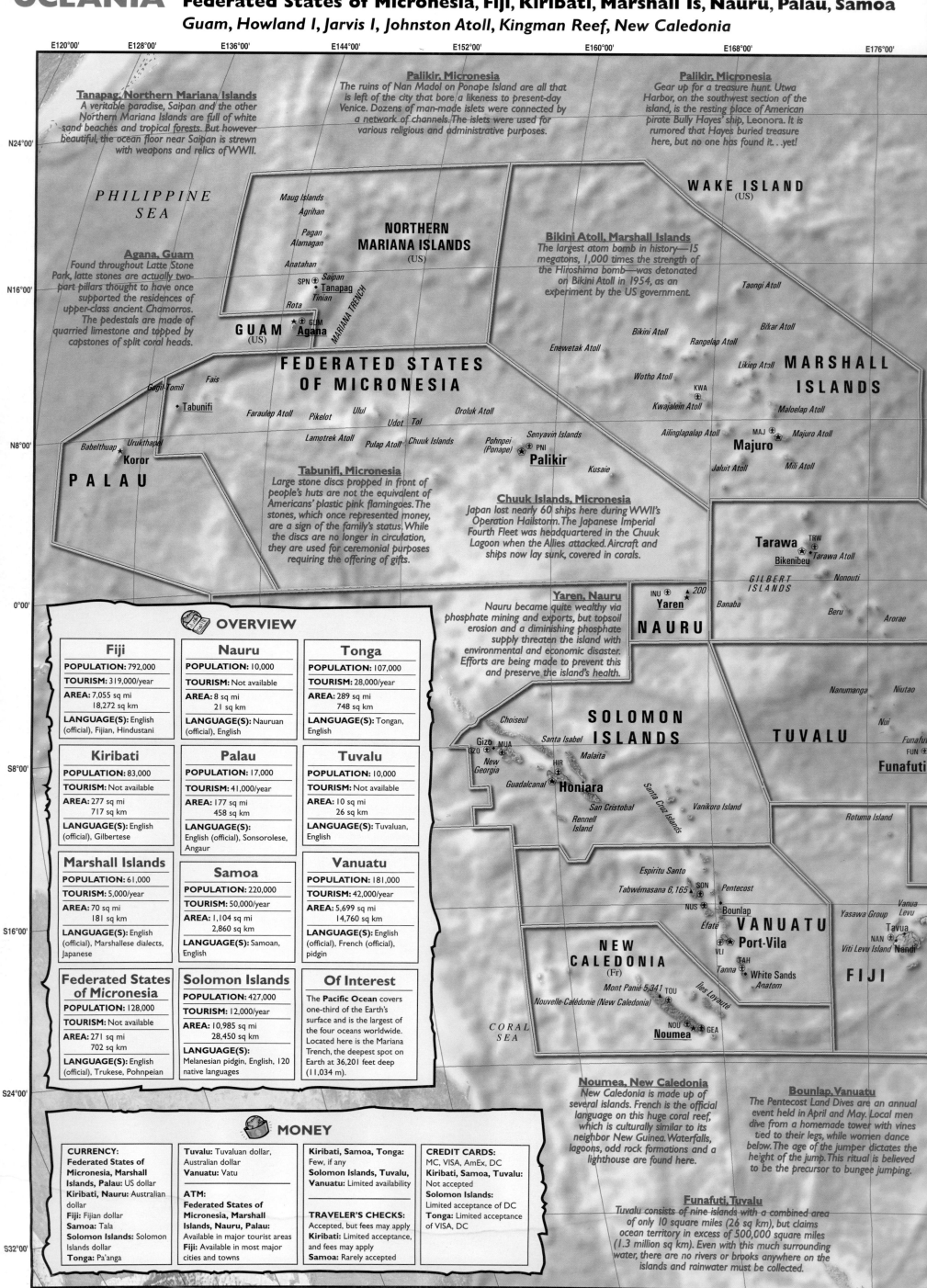

Tanapag, Northern Mariana Islands
A veritable paradise, Saipan and the other Northern Mariana Islands are full of white sand beaches and tropical forests. But however beautiful, the ocean floor near Saipan is strewn with weapons and relics of WWII.

Palikir, Micronesia
The ruins of Nan Madol on Ponape Island are all that is left of the city that bore a likeness to present-day Venice. Dozens of man-made islets were connected by a network of channels. The islets were used for various religious and administrative purposes.

Palikir, Micronesia
Gear up for a treasure hunt. Utwa Harbor, on the southwest section of the island, is the resting place of American pirate Bully Hayes' ship, Leonora. It is rumored that Hayes buried treasure here, but no one has found it...yet!

Agana, Guam
Found throughout Latte Stone Park, latte stones are actually two-part pillars thought to have once supported the residences of upper-class ancient Chamorros. The pedestals are made of quarried limestone and topped by capstones of split coral heads.

Bikini Atoll, Marshall Islands
The largest atom bomb in history—15 megatons, 1,000 times the strength of the Hiroshima bomb—was detonated on Bikini Atoll in 1954, as an experiment by the US government.

Tabunifi, Micronesia
Large stone discs propped in front of people's huts are not the equivalent of Americans' plastic pink flamingoes. The stones, which once represented money, are a sign of the family's status. While the discs are no longer in circulation, they are used for ceremonial purposes requiring the offering of gifts.

Chuuk Islands, Micronesia
Japan lost nearly 60 ships here during WWII's Operation Hailstorm. The Japanese Imperial Fourth Fleet was headquartered in the Chuuk Lagoon when the Allies attacked. Aircraft and ships now lay sunk, covered in corals.

Yaren, Nauru
Nauru became quite wealthy via phosphate mining and exports, but topsoil erosion and a diminishing phosphate supply threaten the island with environmental and economic disaster. Efforts are being made to prevent this and preserve the island's health.

Noumea, New Caledonia
New Caledonia is made up of several islands. French is the official language on this huge coral reef, which is culturally similar to its neighbor New Guinea. Waterfalls, lagoons, odd rock formations and a lighthouse are found here.

Bounlap, Vanuatu
The Pentecost Land Dives are an annual event held in April and May. Local men dive from a homemade tower with vines tied to their legs, while women dance below. The age of the jumper dictates the height of the jump. This ritual is believed to be the precursor to bungee jumping.

Funafuti, Tuvalu
Tuvalu consists of nine islands with a combined area of only 10 square miles (26 sq km), but claims ocean territory in excess of 500,000 square miles (1.3 million sq km). Even with this much surrounding water, there are no rivers or brooks anywhere on the islands and rainwater must be collected.

OVERVIEW

Fiji
POPULATION: 792,000
TOURISM: 319,000/year
AREA: 7,055 sq mi / 18,272 sq km
LANGUAGE(S): English (official), Fijian, Hindustani

Nauru
POPULATION: 10,000
TOURISM: Not available
AREA: 8 sq mi / 21 sq km
LANGUAGE(S): Nauruan (official), English

Tonga
POPULATION: 107,000
TOURISM: 28,000/year
AREA: 289 sq mi / 748 sq km
LANGUAGE(S): Tongan, English

Kiribati
POPULATION: 83,000
TOURISM: Not available
AREA: 277 sq mi / 717 sq km
LANGUAGE(S): English (official), Gilbertese

Palau
POPULATION: 17,000
TOURISM: 41,000/year
AREA: 177 sq mi / 458 sq km
LANGUAGE(S): English (official), Sonsorolese, Angaur

Tuvalu
POPULATION: 10,000
TOURISM: Not available
AREA: 10 sq mi / 26 sq km
LANGUAGE(S): Tuvaluan, English

Marshall Islands
POPULATION: 61,000
TOURISM: 5,000/year
AREA: 70 sq mi / 181 sq km
LANGUAGE(S): English (official), Marshallese dialects, Japanese

Samoa
POPULATION: 220,000
TOURISM: 50,000/year
AREA: 1,104 sq mi / 2,860 sq km
LANGUAGE(S): Samoan, English

Vanuatu
POPULATION: 181,000
TOURISM: 42,000/year
AREA: 5,699 sq mi / 14,760 sq km
LANGUAGE(S): English (official), French (official), pidgin

Federated States of Micronesia
POPULATION: 128,000
TOURISM: Not available
AREA: 271 sq mi / 702 sq km
LANGUAGE(S): English (official), Trukese, Pohnpeian

Solomon Islands
POPULATION: 427,000
TOURISM: 12,000/year
AREA: 10,985 sq mi / 28,450 sq km
LANGUAGE(S): Melanesian pidgin, English, 120 native languages

Of Interest
The Pacific Ocean covers one-third of the Earth's surface and is the largest of the four oceans worldwide. Located here is the Mariana Trench, the deepest spot on Earth at 36,201 feet deep (11,034 m).

MONEY

CURRENCY:
Federated States of Micronesia, Marshall Islands, Palau: US dollar
Kiribati, Nauru: Australian dollar
Fiji: Fijian dollar
Samoa: Tala
Solomon Islands: Solomon Islands dollar
Tonga: Pa'anga

Tuvalu: Tuvaluan dollar, Australian dollar
Vanuatu: Vatu

ATM:
Federated States of Micronesia, Marshall Islands, Nauru, Palau: Available in major tourist areas
Fiji: Available in most major cities and towns

TRAVELER'S CHECKS:
Accepted, but fees may apply
Kiribati: Limited acceptance, and fees may apply
Samoa: Rarely accepted

Kiribati, Samoa, Tonga: Few, if any
Solomon Islands, Tuvalu, Vanuatu: Limited availability

CREDIT CARDS:
MC, VISA, AmEx, DC
Kiribati, Samoa, Tuvalu: Not accepted
Solomon Islands: Limited acceptance of DC
Tonga: Limited acceptance of VISA, DC

Map labels:
E120°00' E128°00' E136°00' E144°00' E152°00' E160°00' E168°00' E176°00'
N24°00' N16°00' N8°00' 0°00' S8°00' S16°00' S24°00' S32°00'

PHILIPPINE SEA
WAKE ISLAND (US)
Maug Islands
Agrihan
Pagan
Alamagan
Anatahan
NORTHERN MARIANA ISLANDS (US)
Saipan
SPN Tanapag
Tinian
Rota
MARIANA TRENCH
GUAM (US) GUM Agana
Taongi Atoll
Bikar Atoll
Rangelap Atoll
Bikini Atoll
Enewetak Atoll
Likiep Atoll
Wotho Atoll
KWA Kwajalein Atoll
MARSHALL ISLANDS
Maloelap Atoll
Fais
Gagil-Tomil
Tabunifi
Faraulep Atoll
Pikelot
Ulul
Oroluk Atoll
Ailinglapalap Atoll
MAJ Majuro Atoll
Majuro
FEDERATED STATES OF MICRONESIA
Lamotrek Atoll
Pulap Atoll
Chuuk Islands
Udot Tol
Senyavin Islands
Pohnpei (Ponape) PNI Palikir
Kusaie
Jaluit Atoll
Mili Atoll
Babelthuap
Urukthapel
Koror
Urukthapel
PALAU
Tarawa TRW
Bikenibeu Tarawa Atoll
GILBERT ISLANDS
Nonouti
INU 200 Yaren
Banaba
Beru
Arorae
NAURU
Nanumanga
Niutao
Nui
SOLOMON ISLANDS
Choiseul
Santa Isabel
Gizo MUA
GZO New Georgia
Malaita
HIR Honiara
Guadalcanal
San Cristobal
Rennell Island
Vanikoro Island
Santa Cruz Islands
Funafuti FUN Funafuti
TUVALU
Rotuma Island
Espiritu Santo
Tabwémasana 6,165
SON Pentecost
NUS Bounlap
Yasawa Group
Vanua Levu
Tavua
NAN Nandi
Viti Levu Island
Éfaté VANUATU
VLI Port-Vila
TAH
Tanna White Sands
Anatom
FIJI
NEW CALEDONIA (Fr)
Mont Panié 5,341 TOU
Nouvelle-Calédonie (New Caledonia)
Îles Loyauté
CORAL SEA
NOU GEA Noumea

Scale 1:19,000,000 at map center

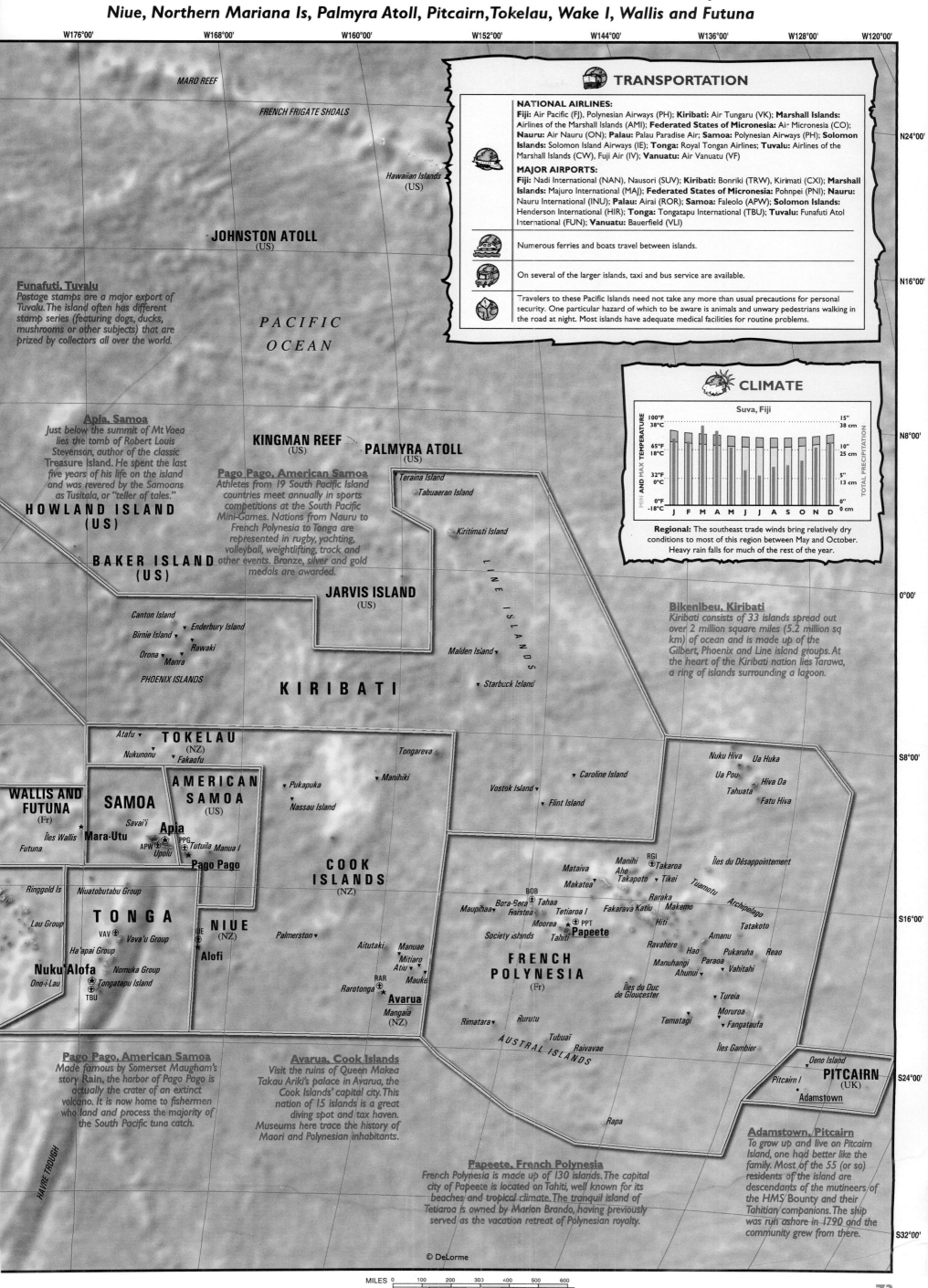

OCEANIA

Solomon Is, Tonga, Tuvalu, Vanuatu, American Samoa, Baker I, Cook Is, French Polynesia
Niue, Northern Mariana Is, Palmyra Atoll, Pitcairn, Tokelau, Wake I, Wallis and Futuna

TRANSPORTATION

NATIONAL AIRLINES:
Fiji: Air Pacific (FJ), Polynesian Airways (PH); **Kiribati:** Air Tungaru (VK); **Marshall Islands:** Airlines of the Marshall Islands (AMI); **Federated States of Micronesia:** Air Micronesia (CO); **Nauru:** Air Nauru (ON); **Palau:** Palau Paradise Air; **Samoa:** Polynesian Airways (PH); **Solomon Islands:** Solomon Island Airways (IE); **Tonga:** Royal Tongan Airlines; **Tuvalu:** Airlines of the Marshall Islands (CW), Fuji Air (IV); **Vanuatu:** Air Vanuatu (VF)

MAJOR AIRPORTS:
Fiji: Nadi International (NAN), Nausori (SUV); **Kiribati:** Bonriki (TRW), Kirimati (CXI); **Marshall Islands:** Majuro International (MAJ); **Federated States of Micronesia:** Pohnpei (PNI); **Nauru:** Nauru International (INU); **Palau:** Airai (ROR); **Samoa:** Faleolo (APW); **Solomon Islands:** Henderson International (HIR); **Tonga:** Tongatapu International (TBU); **Tuvalu:** Funafuti Atoll International (FUN); **Vanuatu:** Bauerfield (VLI)

Numerous ferries and boats travel between islands.

On several of the larger islands, taxi and bus service are available.

Travelers to these Pacific Islands need not take any more than usual precautions for personal security. One particular hazard of which to be aware is animals and unwary pedestrians walking in the road at night. Most islands have adequate medical facilities for routine problems.

CLIMATE

Suva, Fiji

Regional: The southeast trade winds bring relatively dry conditions to most of this region between May and October. Heavy rain falls for much of the rest of the year.

Funafuti, Tuvalu
Postage stamps are a major export of Tuvalu. The island often has different stamp series (featuring dogs, ducks, mushrooms or other subjects) that are prized by collectors all over the world.

Apia, Samoa
Just below the summit of Mt Vaea lies the tomb of Robert Louis Stevenson, author of the classic Treasure Island. He spent the last five years of his life on the island and was revered by the Samoans as Tusitala, or "teller of tales."

Pago Pago, American Samoa
Athletes from 19 South Pacific Island countries meet annually in sports competitions at the South Pacific Mini-Games. Nations from Nauru to French Polynesia to Tonga are represented in rugby, yachting, volleyball, weightlifting, track and other events. Bronze, silver and gold medals are awarded.

Bikenibeu, Kiribati
Kiribati consists of 33 islands spread out over 2 million square miles (5.2 million sq km) of ocean and is made up of the Gilbert, Phoenix and Line island groups. At the heart of the Kiribati nation lies Tarawa, a ring of islands surrounding a lagoon.

Pago Pago, American Samoa
Made famous by Somerset Maugham's story Rain, the harbor of Pago Pago is actually the crater of an extinct volcano. It is now home to fishermen who land and process the majority of the South Pacific tuna catch.

Avarua, Cook Islands
Visit the ruins of Queen Makea Takau Ariki's palace in Avarua, the Cook Islands' capital city. This nation of 15 islands is a great diving spot and tax haven. Museums here trace the history of Maori and Polynesian inhabitants.

Papeete, French Polynesia
French Polynesia is made up of 130 islands. The capital city of Papeete is located on Tahiti, well known for its beaches and tropical climate. The tranquil island of Tetiaroa is owned by Marlon Brando, having previously served as the vacation retreat of Polynesian royalty.

Adamstown, Pitcairn
To grow up and live on Pitcairn Island, one had better like the family. Most of the 55 (or so) residents of the island are descendants of the mutineers of the HMS Bounty and their Tahitian companions. The ship was run ashore in 1790 and the community grew from there.

PACIFIC OCEAN

MARO REEF
FRENCH FRIGATE SHOALS
Hawaiian Islands (US)
JOHNSTON ATOLL (US)
KINGMAN REEF (US)
PALMYRA ATOLL (US)
Teraina Island
Tabuaeran Island
Kiritimati Island
HOWLAND ISLAND (US)
BAKER ISLAND (US)
JARVIS ISLAND (US)
LINE ISLANDS
Malden Island
Starbuck Island
Canton Island
Birnie Island
Enderbury Island
Orona
Rawaki
Manra
PHOENIX ISLANDS
KIRIBATI
Atafu
Nukunonu
Fakaofu
TOKELAU (NZ)
Tongareva
Caroline Island
Vostok Island
Flint Island
Nuku Hiva Ua Huka
Ua Pou Hiva Oa
Tahuata
Fatu Hiva
WALLIS AND FUTUNA (Fr)
Îles Wallis
Futuna
SAMOA
Savai'i
Apia
APW Upolu
Mara-Utu
PPG
AMERICAN SAMOA (US)
Tutuila Manua I
Pago Pago
Pukapuka
Nassau Island
Manihiki
Ringgold Is
Niuatobutabu Group
TONGA
Lau Group
VAV Vava'u Group
Ha'apai Group
Nuku'Alofa
Nomuka Group
Ono-i-Lau Tongatapu Island
TBU
NIUE (NZ)
Alofi
COOK ISLANDS (NZ)
Palmerston
Aitutaki
Manuae
Mitiaro
Atiu
Mauke
Rarotonga
Avarua
RAR
Mangaia (NZ)
Mataiva
Makatea
Maupihaa
Bora-Bora Tahaa
Raiatea
Moorea
Society islands
Tahiti
Papeete
PPT
BOB
Manihi RGI Takaroa
Ahe
Takapoto Tikei
Raraka
Fakarava Katiu Makemo
Hiti
Ravahere
Hao
Manuhangi Paraoa
Ahunui
Îles du Duc de Gloucester
Tuamotu Archipelago
Tatakoto
Amanu
Pukaruha Reao
Vahitahi
Tureia
FRENCH POLYNESIA (Fr)
Îles du Désappointement
Moruroa
Tematagi Fangataufa
Îles Gambier
Rimatara Rurutu
Tubuai
Raivavae
AUSTRAL ISLANDS
Rapa
Oeno Island
Pitcairn I
PITCAIRN (UK)
Adamstown
HAVRE TROUGH

© DeLorme

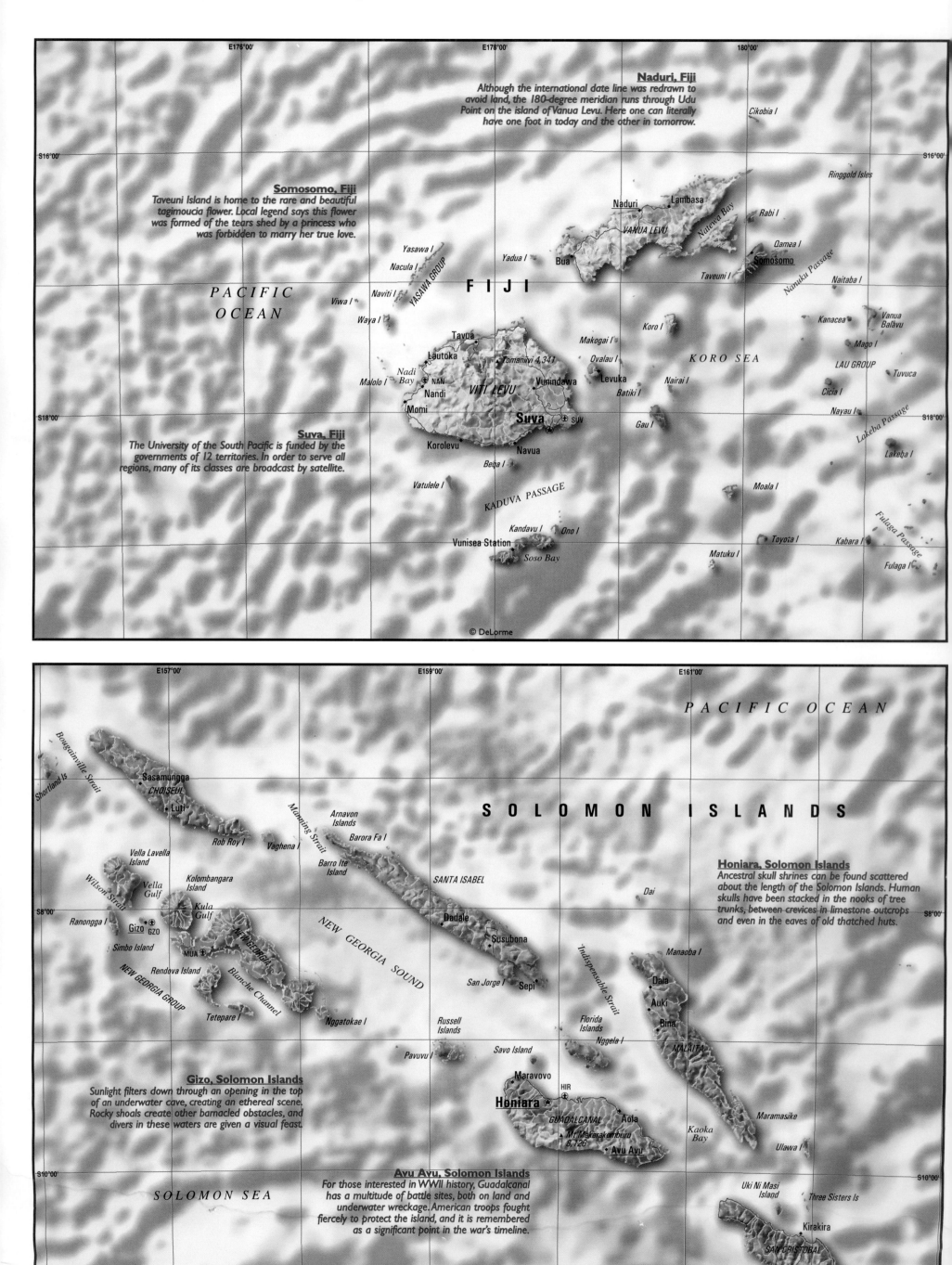

Naduri, Fiji
Although the international date line was redrawn to avoid land, the 180-degree meridian runs through Udu Point on the island of Vanua Levu. Here one can literally have one foot in today and the other in tomorrow.

Somosomo, Fiji
Taveuni Island is home to the rare and beautiful tagimoucia flower. Local legend says this flower was formed of the tears shed by a princess who was forbidden to marry her true love.

PACIFIC OCEAN

Suva, Fiji
The University of the South Pacific is funded by the governments of 12 territories. In order to serve all regions, many of its classes are broadcast by satellite.

© DeLorme

PACIFIC OCEAN

SOLOMON ISLANDS

Honiara, Solomon Islands
Ancestral skull shrines can be found scattered about the length of the Solomon Islands. Human skulls have been stacked in the nooks of tree trunks, between crevices in limestone outcrops and even in the eaves of old thatched huts.

Gizo, Solomon Islands
Sunlight filters down through an opening in the top of an underwater cave, creating an ethereal scene. Rocky shoals create other barnacled obstacles, and divers in these waters are given a visual feast.

Avu Avu, Solomon Islands
For those interested in WWII history, Guadalcanal has a multitude of battle sites, both on land and underwater wreckage. American troops fought fiercely to protect the island, and it is remembered as a significant point in the war's timeline.

SOLOMON SEA

© DeLorme

Scale 1:3,000,000 at map center

MILES
KILOMETERS

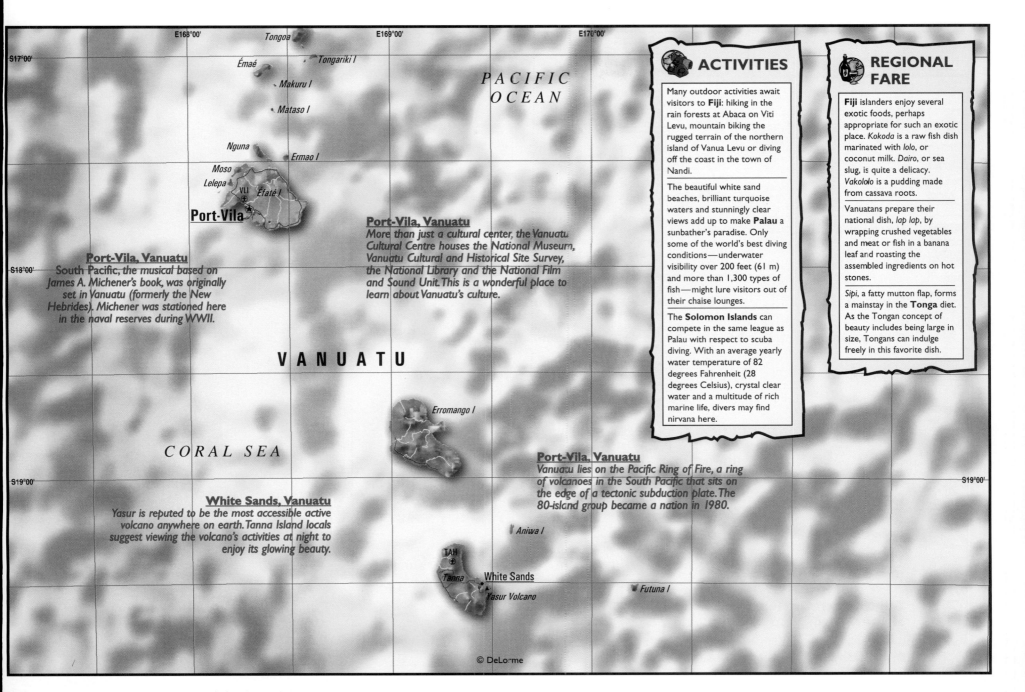

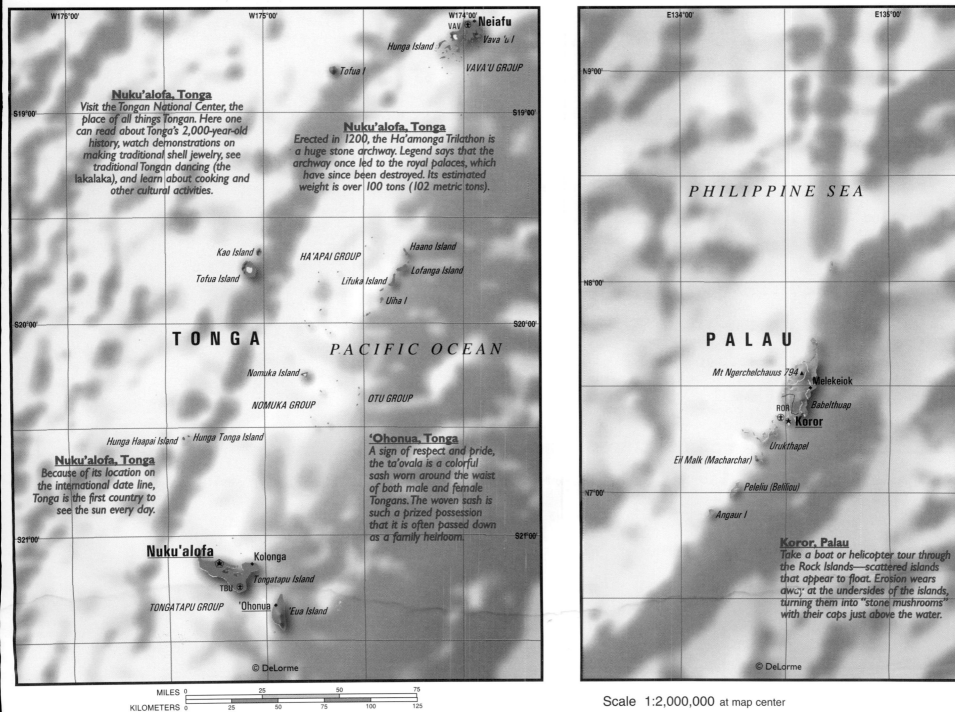

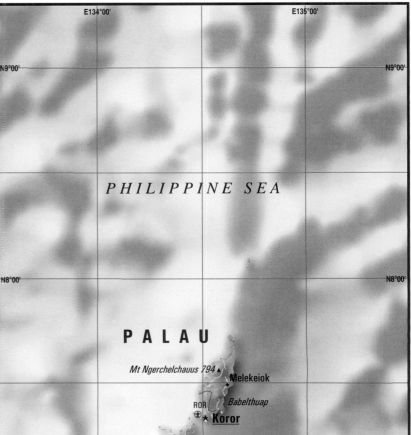

PACIFIC OCEAN

E168°00' E169°00' E170°00'

S17°00'

Tongoa

Émaé Tongariki I

Makuru I

Mataso I

Nguna

Ermao I

Moso

Lelepa

VLI Efaté I

Port-Vila

Port-Vila, Vanuatu
South Pacific, the musical based on James A. Michener's book, was originally set in Vanuatu (formerly the New Hebrides). Michener was stationed here in the naval reserves during WWII.

S18°00'

Port-Vila, Vanuatu
More than just a cultural center, the Vanuatu Cultural Centre houses the National Museum, Vanuatu Cultural and Historical Site Survey, the National Library and the National Film and Sound Unit. This is a wonderful place to learn about Vanuatu's culture.

VANUATU

Erromango I

CORAL SEA

White Sands, Vanuatu
Yasur is reputed to be the most accessible active volcano anywhere on earth. Tanna Island locals suggest viewing the volcano's activities at night to enjoy its glowing beauty.

Port-Vila, Vanuatu
Vanuatu lies on the Pacific Ring of Fire, a ring of volcanoes in the South Pacific that sits on the edge of a tectonic subduction plate. The 80-island group became a nation in 1980.

S19°00'

Aniwa I

TAH

Tanna White Sands

Yasur Volcano

Futuna I

© DeLorme

W175°00' W175°00' W174°00'

VAV **Neiafu**

Hunga Island Vava'u I

Tofua I **VAVA'U GROUP**

Nuku'alofa, Tonga
Visit the Tongan National Center, the place of all things Tongan. Here one can read about Tonga's 2,000-year-old history, watch demonstrations on making traditional shell jewelry, see traditional Tongan dancing (the lakalaka), and learn about cooking and other cultural activities.

S19°00'

Nuku'alofa, Tonga
Erected in 1200, the Ha'amonga Trilathon is a huge stone archway. Legend says that the archway once led to the royal palaces, which have since been destroyed. Its estimated weight is over 100 tons (102 metric tons).

Kao Island

Tofua Island

Haano Island

HA'APAI GROUP

Lofanga Island

Lifuka Island

Uiha I

S20°00'

TONGA

PACIFIC OCEAN

Nomuka Island

NOMUKA GROUP

OTU GROUP

Hunga Haapai Island Hunga Tonga Island

Nuku'alofa, Tonga
Because of its location on the international date line, Tonga is the first country to see the sun every day.

'Ohonua, Tonga
A sign of respect and pride, the ta'ovala is a colorful sash worn around the waist of both male and female Tongans. The woven sash is such a prized possession that it is often passed down as a family heirloom.

S21°00'

Nuku'alofa Kolonga

TBU Tongatapu Island

TONGATAPU GROUP 'Ohonua 'Eua Island

© DeLorme

E134°00' E135°00'

N9°00'

PHILIPPINE SEA

N8°00'

PALAU

Mt Ngerchelchauus 794

Melekeiok

ROR Babelthuap

Koror

Urukthapel

Eil Malk (Macharchar)

N7°00'

Peleliu (Beliliou)

Angaur I

Koror, Palau
Take a boat or helicopter tour through the Rock Islands—scattered islands that appear to float. Erosion wears away at the undersides of the islands, turning them into "stone mushrooms" with their caps just above the water.

© DeLorme

MILES 0 25 50 75

KILOMETERS 0 25 50 75 100 125

Scale 1:2,000,000 at map center

Countries

Territories and Featured Lands

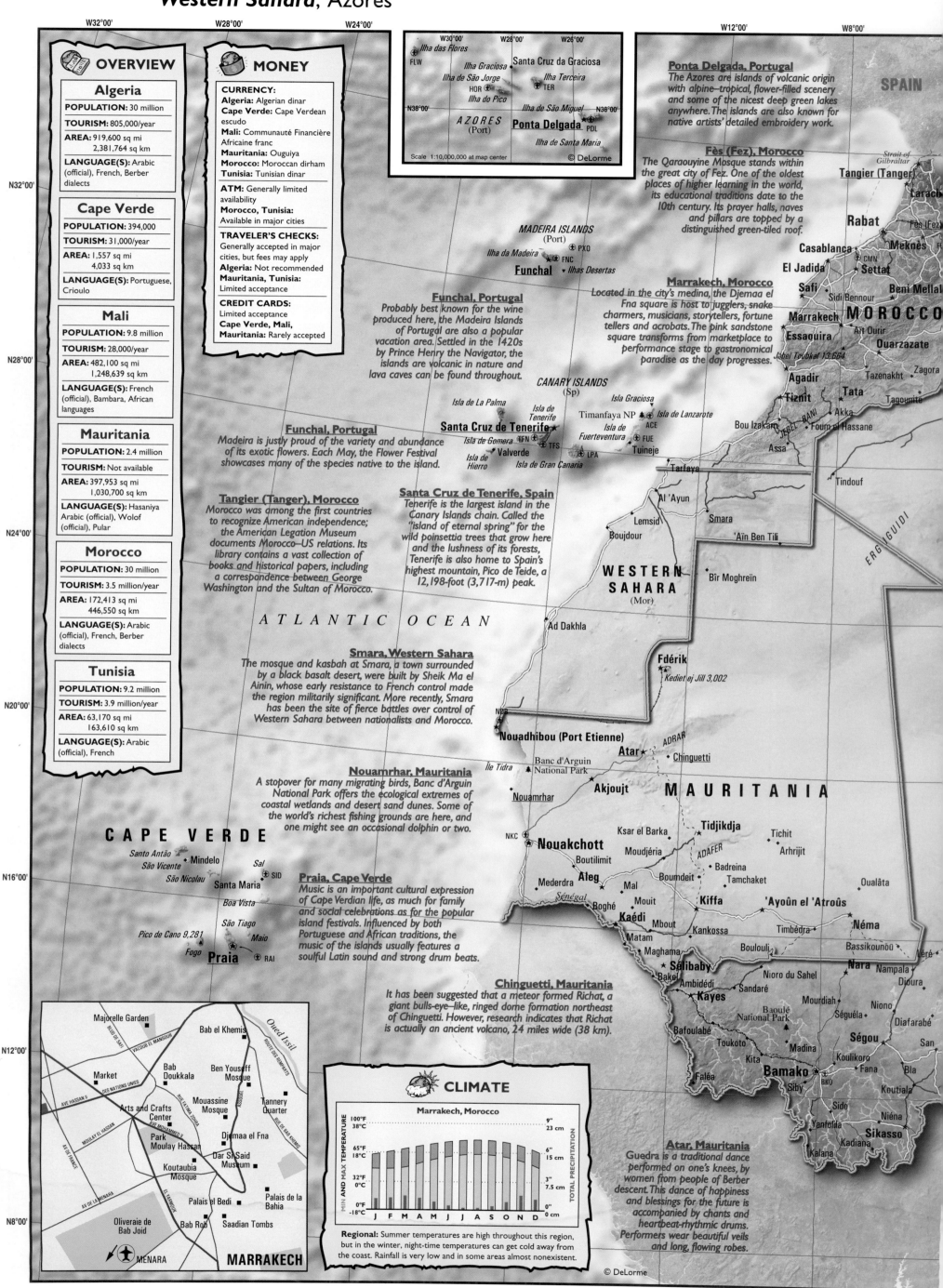

OVERVIEW

Algeria
POPULATION: 30 million
TOURISM: 805,000/year
AREA: 919,600 sq mi
2,381,764 sq km
LANGUAGE(S): Arabic (official), French, Berber dialects

Cape Verde
POPULATION: 394,000
TOURISM: 31,000/year
AREA: 1,557 sq mi
4,033 sq km
LANGUAGE(S): Portuguese, Crioulo

Mali
POPULATION: 9.8 million
TOURISM: 28,000/year
AREA: 482,100 sq mi
1,248,639 sq km
LANGUAGE(S): French (official), Bambara, African languages

Mauritania
POPULATION: 2.4 million
TOURISM: Not available
AREA: 397,953 sq mi
1,030,700 sq km
LANGUAGE(S): Hasaniya Arabic (official), Wolof (official), Pular

Morocco
POPULATION: 30 million
TOURISM: 3.5 million/year
AREA: 172,413 sq mi
446,550 sq km
LANGUAGE(S): Arabic (official), French, Berber dialects

Tunisia
POPULATION: 9.2 million
TOURISM: 3.9 million/year
AREA: 63,170 sq mi
163,610 sq km
LANGUAGE(S): Arabic (official), French

MONEY

CURRENCY:
Algeria: Algerian dinar
Cape Verde: Cape Verdean escudo
Mali: Communauté Financière Africaine franc
Mauritania: Ouguiya
Morocco: Moroccan dirham
Tunisia: Tunisian dinar

ATM: Generally limited availability
Morocco, Tunisia: Available in major cities

TRAVELER'S CHECKS: Generally accepted in major cities, but fees may apply
Algeria: Not recommended
Mauritania, Tunisia: Limited acceptance

CREDIT CARDS: Limited acceptance
Cape Verde, Mali, Mauritania: Rarely accepted

Ponta Delgada, Portugal
The Azores are islands of volcanic origin with alpine–tropical, flower-filled scenery and some of the nicest deep green lakes anywhere. The islands are also known for native artists' detailed embroidery work.

Fès (Fez), Morocco
The Qaraouyine Mosque stands within the great city of Fez. One of the oldest places of higher learning in the world, its educational traditions date to the 10th century. Its prayer halls, naves and pillars are topped by a distinguished green-tiled roof.

Marrakech, Morocco
Located in the city's medina, the Djemaa el Fna square is host to jugglers, snake charmers, musicians, storytellers, fortune tellers and acrobats. The pink sandstone square transforms from marketplace to performance stage to gastronomical paradise as the day progresses.

Funchal, Portugal
Probably best known for the wine produced here, the Madeira Islands of Portugal are also a popular vacation area. Settled in the 1420s by Prince Henry the Navigator, the islands are volcanic in nature and lava caves can be found throughout.

Funchal, Portugal
Madeira is justly proud of the variety and abundance of its exotic flowers. Each May, the Flower Festival showcases many of the species native to the island.

Tangier (Tanger), Morocco
Morocco was among the first countries to recognize American independence; the American Legation Museum documents Morocco–US relations. Its library contains a vast collection of books and historical papers, including a correspondence between George Washington and the Sultan of Morocco.

Santa Cruz de Tenerife, Spain
Tenerife is the largest island in the Canary Islands chain. Called the "island of eternal spring" for the wild poinsettia trees that grow here and the lushness of its forests, Tenerife is also home to Spain's highest mountain, Pico de Teide, a 12,198-foot (3,717-m) peak.

Smara, Western Sahara
The mosque and kasbah at Smara, a town surrounded by a black basalt desert, were built by Sheik Ma el Ainin, whose early resistance to French control made the region militarily significant. More recently, Smara has been the site of fierce battles over control of Western Sahara between nationalists and Morocco.

Nouamrhar, Mauritania
A stopover for many migrating birds, Banc d'Arguin National Park offers the ecological extremes of coastal wetlands and desert sand dunes. Some of the world's richest fishing grounds are here, and one might see an occasional dolphin or two.

Praia, Cape Verde
Music is an important cultural expression of Cape Verdian life, as much for family and social celebrations as for the popular island festivals. Influenced by both Portuguese and African traditions, the music of the islands usually features a soulful Latin sound and strong drum beats.

Chinguetti, Mauritania
It has been suggested that a meteor formed Richat, a giant bulls-eye–like, ringed dome formation northeast of Chinguetti. However, research indicates that Richat is actually an ancient volcano, 24 miles wide (38 km).

Atar, Mauritania
Guedra is a traditional dance performed on one's knees, by women from people of Berber descent. This dance of happiness and blessings for the future is accompanied by chants and heartbeat-rhythmic drums. Performers wear beautiful veils and long, flowing robes.

CLIMATE
Marrakech, Morocco

Regional: Summer temperatures are high throughout this region, but in the winter, night-time temperatures can get cold away from the coast. Rainfall is very low and in some areas almost nonexistent.

MARRAKECH

Map labels: Majorelle Garden, Oued Issil, Bab el Khemis, Market, Bab Doukkala, Ben Youssef Mosque, Mouassine Mosque, Tannery Quarter, Arts and Crafts Center, Park Moulay Hassan, Djemaa el Fna, Dar Si Said Museum, Koutoubia Mosque, Palais el Bedi, Palais de la Bahia, Oliveraie de Bab Joid, Bab Rob, Saadian Tombs, MENARA

Azores inset: Ilha das Flores, FLW, Santa Cruz da Graciosa, Ilha Graciosa, Ilha de São Jorge, HOR, Ilha Terceira, TER, Ilha do Pico, Ilha de São Miguel, Ponta Delgada, PDL, Ilha de Santa Maria, AZORES (Port), Scale 1:10,000,000 at map center, © DeLorme

Main map labels: SPAIN, Strait of Gibraltar, Tangier (Tanger), Larach, Rabat, Fès (Fez), Meknès, Casablanca, CMN, Settat, El Jadida, Safi, Sidi Bennour, Beni Mellal, Marrakech, Essaouira, MOROCCO, Aït Ourir, Jbel Toubkal 13,664, Ouarzazate, Agadir, Tazenakht, Zagora, Tiznit, Tata, Tagounite, Akka, Bou Izakarn, Foum el Hassane, Assa, JBEL BANI, MADEIRA ISLANDS (Port), Ilha da Madeira, PXO, FNC, Funchal, Ilhas Desertas, CANARY ISLANDS (Sp), Isla de La Palma, Isla de Tenerife, Isla Graciosa, Timanfaya NP, Isla de Lanzarote, ACE, Santa Cruz de Tenerife, TFN, TFS, Isla de Gomera, Isla de Fuerteventura, FUE, Valverde, Tuineje, LPA, Isla de Hierro, Isla de Gran Canaria, Tarfaya, Tindouf, Al 'Ayun, Smara, Lemsid, 'Aïn Ben Tili, Boujdour, ERG IGUIDI, WESTERN SAHARA (Mor), ATLANTIC OCEAN, Ad Dakhla, Fdérik, Kediet ej Jill 3,002, Bîr Moghreïn, NDB, Nouadhibou (Port Etienne), Atar, ADRAR, Chinguetti, Île Tidra, Banc d'Arguin National Park, Nouamrhar, Akjoujt, MAURITANIA, NKC, Nouakchott, Ksar el Barka, Tidjikdja, Tichit, Moudjéria, ADAFER, Arhrijit, Boutilimit, Badreina, Aleg, Mederdra, Boumdeit, Tamchaket, Mouit, Kiffa, 'Ayoûn el 'Atroûs, Oualâta, Sénégal, Boghé, Mal, Néma, Kaédi, Kankossa, Timbédra, Bassikounou, Mbout, Matam, Boulouli, Maghama, Nara, Nampala, Salibaby, Bakel, Nioro du Sahel, Dioura, Ambidédi, Sandaré, Kayes, Baoulé National Park, Mourdiah, Niono, Bafoulabé, Madina, Séguéla, Diafarabé, Toukoto, Kita, Ségou, San, Faléa, Koulikoro, Fana, Bla, CAPE VERDE, Santo Antão, Mindelo, São Vicente, Sal, SID, São Nicolau, Santa Maria, Boa Vista, São Tiago, Maio, Pico de Cano 9,281, Fogo, Praia, RAI, Bamako, BKO, Siby, Sido, Niéna, Koutiala, Kalana, Kadiana, Yanfolila, Sikasso

© DeLorme

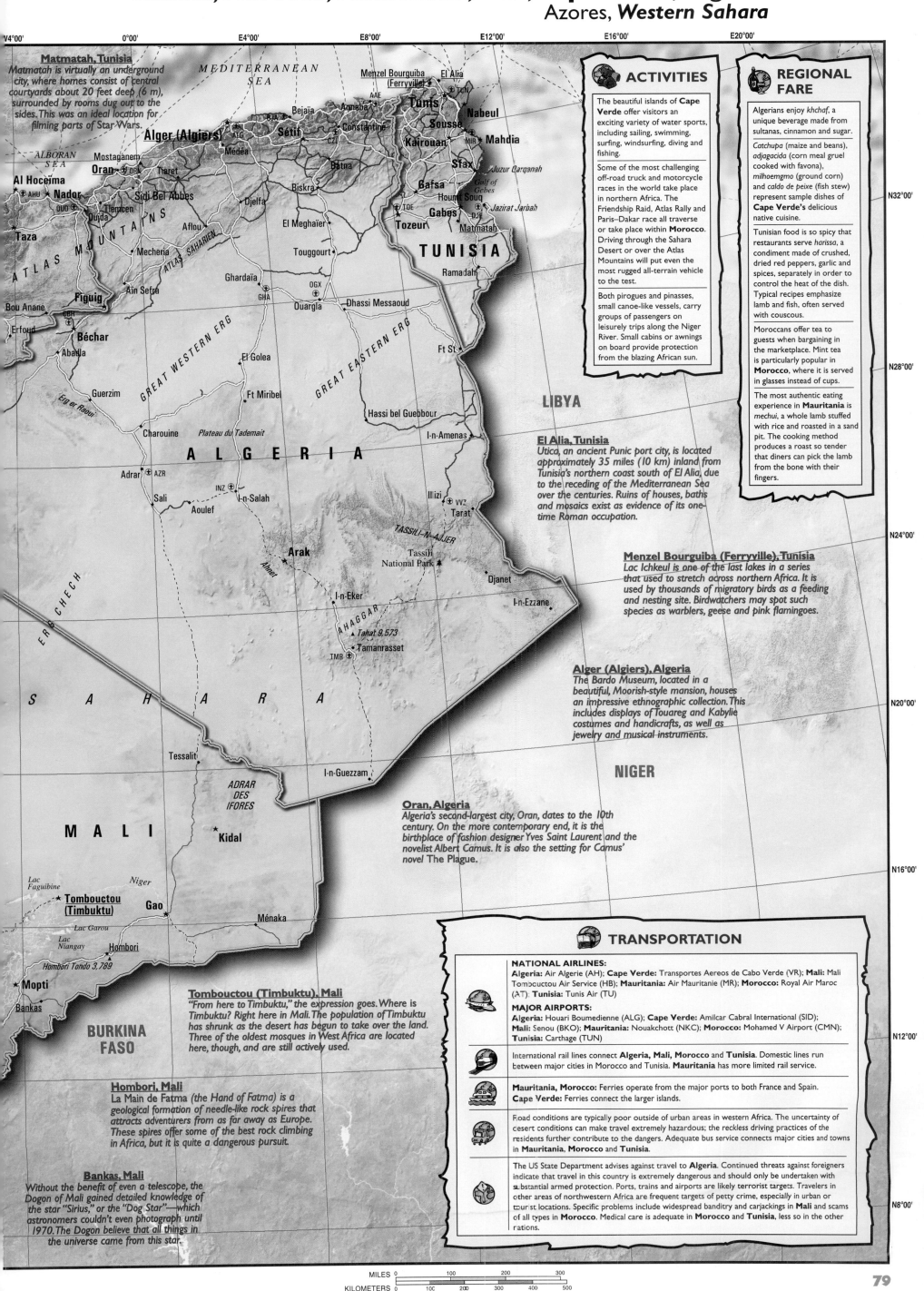

Matmatah, Tunisia
Matmatah is virtually an underground city, where homes consist of central courtyards about 20 feet deep (6 m), surrounded by rooms dug out to the sides. This was an ideal location for filming parts of Star Wars.

ACTIVITIES

The beautiful islands of **Cape Verde** offer visitors an exciting variety of water sports, including sailing, swimming, surfing, windsurfing, diving and fishing.

Some of the most challenging off-road truck and motorcycle races in the world take place in northern Africa. The Friendship Raid, Atlas Rally and Paris–Dakar race all traverse or take place within **Morocco**. Driving through the Sahara Desert or over the Atlas Mountains will put even the most rugged all-terrain vehicle to the test.

Both pirogues and pinasses, small canoe-like vessels, carry groups of passengers on leisurely trips along the Niger River. Small cabins or awnings on board provide protection from the blazing African sun.

REGIONAL FARE

Algerians enjoy *khchaf*, a unique beverage made from sultanas, cinnamon and sugar.

Catchupa (maize and beans), *adjagacida* (corn meal gruel cooked with favona), *milhoemgmo* (ground corn) and *caldo de peixe* (fish stew) represent sample dishes of **Cape Verde's** delicious native cuisine.

Tunisian food is so spicy that restaurants serve *harissa*, a condiment made of crushed, dried red peppers, garlic and spices, separately in order to control the heat of the dish. Typical recipes emphasize lamb and fish, often served with couscous.

Moroccans offer tea to guests when bargaining in the marketplace. Mint tea is particularly popular in **Morocco**, where it is served in glasses instead of cups.

The most authentic eating experience in **Mauritania** is *mechui*, a whole lamb stuffed with rice and roasted in a sand pit. The cooking method produces a roast so tender that diners can pick the lamb from the bone with their fingers.

El Alia, Tunisia
Utica, an ancient Punic port city, is located approximately 35 miles (10 km) inland from Tunisia's northern coast south of El Alia, due to the receding of the Mediterranean Sea over the centuries. Ruins of houses, baths and mosaics exist as evidence of its one-time Roman occupation.

Menzel Bourguiba (Ferryville), Tunisia
Lac Ichkeul is one of the last lakes in a series that used to stretch across northern Africa. It is used by thousands of migratory birds as a feeding and nesting site. Birdwatchers may spot such species as warblers, geese and pink flamingoes.

Alger (Algiers), Algeria
The Bardo Museum, located in a beautiful, Moorish-style mansion, houses an impressive ethnographic collection. This includes displays of Touareg and Kabylie costumes and handicrafts, as well as jewelry and musical instruments.

Oran, Algeria
Algeria's second-largest city, Oran, dates to the 10th century. On the more contemporary end, it is the birthplace of fashion designer Yves Saint Laurent and the novelist Albert Camus. It is also the setting for Camus' novel The Plague.

Tombouctou (Timbuktu), Mali
"From here to Timbuktu," the expression goes. Where is Timbuktu? Right here in Mali. The population of Timbuktu has shrunk as the desert has begun to take over the land. Three of the oldest mosques in West Africa are located here, though, and are still actively used.

Hombori, Mali
La Main de Fatma (the Hand of Fatma) is a geological formation of needle-like rock spires that attracts adventurers from as far away as Europe. These spires offer some of the best rock climbing in Africa, but it is quite a dangerous pursuit.

Bankas, Mali
Without the benefit of even a telescope, the Dogon of Mali gained detailed knowledge of the star "Sirius," or the "Dog Star"—which astronomers couldn't even photograph until 1970. The Dogon believe that all things in the universe came from this star.

TRANSPORTATION

NATIONAL AIRLINES:
Algeria: Air Algerie (AH); **Cape Verde:** Transportes Aereos de Cabo Verde (VR); **Mali:** Mali Tombouctou Air Service (HB); **Mauritania:** Air Mauritanie (MR); **Morocco:** Royal Air Maroc (AT). **Tunisia:** Tunis Air (TU)

MAJOR AIRPORTS:
Algeria: Houari Boumedienne (ALG); **Cape Verde:** Amilcar Cabral International (SID); **Mali:** Senou (BKO); **Mauritania:** Nouakchott (NKC); **Morocco:** Mohamed V Airport (CMN); **Tunisia:** Carthage (TUN)

International rail lines connect **Algeria, Mali, Morocco** and **Tunisia**. Domestic lines run between major cities in Morocco and Tunisia. **Mauritania** has more limited rail service.

Mauritania, Morocco: Ferries operate from the major ports to both France and Spain. **Cape Verde:** Ferries connect the larger islands.

Road conditions are typically poor outside of urban areas in western Africa. The uncertainty of desert conditions can make travel extremely hazardous; the reckless driving practices of the residents further contribute to the dangers. Adequate bus service connects major cities and towns in **Mauritania, Morocco** and **Tunisia**.

The US State Department advises against travel to **Algeria**. Continued threats against foreigners indicate that travel in this country is extremely dangerous and should only be undertaken with substantial armed protection. Ports, trains and airports are likely terrorist targets. Travelers in other areas of northwestern Africa are frequent targets of petty crime, especially in urban or tourist locations. Specific problems include widespread banditry and carjackings in **Mali** and scams of all types in **Morocco**. Medical care is adequate in **Morocco** and **Tunisia**, less so in the other nations.

MILES 0   100   200   300
KILOMETERS 0 100 200 300 400 500

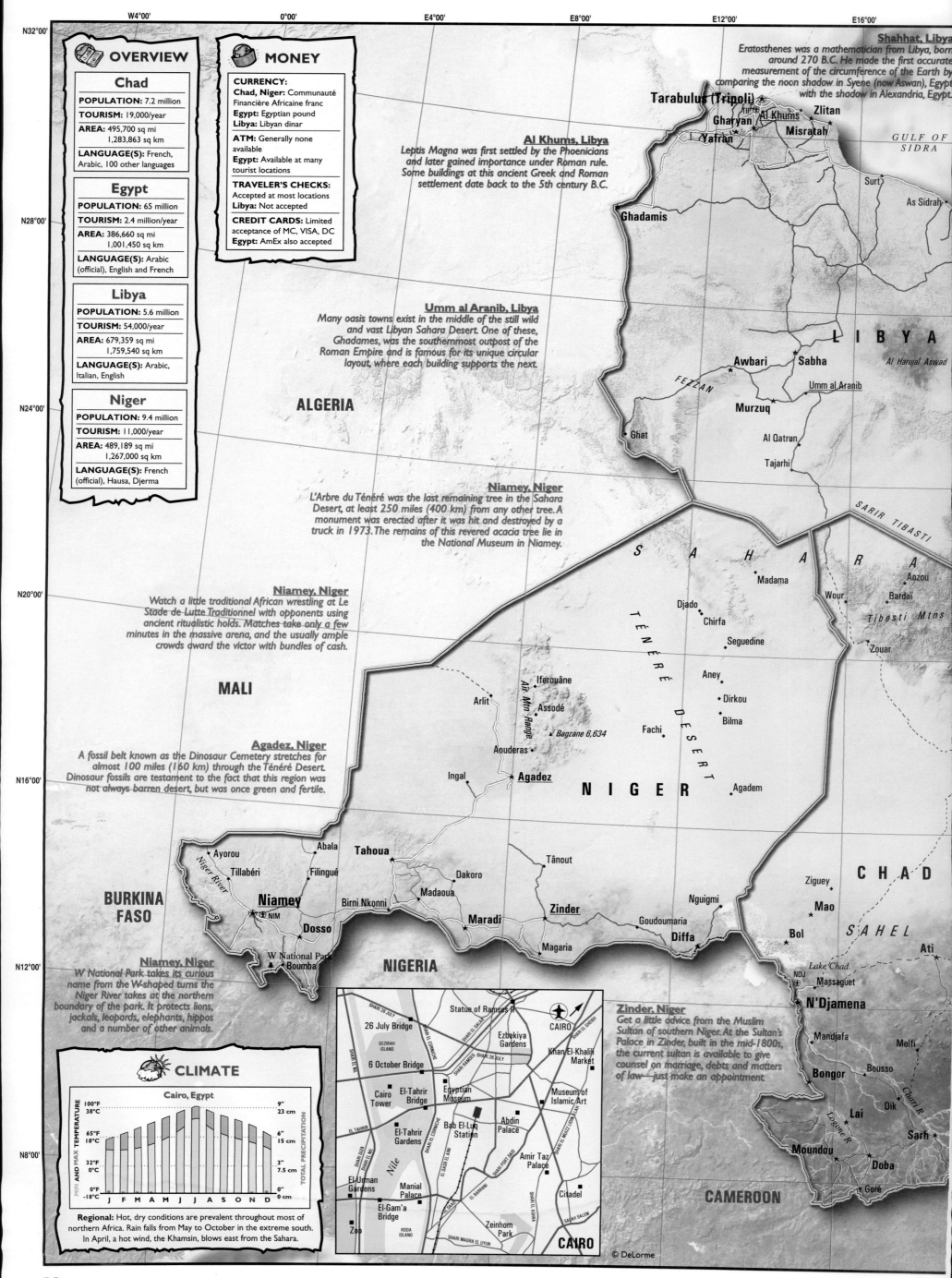

OVERVIEW

Chad
POPULATION: 7.2 million
TOURISM: 19,000/year
AREA: 495,700 sq mi
1,283,863 sq km
LANGUAGE(S): French, Arabic, 100 other languages

Egypt
POPULATION: 65 million
TOURISM: 2.4 million/year
AREA: 386,660 sq mi
1,001,450 sq km
LANGUAGE(S): Arabic (official), English and French

Libya
POPULATION: 5.6 million
TOURISM: 54,000/year
AREA: 679,359 sq mi
1,759,540 sq km
LANGUAGE(S): Arabic, Italian, English

Niger
POPULATION: 9.4 million
TOURISM: 11,000/year
AREA: 489,189 sq mi
1,267,000 sq km
LANGUAGE(S): French (official), Hausa, Djerma

MONEY

CURRENCY:
Chad, Niger: Communauté Financière Africaine franc
Egypt: Egyptian pound
Libya: Libyan dinar
ATM: Generally none available
Egypt: Available at many tourist locations
TRAVELER'S CHECKS: Accepted at most locations
Libya: Not accepted
CREDIT CARDS: Limited acceptance of MC, VISA, DC
Egypt: AmEx also accepted

Shahhat, Libya
Eratosthenes was a mathematician from Libya, born around 270 B.C. He made the first accurate measurement of the circumference of the Earth by comparing the noon shadow in Syene (now Aswan), Egypt with the shadow in Alexandria, Egypt.

Al Khums, Libya
Leptis Magna was first settled by the Phoenicians and later gained importance under Roman rule. Some buildings at this ancient Greek and Roman settlement date back to the 5th century B.C.

Umm al Aranib, Libya
Many oasis towns exist in the middle of the still wild and vast Libyan Sahara Desert. One of these, Ghadames, was the southernmost outpost of the Roman Empire and is famous for its unique circular layout, where each building supports the next.

Niamey, Niger
L'Arbre du Ténéré was the last remaining tree in the Sahara Desert, at least 250 miles (400 km) from any other tree. A monument was erected after it was hit and destroyed by a truck in 1973. The remains of this revered acacia tree lie in the National Museum in Niamey.

Niamey, Niger
Watch a little traditional African wrestling at Le Stade de Lutte Traditionnel with opponents using ancient ritualistic holds. Matches take only a few minutes in the massive arena, and the usually ample crowds award the victor with bundles of cash.

Agadez, Niger
A fossil belt known as the Dinosaur Cemetery stretches for almost 100 miles (160 km) through the Ténéré Desert. Dinosaur fossils are testament to the fact that this region was not always barren desert, but was once green and fertile.

Niamey, Niger
W National Park takes its curious name from the W-shaped turns the Niger River takes at the northern boundary of the park. It protects lions, jackals, leopards, elephants, hippos and a number of other animals.

Zinder, Niger
Get a little advice from the Muslim Sultan of southern Niger. At the Sultan's Palace in Zinder, built in the mid-1800s, the current sultan is available to give counsel on marriage, debts and matters of law — just make an appointment.

CLIMATE

Cairo, Egypt

Regional: Hot, dry conditions are prevalent throughout most of northern Africa. Rain falls from May to October in the extreme south. In April, a hot wind, the Khamsin, blows east from the Sahara.

Cairo inset map labels
Statue of Ramses II
26 July Bridge
6 October Bridge
Ezbekiya Gardens
Khan El-Khalili Market
Cairo Tower
El-Tahrir Bridge
Egyptian Museum
Museum of Islamic Art
El-Tahrir Gardens
Bab El-Luq Station
Abdin Palace
Amir Taz Palace
El-Urman Gardens
Manial Palace
Citadel
El-Gam'a Bridge
Zeinhom Park
Zoo
RODA ISLAND
GEZIRAH ISLAND
CAIRO

© DeLorme

Map place labels
LIBYA
Tarabulus (Tripoli)
Gharyan, Al Khums, Zlitan
Yafran, Misratah
GULF OF SIDRA
Surt
As Sidrah
Ghadamis
Awbari, Sabha
Al Harujal Aswad
Murzuq
Umm al Aranib
Ghat
Al Qatrun
Tajarhi
FEZZAN
ALGERIA
MALI
BURKINA FASO
SAHARA
SARIR TIBASTI
Madama
Djado, Chirfa
Seguedine
Aney
Dirkou
Bilma
Aozou
Wour, Bardai
Tibesti Mtns
Zouar
TÉNÉRÉ DESERT
Iferouâne
Arlit, Assodé
Aïr Mtn Range
Bagzane 6,634
Fachi
Aouderas
Ingal, Agadez
NIGER
Agadem
Ayorou
Tillabéri
Abala
Tahoua
Tânout
Ziguey
Niger River
Filingué
Dakoro
Madaoua
Nguigmi
Mao
CHAD
Niamey, NIM
Birni Nkonni
Maradi
Zinder
Goudoumaria
Diffa
Bol
SAHEL
Ati
Dosso
Magaria
Lake Chad
W National Park
Boumba
NIGERIA
NDJ, Massaguet
N'Djamena
Mandjafa
Melfi
Bousso
Bongor
Lai, Dik
Charl R
Logone R
Moundou
Doba, Goré
Sarh
CAMEROON

Scale 1:9,000,000 at map center

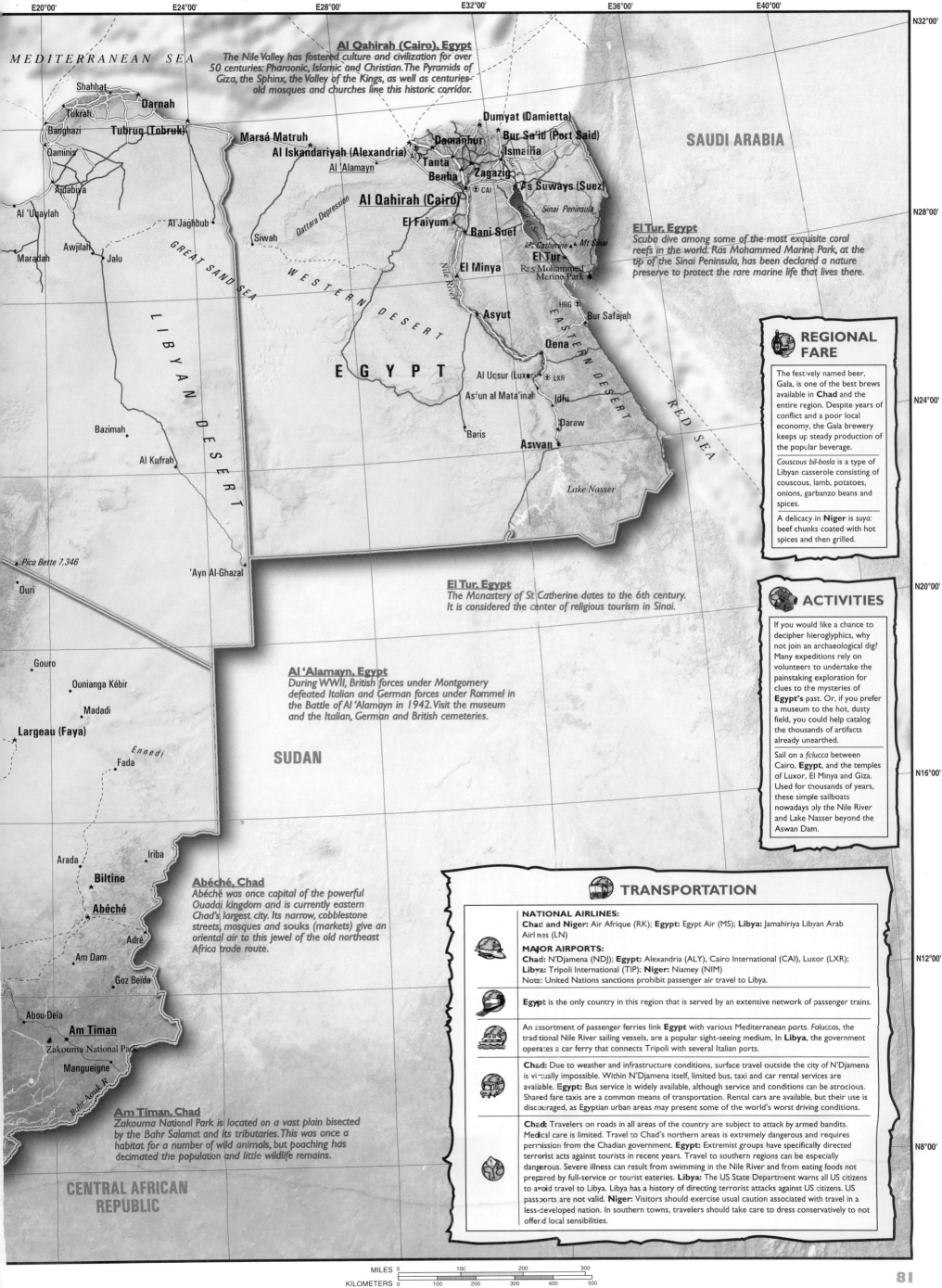

MEDITERRANEAN SEA

Al Qahirah (Cairo), Egypt
The Nile Valley has fostered culture and civilization for over 50 centuries: Pharaonic, Islamic and Christian. The Pyramids of Giza, the Sphinx, the Valley of the Kings, as well as centuries-old mosques and churches line this historic corridor.

SAUDI ARABIA

Shahhat
Darnah
Tukrah
Banghazi
Tubruq (Tobruk)
Qaminis
Al 'Uqaylah
Ajdabiya
Awjilah   Jalu
Maradah

Marsá Matruh
Al Iskandariyah (Alexandria)
Al 'Alamayn
Tanta
Benha
Damanhur
Dumyat (Damietta)
Bur Sa'id (Port Said)
Ismailia
Zagazig
As Suways (Suez)
Al Qahirah (Cairo)
CAI
El Faiyum
Bani Suef
Sinai Peninsula

Al Jaghbub
Siwah
Qattara Depression
WESTERN DESERT
El Minya
Mt. Catherine Mt Sinai
El Tur
Ras Mohammed Marine Park

El Tur, Egypt
Scuba dive among some of the most exquisite coral reefs in the world. Ras Mohammed Marine Park, at the tip of the Sinai Peninsula, has been declared a nature preserve to protect the rare marine life that lives there.

GREAT SAND SEA

LIBYAN DESERT

Bazimah
Al Kufrah

Nile River
Asyut
HRG
Bur Safajah

EASTERN DESERT

EGYPT
Qena
Al Uqsur (Luxor)
LXR
Asfun al Mata'inah
Idfu
Daraw
Baris
Aswan

RED SEA

Pico Bette 7,346
Ouri
'Ayn Al-Ghazal

Lake Nasser

El Tur, Egypt
The Monastery of St. Catherine dates to the 6th century. It is considered the center of religious tourism in Sinai.

ACTIVITIES

If you would like a chance to decipher hieroglyphics, why not join an archaeological dig? Many expeditions rely on volunteers to undertake the painstaking exploration for clues to the mysteries of **Egypt's** past. Or, if you prefer a museum to the hot, dusty field, you could help catalog the thousands of artifacts already unearthed.

Sail on a *felucca* between Cairo, **Egypt**, and the temples of Luxor, El Minya and Giza. Used for thousands of years, these simple sailboats nowadays ply the Nile River and Lake Nasser beyond the Aswan Dam.

Al 'Alamayn, Egypt
During WWII, British forces under Montgomery defeated Italian and German forces under Rommel in the Battle of Al 'Alamayn in 1942. Visit the museum and the Italian, German and British cemeteries.

SUDAN

Gouro
Ounianga Kébir
Madadi
Largeau (Faya)
Ennedi
Fada

Arada   Iriba
Biltine
Abéché
Adré
Am Dam
Goz Beïda
Abou-Deïa
Am Timan
Zakouma National Park
Mangueigne
Bahr Aouk R.

Abéché, Chad
Abéché was once capital of the powerful Ouadaï kingdom and is currently eastern Chad's largest city. Its narrow, cobblestone streets, mosques and souks (markets) give an oriental air to this jewel of the old northeast Africa trade route.

Am Timan, Chad
Zakouma National Park is located on a vast plain bisected by the Bahr Salamat and its tributaries. This was once a habitat for a number of wild animals, but poaching has decimated the population and little wildlife remains.

CENTRAL AFRICAN REPUBLIC

TRANSPORTATION

NATIONAL AIRLINES:
Chad and Niger: Air Afrique (RK); **Egypt:** Egypt Air (MS); **Libya:** Jamahiriya Libyan Arab Airlines (LN)

MAJOR AIRPORTS:
Chad: N'Djamena (NDJ); **Egypt:** Alexandria (ALY), Cairo International (CAI), Luxor (LXR); **Libya:** Tripoli International (TIP); **Niger:** Niamey (NIM)
Note: United Nations sanctions prohibit passenger air travel to Libya.

Egypt is the only country in this region that is served by an extensive network of passenger trains.

An assortment of passenger ferries link **Egypt** with various Mediterranean ports. Faluccas, the traditional Nile River sailing vessels, are a popular sight-seeing medium. In **Libya**, the government operates a car ferry that connects Tripoli with several Italian ports.

Chad: Due to weather and infrastructure conditions, surface travel outside the city of N'Djamena is virtually impossible. Within N'Djamena itself, limited bus, taxi and car rental services are available. **Egypt:** Bus service is widely available, although service and conditions can be atrocious. Shared fare taxis are a common means of transportation. Rental cars are available, but their use is discouraged, as Egyptian urban areas may present some of the world's worst driving conditions.

Chad: Travelers on roads in all areas of the country are subject to attack by armed bandits. Medical care is limited. Travel to Chad's northern areas is extremely dangerous and requires permission from the Chadian government. **Egypt:** Extremist groups have specifically directed terrorist acts against tourists in recent years. Travel to southern regions can be especially dangerous. Severe illness can result from swimming in the Nile River and from eating foods not prepared by full-service or tourist eateries. **Libya:** The US State Department warns all US citizens to avoid travel to Libya. Libya has a history of directing terrorist attacks against US citizens. US passports are not valid. **Niger:** Visitors should exercise usual caution associated with travel in a less-developed nation. In southern towns, travelers should take care to dress conservatively to not offend local sensibilities.

MILES   0   100   200   300
KILOMETERS   0   100   200   300   400   500

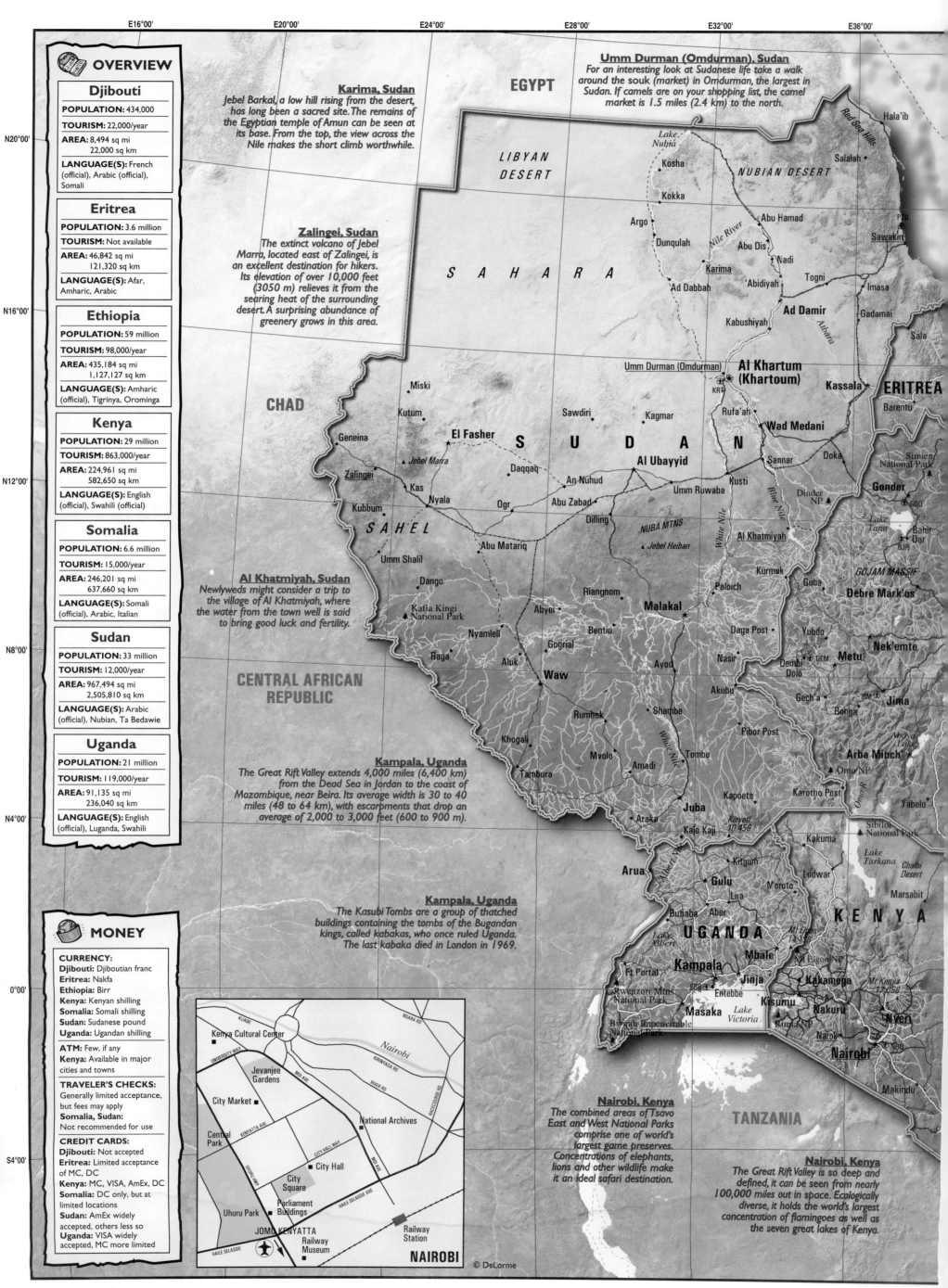

Scale 1:10,000,000 at map center

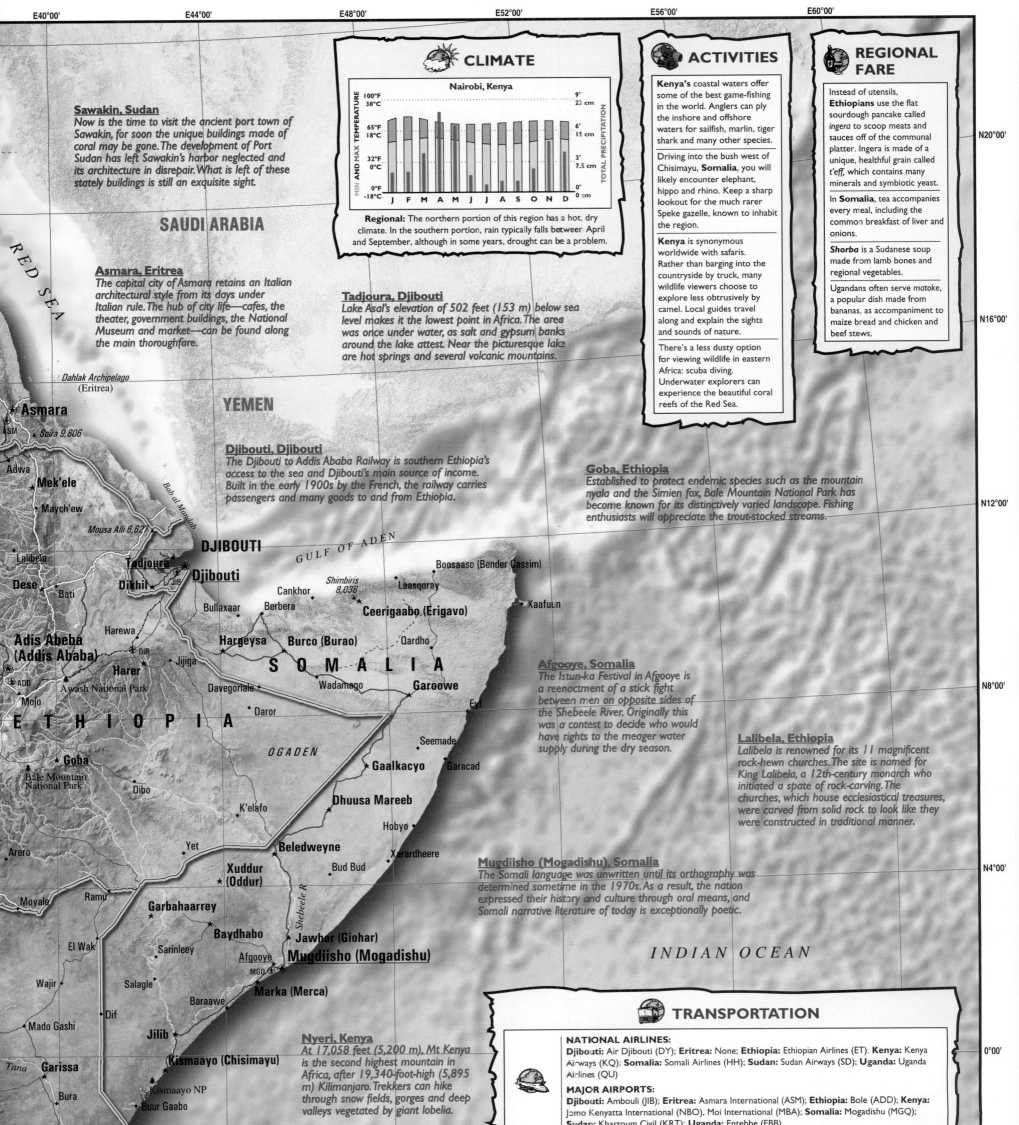

E40°00'   E44°00'   E48°00'   E52°00'   E56°00'   E60°00'

Sawakin, Sudan
Now is the time to visit the ancient port town of Sawakin, for soon the unique buildings made of coral may be gone. The development of Port Sudan has left Sawakin's harbor neglected and its architecture in disrepair. What is left of these stately buildings is still an exquisite sight.

CLIMATE

Nairobi, Kenya

100°F 38°C		9" 23 cm
65°F 18°C		6" 15 cm
32°F 0°C		3" 7.5 cm
0°F -18°C	J F M A M J J A S O N D	0" 0 cm

MIN AND MAX TEMPERATURE / TOTAL PRECIPITATION

Regional: The northern portion of this region has a hot, dry climate. In the southern portion, rain typically falls between April and September, although in some years, drought can be a problem.

ACTIVITIES

Kenya's coastal waters offer some of the best game-fishing in the world. Anglers can ply the inshore and offshore waters for sailfish, marlin, tiger shark and many other species.

Driving into the bush west of Chisimayu, **Somalia**, you will likely encounter elephant, hippo and rhino. Keep a sharp lookout for the much rarer Speke gazelle, known to inhabit the region.

Kenya is synonymous worldwide with safaris. Rather than barging into the countryside by truck, many wildlife viewers choose to explore less obtrusively by camel. Local guides travel along and explain the sights and sounds of nature.

There's a less dusty option for viewing wildlife in eastern Africa: scuba diving. Underwater explorers can experience the beautiful coral reefs of the Red Sea.

REGIONAL FARE

Instead of utensils, **Ethiopians** use the flat sourdough pancake called *ingera* to scoop meats and sauces off of the communal platter. Ingera is made of a unique, healthful grain called *t'eff*, which contains many minerals and symbiotic yeast.

In **Somalia**, tea accompanies every meal, including the common breakfast of liver and onions.

Shorba is a Sudanese soup made from lamb bones and regional vegetables.

Ugandans often serve *matoke*, a popular dish made from bananas, as accompaniment to maize bread and chicken and beef stews.

SAUDI ARABIA

Asmara, Eritrea
The capital city of Asmara retains an Italian architectural style from its days under Italian rule. The hub of city life—cafes, the theater, government buildings, the National Museum and market—can be found along the main thoroughfare.

Tadjoura, Djibouti
Lake Asal's elevation of 502 feet (153 m) below sea level makes it the lowest point in Africa. The area was once under water, as salt and gypsum banks around the lake attest. Near the picturesque lake are hot springs and several volcanic mountains.

RED SEA

Dahlak Archipelago (Eritrea)

YEMEN

Djibouti, Djibouti
The Djibouti to Addis Ababa Railway is southern Ethiopia's access to the sea and Djibouti's main source of income. Built in the early 1900s by the French, the railway carries passengers and many goods to and from Ethiopia.

Goba, Ethiopia
Established to protect endemic species such as the mountain nyala and the Simien fox, Bale Mountain National Park has become known for its distinctively varied landscape. Fishing enthusiasts will appreciate the trout-stocked streams.

Asmara
ASM
Soira 9,806

Adwa
Mek'ele
Maych'ew
Mousa Ali 6,627

Lalibela
Dese
Bati
Harewa

Adis Abeba (Addis Ababa)
ADD
Harer
DIR
Jijiga
Mojo
Awash National Park

E T H I O P I A

Arero
Moyale
Ramu
El Wak
Wajir

Goba
Bale Mountain National Park
Dibo
K'elafo
Yet
Ramu

Tadjoura
Dikhil
JIB
Bullaxaar
Berbera
Cankhor
Shimbiris 8,058

DJIBOUTI
Djibouti

GULF OF ADEN

Boosaaso (Bender Cassim)
Laasqoray

Ceerigaabo (Erigavo)
Xaafuun

Hargeysa
Burco (Burao)
Qardho

S O M A L I A

Davegoriale
Wadamago
Garoowe
Eyl
Daror

OGADEN

Seemade

Gaalkacyo
Garacad

Dhuusa Mareeb

Hobyo
Xarardheere

Beledweyne
Bud Bud

Xuddur (Oddur)

Afgooye, Somalia
The Istun-ka Festival in Afgooye is a reenactment of a stick fight between men on opposite sides of the Shebeele River. Originally this was a contest to decide who would have rights to the meager water supply during the dry season.

Lalibela, Ethiopia
Lalibela is renowned for its 11 magnificent rock-hewn churches. The site is named for King Lalibela, a 12th-century monarch who initiated a spate of rock-carving. The churches, which house ecclesiastical treasures, were carved from solid rock to look like they were constructed in traditional manner.

Mugdiisho (Mogadishu), Somalia
The Somali language was unwritten until its orthography was determined sometime in the 1970s. As a result, the nation expressed their history and culture through oral means, and Somali narrative literature of today is exceptionally poetic.

I N D I A N   O C E A N

Garbahaarrey
Sarinleey
Baydhabo
Afgooye
Jawhar (Giohar)
MGO
Mugdiisho (Mogadishu)
Salagle
Marka (Merca)
Baraawe
Dif

Shebeele R.

Nyeri, Kenya
At 17,058 feet (5,200 m), Mt Kenya is the second highest mountain in Africa, after 19,340-foot-high (5,895 m) Kilimanjaro. Trekkers can hike through snow fields, gorges and deep valleys vegetated by giant lobelia.

Mado Gashi
Jilib
Tana
Garissa
Bura
(Kismaayo (Chisimayu)
Kismaayo NP
Buur Gaabo

TRANSPORTATION

NATIONAL AIRLINES:
Djibouti: Air Djibouti (DY); **Eritrea:** None; **Ethiopia:** Ethiopian Airlines (ET); **Kenya:** Kenya Airways (KQ); **Somalia:** Somali Airlines (HH); **Sudan:** Sudan Airways (SD); **Uganda:** Uganda Airlines (QU)

MAJOR AIRPORTS:
Djibouti: Ambouli (JIB); **Eritrea:** Asmara International (ASM); **Ethiopia:** Bole (ADD); **Kenya:** Jomo Kenyatta International (NBO), Moi International (MBA); **Somalia:** Mogadishu (MGQ); **Sudan:** Khartoum Civil (KRT); **Uganda:** Entebbe (EBB)

Limited passenger rail lines serve these East African nations. Only **Kenya** has a well-developed system. Main lines lead out from Nairobi to the Indian Ocean port of Mombasa or to Kisumu on Lake Victoria.

Kenya also has regular coastal ferries between Mombasa, Malindi and Lamu. **Uganda** has limited ferry service on Lake Victoria.

Bus services of varying efficiency and comfort travel between most major cities and towns within each nation. Travelers will find taxi service available in major cities.

The US State Department recommends against travel to **Somalia** or **Sudan**. Civil conflict in both nations has created an unstable and violent environment. In Somalia, kidnappings and other threats to foreigners occur unpredictably in virtually all regions, while in Sudan, terrorists have targeted Western interests in Khartoum several times in recent years. Armed attackers, some rebels and others bandits, have targeted foreigners in **Ethiopia** and **Uganda**. Vehicle hijackings and armed highway robbery are especially frequent in Uganda. Although travel is somewhat safer in **Djibouti**, **Eritrea** and **Kenya**, land mines from prior civil conflicts, street crime, border tensions and limited medical facilities all pose hazards to visitors to this region.

Lamu, Kenya
Explore the exotic waterfront of Lamu, Kenya's oldest active town. This island town has retained a great deal of its ancient character, and is a favorite resting point for adventure travelers.

Tsavo National Park
Lamu
Watamu Marine National Park
Kasigau Hill
Mombasa
MBA
Vanga

Narok, Kenya
Sprawling Masai Mara Game Reserve contains Africa's biggest concentration of wildlife. Its prime attraction, the annual migration of over one million wildebeests and zebras, stands as one of nature's grandest spectacles.

MILES 0   100   200   300
KILOMETERS 0 100 200 300 400 500

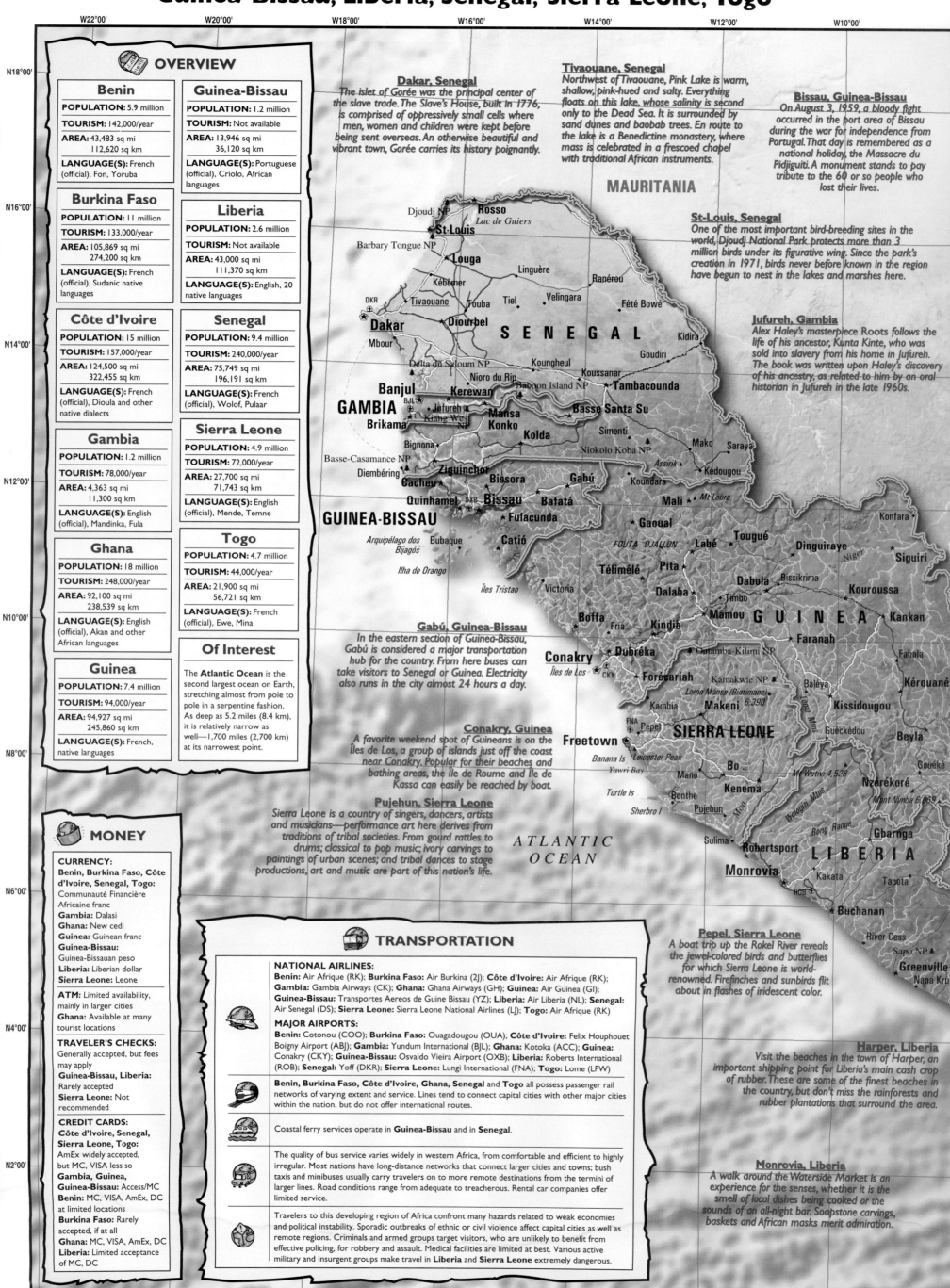

OVERVIEW

Benin
POPULATION: 5.9 million
TOURISM: 142,000/year
AREA: 43,483 sq mi
112,620 sq km
LANGUAGE(S): French (official), Fon, Yoruba

Burkina Faso
POPULATION: 11 million
TOURISM: 133,000/year
AREA: 105,869 sq mi
274,200 sq km
LANGUAGE(S): French (official), Sudanic native languages

Côte d'Ivoire
POPULATION: 15 million
TOURISM: 157,000/year
AREA: 124,500 sq mi
322,455 sq km
LANGUAGE(S): French (official), Dioula and other native dialects

Gambia
POPULATION: 1.2 million
TOURISM: 78,000/year
AREA: 4,363 sq mi
11,300 sq km
LANGUAGE(S): English (official), Mandinka, Fula

Ghana
POPULATION: 18 million
TOURISM: 248,000/year
AREA: 92,100 sq mi
238,539 sq km
LANGUAGE(S): English (official), Akan and other African languages

Guinea
POPULATION: 7.4 million
TOURISM: 94,000/year
AREA: 94,927 sq mi
245,860 sq km
LANGUAGE(S): French, native languages

Guinea-Bissau
POPULATION: 1.2 million
TOURISM: Not available
AREA: 13,946 sq mi
36,120 sq km
LANGUAGE(S): Portuguese (official), Criolo, African languages

Liberia
POPULATION: 2.6 million
TOURISM: Not available
AREA: 43,000 sq mi
111,370 sq km
LANGUAGE(S): English, 20 native languages

Senegal
POPULATION: 9.4 million
TOURISM: 240,000/year
AREA: 75,749 sq mi
196,191 sq km
LANGUAGE(S): French (official), Wolof, Pulaar

Sierra Leone
POPULATION: 4.9 million
TOURISM: 72,000/year
AREA: 27,700 sq mi
71,743 sq km
LANGUAGE(S): English (official), Mende, Temne

Togo
POPULATION: 4.7 million
TOURISM: 44,000/year
AREA: 21,900 sq mi
56,721 sq km
LANGUAGE(S): French (official), Ewe, Mina

Of Interest
The **Atlantic Ocean** is the second largest ocean on Earth, stretching almost from pole to pole in a serpentine fashion. As deep as 5.2 miles (8.4 km), it is relatively narrow as well—1,700 miles (2,700 km) at its narrowest point.

MONEY

CURRENCY:
Benin, Burkina Faso, Côte d'Ivoire, Senegal, Togo: Communauté Financière Africaine franc
Gambia: Dalasi
Ghana: New cedi
Guinea: Guinean franc
Guinea-Bissau: Guinea-Bissauan peso
Liberia: Liberian dollar
Sierra Leone: Leone

ATM: Limited availability, mainly in larger cities
Ghana: Available at many tourist locations

TRAVELER'S CHECKS: Generally accepted, but fees may apply
Guinea-Bissau, Liberia: Rarely accepted
Sierra Leone: Not recommended

CREDIT CARDS:
Côte d'Ivoire, Senegal, Sierra Leone, Togo: AmEx widely accepted, but MC, VISA less so
Gambia, Guinea, Guinea-Bissau: Access/MC
Benin: MC, VISA, AmEx, DC at limited locations
Burkina Faso: Rarely accepted, if at all
Ghana: MC, VISA, AmEx, DC
Liberia: Limited acceptance of MC, DC

Dakar, Senegal
The islet of Gorée was the principal center of the slave trade. The Slave's House, built in 1776, is comprised of oppressively small cells where men, women and children were kept before being sent overseas. An otherwise beautiful and vibrant town, Gorée carries its history poignantly.

Tivaouane, Senegal
Northwest of Tivaouane, Pink Lake is warm, shallow, pink-hued and salty. Everything floats on this lake, whose salinity is second only to the Dead Sea. It is surrounded by sand dunes and baobab trees. En route to the lake is a Benedictine monastery, where mass is celebrated in a frescoed chapel with traditional African instruments.

Bissau, Guinea-Bissau
On August 3, 1959, a bloody fight occurred in the port area of Bissau during the war for independence from Portugal. That day is remembered as a national holiday, the Massacre du Pidjiguiti. A monument stands to pay tribute to the 60 or so people who lost their lives.

St-Louis, Senegal
One of the most important bird-breeding sites in the world, Djoudj National Park protects more than 3 million birds under its figurative wing. Since the park's creation in 1971, birds never before known in the region have begun to nest in the lakes and marshes here.

Jufureh, Gambia
Alex Haley's masterpiece Roots follows the life of his ancestor, Kunta Kinte, who was sold into slavery from his home in Jufureh. The book was written upon Haley's discovery of his ancestry, as related to him by an oral historian in Jufureh in the late 1960s.

Gabú, Guinea-Bissau
In the eastern section of Guinea-Bissau, Gabú is considered a major transportation hub for the country. From here buses can take visitors to Senegal or Guinea. Electricity also runs in the city almost 24 hours a day.

Conakry, Guinea
A favorite weekend spot of Guineans is on the Îles de Los, a group of islands just off the coast near Conakry. Popular for their beaches and bathing areas, the Île de Roume and Île de Kassa can easily be reached by boat.

Pujehun, Sierra Leone
Sierra Leone is a country of singers, dancers, artists and musicians—performance art here derives from traditions of tribal societies. From gourd rattles to drums; classical to pop music; ivory carvings to paintings of urban scenes; and tribal dances to stage productions, art and music are part of this nation's life.

Pepel, Sierra Leone
A boat trip up the Rokel River reveals the jewel-colored birds and butterflies for which Sierra Leone is world-renowned. Firefinches and sunbirds flit about in flashes of iridescent color.

Harper, Liberia
Visit the beaches in the town of Harper, an important shipping point for Liberia's main cash crop of rubber. These are some of the finest beaches in the country, but don't miss the rainforests and rubber plantations that surround the area.

Monrovia, Liberia
A walk around the Waterside Market is an experience for the senses, whether it is the smell of local dishes being cooked or the sounds of an all-night bar. Soapstone carvings, baskets and African masks merit admiration.

TRANSPORTATION

NATIONAL AIRLINES:
Benin: Air Afrique (RK); **Burkina Faso:** Air Burkina (2J); **Côte d'Ivoire:** Air Afrique (RK); **Gambia:** Gambia Airways (CK); **Ghana:** Ghana Airways (GH); **Guinea:** Air Guinea (GI); **Guinea-Bissau:** Transportes Aereos de Guine Bissau (YZ); **Liberia:** Air Liberia (NL); **Senegal:** Air Senegal (DS); **Sierra Leone:** Sierra Leone National Airlines (LJ); **Togo:** Air Afrique (RK)

MAJOR AIRPORTS:
Benin: Cotonou (COO); **Burkina Faso:** Ouagadougou (OUA); **Côte d'Ivoire:** Felix Houphouet Boigny Airport (ABJ); **Gambia:** Yundum International (BJL); **Ghana:** Kotoka (ACC); **Guinea:** Conakry (CKY); **Guinea-Bissau:** Osvaldo Vieira Airport (OXB); **Liberia:** Roberts International (ROB); **Senegal:** Yoff (DKR); **Sierra Leone:** Lungi International (FNA); **Togo:** Lome (LFW)

Benin, Burkina Faso, Côte d'Ivoire, Ghana, Senegal and **Togo** all possess passenger rail networks of varying extent and service. Lines tend to connect capital cities with other major cities within the nation, but do not offer international routes.

Coastal ferry services operate in **Guinea-Bissau** and in **Senegal.**

The quality of bus service varies widely in western Africa, from comfortable and efficient to highly irregular. Most nations have long-distance networks that connect larger cities and towns; bush taxis and minibuses usually carry travelers on to more remote destinations from the termini of larger lines. Road conditions range from adequate to treacherous. Rental car companies offer limited service.

Travelers to this developing region of Africa confront many hazards related to weak economies and political instability. Sporadic outbreaks of ethnic or civil violence affect capital cities as well as remote regions. Criminals and armed groups target visitors, who are unlikely to benefit from effective policing, for robbery and assault. Medical facilities are limited at best. Various active military and insurgent groups make travel in **Liberia** and **Sierra Leone** extremely dangerous.

Scale 1:6,000,000 at map center

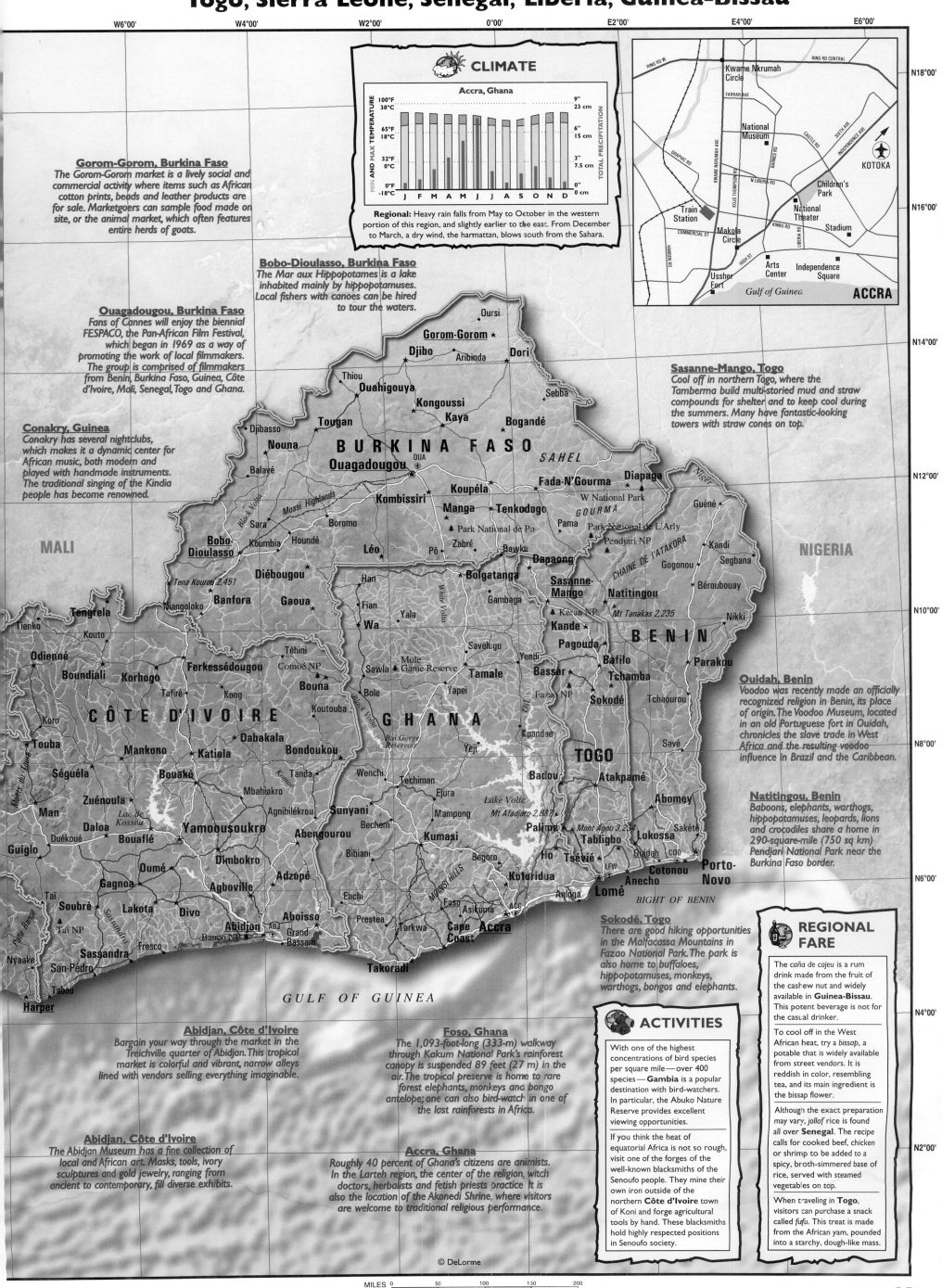

Gorom-Gorom, Burkina Faso
The Gorom-Gorom market is a lively social and commercial activity where items such as African cotton prints, beads and leather products are for sale. Marketgoers can sample food made on site, or the animal market, which often features entire herds of goats.

Ouagadougou, Burkina Faso
Fans of Cannes will enjoy the biennial FESPACO, the Pan-African Film Festival, which began in 1969 as a way of promoting the work of local filmmakers. The group is comprised of filmmakers from Benin, Burkina Faso, Guinea, Côte d'Ivoire, Mali, Senegal, Togo and Ghana.

Conakry, Guinea
Conakry has several nightclubs, which makes it a dynamic center for African music, both modern and played with handmade instruments. The traditional singing of the Kindia people has become renowned.

Bobo-Dioulasso, Burkina Faso
The Mar aux Hippopotames is a lake inhabited mainly by hippopotamuses. Local fishers with canoes can be hired to tour the waters.

Sasanne-Mango, Togo
Cool off in northern Togo, where the Tamberma build multi-storied mud and straw compounds for shelter and to keep cool during the summers. Many have fantastic-looking towers with straw cones on top.

Ouidah, Benin
Voodoo was recently made an officially recognized religion in Benin, its place of origin. The Voodoo Museum, located in an old Portuguese fort in Ouidah, chronicles the slave trade in West Africa and the resulting voodoo influence in Brazil and the Caribbean.

Natitingou, Benin
Baboons, elephants, warthogs, hippopotamuses, leopards, lions and crocodiles share a home in 290-square-mile (750 sq km) Pendjari National Park near the Burkina Faso border.

CLIMATE
Accra, Ghana

Regional: Heavy rain falls from May to October in the western portion of this region, and slightly earlier to the east. From December to March, a dry wind, the harmattan, blows south from the Sahara.

Abidjan, Côte d'Ivoire
Bargain your way through the market in the Treichville quarter of Abidjan. This tropical market is colorful and vibrant, narrow alleys lined with vendors selling everything imaginable.

Abidjan, Côte d'Ivoire
The Abidjan Museum has a fine collection of local and African art. Masks, tools, ivory sculptures and gold jewelry, ranging from ancient to contemporary, fill diverse exhibits.

Foso, Ghana
The 1,093-foot-long (333-m) walkway through Kakum National Park's rainforest canopy is suspended 89 feet (27 m) in the air. The tropical preserve is home to rare forest elephants, monkeys and bongo antelope; one can also bird-watch in one of the last rainforests in Africa.

Accra, Ghana
Roughly 40 percent of Ghana's citizens are animists. In the Larteh region, the center of the religion, witch doctors, herbalists and fetish priests practice. It is also the location of the Akonedi Shrine, where visitors are welcome to traditional religious performance.

Sokodé, Togo
There are good hiking opportunities in the Malfacassa Mountains in Fazao National Park. The park is also home to buffaloes, hippopotamuses, monkeys, warthogs, bongos and elephants.

ACTIVITIES
With one of the highest concentrations of bird species per square mile—over 400 species—**Gambia** is a popular destination with bird-watchers. In particular, the Abuko Nature Reserve provides excellent viewing opportunities.

If you think the heat of equatorial Africa is not so rough, visit one of the forges of the well-known blacksmiths of the Senoufo people. They mine their own iron outside of the northern **Côte d'Ivoire** town of Koni and forge agricultural tools by hand. These blacksmiths hold highly respected positions in Senoufo society.

REGIONAL FARE
The *caña de cajeu* is a rum drink made from the fruit of the cashew nut and widely available in **Guinea-Bissau**. This potent beverage is not for the casual drinker.

To cool off in the West African heat, try a *bissap*, a potable that is widely available from street vendors. It is reddish in color, resembling tea, and its main ingredient is the bissap flower.

Although the exact preparation may vary, *jollof* rice is found all over **Senegal**. The recipe calls for cooked beef, chicken or shrimp to be added to a spicy, broth-simmered base of rice, served with steamed vegetables on top.

When traveling in **Togo**, visitors can purchase a snack called *fufu*. This treat is made from the African yam, pounded into a starchy, dough-like mass.

© DeLorme

MILES
KILOMETERS

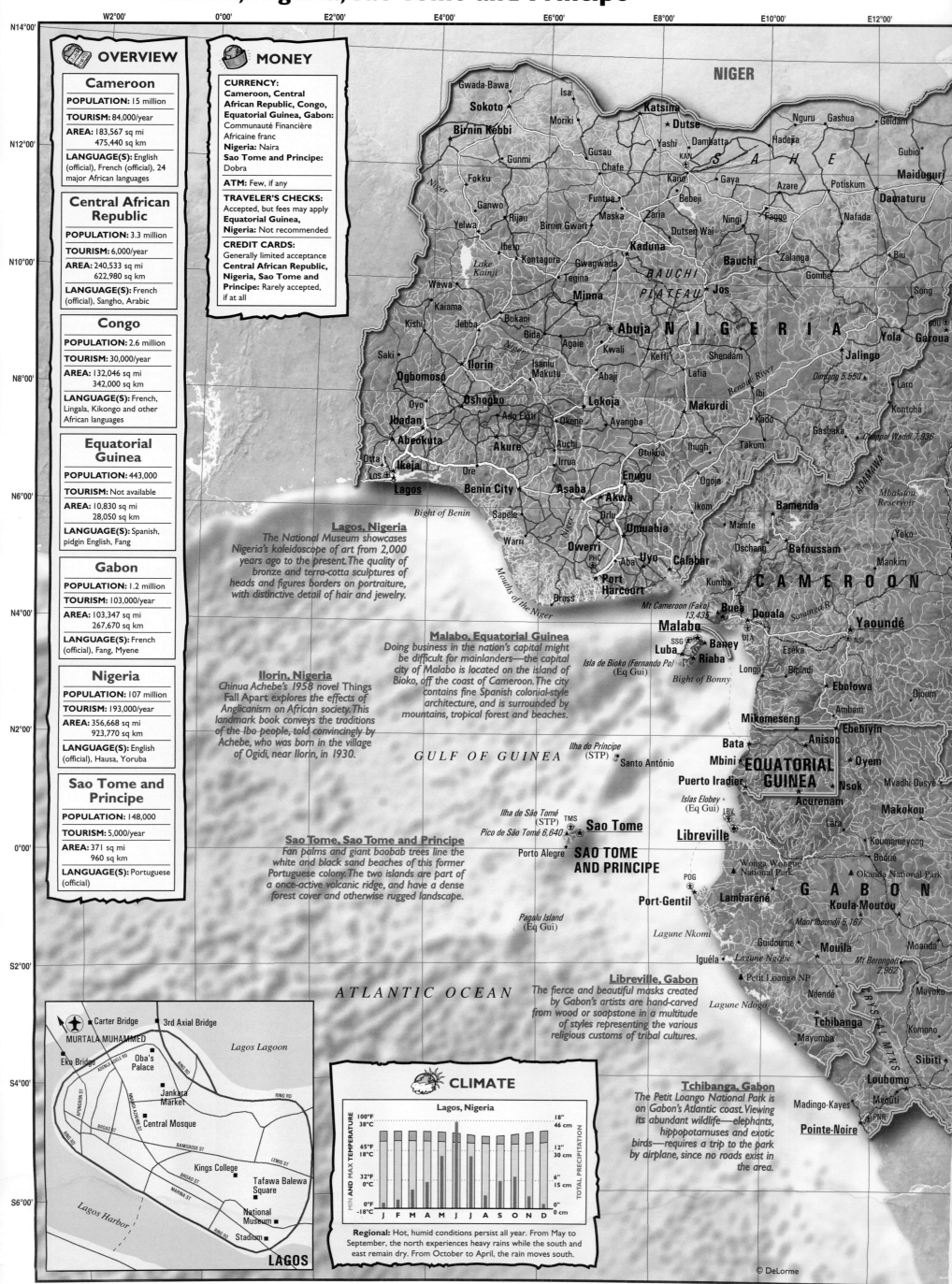

OVERVIEW

Cameroon
POPULATION: 15 million
TOURISM: 84,000/year
AREA: 183,567 sq mi
475,440 sq km
LANGUAGE(S): English (official), French (official), 24 major African languages

Central African Republic
POPULATION: 3.3 million
TOURISM: 6,000/year
AREA: 240,533 sq mi
622,980 sq km
LANGUAGE(S): French (official), Sangho, Arabic

Congo
POPULATION: 2.6 million
TOURISM: 30,000/year
AREA: 132,046 sq mi
342,000 sq km
LANGUAGE(S): French, Lingala, Kikongo and other African languages

Equatorial Guinea
POPULATION: 443,000
TOURISM: Not available
AREA: 10,830 sq mi
28,050 sq km
LANGUAGE(S): Spanish, pidgin English, Fang

Gabon
POPULATION: 1.2 million
TOURISM: 103,000/year
AREA: 103,347 sq mi
267,670 sq km
LANGUAGE(S): French (official), Fang, Myene

Nigeria
POPULATION: 107 million
TOURISM: 193,000/year
AREA: 356,668 sq mi
923,770 sq km
LANGUAGE(S): English (official), Hausa, Yoruba

Sao Tome and Principe
POPULATION: 148,000
TOURISM: 5,000/year
AREA: 371 sq mi
960 sq km
LANGUAGE(S): Portuguese (official)

MONEY

CURRENCY:
Cameroon, Central African Republic, Congo, Equatorial Guinea, Gabon: Communauté Financière Africaine franc
Nigeria: Naira
Sao Tome and Principe: Dobra

ATM: Few, if any

TRAVELER'S CHECKS: Accepted, but fees may apply
Equatorial Guinea, Nigeria: Not recommended

CREDIT CARDS: Generally limited acceptance
Central African Republic, Nigeria, Sao Tome and Principe: Rarely accepted, if at all

Lagos, Nigeria
The National Museum showcases Nigeria's kaleidoscope of art from 2,000 years ago to the present. The quality of bronze and terra-cotta sculptures of heads and figures borders on portraiture, with distinctive detail of hair and jewelry.

Ilorin, Nigeria
Chinua Achebe's 1958 novel Things Fall Apart explores the effects of Anglicanism on African society. This landmark book conveys the traditions of the Ibo people, told convincingly by Achebe, who was born in the village of Ogidi, near Ilorin, in 1930.

Malabo, Equatorial Guinea
Doing business in the nation's capital might be difficult for mainlanders—the capital city of Malabo is located on the island of Bioko, off the coast of Cameroon. The city contains fine Spanish colonial-style architecture, and is surrounded by mountains, tropical forest and beaches.

Sao Tome, Sao Tome and Principe
Fan palms and giant baobab trees line the white and black sand beaches of this former Portuguese colony. The two islands are part of a once-active volcanic ridge, and have a dense forest cover and otherwise rugged landscape.

Libreville, Gabon
The fierce and beautiful masks created by Gabon's artists are hand-carved from wood or soapstone in a multitude of styles representing the various religious customs of tribal cultures.

Tchibanga, Gabon
The Petit Loango National Park is on Gabon's Atlantic coast. Viewing its abundant wildlife—elephants, hippopotamuses and exotic birds—requires a trip to the park by airplane, since no roads exist in the area.

CLIMATE
Lagos, Nigeria

Regional: Hot, humid conditions persist all year. From May to September, the north experiences heavy rains while the south and east remain dry. From October to April, the rain moves south.

© DeLorme

Scale 1:7,000,000 at map center

Oshogbo, Nigeria
Oshun River is named for the Yoruba deity of water, love and fertility—greatly revered for her wisdom and compassion. There is a shrine to her along the banks of this river in a sacred grove.

Yaoundé, Cameroon
In the early 1970s Manu Dibango came out with the still-popular album Soul Makossa, spawning a major style of modern African music. The work of artists like Moni Bile and Ekambi Brillant carry on the beat.

Buea, Cameroon
The highest peak in West Africa, Mt Cameroon (Fako) is a volcanic monolith of more than 13,435 feet (4,095 m). It last erupted in 1959, and has since had light and sporadic activity. It is a popular destination for hikers.

🌍 REGIONAL FARE

The itanga is a unique-tasting local fruit of **Gabon** that is abundant in season. It is egg-shaped, about 4 inches (10 cm) long, and turns violet-colored when ripe. The itanga has the consistency of a cooked yam.

The almost-constant rainfall and the dark volcanic soil found in the higher elevations of **Cameroon** are perfect conditions for growing the rich arabica coffee bean prized all over the world.

In the **Central African Republic**, hydromiel is a popular and inexpensive alcoholic beverage resembling honey beer. To the west, in **Equatorial Guinea**, inhabitants drink malamba, a potent alcoholic beverage made from sugar cane.

🪨 ACTIVITIES

The waters of the Bight of Bonney, the narrow body of water that separates the **Cameroon** coast from volcanic Bioko Island, make for excellent sailing. The sharks in the area make this an expert-only activity.

If you're interested in carved wooden art, native metal crafts or yards and yards of fabulous fabrics, take time to visit the Kurmi Market in the thousand-year-old city of Kano, **Nigeria**. This is one of the largest shopping areas in Africa, covering over 40 acres (16 ha).

Explore an archaeological site outside of Bouar in the **Central African Republic**, which may leave you with more questions than answers. Seventy or so groups of standing stones, some of which weigh 3 to 4 tons (2,700 to 3,600 kg) each, are mysterious evidence of an ancient culture.

Bangui, Central African Republic
The rambling Chutes de Boali are a series of waterfalls that make a good day trip from Bangui. The falls are spectacular, mainly so during the rainy season.

Bangui, Central African Republic
The Bayaka pygmy people are one of the few remaining tribes that live in the dwindling African rainforests. Traditionally nomadic, they hunt with bow and arrow in one area for several weeks and then move elsewhere. The Bayaka are best known for their music, played on flutes and stringed instruments before battle or ceremonies.

Yaoundé, Cameroon
The National Museum of Yaoundé boasts a superb collection of Cameroon art, both primitive and modern. Archaeological artifacts, bronze sculptures, statues and masks dominate the collection.

Brazzaville, Congo
The infectious beat of Congo music originated when African pop musicians began blending Latin American and Caribbean styles with their own. This music is very popular all over Central and West Africa.

Pointe-Noire, Congo
Try fishing for tuna, barracuda or tarpon while sitting on the beach in Pointe-Noire, or take a ride on the Congo–Ocean Railway, started by the French in the 1920s to gain access to the African interior. A center for shipping and oil industries of the area, Pointe-Noire offers a great deal for anyone visiting.

🚠 TRANSPORTATION

NATIONAL AIRLINES:
Cameroon: Cameroon Airlines (UY); **Central African Republic:** Air Afrique (RK); **Equatorial Guinea:** Ecuato Guineana de Aviacion (8Y); **Gabon:** Air Gabon (GN); **Nigeria:** Nigeria Airways (WT); **Congo:** Air Afrique (RK); **Sao Tome and Principe:** Air Sao Tome (GJ)

MAJOR AIRPORTS:
Cameroon: Douala (DLA); **Central African Republic:** Bangui (BGF); **Congo:** Maya Maya (BZV); **Equatorial Guinea:** Santa Isabel (SSG); **Gabon:** Libreville (LBV); **Nigeria:** Aminu Kano International (KAN), Murtala Muhammed Airport (LOS), Port Harcourt International (PHC); **Sao Tome and Principe:** Sao Tome International (TMS)

These nations of equatorial Africa possess only limited train service. In **Cameroon**, trains link the coastal city of Douala and the interior city of Ngaoundéré with the capital of Yaoundé. The Trans-Gabon railway in **Gabon** links Libreville, Franceville and several other cities. Train routes connect **Nigeria's** major cities of Lagos, Kano and Port Harcourt, and in **Congo**, they connect the southern cities of Brazzaville and Pointe-Noire.

Limited passenger ferry service exists in these coastal nations. **Equatorial Guinea, Gabon** and **Nigeria** have ferry lines that connect coastal cities. Scheduled service also links the islands of **Sao Tome and Principe**. Travelers are likely to find ferry service on the rivers leading from the coasts into the interior, such as along the Ubangi River in the **Central African Republic** or on the Benue and Niger rivers in **Nigeria**.

Buses, taxis and bush taxis provide transportation between most cities and many towns in equatorial Africa. Travelers should expect poor road conditions.

The US State Department discourages travel to the **Central African Republic** due to recent military and civil unrest. An uncertain security situation makes travel dangerous, especially in the central and northern regions. In the highly unstable nation of **Nigeria**, criminal elements of the military and police forces as well as the business community deliberately target foreigners for harassment, robbery, assault, violence, extortion and fraud. Poorly run domestic airlines and insecure airports make air travel within Nigeria very risky. Throughout this region, limited medical care exists, and foreigners are frequently the targets of street crime. Visitors should avoid travel at night in unfamiliar or remote areas.

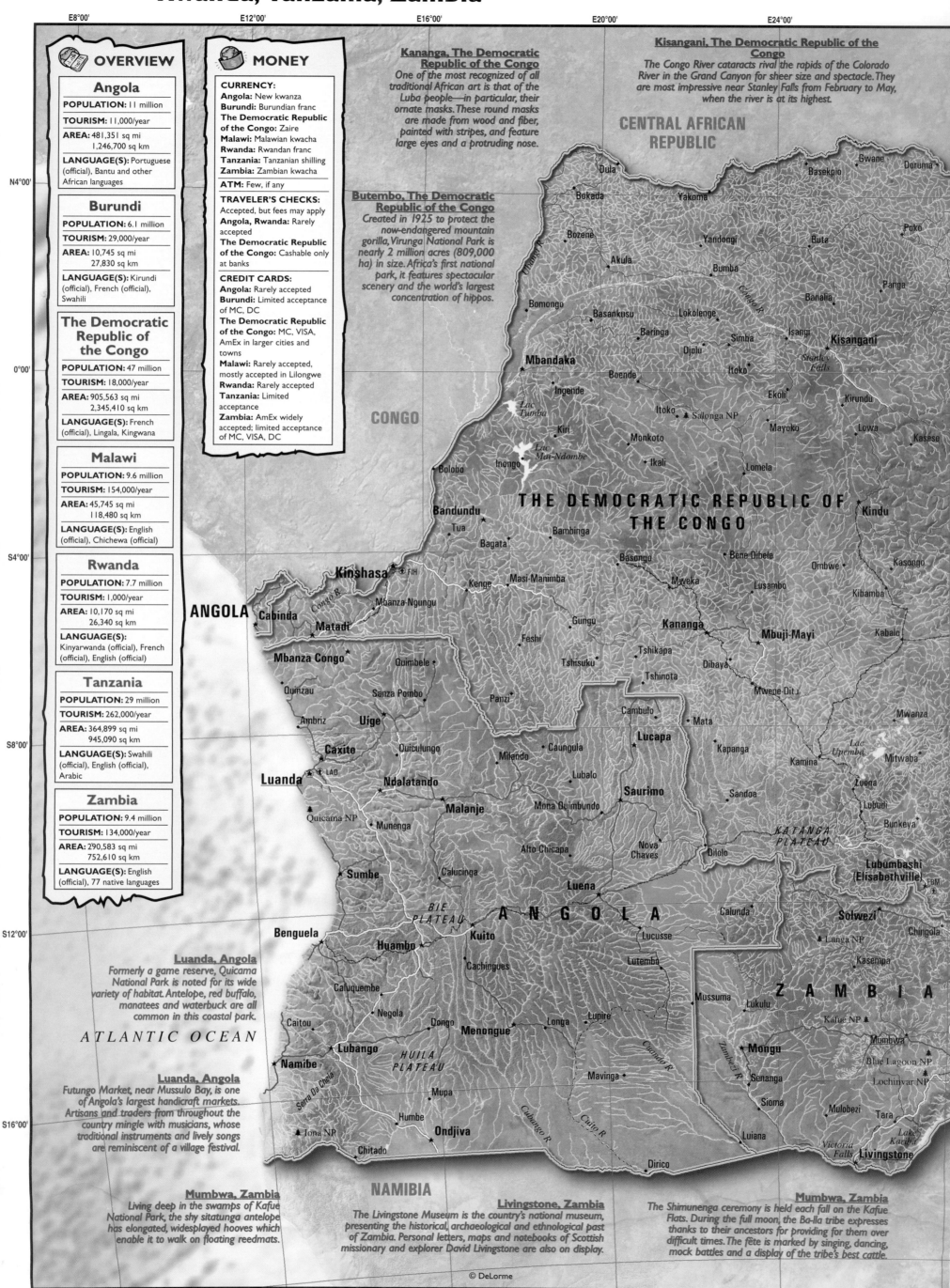

OVERVIEW

Angola
POPULATION: 11 million
TOURISM: 11,000/year
AREA: 481,351 sq mi
1,246,700 sq km
LANGUAGE(S): Portuguese (official), Bantu and other African languages

Burundi
POPULATION: 6.1 million
TOURISM: 29,000/year
AREA: 10,745 sq mi
27,830 sq km
LANGUAGE(S): Kirundi (official), French (official), Swahili

The Democratic Republic of the Congo
POPULATION: 47 million
TOURISM: 18,000/year
AREA: 905,563 sq mi
2,345,410 sq km
LANGUAGE(S): French (official), Lingala, Kingwana

Malawi
POPULATION: 9.6 million
TOURISM: 154,000/year
AREA: 45,745 sq mi
118,480 sq km
LANGUAGE(S): English (official), Chichewa (official)

Rwanda
POPULATION: 7.7 million
TOURISM: 1,000/year
AREA: 10,170 sq mi
26,340 sq km
LANGUAGE(S): Kinyarwanda (official), French (official), English (official)

Tanzania
POPULATION: 29 million
TOURISM: 262,000/year
AREA: 364,899 sq mi
945,090 sq km
LANGUAGE(S): Swahili (official), English (official), Arabic

Zambia
POPULATION: 9.4 million
TOURISM: 134,000/year
AREA: 290,583 sq mi
752,610 sq km
LANGUAGE(S): English (official), 77 native languages

MONEY

CURRENCY:
Angola: New kwanza
Burundi: Burundian franc
The Democratic Republic of the Congo: Zaire
Malawi: Malawian kwacha
Rwanda: Rwandan franc
Tanzania: Tanzanian shilling
Zambia: Zambian kwacha
ATM: Few, if any
TRAVELER'S CHECKS:
Accepted, but fees may apply
Angola, Rwanda: Rarely accepted
The Democratic Republic of the Congo: Cashable only at banks
CREDIT CARDS:
Angola: Rarely accepted
Burundi: Limited acceptance of MC, DC
The Democratic Republic of the Congo: MC, VISA, AmEx in larger cities and towns
Malawi: Rarely accepted, mostly accepted in Lilongwe
Rwanda: Rarely accepted
Tanzania: Limited acceptance
Zambia: AmEx widely accepted; limited acceptance of MC, VISA, DC

Kananga, The Democratic Republic of the Congo
One of the most recognized of all traditional African art is that of the Luba people—in particular, their ornate masks. These round masks are made from wood and fiber, painted with stripes, and feature large eyes and a protruding nose.

Butembo, The Democratic Republic of the Congo
Created in 1925 to protect the now-endangered mountain gorilla, Virunga National Park is nearly 2 million acres (809,000 ha) in size. Africa's first national park, it features spectacular scenery and the world's largest concentration of hippos.

Kisangani, The Democratic Republic of the Congo
The Congo River cataracts rival the rapids of the Colorado River in the Grand Canyon for sheer size and spectacle. They are most impressive near Stanley Falls from February to May, when the river is at its highest.

Luanda, Angola
Formerly a game reserve, Quicama National Park is noted for its wide variety of habitat. Antelope, red buffalo, manatees and waterbuck are all common in this coastal park.

Luanda, Angola
Futungo Market, near Mussulo Bay, is one of Angola's largest handicraft markets. Artisans and traders from throughout the country mingle with musicians, whose traditional instruments and lively songs are reminiscent of a village festival.

Mumbwa, Zambia
Living deep in the swamps of Kafue National Park, the shy sitatunga antelope has elongated, widesplayed hooves which enable it to walk on floating reedmats.

Livingstone, Zambia
The Livingstone Museum is the country's national museum, presenting the historical, archaeological and ethnological past of Zambia. Personal letters, maps and notebooks of Scottish missionary and explorer David Livingstone are also on display.

Mumbwa, Zambia
The Shimunenga ceremony is held each fall on the Kafue Flats. During the full moon, the Ba-Ila tribe expresses thanks to their ancestors for providing for them over difficult times. The fête is marked by singing, dancing, mock battles and a display of the tribe's best cattle.

© DeLorme

Scale 1:9,000,000 at map center

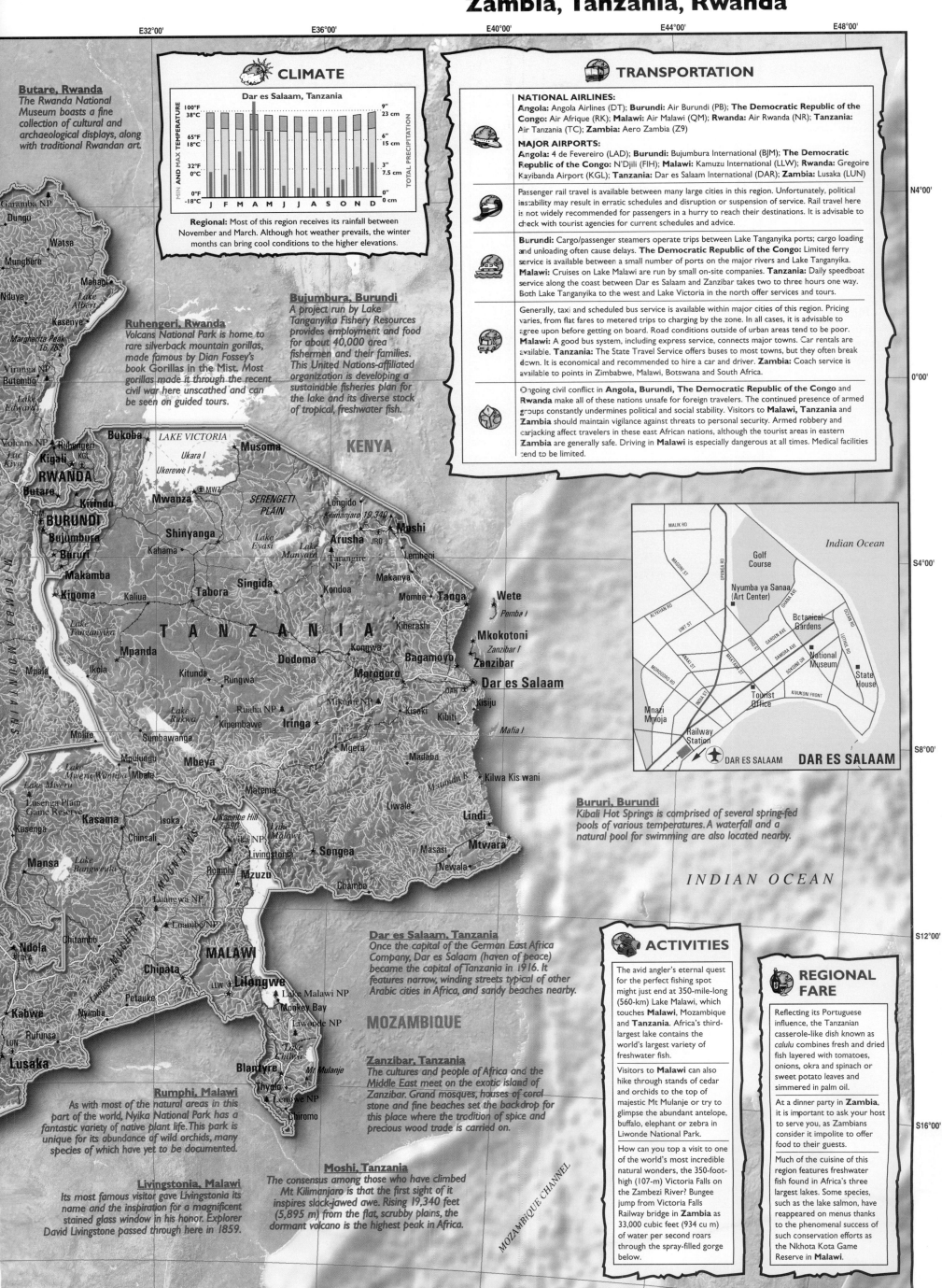

Butare, Rwanda
The Rwanda National Museum boasts a fine collection of cultural and archaeological displays, along with traditional Rwandan art.

CLIMATE

Dar es Salaam, Tanzania

(climate chart: MIN AND MAX TEMPERATURE / TOTAL PRECIPITATION; months J F M A M J J A S O N D; temperature scale 100°F 38°C, 65°F 18°C, 32°F 0°C, 0°F -18°C; precipitation scale 9" 23 cm, 6" 15 cm, 3" 7.5 cm, 0 cm)

Regional: Most of this region receives its rainfall between November and March. Although hot weather prevails, the winter months can bring cool conditions to the higher elevations.

TRANSPORTATION

NATIONAL AIRLINES:
Angola: Angola Airlines (DT); **Burundi:** Air Burundi (PB); **The Democratic Republic of the Congo:** Air Afrique (RK); **Malawi:** Air Malawi (QM); **Rwanda:** Air Rwanda (NR); **Tanzania:** Air Tanzania (TC); **Zambia:** Aero Zambia (Z9)

MAJOR AIRPORTS:
Angola: 4 de Fevereiro (LAD); **Burundi:** Bujumbura International (BJM); **The Democratic Republic of the Congo:** N'Djili (FIH); **Malawi:** Kamuzu International (LLW); **Rwanda:** Gregoire Kayibanda Airport (KGL); **Tanzania:** Dar es Salaam International (DAR); **Zambia:** Lusaka (LUN)

Passenger rail travel is available between many large cities in this region. Unfortunately, political instability may result in erratic schedules and disruption or suspension of service. Rail travel here is not widely recommended for passengers in a hurry to reach their destinations. It is advisable to check with tourist agencies for current schedules and advice.

Burundi: Cargo/passenger steamers operate trips between Lake Tanganyika ports; cargo loading and unloading often cause delays. **The Democratic Republic of the Congo:** Limited ferry service is available between a small number of ports on the major rivers and Lake Tanganyika. **Malawi:** Cruises on Lake Malawi are run by small on-site companies. **Tanzania:** Daily speedboat service along the coast between Dar es Salaam and Zanzibar takes two to three hours one way. Both Lake Tanganyika to the west and Lake Victoria in the north offer services and tours.

Generally, taxi and scheduled bus service is available within major cities of this region. Pricing varies, from flat fares to metered trips to charging by the zone. In all cases, it is advisable to agree upon before getting on board. Road conditions outside of urban areas tend to be poor. **Malawi:** A good bus system, including express service, connects major towns. Car rentals are available. **Tanzania:** The State Travel Service offers buses to most towns, but they often break down. It is economical and recommended to hire a car and driver. **Zambia:** Coach service is available to points in Zimbabwe, Malawi, Botswana and South Africa.

Ongoing civil conflict in **Angola, Burundi, The Democratic Republic of the Congo** and **Rwanda** make all of these nations unsafe for foreign travelers. The continued presence of armed groups constantly undermines political and social stability. Visitors to **Malawi, Tanzania** and **Zambia** should maintain vigilance against threats to personal security. Armed robbery and carjacking affect travelers in these east African nations, although the tourist areas in eastern **Zambia** are generally safe. Driving in **Malawi** is especially dangerous at all times. Medical facilities tend to be limited.

Ruhengeri, Rwanda
Volcans National Park is home to rare silverback mountain gorillas, made famous by Dian Fossey's book Gorillas in the Mist. Most gorillas made it through the recent civil war here unscathed and can be seen on guided tours.

Bujumbura, Burundi
A project run by Lake Tanganyika Fishery Resources provides employment and food for about 40,000 area fishermen and their families. This United Nations-affiliated organization is developing a sustainable fisheries plan for the lake and its diverse stock of tropical, freshwater fish.

DAR ES SALAAM

(inset city map labels: MALIK RD, UPANGA RD, MASOMO ST, Golf Course, Indian Ocean, ALYKHAN RD, UWT ST, Nyumba ya Sanaa (Art Center), GARDEN AVE, GUINEA AVE, Botanical Gardens, BIBI TITI RD, SAMORA AVE, SOKOINE DR, National Museum, LUTHULI RD, MONGOBORO RD, MAKTABA ST, BRIDGE ST, BAKERY ST, INDIA ST, KIVUKONI FRONT, Tourist Office, State House, Mnazi Mmoja, Railway Station, DAR ES SALAAM)

Bururi, Burundi
Kibali Hot Springs is comprised of several spring-fed pools of various temperatures. A waterfall and a natural pool for swimming are also located nearby.

Dar es Salaam, Tanzania
Once the capital of the German East Africa Company, Dar es Salaam (haven of peace) became the capital of Tanzania in 1916. It features narrow, winding streets typical of other Arabic cities in Africa, and sandy beaches nearby.

Zanzibar, Tanzania
The cultures and people of Africa and the Middle East meet on the exotic island of Zanzibar. Grand mosques, houses of coral stone and fine beaches set the backdrop for this place where the tradition of spice and precious wood trade is carried on.

Rumphi, Malawi
As with most of the natural areas in this part of the world, Nyika National Park has a fantastic variety of native plant life. This park is unique for its abundance of wild orchids, many species of which have yet to be documented.

Livingstonia, Malawi
Its most famous visitor gave Livingstonia its name and the inspiration for a magnificent stained glass window in his honor. Explorer David Livingstone passed through here in 1859.

Moshi, Tanzania
The consensus among those who have climbed Mt Kilimanjaro is that the first sight of it inspires slack-jawed awe. Rising 19,340 feet (5,895 m) from the flat, scrubby plains, the dormant volcano is the highest peak in Africa.

ACTIVITIES

The avid angler's eternal quest for the perfect fishing spot might just end at 350-mile-long (560-km) Lake Malawi, which touches **Malawi**, Mozambique and **Tanzania**. Africa's third-largest lake contains the world's largest variety of freshwater fish.

Visitors to **Malawi** can also hike through stands of cedar and orchids to the top of majestic Mt Mulanje or try to glimpse the abundant antelope, buffalo, elephant or zebra in Liwonde National Park.

How can you top a visit to one of the world's most incredible natural wonders, the 350-foot-high (107-m) Victoria Falls on the Zambezi River? Bungee jump from Victoria Falls Railway bridge in **Zambia** as 33,000 cubic feet (934 cu m) of water per second roars through the spray-filled gorge below.

REGIONAL FARE

Reflecting its Portuguese influence, the Tanzanian casserole-like dish known as *calulu* combines fresh and dried fish layered with tomatoes, onions, okra and spinach or sweet potato leaves and simmered in palm oil.

At a dinner party in **Zambia**, it is important to ask your host to serve you, as Zambians consider it impolite to offer food to their guests.

Much of the cuisine of this region features freshwater fish found in Africa's three largest lakes. Some species, such as the lake salmon, have reappeared on menus thanks to the phenomenal success of such conservation efforts as the Nkhota Kota Game Reserve in **Malawi**.

(map scale: MILES 0 100 200 300; KILOMETERS 0 100 200 300 400 500)

AFRICA Botswana, Lesotho, Mozambique, Namibia, South Africa Swaziland, Zimbabwe

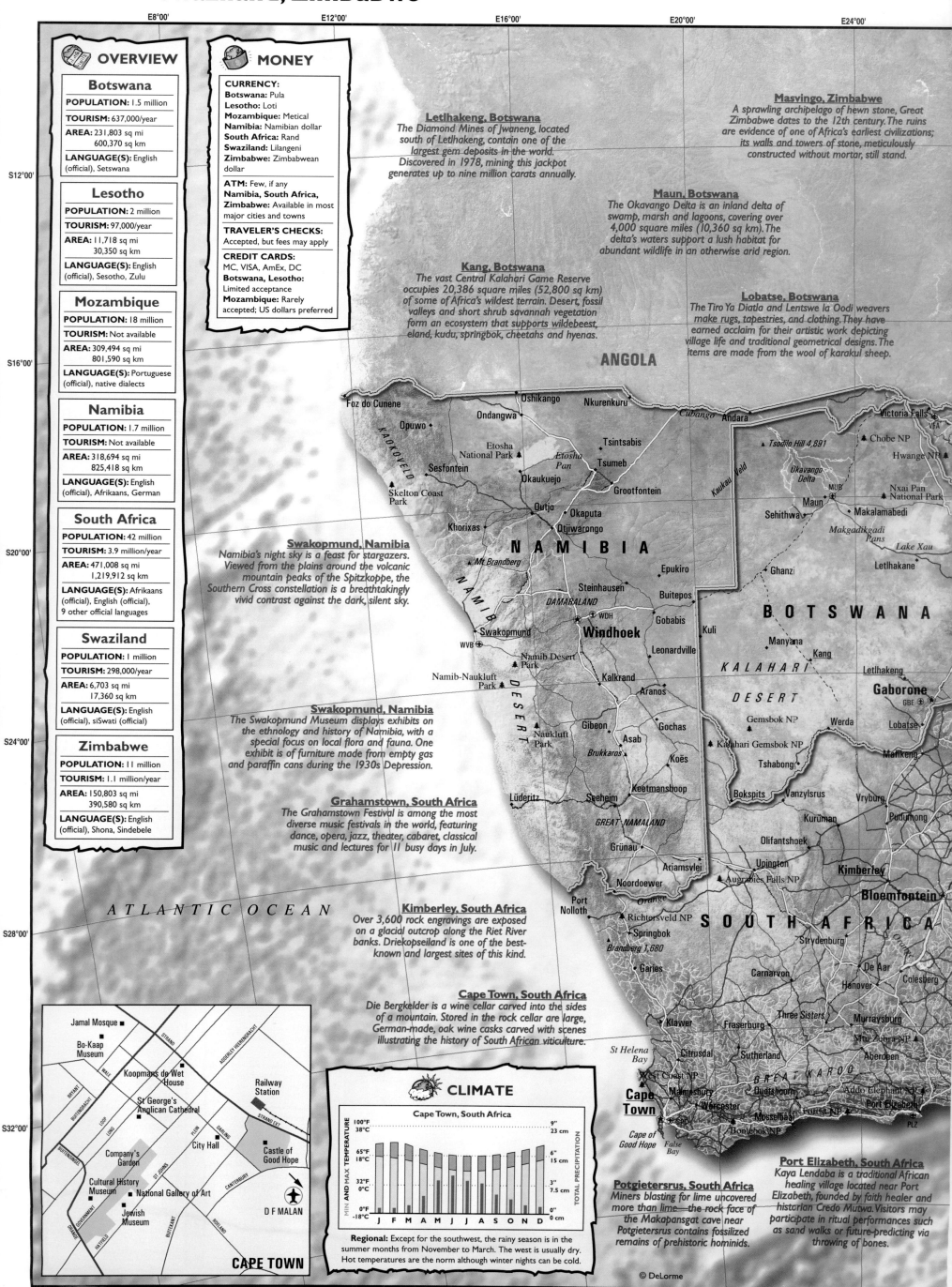

OVERVIEW

Botswana
POPULATION: 1.5 million
TOURISM: 637,000/year
AREA: 231,803 sq mi
600,370 sq km
LANGUAGE(S): English
(official), Setswana

Lesotho
POPULATION: 2 million
TOURISM: 97,000/year
AREA: 11,718 sq mi
30,350 sq km
LANGUAGE(S): English
(official), Sesotho, Zulu

Mozambique
POPULATION: 18 million
TOURISM: Not available
AREA: 309,494 sq mi
801,590 sq km
LANGUAGE(S): Portuguese
(official), native dialects

Namibia
POPULATION: 1.7 million
TOURISM: Not available
AREA: 318,694 sq mi
825,418 sq km
LANGUAGE(S): English
(official), Afrikaans, German

South Africa
POPULATION: 42 million
TOURISM: 3.9 million/year
AREA: 471,008 sq mi
1,219,912 sq km
LANGUAGE(S): Afrikaans
(official), English (official),
9 other official languages

Swaziland
POPULATION: 1 million
TOURISM: 298,000/year
AREA: 6,703 sq mi
17,360 sq km
LANGUAGE(S): English
(official), siSwati (official)

Zimbabwe
POPULATION: 11 million
TOURISM: 1.1 million/year
AREA: 150,803 sq mi
390,580 sq km
LANGUAGE(S): English
(official), Shona, Sindebele

MONEY

CURRENCY:
Botswana: Pula
Lesotho: Loti
Mozambique: Metical
Namibia: Namibian dollar
South Africa: Rand
Swaziland: Lilangeni
Zimbabwe: Zimbabwean
dollar

ATM: Few, if any
**Namibia, South Africa,
Zimbabwe:** Available in most
major cities and towns

TRAVELER'S CHECKS:
Accepted, but fees may apply

CREDIT CARDS:
MC, VISA, AmEx, DC
Botswana, Lesotho:
Limited acceptance
Mozambique: Rarely
accepted; US dollars preferred

Letlhakeng, Botswana
The Diamond Mines of Jwaneng, located south of Letlhakeng, contain one of the largest gem deposits in the world. Discovered in 1978, mining this jackpot generates up to nine million carats annually.

Kang, Botswana
The vast Central Kalahari Game Reserve occupies 20,386 square miles (52,800 sq km) of some of Africa's wildest terrain. Desert, fossil valleys and short shrub savannah vegetation form an ecosystem that supports wildebeest, eland, kudu, springbok, cheetahs and hyenas.

Masvingo, Zimbabwe
A sprawling archipelago of hewn stone, Great Zimbabwe dates to the 12th century. The ruins are evidence of one of Africa's earliest civilizations; its walls and towers of stone, meticulously constructed without mortar, still stand.

Maun, Botswana
The Okavango Delta is an inland delta of swamp, marsh and lagoons, covering over 4,000 square miles (10,360 sq km). The delta's waters support a lush habitat for abundant wildlife in an otherwise arid region.

Lobatse, Botswana
The Tiro Ya Diatla and Lentswe la Oodi weavers make rugs, tapestries, and clothing. They have earned acclaim for their artistic work depicting village life and traditional geometrical designs. The items are made from the wool of karakul sheep.

Swakopmund, Namibia
Namibia's night sky is a feast for stargazers. Viewed from the plains around the volcanic mountain peaks of the Spitzkoppe, the Southern Cross constellation is a breathtakingly vivid contrast against the dark, silent sky.

Swakopmund, Namibia
The Swakopmund Museum displays exhibits on the ethnology and history of Namibia, with a special focus on local flora and fauna. One exhibit is of furniture made from empty gas and paraffin cans during the 1930s Depression.

Grahamstown, South Africa
The Grahamstown Festival is among the most diverse music festivals in the world, featuring dance, opera, jazz, theater, cabaret, classical music and lectures for 11 busy days in July.

Kimberley, South Africa
Over 3,600 rock engravings are exposed on a glacial outcrop along the Riet River banks. Driekopseiland is one of the best-known and largest sites of this kind.

Cape Town, South Africa
Die Bergkelder is a wine cellar carved into the sides of a mountain. Stored in the rock cellar are large, German-made, oak wine casks carved with scenes illustrating the history of South African viticulture.

Potgietersrus, South Africa
Miners blasting for lime uncovered more than lime—the rock face of the Makapansgat cave near Potgietersrus contains fossilized remains of prehistoric hominids.

Port Elizabeth, South Africa
Kaya Lendaba is a traditional African healing village located near Port Elizabeth, founded by faith healer and historian Credo Mutwa. Visitors may participate in ritual performances such as sand walks or future-predicting via throwing of bones.

CLIMATE
Cape Town, South Africa

Regional: Except for the southwest, the rainy season is in the summer months from November to March. The west is usually dry. Hot temperatures are the norm although winter nights can be cold.

CAPE TOWN
Jamal Mosque
Bo-Kaap Museum
Koopmans de Wet House
Railway Station
St George's Anglican Cathedral
City Hall
Castle of Good Hope
Company's Garden
Cultural History Museum
National Gallery of Art
Jewish Museum
D F MALAN

© DeLorme

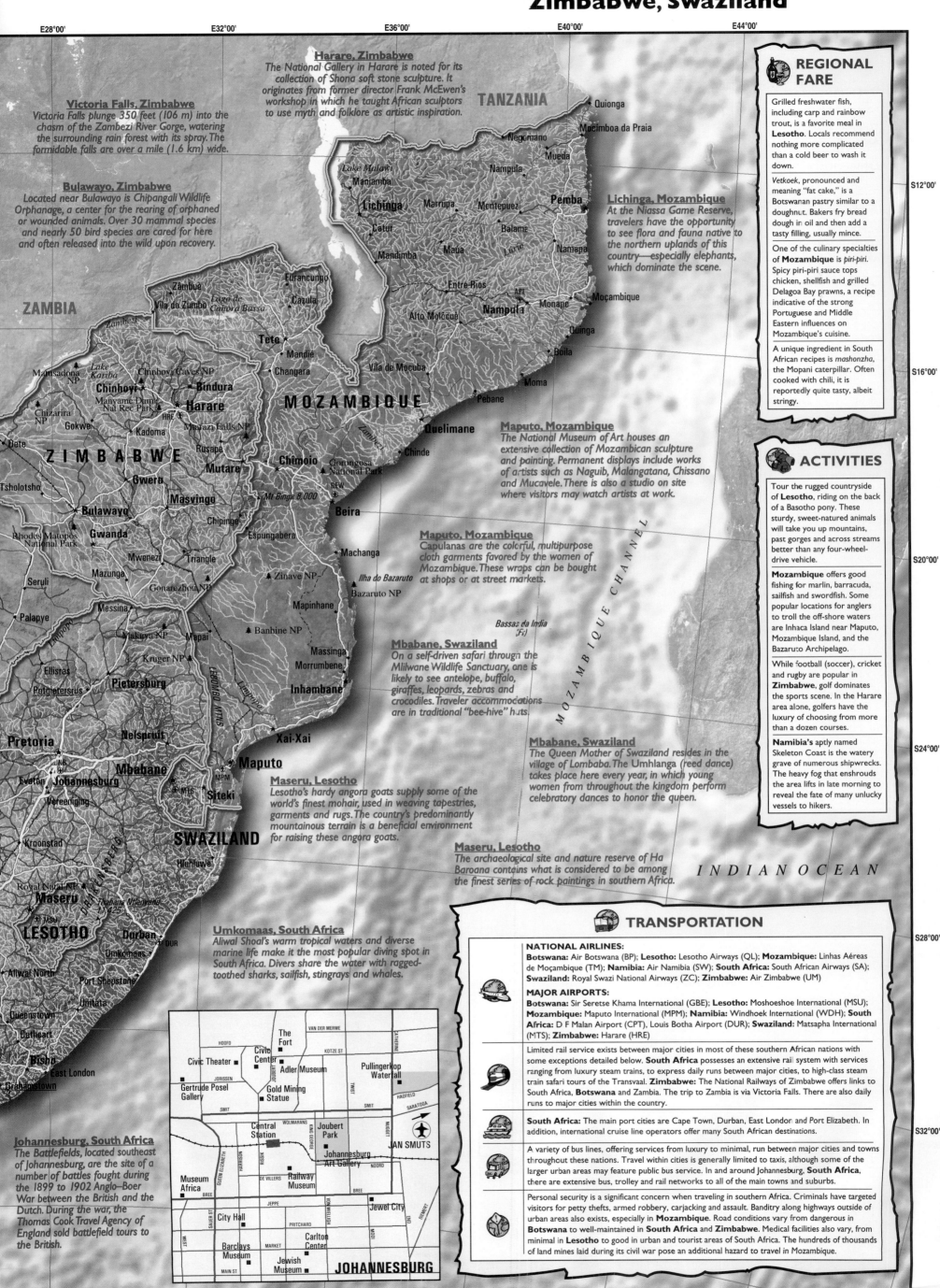

Harare, Zimbabwe
The National Gallery in Harare is noted for its collection of Shona soft stone sculpture. It originates from former director Frank McEwen's workshop in which he taught African sculptors to use myth and folklore as artistic inspiration.

Victoria Falls, Zimbabwe
Victoria Falls plunge 350 feet (106 m) into the chasm of the Zambezi River Gorge, watering the surrounding rain forest with its spray. The formidable falls are over a mile (1.6 km) wide.

Bulawayo, Zimbabwe
Located near Bulawayo is Chipangali Wildlife Orphanage, a center for the rearing of orphaned or wounded animals. Over 30 mammal species and nearly 50 bird species are cared for here and often released into the wild upon recovery.

Lichinga, Mozambique
At the Niassa Game Reserve, travelers have the opportunity to see flora and fauna native to the northern uplands of this country—especially elephants, which dominate the scene.

Maputo, Mozambique
The National Museum of Art houses an extensive collection of Mozambican sculpture and painting. Permanent displays include works of artists such as Naguib, Malangatana, Chissano and Mucavele. There is also a studio on site where visitors may watch artists at work.

Maputo, Mozambique
Capulanas are the colorful, multipurpose cloth garments favored by the women of Mozambique. These wraps can be bought at shops or at street markets.

Mbabane, Swaziland
On a self-driven safari through the Mlilwane Wildlife Sanctuary, one is likely to see antelope, buffalo, giraffes, leopards, zebras and crocodiles. Traveler accommodations are in traditional "bee-hive" huts.

Mbabane, Swaziland
The Queen Mother of Swaziland resides in the village of Lombaba. The Umhlanga (reed dance) takes place here every year, in which young women from throughout the kingdom perform celebratory dances to honor the queen.

Maseru, Lesotho
Lesotho's hardy angora goats supply some of the world's finest mohair, used in weaving tapestries, garments and rugs. The country's predominantly mountainous terrain is a beneficial environment for raising these angora goats.

Maseru, Lesotho
The archaeological site and nature reserve of Ha Baroana contains what is considered to be among the finest series of rock paintings in southern Africa.

Umkomaas, South Africa
Aliwal Shoal's warm tropical waters and diverse marine life make it the most popular diving spot in South Africa. Divers share the water with ragged-toothed sharks, sailfish, stingrays and whales.

Johannesburg, South Africa
The Battlefields, located southeast of Johannesburg, are the site of a number of battles fought during the 1899 to 1902 Anglo–Boer War between the British and the Dutch. During the war, the Thomas Cook Travel Agency of England sold battlefield tours to the British.

REGIONAL FARE

Grilled freshwater fish, including carp and rainbow trout, is a favorite meal in **Lesotho**. Locals recommend nothing more complicated than a cold beer to wash it down.

Vetkoek, pronounced and meaning "fat cake," is a Botswaran pastry similar to a doughnut. Bakers fry bread dough in oil and then add a tasty filling, usually mince.

One of the culinary specialties of **Mozambique** is piri-piri. Spicy piri-piri sauce tops chicken, shellfish and grilled Delagoa Bay prawns, a recipe indicative of the strong Portuguese and Middle Eastern influences on Mozambique's cuisine.

A unique ingredient in South African recipes is mashonzha, the Mopani caterpillar. Often cooked with chili, it is reportedly quite tasty, albeit stringy.

ACTIVITIES

Tour the rugged countryside of **Lesotho**, riding on the back of a Basotho pony. These sturdy, sweet-natured animals will take you up mountains, past gorges and across streams better than any four-wheel-drive vehicle.

Mozambique offers good fishing for marlin, barracuda, sailfish and swordfish. Some popular locations for anglers are to troll the off-shore waters are Inhaca Island near Maputo, Mozambique Island, and the Bazaruto Archipelago.

While football (soccer), cricket and rugby are popular in **Zimbabwe**, golf dominates the sports scene. In the Harare area alone, golfers have the luxury of choosing from more than a dozen courses.

Namibia's aptly named Skeleton Coast is the watery grave of numerous shipwrecks. The heavy fog that enshrouds the area lifts in late morning to reveal the fate of many unlucky vessels to hikers.

TRANSPORTATION

NATIONAL AIRLINES:
Botswana: Air Botswana (BP); **Lesotho:** Lesotho Airways (QL); **Mozambique:** Linhas Aéreas de Moçambique (TM); **Namibia:** Air Namibia (SW); **South Africa:** South African Airways (SA); **Swaziland:** Royal Swazi National Airways (ZC); **Zimbabwe:** Air Zimbabwe (UM)

MAJOR AIRPORTS:
Botswana: Sir Seretse Khama International (GBE); **Lesotho:** Moshoeshoe International (MSU); **Mozambique:** Maputo International (MPM); **Namibia:** Windhoek International (WDH); **South Africa:** D F Malan Airport (CPT), Louis Botha Airport (DUR); **Swaziland:** Matsapha International (MTS); **Zimbabwe:** Harare (HRE)

Limited rail service exists between major cities in most of these southern African nations with some exceptions detailed below. **South Africa** possesses an extensive rail system with services ranging from luxury steam trains, to express daily runs between major cities, to high-class steam train safari tours of the Transvaal. **Zimbabwe:** The National Railways of Zimbabwe offers links to South Africa, Botswana and Zambia. The trip to Zambia is via Victoria Falls. There are also daily runs to major cities within the country.

South Africa: The main port cities are Cape Town, Durban, East London and Port Elizabeth. In addition, international cruise line operators offer many South African destinations.

A variety of bus lines, offering services from luxury to minimal, run between major cities and towns throughout these nations. Travel within cities is generally limited to taxis, although some of the larger urban areas may feature public bus service. In and around Johannesburg, **South Africa**, there are extensive bus, trolley and rail networks to all of the main towns and suburbs.

Personal security is a significant concern when traveling in southern Africa. Criminals have targeted visitors for petty thefts, armed robbery, carjacking and assault. Banditry along highways outside of urban areas also exists, especially in **Mozambique**. Road conditions vary from dangerous in **Botswana** to well-maintained in **South Africa** and **Zimbabwe**. Medical facilities also vary, from minimal in **Lesotho** to good in urban and tourist areas of South Africa. The hundreds of thousands of land mines laid during its civil war pose an additional hazard to travel in Mozambique.

91

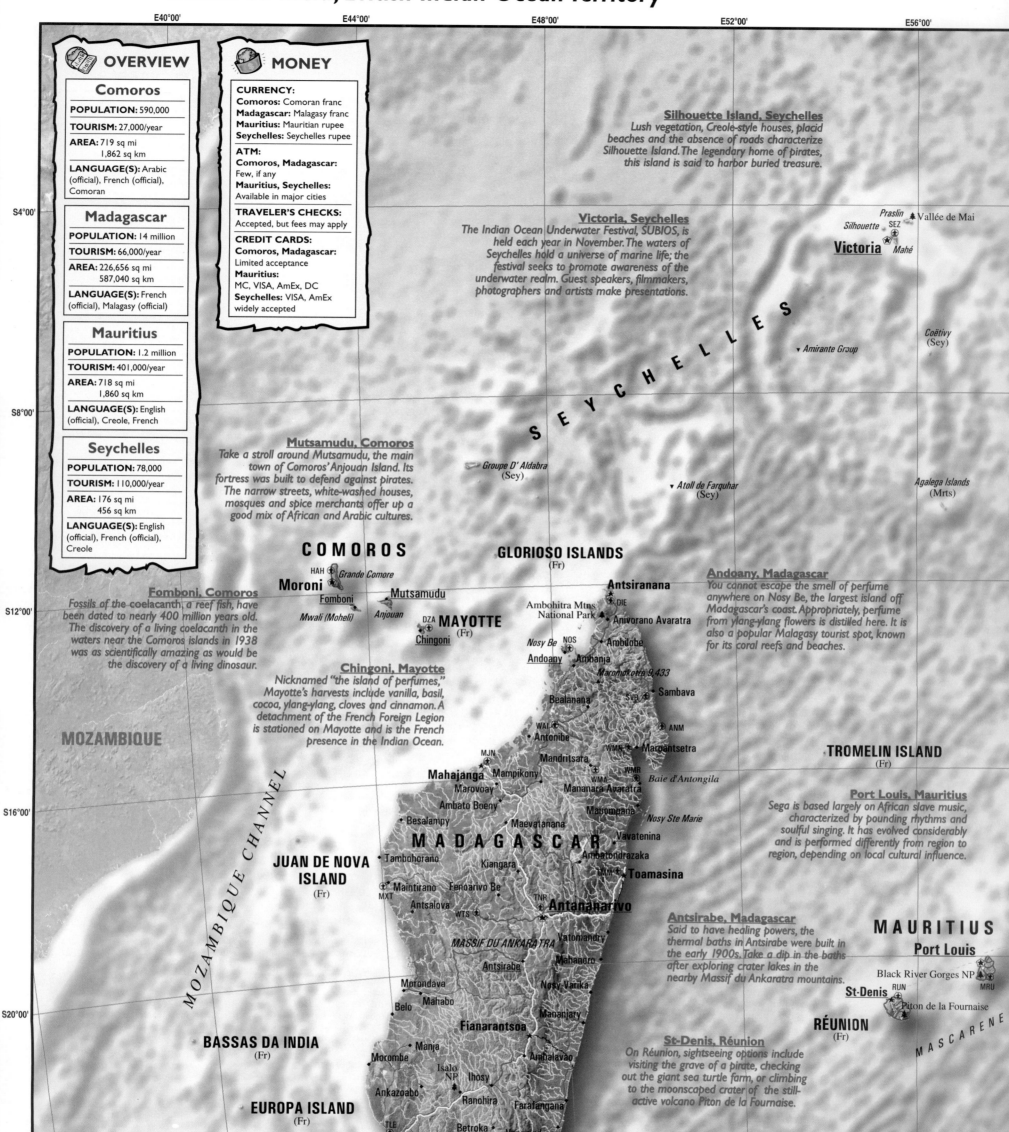

OVERVIEW

Comoros
POPULATION: 590,000
TOURISM: 27,000/year
AREA: 719 sq mi
1,862 sq km
LANGUAGE(S): Arabic (official), French (official), Comoran

Madagascar
POPULATION: 14 million
TOURISM: 66,000/year
AREA: 226,656 sq mi
587,040 sq km
LANGUAGE(S): French (official), Malagasy (official)

Mauritius
POPULATION: 1.2 million
TOURISM: 401,000/year
AREA: 718 sq mi
1,860 sq km
LANGUAGE(S): English (official), Creole, French

Seychelles
POPULATION: 78,000
TOURISM: 110,000/year
AREA: 176 sq mi
456 sq km
LANGUAGE(S): English (official), French (official), Creole

MONEY

CURRENCY:
Comoros: Comoran franc
Madagascar: Malagasy franc
Mauritius: Mauritian rupee
Seychelles: Seychelles rupee

ATM:
Comoros, Madagascar: Few, if any
Mauritius, Seychelles: Available in major cities

TRAVELER'S CHECKS: Accepted, but fees may apply

CREDIT CARDS:
Comoros, Madagascar: Limited acceptance
Mauritius: MC, VISA, AmEx, DC
Seychelles: VISA, AmEx widely accepted

Silhouette Island, Seychelles
Lush vegetation, Creole-style houses, placid beaches and the absence of roads characterize Silhouette Island. The legendary home of pirates, this island is said to harbor buried treasure.

Victoria, Seychelles
The Indian Ocean Underwater Festival, SUBIOS, is held each year in November. The waters of Seychelles hold a universe of marine life; the festival seeks to promote awareness of the underwater realm. Guest speakers, filmmakers, photographers and artists make presentations.

Mutsamudu, Comoros
Take a stroll around Mutsamudu, the main town of Comoros'Anjouan Island. Its fortress was built to defend against pirates. The narrow streets, white-washed houses, mosques and spice merchants offer up a good mix of African and Arabic cultures.

Fomboni, Comoros
Fossils of the coelacanth, a reef fish, have been dated to nearly 400 million years old. The discovery of a living coelacanth in the waters near the Comoros islands in 1938 was as scientifically amazing as would be the discovery of a living dinosaur.

Chingoni, Mayotte
Nicknamed "the island of perfumes," Mayotte's harvests include vanilla, basil, cocoa, ylang-ylang, cloves and cinnamon. A detachment of the French Foreign Legion is stationed on Mayotte and is the French presence in the Indian Ocean.

Andoany, Madagascar
You cannot escape the smell of perfume anywhere on Nosy Be, the largest island off Madagascar's coast. Appropriately, perfume from ylang-ylang flowers is distilled here. It is also a popular Malagasy tourist spot, known for its coral reefs and beaches.

Port Louis, Mauritius
Sega is based largely on African slave music, characterized by pounding rhythms and soulful singing. It has evolved considerably and is performed differently from region to region, depending on local cultural influence.

Antsirabe, Madagascar
Said to have healing powers, the thermal baths in Antsirabe were built in the early 1900s. Take a dip in the baths after exploring crater lakes in the nearby Massif du Ankaratra mountains.

St-Denis, Réunion
On Réunion, sightseeing options include visiting the grave of a pirate, checking out the giant sea turtle farm, or climbing to the moonscaped crater of the still-active volcano Piton de la Fournaise.

Antananarivo, Madagascar
It could be called a bus or a train. The Micheline is a vehicle on rubber wheels that follow steel tracks, built by Michelin in the 1930s. The 19-seater, of which only two remain in Madagascar, still carries passengers from Antananarivo to Toamasina.

Antananarivo, Madagascar
Hanging from trees or dancing on the ground, the lemur, unique to Madagascar and neighboring Indian Ocean islands, is a nocturnal monkey with exceptionally large eyes. It can be seen in several of the national parks and reserves here.

© DeLorme

Scale 1:9,000,000 at map center

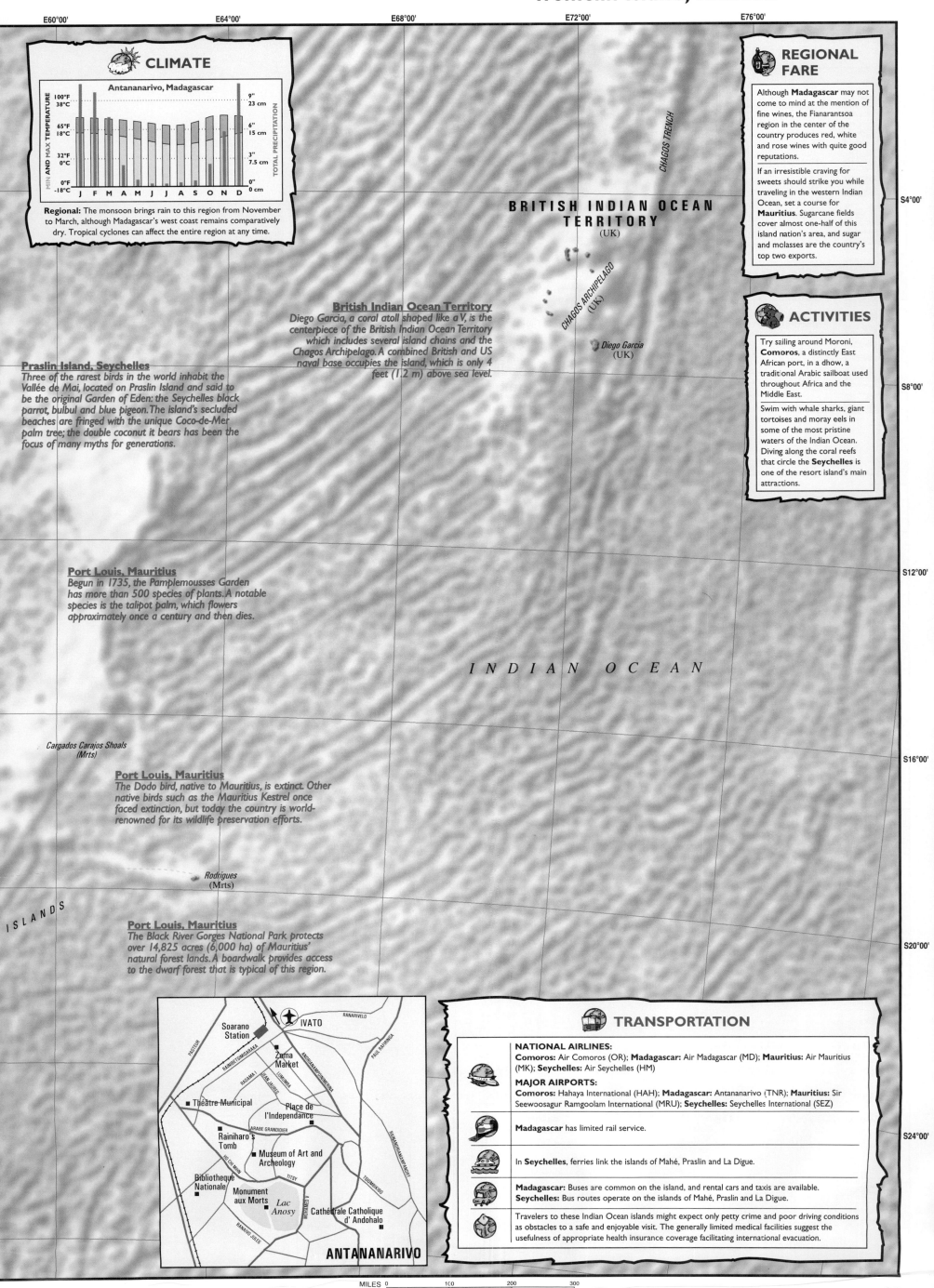

E60°00' E64°00' E68°00' E72°00' E76°00'

S4°00'
S8°00'
S12°00'
S16°00'
S20°00'
S24°00'

CLIMATE

Antananarivo, Madagascar

MIN AND MAX TEMPERATURE

100°F 38°C
65°F 18°C
32°F 0°C
0°F -18°C

J F M A M J J A S O N D

TOTAL PRECIPITATION

9" 23 cm
6" 15 cm
3" 7.5 cm
0" 0 cm

Regional: The monsoon brings rain to this region from November to March, although Madagascar's west coast remains comparatively dry. Tropical cyclones can affect the entire region at any time.

REGIONAL FARE

Although **Madagascar** may not come to mind at the mention of fine wines, the Fianarantsoa region in the center of the country produces red, white and rose wines with quite good reputations.

If an irresistible craving for sweets should strike you while traveling in the western Indian Ocean, set a course for **Mauritius**. Sugarcane fields cover almost one-half of this island nation's area, and sugar and molasses are the country's top two exports.

ACTIVITIES

Try sailing around Moroni, **Comoros**, a distinctly East African port, in a dhow, a traditional Arabic sailboat used throughout Africa and the Middle East.

Swim with whale sharks, giant tortoises and moray eels in some of the most pristine waters of the Indian Ocean. Diving along the coral reefs that circle the **Seychelles** is one of the resort island's main attractions.

BRITISH INDIAN OCEAN TERRITORY
(UK)

CHAGOS TRENCH

CHAGOS ARCHIPELAGO
(UK)

Diego Garcia
(UK)

British Indian Ocean Territory
Diego Garcia, a coral atoll shaped like a V, is the centerpiece of the British Indian Ocean Territory which includes several island chains and the Chagos Archipelago. A combined British and US naval base occupies the island, which is only 4 feet (1.2 m) above sea level.

Praslin Island, Seychelles
Three of the rarest birds in the world inhabit the Vallée de Mai, located on Praslin Island and said to be the original Garden of Eden: the Seychelles black parrot, bulbul and blue pigeon. The island's secluded beaches are fringed with the unique Coco-de-Mer palm tree; the double coconut it bears has been the focus of many myths for generations.

Port Louis, Mauritius
Begun in 1735, the Pamplemousses Garden has more than 500 species of plants. A notable species is the talipot palm, which flowers approximately once a century and then dies.

INDIAN OCEAN

Cargados Carajos Shoals
(Mrts)

Port Louis, Mauritius
The Dodo bird, native to Mauritius, is extinct. Other native birds such as the Mauritius Kestrel once faced extinction, but today the country is world-renowned for its wildlife preservation efforts.

Rodrigues
(Mrts)

ISLANDS

Port Louis, Mauritius
The Black River Gorges National Park protects over 14,825 acres (6,000 ha) of Mauritius' natural forest lands. A boardwalk provides access to the dwarf forest that is typical of this region.

ANTANANARIVO

RANARIVELO
Soarano Station
IVATO
RASETOR
RAINIBETSIMISARAKA
RAJAMA 1
ANDRIANAMPOINIMERINA
PAUL BATHINEA
Zama Market
LUMIMIRA
JEAN RALSES
Théâtre Municipal
Place de l'Independance
ARABE GRANDIDIER
Rainiharo's Tomb
HO CHI MINH
Museum of Art and Archeology
Bibliotheque Nationale
TITSY
Monument aux Morts
RANAVALO JULES
MOHAMAD V
Lac Anosy
RANAVALONANDRIANA
Cathédrale Catholique d' Andohalo
TSIOMBIKIBO

TRANSPORTATION

NATIONAL AIRLINES:
Comoros: Air Comoros (OR); **Madagascar:** Air Madagascar (MD); **Mauritius:** Air Mauritius (MK); **Seychelles:** Air Seychelles (HM)

MAJOR AIRPORTS:
Comoros: Hahaya International (HAH); **Madagascar:** Antananarivo (TNR); **Mauritius:** Sir Seewoosagur Ramgoolam International (MRU); **Seychelles:** Seychelles International (SEZ)

Madagascar has limited rail service.

In **Seychelles**, ferries link the islands of Mahé, Praslin and La Digue.

Madagascar: Buses are common on the island, and rental cars and taxis are available.
Seychelles: Bus routes operate on the islands of Mahé, Praslin and La Digue.

Travelers to these Indian Ocean islands might expect only petty crime and poor driving conditions as obstacles to a safe and enjoyable visit. The generally limited medical facilities suggest the usefulness of appropriate health insurance coverage facilitating international evacuation.

MILES 0   100   200   300
KILOMETERS 0   100   200   300   400   500

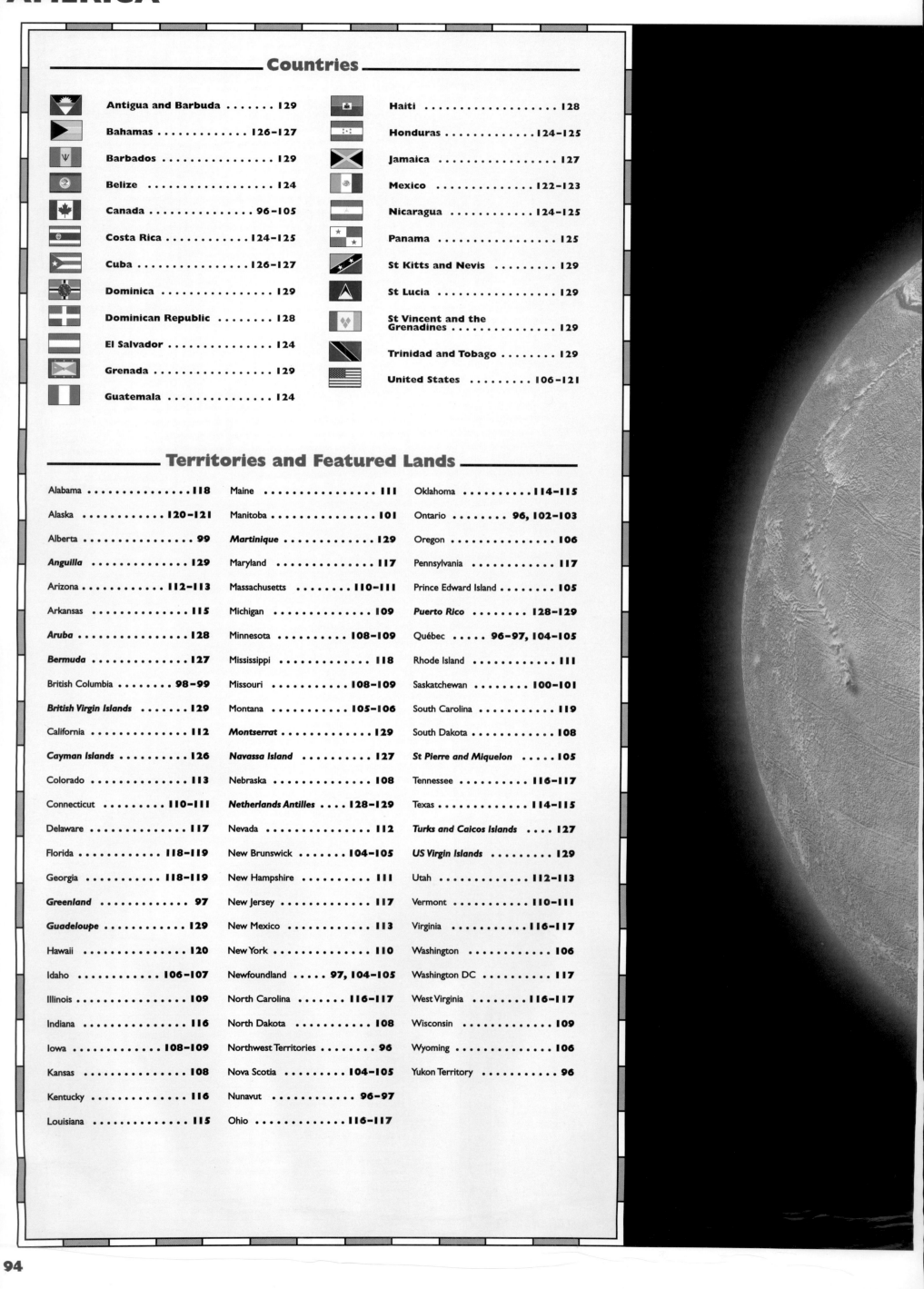

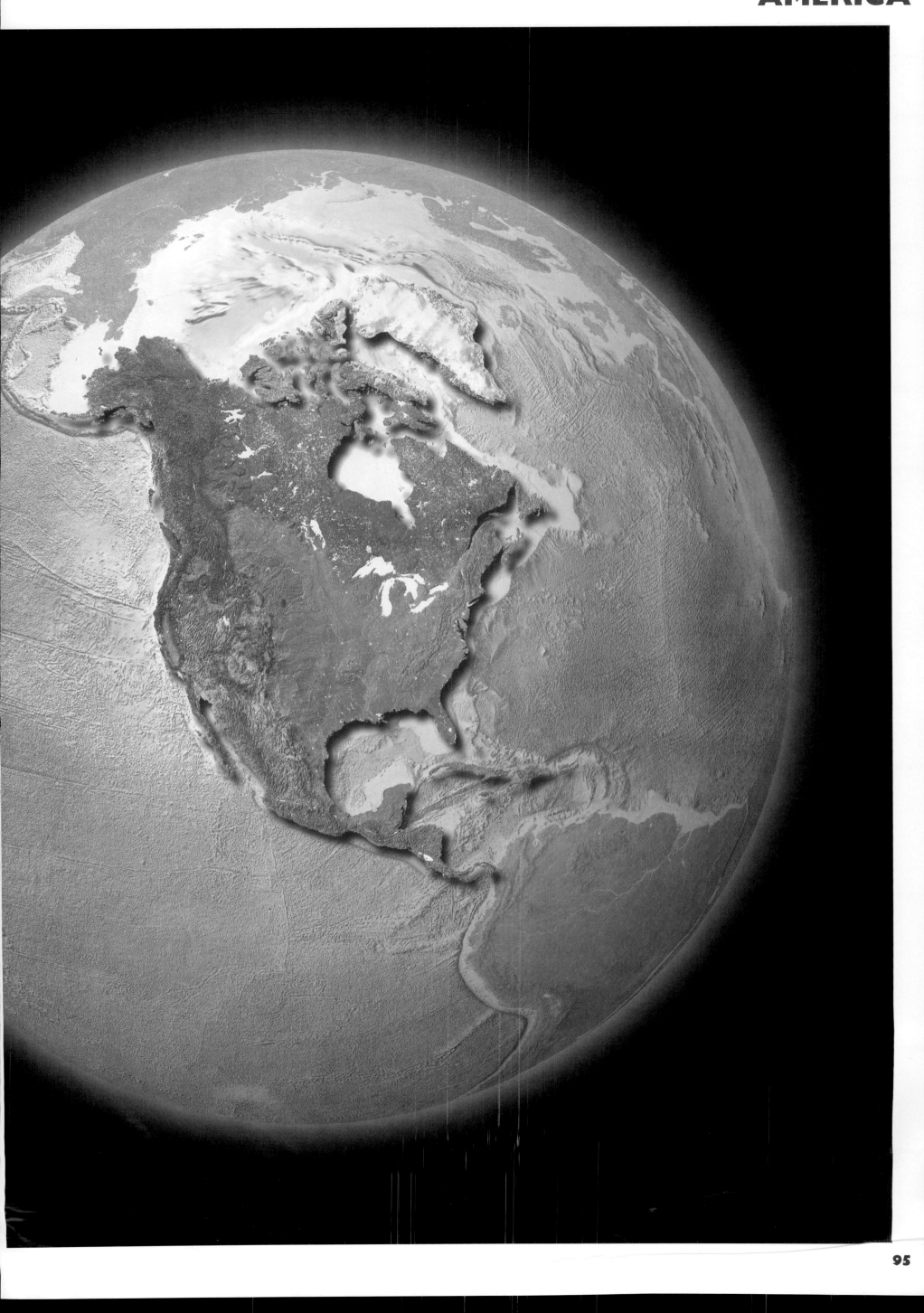

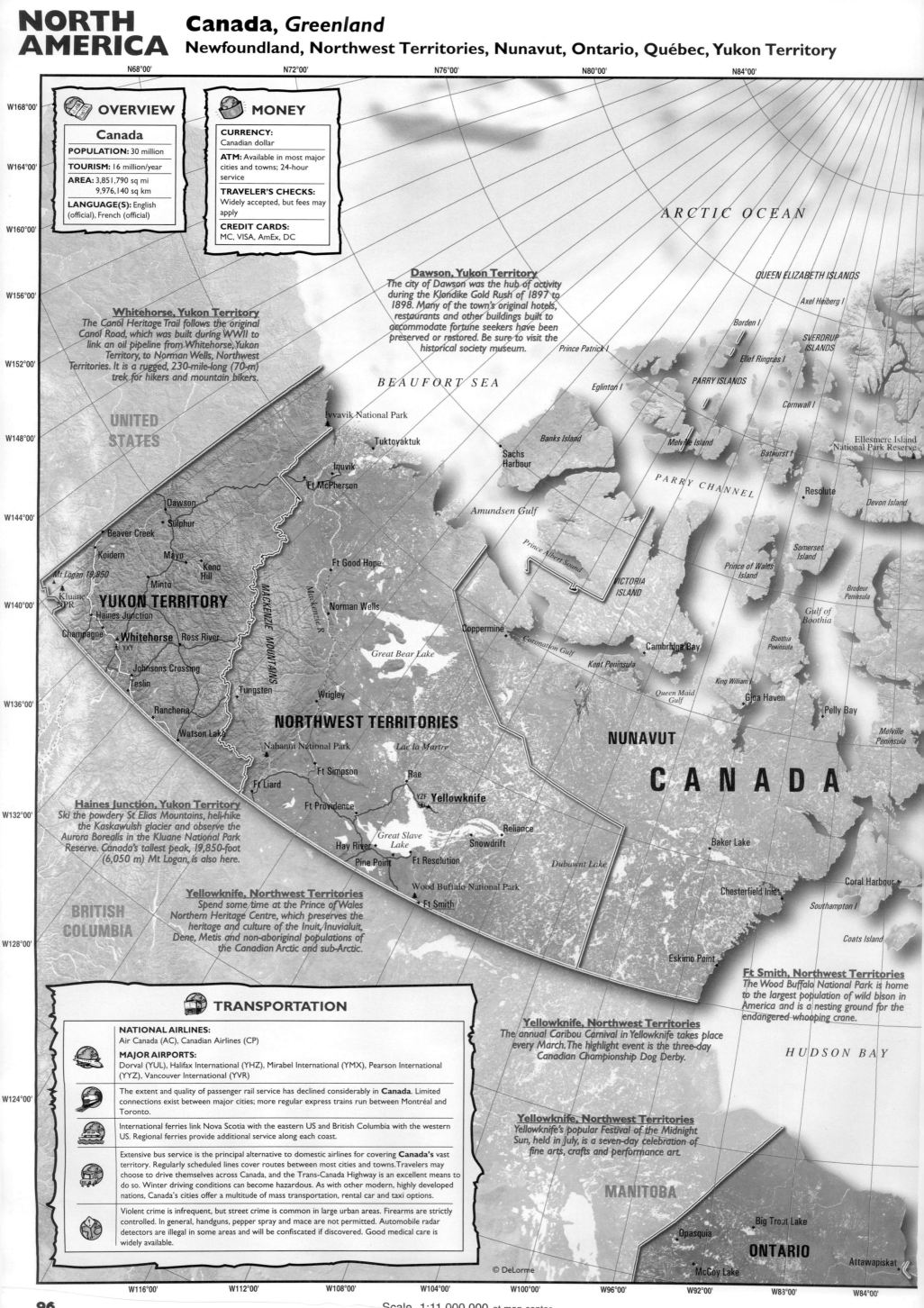

Scale 1:11,000,000 at map center

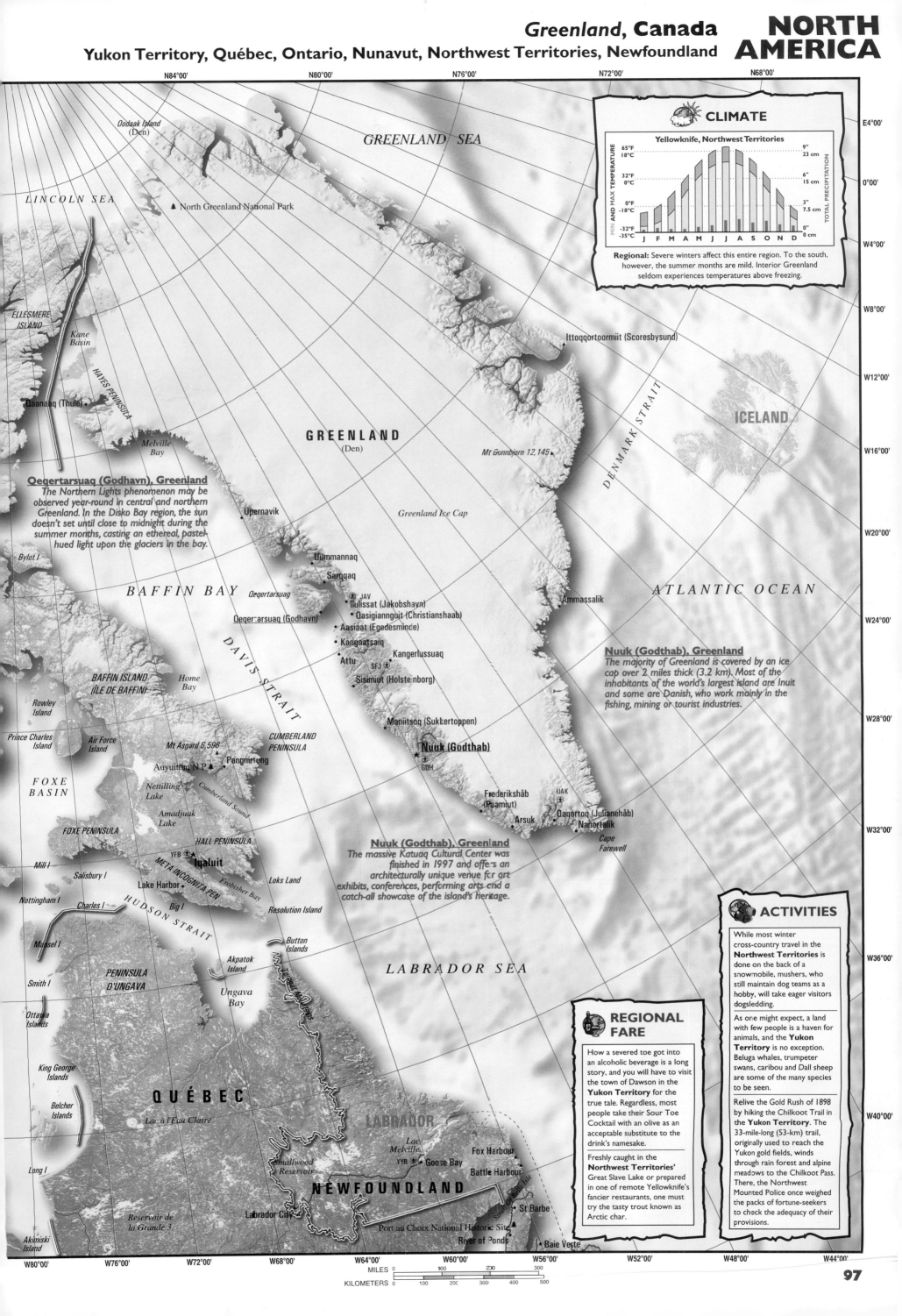

GREENLAND SEA

LINCOLN SEA

Oodaak Island (Den)

⚲ North Greenland National Park

CLIMATE

Yellowknife, Northwest Territories

Regional: Severe winters affect this entire region. To the south, however, the summer months are mild. Interior Greenland seldom experiences temperatures above freezing.

ELLESMERE ISLAND

Kane Basin

Qaanaaq (Thule)

HAYES PENINSULA

Melville Bay

Ittoqqortoormiit (Scoresbysund)

GREENLAND (Den)

Mt Gunnbjorn 12,145 ▲

DENMARK STRAIT

ICELAND

Qeqertarsuaq (Godhavn), Greenland
The Northern Lights phenomenon may be observed year-round in central and northern Greenland. In the Disko Bay region, the sun doesn't set until close to midnight during the summer months, casting an ethereal, pastel-hued light upon the glaciers in the bay.

Upernavik

Greenland Ice Cap

Bylot I

BAFFIN BAY

Uummannaq

Sarqaq

Qeqertarsuaq

Qeqertarsuaq (Godhavn)

● JAV
● Ilulissat (Jakobshavn)
● Qasigianguit (Christianshaab)
● Aasiaat (Egedesminde)
● Kangaatsiaq

Attu
● Kangerlussuaq

SFJ

Sisimiut (Holsteinborg)

ATLANTIC OCEAN

Ammassalik

DAVIS STRAIT

BAFFIN ISLAND (ÎLE DE BAFFIN)

Home Bay

Rowley Island

Prince Charles Island

Air Force Island

Mt Asgard 6,598 ▲

CUMBERLAND PENINSULA

Pangnirtung

Auyuittuq N P ▲

Nuuk (Godthab), Greenland
The majority of Greenland is covered by an ice cap over 2 miles thick (3.2 km). Most of the inhabitants of the world's largest island are Inuit and some are Danish, who work mainly in the fishing, mining or tourist industries.

Maniitsoq (Sukkertoppen)

Nuuk (Godthab) ✦
GOH

FOXE BASIN

Nettilling Lake

Amadjuak Lake

FOXE PENINSULA

Cumberland Sound

HALL PENINSULA

Mill I

Salisbury I

YFB ✦ ★ **Iqaluit**

META INCOGNITA PEN.

Lake Harbor

Frobisher Bay

Loks Land

Frederikshåb (Paamiut)

UAK

Qaqortoq (Julianehåb)

Arsuk

Nanortalik

Cape Farewell

Nottingham I

HUDSON STRAIT

Charles I

Big I

Resolution Island

Nuuk (Godthab), Greenland
The massive Katuaq Cultural Center was finished in 1997 and offers an architecturally unique venue for art exhibits, conferences, performing arts and a catch-all showcase of the island's heritage.

Mansel I

Button Islands

Smith I

PENINSULA D'UNGAVA

Akpatok Island

LABRADOR SEA

Ottawa Islands

Ungava Bay

ACTIVITIES

While most winter cross-country travel in the **Northwest Territories** is done on the back of a snowmobile, mushers, who still maintain dog teams as a hobby, will take eager visitors dogsledding.

King George Islands

Belcher Islands

REGIONAL FARE

How a severed toe got into an alcoholic beverage is a long story, and you will have to visit the town of Dawson in the **Yukon Territory** for the true tale. Regardless, most people take their Sour Toe Cocktail with an olive as an acceptable substitute to the drink's namesake.

As one might expect, a land with few people is a haven for animals, and the **Yukon Territory** is no exception. Beluga whales, trumpeter swans, caribou and Dall sheep are some of the many species to be seen.

QUÉBEC

Long I

Lac à l'Eau Claire

LABRADOR

Lac Melville

Fox Harbour

Freshly caught in the **Northwest Territories'** Great Slave Lake or prepared in one of remote Yellowknife's fancier restaurants, one must try the tasty trout known as Arctic char.

Relive the Gold Rush of 1898 by hiking the Chilkoot Trail in the **Yukon Territory**. The 33-mile-long (53-km) trail, originally used to reach the Yukon gold fields, winds through rain forest and alpine meadows to the Chilkoot Pass. There, the Northwest Mounted Police once weighed the packs of fortune-seekers to check the adequacy of their provisions.

YYR ✦ ★ Goose Bay

Battle Harbour

Akimiski Island

Smallwood Reservoir

NEWFOUNDLAND

St Barbe

Reservoir de la Grande 3

Labrador City

Port au Choix National Historic Site

River of Ponds

Baie Verte

MILES 0   100   200   300

KILOMETERS 0 100 200 300 400 500

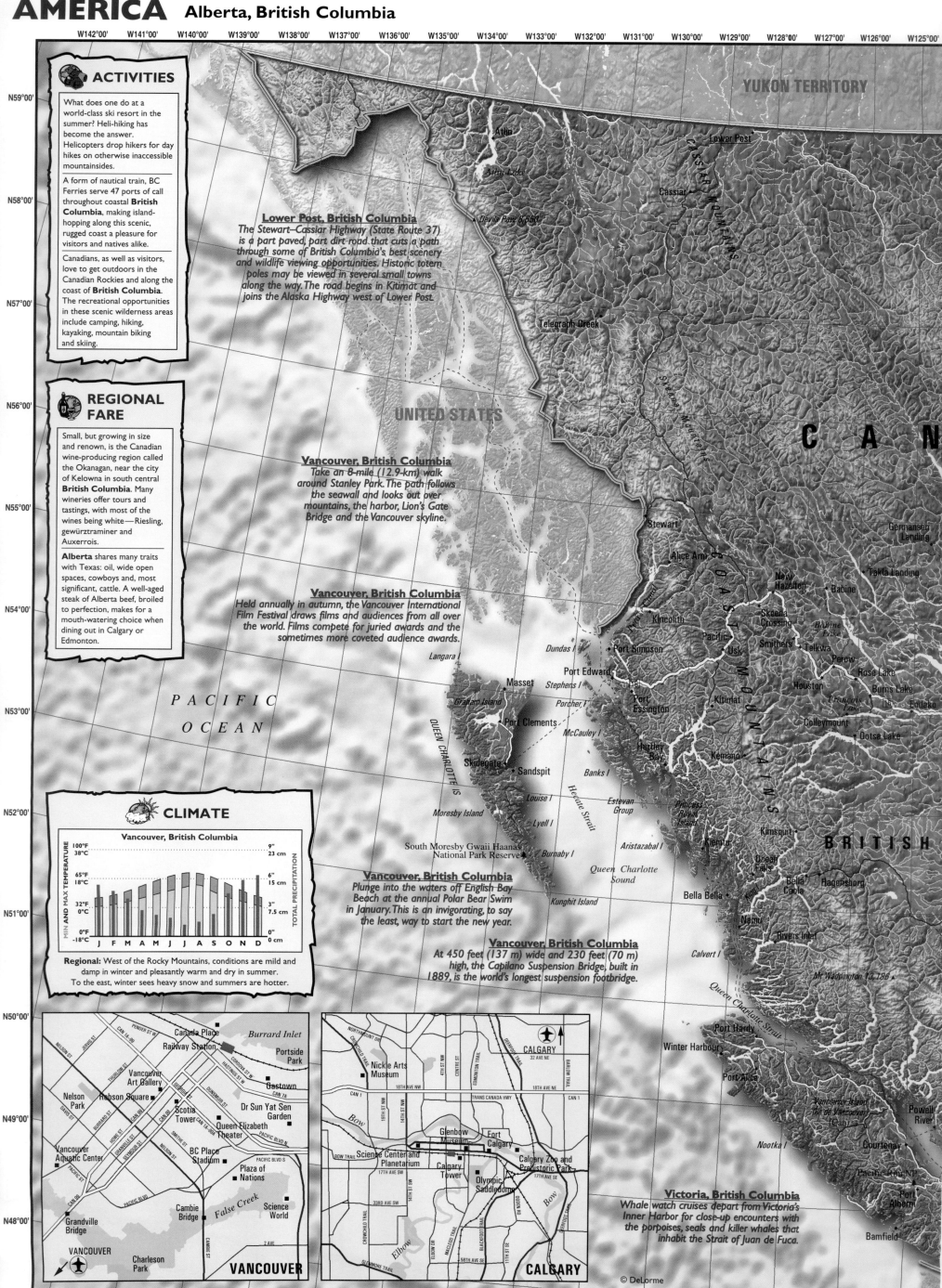

ACTIVITIES

What does one do at a world-class ski resort in the summer? Heli-hiking has become the answer. Helicopters drop hikers for day hikes on otherwise inaccessible mountainsides.

A form of nautical train, BC Ferries serve 47 ports of call throughout coastal **British Columbia**, making island-hopping along this scenic, rugged coast a pleasure for visitors and natives alike.

Canadians, as well as visitors, love to get outdoors in the Canadian Rockies and along the coast of **British Columbia**. The recreational opportunities in these scenic wilderness areas include camping, hiking, kayaking, mountain biking and skiing.

REGIONAL FARE

Small, but growing in size and renown, is the Canadian wine-producing region called the Okanagan, near the city of Kelowna in south central **British Columbia**. Many wineries offer tours and tastings, with most of the wines being white—Riesling, gewürztraminer and Auxerrois.

Alberta shares many traits with Texas: oil, wide open spaces, cowboys and, most significant, cattle. A well-aged steak of Alberta beef, broiled to perfection, makes for a mouth-watering choice when dining out in Calgary or Edmonton.

Lower Post, British Columbia
The Stewart–Cassiar Highway (State Route 37) is a part paved, part dirt road that cuts a path through some of British Columbia's best scenery and wildlife viewing opportunities. Historic totem poles may be viewed in several small towns along the way. The road begins in Kitimat and joins the Alaska Highway west of Lower Post.

Vancouver, British Columbia
Take an 8-mile (12.9-km) walk around Stanley Park. The path follows the seawall and looks out over mountains, the harbor, Lion's Gate Bridge and the Vancouver skyline.

Vancouver, British Columbia
Held annually in autumn, the Vancouver International Film Festival draws films and audiences from all over the world. Films compete for juried awards and the sometimes more coveted audience awards.

Vancouver, British Columbia
Plunge into the waters off English Bay Beach at the annual Polar Bear Swim in January. This is an invigorating, to say the least, way to start the new year.

Vancouver, British Columbia
At 450 feet (137 m) wide and 230 feet (70 m) high, the Capilano Suspension Bridge, built in 1889, is the world's longest suspension footbridge.

Victoria, British Columbia
Whale watch cruises depart from Victoria's Inner Harbor for close-up encounters with the porpoises, seals and killer whales that inhabit the Strait of Juan de Fuca.

CLIMATE

Vancouver, British Columbia

Regional: West of the Rocky Mountains, conditions are mild and damp in winter and pleasantly warm and dry in summer. To the east, winter sees heavy snow and summers are hotter.

© DeLorme

Scale 1:4,000,000 at map center

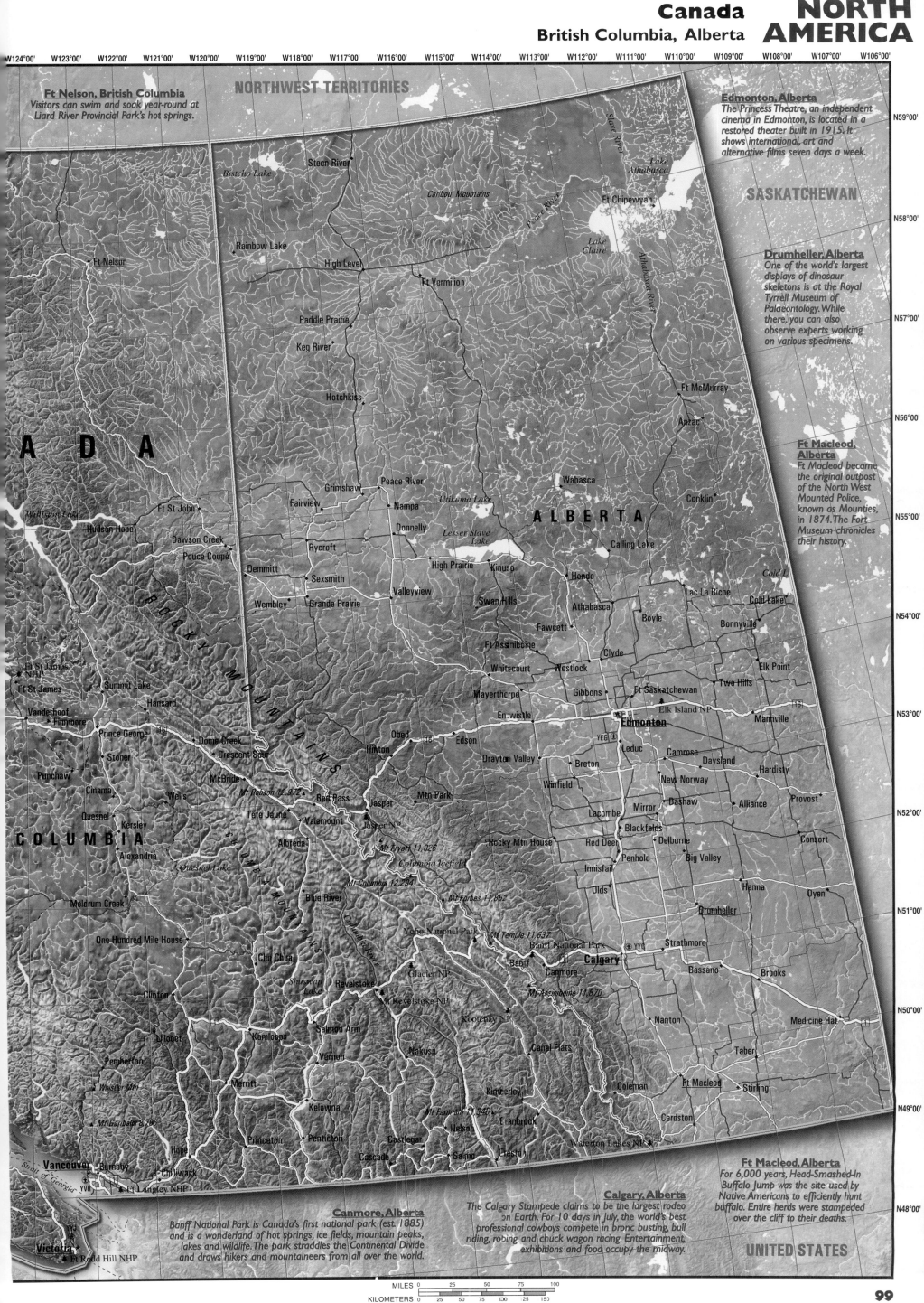

W124°00' W123°00' W122°00' W121°00' W120°00' W119°00' W118°00' W117°00' W116°00' W115°00' W114°00' W113°00' W112°00' W111°00' W110°00' W109°00' W108°00' W107°00' W106°00'

NORTHWEST TERRITORIES

Ft Nelson, British Columbia
Visitors can swim and soak year-round at
Liard River Provincial Park's hot springs.

Edmonton, Alberta
The Princess Theatre, an independent
cinema in Edmonton, is located in a
restored theater built in 1915. It
shows international, art and
alternative films seven days a week.

SASKATCHEWAN

Drumheller, Alberta
One of the world's largest
displays of dinosaur
skeletons is at the Royal
Tyrrell Museum of
Palaeontology. While
there, you can also
observe experts working
on various specimens.

**Ft Macleod,
Alberta**
Ft Macleod became
the original outpost
of the North West
Mounted Police,
known as Mounties,
in 1874. The Fort
Museum chronicles
their history.

N59°00'
N58°00'
N57°00'
N56°00'
N55°00'
N54°00'
N53°00'
N52°00'
N51°00'
N50°00'
N49°00'
N48°00'

ALBERTA

COLUMBIA

ROCKY MOUNTAINS

Vancouver
Victoria

Canmore, Alberta
Banff National Park is Canada's first national park (est. 1885)
and is a wonderland of hot springs, ice fields, mountain peaks,
lakes and wildlife. The park straddles the Continental Divide
and draws hikers and mountaineers from all over the world.

Calgary, Alberta
The Calgary Stampede claims to be the largest rodeo
on Earth. For 10 days in July, the world's best
professional cowboys compete in bronc busting, bull
riding, roping and chuck wagon racing. Entertainment,
exhibitions and food occupy the midway.

Ft Macleod, Alberta
For 6,000 years, Head-Smashed-In
Buffalo Jump was the site used by
Native Americans to efficiently hunt
buffalo. Entire herds were stampeded
over the cliff to their deaths.

UNITED STATES

MILES   0   25   50   75   100
KILOMETERS 0 25 50 75 100 125 150

99

W121°00' W120°00' W119°00' W118°00' W117°00' W116°00' W115°00' W114°00' W113°00' W112°00' W111°00' W110°00' W109°00' W108°00' W107°00' W106°00' W105°00' W104°00'

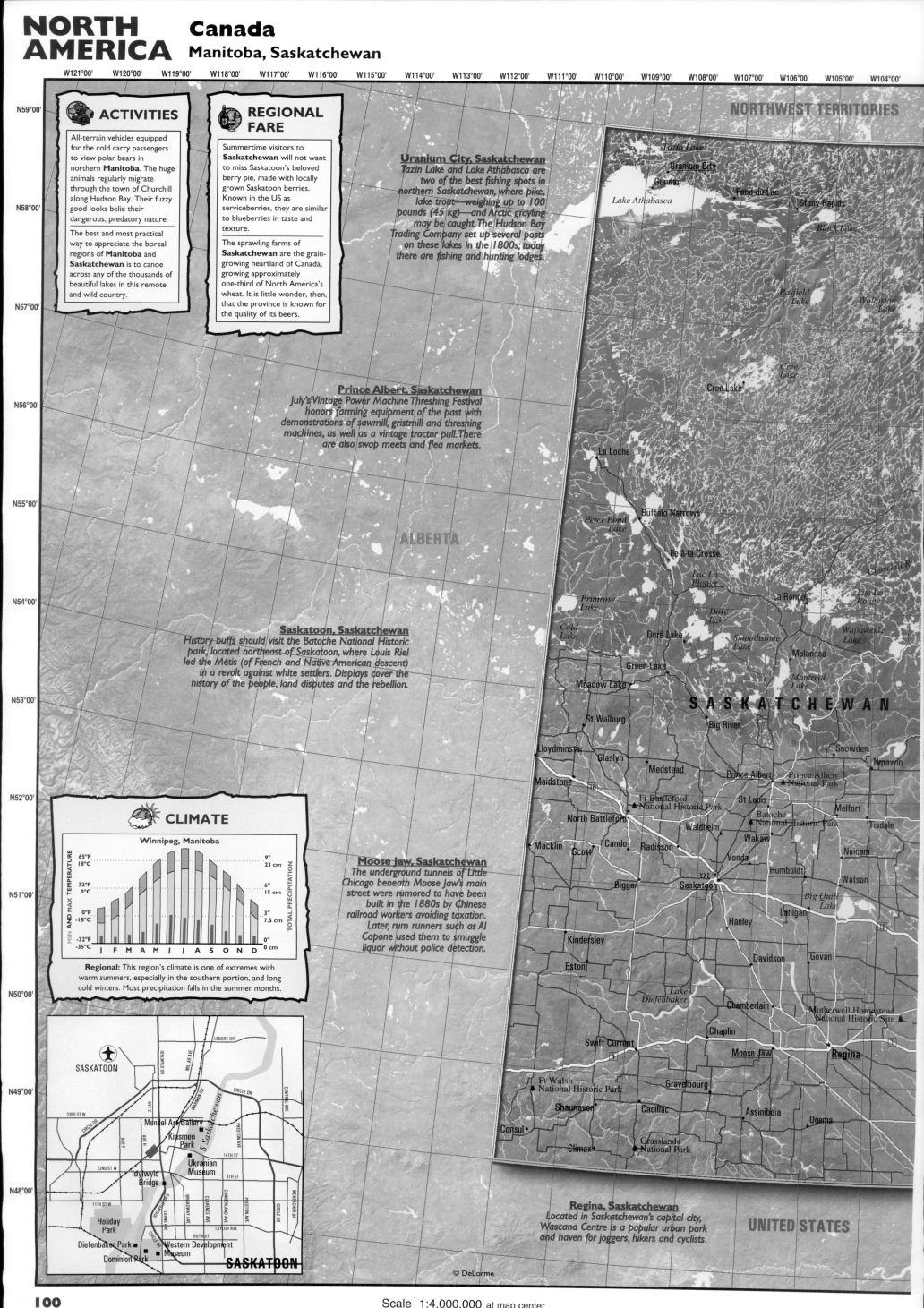

ACTIVITIES

All-terrain vehicles equipped for the cold carry passengers to view polar bears in northern **Manitoba**. The huge animals regularly migrate through the town of Churchill along Hudson Bay. Their fuzzy good looks belie their dangerous, predatory nature.

The best and most practical way to appreciate the boreal regions of **Manitoba** and **Saskatchewan** is to canoe across any of the thousands of beautiful lakes in this remote and wild country.

REGIONAL FARE

Summertime visitors to **Saskatchewan** will not want to miss Saskatoon's beloved berry pie, made with locally grown Saskatoon berries. Known in the US as serviceberries, they are similar to blueberries in taste and texture.

The sprawling farms of **Saskatchewan** are the grain-growing heartland of Canada, growing approximately one-third of North America's wheat. It is little wonder, then, that the province is known for the quality of its beers.

Uranium City, Saskatchewan
Tazin Lake and Lake Athabasca are two of the best fishing spots in northern Saskatchewan, where pike, lake trout—weighing up to 100 pounds (45 kg)—and Arctic grayling may be caught. The Hudson Bay Trading Company set up several posts on these lakes in the 1800s; today there are fishing and hunting lodges.

Prince Albert, Saskatchewan
July's Vintage Power Machine Threshing Festival honors farming equipment of the past with demonstrations of sawmill, gristmill and threshing machines, as well as a vintage tractor pull. There are also swap meets and flea markets.

Saskatoon, Saskatchewan
History buffs should visit the Batoche National Historic park, located northeast of Saskatoon, where Louis Riel led the Métis (of French and Native American descent) in a revolt against white settlers. Displays cover the history of the people, land disputes and the rebellion.

Moose Jaw, Saskatchewan
The underground tunnels of Little Chicago beneath Moose Jaw's main street were rumored to have been built in the 1880s by Chinese railroad workers avoiding taxation. Later, rum runners such as Al Capone used them to smuggle liquor without police detection.

Regina, Saskatchewan
Located in Saskatchewan's capital city, Wascana Centre is a popular urban park and haven for joggers, hikers and cyclists.

CLIMATE

Winnipeg, Manitoba

MIN AND MAX TEMPERATURE		TOTAL PRECIPITATION
65°F 18°C		9" 23 cm
32°F 0°C		6" 15 cm
0°F -18°C		3" 7.5 cm
-32°F -35°C	J F M A M J J A S O N D	0" 0 cm

Regional: This region's climate is one of extremes with warm summers, especially in the southern portion, and long cold winters. Most precipitation falls in the summer months.

SASKATOON

SASKATOON

33RD ST W
LENORE DR
IDYLWYLD DR
MILLAR AVE
WANUSKEWIN RD
CIRCLE DR
CENTRAL AVE
Mendel Art Gallery
Kinsmen Park
22ND ST W
Idylwyld Bridge
Ukranian Museum
AVE C
AVE P
AVE H
11TH ST W
Holiday Park
Diefenbaker Park
Dominion Park
Western Development Museum
S Saskatchewan
PRESTON AVE
8TH ST
14TH ST
BROADWAY AVE
LORNE AVE
CLARENCE AVE
CUMBERLAND AVE
RUTH ST
TAYLOR AVE
PRESTON AVE
CIRCLE DR
McKERCHER DR

Map labels

NORTHWEST TERRITORIES

Tazin Lake
Uranium City
Gunnar
Lake Athabasca
Fond-du-Lac
Stony Rapids
Black Lake
Pasfield Lake
Wollaston Lake
Cree Lake
Cree Lake
La Loche
Buffalo Narrows
Peter Pond Lake
Ile-à-la-Crosse
Churchill R
Lac La Plonge
La Ronge
Lac La Ronge
ALBERTA
Primrose Lake
Doré Lake
Doré Lake
Smoothstone Lake
Wapawekka Lake
Cold Lake
Green Lake
Molanosa
Montreal Lake
Meadow Lake
SASKATCHEWAN
St Walburg
Big River
Snowden
Lloydminster
Glaslyn
Medstead
Prince Albert
Prince Albert National Park
Nipawin
Maidstone
Ft Battleford National Historic Park
St Louis
Melfort
North Battleford
Waldheim
Batoche National Historic Park
Tisdale
Macklin
Scott
Cando
Radisson
Wakaw
Naicam
Biggar
Vonda
YXE
Saskatoon
Humboldt
Watson
Hanley
Lanigan
Big Quill Lake
Kindersley
Eston
Davidson
Govan
Lake Diefenbaker
Chamberlain
Motherwell Homestead National Historic Site
Chaplin
Swift Current
Moose Jaw
Regina
Ft Walsh National Historic Park
Gravelbourg
Shaunavon
Cadillac
Assiniboia
Consul
Ogema
Climax
Grasslands National Park

© DeLorme

UNITED STATES

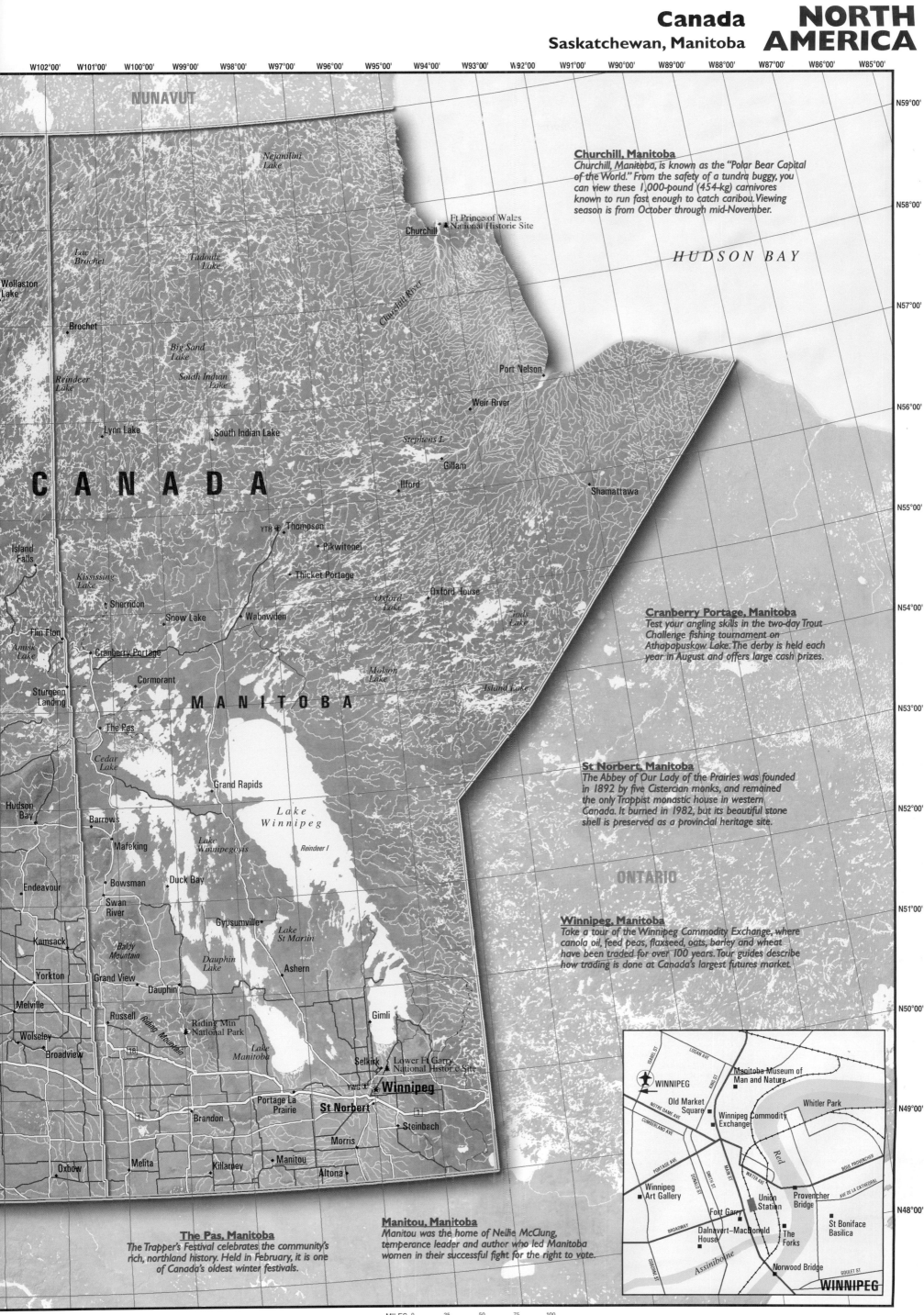

W102°00' W101°00' W100°00' W99°00' W98°00' W97°00' W96°00' W95°00' W94°00' W93°00' W92°00 W91°00' W90°00' W89°00' W88°00' W87°00' W86°00' W85°00'

N59°00'
N58°00'
N57°00'
N56°00'
N55°00'
N54°00'
N53°00'
N52°00'
N51°00'
N50°00'
N49°00'
N48°00'

NUNAVUT

Churchill, Manitoba
Churchill, Manitoba, is known as the "Polar Bear Capital of the World." From the safety of a tundra buggy, you can view these 1,000-pound (454-kg) carnivores known to run fast enough to catch caribou. Viewing season is from October through mid-November.

HUDSON BAY

Nejanilini Lake

Lac Brochet
Tadoule Lake
Wollaston Lake

Ft Prince of Wales National Historic Site
Churchill

Brochet
Big Sand Lake
South Indian Lake
Port Nelson

Reindeer Lake
Weir River

Lynn Lake
South Indian Lake
Stephens I.
Gillam
Ilford
Shamattawa

C A N A D A
YTH Thompson
Pikwitonei
Oxford House

Island Falls
Kississing Lake
Thicket Portage
Oxford Lake
Gods Lake

Sherridon
Snow Lake
Wabowden

Cranberry Portage, Manitoba
Test your angling skills in the two-day Trout Challenge fishing tournament on Athapapuskow Lake. The derby is held each year in August and offers large cash prizes.

Flin Flon
Amisk Lake
Cranberry Portage
Molson Lake
Island Lake

Sturgeon Landing
Cormorant

M A N I T O B A

The Pas

Cedar Lake
Grand Rapids

St Norbert, Manitoba
The Abbey of Our Lady of the Prairies was founded in 1892 by five Cistercian monks, and remained the only Trappist monastic house in western Canada. It burned in 1982, but its beautiful stone shell is preserved as a provincial heritage site.

Hudson Bay
Barrows

Lake Winnipeg

ONTARIO

Mafeking
Lake Winnipegosis
Reindeer I.

Bowsman
Duck Bay

Winnipeg, Manitoba
Take a tour of the Winnipeg Commodity Exchange, where canola oil, feed peas, flaxseed, oats, barley and wheat have been traded for over 100 years. Tour guides describe how trading is done at Canada's largest futures market.

Endeavour
Swan River
Gypsumville
Lake St Martin

Kamsack
Baldy Mountain
Dauphin Lake
Ashern

Yorkton
Grand View
Dauphin

Melville
Russell
Gimli

Wolseley
Riding Mtn National Park
Lake Manitoba

Broadview
Selkirk
Lower Ft Garry National Historic Site

Winnipeg

Portage La Prairie
St Norbert

Brandon
Steinbach

Oxbow
Melita
Killarney
Manitou
Morris
Altona

The Pas, Manitoba
The Trapper's Festival celebrates the community's rich, northland history. Held in February, it is one of Canada's oldest winter festivals.

Manitou, Manitoba
Manitou was the home of Nellie McClung, temperance leader and author who led Manitoba women in their successful fight for the right to vote.

Logan Ave
ISABEL ST
KING ST
Manitoba Museum of Man and Nature
Whitler Park

WINNIPEG
Old Market Square
NOTRE DAME AVE
Winnipeg Commodity Exchange
CUMBERLAND AVE

PORTAGE AVE
MAIN ST
DONALD ST
SMITH ST
Red

Winnipeg Art Gallery
Fort Garry
Union Station
Provencher Bridge
AVE DE LA CATHEDRALE

BROADWAY
Dalnavert-Macdonald House
The Forks
St Boniface Basilica

OSBORNE ST
Assiniboine
Norwood Bridge
GOULET ST

WINNIPEG

MILES 0 25 50 75 100
KILOMETERS 0 25 50 75 100 125 150

Atikokan, Ontario
Paddle through miles and miles of serene wilderness waterways in Quetico Provincial Park—considered by many to be a canoeist's paradise. The interconnected system of lakes and bogs is the northern portion of Minnesota's Boundary Waters Canoe Area.

Thunder Bay, Ontario
Having lost a leg to cancer, Terry Fox ran his "Marathon of Hope" from the Atlantic coast to Thunder Bay to fund cancer research. Originally intending to cross the nation and finish in British Columbia, Fox's run was cut short by a recurrence of the cancer. A year later, in 1982, a section of the Trans-Canadian Highway was named "Terry Fox Courage Highway" in his honor.

Tobermory, Ontario
Take a day trip aboard the MS Chi-Cheemaun (Big Canoe) from Tobermory across Lake Huron to Manitoulin Island, where quaint villages, hiking trails and waterfalls await. The Big Canoe is one of the largest ferries ever built for Great Lakes service.

St Catharines, Ontario
A tradition for over 100 years, the Royal Canadian Henley Regatta is one of the world's premier rowing events. The week-long competition takes place on the placid waters of Martindale Pond.

REGIONAL FARE

Reflecting the diversity of its recent immigrants, Toronto's restaurants cater to tastes from every continent. Whether you crave Caribbean, Indonesian, Irish, Japanese, Lebanese, Portugese, Tibetan or West African cuisine, chefs in this cosmopolitan city more than likely can satisfy your hunger.

The city of Thunder Bay is a center for the production of Cheddar, Gouda and cottage cheeses originally introduced to the area by Dutch arrivals. Notably, the largest population of Finns outside of Finland have joined the Dutch immigrants in the cheese trade of Thunder Bay.

ACTIVITIES

Fish for Arctic grayling and northern pike at numerous roadside access points across Canada. A valid fishing license is required.

Walk on air at the world's tallest free-standing structure. The CN Tower in Toronto, **Ontario**, features indoor and outdoor observation decks and a glass floor, 113 stories above the ground.

Boat along sections of the Rideau Canal, built to connect Ottawa on the Ottawa River to Kingston on Lake Ontario 124 miles (200 km) away. In winter, ice skating along the canal's frozen sections within Ottawa affords excellent views of the city.

Scale 1:4,000,000 at map center

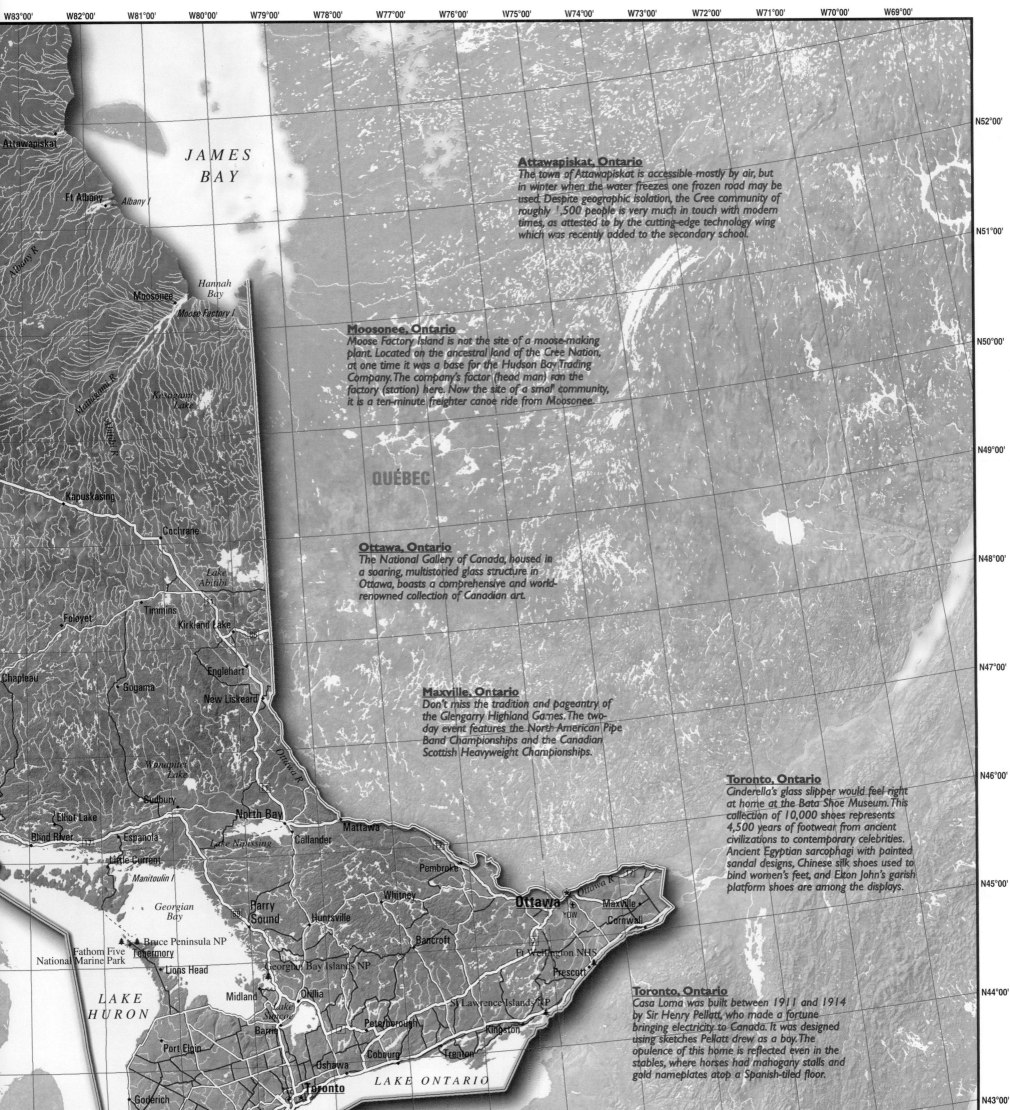

W83°00' **W82°00'** **W81°00'** **W80°00'** **W79°00'** **W78°00'** **W77°00'** **W76°00'** **W75°00'** **W74°00'** **W73°00'** **W72°00'** **W71°00'** **W70°00'** **W69°00'**

N52°00'

N51°00'

N50°00'

N49°00'

N48°00'

N47°00'

N46°00'

N45°00'

N44°00'

N43°00'

N42°00'

N41°00'

JAMES BAY

Attawapiskat

Ft Albany • Albany I
Albany R

Hannah Bay
Moosonee •
Moose Factory I

Kapuskasing •

Cochrane •

QUÉBEC

Foleyet •

Timmins •
Kirkland Lake •

Chapleau •

Gogama •

New Liskeard •

Wanapitei Lake

Elliot Lake •
Sudbury •

Blind River •
North Bay •

Espanola •
Lake Nipissing
Little Current •
Callander •
Mattawa

Manitoulin I

Pembroke •

Whitney •

Georgian Bay

Parry Sound •
Huntsville •

Bruce Peninsula NP

Fathom Five
National Marine Park
Tobermory

Lions Head •

Georgian Bay Islands NP

Bancroft •

Orillia •

Midland •
Lake Simcoe

Ottawa
YOW
Maxville •
Cornwall •

Ft Wellington NHS
Prescott •

St Lawrence Islands NP

LAKE HURON

Port Elgin •

Barrie •

Peterborough •

Kingston •

Goderich •

Oshawa •

Cobourg •

Trenton •

Waterloo • Woodside NHS
Stratford •
Hamilton •
George NHS

Toronto

LAKE ONTARIO

Sarnia •
London •
Brantford •

St Catherines •
Niagara Falls

St Thomas •

UNITED STATES

Wallaceburg •

Windsor •
Lake St Clair
Chatham •

Leamington •
Point Pelee NP

LAKE ERIE

Attawapiskat, Ontario
The town of Attawapiskat is accessible mostly by air, but in winter when the water freezes one frozen road may be used. Despite geographic isolation, the Cree community of roughly 1,500 people is very much in touch with modern times, as attested to by the cutting-edge technology wing which was recently added to the secondary school.

Moosonee, Ontario
Moose Factory Island is not the site of a moose-making plant. Located on the ancestral land of the Cree Nation, at one time it was a base for the Hudson Bay Trading Company. The company's factor (head man) ran the factory (station) here. Now the site of a small community, it is a ten-minute freighter canoe ride from Moosonee.

Ottawa, Ontario
The National Gallery of Canada, housed in a soaring, multistoried glass structure in Ottawa, boasts a comprehensive and world-renowned collection of Canadian art.

Maxville, Ontario
Don't miss the tradition and pageantry of the Glengarry Highland Games. The two-day event features the North American Pipe Band Championships and the Canadian Scottish Heavyweight Championships.

Toronto, Ontario
Cinderella's glass slipper would feel right at home at the Bata Shoe Museum. This collection of 10,000 shoes represents 4,500 years of footwear from ancient civilizations to contemporary celebrities. Ancient Egyptian sarcophagi with painted sandal designs, Chinese silk shoes used to bind women's feet, and Elton John's garish platform shoes are among the displays.

Toronto, Ontario
Casa Loma was built between 1911 and 1914 by Sir Henry Pellatt, who made a fortune bringing electricity to Canada. It was designed using sketches Pellatt drew as a boy. The opulence of this home is reflected even in the stables, where horses had mahogany stalls and gold nameplates atop a Spanish-tiled floor.

Niagara Falls, Ontario
Although commercialized and enhanced by artificial lighting, Niagara Falls is still a natural wonder worth seeing any time of year. It is said that the site's popularity as a honeymoon location began when Napoleon's brother brought his bride here.

© DeLorme

CLIMATE

Toronto, Ontario

MIN AND MAX TEMPERATURE
100°F 38°C
65°F 18°C
32°F 0°C
0°F -18°C

TOTAL PRECIPITATION
9" 23 cm
6" 15 cm
3" 7.5 cm
0" 0 cm

J F M A M J J A S O N D

Regional: Cold winters give way to pleasant summer weather across this region. Precipitation is moderate throughout the year. Further north, the winter conditions are much more severe.

MILES 0 25 50 75 100
KILOMETERS 0 25 50 75 100 125 150

Montréal (Montreal), Québec
In a form of metropolitan Darwinism, Montreal has adapted to the chilly northern climate by creating a vast network of offices, restaurants, shops, theaters and hotels. The network is connected via the Métro and covered passageways, and is known as the "Underground City."

Québec, Québec
The first North American city to be declared a UNESCO World Heritage site, Québec is also the only walled city in North America. The restored historic architecture of the Old City, complete with its stone stairways, cobblestone streets and breathtaking views, gives the city a distinctly European air.

Edmundston, New Brunswick
Tired of the bickering between the US and Canada over the exact location of the border, citizens of Edmundston declared themselves Brayons who resided in the République de Madawaska. Edmundston, on the Maine–Canada border, is still its capital.

Sackville, New Brunswick
There are few places in the world with tides more dramatic than the Bay of Fundy. This is made apparent by the Hopewell Rocks, five-story-tall "flowerpots" carved by the sea. When the tide is in they become islands.

Scale 1:4,000,000 at map center

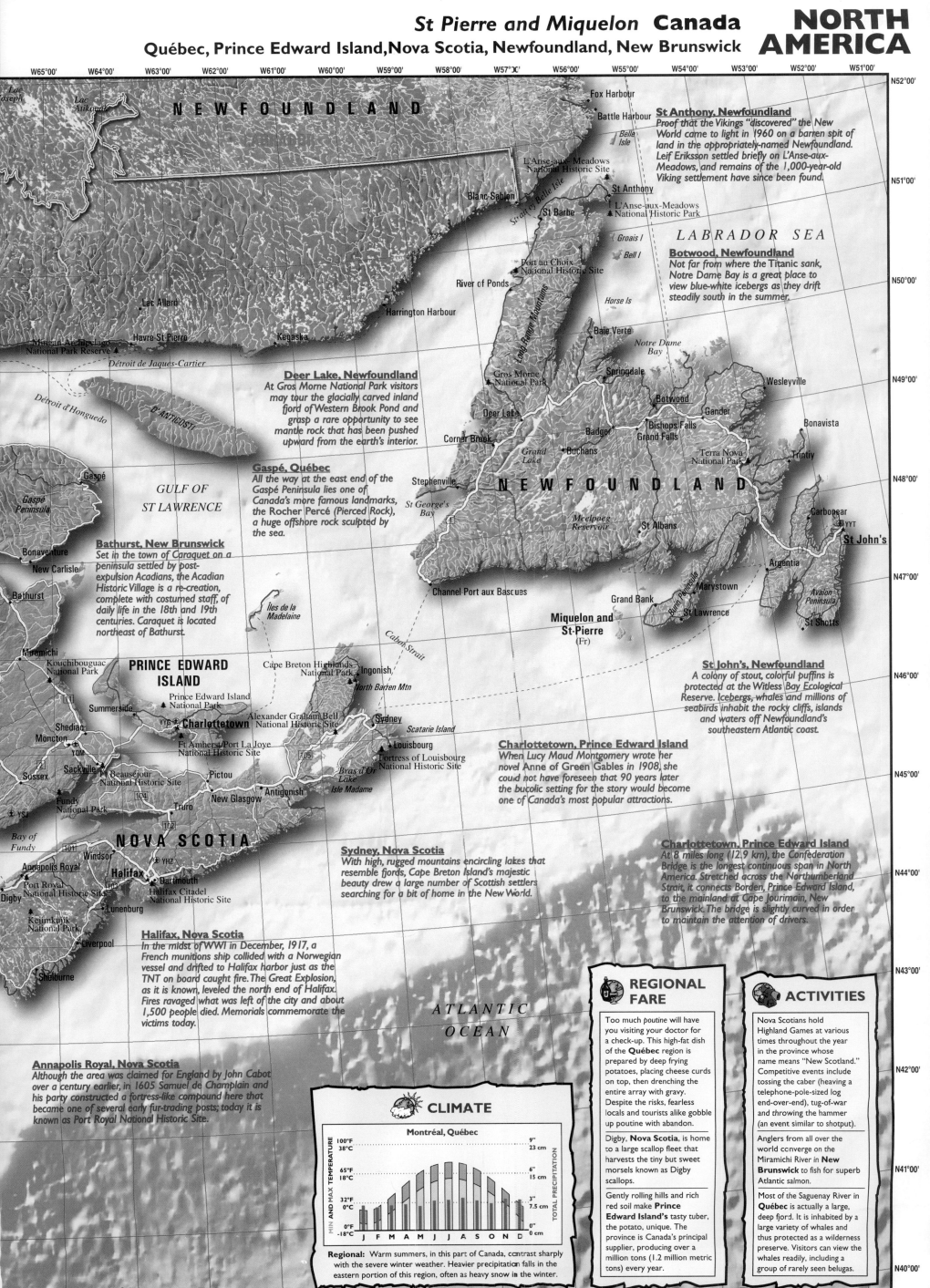

St Anthony, Newfoundland
Proof that the Vikings "discovered" the New World came to light in 1960 on a barren spit of land in the appropriately-named Newfoundland. Leif Eriksson settled briefly on L'Anse-aux-Meadows, and remains of the 1,000-year-old Viking settlement have since been found.

Botwood, Newfoundland
Not far from where the Titanic sank, Notre Dame Bay is a great place to view blue-white icebergs as they drift steadily south in the summer.

Deer Lake, Newfoundland
At Gros Morne National Park visitors may tour the glacially carved inland fjord of Western Brook Pond and grasp a rare opportunity to see mantle rock that has been pushed upward from the earth's interior.

Gaspé, Québec
All the way at the east end of the Gaspé Peninsula lies one of Canada's more famous landmarks, the Rocher Percé (Pierced Rock), a huge offshore rock sculpted by the sea.

Bathurst, New Brunswick
Set in the town of Caraquet on a peninsula settled by post-expulsion Acadians, the Acadian Historic Village is a re-creation, complete with costumed staff, of daily life in the 18th and 19th centuries. Caraquet is located northeast of Bathurst.

St John's, Newfoundland
A colony of stout, colorful puffins is protected at the Witless Bay Ecological Reserve. Icebergs, whales and millions of seabirds inhabit the rocky cliffs, islands and waters off Newfoundland's southeastern Atlantic coast.

Charlottetown, Prince Edward Island
When Lucy Maud Montgomery wrote her novel Anne of Green Gables in 1908, she could not have foreseen that 90 years later the bucolic setting for the story would become one of Canada's most popular attractions.

Charlottetown, Prince Edward Island
At 8 miles long (12.9 km), the Confederation Bridge is the longest continuous span in North America. Stretched across the Northumberland Strait, it connects Borden, Prince Edward Island, to the mainland at Cape Jourimain, New Brunswick. The bridge is slightly curved in order to maintain the attention of drivers.

Sydney, Nova Scotia
With high, rugged mountains encircling lakes that resemble fjords, Cape Breton Island's majestic beauty drew a large number of Scottish settlers searching for a bit of home in the New World.

Halifax, Nova Scotia
In the midst of WWI in December, 1917, a French munitions ship collided with a Norwegian vessel and drifted to Halifax harbor just as the TNT on board caught fire. The Great Explosion, as it is known, leveled the north end of Halifax. Fires ravaged what was left of the city and about 1,500 people died. Memorials commemorate the victims today.

Annapolis Royal, Nova Scotia
Although the area was claimed for England by John Cabot over a century earlier, in 1605 Samuel de Champlain and his party constructed a fortress-like compound here that became one of several early fur-trading posts; today it is known as Port Royal National Historic Site.

REGIONAL FARE

Too much poutine will have you visiting your doctor for a check-up. This high-fat dish of the **Québec** region is prepared by deep frying potatoes, placing cheese curds on top, then drenching the entire array with gravy. Despite the risks, fearless locals and tourists alike gobble up poutine with abandon.

Digby, **Nova Scotia**, is home to a large scallop fleet that harvests the tiny but sweet morsels known as Digby scallops.

Gently rolling hills and rich red soil make **Prince Edward Island's** tasty tuber, the potato, unique. The province is Canada's principal supplier, producing over a million tons (1.2 million metric tons) every year.

ACTIVITIES

Nova Scotians hold Highland Games at various times throughout the year in the province whose name means "New Scotland." Competitive events include tossing the caber (heaving a telephone-pole-sized log end-over-end), tug-of-war and throwing the hammer (an event similar to shotput).

Anglers from all over the world converge on the Miramichi River in **New Brunswick** to fish for superb Atlantic salmon.

Most of the Saguenay River in **Québec** is actually a large, deep fjord. It is inhabited by a large variety of whales and thus protected as a wilderness preserve. Visitors can view the whales readily, including a group of rarely seen belugas.

CLIMATE

Montréal, Québec

Regional: Warm summers, in this part of Canada, contrast sharply with the severe winter weather. Heavier precipitation falls in the eastern portion of this region, often as heavy snow in the winter.

© DeLorme

MILES 0 25 50 75 100
KILOMETERS 0 25 50 75 100 125 150

United States
Idaho, Montana, Oregon, Washington, Wyoming

OVERVIEW

United States

POPULATION: 268 million

TOURISM: 46 million/year

AREA: 3,717,794 sq mi
9,629,091 sq km

LANGUAGE(S): English, Spanish, many other languages in native and ethnic communities

MONEY

CURRENCY: US dollar

ATM: Widespread availability; 24-hour service

TRAVELER'S CHECKS: Accepted, but fees may apply

CREDIT CARDS: MC, VISA, AmEx, DC

Port Angeles, Washington
The gorgeous, rugged Olympic Mountains are so sky-high, they literally block the path of most Pacific Ocean storms. Rainfall on the west side is up to 200 inches (508 cm) per year; on the east side it drops to 20 inches (51 cm).

Seattle, Washington
Ye Olde Curiosity Shop caters to the American fascination with the bizarre. Shrunken heads, a mummy, the Lord's Prayer inscribed on a grain of rice, and a two-headed cow are among the many oddities collected and displayed at this waterfront shop since 1899.

Olympia, Washington
Each August, Bon Odori Festival participants dance in traditional Japanese dress such as kimonos and hopi coats (short coats similar to kimono tops). Dancers use fans and castinets in this heritage celebration.

Vancouver, Washington
Join the search for the only skyjacker who has escaped from the FBI: D. B. Cooper. There has been no trace of Cooper since 1971, when he hijacked a flight from Portland, Oregon to Seattle, and parachuted off the 727 jet with $200,000 in tow.

PACIFIC OCEAN

Vancouver, Washington
When the hunt for D. B. Cooper grows tiresome, head for "Bigfoot Country" near Lake Merwin, an area of the state haunted by stories of a 9-foot-tall (3-m) hairy creature. Ever since Pacific Indian tribes were the area's only human inhabitants, the sasquatch (a Native American word for "hairy giant") has eluded all attempts to confirm its existence.

Weiser, Idaho
Each summer during the third week in June, several hundred of the nation's best country fiddlers converge on this small town to play until dawn at the National Old-Time Fiddlers' Contest. Bluegrass, country and folk fiddling is expertly performed before enthusiastic crowds.

Klamath Falls, Oregon
Nearly 60,000 arrowheads, countless pottery pieces, carvings and hundreds of miniature guns of Native Americans from all over the continent can be seen at the Favell Museum of Western Art and Indian Artifacts.

Boise, Idaho
It may seem spooky, but Silver City (the "Queen of Ghost Towns"), located southwest of Boise, is a pretty interesting place to visit. Founded in 1863 as a mining town, its population grew to 2,000 before being abandoned when the mine ran out.

Portland, Oregon
See how we've been sold to from the very beginning, at the American Advertising Museum. At one of the only museums in the US dedicated to the history of advertising, exhibits range from radio and television ads to print ads, some dating as far back as the 1680s.

Mitchell, Oregon
Hike through the Painted Hills of Oregon—hills formed by striated volcanic ash deposits in bright red, yellow and brown hues. The hills are located within the John Day Fossil Beds National Monument, where fossilized remains of plants and animals date back to million years.

© DeLorme

Scale 1:5,000,000 at map center

Kalispell, Montana
Glacier National Park is more than its name implies. With only one road, it has 700 miles (1,127 km) of forested trails and the largest grizzly bear population in the lower 48 states. Iceberg Lake, in the middle of the park, is choked with large chunks of ice—even in summertime.

Boulder, Montana
A few defunct gold and uranium mines attract ailing people to bask in radioactive radon gas and drink radioactive water to improve their health. Located in the vicinity of Boulder, radon therapy mines are praised by some as curative of the likes of diabetes, eczema and arthritis.

ACTIVITIES

The Grand Tetons of **Wyoming** challenge climbers with some of the most rugged mountains in the West. Rock climbing can be learned or perfected on Grand Teton itself, for which the range and National Park are named, or on many other peaks nearby.

Windsurfers will find an unusual site to practice their sport in the Columbia River Gorge in **Oregon**. Well known for its strong winds and serious waves, the gorge hosts regular competitions in the difficult conditions to see which surfer can ride the longest into the wind while maintaining balance.

REGIONAL FARE

Where else would there be a Potato Hall of Fame event held every year? **Idaho** grows more potatoes than any other state in the US, and potatoes are a staple on nearly every restaurant menu in the state.

Residents of southeastern **Washington** drink "red beer," an unusual blend of tap beer and tomato juice. Bartenders vary the proportions to suit individual tastes, from five parts beer to one part juice down to two to one, which tastes more like a fruit drink.

They may look like regular clams, but they are usually five times the size. Geoduck clams are found in abundance in the Pacific Northwest, and, with an average weight of nearly 2 pounds (1 kg), each makes a substantial meal.

Bozeman, Montana
Every August Bozeman celebrates the Sweet Pea Festival of the Arts. This full-blown festival of music, arts and crafts features bands, running races and a homegrown parade.

Billings, Montana
In 1876 Cheyenne and Sioux warriors wiped out Colonel George Custer and the 262 men in his command at the Battle of Little Big Horn. This battle was one of the last armed efforts of Northern Plains tribes to resist the encroachment of modern civilization. There is a national cemetery in Crow Agency, south of Billings.

Cheyenne, Wyoming
The Cold War lives on at the F. E. Warren Air Force Base where the nation's largest nuclear and ballistic missile group resides. The Intercontinental Ballistic Missile and Heritage Museum at the base focuses on the history of ICBMs and their central, though mostly symbolic, role in nuclear competition with the former Soviet Union.

Cody, Wyoming
The boardwalks at the Norris Geyser Basin in Yellowstone National Park are not necessarily conducive to a relaxing stroll. They lead through one of the most volatile geothermal areas in North America, with hundreds of hot springs, thermal pools and constantly erupting geysers.

Blackfoot, Idaho
Take a walk on the moon in your shorts and sandals at Craters of the Moon National Monument. The park was opened in 1924 to protect 82,000 sq miles (212,380 sq km) of lava flows, craters, volcanic cones and lava caves. Located in Arco, northeast of Blackfoot.

Guernsey, Wyoming
Register Cliff is a soft sandstone outcropping where thousands of pioneers traveling westward carved their names, intended destinations and dates. This is not far from an area where wagon wheel ruts from mid-1800s Oregon Trail emigration are still starkly visible in the stone.

TRANSPORTATION

NATIONAL AIRLINES: American Airlines (AA), Delta Airlines (DL), United Airlines (UA)

MAJOR AIRPORTS: Dallas/Ft Worth International (DFW), Dulles International (IAD), John F Kennedy International (JFK), Logan International (BOS), Los Angeles International (LAX), Miami International (MIA), O'Hare International (ORD), W B Hartsfield International (ATL) National and regional carriers provide regularly scheduled air service to all parts of the country.

Amtrak runs most of the regularly scheduled passenger trains in the **United States** (aside from regional commuter lines). Information on fares, schedules, stations and routes is provided in publications from Amtrak.

Regional ferry lines operate along the Atlantic and Pacific coasts, especially in Maine and Washington where ships connect the residents of scattered islands to the mainland. Numerous cruise ships depart from major ports for destinations in the **United States**, Canada, Mexico and the Caribbean.

Ground transportation of all types—buses, taxis and rental cars—is readily available for travel within and between most cities and towns. Many larger urban areas have efficient and extensive mass transportation networks and offer hired car services. An interstate highway system of four-lane, divided, limited-access highways connects all major urban areas and traverses the entire country.

Visitors to urban areas should take usual precautions regarding personal security. Driving conditions between cities are good; urban areas are prone to congestion. Good medical services are widely available.

CLIMATE

Seattle, Washington

Regional: The west coast has mild and damp conditions for much of the year, although summers are pleasant. East of the Cascades, winters are more severe, and precipitation is minimal.

107

NORTH AMERICA

United States
Illinois, Iowa, Kansas, Michigan, Minnesota, Missouri, Nebraska
North Dakota, South Dakota, Wisconsin

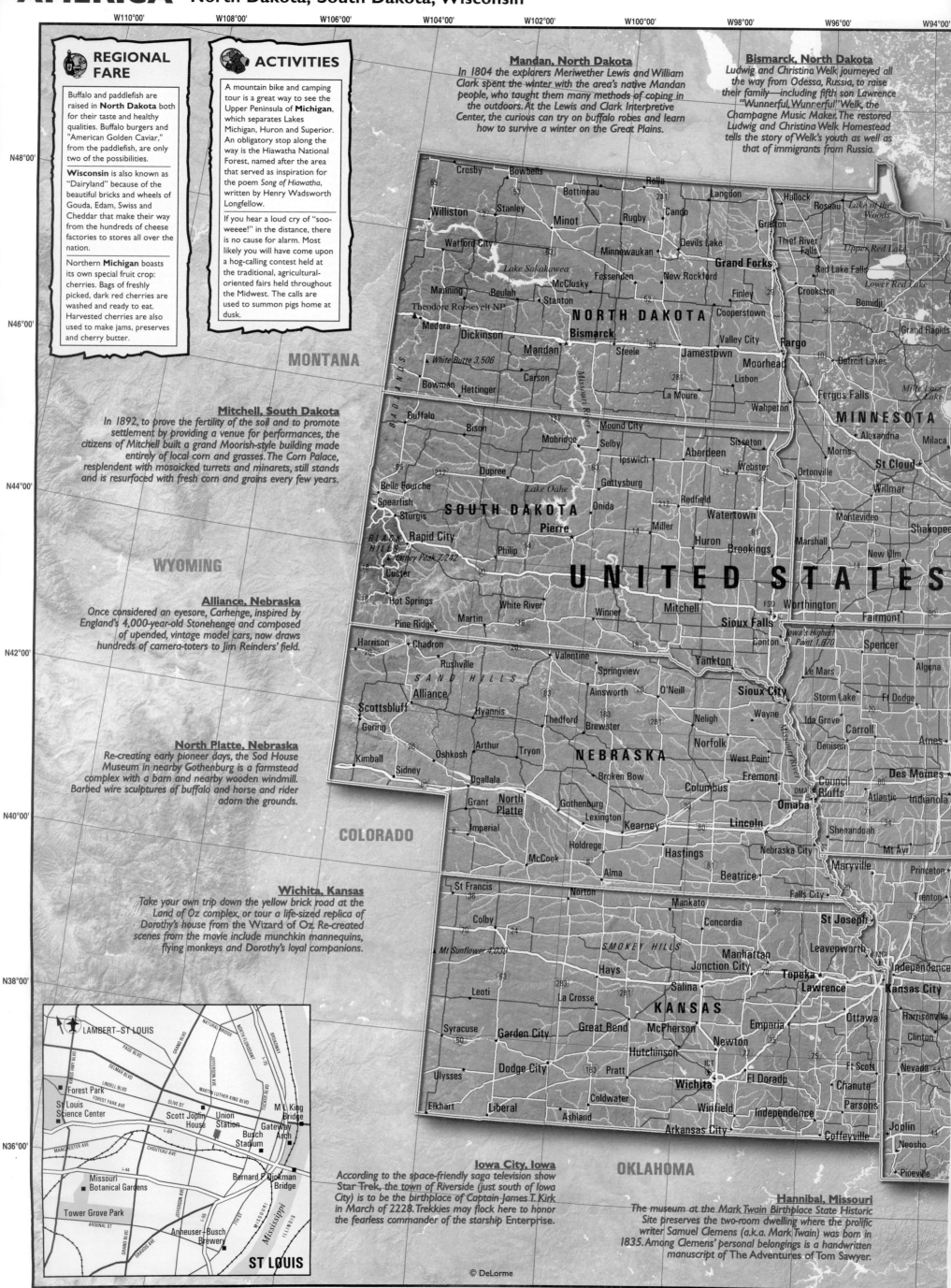

REGIONAL FARE

Buffalo and paddlefish are raised in **North Dakota** both for their taste and healthy qualities. Buffalo burgers and "American Golden Caviar," from the paddlefish, are only two of the possibilities.

Wisconsin is also known as "Dairyland" because of the beautiful bricks and wheels of Gouda, Edam, Swiss and Cheddar that make their way from the hundreds of cheese factories to stores all over the nation.

Northern **Michigan** boasts its own special fruit crop: cherries. Bags of freshly picked, dark red cherries are washed and ready to eat. Harvested cherries are also used to make jams, preserves and cherry butter.

ACTIVITIES

A mountain bike and camping tour is a great way to see the Upper Peninsula of **Michigan**, which separates Lakes Michigan, Huron and Superior. An obligatory stop along the way is the Hiawatha National Forest, named after the area that served as inspiration for the poem *Song of Hiawatha*, written by Henry Wadsworth Longfellow.

If you hear a loud cry of "soo-weeee!" in the distance, there is no cause for alarm. Most likely you will have come upon a hog-calling contest held at the traditional, agricultural-oriented fairs held throughout the Midwest. The calls are used to summon pigs home at dusk.

Mandan, North Dakota
In 1804 the explorers Meriwether Lewis and William Clark spent the winter with the area's native Mandan people, who taught them many methods of coping in the outdoors. At the Lewis and Clark Interpretive Center, the curious can try on buffalo robes and learn how to survive a winter on the Great Plains.

Bismarck, North Dakota
Ludwig and Christina Welk journeyed all the way from Odessa, Russia, to raise their family—including fifth son Lawrence "Wunnerful, Wunnerful" Welk, the Champagne Music Maker. The restored Ludwig and Christina Welk Homestead tells the story of Welk's youth as well as that of immigrants from Russia.

Mitchell, South Dakota
In 1892, to prove the fertility of the soil and to promote settlement by providing a venue for performances, the citizens of Mitchell built a grand Moorish-style building made entirely of local corn and grasses. The Corn Palace, resplendent with mosaicked turrets and minarets, still stands and is resurfaced with fresh corn and grains every few years.

Alliance, Nebraska
Once considered an eyesore, Carhenge, inspired by England's 4,000-year-old Stonehenge and composed of upended, vintage model cars, now draws hundreds of camera-toters to Jim Reinders' field.

North Platte, Nebraska
Re-creating early pioneer days, the Sod House Museum in nearby Gothenburg is a farmstead complex with a barn and nearby wooden windmill. Barbed wire sculptures of buffalo and horse and rider adorn the grounds.

Wichita, Kansas
Take your own trip down the yellow brick road at the Land of Oz complex, or tour a life-sized replica of Dorothy's house from the Wizard of Oz. Re-created scenes from the movie include munchkin mannequins, flying monkeys and Dorothy's loyal companions.

Iowa City, Iowa
According to the space-friendly saga television show Star Trek, the town of Riverside (just south of Iowa City) is to be the birthplace of Captain James T. Kirk in March of 2228. Trekkies may flock here to honor the fearless commander of the starship Enterprise.

Hannibal, Missouri
The museum at the Mark Twain Birthplace State Historic Site preserves the two-room dwelling where the prolific writer Samuel Clemens (a.k.a. Mark Twain) was born in 1835. Among Clemens' personal belongings is a handwritten manuscript of The Adventures of Tom Sawyer.

© DeLorme

Scale 1:5,000,000 at map center

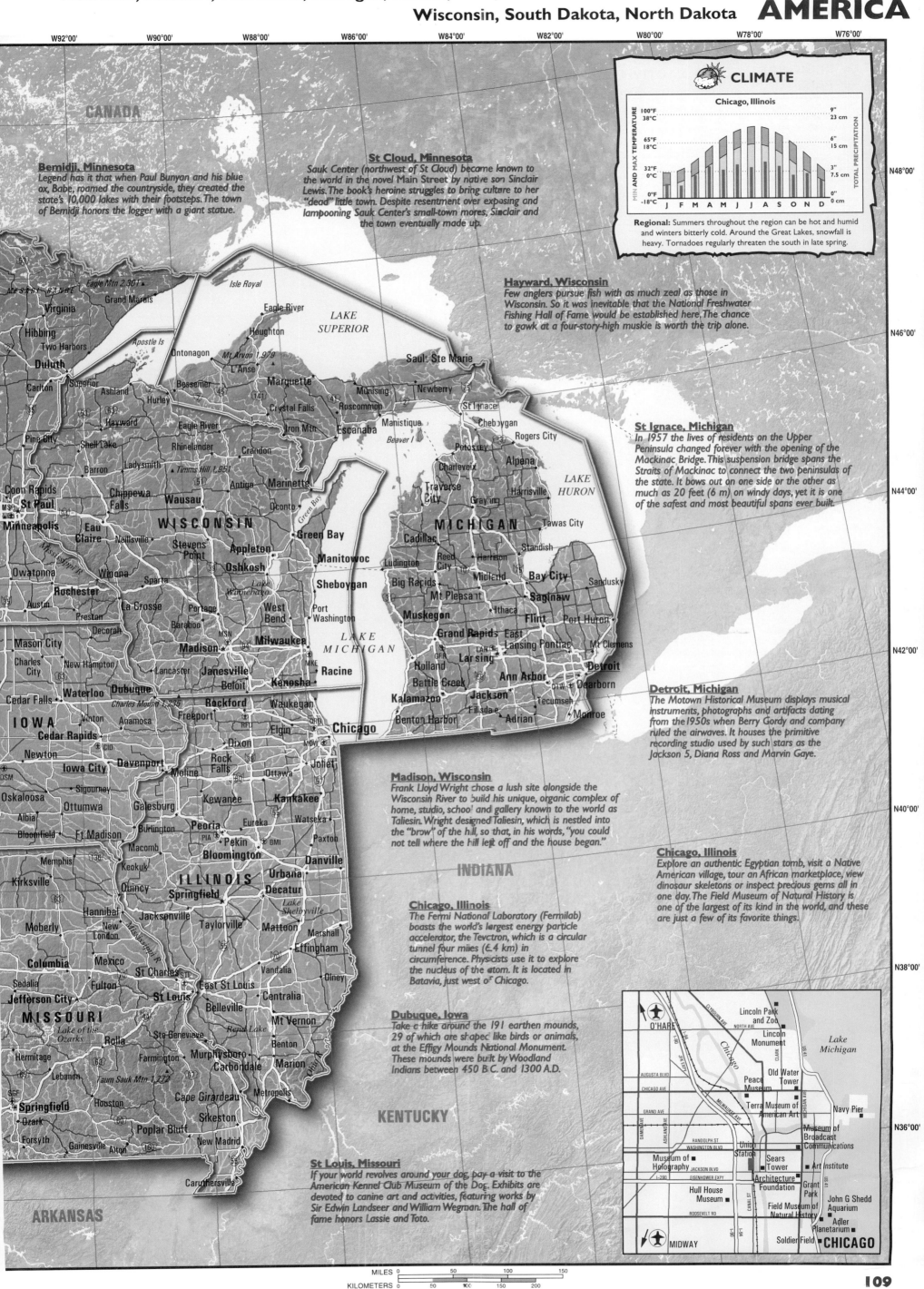

CLIMATE

Chicago, Illinois

Regional: Summers throughout the region can be hot and humid and winters bitterly cold. Around the Great Lakes, snowfall is heavy. Tornadoes regularly threaten the south in late spring.

Bemidji, Minnesota
Legend has it that when Paul Bunyan and his blue ox, Babe, roamed the countryside, they created the state's 10,000 lakes with their footsteps. The town of Bemidji honors the logger with a giant statue.

St Cloud, Minnesota
Sauk Center (northwest of St Cloud) became known to the world in the novel Main Street by native son Sinclair Lewis. The book's heroine struggles to bring culture to her "dead" little town. Despite resentment over exposing and lampooning Sauk Center's small-town mores, Sinclair and the town eventually made up.

Hayward, Wisconsin
Few anglers pursue fish with as much zeal as those in Wisconsin. So it was inevitable that the National Freshwater Fishing Hall of Fame would be established here. The chance to gawk at a four-story-high muskie is worth the trip alone.

St Ignace, Michigan
In 1957 the lives of residents on the Upper Peninsula changed forever with the opening of the Mackinac Bridge. This suspension bridge spans the Straits of Mackinac to connect the two peninsulas of the state. It bows out on one side or the other as much as 20 feet (6 m) on windy days, yet it is one of the safest and most beautiful spans ever built.

Detroit, Michigan
The Motown Historical Museum displays musical instruments, photographs and artifacts dating from the 1950s when Berry Gordy and company ruled the airwaves. It houses the primitive recording studio used by such stars as the Jackson 5, Diana Ross and Marvin Gaye.

Madison, Wisconsin
Frank Lloyd Wright chose a lush site alongside the Wisconsin River to build his unique, organic complex of home, studio, school and gallery known to the world as Taliesin. Wright designed Taliesin, which is nestled into the "brow" of the hill, so that, in his words, "you could not tell where the hill left off and the house began."

Chicago, Illinois
Explore an authentic Egyptian tomb, visit a Native American village, tour an African marketplace, view dinosaur skeletons or inspect precious gems all in one day. The Field Museum of Natural History is one of the largest of its kind in the world, and these are just a few of its favorite things.

Chicago, Illinois
The Fermi National Laboratory (Fermilab) boasts the world's largest energy particle accelerator, the Tevctron, which is a circular tunnel four miles (6.4 km) in circumference. Physicists use it to explore the nucleus of the atom. It is located in Batavia, just west of Chicago.

Dubuque, Iowa
Take a hike around the 191 earthen mounds, 29 of which are shaped like birds or animals, at the Effigy Mounds National Monument. These mounds were built by Woodland Indians between 450 B.C. and 1300 A.D.

St Louis, Missouri
If your world revolves around your dog, pay a visit to the American Kennel Club Museum of the Dog. Exhibits are devoted to canine art and activities, featuring works by Sir Edwin Landseer and William Wegman. The hall of fame honors Lassie and Toto.

MILES / KILOMETERS

REGIONAL FARE

The very trees that make for splendid fall foliage contribute to **Vermont's** rite of spring—maple sugaring. An average tree yields 10 gallons (38 liters) of sap in one season. It takes approximately 40 gallons (151 liters) of sap to make one gallon (4 liters) of "liquid sunshine."

Maine is well known for its seafood, especially the king of all sea delicacies, the lobster. Found on menus throughout the state in many forms, it is most popularly served boiled, baked, stewed, in a hotdog roll—and even on a pizza.

Over 350 years ago, Dutch settlers planted grape vines in their new world. Today, the state of **New York** boasts over 100 wineries, spread over four regions with some even using the native American grape.

ACTIVITIES

Less than an hour from New York City, the Shawangunk Mountains, or "Gunks," offer some of the best rock climbing in the eastern US.

Spot black bear and moose while canoeing down the St John River along **Maine's** border with Canada. The best time to go is in early June when the river runs highest, buoyed by melting snow.

New Englanders love a parade, even if it consists only of the town fire truck, a couple of Scout troops and a ragtag fife and drums corps. Nonetheless, parades and accompanying festivals, especially on Independence Day, bring communities together for family-oriented fun.

Bennington, Vermont
Illustrator Norman Rockwell lived in this area from 1939 to 1953. Many of the area's inhabitants, buildings and vistas appear in his work—rendering towns like Arlington and Bennington metaphors for America's small town.

Waterbury, Vermont
Ben Cohen and Jerry Greenfield opened their first ice cream store in a renovated gas station in 1978. Today Ben & Jerry's is as well known for its philanthropy as its quirky flavors. Tour the factory and purchase "second-quality" goods—for example, chocolate chip ice cream with too many chips—at the factory store.

Penn Yan, New York
Vintner Walter S. Taylor was barred from using his name on his own wine labels after a court decision favoring a prior claim to the name. Undaunted, Mr. Taylor still produces wine at Bully Hill Vineyards, south of Penn Yan in Hammondsport, which are gussied up by his own fanciful labels and signed Walter S. XXXXXX.

Watkins Glen, New York
Automobile aficionados from all over the country converge on the small town of Watkins Glen each fall for the Grand Prix Festival. Swap meets, road rallies and a Concours d'Elegance are shoehorned into this one-day event.

New York, New York
So often has it been photographed, painted and drawn, the graceful span over the East River known as the Brooklyn Bridge, is now an icon for the urban experience called New York City.

CLIMATE

New York, New York

Regional: This region's interior experiences much hotter summers and colder winters than its more moderate coast. Snowfall is greatest close to the Great Lakes. Summer thunderstorms are common.

© DeLorme

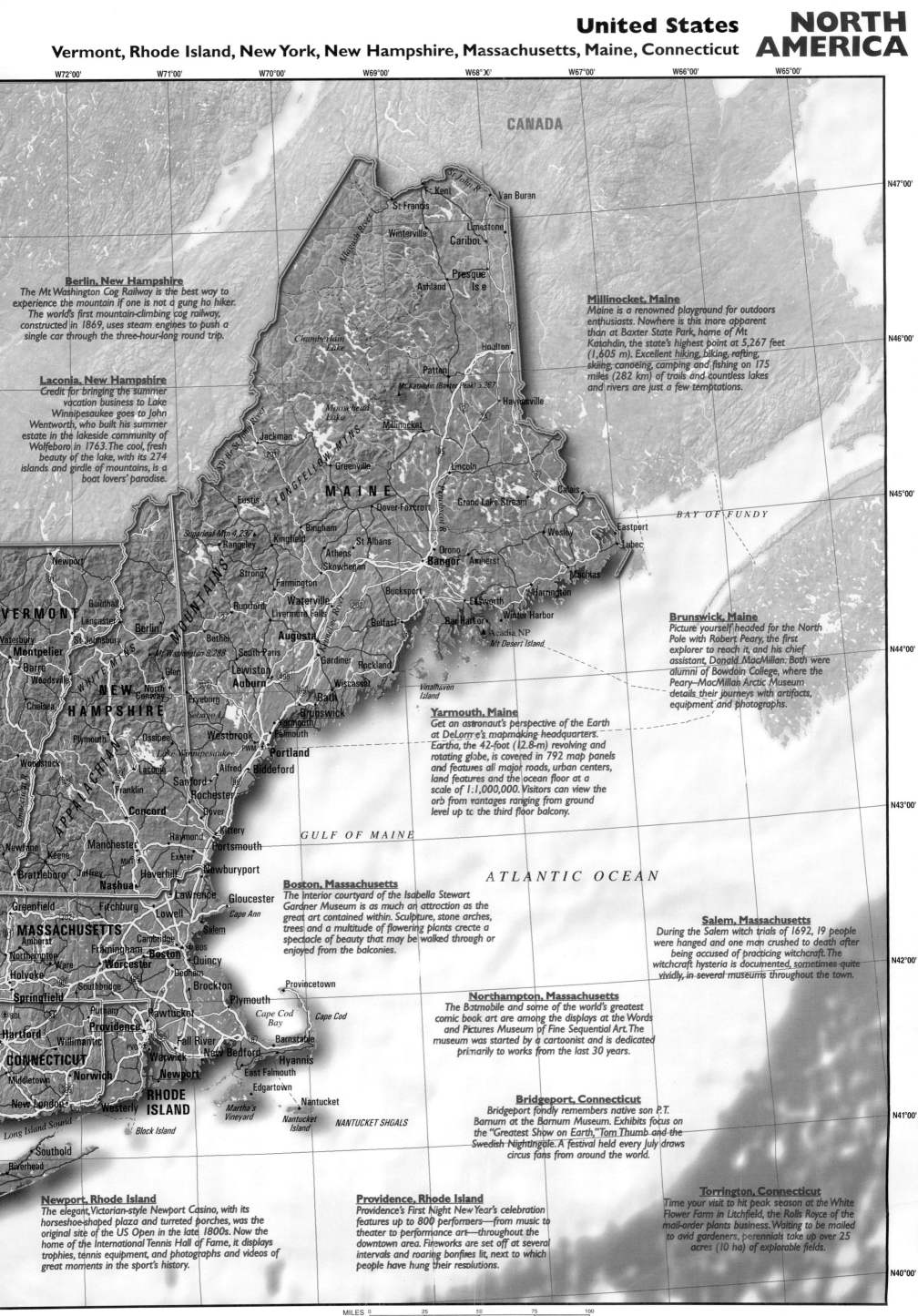

Berlin, New Hampshire
The Mt Washington Cog Railway is the best way to experience the mountain if one is not a gung ho hiker. The world's first mountain-climbing cog railway, constructed in 1869, uses steam engines to push a single car through the three-hour-long round trip.

Laconia, New Hampshire
Credit for bringing the summer vacation business to Lake Winnipesaukee goes to John Wentworth, who built his summer estate in the lakeside community of Wolfeboro in 1763. The cool, fresh beauty of the lake, with its 274 islands and girdle of mountains, is a boat lovers' paradise.

Millinocket, Maine
Maine is a renowned playground for outdoors enthusiasts. Nowhere is this more apparent than at Baxter State Park, home of Mt Katahdin, the state's highest point at 5,267 feet (1,605 m). Excellent hiking, biking, rafting, skiing, canoeing, camping and fishing on 175 miles (282 km) of trails and countless lakes and rivers are just a few temptations.

Brunswick, Maine
Picture yourself headed for the North Pole with Robert Peary, the first explorer to reach it, and his chief assistant, Donald MacMillan. Both were alumni of Bowdoin College, where the Peary–MacMillan Arctic Museum details their journeys with artifacts, equipment and photographs.

Yarmouth, Maine
Get an astronaut's perspective of the Earth at DeLorme's mapmaking headquarters. Eartha, the 42-foot (12.8-m) revolving and rotating globe, is covered in 792 map panels and features all major roads, urban centers, land features and the ocean floor at a scale of 1:1,000,000. Visitors can view the orb from vantages ranging from ground level up to the third floor balcony.

Boston, Massachusetts
The interior courtyard of the Isabella Stewart Gardner Museum is as much an attraction as the great art contained within. Sculpture, stone arches, trees and a multitude of flowering plants create a spectacle of beauty that may be walked through or enjoyed from the balconies.

Salem, Massachusetts
During the Salem witch trials of 1692, 19 people were hanged and one man crushed to death after being accused of practicing witchcraft. The witchcraft hysteria is documented, sometimes quite vividly, in several museums throughout the town.

Northampton, Massachusetts
The Batmobile and some of the world's greatest comic book art are among the displays at the Words and Pictures Museum of Fine Sequential Art. The museum was started by a cartoonist and is dedicated primarily to works from the last 30 years.

Bridgeport, Connecticut
Bridgeport fondly remembers native son P.T. Barnum at the Barnum Museum. Exhibits focus on the "Greatest Show on Earth," Tom Thumb and the Swedish Nightingale. A festival held every July draws circus fans from around the world.

Newport, Rhode Island
The elegant, Victorian-style Newport Casino, with its horseshoe-shaped plaza and turreted porches, was the original site of the US Open in the late 1800s. Now the home of the International Tennis Hall of Fame, it displays trophies, tennis equipment, and photographs and videos of great moments in the sport's history.

Providence, Rhode Island
Providence's First Night New Year's celebration features up to 800 performers—from music to theater to performance art—throughout the downtown area. Fireworks are set off at several intervals and roaring bonfires lit, next to which people have hung their resolutions.

Torrington, Connecticut
Time your visit to hit peak season at the White Flower Farm in Litchfield, the Rolls Royce of the mail-order plants business. Waiting to be mailed to avid gardeners, perennials take up over 25 acres (10 ha) of explorable fields.

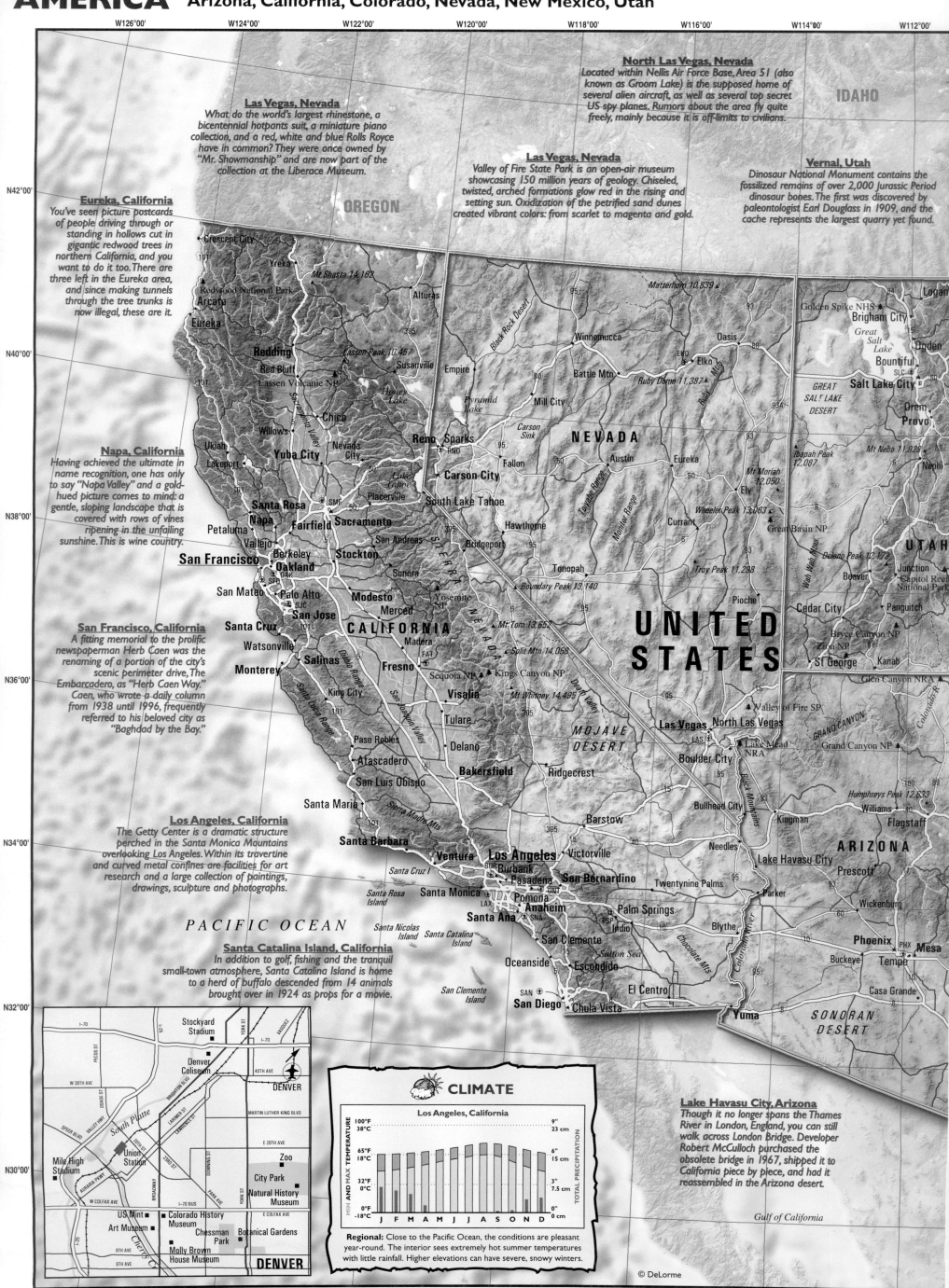

Las Vegas, Nevada
What do the world's largest rhinestone, a bicentennial hotpants suit, a miniature piano collection, and a red, white and blue Rolls Royce have in common? They were once owned by "Mr. Showmanship" and are now part of the collection at the Liberace Museum.

North Las Vegas, Nevada
Located within Nellis Air Force Base, Area 51 (also known as Groom Lake) is the supposed home of several alien aircraft, as well as several top secret US spy planes. Rumors about the area fly quite freely, mainly because it is off-limits to civilians.

Las Vegas, Nevada
Valley of Fire State Park is an open-air museum showcasing 150 million years of geology. Chiseled, twisted, arched formations glow red in the rising and setting sun. Oxidization of the petrified sand dunes created vibrant colors: from scarlet to magenta and gold.

Vernal, Utah
Dinosaur National Monument contains the fossilized remains of over 2,000 Jurassic Period dinosaur bones. The first was discovered by paleontologist Earl Douglass in 1909, and the cache represents the largest quarry yet found.

Eureka, California
You've seen picture postcards of people driving through or standing in hollows cut in gigantic redwood trees in northern California, and you want to do it too. There are three left in the Eureka area, and since making tunnels through the tree trunks is now illegal, these are it.

Napa, California
Having achieved the ultimate in name recognition, one has only to say "Napa Valley" and a gold-hued picture comes to mind: a gentle, sloping landscape that is covered with rows of vines ripening in the unfailing sunshine. This is wine country.

San Francisco, California
A fitting memorial to the prolific newspaperman Herb Caen was the renaming of a portion of the city's scenic perimeter drive, The Embarcadero, as "Herb Caen Way." Caen, who wrote a daily column from 1938 until 1996, frequently referred to his beloved city as "Baghdad by the Bay."

Los Angeles, California
The Getty Center is a dramatic structure perched in the Santa Monica Mountains overlooking Los Angeles. Within its travertine and curved metal confines are facilities for art research and a large collection of paintings, drawings, sculpture and photographs.

Santa Catalina Island, California
In addition to golf, fishing and the tranquil small-town atmosphere, Santa Catalina Island is home to a herd of buffalo descended from 14 animals brought over in 1924 as props for a movie.

Lake Havasu City, Arizona
Though it no longer spans the Thames River in London, England, you can still walk across London Bridge. Developer Robert McCulloch purchased the obsolete bridge in 1967, shipped it to California piece by piece, and had it reassembled in the Arizona desert.

CLIMATE

Los Angeles, California

Regional: Close to the Pacific Ocean, the conditions are pleasant year-round. The interior sees extremely hot summer temperatures with little rainfall. Higher elevations can have severe, snowy winters.

© DeLorme

Scale 1:5,000,000 at map center

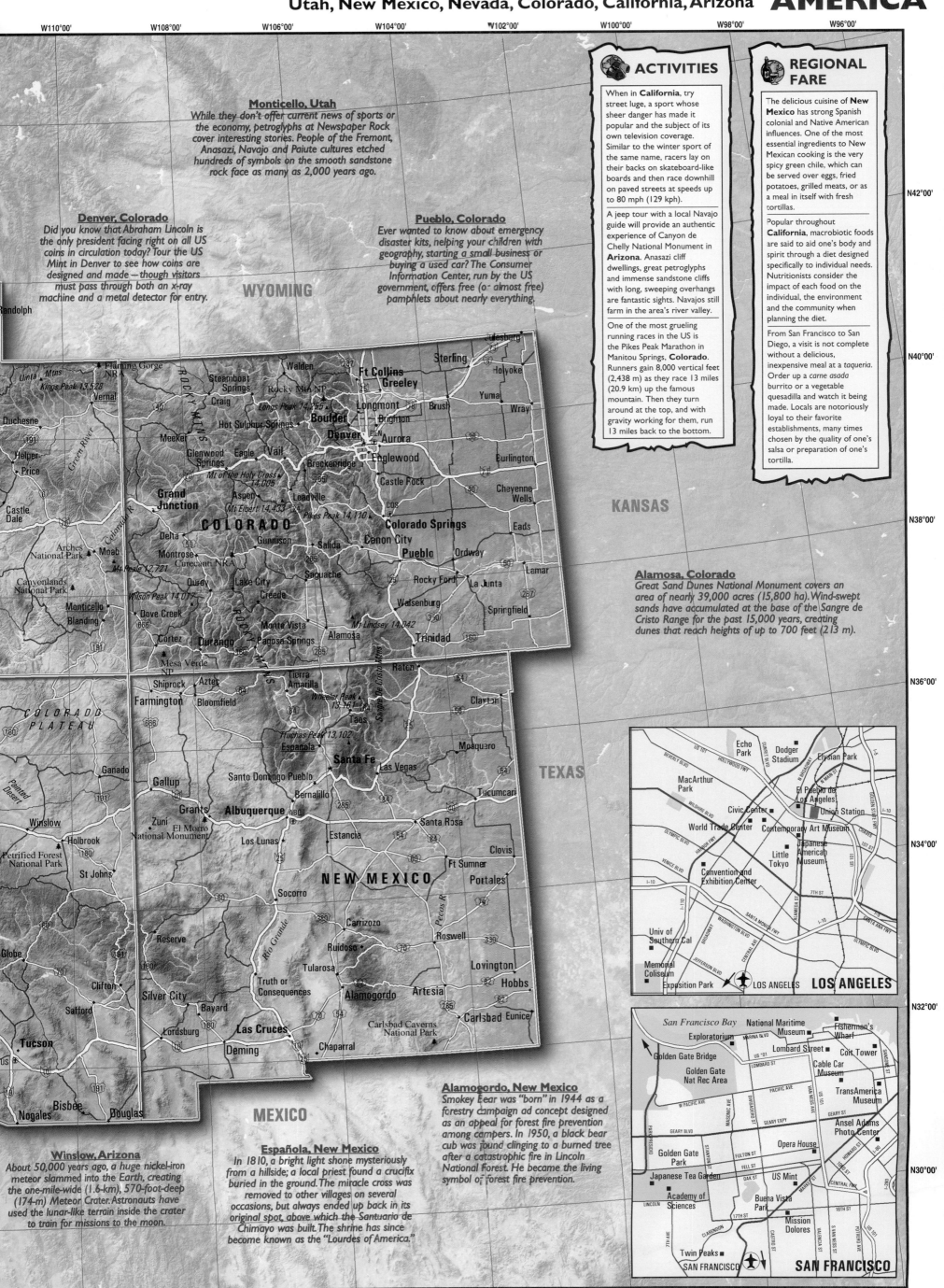

W110°00' W108°00' W106°00' W104°00' W102°00' W100°00' W98°00' W96°00'

Monticello, Utah
While they don't offer current news of sports or the economy, petroglyphs at Newspaper Rock cover interesting stories. People of the Fremont, Anasazi, Navajo and Paiute cultures etched hundreds of symbols on the smooth sandstone rock face as many as 2,000 years ago.

Denver, Colorado
Did you know that Abraham Lincoln is the only president facing right on all US coins in circulation today? Tour the US Mint in Denver to see how coins are designed and made—though visitors must pass through both an x-ray machine and a metal detector for entry.

Pueblo, Colorado
Ever wanted to know about emergency disaster kits, helping your children with geography, starting a small business or buying a used car? The Consumer Information Center, run by the US government, offers free (or almost free) pamphlets about nearly everything.

ACTIVITIES
When in **California**, try street luge, a sport whose sheer danger has made it popular and the subject of its own television coverage. Similar to the winter sport of the same name, racers lay on their backs on skateboard-like boards and then race downhill on paved streets at speeds up to 80 mph (129 kph).

A jeep tour with a local Navajo guide will provide an authentic experience of Canyon de Chelly National Monument in **Arizona**. Anasazi cliff dwellings, great petroglyphs and immense sandstone cliffs with long, sweeping overhangs are fantastic sights. Navajos still farm in the area's river valley.

One of the most grueling running races in the US is the Pikes Peak Marathon in Manitou Springs, **Colorado**. Runners gain 8,000 vertical feet (2,438 m) as they race 13 miles (20.9 km) up the famous mountain. Then they turn around at the top, and with gravity working for them, run 13 miles back to the bottom.

REGIONAL FARE
The delicious cuisine of **New Mexico** has strong Spanish colonial and Native American influences. One of the most essential ingredients to New Mexican cooking is the very spicy green chile, which can be served over eggs, fried potatoes, grilled meats, or as a meal in itself with fresh tortillas.

Popular throughout **California**, macrobiotic foods are said to aid one's body and spirit through a diet designed specifically to individual needs. Nutritionists consider the impact of each food on the individual, the environment and the community when planning the diet.

From San Francisco to San Diego, a visit is not complete without a delicious, inexpensive meal at a *taqueria*. Order up a *carne asada* burrito or a vegetable quesadilla and watch it being made. Locals are notoriously loyal to their favorite establishments, many times chosen by the quality of one's salsa or preparation of one's tortilla.

Alamosa, Colorado
Great Sand Dunes National Monument covers an area of nearly 39,000 acres (15,800 ha). Wind-swept sands have accumulated at the base of the Sangre de Cristo Range for the past 15,000 years, creating dunes that reach heights of up to 700 feet (213 m).

Alamogordo, New Mexico
Smokey Bear was "born" in 1944 as a forestry campaign ad concept designed as an appeal for forest fire prevention among campers. In 1950, a black bear cub was found clinging to a burned tree after a catastrophic fire in Lincoln National Forest. He became the living symbol of forest fire prevention.

Española, New Mexico
In 1810, a bright light shone mysteriously from a hillside; a local priest found a crucifix buried in the ground. The miracle cross was removed to other villages on several occasions, but always ended up back in its original spot, above which the Santuario de Chimayo was built. The shrine has since become known as the "Lourdes of America."

Winslow, Arizona
About 50,000 years ago, a huge nickel-iron meteor slammed into the Earth, creating the one-mile-wide (1.6-km), 570-foot-deep (174-m) Meteor Crater. Astronauts have used the lunar-like terrain inside the crater to train for missions to the moon.

LOS ANGELES

SAN FRANCISCO

MILES 0   50   100   150
KILOMETERS 0   50   100   150   200

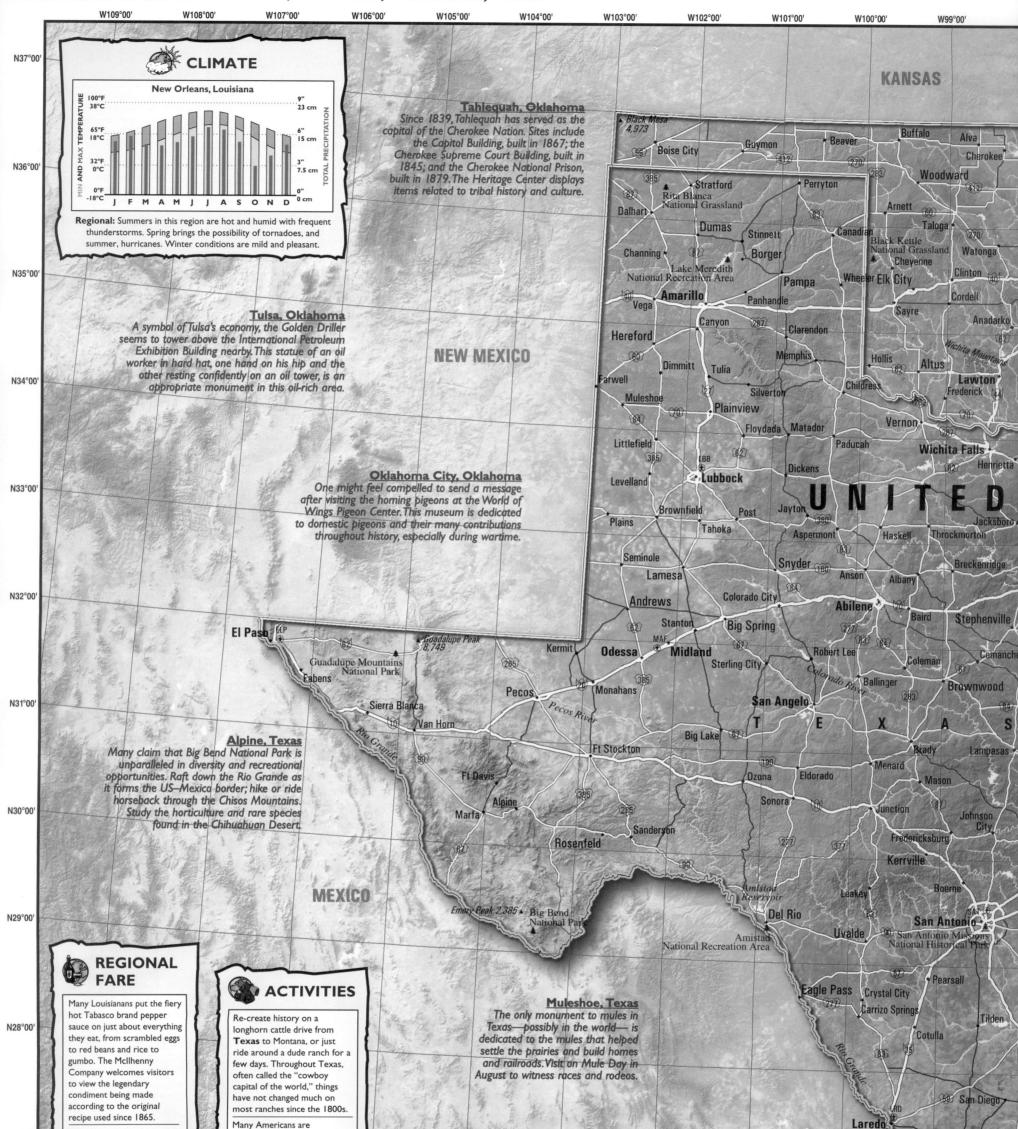

CLIMATE

New Orleans, Louisiana

Regional: Summers in this region are hot and humid with frequent thunderstorms. Spring brings the possibility of tornadoes, and summer, hurricanes. Winter conditions are mild and pleasant.

Tahlequah, Oklahoma
Since 1839, Tahlequah has served as the capital of the Cherokee Nation. Sites include the Capitol Building, built in 1867; the Cherokee Supreme Court Building, built in 1845; and the Cherokee National Prison, built in 1879. The Heritage Center displays items related to tribal history and culture.

Tulsa, Oklahoma
A symbol of Tulsa's economy, the Golden Driller seems to tower above the International Petroleum Exhibition Building nearby. This statue of an oil worker in hard hat, one hand on his hip and the other resting confidently on an oil tower, is an appropriate monument in this oil-rich area.

Oklahoma City, Oklahoma
One might feel compelled to send a message after visiting the homing pigeons at the World of Wings Pigeon Center. This museum is dedicated to domestic pigeons and their many contributions throughout history, especially during wartime.

Alpine, Texas
Many claim that Big Bend National Park is unparalleled in diversity and recreational opportunities. Raft down the Rio Grande as it forms the US–Mexico border; hike or ride horseback through the Chisos Mountains. Study the horticulture and rare species found in the Chihuahuan Desert.

REGIONAL FARE

Many Louisianans put the fiery hot Tabasco brand pepper sauce on just about everything they eat, from scrambled eggs to red beans and rice to gumbo. The McIlhenny Company welcomes visitors to view the legendary condiment being made according to the original recipe used since 1865.

Texas likes to boast that it is "a whole other country," and its distinctive cuisine just might prove the claim. One favorite dish is chicken-fried steak: a lesser-quality cut of meat, dunked in batter, deep fried and served with cream gravy.

Texans also pride themselves on their chili, a fiery stew of chunks of beef cooked with tomatoes, spices and other, often "secret," ingredients. A bona fide chili will scorch your tongue, clear the sinuses and leave you gasping for a cold beer.

ACTIVITIES

Re-create history on a longhorn cattle drive from **Texas** to Montana, or just ride around a dude ranch for a few days. Throughout Texas, often called the "cowboy capital of the world," things have not changed much on most ranches since the 1800s.

Many Americans are unaware of the scenic beauty of the Ozark Mountains of **Arkansas**. Visitors and residents alike enjoy hiking, camping and mountain biking in the hardwood forests here. After a strenuous outing, a recuperative visit to the famous spas in Hot Springs may be in order.

In **Louisiana**, take a tour of the bayou with a Cajun guide and learn about French Acadian folklore and tradition. Alligators, egrets and herons may be spotted under the Spanish moss-covered cypress and oak trees.

Muleshoe, Texas
The only monument to mules in Texas—possibly in the world— is dedicated to the mules that helped settle the prairies and build homes and railroads. Visit on Mule Day in August to witness races and rodeos.

Ft Worth, Texas
Do you find yourself intrigued by snakes, despite their bad press? At Bayou Bob's Brazos River Rattlesnake Ranch, visitors are treated to herpetologist-certified information on venomous snakes such as rattlesnakes, copperheads and anacondas. Safety tips and cures for bites are touted as well.

© DeLorme

Scale 1:4,000,000 at map center

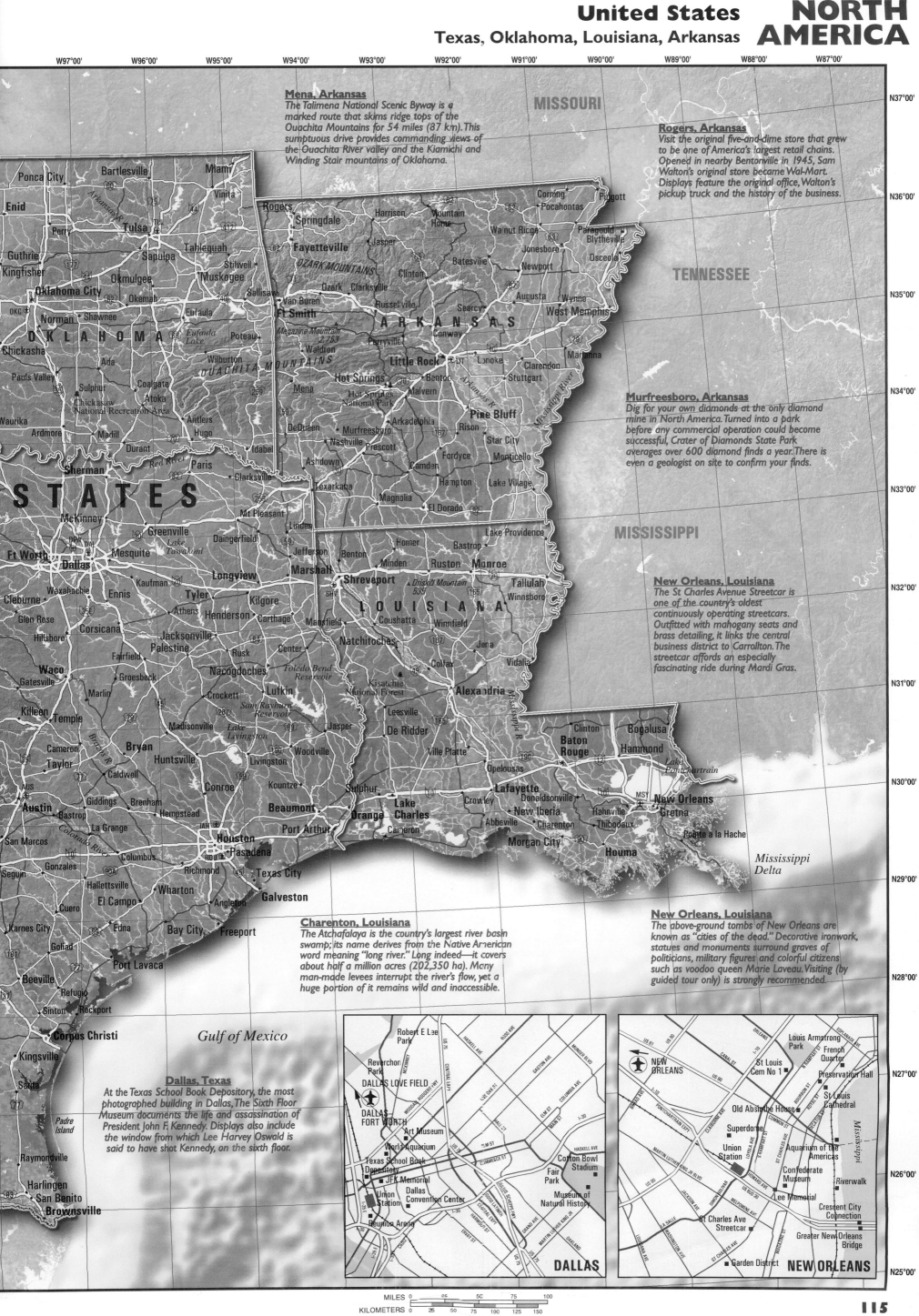

Mena, Arkansas
The Talimena National Scenic Byway is a marked route that skims ridge tops of the Ouachita Mountains for 54 miles (87 km). This sumptuous drive provides commanding views of the Ouachita River valley and the Kiamichi and Winding Stair mountains of Oklahoma.

Rogers, Arkansas
Visit the original five-and-dime store that grew to be one of America's largest retail chains. Opened in nearby Bentonville in 1945, Sam Walton's original store became Wal-Mart. Displays feature the original office, Walton's pickup truck and the history of the business.

Murfreesboro, Arkansas
Dig for your own diamonds at the only diamond mine in North America. Turned into a park before any commercial operation could become successful, Crater of Diamonds State Park averages over 600 diamond finds a year. There is even a geologist on site to confirm your finds.

New Orleans, Louisiana
The St Charles Avenue Streetcar is one of the country's oldest continuously operating streetcars. Outfitted with mahogany seats and brass detailing, it links the central business district to Carrollton. The streetcar affords an especially fascinating ride during Mardi Gras.

Charenton, Louisiana
The Atchafalaya is the country's largest river basin swamp; its name derives from the Native American word meaning "long river." Long indeed—it covers about half a million acres (202,350 ha). Many man-made levees interrupt the river's flow, yet a huge portion of it remains wild and inaccessible.

New Orleans, Louisiana
The above-ground tombs of New Orleans are known as "cities of the dead." Decorative ironwork, statues and monuments surround graves of politicians, military figures and colorful citizens such as voodoo queen Marie Laveau. Visiting (by guided tour only) is strongly recommended.

Dallas, Texas
At the Texas School Book Depository, the most photographed building in Dallas, The Sixth Floor Museum documents the life and assassination of President John F. Kennedy. Displays also include the window from which Lee Harvey Oswald is said to have shot Kennedy, on the sixth floor.

MILES 0 25 50 75 100
KILOMETERS 0 25 50 75 100 125 150

DALLAS

NEW ORLEANS

NORTH AMERICA

United States

Delaware, Indiana, Kentucky, Maryland, New Jersey, North Carolina Ohio, Pennsylvania, Tennessee, Virginia, West Virginia, Washington, DC

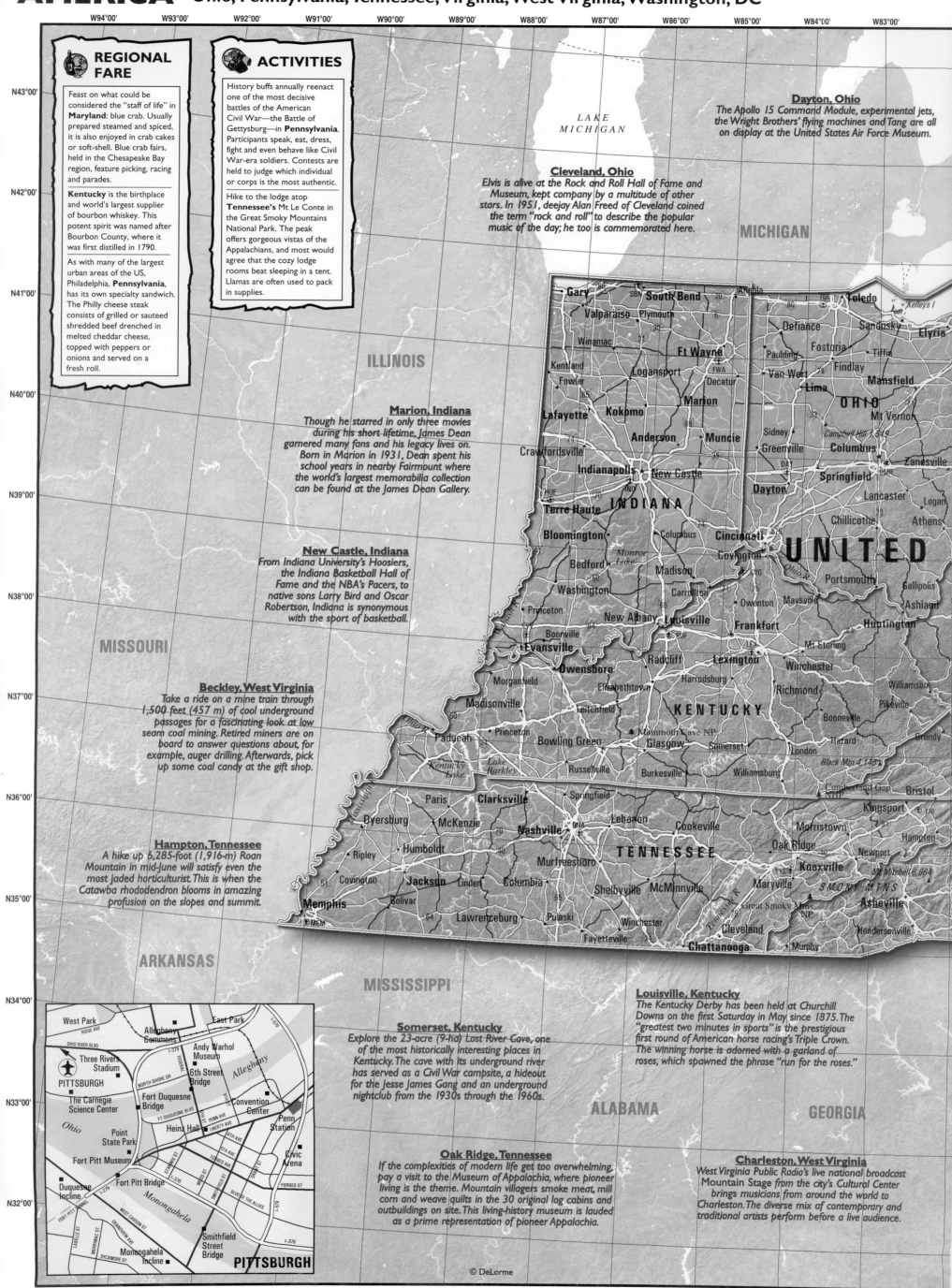

REGIONAL FARE

Feast on what could be considered the "staff of life" in **Maryland**: blue crab. Usually prepared steamed and spiced, it is also enjoyed in crab cakes or soft-shell. Blue crab fairs, held in the Chesapeake Bay region, feature picking, racing and parades.

Kentucky is the birthplace and world's largest supplier of bourbon whiskey. This potent spirit was named after Bourbon County, where it was first distilled in 1790.

As with many of the largest urban areas of the US, Philadelphia, **Pennsylvania**, has its own specialty sandwich. The Philly cheese steak consists of grilled or sauteed shredded beef drenched in melted cheddar cheese, topped with peppers or onions and served on a fresh roll.

ACTIVITIES

History buffs annually reenact one of the most decisive battles of the American Civil War—the Battle of Gettysburg—in **Pennsylvania**. Participants speak, eat, dress, fight and even behave like Civil War-era soldiers. Contests are held to judge which individual or corps is the most authentic.

Hike to the lodge atop **Tennessee's** Mt Le Conte in the Great Smoky Mountains National Park. The peak offers gorgeous vistas of the Appalachians, and most would agree that the cozy lodge rooms beat sleeping in a tent. Llamas are often used to pack in supplies.

Dayton, Ohio
The Apollo 15 Command Module, experimental jets, the Wright Brothers' flying machines and Tang are all on display at the United States Air Force Museum.

Cleveland, Ohio
Elvis is alive at the Rock and Roll Hall of Fame and Museum, kept company by a multitude of other stars. In 1951, deejay Alan Freed of Cleveland coined the term "rock and roll" to describe the popular music of the day; he too is commemorated here.

Marion, Indiana
Though he starred in only three movies during his short lifetime, James Dean garnered many fans and his legacy lives on. Born in Marion in 1931, Dean spent his school years in nearby Fairmount where the world's largest memorabilia collection can be found at the James Dean Gallery.

New Castle, Indiana
From Indiana University's Hoosiers, the Indiana Basketball Hall of Fame and the NBA's Pacers, to native sons Larry Bird and Oscar Robertson, Indiana is synonymous with the sport of basketball.

Beckley, West Virginia
Take a ride on a mine train through 1,500 feet (457 m) of cool underground passages for a fascinating look at low seam coal mining. Retired miners are on board to answer questions about, for example, auger drilling. Afterwards, pick up some coal candy at the gift shop.

Hampton, Tennessee
A hike up 6,285-foot (1,916-m) Roan Mountain in mid-June will satisfy even the most jaded horticulturist. This is when the Catawba rhododendron blooms in amazing profusion on the slopes and summit.

Somerset, Kentucky
Explore the 23-acre (9-ha) Lost River Cave, one of the most historically interesting places in Kentucky. The cave with its underground river has served as a Civil War campsite, a hideout for the Jesse James Gang and an underground nightclub from the 1930s through the 1960s.

Louisville, Kentucky
The Kentucky Derby has been held at Churchill Downs on the first Saturday in May since 1875. The "greatest two minutes in sports" is the prestigious first round of American horse racing's Triple Crown. The winning horse is adorned with a garland of roses, which spawned the phrase "run for the roses."

Oak Ridge, Tennessee
If the complexities of modern life get too overwhelming, pay a visit to the Museum of Appalachia, where pioneer living is the theme. Mountain villagers smoke meat, mill corn and weave quilts in the 30 original log cabins and outbuildings on site. This living-history museum is lauded as a prime representation of pioneer Appalachia.

Charleston, West Virginia
West Virginia Public Radio's live national broadcast Mountain Stage from the city's Cultural Center brings musicians from around the world to Charleston. The diverse mix of contemporary and traditional artists perform before a live audience.

© DeLorme

Scale 1:4,000,000 at map center

North Carolina, New Jersey, Maryland, Kentucky, Indiana, Delaware
Washington, DC, West Virginia, Virginia, Tennessee, Pennsylvania, Ohio

United States

NORTH AMERICA

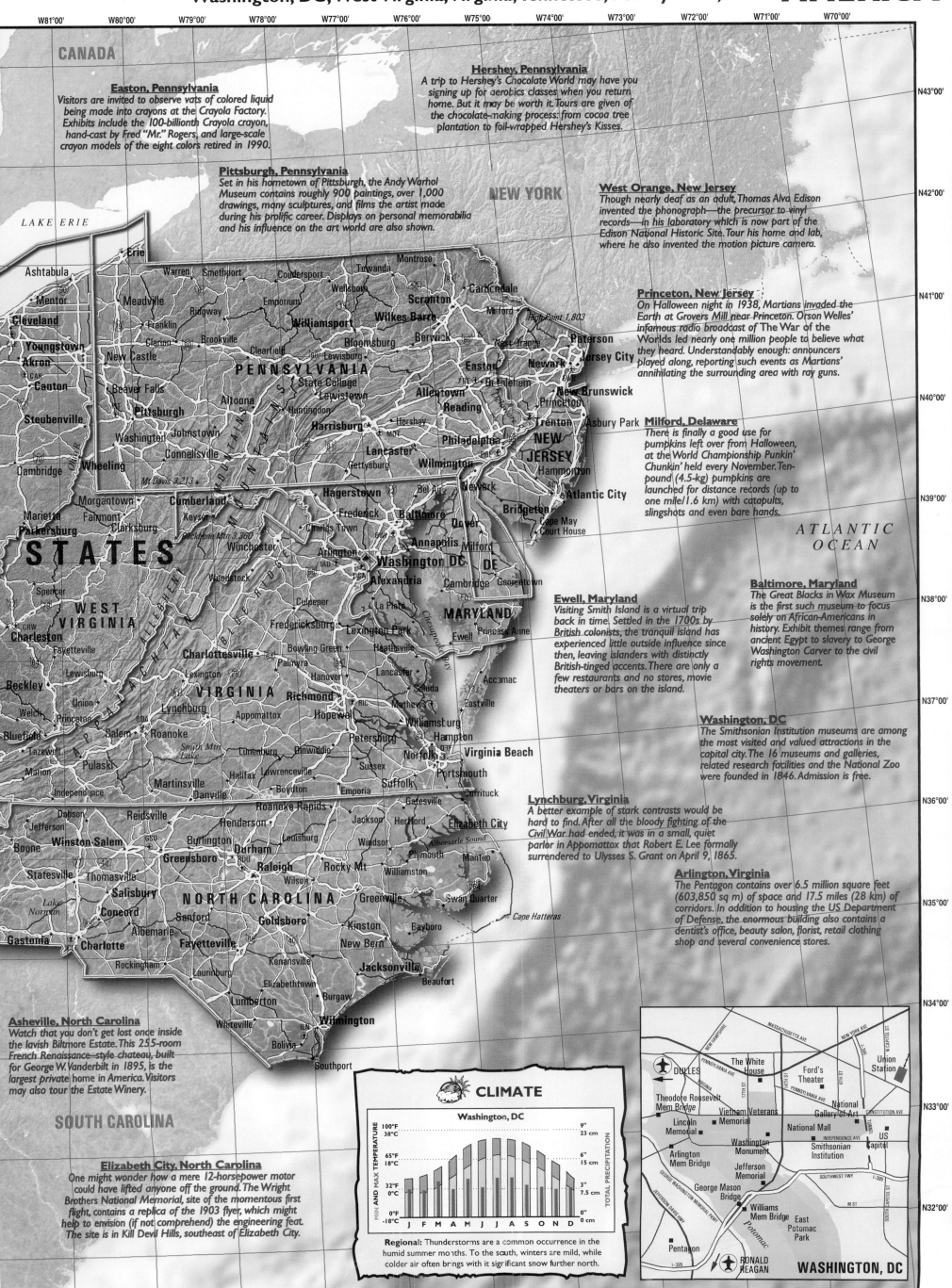

Easton, Pennsylvania
Visitors are invited to observe vats of colored liquid being made into crayons at the Crayola Factory. Exhibits include the 100-billionth Crayola crayon, hand-cast by Fred "Mr." Rogers, and large-scale crayon models of the eight colors retired in 1990.

Hershey, Pennsylvania
A trip to Hershey's Chocolate World may have you signing up for aerobics classes when you return home. But it may be worth it. Tours are given of the chocolate-making process: from cocoa tree plantation to foil-wrapped Hershey's Kisses.

Pittsburgh, Pennsylvania
Set in his hometown of Pittsburgh, the Andy Warhol Museum contains roughly 900 paintings, over 1,000 drawings, many sculptures, and films the artist made during his prolific career. Displays on personal memorabilia and his influence on the art world are also shown.

West Orange, New Jersey
Though nearly deaf as an adult, Thomas Alva Edison invented the phonograph—the precursor to vinyl records—in his laboratory which is now part of the Edison National Historic Site. Tour his home and lab, where he also invented the motion picture camera.

Princeton, New Jersey
On Halloween night in 1938, Martians invaded the Earth at Grovers Mill near Princeton. Orson Welles' infamous radio broadcast of The War of the Worlds led nearly one million people to believe what they heard. Understandably enough: announcers played along, reporting such events as Martians' annihilating the surrounding area with ray guns.

Milford, Delaware
There is finally a good use for pumpkins left over from Halloween, at the World Championship Punkin' Chunkin' held every November. Ten-pound (4.5-kg) pumpkins are launched for distance records (up to one mile/1.6 km) with catapults, slingshots and even bare hands.

Ewell, Maryland
Visiting Smith Island is a virtual trip back in time. Settled in the 1700s by British colonists, the tranquil island has experienced little outside influence since then, leaving islanders with distinctly British-tinged accents. There are only a few restaurants and no stores, movie theaters or bars on the island.

Baltimore, Maryland
The Great Blacks in Wax Museum is the first such museum to focus solely on African-Americans in history. Exhibit themes range from ancient Egypt to slavery to George Washington Carver to the civil rights movement.

Washington, DC
The Smithsonian Institution museums are among the most visited and valued attractions in the capital city. The 16 museums and galleries, related research facilities and the National Zoo were founded in 1846. Admission is free.

Lynchburg, Virginia
A better example of stark contrasts would be hard to find. After all the bloody fighting of the Civil War had ended, it was in a small, quiet parlor in Appomattox that Robert E. Lee formally surrendered to Ulysses S. Grant on April 9, 1865.

Arlington, Virginia
The Pentagon contains over 6.5 million square feet (603,850 sq m) of space and 17.5 miles (28 km) of corridors. In addition to housing the US Department of Defense, the enormous building also contains a dentist's office, beauty salon, florist, retail clothing shop and several convenience stores.

Asheville, North Carolina
Watch that you don't get lost once inside the lavish Biltmore Estate. This 255-room French Renaissance–style chateau, built for George W. Vanderbilt in 1895, is the largest private home in America. Visitors may also tour the Estate Winery.

Elizabeth City, North Carolina
One might wonder how a mere 12-horsepower motor could have lifted anyone off the ground. The Wright Brothers National Memorial, site of the momentous first flight, contains a replica of the 1903 flyer, which might help to envision (if not comprehend) the engineering feat. The site is in Kill Devil Hills, southeast of Elizabeth City.

CLIMATE

Washington, DC

MIN AND MAX TEMPERATURE / TOTAL PRECIPITATION
100°F 38°C / 9" 23 cm
65°F 18°C / 6" 15 cm
32°F 0°C / 3" 7.5 cm
0°F -18°C / 0" 0 cm
J F M A M J J A S O N D

Regional: Thunderstorms are a common occurrence in the humid summer months. To the south, winters are mild, while colder air often brings with it significant snow further north.

WASHINGTON, DC

MILES 0 25 50 75 100
KILOMETERS 0 25 50 75 100 125 150

REGIONAL FARE

A fortunate combination of soil and climate created an unexpectedly sweet onion in central **Georgia**: the Vidalia onion, named for the town at the center of the growing area. Local farmers now sell Vidalias nationwide, and the state legislature has designated the Vidalia onion as Georgia's official state vegetable.

They can be boiled or fried, eaten with hot sauce or without, but they must be made of pig intestine. Chitlins, or chitterlings, have a big following in the southeastern US. They are usually served on top of rice and accompanied by other southern favorites such as corn-on-the-cob, black-eyed peas and collard greens.

From the **Florida** coral islands that trail into the Gulf of Mexico comes a refreshing citrus dessert: key lime pie. The graham cracker crust contains chilled lime custard topped with meringue. The limes are usually grown in the Florida Keys.

ACTIVITIES

Search along the beaches or dive for treasure on the reefs off **Florida**, **Georgia**, **North Carolina** and **South Carolina**. Many wrecks of Spanish galleons and pirate ships have never been found or are only partially recovered.

Although the South is already well-known for golf, **Alabama** has established the Robert Trent Jones Golf Trail, which traverses the whole state. Consisting of seven major courses totaling 324 holes, the trail is connected by major highways.

Oxford, Mississippi
Author William Faulkner peopled his books with street scenes and characters drawn from daily life in Oxford, a classic Southern town complete with courthouse-dominated square.

Tuscumbia, Alabama
Nestled in the town of Tuscumbia, deep in hunting country, is the final resting place of over 100 beloved coon hounds: the Key Underwood Coon Dog Memorial Graveyard. It was established in 1937 when Underwood buried his favorite coon dog, Troop.

Indianola, Mississippi
Part museum with exhibits and video, part art gallery with pieces in all media, the Catfish Capitol serves as a repository for the history and cultivation of the tasty bewhiskered fish. Outside, sculptures fashioned from spawning cans, hatchery tanks and seining nets decorate the grounds. Located in Belzoni, south of Indianola.

Warrior, Alabama
At Rickwood Caverns State Park, one mile (1.6 km) of underground passageways reveals 260-million-year-old limestone formations. Some of the underground pools are populated by blind cave fish.

Tuscaloosa, Alabama
The Paul W Bryant Museum at the University of Alabama—Tuscaloosa highlights over 100 years of football history. Even if you have never heard of coach "Bear" Bryant, you will certainly notice how proud Alabamans are of their team, the Crimson Tide.

GULF OF MEXICO

ATLANTA

Science and Technology Museum · Civic Center · Centennial Olympic Park · World Congress Center · Omni Coliseum · Georgia Dome · CNN Center · High Museum of Art · Sweet Auburn Preservation District · M L King Jr Nat Hist Site · Butler Park · World of Coca-Cola · WILLIAM B HARTSFIELD

MIAMI

Miami Stadium · Orange Bowl · Miami Arena · Bicentennial Park · JFK Torch of Friendship · Bay Front Park · Cultural Center · Bayside Amphitheater

Scale 1:4,000,000 at map center

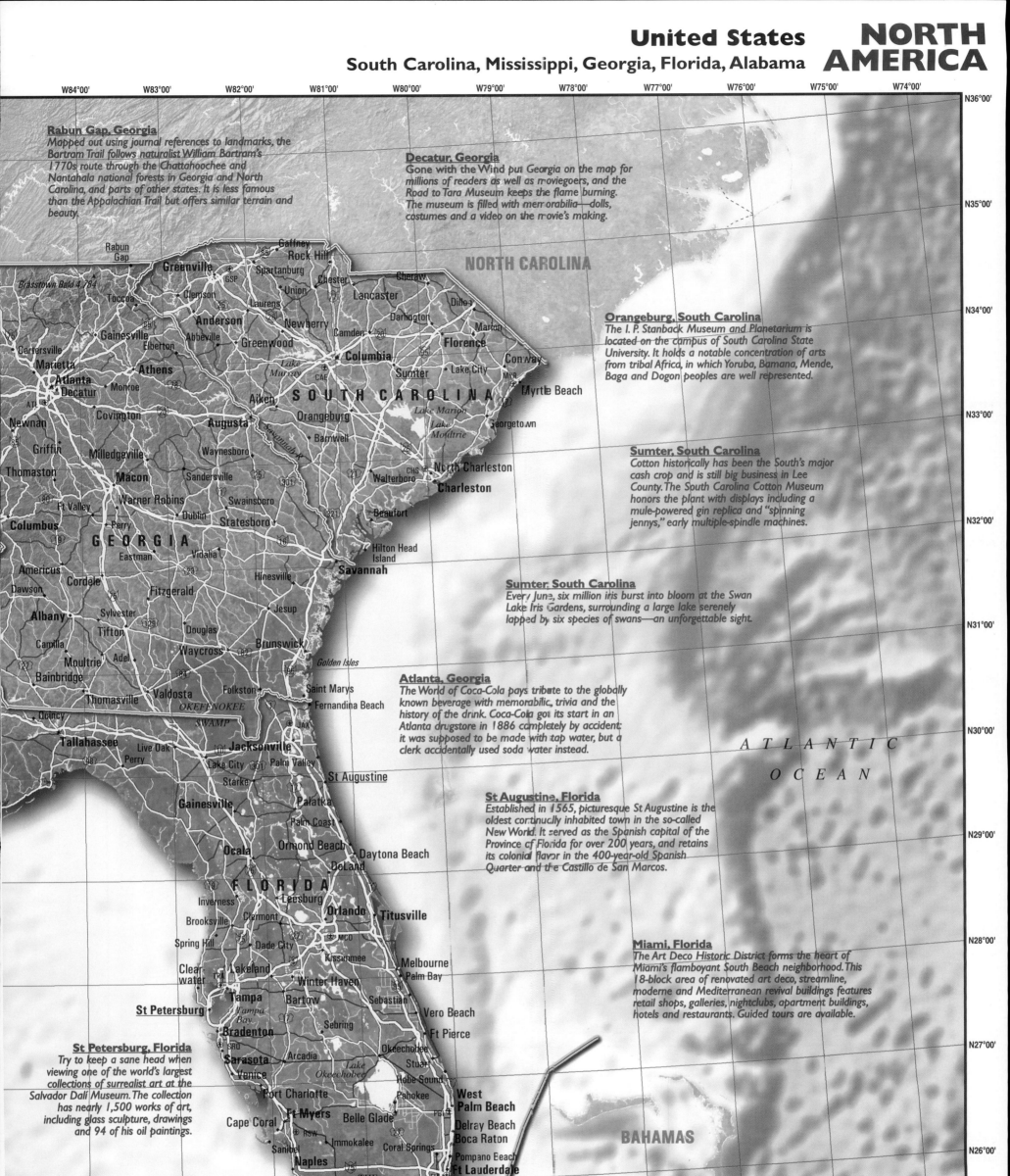

Rabun Gap, Georgia
Mapped out using journal references to landmarks, the Bartram Trail follows naturalist William Bartram's 1770s route through the Chattahoochee and Nantahala national forests in Georgia and North Carolina, and parts of other states. It is less famous than the Appalachian Trail but offers similar terrain and beauty.

Decatur, Georgia
Gone with the Wind put Georgia on the map for millions of readers as well as moviegoers, and the Road to Tara Museum keeps the flame burning. The museum is filled with memorabilia—dolls, costumes and a video on the movie's making.

Orangeburg, South Carolina
The I. P. Stanback Museum and Planetarium is located on the campus of South Carolina State University. It holds a notable concentration of arts from tribal Africa, in which Yoruba, Bamana, Mende, Baga and Dogon peoples are well represented.

Sumter, South Carolina
Cotton historically has been the South's major cash crop and is still big business in Lee County. The South Carolina Cotton Museum honors the plant with displays including a mule-powered gin replica and "spinning jennys," early multiple-spindle machines.

Sumter, South Carolina
Every June, six million iris burst into bloom at the Swan Lake Iris Gardens, surrounding a large lake serenely lapped by six species of swans—an unforgettable sight.

Atlanta, Georgia
The World of Coca-Cola pays tribute to the globally known beverage with memorabilia, trivia and the history of the drink. Coca-Cola got its start in an Atlanta drugstore in 1886 completely by accident: it was supposed to be made with tap water, but a clerk accidentally used soda water instead.

St Augustine, Florida
Established in 1565, picturesque St Augustine is the oldest continually inhabited town in the so-called New World. It served as the Spanish capital of the Province of Florida for over 200 years, and retains its colonial flavor in the 400-year-old Spanish Quarter and the Castillo de San Marcos.

Miami, Florida
The Art Deco Historic District forms the heart of Miami's flamboyant South Beach neighborhood. This 18-block area of renovated art deco, streamline, moderne and Mediterranean revival buildings features retail shops, galleries, nightclubs, apartment buildings, hotels and restaurants. Guided tours are available.

St Petersburg, Florida
Try to keep a sane head when viewing one of the world's largest collections of surrealist art at the Salvador Dalí Museum. The collection has nearly 1,500 works of art, including glass sculpture, drawings and 94 of his oil paintings.

Homestead, Florida
Unless its decline is reversed, Everglades National Park may become another paved-over theme park. Development has encroached on this marshy home to many endangered or threatened animal and plant species, including the American crocodile and the Florida panther.

NORTH CAROLINA
SOUTH CAROLINA
GEORGIA
FLORIDA
ATLANTIC OCEAN
BAHAMAS

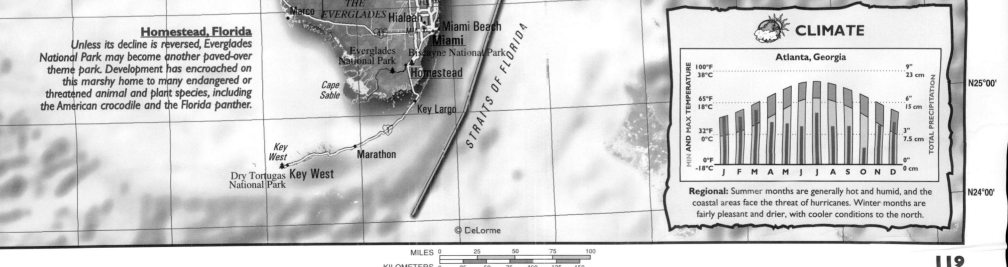

CLIMATE

Atlanta, Georgia

MIN AND MAX TEMPERATURE — TOTAL PRECIPITATION

J F M A M J J A S O N D

Regional: Summer months are generally hot and humid, and the coastal areas face the threat of hurricanes. Winter months are fairly pleasant and drier, with cooler conditions to the north.

© DeLorme

MILES 0 25 50 75 100
KILOMETERS 0 25 50 75 100 125 150

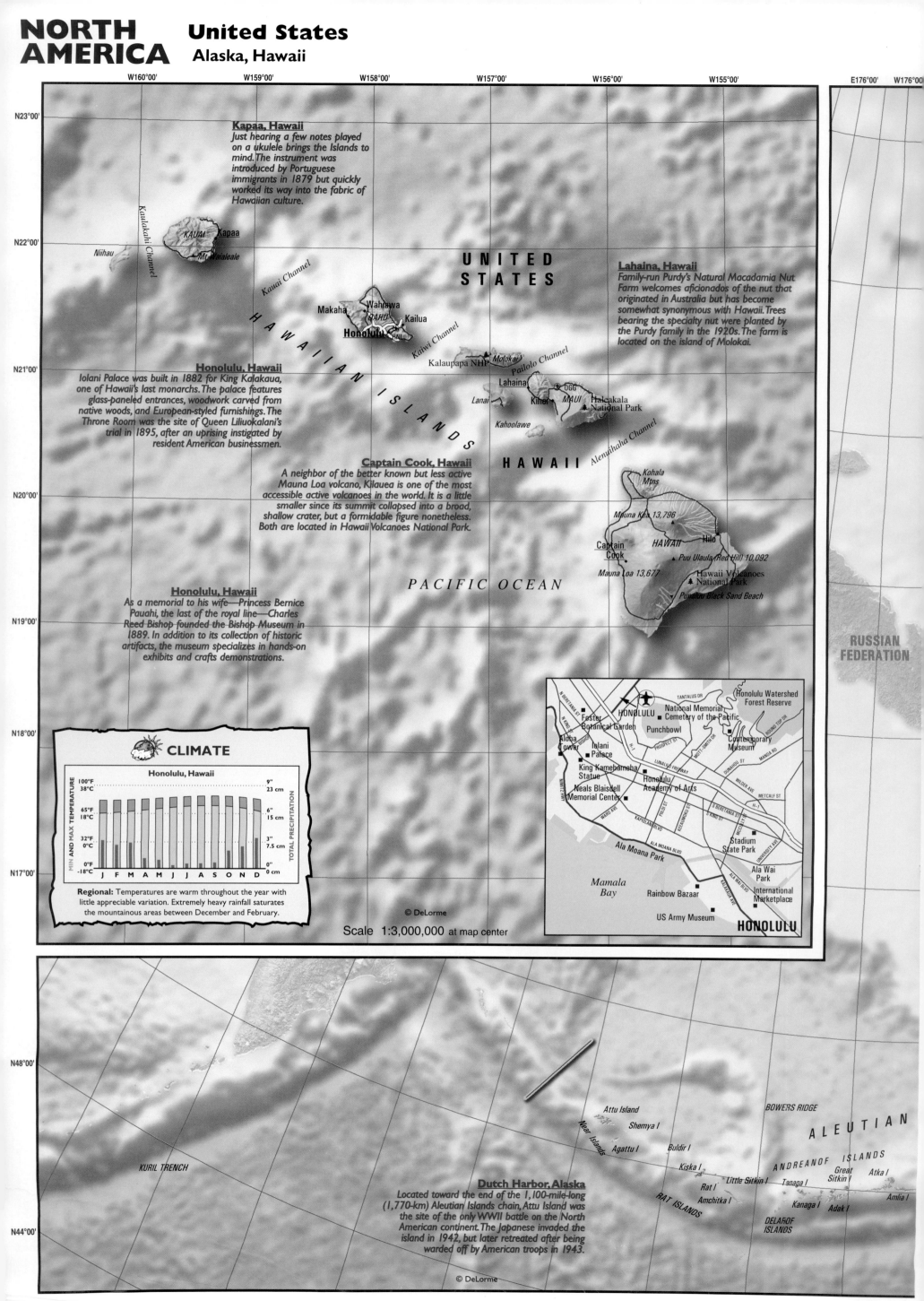

W160°00' W159°00' W158°00' W157°00' W156°00' W155°00' E176°00' W176°00'

N23°00' N22°00' N21°00' N20°00' N19°00' N18°00' N17°00'

Kapaa, Hawaii
Just hearing a few notes played on a ukulele brings the Islands to mind. The instrument was introduced by Portuguese immigrants in 1879 but quickly worked its way into the fabric of Hawaiian culture.

Lahaina, Hawaii
Family-run Purdy's Natural Macadamia Nut Farm welcomes aficionados of the nut that originated in Australia but has become somewhat synonymous with Hawaii. Trees bearing the specialty nut were planted by the Purdy family in the 1920s. The farm is located on the island of Molokai.

Honolulu, Hawaii
Iolani Palace was built in 1882 for King Kalakaua, one of Hawaii's last monarchs. The palace features glass-paneled entrances, woodwork carved from native woods, and European-styled furnishings. The Throne Room was the site of Queen Liliuokalani's trial in 1895, after an uprising instigated by resident American businessmen.

Captain Cook, Hawaii
A neighbor of the better known but less active Mauna Loa volcano, Kilauea is one of the most accessible active volcanoes in the world. It is a little smaller since its summit collapsed into a broad, shallow crater, but a formidable figure nonetheless. Both are located in Hawaii Volcanoes National Park.

Honolulu, Hawaii
As a memorial to his wife—Princess Bernice Pauahi, the last of the royal line—Charles Reed Bishop founded the Bishop Museum in 1889. In addition to its collection of historic artifacts, the museum specializes in hands-on exhibits and crafts demonstrations.

UNITED STATES

HAWAIIAN ISLANDS

HAWAII

PACIFIC OCEAN

Kauai
Kapaa
Niihau
Mt. Waialeale
Kaulakahi Channel
Kauai Channel
Makaha
Wahiawa
OAHU
Kailua
Honolulu
HNL
Kaiwi Channel
Molokai
Kalaupapa NHP
Pailolo Channel
Lahaina
Lanai
Kihei
MAUI
OGG
Haleakala National Park
Kahoolawe
Alenuihaha Channel
Kohala Mtns
Mauna Kea 13,796
Hilo
HAWAII
Captain Cook
Puu Ulaula (Red Hill) 10,092
Mauna Loa 13,677
Hawaii Volcanoes National Park
Punaluu Black Sand Beach

RUSSIAN FEDERATION

CLIMATE

Honolulu, Hawaii

MIN AND MAX TEMPERATURE
100°F / 38°C
65°F / 18°C
32°F / 0°C
0°F / -18°C

TOTAL PRECIPITATION
9" / 23 cm
6" / 15 cm
3" / 7.5 cm
0" / 0 cm

J F M A M J J A S O N D

Regional: Temperatures are warm throughout the year with little appreciable variation. Extremely heavy rainfall saturates the mountainous areas between December and February.

© DeLorme

Scale 1:3,000,000 at map center

HONOLULU

N Beretania St
Tantalus Dr
Honolulu Watershed Forest Reserve
Foster Botanical Garden
N King St
HONOLULU
Punchbowl
National Memorial Cemetery of the Pacific
Contemporary Museum
Aloha Tower
Iolani Palace
Prospect St
H-1
King Kamehameha Statue
Honolulu Academy of Arts
S Beretania St
Neals Blaisdell Memorial Center
Ward Ave
Kapiolani Blvd
Stadium State Park
Ala Moana Park
Ala Moana Blvd
Ala Wai Park
Mamala Bay
Rainbow Bazaar
International Marketplace
US Army Museum

N48°00' N44°00'

Attu Island
Shemya I
Near Islands
Agattu I
Buldir I
BOWERS RIDGE
ALEUTIAN
ANDREANOF ISLANDS
Great Sitkin I
Atka I
KURIL TRENCH
Kiska I
Little Sitkin I
Tanaga I
Amlia I
Rat I
Amchitka I
Kanaga I
Adak I
RAT ISLANDS
DELAROF ISLANDS

Dutch Harbor, Alaska
Located toward the end of the 1,100-mile-long (1,770-km) Aleutian Islands chain, Attu Island was the site of the only WWII battle on the North American continent. The Japanese invaded the island in 1942, but later retreated after being warded off by American troops in 1943.

© DeLorme

Scale 1:10,000,000 at map center

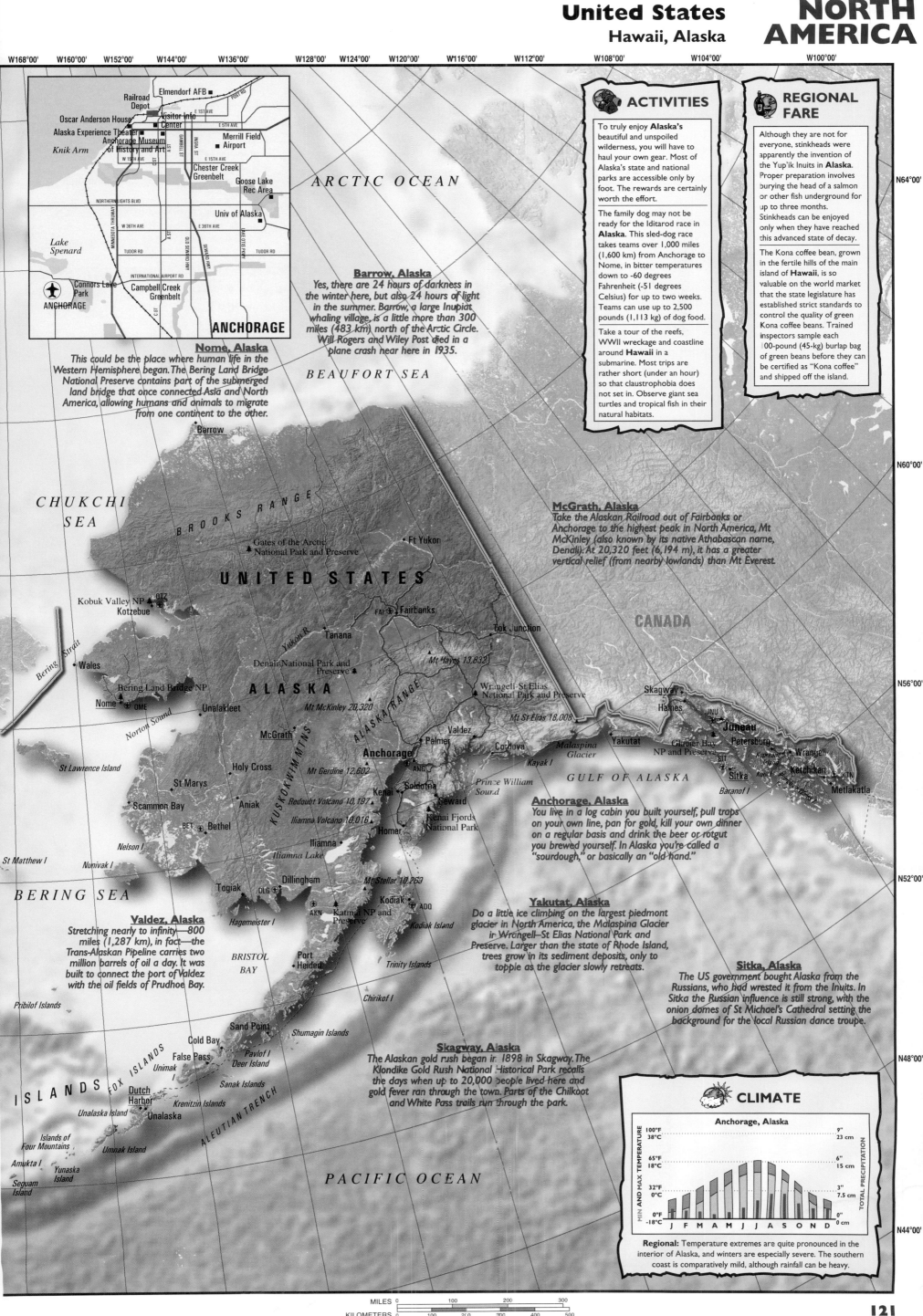

ANCHORAGE (inset map)

Railroad Depot · Elmendorf AFB · PORT RD · E 5TH AVE · Oscar Anderson House · Visitor Info Center · Alaska Experience Theater · Anchorage Museum of History and Art · Merrill Field Airport · W 15TH AVE · E 15TH AVE · Chester Creek Greenbelt · Goose Lake Rec Area · Knik Arm · Lake Spenard · W 36TH AVE · E 36TH AVE · Univ of Alaska · TUDOR RD · NORTHERN LIGHTS BLVD · MINNESOTA THRUWAY · INTERNATIONAL AIRPORT RD · Connors Lake Park · Campbell Creek Greenbelt · ANCHORAGE

ACTIVITIES

To truly enjoy **Alaska's** beautiful and unspoiled wilderness, you will have to haul your own gear. Most of Alaska's state and national parks are accessible only by foot. The rewards are certainly worth the effort.

The family dog may not be ready for the Iditarod race in **Alaska**. This sled-dog race takes teams over 1,000 miles (1,600 km) from Anchorage to Nome, in bitter temperatures down to -60 degrees Fahrenheit (-51 degrees Celsius) for up to two weeks. Teams can use up to 2,500 pounds (1,113 kg) of dog food.

Take a tour of the reefs, WWII wreckage and coastline around **Hawaii** in a submarine. Most trips are rather short (under an hour) so that claustrophobia does not set in. Observe giant sea turtles and tropical fish in their natural habitats.

REGIONAL FARE

Although they are not for everyone, stinkheads were apparently the invention of the Yup'ik Inuits in **Alaska**. Proper preparation involves burying the head of a salmon or other fish underground for up to three months. Stinkheads can be enjoyed only when they have reached this advanced state of decay.

The Kona coffee bean, grown in the fertile hills of the main island of **Hawaii**, is so valuable on the world market that the state legislature has established strict standards to control the quality of green Kona coffee beans. Trained inspectors sample each 100-pound (45-kg) burlap bag of green beans before they can be certified as "Kona coffee" and shipped off the island.

Barrow, Alaska
Yes, there are 24 hours of darkness in the winter here, but also 24 hours of light in the summer. Barrow, a large Inupiat whaling village, is a little more than 300 miles (483 km) north of the Arctic Circle. Will Rogers and Wiley Post died in a plane crash near here in 1935.

Nome, Alaska
This could be the place where human life in the Western Hemisphere began. The Bering Land Bridge National Preserve contains part of the submerged land bridge that once connected Asia and North America, allowing humans and animals to migrate from one continent to the other.

McGrath, Alaska
Take the Alaskan Railroad out of Fairbanks or Anchorage to the highest peak in North America, Mt McKinley (also known by its native Athabascan name, Denali). At 20,320 feet (6,194 m), it has a greater vertical relief (from nearby lowlands) than Mt Everest.

Anchorage, Alaska
You live in a log cabin you built yourself, pull traps on your own line, pan for gold, kill your own dinner on a regular basis and drink the beer or rotgut you brewed yourself. In Alaska you're called a "sourdough," or basically an "old hand."

Valdez, Alaska
Stretching nearly to infinity—800 miles (1,287 km), in fact—the Trans-Alaskan Pipeline carries two million barrels of oil a day. It was built to connect the port of Valdez with the oil fields of Prudhoe Bay.

Yakutat, Alaska
Do a little ice climbing on the largest piedmont glacier in North America, the Malaspina Glacier in Wrangell–St Elias National Park and Preserve. Larger than the state of Rhode Island, trees grow in its sediment deposits, only to topple as the glacier slowly retreats.

Sitka, Alaska
The US government bought Alaska from the Russians, who had wrested it from the Inuits. In Sitka the Russian influence is still strong, with the onion domes of St Michael's Cathedral setting the background for the local Russian dance troupe.

Skagway, Alaska
The Alaskan gold rush began in 1898 in Skagway. The Klondike Gold Rush National Historical Park recalls the days when up to 20,000 people lived here and gold fever ran through the town. Parts of the Chilkoot and White Pass trails run through the park.

CLIMATE

Anchorage, Alaska

Regional: Temperature extremes are quite pronounced in the interior of Alaska, and winters are especially severe. The southern coast is comparatively mild, although rainfall can be heavy.

MILES 0 · 100 · 200 · 300
KILOMETERS 0 · 100 · 200 · 300 · 400 · 500

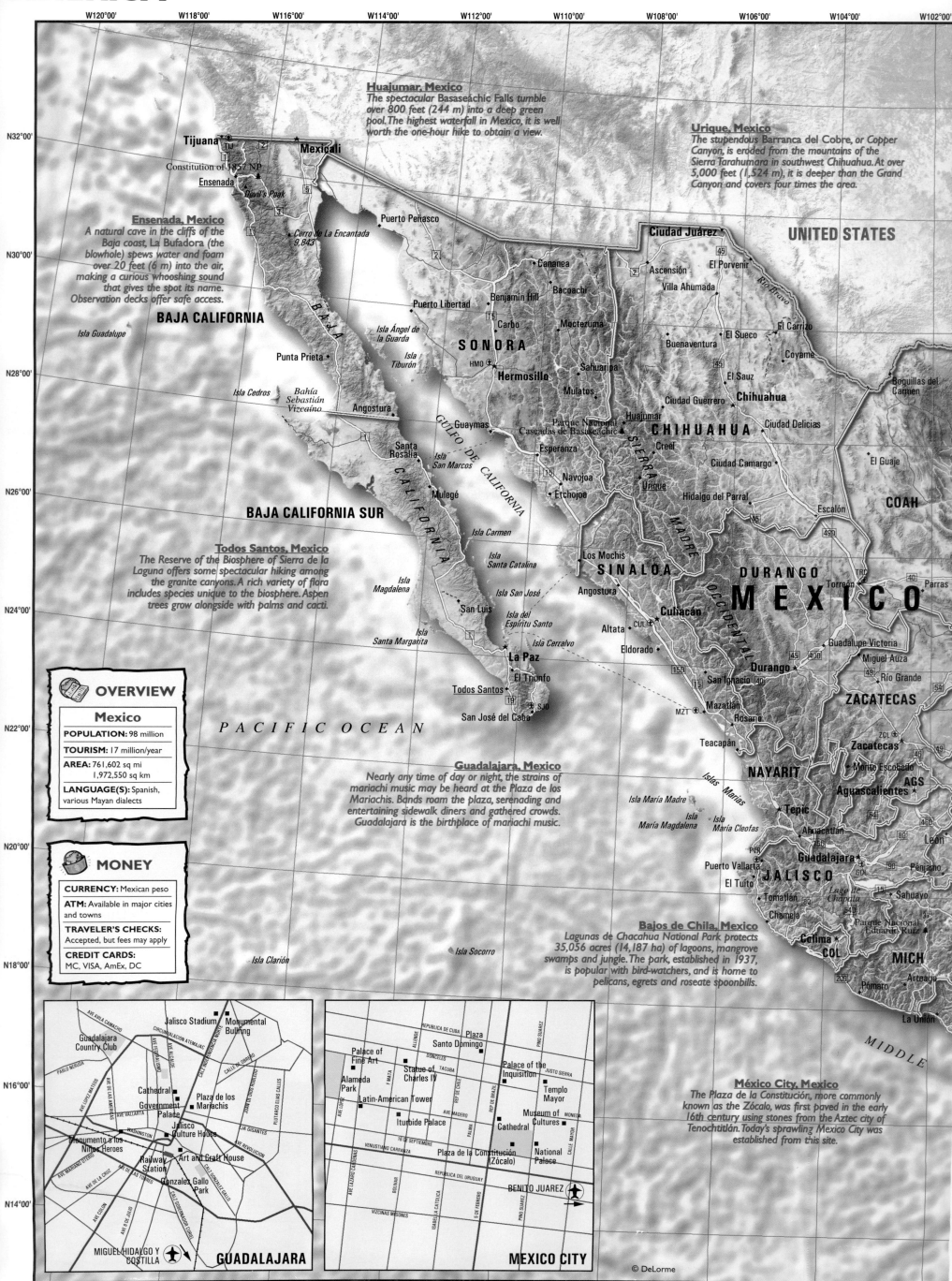

Huajumar, Mexico
The spectacular Basaseáchic Falls tumble over 800 feet (244 m) into a deep green pool. The highest waterfall in Mexico, it is well worth the one-hour hike to obtain a view.

Urique, Mexico
The stupendous Barranca del Cobre, or Copper Canyon, is eroded from the mountains of the Sierra Tarahumara in southwest Chihuahua. At over 5,000 feet (1,524 m), it is deeper than the Grand Canyon and covers four times the area.

Ensenada, Mexico
A natural cave in the cliffs of the Baja coast, La Bufadora (the blowhole) spews water and foam over 20 feet (6 m) into the air, making a curious whooshing sound that gives the spot its name. Observation decks offer safe access.

UNITED STATES

Todos Santos, Mexico
The Reserve of the Biosphere of Sierra de la Laguna offers some spectacular hiking among the granite canyons. A rich variety of flora includes species unique to the biosphere. Aspen trees grow alongside with palms and cacti.

OVERVIEW

Mexico

POPULATION: 98 million

TOURISM: 17 million/year

AREA: 761,602 sq mi
1,972,550 sq km

LANGUAGE(S): Spanish, various Mayan dialects

MONEY

CURRENCY: Mexican peso

ATM: Available in major cities and towns

TRAVELER'S CHECKS: Accepted, but fees may apply

CREDIT CARDS: MC, VISA, AmEx, DC

PACIFIC OCEAN

Guadalajara, Mexico
Nearly any time of day or night, the strains of mariachi music may be heard at the Plaza de los Mariachis. Bands roam the plaza, serenading and entertaining sidewalk diners and gathered crowds. Guadalajara is the birthplace of mariachi music.

Bajos de Chila, Mexico
Lagunas de Chacahua National Park protects 35,056 acres (14,187 ha) of lagoons, mangrove swamps and jungle. The park, established in 1937, is popular with bird-watchers, and is home to pelicans, egrets and roseate spoonbills.

México City, Mexico
The Plaza de la Constitución, more commonly known as the Zócalo, was first paved in the early 16th century using stones from the Aztec city of Tenochtitlán. Today's sprawling Mexico City was established from this site.

GUADALAJARA

MEXICO CITY

© DeLorme

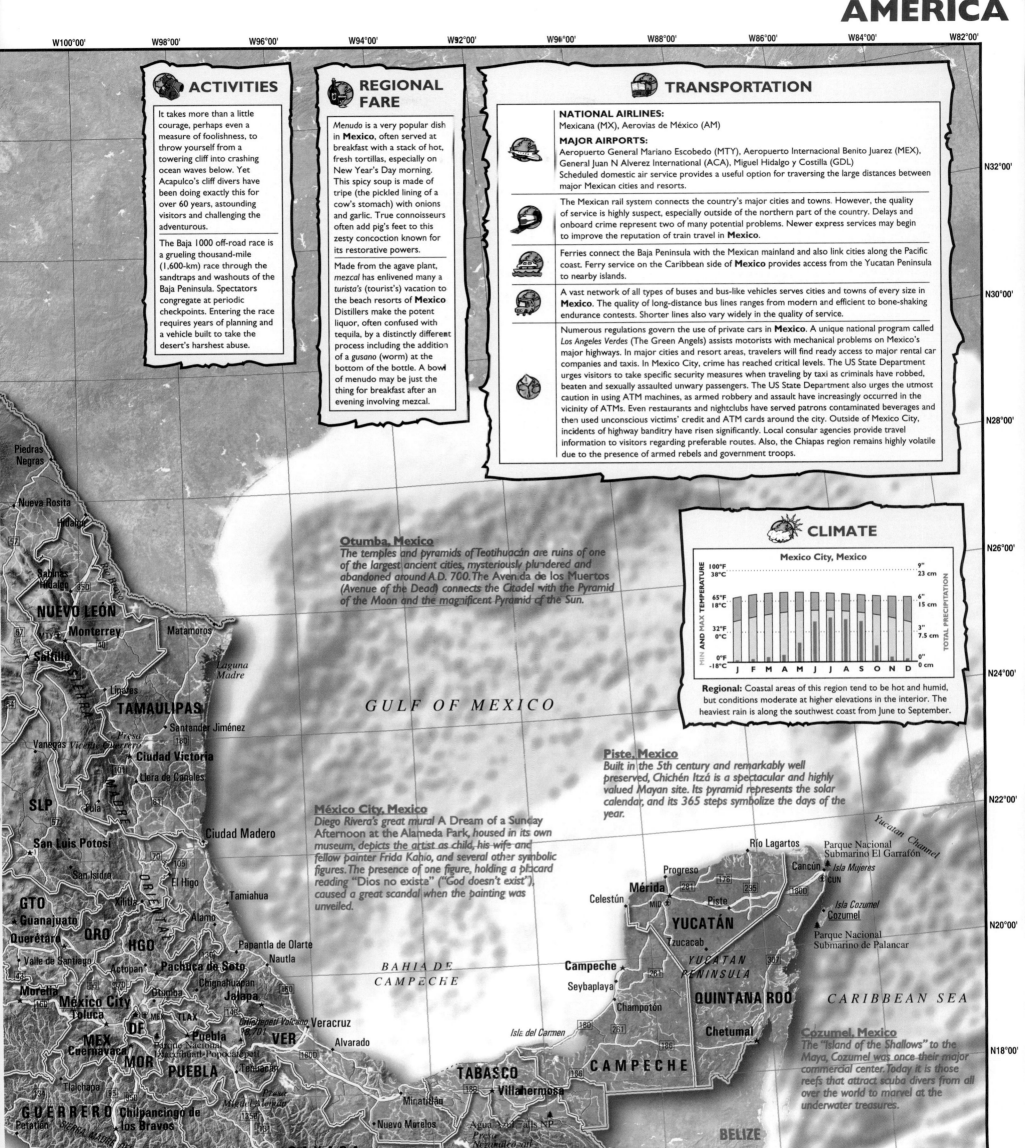

ACTIVITIES

It takes more than a little courage, perhaps even a measure of foolishness, to throw yourself from a towering cliff into crashing ocean waves below. Yet Acapulco's cliff divers have been doing exactly this for over 60 years, astounding visitors and challenging the adventurous.

The Baja 1000 off-road race is a grueling thousand-mile (1,600-km) race through the sandtraps and washouts of the Baja Peninsula. Spectators congregate at periodic checkpoints. Entering the race requires years of planning and a vehicle built to take the desert's harshest abuse.

REGIONAL FARE

Menudo is a very popular dish in **Mexico**, often served at breakfast with a stack of hot, fresh tortillas, especially on New Year's Day morning. This spicy soup is made of tripe (the pickled lining of a cow's stomach) with onions and garlic. True connoisseurs often add pig's feet to this zesty concoction known for its restorative powers.

Made from the agave plant, *mezcal* has enlivened many a *turista's* (tourist's) vacation to the beach resorts of **Mexico** Distillers make the potent liquor, often confused with tequila, by a distinctly different process including the addition of a *gusano* (worm) at the bottom of the bottle. A bowl of menudo may be just the thing for breakfast after an evening involving mezcal.

TRANSPORTATION

NATIONAL AIRLINES:
Mexicana (MX), Aerovias de México (AM)

MAJOR AIRPORTS:
Aeropuerto General Mariano Escobedo (MTY), Aeropuerto Internacional Benito Juarez (MEX), General Juan N Alverez International (ACA), Miguel Hidalgo y Costilla (GDL)
Scheduled domestic air service provides a useful option for traversing the large distances between major Mexican cities and resorts.

The Mexican rail system connects the country's major cities and towns. However, the quality of service is highly suspect, especially outside of the northern part of the country. Delays and onboard crime represent two of many potential problems. Newer express services may begin to improve the reputation of train travel in **Mexico**.

Ferries connect the Baja Peninsula with the Mexican mainland and also link cities along the Pacific coast. Ferry service on the Caribbean side of **Mexico** provides access from the Yucatan Peninsula to nearby islands.

A vast network of all types of buses and bus-like vehicles serves cities and towns of every size in **Mexico**. The quality of long-distance bus lines ranges from modern and efficient to bone-shaking endurance contests. Shorter lines also vary widely in the quality of service.

Numerous regulations govern the use of private cars in **Mexico**. A unique national program called *Los Angeles Verdes* (The Green Angels) assists motorists with mechanical problems on Mexico's major highways. In major cities and resort areas, travelers will find ready access to major rental car companies and taxis. In Mexico City, crime has reached critical levels. The US State Department urges visitors to take specific security measures when traveling by taxi as criminals have robbed, beaten and sexually assaulted unwary passengers. The US State Department also urges the utmost caution in using ATM machines, as armed robbery and assault have increasingly occurred in the vicinity of ATMs. Even restaurants and nightclubs have served patrons contaminated beverages and then used unconscious victims' credit and ATM cards around the city. Outside of Mexico City, incidents of highway banditry have risen significantly. Local consular agencies provide travel information to visitors regarding preferable routes. Also, the Chiapas region remains highly volatile due to the presence of armed rebels and government troops.

CLIMATE

Mexico City, Mexico

Regional: Coastal areas of this region tend to be hot and humid, but conditions moderate at higher elevations in the interior. The heaviest rain is along the southwest coast from June to September.

Otumba, Mexico
The temples and pyramids of *Teotihuacán* are ruins of one of the largest ancient cities, mysteriously plundered and abandoned around A.D. 700. The Avenida de los Muertos (Avenue of the Dead) connects the Citadel with the Pyramid of the Moon and the magnificent Pyramid of the Sun.

México City, Mexico
Diego Rivera's great mural *A Dream of a Sunday Afternoon at the Alameda Park*, housed in its own museum, depicts the artist as child, his wife and fellow painter Frida Kahlo, and several other symbolic figures. The presence of one figure, holding a placard reading "Dios no existe" ("God doesn't exist"), caused a great scandal when the painting was unveiled.

Piste, Mexico
Built in the 5th century and remarkably well preserved, Chichén Itzá is a spectacular and highly valued Mayan site. Its pyramid represents the solar calendar, and its 365 steps symbolize the days of the year.

Cozumel, Mexico
The "Island of the Shallows" to the Maya, Cozumel was once their major commercial center. Today it is those reefs that attract scuba divers from all over the world to marvel at the underwater treasures.

Oaxaca, Mexico
Oaxaca is famous for its Dia de los Muertos (Day of the Dead) festival held the day after All Saints Day. Food and crafts shaped in the form of skulls and skeletons are sold on the streets. This celebration of death and life is marked throughout Mexico.

GULF OF MEXICO

BAHIA DE CAMPECHE

CARIBBEAN SEA

GULFO DE TEHUANTEPEC

GUATEMALA

HONDURAS

BELIZE

MILES 0 50 100 150 200
KILOMETERS 0 50 100 150 200 250 300

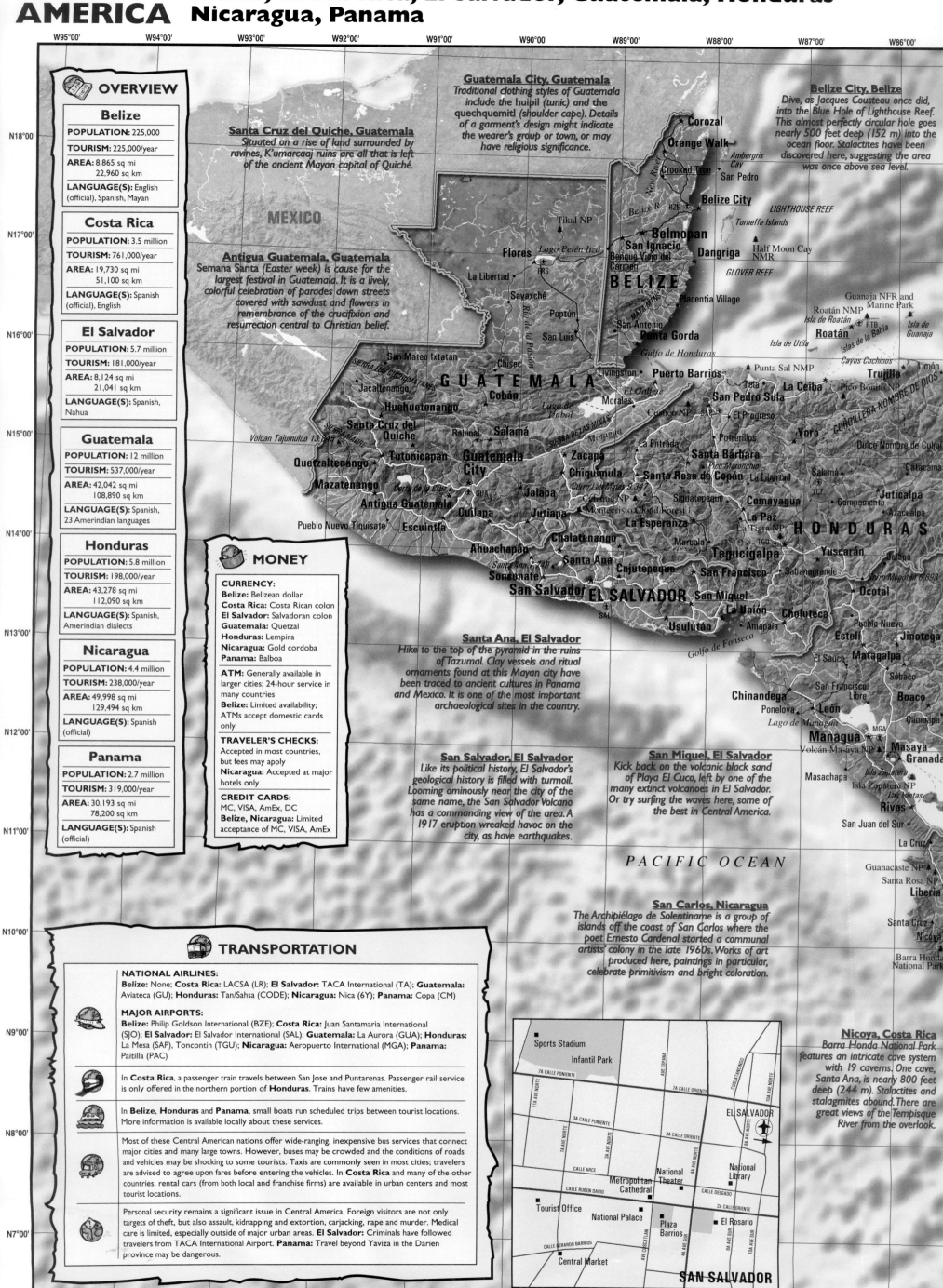

OVERVIEW

Belize
POPULATION: 225,000
TOURISM: 225,000/year
AREA: 8,865 sq mi 22,960 sq km
LANGUAGE(S): English (official), Spanish, Mayan

Costa Rica
POPULATION: 3.5 million
TOURISM: 761,000/year
AREA: 19,730 sq mi 51,100 sq km
LANGUAGE(S): Spanish (official), English

El Salvador
POPULATION: 5.7 million
TOURISM: 181,000/year
AREA: 8,124 sq mi 21,041 sq km
LANGUAGE(S): Spanish, Nahua

Guatemala
POPULATION: 12 million
TOURISM: 537,000/year
AREA: 42,042 sq mi 108,890 sq km
LANGUAGE(S): Spanish, 23 Amerindian languages

Honduras
POPULATION: 5.8 million
TOURISM: 198,000/year
AREA: 43,278 sq mi 112,090 sq km
LANGUAGE(S): Spanish, Amerindian dialects

Nicaragua
POPULATION: 4.4 million
TOURISM: 238,000/year
AREA: 49,998 sq mi 129,494 sq km
LANGUAGE(S): Spanish (official)

Panama
POPULATION: 2.7 million
TOURISM: 319,000/year
AREA: 30,193 sq mi 78,200 sq km
LANGUAGE(S): Spanish (official)

MONEY

CURRENCY:
Belize: Belizean dollar
Costa Rica: Costa Rican colon
El Salvador: Salvadoran colon
Guatemala: Quetzal
Honduras: Lempira
Nicaragua: Gold cordoba
Panama: Balboa

ATM: Generally available in larger cities; 24-hour service in many countries
Belize: Limited availability; ATMs accept domestic cards only

TRAVELER'S CHECKS:
Accepted in most countries, but fees may apply
Nicaragua: Accepted at major hotels only

CREDIT CARDS:
MC, VISA, AmEx, DC
Belize, Nicaragua: Limited acceptance of MC, VISA, AmEx

TRANSPORTATION

NATIONAL AIRLINES:
Belize: None; **Costa Rica:** LACSA (LR); **El Salvador:** TACA International (TA); **Guatemala:** Aviateca (GU); **Honduras:** Tan/Sahsa (CODE); **Nicaragua:** Nica (6Y); **Panama:** Copa (CM)

MAJOR AIRPORTS:
Belize: Philip Goldson International (BZE); **Costa Rica:** Juan Santamaria International (SJO); **El Salvador:** El Salvador International (SAL); **Guatemala:** La Aurora (GUA); **Honduras:** La Mesa (SAP), Toncontin (TGU); **Nicaragua:** Aeropuerto International (MGA); **Panama:** Paitilla (PAC)

In **Costa Rica**, a passenger train travels between San Jose and Puntarenas. Passenger rail service is only offered in the northern portion of **Honduras**. Trains have few amenities.

In **Belize, Honduras** and **Panama**, small boats run scheduled trips between tourist locations. More information is available locally about these services.

Most of these Central American nations offer wide-ranging, inexpensive bus services that connect major cities and many large towns. However, buses may be crowded and the conditions of roads and vehicles may be shocking to some tourists. Taxis are commonly seen in most cities; travelers are advised to agree upon fares before entering the vehicles. In **Costa Rica** and many of the other countries, rental cars (from both local and franchise firms) are available in urban centers and most tourist locations.

Personal security remains a significant issue in Central America. Foreign visitors are not only targets of theft, but also assault, kidnapping and extortion, carjacking, rape and murder. Medical care is limited, especially outside of major urban areas. **El Salvador:** Criminals have followed travelers from TACA International Airport. **Panama:** Travel beyond Yaviza in the Darien province may be dangerous.

Guatemala City, Guatemala
Traditional clothing styles of Guatemala include the huipil (tunic) and the quechquemitl (shoulder cape). Details of a garment's design might indicate the wearer's group or town, or may have religious significance.

Santa Cruz del Quiche, Guatemala
Situated on a rise of land surrounded by ravines, K'umarcaaj ruins are all that is left of the ancient Mayan capital of Quiché.

Antigua Guatemala, Guatemala
Semana Santa (Easter week) is cause for the largest festival in Guatemala. It is a lively, colorful celebration of parades down streets covered with sawdust and flowers in remembrance of the crucifixion and resurrection central to Christian belief.

Belize City, Belize
Dive, as Jacques Cousteau once did, into the Blue Hole of Lighthouse Reef. This almost perfectly circular hole goes nearly 500 feet deep (152 m) into the ocean floor. Stalactites have been discovered here, suggesting the area was once above sea level.

Santa Ana, El Salvador
Hike to the top of the pyramid in the ruins of Tazumal. Clay vessels and ritual ornaments found at this Mayan city have been traced to ancient cultures in Panama and Mexico. It is one of the most important archaeological sites in the country.

San Salvador, El Salvador
Like its political history, El Salvador's geological history is filled with turmoil. Looming ominously near the city of the same name, the San Salvador Volcano has a commanding view of the area. A 1917 eruption wreaked havoc on the city, as have earthquakes.

San Miguel, El Salvador
Kick back on the volcanic black sand of Playa El Cuco, left by one of the many extinct volcanoes in El Salvador. Or try surfing the waves here, some of the best in Central America.

San Carlos, Nicaragua
The Archipiélago de Solentiname is a group of islands off the coast of San Carlos where the poet Ernesto Cardenal started a communal artists' colony in the late 1960s. Works of art produced here, paintings in particular, celebrate primitivism and bright coloration.

Nicoya, Costa Rica
Barra Honda National Park features an intricate cave system with 19 caverns. One cave, Santa Ana, is nearly 800 feet deep (244 m). Stalactites and stalagmites abound. There are great views of the Tempisque River from the overlook.

Map labels include: MEXICO, BELIZE, GUATEMALA, HONDURAS, EL SALVADOR, Corozal, Orange Walk, Belize City, Belmopan, San Ignacio, Dangriga, Tikal NP, Flores, Lago Petén Itzá, La Libertad, Sayaxché, Poptún, San Luis, Punta Gorda, Cobán, Huehuetenango, Santa Cruz del Quiche, Quetzaltenango, Totonicapán, Guatemala City, Mazatenango, Antigua Guatemala, Escuintla, Puerto Barrios, La Ceiba, San Pedro Sula, Comayagua, Tegucigalpa, Juticalpa, Ocotal, Estelí, Jinotega, Matagalpa, Managua, Masaya, Granada, Rivas, San Juan del Sur, Liberia, Nicoya, Roatán, Lighthouse Reef, Glover Reef, PACIFIC OCEAN, Gulf of Honduras, Golfo de Fonseca

MONEY / Money map detail (San Salvador inset)
Sports Stadium, Infantil Park, EL SALVADOR, National Theater, National Library, Metropolitan Cathedral, Tourist Office, National Palace, Plaza Barrios, El Rosario, Central Market, SAN SALVADOR

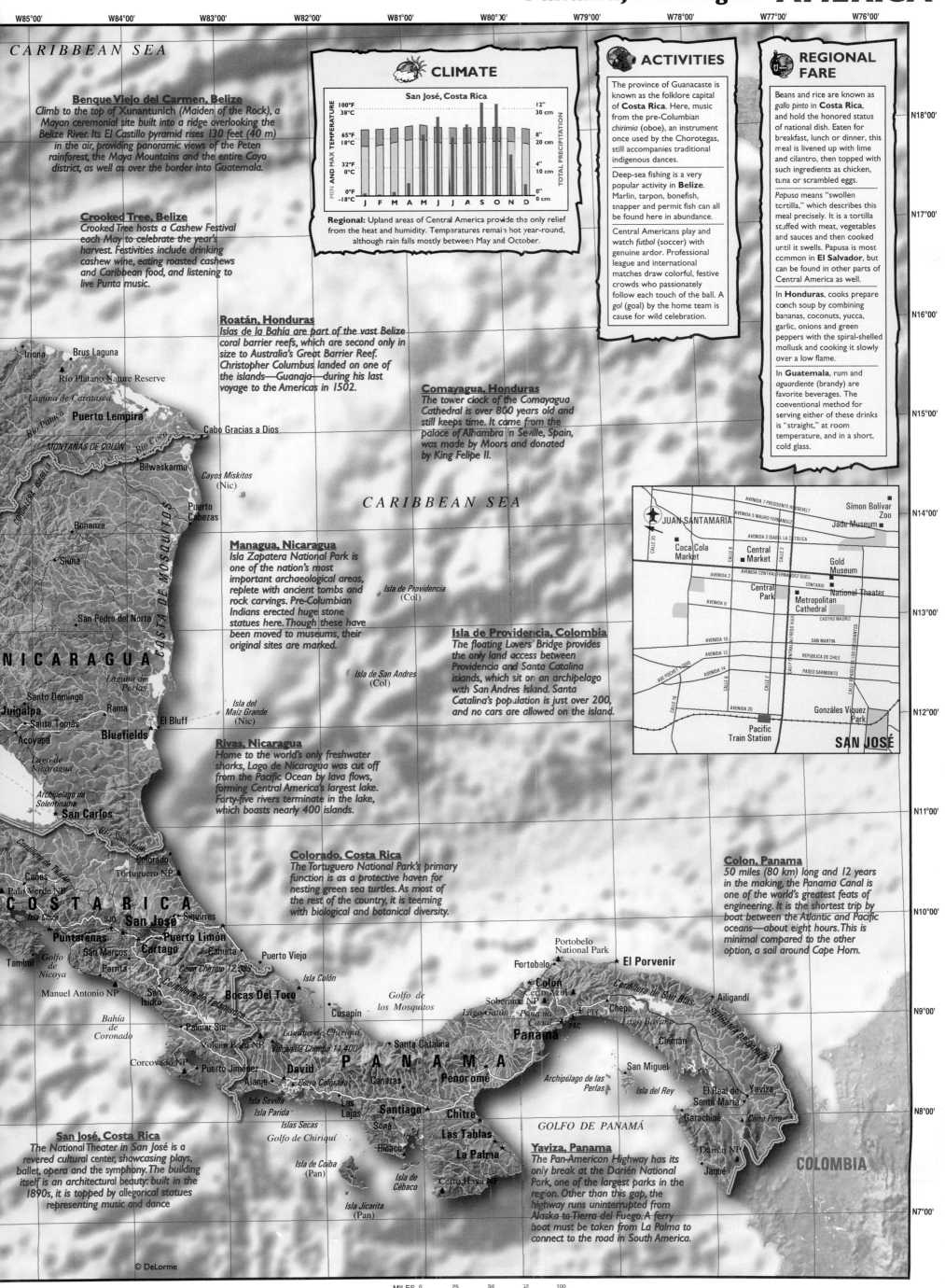

CARIBBEAN SEA

Benque Viejo del Carmen, Belize
Climb to the top of Xunantunich (Maiden of the Rock), a Mayan ceremonial site built into a ridge overlooking the Belize River. Its El Castillo pyramid rises 130 feet (40 m) in the air, providing panoramic views of the Peten rainforest, the Maya Mountains and the entire Cayo district, as well as over the border into Guatemala.

Crooked Tree, Belize
Crooked Tree hosts a Cashew Festival each May to celebrate the year's harvest. Festivities include drinking cashew wine, eating roasted cashews and Caribbean food, and listening to live Punta music.

Roatán, Honduras
Islas de la Bahía are part of the vast Belize coral barrier reefs, which are second only in size to Australia's Great Barrier Reef. Christopher Columbus landed on one of the islands—Guanaja—during his last voyage to the Americas in 1502.

Comayagua, Honduras
The tower clock of the Comayagua Cathedral is over 800 years old and still keeps time. It came from the palace of Alhambra in Seville, Spain, was made by Moors and donated by King Felipe II.

CARIBBEAN SEA

Managua, Nicaragua
Isla Zapatera National Park is one of the nation's most important archaeological areas, replete with ancient tombs and rock carvings. Pre-Columbian Indians erected huge stone statues here. Though these have been moved to museums, their original sites are marked.

Isla de Providencia, Colombia
The floating Lovers' Bridge provides the only land access between Providencia and Santa Catalina islands, which sit on an archipelago with San Andres Island. Santa Catalina's population is just over 200, and no cars are allowed on the island.

Rivas, Nicaragua
Home to the world's only freshwater sharks, Lago de Nicaragua was cut off from the Pacific Ocean by lava flows, forming Central America's largest lake. Forty-five rivers terminate in the lake, which boasts nearly 400 islands.

Colorado, Costa Rica
The Tortuguero National Park's primary function is as a protective haven for nesting green sea turtles. As most of the rest of the country, it is teeming with biological and botanical diversity.

Colon, Panama
50 miles (80 km) long and 12 years in the making, the Panama Canal is one of the world's greatest feats of engineering. It is the shortest trip by boat between the Atlantic and Pacific oceans—about eight hours. This is minimal compared to the other option, a sail around Cape Horn.

San José, Costa Rica
The National Theater in San José is a revered cultural center, showcasing plays, ballet, opera and the symphony. The building itself is an architectural beauty: built in the 1890s, it is topped by allegorical statues representing music and dance.

Yaviza, Panama
The Pan-American Highway has its only break at the Darién National Park, one of the largest parks in the region. Other than this gap, the highway runs uninterrupted from Alaska to Tierra del Fuego. A ferry boat must be taken from La Palma to connect to the road in South America.

CLIMATE
San José, Costa Rica

Regional: Upland areas of Central America provide the only relief from the heat and humidity. Temperatures remain hot year-round, although rain falls mostly between May and October.

ACTIVITIES
The province of Guanacaste is known as the folklore capital of **Costa Rica**. Here, music from the pre-Columbian *chirimia* (oboe), an instrument once used by the Chorotegas, still accompanies traditional indigenous dances.

Deep-sea fishing is a very popular activity in **Belize**. Marlin, tarpon, bonefish, snapper and permit fish can all be found here in abundance.

Central Americans play and watch *futbol* (soccer) with genuine ardor. Professional league and international matches draw colorful, festive crowds who passionately follow each touch of the ball. A *gol* (goal) by the home team is cause for wild celebration.

REGIONAL FARE
Beans and rice are known as *gallo pinto* in **Costa Rica**, and hold the honored status of national dish. Eaten for breakfast, lunch or dinner, this meal is livened up with lime and cilantro, then topped with such ingredients as chicken, tuna or scrambled eggs.

Papusa means "swollen tortilla," which describes this meal precisely. It is a tortilla stuffed with meat, vegetables and sauces and then cooked until it swells. Papusa is most common in **El Salvador**, but can be found in other parts of Central America as well.

In **Honduras**, cooks prepare conch soup by combining bananas, coconuts, yucca, garlic, onions and green peppers with the spiral-shelled mollusk and cooking it slowly over a low flame.

In **Guatemala**, rum and *aguardiente* (brandy) are favorite beverages. The conventional method for serving either of these drinks is "straight," at room temperature, and in a short, cold glass.

© DeLorme

MILES
KILOMETERS

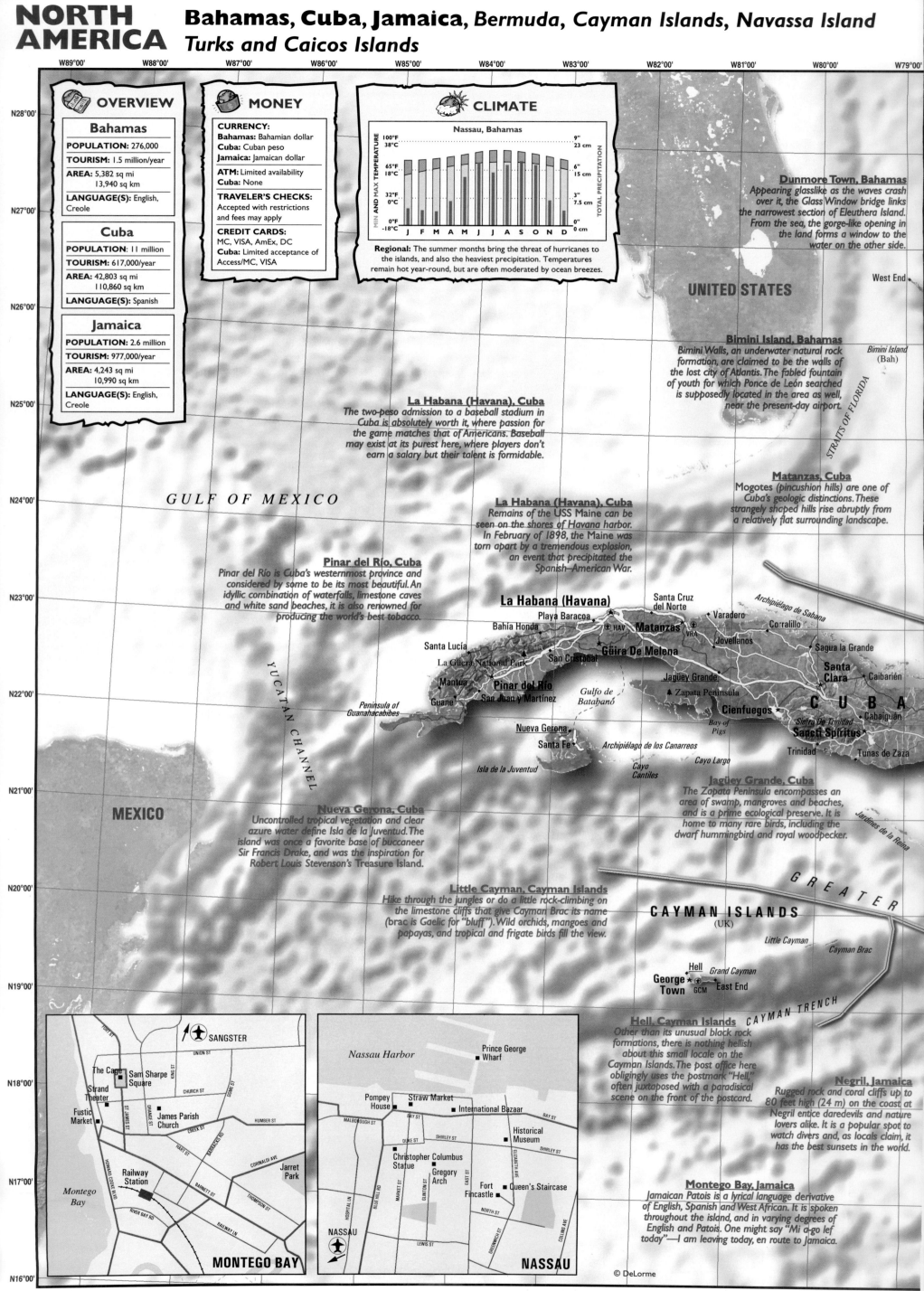

OVERVIEW

Bahamas
POPULATION: 276,000
TOURISM: 1.5 million/year
AREA: 5,382 sq mi
13,940 sq km
LANGUAGE(S): English, Creole

Cuba
POPULATION: 11 million
TOURISM: 617,000/year
AREA: 42,803 sq mi
110,860 sq km
LANGUAGE(S): Spanish

Jamaica
POPULATION: 2.6 million
TOURISM: 977,000/year
AREA: 4,243 sq mi
10,990 sq km
LANGUAGE(S): English, Creole

MONEY

CURRENCY:
Bahamas: Bahamian dollar
Cuba: Cuban peso
Jamaica: Jamaican dollar
ATM: Limited availability
Cuba: None
TRAVELER'S CHECKS: Accepted with restrictions and fees may apply
CREDIT CARDS: MC, VISA, AmEx, DC
Cuba: Limited acceptance of Access/MC, VISA

CLIMATE

Nassau, Bahamas

Regional: The summer months bring the threat of hurricanes to the islands, and also the heaviest precipitation. Temperatures remain hot year-round, but are often moderated by ocean breezes.

Dunmore Town, Bahamas
Appearing glasslike as the waves crash over it, the Glass Window bridge links the narrowest section of Eleuthera Island. From the sea, the gorge-like opening in the land forms a window to the water on the other side.

Bimini Island, Bahamas
Bimini Walls, an underwater natural rock formation, are claimed to be the walls of the lost city of Atlantis. The fabled fountain of youth for which Ponce de León searched is supposedly located in the area as well, near the present-day airport.

La Habana (Havana), Cuba
The two-peso admission to a baseball stadium in Cuba is absolutely worth it, where passion for the game matches that of the Americans. Baseball may exist at its purest here, where players don't earn a salary but their talent is formidable.

Matanzas, Cuba
Mogotes (pincushion hills) are one of Cuba's geologic distinctions. These strangely shaped hills rise abruptly from a relatively flat surrounding landscape.

La Habana (Havana), Cuba
Remains of the USS Maine can be seen on the shores of Havana harbor. In February of 1898, the Maine was torn apart by a tremendous explosion, an event that precipitated the Spanish–American War.

Pinar del Río, Cuba
Pinar del Río is Cuba's westernmost province and considered by some to be its most beautiful. An idyllic combination of waterfalls, limestone caves and white sand beaches, it is also renowned for producing the world's best tobacco.

Nueva Gerona, Cuba
Uncontrolled tropical vegetation and clear azure water define Isla de la Juventud. The island was once a favorite base of buccaneer Sir Francis Drake, and was the inspiration for Robert Louis Stevenson's Treasure Island.

Little Cayman, Cayman Islands
Hike through the jungles or do a little rock-climbing on the limestone cliffs that give Cayman Brac its name (brac is Gaelic for "bluff"). Wild orchids, mangoes and papayas, and tropical and frigate birds fill the view.

Jagüey Grande, Cuba
The Zapata Peninsula encompasses an area of swamp, mangroves and beaches, and is a prime ecological preserve. It is home to many rare birds, including the dwarf hummingbird and royal woodpecker.

Hell, Cayman Islands
Other than its unusual black rock formations, there is nothing hellish about this small locale on the Cayman Islands. The post office here obligingly uses the postmark "Hell" often juxtaposed with a paradisical scene on the front of the postcard.

Negril, Jamaica
Rugged rock and coral cliffs up to 80 feet high (24 m) on the coast at Negril entice daredevils and nature lovers alike. It is a popular spot to watch divers and, as locals claim, it has the best sunsets in the world.

Montego Bay, Jamaica
Jamaican Patois is a lyrical language derivative of English, Spanish and West African. It is spoken throughout the island, and in varying degrees of English and Patois. One might say "Mi a-go lef today"—I am leaving today, en route to Jamaica.

Map labels:
UNITED STATES
West End
Bimini Island (Bah)
STRAITS OF FLORIDA
GULF OF MEXICO
YUCATAN CHANNEL
MEXICO
Peninsula of Guanahacabibes
Mantua
Guane
San Juan y Martínez
Santa Lucía
La Güira National Park
Bahía Honda
Playa Baracoa
La Habana (Havana)
HAV
Santa Cruz del Norte
Varadero
VRA
Corralillo
Archipiélago de Sabana
Matanzas
Jovellanos
Sagua la Grande
San Cristóbal
Güira De Melena
Pinar del Río
Jagüey Grande
Santa Clara
Caibarién
Nueva Gerona
Gulfo de Batabanó
Zapata Peninsula
Cienfuegos
Sierra De Trinidad
Cabaiguán
CUBA
Santa Fe
Archipiélago de los Canarreos
Bay of Pigs
Sancti Spíritus
Isla de la Juventud
Cayo Largo
Cayo Cantiles
Trinidad
Tunas de Zaza
Jardines de la Reina
GREATER
CAYMAN ISLANDS (UK)
Little Cayman
Cayman Brac
Hell
Grand Cayman
George Town
GCM
East End
CAYMAN TRENCH

MONTEGO BAY (inset map)
SANGSTER
FORT ST
UNION ST
The Cage
Sam Sharpe Square
Strand Theater
Fustic Market
James Parish Church
CHURCH ST
CREEK ST
HUMBER ST
HART ST
BARRACKS RD
CORINALDI AVE
Railway Station
Jarret Park
Montego Bay
HOWARD COOKE BLVD
RIVER BAY RD
BARNETT ST
THOMPSON ST
RAILWAY LN
ST JAMES ST
ORANGE ST
ST JAMES ST
DUKE ST

NASSAU (inset map)
Nassau Harbor
Prince George Wharf
Pompey House
Straw Market
International Bazaar
Christopher Columbus Statue
Gregory Arch
Historical Museum
Fort Fincastle
Queen's Staircase
BAY ST
MALBOROUGH ST
SHIRLEY ST
MARKET ST
GEORGE ST
EAST ST
ELIZABETH ST
NORTH ST
LEWIS ST
COLLINS AVE
HOSPITAL LN
BLUE HILL RD
DUKE ST
GREENWOOD ST
NASSAU

© DeLorme

Scale 1:4,000,000 at map center

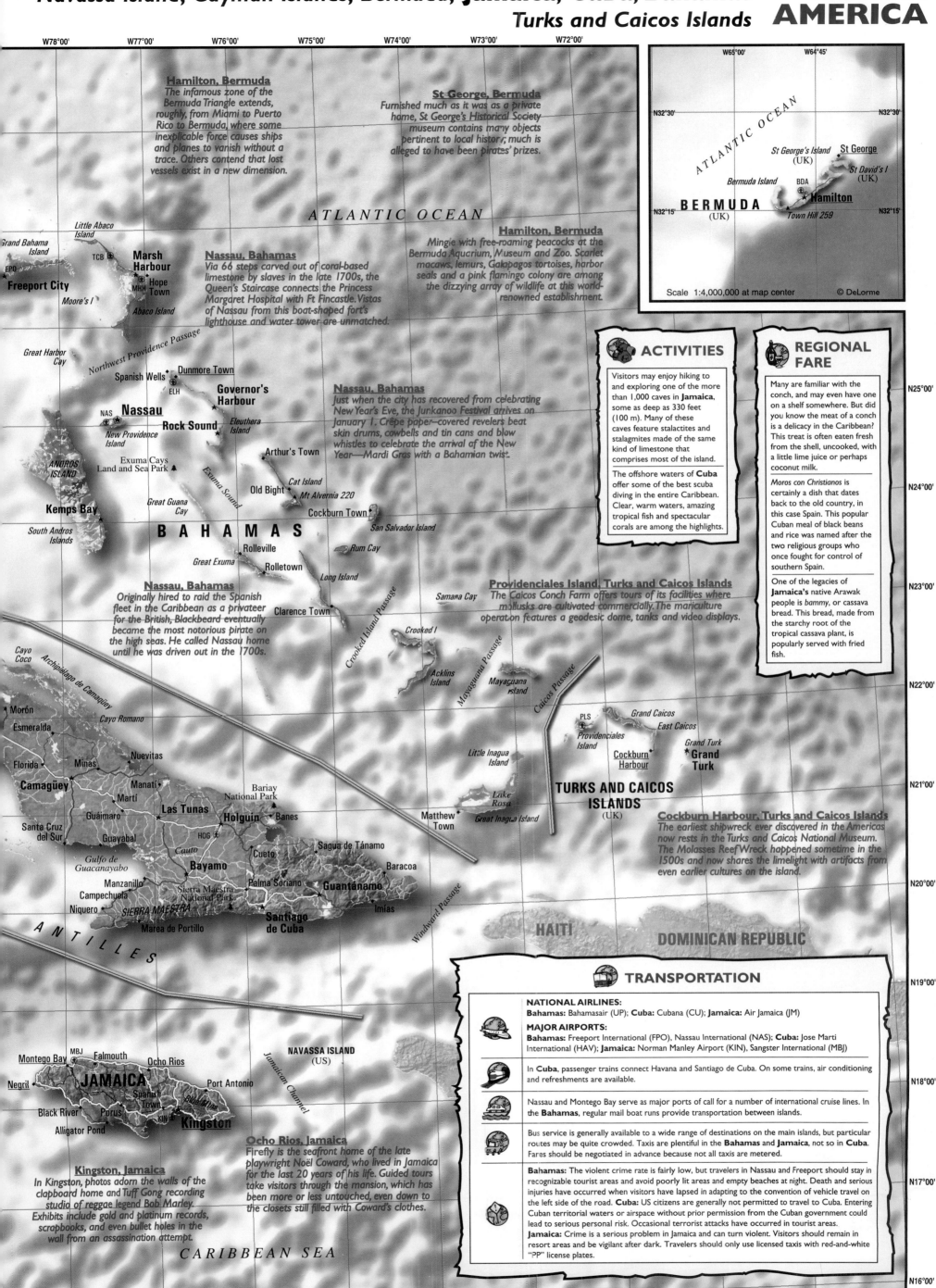

W78°00' W77°00' W76°00' W75°00' W74°00' W73°00' W72°00'

W65°00' W64°45'

Hamilton, Bermuda
The infamous zone of the Bermuda Triangle extends, roughly, from Miami to Puerto Rico to Bermuda, where some inexplicable force causes ships and planes to vanish without a trace. Others contend that lost vessels exist in a new dimension.

St George, Bermuda
Furnished much as it was as a private home, St George's Historical Society museum contains many objects pertinent to local history; much is alleged to have been pirates' prizes.

ATLANTIC OCEAN

N32°30'

N32°30'

St George's Island (UK) St George

Bermuda Island BDA St David's I (UK)

BERMUDA (UK) Hamilton

N32°15' Town Hill 259 **N32°15'**

Scale 1:4,000,000 at map center © DeLorme

Grand Bahama Island Little Abaco Island
EPO TCB Marsh Harbour
Freeport City MHH Hope Town
Moore's I Abaco Island

Nassau, Bahamas
Via 66 steps carved out of coral-based limestone by slaves in the late 1700s, the Queen's Staircase connects the Princess Margaret Hospital with Ft Fincastle. Vistas of Nassau from this boat-shaped fort's lighthouse and water tower are unmatched.

Hamilton, Bermuda
Mingle with free-roaming peacocks at the Bermuda Aquarium, Museum and Zoo. Scarlet macaws, lemurs, Galapagos tortoises, harbor seals and a pink flamingo colony are among the dizzying array of wildlife at this world-renowned establishment.

Great Harbor Cay
Northwest Providence Passage
Spanish Wells Dunmore Town
ELH **Governor's Harbour**
NAS **Nassau**
Rock Sound Eleuthera Island
New Providence Island
Exuma Cays Land and Sea Park
ANDROS ISLAND
Kemps Bay
South Andros Islands
BAHAMAS
Great Guana Cay
Rolleville
Great Exuma Rolletown
Long Island

Nassau, Bahamas
Just when the city has recovered from celebrating New Year's Eve, the Junkanoo Festival arrives on January 1. Crêpe paper–covered revelers beat skin drums, cowbells and tin cans and blow whistles to celebrate the arrival of the New Year—Mardi Gras with a Bahamian twist.

Arthur's Town
Cat Island
Old Bight Mt Alvernia 220
Cockburn Town
San Salvador Island
Rum Cay

ACTIVITIES
Visitors may enjoy hiking to and exploring one of the more than 1,000 caves in **Jamaica**, some as deep as 330 feet (100 m). Many of these caves feature stalactites and stalagmites made of the same kind of limestone that comprises most of the island.

The offshore waters of **Cuba** offer some of the best scuba diving in the entire Caribbean. Clear, warm waters, amazing tropical fish and spectacular corals are among the highlights.

REGIONAL FARE
Many are familiar with the conch, and may even have one on a shelf somewhere. But did you know the meat of a conch is a delicacy in the Caribbean? This treat is often eaten fresh from the shell, uncooked, with a little lime juice or perhaps coconut milk.

Moros con Christianos is certainly a dish that dates back to the old country, in this case Spain. This popular Cuban meal of black beans and rice was named after the two religious groups who once fought for control of southern Spain.

One of the legacies of **Jamaica's** native Arawak people is *bammy*, or cassava bread. This bread, made from the starchy root of the tropical cassava plant, is popularly served with fried fish.

Nassau, Bahamas
Originally hired to raid the Spanish fleet in the Caribbean as a privateer for the British, Blackbeard eventually became the most notorious pirate on the high seas. He called Nassau home until he was driven out in the 1700s.

Providenciales Island, Turks and Caicos Islands
The Caicos Conch Farm offers tours of its facilities where mollusks are cultivated commercially. The mariculture operation features a geodesic dome, tanks and video displays.

Clarence Town
Crooked Island Passage
Samana Cay
Crooked I
Acklins Island
Mayaguana Passage
Mayaguana Island
Caicos Passage
PLS Grand Caicos East Caicos
Providenciales Island Grand Turk
Cockburn Harbour **Grand Turk**

Cayo Coco
Archipiélago de Camagüey
Morón
Esmeralda
Florida
Camagüey Minas
Nuevitas
Manatí
Las Tunas Martí
Guáimaro HOG Holguín Banes
Santa Cruz del Sur
Guayabal
Gulfo de Guacanayabo Cauto Cueto Sagua de Tánamo
Manzanillo **Bayamo** Palma Soriano Baracoa
Campechuela Sierra Maestra National Park **Guantánamo**
Niquero SIERRA MAESTRA Imías
A N T I L L E S Marea de Portillo **Santiago de Cuba**

Little Inagua Island
Lake Rosa
Matthew Town
Great Inagua Island

TURKS AND CAICOS ISLANDS (UK)

Cockburn Harbour, Turks and Caicos Islands
The earliest shipwreck ever discovered in the Americas now rests in the Turks and Caicos National Museum. The Molasses Reef Wreck happened sometime in the 1500s and now shares the limelight with artifacts from even earlier cultures on the island.

Windward Passage

HAITI **DOMINICAN REPUBLIC**

N25°00'
N24°00'
N23°00'
N22°00'
N21°00'
N20°00'
N19°00'

TRANSPORTATION
NATIONAL AIRLINES:
Bahamas: Bahamasair (UP); **Cuba:** Cubana (CU); **Jamaica:** Air Jamaica (JM)

MAJOR AIRPORTS:
Bahamas: Freeport International (FPO), Nassau International (NAS); **Cuba:** Jose Marti International (HAV); **Jamaica:** Norman Manley Airport (KIN), Sangster International (MBJ)

In **Cuba**, passenger trains connect Havana and Santiago de Cuba. On some trains, air conditioning and refreshments are available.

Nassau and Montego Bay serve as major ports of call for a number of international cruise lines. In the **Bahamas**, regular mail boat runs provide transportation between islands.

Bus service is generally available to a wide range of destinations on the main islands, but particular routes may be quite crowded. Taxis are plentiful in the **Bahamas** and **Jamaica**, not so in **Cuba**. Fares should be negotiated in advance because not all taxis are metered.

Bahamas: The violent crime rate is fairly low, but travelers in Nassau and Freeport should stay in recognizable tourist areas and avoid poorly lit areas and empty beaches at night. Death and serious injuries have occurred when visitors have lapsed in adapting to the convention of vehicle travel on the left side of the road. **Cuba:** US citizens are generally not permitted to travel to Cuba. Entering Cuban territorial waters or airspace without prior permission from the Cuban government could lead to serious personal risk. Occasional terrorist attacks have occurred in tourist areas. **Jamaica:** Crime is a serious problem in Jamaica and can turn violent. Visitors should remain in resort areas and be vigilant after dark. Travelers should only use licensed taxis with red-and-white "PP" license plates.

MBJ Falmouth Ocho Rios
Montego Bay
Negril **JAMAICA** Spanish Town Port Antonio
Black River Porus KIN
Alligator Pond **Kingston**

NAVASSA ISLAND (US)
Jamaican Channel

Ocho Rios, Jamaica
Firefly is the seafront home of the late playwright Noël Coward, who lived in Jamaica for the last 20 years of his life. Guided tours take visitors through the mansion, which has been more or less untouched, even down to the closets still filled with Coward's clothes.

Kingston, Jamaica
In Kingston, photos adorn the walls of the clapboard home and Tuff Gong recording studio of reggae legend Bob Marley. Exhibits include gold and platinum records, scrapbooks, and even bullet holes in the wall from an assassination attempt.

CARIBBEAN SEA

N18°00'
N17°00'
N16°00'

MILES 0   25   50   75   100
KILOMETERS 0 25 50 75 100 125 150

NORTH AMERICA

Antigua and Barbuda, Barbados, Dominica, Dominican Republic, Grenada
Trinidad and Tobago, *Anguilla, Aruba, British Virgin Islands, Guadeloupe*

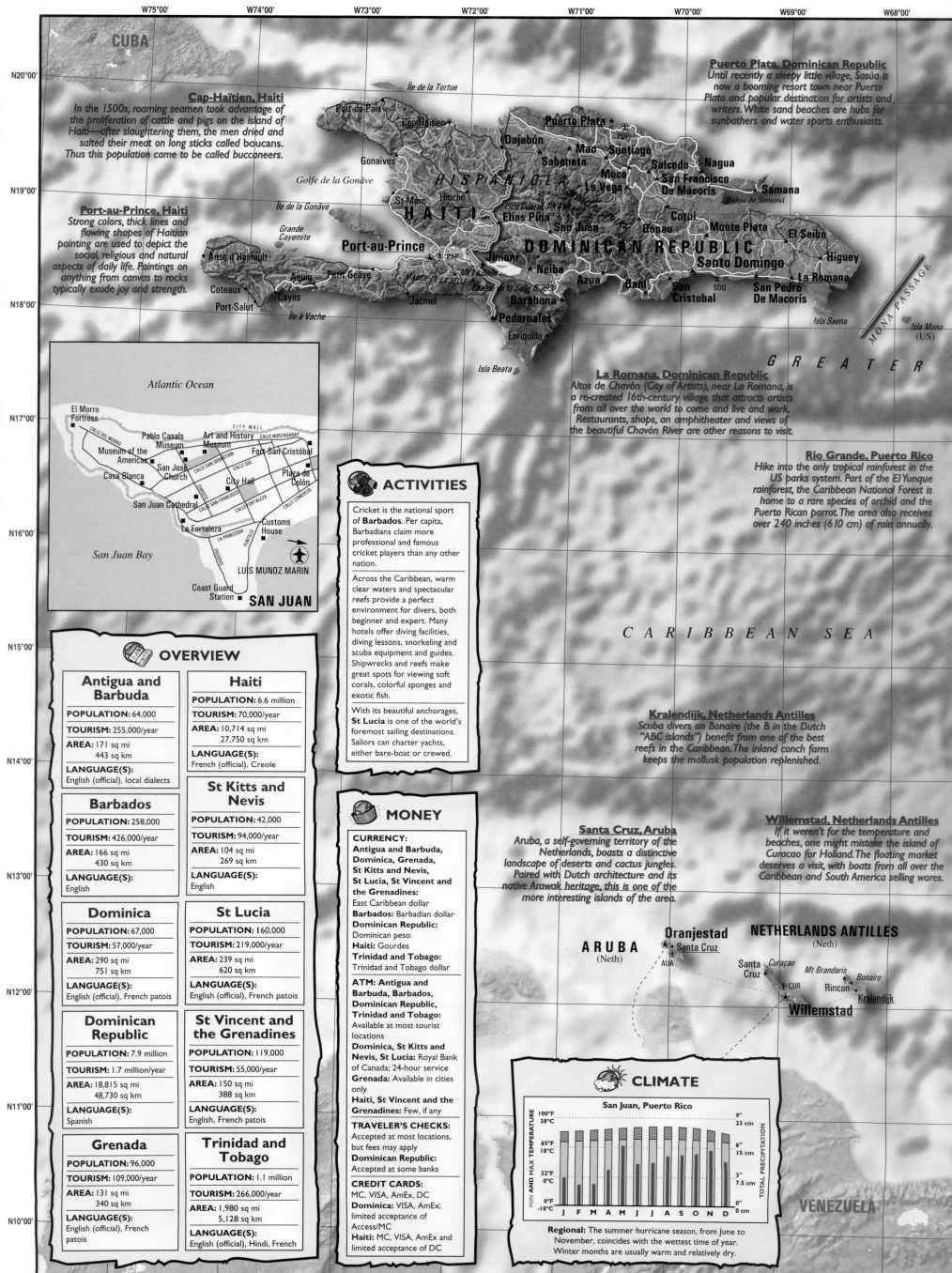

CUBA

Cap-Haïtien, Haiti
In the 1500s, roaming seamen took advantage of the proliferation of cattle and pigs on the island of Haiti—after slaughtering them, the men dried and salted their meat on long sticks called boucans. Thus this population came to be called buccaneers.

Port-au-Prince, Haiti
Strong colors, thick lines and flowing shapes of Haitian painting are used to depict the social, religious and natural aspects of daily life. Paintings on anything from canvas to rocks typically exude joy and strength.

Puerto Plata, Dominican Republic
Until recently a sleepy little village, Sosúa is now a booming resort town near Puerto Plata and popular destination for artists and writers. White sand beaches are hubs for sunbathers and water sports enthusiasts.

La Romana, Dominican Republic
Altos de Chavón (City of Artists), near La Romana, is a re-created 16th-century village that attracts artists from all over the world to come and live and work. Restaurants, shops, an amphitheater and views of the beautiful Chavón River are other reasons to visit.

Rio Grande, Puerto Rico
Hike into the only tropical rainforest in the US parks system. Part of the El Yunque rainforest, the Caribbean National Forest is home to a rare species of orchid and the Puerto Rican parrot. The area also receives over 240 inches (610 cm) of rain annually.

Kralendijk, Netherlands Antilles
Scuba divers on Bonaire (the B in the Dutch "ABC islands") benefit from one of the best reefs in the Caribbean. The inland conch farm keeps the mollusk population replenished.

Santa Cruz, Aruba
Aruba, a self-governing territory of the Netherlands, boasts a distinctive landscape of deserts and cactus jungles. Paired with Dutch architecture and its native Arawak heritage, this is one of the more interesting islands of the area.

Willemstad, Netherlands Antilles
If it weren't for the temperature and beaches, one might mistake the island of Curaçao for Holland. The floating market deserves a visit, with boats from all over the Caribbean and South America selling wares.

Inset map (San Juan)
Atlantic Ocean
El Morro Fortress
Pablo Casals Museum
Museum of the Americas
Casa Blanca
San José Church
Art and History Museum
Fort San Cristóbal
City Hall
Plaza de Colón
San Juan Cathedral
La Fortaleza
Customs House
San Juan Bay
LUIS MUÑOZ MARIN
Coast Guard Station
SAN JUAN

ACTIVITIES

Cricket is the national sport of **Barbados**. Per capita, Barbadians claim more professional and famous cricket players than any other nation.

Across the Caribbean, warm clear waters and spectacular reefs provide a perfect environment for divers, both beginner and expert. Many hotels offer diving facilities, diving lessons, snorkeling and scuba equipment and guides. Shipwrecks and reefs make great spots for viewing soft corals, colorful sponges and exotic fish.

With its beautiful anchorages, **St Lucia** is one of the world's foremost sailing destinations. Sailors can charter yachts, either bare-boat or crewed.

MONEY

CURRENCY:
Antigua and Barbuda, Dominica, Grenada, St Kitts and Nevis, St Lucia, St Vincent and the Grenadines: East Caribbean dollar
Barbados: Barbadian dollar
Dominican Republic: Dominican peso
Haiti: Gourdes
Trinidad and Tobago: Trinidad and Tobago dollar

ATM: Antigua and Barbuda, Barbados, Dominican Republic, Trinidad and Tobago: Available at most tourist locations
Dominica, St Kitts and Nevis, St Lucia: Royal Bank of Canada; 24-hour service
Grenada: Available in cities only
Haiti, St Vincent and the Grenadines: Few, if any

TRAVELER'S CHECKS: Accepted at most locations, but fees may apply
Dominican Republic: Accepted at some banks

CREDIT CARDS:
MC, VISA, AmEx, DC
Dominica: VISA, AmEx; limited acceptance of Access/MC
Haiti: MC, VISA, AmEx and limited acceptance of DC

OVERVIEW

Antigua and Barbuda
POPULATION: 64,000
TOURISM: 255,000/year
AREA: 171 sq mi / 443 sq km
LANGUAGE(S): English (official), local dialects

Haiti
POPULATION: 6.6 million
TOURISM: 70,000/year
AREA: 10,714 sq mi / 27,750 sq km
LANGUAGE(S): French (official), Creole

Barbados
POPULATION: 258,000
TOURISM: 426,000/year
AREA: 166 sq mi / 430 sq km
LANGUAGE(S): English

St Kitts and Nevis
POPULATION: 42,000
TOURISM: 94,000/year
AREA: 104 sq mi / 269 sq km
LANGUAGE(S): English

Dominica
POPULATION: 67,000
TOURISM: 57,000/year
AREA: 290 sq mi / 751 sq km
LANGUAGE(S): English (official), French patois

St Lucia
POPULATION: 160,000
TOURISM: 219,000/year
AREA: 239 sq mi / 620 sq km
LANGUAGE(S): English (official), French patois

Dominican Republic
POPULATION: 7.9 million
TOURISM: 1.7 million/year
AREA: 18,815 sq mi / 48,730 sq km
LANGUAGE(S): Spanish

St Vincent and the Grenadines
POPULATION: 119,000
TOURISM: 55,000/year
AREA: 150 sq mi / 388 sq km
LANGUAGE(S): English, French patois

Grenada
POPULATION: 96,000
TOURISM: 109,000/year
AREA: 131 sq mi / 340 sq km
LANGUAGE(S): English (official), French patois

Trinidad and Tobago
POPULATION: 1.1 million
TOURISM: 266,000/year
AREA: 1,980 sq mi / 5,128 sq km
LANGUAGE(S): English (official), Hindi, French

CLIMATE

San Juan, Puerto Rico

J F M A M J J A S O N D

Regional: The summer hurricane season, from June to November, coincides with the wettest time of year. Winter months are usually warm and relatively dry.

Haiti, St Kitts and Nevis, St Lucia, St Vincent and the Grenadines
Martinique, Montserrat, Netherlands Antilles, Puerto Rico, US Virgin Islands

NORTH AMERICA

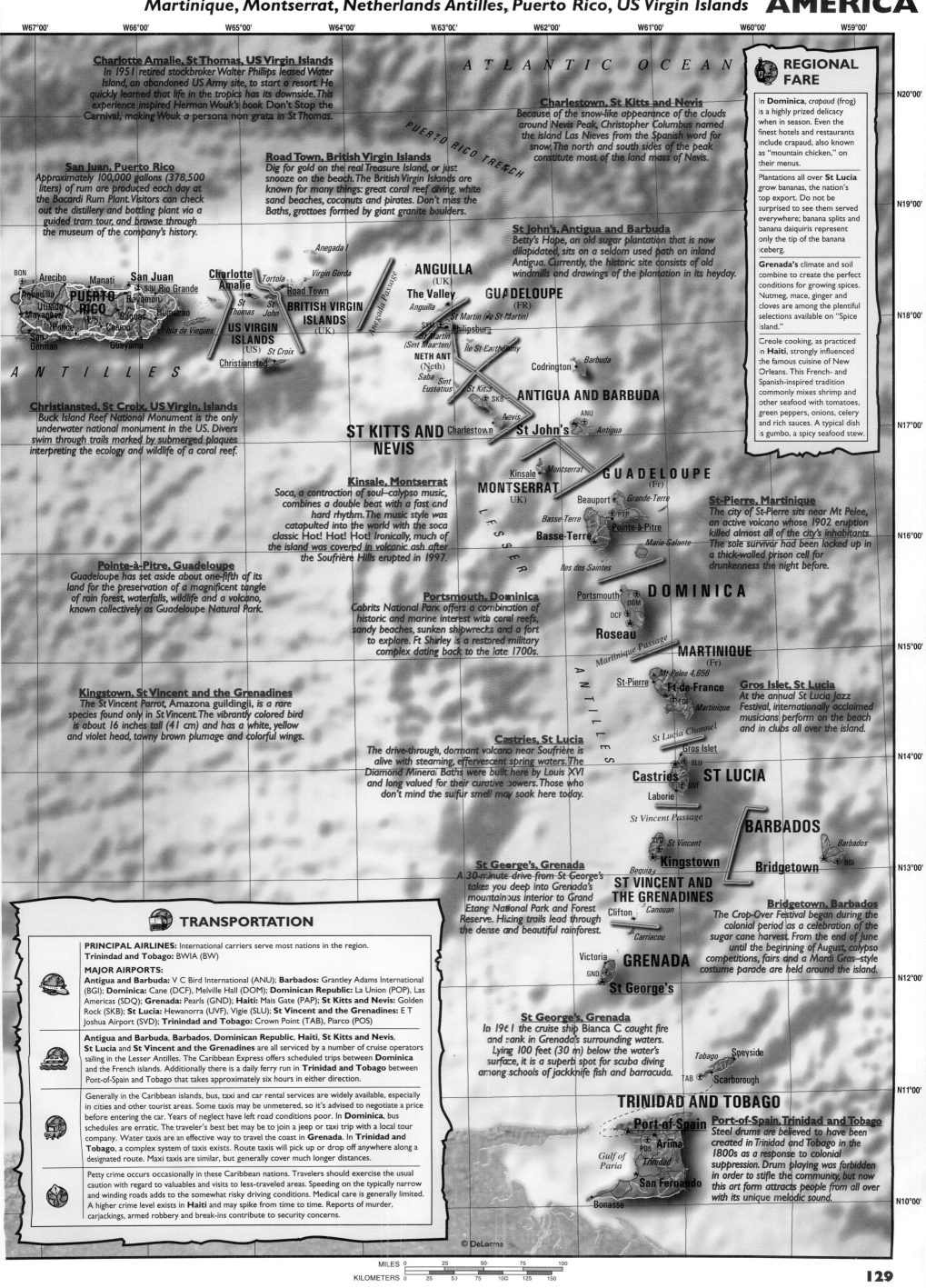

Charlotte Amalie, St Thomas, US Virgin Islands
In 1951 retired stockbroker Walter Phillips leased Water Island, an abandoned US Army site, to start a resort. He quickly learned that life in the tropics has its downside. This experience inspired Herman Wouk's book Don't Stop the Carnival, making Wouk a persona non grata in St Thomas.

San Juan, Puerto Rico
Approximately 100,000 gallons (378,500 liters) of rum are produced each day at the Bacardi Rum Plant. Visitors can check out the distillery and bottling plant via a guided tram tour, and browse through the museum of the company's history.

Road Town, British Virgin Islands
Dig for gold on the real Treasure Island, or just snooze on the beach. The British Virgin Islands are known for many things: great coral reef diving, white sand beaches, coconuts and pirates. Don't miss the Baths, grottoes formed by giant granite boulders.

Charlestown, St Kitts and Nevis
Because of the snow-like appearance of the clouds around Nevis Peak, Christopher Columbus named the island Las Nieves from the Spanish word for snow. The north and south sides of the peak constitute most of the land mass of Nevis.

St John's, Antigua and Barbuda
Betty's Hope, an old sugar plantation that is now dilapidated, sits on a seldom used path on inland Antigua. Currently, the historic site consists of old windmills and drawings of the plantation in its heyday.

Christiansted, St Croix, US Virgin Islands
Buck Island Reef National Monument is the only underwater national monument in the US. Divers swim through trails marked by submerged plaques interpreting the ecology and wildlife of a coral reef.

Kinsale, Montserrat
Soca, a contraction of soul—calypso music, combines a double beat with a fast and hard rhythm. The music style was catapulted into the world with the soca classic Hot! Hot! Hot! Ironically, much of the island was covered in volcanic ash after the Soufrière Hills erupted in 1997.

Pointe-à-Pitre, Guadeloupe
Guadeloupe has set aside about one-fifth of its land for the preservation of a magnificent tangle of rain forest, waterfalls, wildlife and a volcano, known collectively as Guadeloupe Natural Park.

Portsmouth, Dominica
Cabrits National Park offers a combination of historic and marine interest with coral reefs, sandy beaches, sunken shipwrecks and a fort to explore. Ft Shirley is a restored military complex dating back to the late 1700s.

St-Pierre, Martinique
The city of St-Pierre sits near Mt Pelee, an active volcano whose 1902 eruption killed almost all of the city's inhabitants. The sole survivor had been locked up in a thick-walled prison cell for drunkenness the night before.

Kingstown, St Vincent and the Grenadines
The St Vincent Parrot, Amazona guildingii, is a rare species found only in St Vincent. The vibrantly colored bird is about 16 inches tall (41 cm) and has a white, yellow and violet head, tawny brown plumage and colorful wings.

Castries, St Lucia
The drive-through, dormant volcano near Soufrière is alive with steaming, effervescent spring waters. The Diamond Mineral Baths were built here by Louis XVI and long valued for their curative powers. Those who don't mind the sulfur smell may soak here today.

Gros Islet, St Lucia
At the annual St Lucia Jazz Festival, internationally acclaimed musicians perform on the beach and in clubs all over the island.

St George's, Grenada
A 30-minute drive from St George's takes you deep into Grenada's mountainous interior to Grand Etang National Park and Forest Reserve. Hiking trails lead through the dense and beautiful rainforest.

Bridgetown, Barbados
The Crop-Over Festival began during the colonial period as a celebration of the sugar cane harvest. From the end of June until the beginning of August, calypso competitions, fairs and a Mardi Gras–style costume parade are held around the island.

St George's, Grenada
In 1961 the cruise ship Bianca C caught fire and sank in Grenada's surrounding waters. Lying 100 feet (30 m) below the water's surface, it is a superb spot for scuba diving among schools of jackknife fish and barracuda.

Port-of-Spain, Trinidad and Tobago
Steel drums are believed to have been created in Trinidad and Tobago in the 1800s as a response to colonial suppression. Drum playing was forbidden in order to stifle the community, but now this art form attracts people from all over with its unique melodic sound.

REGIONAL FARE

In **Dominica**, crapaud (frog) is a highly prized delicacy when in season. Even the finest hotels and restaurants include crapaud, also known as "mountain chicken," on their menus.

Plantations all over **St Lucia** grow bananas, the nation's top export. Do not be surprised to see them served everywhere; banana splits and banana daiquiris represent only the tip of the banana iceberg.

Grenada's climate and soil combine to create the perfect conditions for growing spices. Nutmeg, mace, ginger and cloves are among the plentiful selections available on "Spice island."

Creole cooking, as practiced in **Haiti**, strongly influenced the famous cuisine of New Orleans. This French- and Spanish-inspired tradition commonly mixes shrimp and other seafood with tomatoes, green peppers, onions, celery and rich sauces. A typical dish is gumbo, a spicy seafood stew.

TRANSPORTATION

PRINCIPAL AIRLINES: International carriers serve most nations in the region.
Trinidad and Tobago: BWIA (BW)

MAJOR AIRPORTS:
Antigua and Barbuda: V C Bird International (ANU); **Barbados:** Grantley Adams International (BGI); **Dominica:** Cane (DCF), Melville Hall (DOM); **Dominican Republic:** La Union (POP), Las Americas (SDQ); **Grenada:** Pearls (GND); **Haiti:** Mais Gate (PAP); **St Kitts and Nevis:** Golden Rock (SKB); **St Lucia:** Hewanorra (UVF), Vigie (SLU); **St Vincent and the Grenadines:** E T Joshua Airport (SVD); **Trinidad and Tobago:** Crown Point (TAB), Piarco (POS)

Antigua and Barbuda, Barbados, Dominica, Haiti, St Kitts and Nevis, St Lucia and **St Vincent and the Grenadines** are all serviced by a number of cruise operators sailing in the Lesser Antilles. The Caribbean Express offers scheduled trips between **Dominica** and the French islands. Additionally there is a daily ferry run in **Trinidad and Tobago** between Port-of-Spain and Tobago that takes approximately six hours in either direction.

Generally in the Caribbean islands, bus, taxi and car rental services are widely available, especially in cities and other tourist areas. Some taxis may be unmetered, so it's advised to negotiate a price before entering the car. Years of neglect have left road conditions poor. In **Dominica**, bus schedules are erratic. The traveler's best bet may be to join a jeep or taxi trip with a local tour company. Water taxis are an effective way to travel the coast in **Grenada**. In **Trinidad and Tobago**, a complex system of taxis exists. Route taxis will pick up or drop off anywhere along a designated route. Maxi taxis are similar, but generally cover much longer distances.

Petty crime occurs occasionally in these Caribbean nations. Travelers should exercise the usual caution with regard to valuables and visits to less-traveled areas. Speeding on the typically narrow and winding roads adds to the somewhat risky driving conditions. Medical care is generally limited. A higher crime level exists in **Haiti** and may spike from time to time. Reports of murder, carjackings, armed robbery and break-ins contribute to security concerns.

© DeLorme

MILES 0 25 50 75 100
KILOMETERS 0 25 50 75 100 125 150

Countries

Territories and Featured Lands

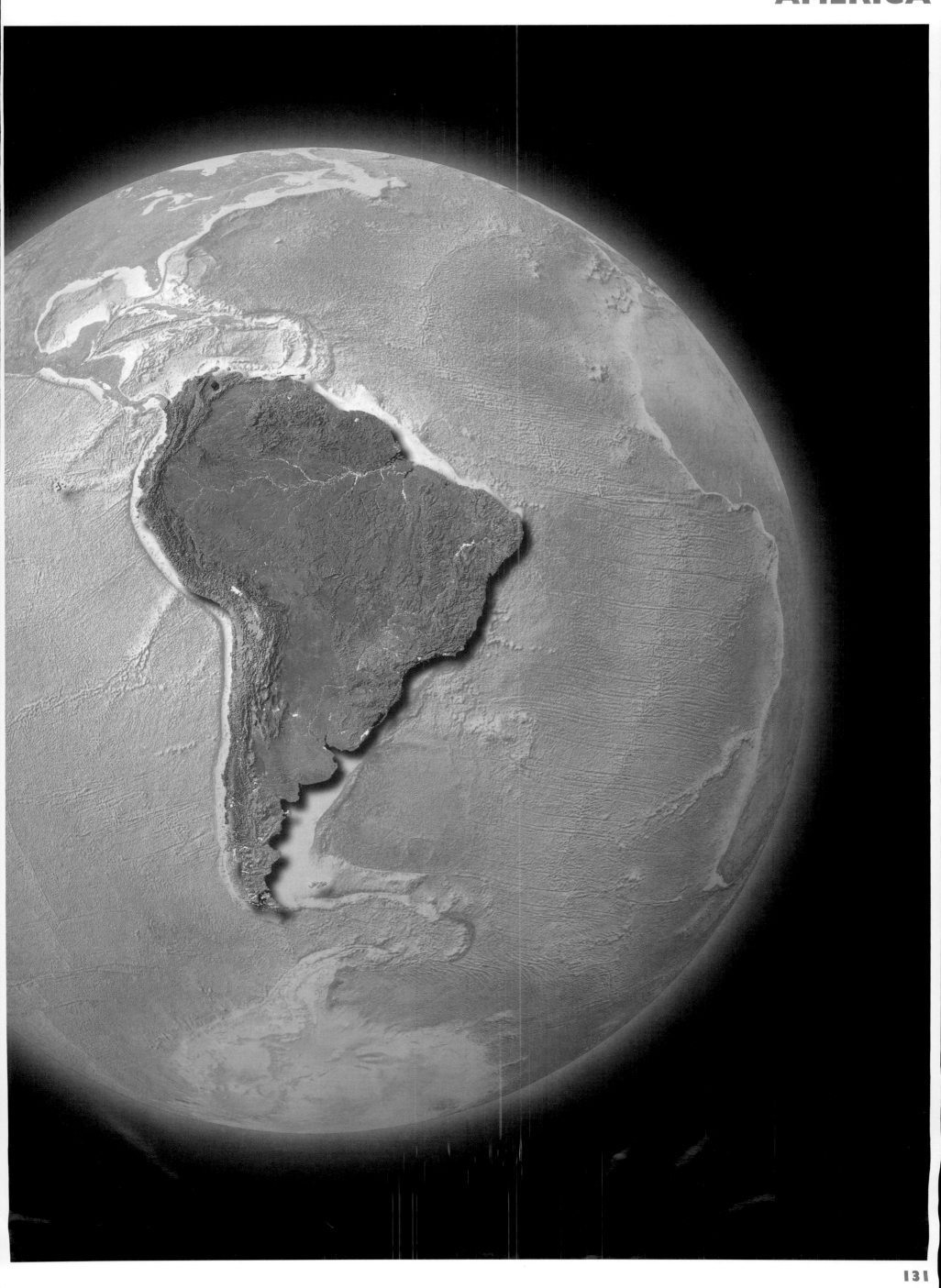

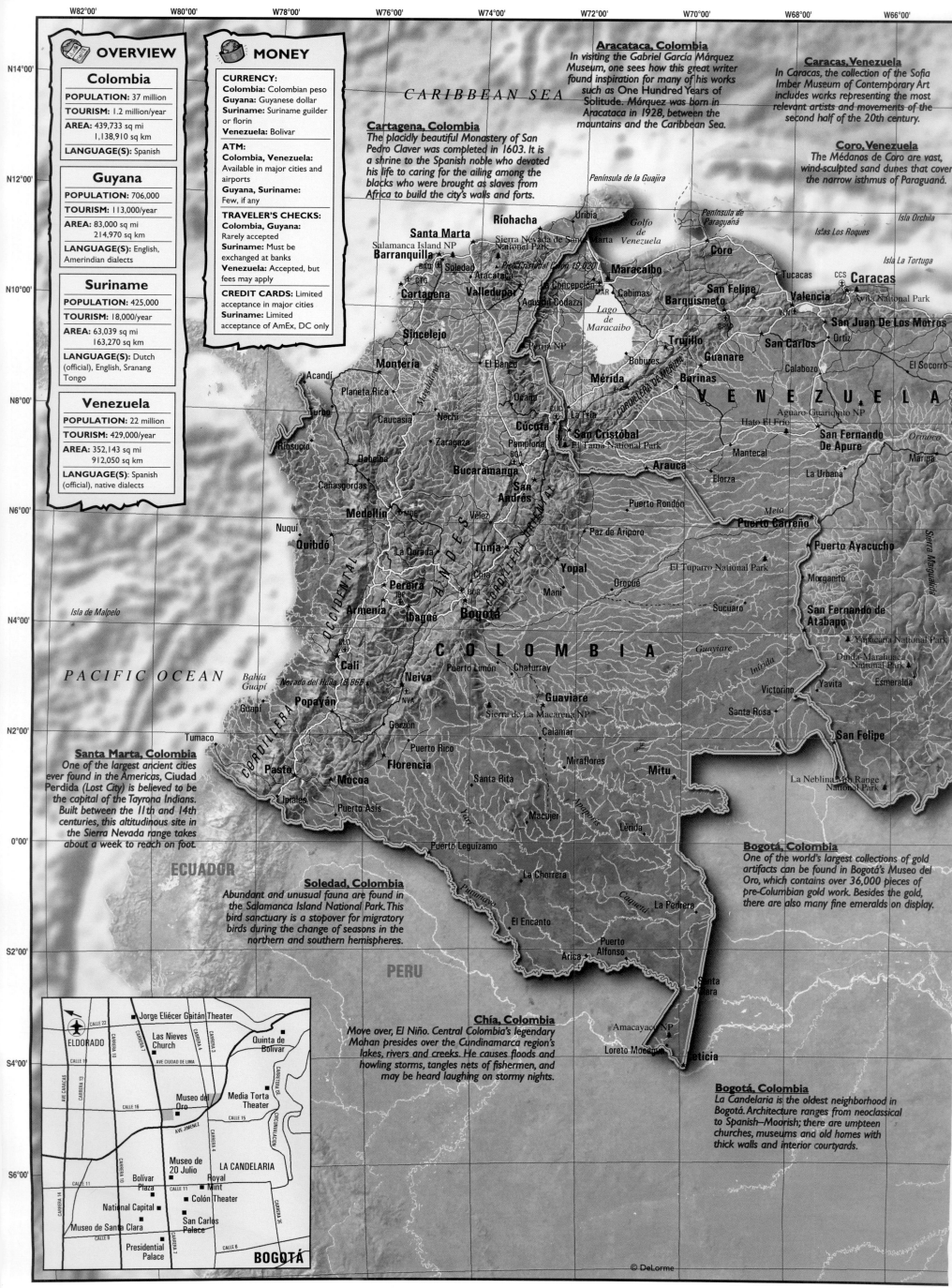

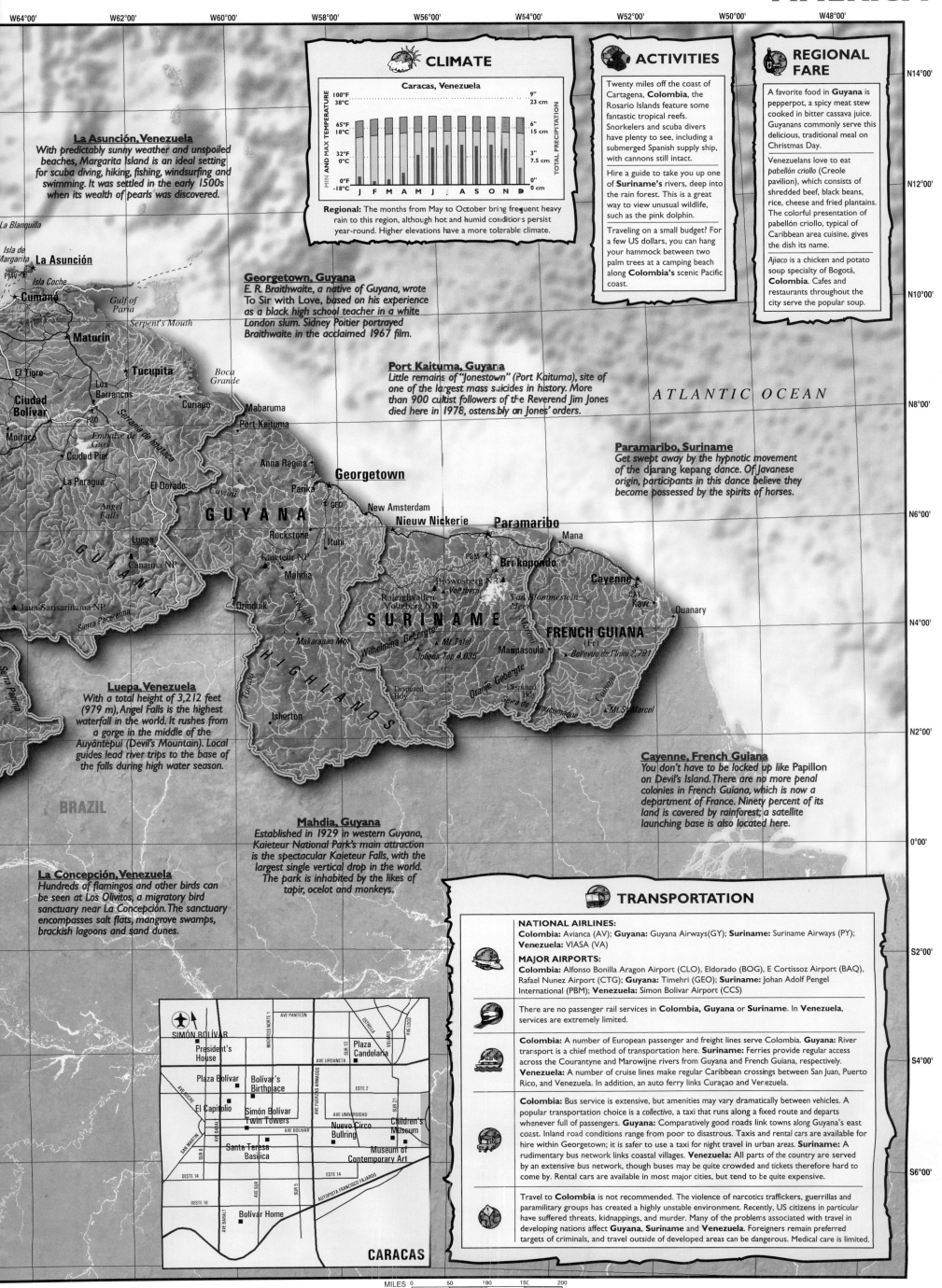

CLIMATE

Caracas, Venezuela

Regional: The months from May to October bring frequent heavy rain to this region, although hot and humid conditions persist year-round. Higher elevations have a more tolerable climate.

ACTIVITIES

Twenty miles off the coast of Cartagena, **Colombia**, the Rosario Islands feature some fantastic tropical reefs. Snorkelers and scuba divers have plenty to see, including a submerged Spanish supply ship, with cannons still intact.

Hire a guide to take you up one of **Suriname's** rivers, deep into the rain forest. This is a great way to view unusual wildlife, such as the pink dolphin.

Traveling on a small budget? For a few US dollars, you can hang your hammock between two palm trees at a camping beach along **Colombia's** scenic Pacific coast.

REGIONAL FARE

A favorite food in **Guyana** is pepperpot, a spicy meat stew cooked in bitter cassava juice. Guyanans commonly serve this delicious, traditional meal on Christmas Day.

Venezuelans love to eat *pabellón criollo* (Creole pavilion), which consists of shredded beef, black beans, rice, cheese and fried plantains. The colorful presentation of pabellón criollo, typical of Caribbean area cuisine, gives the dish its name.

Ajiaco is a chicken and potato soup specialty of Bogotá, **Colombia**. Cafes and restaurants throughout the city serve the popular soup.

La Asunción, Venezuela
With predictably sunny weather and unspoiled beaches, Margarita Island is an ideal setting for scuba diving, hiking, fishing, windsurfing and swimming. It was settled in the early 1500s when its wealth of pearls was discovered.

Georgetown, Guyana
E. R. Braithwaite, a native of Guyana, wrote *To Sir with Love*, based on his experience as a black high school teacher in a white London slum. Sidney Poitier portrayed Braithwaite in the acclaimed 1967 film.

Port Kaituma, Guyana
Little remains of "Jonestown" (Port Kaituma), site of one of the largest mass suicides in history. More than 900 cultist followers of the Reverend Jim Jones died here in 1978, ostensibly on Jones' orders.

Paramaribo, Suriname
Get swept away by the hypnotic movement of the djarang kepang dance. Of Javanese origin, participants in this dance believe they become possessed by the spirits of horses.

Luepa, Venezuela
With a total height of 3,212 feet (979 m), Angel Falls is the highest waterfall in the world. It rushes from a gorge in the middle of the Auyántepui (Devil's Mountain). Local guides lead river trips to the base of the falls during high water season.

Cayenne, French Guiana
You don't have to be locked up like Papillon on Devil's Island. There are no more penal colonies in French Guiana, which is now a department of France. Ninety percent of its land is covered by rainforest; a satellite launching base is also located here.

Mahdia, Guyana
Established in 1929 in western Guyana, Kaieteur National Park's main attraction is the spectacular Kaieteur Falls, with the largest single vertical drop in the world. The park is inhabited by the likes of tapir, ocelot and monkeys.

La Concepción, Venezuela
Hundreds of flamingos and other birds can be seen at Los Olivitos, a migratory bird sanctuary near La Concepción. The sanctuary encompasses salt flats, mangrove swamps, brackish lagoons and sand dunes.

ATLANTIC OCEAN

BRAZIL

TRANSPORTATION

NATIONAL AIRLINES:
Colombia: Avianca (AV); **Guyana:** Guyana Airways(GY); **Suriname:** Suriname Airways (PY); **Venezuela:** VIASA (VA)

MAJOR AIRPORTS:
Colombia: Alfonso Bonilla Aragon Airport (CLO), Eldorado (BOG), E Cortissoz Airport (BAQ), Rafael Nunez Airport (CTG); **Guyana:** Timehri (GEO); **Suriname:** Johan Adolf Pengel International (PBM); **Venezuela:** Simon Bolivar Airport (CCS)

There are no passenger rail services in **Colombia, Guyana** or **Suriname**. In **Venezuela**, services are extremely limited.

Colombia: A number of European passenger and freight lines serve Colombia. **Guyana:** River transport is a chief method of transportation here. **Suriname:** Ferries provide regular access across the Courantyne and Marowijne rivers from Guyana and French Guiana, respectively. **Venezuela:** A number of cruise lines make regular Caribbean crossings between San Juan, Puerto Rico, and Venezuela. In addition, an auto ferry links Curaçao and Venezuela.

Colombia: Bus service is extensive, but amenities may vary dramatically between vehicles. A popular transportation choice is a *collectivo*, a taxi that runs along a fixed route and departs whenever full of passengers. **Guyana:** Comparatively good roads link towns along Guyana's east coast. Inland road conditions range from poor to disastrous. Taxis and rental cars are available for hire within Georgetown; it is safer to use a taxi for night travel in urban areas. **Suriname:** A rudimentary bus network links coastal villages. **Venezuela:** All parts of the country are served by an extensive bus network, though buses may be quite crowded and tickets therefore hard to come by. Rental cars are available in most major cities, but tend to be quite expensive.

Travel to **Colombia** is not recommended. The violence of narcotics traffickers, guerrillas and paramilitary groups has created a highly unstable environment. Recently, US citizens in particular have suffered threats, kidnappings, and murder. Many of the problems associated with travel in developing nations affect **Guyana, Suriname** and **Venezuela**. Foreigners remain preferred targets of criminals, and travel outside of developed areas can be dangerous. Medical care is limited.

CARACAS

SIMÓN BOLÍVAR
President's House
Plaza Bolívar
Bolívar's Birthplace
Plaza Candelaria
El Capitolio
Simón Bolívar Twin Towers
Nuevo Circo Bullring
Children's Museum
Santa Teresa Basilica
Museum of Contemporary Art
Bolívar Home

AVE PANTEON
MADRICES NORTE 1
ESTRELLA
AVE NORTE
AVE URDANETA
SUR 13
SUR 17
AVE FUERZAS ARMADAS
ESTE 2
AVE UNIVERSIDAD
ESTE 21
AVE BOLIVAR
SAN MARTIN
AVE BARALT
SUR 8
AVE SUR
SUR 5
OESTE 14
ESTE 14
AUTOPISTA FRANCISCO FAJARDO
OESTE 18

MILES 0 50 100 150 200
KILOMETERS 0 50 100 150 200 250 300

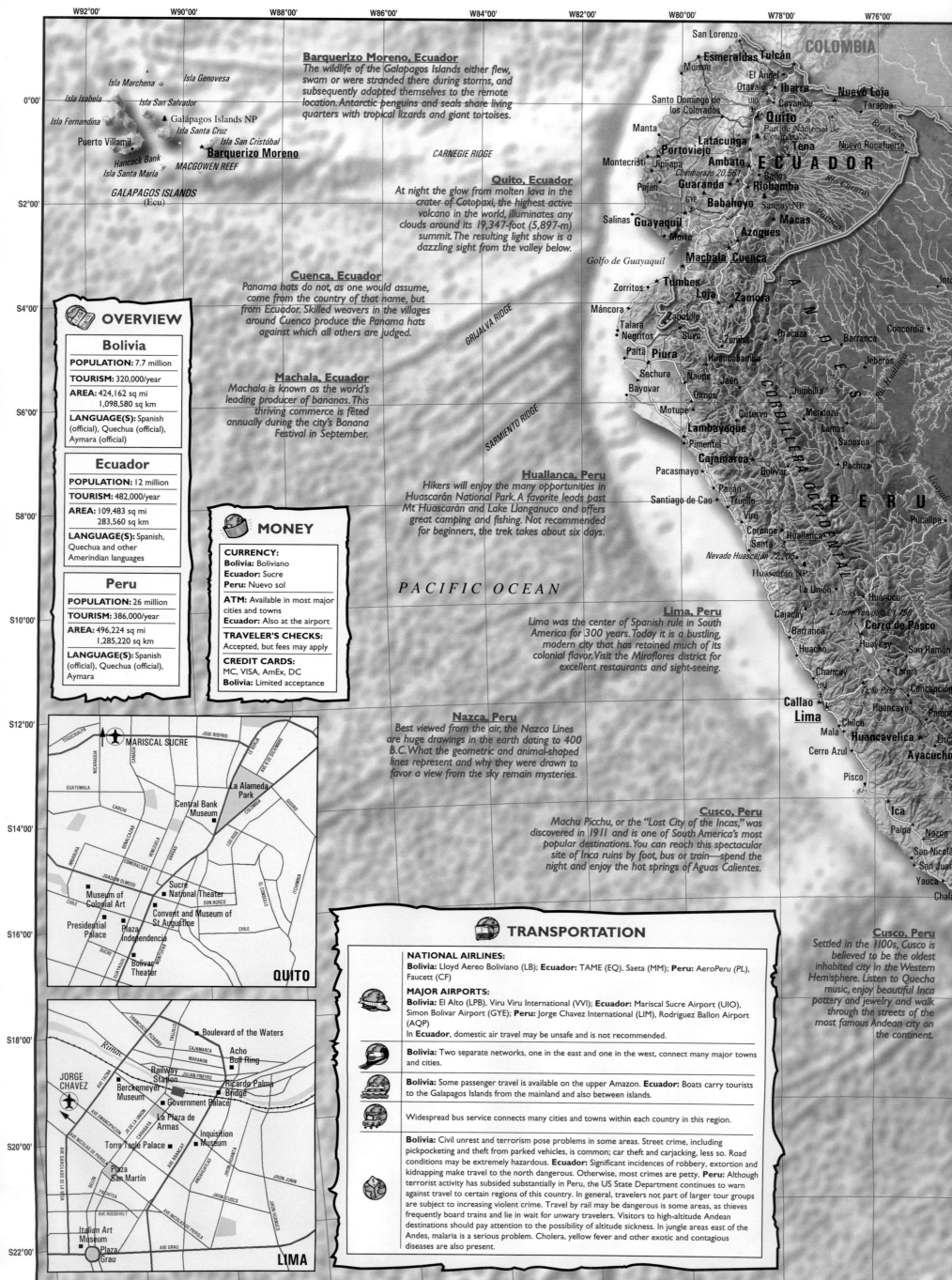

Barquerizo Moreno, Ecuador
The wildlife of the Galapagos Islands either flew, swam or were stranded there during storms, and subsequently adapted themselves to the remote location. Antarctic penguins and seals share living quarters with tropical lizards and giant tortoises.

Quito, Ecuador
At night the glow from molten lava in the crater of Cotopaxi, the highest active volcano in the world, illuminates any clouds around its 19,347-foot (5,897-m) summit. The resulting light show is a dazzling sight from the valley below.

Cuenca, Ecuador
Panama hats do not, as one would assume, come from the country of that name, but from Ecuador. Skilled weavers in the villages around Cuenca produce the Panama hats against which all others are judged.

Machala, Ecuador
Machala is known as the world's leading producer of bananas. This thriving commerce is feted annually during the city's Banana Festival in September.

Huallanca, Peru
Hikers will enjoy the many opportunities in Huascarán National Park. A favorite leads past Mt Huascarán and Lake Llanganuco and offers great camping and fishing. Not recommended for beginners, the trek takes about six days.

Lima, Peru
Lima was the center of Spanish rule in South America for 300 years. Today it is a bustling, modern city that has retained much of its colonial flavor. Visit the Miraflores district for excellent restaurants and sight-seeing.

Nazca, Peru
Best viewed from the air, the Nazca Lines are huge drawings in the earth dating to 400 B.C. What the geometric and animal-shaped lines represent and why they were drawn to favor a view from the sky remain mysteries.

Cusco, Peru
Machu Picchu, or the "Lost City of the Incas," was discovered in 1911 and is one of South America's most popular destinations. You can reach this spectacular site of Inca ruins by foot, bus or train—spend the night and enjoy the hot springs of Aguas Calientes.

Cusco, Peru
Settled in the 1100s, Cusco is believed to be the oldest inhabited city in the Western Hemisphere. Listen to Quecha music, enjoy beautiful Inca pottery and jewelry and walk through the streets of the most famous Andean city on the continent.

OVERVIEW

Bolivia
POPULATION: 7.7 million
TOURISM: 320,000/year
AREA: 424,162 sq mi 1,098,580 sq km
LANGUAGE(S): Spanish (official), Quechua (official), Aymara (official)

Ecuador
POPULATION: 12 million
TOURISM: 482,000/year
AREA: 109,483 sq mi 283,560 sq km
LANGUAGE(S): Spanish, Quechua and other Amerindian languages

Peru
POPULATION: 26 million
TOURISM: 386,000/year
AREA: 496,224 sq mi 1,285,220 sq km
LANGUAGE(S): Spanish (official), Quechua (official), Aymara

MONEY

CURRENCY:
Bolivia: Boliviano
Ecuador: Sucre
Peru: Nuevo sol

ATM: Available in most major cities and towns **Ecuador:** Also at the airport

TRAVELER'S CHECKS: Accepted, but fees may apply

CREDIT CARDS: MC, VISA, AmEx, DC **Bolivia:** Limited acceptance

TRANSPORTATION

NATIONAL AIRLINES:
Bolivia: Lloyd Aereo Boliviano (LB); **Ecuador:** TAME (EQ), Saeta (MM); **Peru:** AeroPeru (PL), Faucett (CF)

MAJOR AIRPORTS:
Bolivia: El Alto (LPB), Viru Viru International (VVI); **Ecuador:** Mariscal Sucre Airport (UIO), Simon Bolivar Airport (GYE); **Peru:** Jorge Chavez International (LIM), Rodriguez Ballon Airport (AQP)
In **Ecuador**, domestic air travel may be unsafe and is not recommended.

Bolivia: Two separate networks, one in the east and one in the west, connect many major towns and cities.

Bolivia: Some passenger travel is available on the upper Amazon. **Ecuador:** Boats carry tourists to the Galapagos Islands from the mainland and also between islands.

Widespread bus service connects many cities and towns within each country in this region.

Bolivia: Civil unrest and terrorism pose problems in some areas. Street crime, including pickpocketing and theft from parked vehicles, is common; car theft and carjacking, less so. Road conditions may be extremely hazardous. **Ecuador:** Significant incidences of robbery, extortion and kidnapping make travel to the north dangerous. Otherwise, most crimes are petty. **Peru:** Although terrorist activity has subsided substantially in Peru, the US State Department continues to warn against travel to certain regions of this country. In general, travelers not part of larger tour groups are subject to increasing violent crime. Travel by rail may be dangerous is some areas, as thieves frequently board trains and lie in wait for unwary travelers. Visitors to high-altitude Andean destinations should pay attention to the possibility of altitude sickness. In jungle areas east of the Andes, malaria is a serious problem. Cholera, yellow fever and other exotic and contagious diseases are also present.

Scale 1:8,000,000 at map center

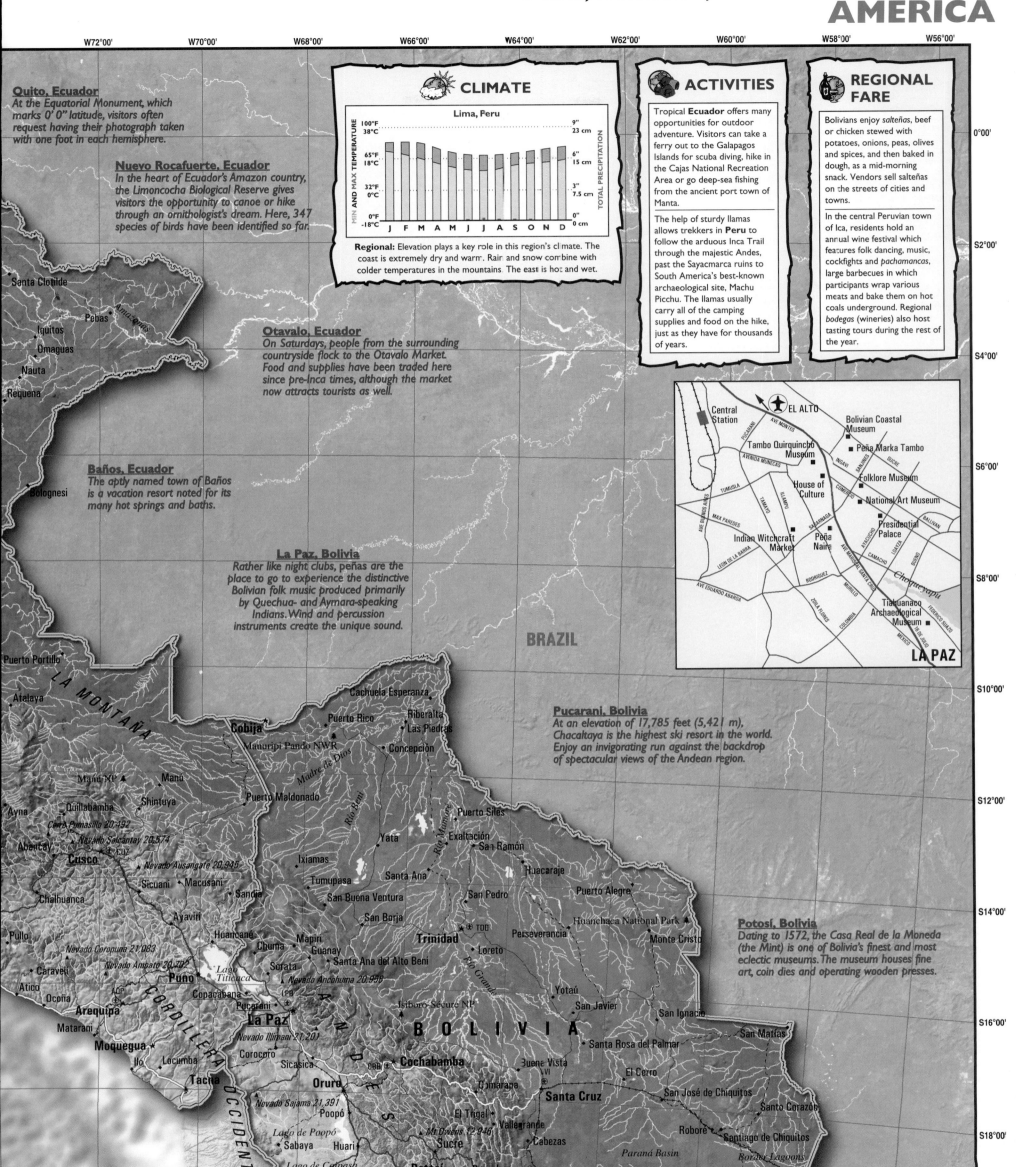

Quito, Ecuador
At the Equatorial Monument, which marks 0° 0" latitude, visitors often request having their photograph taken with one foot in each hemisphere.

Nuevo Rocafuerte, Ecuador
In the heart of Ecuador's Amazon country, the Limoncocha Biological Reserve gives visitors the opportunity to canoe or hike through an ornithologist's dream. Here, 347 species of birds have been identified so far.

Otavalo, Ecuador
On Saturdays, people from the surrounding countryside flock to the Otavalo Market. Food and supplies have been traded here since pre-Inca times, although the market now attracts tourists as well.

Baños, Ecuador
The aptly named town of Baños is a vacation resort noted for its many hot springs and baths.

La Paz, Bolivia
Rather like night clubs, peñas are the place to go to experience the distinctive Bolivian folk music produced primarily by Quechua- and Aymara-speaking Indians. Wind and percussion instruments create the unique sound.

CLIMATE

Lima, Peru

Regional: Elevation plays a key role in this region's climate. The coast is extremely dry and warm. Rain and snow combine with colder temperatures in the mountains. The east is hot and wet.

ACTIVITIES

Tropical **Ecuador** offers many opportunities for outdoor adventure. Visitors can take a ferry out to the Galapagos Islands for scuba diving, hike in the Cajas National Recreation Area or go deep-sea fishing from the ancient port town of Manta.

The help of sturdy llamas allows trekkers in **Peru** to follow the arduous Inca Trail through the majestic Andes, past the Sayacmarca ruins to South America's best-known archaeological site, Machu Picchu. The llamas usually carry all of the camping supplies and food on the hike, just as they have for thousands of years.

REGIONAL FARE

Bolivians enjoy *salteñas*, beef or chicken stewed with potatoes, onions, peas, olives and spices, and then baked in dough, as a mid-morning snack. Vendors sell salteñas on the streets of cities and towns.

In the central Peruvian town of Ica, residents hold an annual wine festival which features folk dancing, music, cockfights and *pachamancas*, large barbecues in which participants wrap various meats and bake them on hot coals underground. Regional *bodegas* (wineries) also host tasting tours during the rest of the year.

Pucarani, Bolivia
At an elevation of 17,785 feet (5,421 m), Chacaltaya is the highest ski resort in the world. Enjoy an invigorating run against the backdrop of spectacular views of the Andean region.

Potosí, Bolivia
Dating to 1572, the Casa Real de la Moneda (the Mint) is one of Bolivia's finest and most eclectic museums. The museum houses fine art, coin dies and operating wooden presses.

Puno, Peru
Only 15 miles (24 km) from Puno, Isla Taquile in Lake Titicaca boasts pre-Inca terracing, traditional clothing and fascinating walks. Boats leave the dock at Puno daily for the four-hour scenic ride to the island.

Copacabana, Bolivia
Lake Titicaca is the world's highest navigable lake, located at 12,500 feet (3,810 m). It is also the site of the Island of the Sun, which plays an important role in Inca creation legends. Interesting boat trips depart from Copacabana or Puno, Peru.

© DeLorme

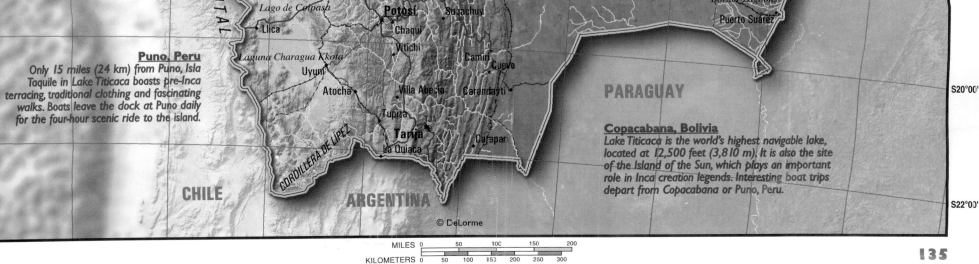

MILES 0 50 100 150 200
KILOMETERS 0 50 100 150 200 250 300

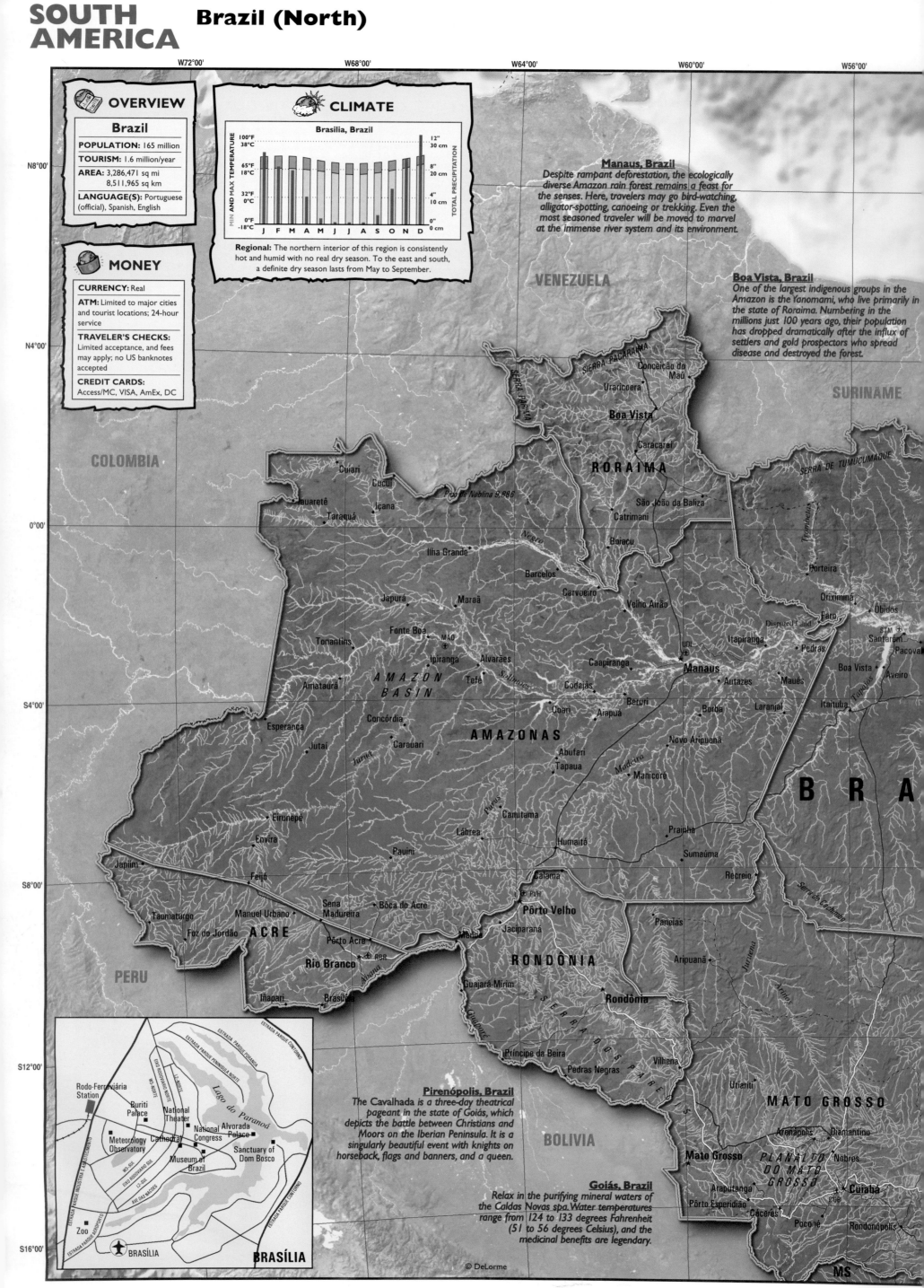

OVERVIEW

Brazil

POPULATION: 165 million

TOURISM: 1.6 million/year

AREA: 3,286,471 sq mi
8,511,965 sq km

LANGUAGE(S): Portuguese
(official), Spanish, English

MONEY

CURRENCY: Real

ATM: Limited to major cities
and tourist locations; 24-hour
service

TRAVELER'S CHECKS:
Limited acceptance, and fees
may apply; no US banknotes
accepted

CREDIT CARDS:
Access/MC, VISA, AmEx, DC

CLIMATE

Brasilia, Brazil

Regional: The northern interior of this region is consistently hot and humid with no real dry season. To the east and south, a definite dry season lasts from May to September.

Manaus, Brazil
Despite rampant deforestation, the ecologically diverse Amazon rain forest remains a feast for the senses. Here, travelers may go bird-watching, alligator-spotting, canoeing or trekking. Even the most seasoned traveler will be moved to marvel at the immense river system and its environment.

Boa Vista, Brazil
One of the largest indigenous groups in the Amazon is the Yanomami, who live primarily in the state of Roraima. Numbering in the millions just 100 years ago, their population has dropped dramatically after the influx of settlers and gold prospectors who spread disease and destroyed the forest.

Pirenópolis, Brazil
The Cavalhada is a three-day theatrical pageant in the state of Goiás, which depicts the battle between Christians and Moors on the Iberian Peninsula. It is a singularly beautiful event with knights on horseback, flags and banners, and a queen.

Goiás, Brazil
Relax in the purifying mineral waters of the Caldas Novas spa. Water temperatures range from 124 to 133 degrees Fahrenheit (51 to 56 degrees Celsius), and the medicinal benefits are legendary.

VENEZUELA

SURINAME

COLOMBIA

PERU

BOLIVIA

RORAIMA

AMAZONAS

AMAZON BASIN

ACRE

RONDÔNIA

MATO GROSSO

PLANALTO DO MATO GROSSO

BRA

Boa Vista
Manaus
Rio Branco
Pôrto Velho
Rondônia
Cuiabá

BRASÍLIA

Rodo-Ferroviária Station
Buriti Palace
National Theater
Meteorology Observatory
Cathedral
National Congress
Alvorada Palace
Museum of Brazil
Sanctuary of Dom Bosco
Zoo
Lago do Paranoá

© DeLorme

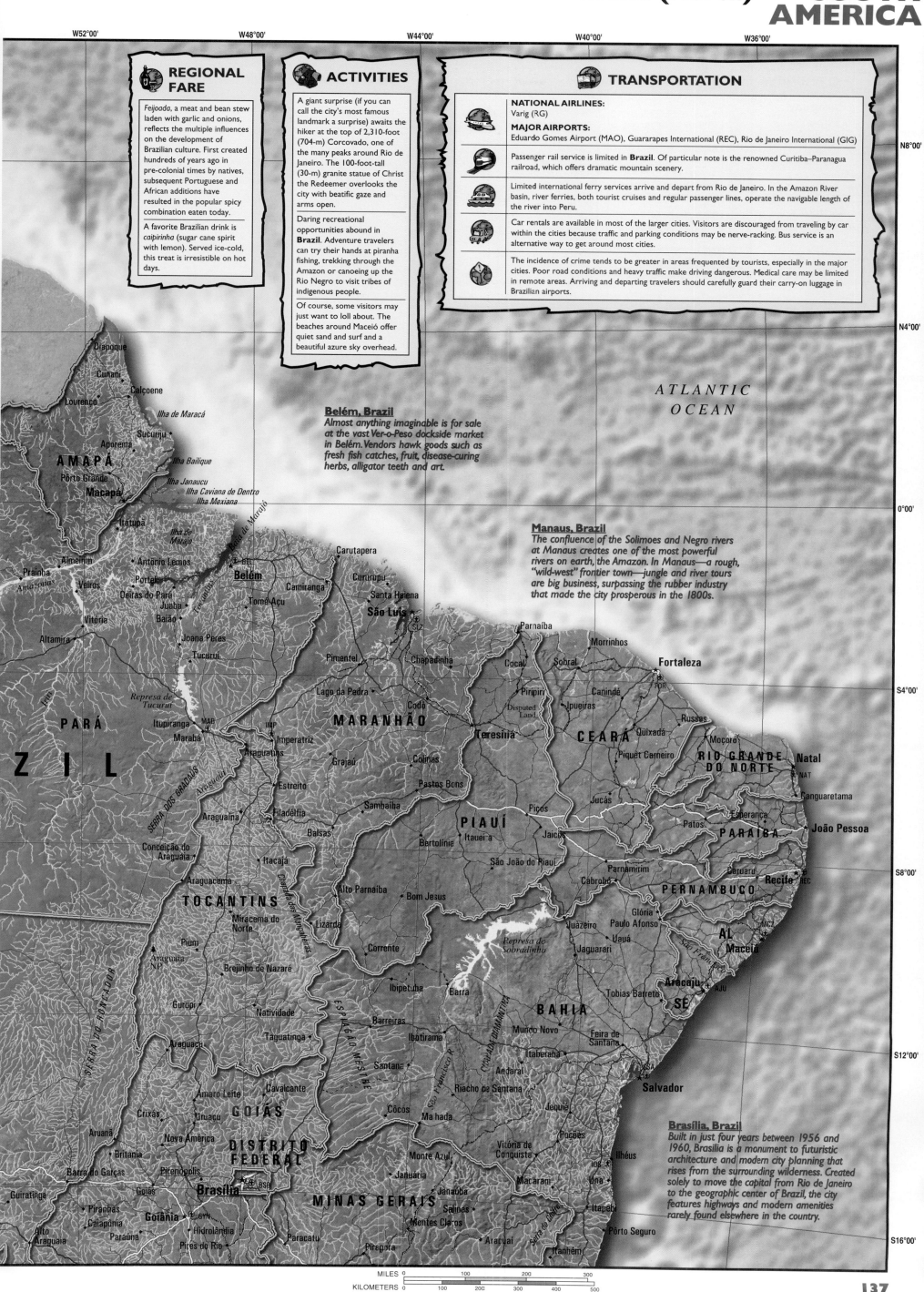

REGIONAL FARE

Feijoada, a meat and bean stew laden with garlic and onions, reflects the multiple influences on the development of Brazilian culture. First created hundreds of years ago in pre-colonial times by natives, subsequent Portuguese and African additions have resulted in the popular spicy combination eaten today.

A favorite Brazilian drink is caipirinha (sugar cane spirit with lemon). Served ice-cold, this treat is irresistible on hot days.

ACTIVITIES

A giant surprise (if you can call the city's most famous landmark a surprise) awaits the hiker at the top of 2,310-foot (704-m) Corcovado, one of the many peaks around Rio de Janeiro. The 100-foot-tall (30-m) granite statue of Christ the Redeemer overlooks the city with beatific gaze and arms open.

Daring recreational opportunities abound in Brazil. Adventure travelers can try their hands at piranha fishing, trekking through the Amazon or canoeing up the Rio Negro to visit tribes of indigenous people.

Of course, some visitors may just want to loll about. The beaches around Maceió offer quiet sand and surf and a beautiful azure sky overhead.

TRANSPORTATION

NATIONAL AIRLINES:
Varig (RG)

MAJOR AIRPORTS:
Eduardo Gomes Airport (MAO), Guararapes International (REC), Rio de Janeiro International (GIG)

Passenger rail service is limited in **Brazil**. Of particular note is the renowned Curitiba–Paranagua railroad, which offers dramatic mountain scenery.

Limited international ferry services arrive and depart from Rio de Janeiro. In the Amazon River basin, river ferries, both tourist cruises and regular passenger lines, operate the navigable length of the river into Peru.

Car rentals are available in most of the larger cities. Visitors are discouraged from traveling by car within the cities because traffic and parking conditions may be nerve-racking. Bus service is an alternative way to get around most cities.

The incidence of crime tends to be greater in areas frequented by tourists, especially in the major cities. Poor road conditions and heavy traffic make driving dangerous. Medical care may be limited in remote areas. Arriving and departing travelers should carefully guard their carry-on luggage in Brazilian airports.

Belém, Brazil
Almost anything imaginable is for sale at the vast Ver-o-Peso dockside market in Belém. Vendors hawk goods such as fresh fish catches, fruit, disease-curing herbs, alligator teeth and art.

Manaus, Brazil
The confluence of the Solimoes and Negro rivers at Manaus creates one of the most powerful rivers on earth, the Amazon. In Manaus—a rough, "wild-west" frontier town—jungle and river tours are big business, surpassing the rubber industry that made the city prosperous in the 1800s.

Brasília, Brazil
Built in just four years between 1956 and 1960, Brasília is a monument to futuristic architecture and modern city planning that rises from the surrounding wilderness. Created solely to move the capital from Rio de Janeiro to the geographic center of Brazil, the city features highways and modern amenities rarely found elsewhere in the country.

ATLANTIC OCEAN

MILES 0   100   200   300
KILOMETERS 0   100   200   300   400   500

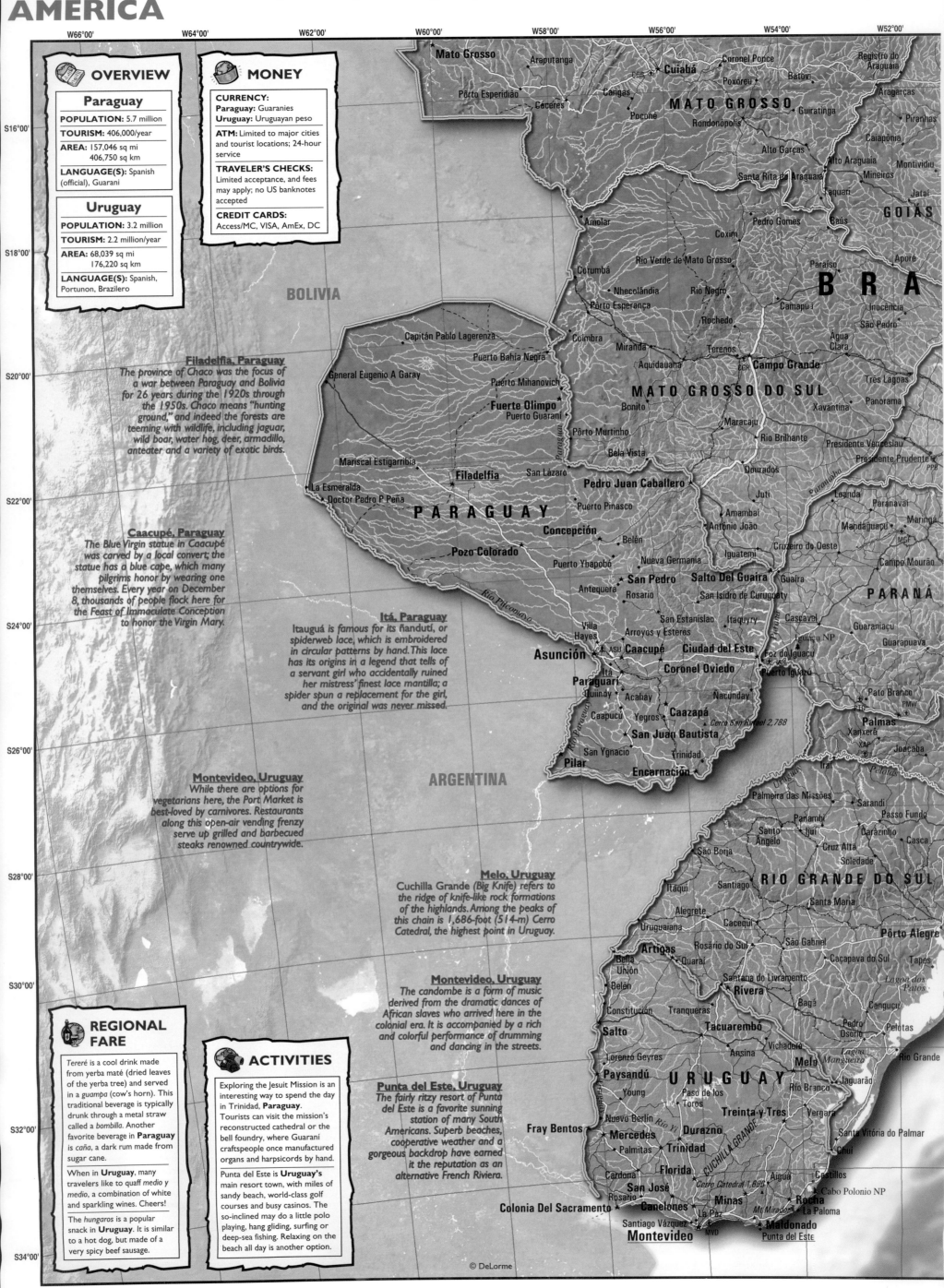

OVERVIEW

Paraguay
POPULATION: 5.7 million
TOURISM: 406,000/year
AREA: 157,046 sq mi
406,750 sq km
LANGUAGE(S): Spanish (official), Guarani

Uruguay
POPULATION: 3.2 million
TOURISM: 2.2 million/year
AREA: 68,039 sq mi
176,220 sq km
LANGUAGE(S): Spanish, Portunon, Brazilero

MONEY

CURRENCY:
Paraguay: Guaranies
Uruguay: Uruguayan peso
ATM: Limited to major cities and tourist locations; 24-hour service
TRAVELER'S CHECKS: Limited acceptance, and fees may apply; no US banknotes accepted
CREDIT CARDS: Access/MC, VISA, AmEx, DC

Filadelfia, Paraguay
The province of Chaco was the focus of a war between Paraguay and Bolivia for 26 years during the 1920s through the 1950s. Chaco means "hunting ground," and indeed the forests are teeming with wildlife, including jaguar, wild boar, water hog, deer, armadillo, anteater and a variety of exotic birds.

Caacupé, Paraguay
The Blue Virgin statue in Caacupé was carved by a local convert; the statue has a blue cape, which many pilgrims honor by wearing one themselves. Every year on December 8, thousands of people flock here for the Feast of Immaculate Conception to honor the Virgin Mary.

Itá, Paraguay
Itauguá is famous for its ñandutí, or spiderweb lace, which is embroidered in circular patterns by hand. This lace has its origins in a legend that tells of a servant girl who accidentally ruined her mistress' finest lace mantilla; a spider spun a replacement for the girl, and the original was never missed.

Montevideo, Uruguay
While there are options for vegetarians here, the Port Market is best-loved by carnivores. Restaurants along this open-air vending frenzy serve up grilled and barbecued steaks renowned countrywide.

Melo, Uruguay
Cuchilla Grande (Big Knife) refers to the ridge of knife-like rock formations of the highlands. Among the peaks of this chain is 1,686-foot (514-m) Cerro Catedral, the highest point in Uruguay.

Montevideo, Uruguay
The candombe is a form of music derived from the dramatic dances of African slaves who arrived here in the colonial era. It is accompanied by a rich and colorful performance of drumming and dancing in the streets.

Punta del Este, Uruguay
The fairly ritzy resort of Punta del Este is a favorite sunning station of many South Americans. Superb beaches, cooperative weather and a gorgeous backdrop have earned it the reputation as an alternative French Riviera.

REGIONAL FARE

Tereré is a cool drink made from yerba maté (dried leaves of the yerba tree) and served in a guampa (cow's horn). This traditional beverage is typically drunk through a metal straw called a bombilla. Another favorite beverage in **Paraguay** is caña, a dark rum made from sugar cane.

When in **Uruguay**, many travelers like to quaff medio y medio, a combination of white and sparkling wines. Cheers!

The hungaros is a popular snack in **Uruguay**. It is similar to a hot dog, but made of a very spicy beef sausage.

ACTIVITIES

Exploring the Jesuit Mission is an interesting way to spend the day in Trinidad, **Paraguay**. Tourists can visit the mission's reconstructed cathedral or the bell foundry, where Guaraní craftspeople once manufactured organs and harpsicords by hand.

Punta del Este is **Uruguay's** main resort town, with miles of sandy beach, world-class golf courses and busy casinos. The so-inclined may do a little polo playing, hang gliding, surfing or deep-sea fishing. Relaxing on the beach all day is another option.

© DeLorme

Scale 1:6,500,000 at map center

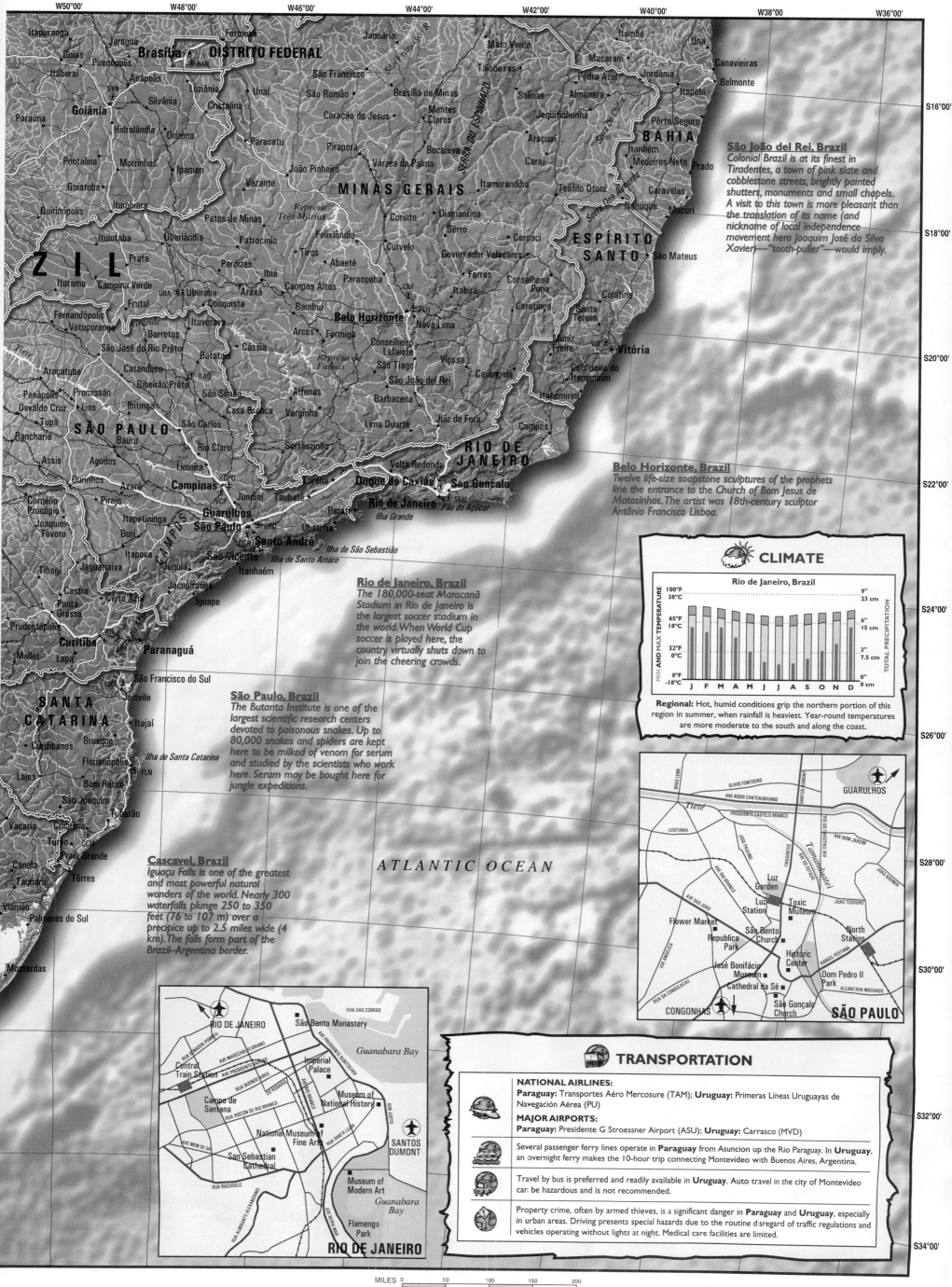

São João del Rei, Brazil
Colonial Brazil is at its finest in Tiradentes, a town of pink slate and cobblestone streets, brightly painted shutters, monuments and small chapels. A visit to this town is more pleasant than the translation of its name (and nickname of local independence movement hero Joaquim José da Silva Xavier—"tooth-puller"—would imply.

Belo Horizonte, Brazil
Twelve life-size soapstone sculptures of the prophets line the entrance to the Church of Bom Jesus de Matosinhos. The artist was 18th-century sculptor Antônio Francisco Lisboa.

Rio de Janeiro, Brazil
The 180,000-seat Maracanã Stadium in Rio de Janeiro is the largest soccer stadium in the world. When World Cup soccer is played here, the country virtually shuts down to join the cheering crowds.

São Paulo, Brazil
The Butanta Institute is one of the largest scientific research centers devoted to poisonous snakes. Up to 80,000 snakes and spiders are kept here to be milked of venom for serum and studied by the scientists who work here. Serum may be bought here for jungle expeditions.

Cascavel, Brazil
Iguaçu Falls is one of the greatest and most powerful natural wonders of the world. Nearly 300 waterfalls plunge 250 to 350 feet (76 to 107 m) over a precipice up to 2.5 miles wide (4 km). The falls form part of the Brazil–Argentina border.

CLIMATE

Rio de Janeiro, Brazil

Regional: Hot, humid conditions grip the northern portion of this region in summer, when rainfall is heaviest. Year-round temperatures are more moderate to the south and along the coast.

TRANSPORTATION

NATIONAL AIRLINES:
Paraguay: Transportes Aéro Mercosure (TAM); **Uruguay:** Primeras Líneas Uruguayas de Navegación Aérea (PU)

MAJOR AIRPORTS:
Paraguay: Presidente G Stroessner Airport (ASU); **Uruguay:** Carrasco (MVD)

Several passenger ferry lines operate in **Paraguay** from Asuncion up the Rio Paraguay. In **Uruguay**, an overnight ferry makes the 10-hour trip connecting Montevideo with Buenos Aires, Argentina.

Travel by bus is preferred and readily available in **Uruguay**. Auto travel in the city of Montevideo can be hazardous and is not recommended.

Property crime, often by armed thieves, is a significant danger in **Paraguay** and **Uruguay**, especially in urban areas. Driving presents special hazards due to the routine disregard of traffic regulations and vehicles operating without lights at night. Medical care facilities are limited.

MILES 0 50 100 150 200
KILOMETERS 0 50 100 150 200 250 300

Argentina, Chile, *Falkland Islands (Malvinas),* Isla de Pascua (Easter Island)

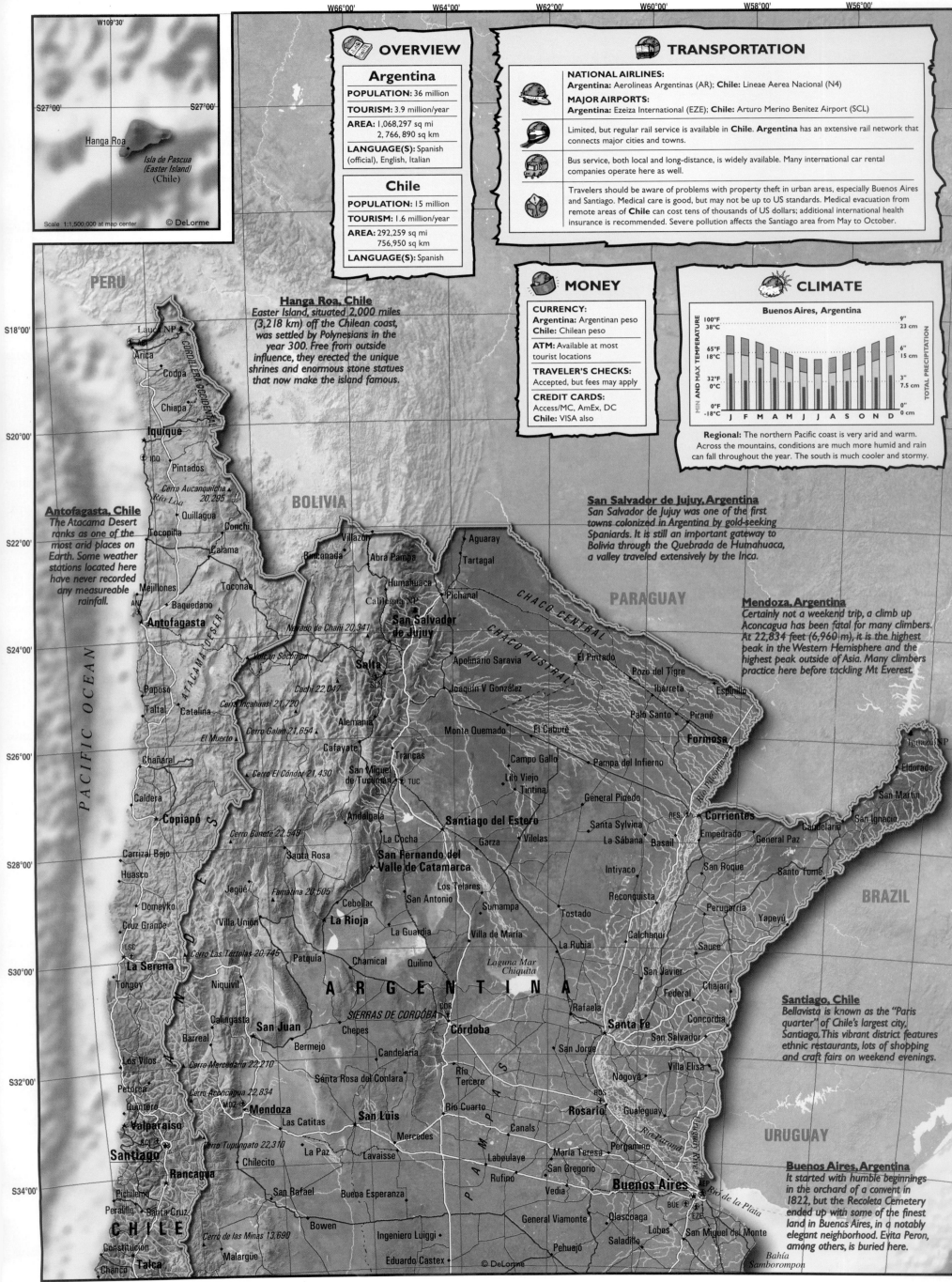

OVERVIEW

Argentina
POPULATION: 36 million
TOURISM: 3.9 million/year
AREA: 1,068,297 sq mi
2,766,890 sq km
LANGUAGE(S): Spanish (official), English, Italian

Chile
POPULATION: 15 million
TOURISM: 1.6 million/year
AREA: 292,259 sq mi
756,950 sq km
LANGUAGE(S): Spanish

TRANSPORTATION

NATIONAL AIRLINES:
Argentina: Aerolineas Argentinas (AR); **Chile:** Lineae Aerea Nacional (N4)
MAJOR AIRPORTS:
Argentina: Ezeiza International (EZE); **Chile:** Arturo Merino Benitez Airport (SCL)

Limited, but regular rail service is available in **Chile**. **Argentina** has an extensive rail network that connects major cities and towns.

Bus service, both local and long-distance, is widely available. Many international car rental companies operate here as well.

Travelers should be aware of problems with property theft in urban areas, especially Buenos Aires and Santiago. Medical care is good, but may not be up to US standards. Medical evacuation from remote areas of **Chile** can cost tens of thousands of US dollars; additional international health insurance is recommended. Severe pollution affects the Santiago area from May to October.

MONEY

CURRENCY:
Argentina: Argentinan peso
Chile: Chilean peso
ATM: Available at most tourist locations
TRAVELER'S CHECKS: Accepted, but fees may apply
CREDIT CARDS:
Access/MC, AmEx, DC
Chile: VISA also

CLIMATE

Buenos Aires, Argentina

Regional: The northern Pacific coast is very arid and warm. Across the mountains, conditions are much more humid and rain can fall throughout the year. The south is much cooler and stormy.

Hanga Roa, Chile
Easter Island, situated 2,000 miles (3,218 km) off the Chilean coast, was settled by Polynesians in the year 300. Free from outside influence, they erected the unique shrines and enormous stone statues that now make the island famous.

Antofagasta, Chile
The Atacama Desert ranks as one of the most arid places on Earth. Some weather stations located here have never recorded any measureable rainfall.

San Salvador de Jujuy, Argentina
San Salvador de Jujuy was one of the first towns colonized in Argentina by gold-seeking Spaniards. It is still an important gateway to Bolivia through the Quebrada de Humahuaca, a valley traveled extensively by the Inca.

Mendoza, Argentina
Certainly not a weekend trip, a climb up Aconcagua has been fatal for many climbers. At 22,834 feet (6,960 m), it is the highest peak in the Western Hemisphere and the highest peak outside of Asia. Many climbers practice here before tackling Mt Everest.

Santiago, Chile
Bellavista is known as the "Paris quarter" of Chile's largest city, Santiago. This vibrant district features ethnic restaurants, lots of shopping and craft fairs on weekend evenings.

Buenos Aires, Argentina
It started with humble beginnings in the orchard of a convent in 1822, but the Recoleta Cemetery ended up with some of the finest land in Buenos Aires, in a notably elegant neighborhood. Evita Peron, among others, is buried here.

Santa Rosa, Argentina
The Pampas region is home to the gauchos (cowboys) of the Argentinian plains, who work on local ranches. They are best known for their roping techniques and their payadas (rhymed musical duels), sung accompanied by guitars.

Ancud, Chile
Historic San Antonio Fort's cannons still stand guard over Ancud's harbor. Built in 1770, this fort was the last stronghold of the Spanish in Chile.

San Carlos de Bariloche, Argentina
Bearing a strong resemblance to Switzerland's surroundings, San Carlos de Bariloche is an alpine resort town with a distinctly European feel. A center for some of the best skiing in Patagonia, it is also a hunting and hiking destination.

Lago Viedma, Argentina
Located against the Chilean border, Los Glaciares National Park holds the Moreno glacier, one of the few advancing glaciers in the world. Icebergs often "calve" off into one of the adjacent lakes.

Stanley, Falkland Islands (Malvinas)
One can hike through the treeless moors or fish off the coast of the Falkland Islands. Possession has been disputed between the United Kingdom and Argentina (resulting in war in 1982). Sheep, penguins, herons, terns and albatross are the true proprietors.

Punta Arenas, Chile
Torres del Paine National Park is a land of superlatives. This 595,000-acre (240,800-ha) ecological reserve is brimming with craggy mountains, crystal clear lakes, waterfalls, glaciers and rare species of wildlife.

Ushuaia, Argentina
One can almost see Antarctica from Ushuaia, the principal city of Tierra del Fuego and the southernmost city in the world. In addition to peering across the horizon towards Antarctica, skiing and dogsledding are among popular activities here.

REGIONAL FARE
Although the beverage may be of Peruvian origin, **Chile** produces more pisco sour than any South American country. A combination of fermented muscatel grapes, lemon juice, egg white and confectioner's sugar, it tastes similar to a very potent and tangy grape soda.

Curanto is a hearty stew made from seafood, pork, beef, lamb, chicken and potato, and eaten with milcao (potato) bread.

ACTIVITIES
Interested in trying a little skiing in the Andes? Las Leñas ski resort, located at an elevation of 7,380 feet (2,250 m), has become a popular spot for extreme skiing. Be careful, though: conditions at the peak (11,250 feet/3,429 m) often present bad weather and danger of avalanches.

Originally regarded as a low-class display of sensuality, the tango has gained acceptance over the years in **Argentina**. The craze is still quite popular in Buenos Aires where it was invented, and so-called tango bars can be found throughout the city.

© DeLorme

| MILES | 0 | | 50 | 100 | 150 | 200 |
| KILOMETERS | 0 | 50 | 100 | 150 | 200 | 250 | 300 |

ANTARCTICA

OVERVIEW

Antarctica

POPULATION: High of 5,000, none indigenous, fluctuates seasonally

TOURISM: 10,000/year

AREA: 5.4 million sq mi 14,000,000 sq km

LANGUAGE(S): Depends on research station. Fifteen different nations operate temporary or permanent stations.

MONEY

CURRENCY: **Antarctica** has no circulating currency. Researchers' needs are met by their governments. US dollars prove useful.

ATM: None available

TRAVELER'S CHECKS: Limited acceptance at base souvenir shops

CREDIT CARDS: Limited acceptance at base souvenir shops

Antarctica

Called Terra Australis Incognita on old sea charts, Antarctica, with an area of 5.4 million square miles (14 million sq km), is both the most isolated continent and the last vast wilderness on the planet.

TRANSPORTATION

AIRLINES:
Private carriers operate charter service from both the southern tip of South America and from Australia, with some flights merely flying over **Antarctica**. Highly variable weather conditions affect flight schedules. Occasionally, helicopters ferry cruise passengers from ship to shore.

MAJOR AIRPORTS:
There are no commercial airports on the continent. Many bases operate gravel or ice air strips for supply planes.

Many cruise lines operate from South America and Australia to **Antarctica**, with trips to the peninsula and other areas around the continent during the austral summer. Depending on conditions, some lines use Zodiac boats to ferry passengers for landings. Occasional space is available on naval or expedition vessels.

Researchers use several modes of surface transportation suited to the cold weather environment. Snowmobiles have replaced sled dogs to haul equipment across the ice. Larger vehicles with wide, rubber crawler tracks do heavier work around the bases. Cross-country skis are also reliable during summer months.

The 1961 Antarctica Treaty governs scientific and other activity on the continent. In addition to the treaty provisions, visitors to **Antarctica** should adhere to additional guidelines established by the nations with permanent bases. The Antarctic natural environment is extremely fragile. All plant and animal life should be treated with extreme care. Other cautions include the following: wear proper cold weather gear, never leave guided groups due to the treacherous landscape, drink adequate fluids to stay hydrated and do not disturb scientific areas or research instruments.

Ross Island, Antarctica
Built by the explorer Robert Falcon Scott in 1902, the Discovery Hut was originally used as a utility shed. The hut is the first historic site on the continent, and is maintained as a museum by the New Zealand Antarctic Society.

Ross Island, Antarctica
Named for its 1841 discoverer, James Clark Ross, Ross Island is accessible only by ship. McMurdo Station, the US center for scientific research on Antarctica, is located here.

South Georgia (UK)

SOUTH SANDWICH ISLANDS (UK)

Montagu Island

Bristol Island

ATLANTIC OCEAN

NEW SCHWABENLAND

SOUTH ORKNEY ISLANDS (UK)

WEDDELL SEA

COATS LAND

SOUTH SHETLAND ISLANDS (UK)

Livingston I

Joinville I

James Ross I

Drake Passage

GRAHAM LAND

Brabant I

Anvers I

Larsen Ice Shelf

ANTARCTIC PENINSULA

CHILE

Vahsel Bay

Filchner Ice Shelf

Adelaide I

Marguerite Bay

Charcot I

PALMER LAND

Berkner I

RONNE ICE SHELF

Alexander Island

Korff Ice Rise

Pensacola Mtns

BELLINGSHAUSEN SEA

TRANSANTARCTIC

▲ Vinson Massif 16,067

South Pole

ELLSWORTH LAND

WEST ANTARCTICA

Whitmore Mtns

MOUNTAINS

PACIFIC OCEAN

Thurston Island

Queen Maude Mtns

Pine Island Bay

AMUNDSEN SEA

MARIE BYRD LAND

Rockefeller Plateau

ROSS ICE SHELF

Roosevelt Island

Siple I

Bay of Whales

ROSS SEA

142

Scale 1:16,000,000 at map center

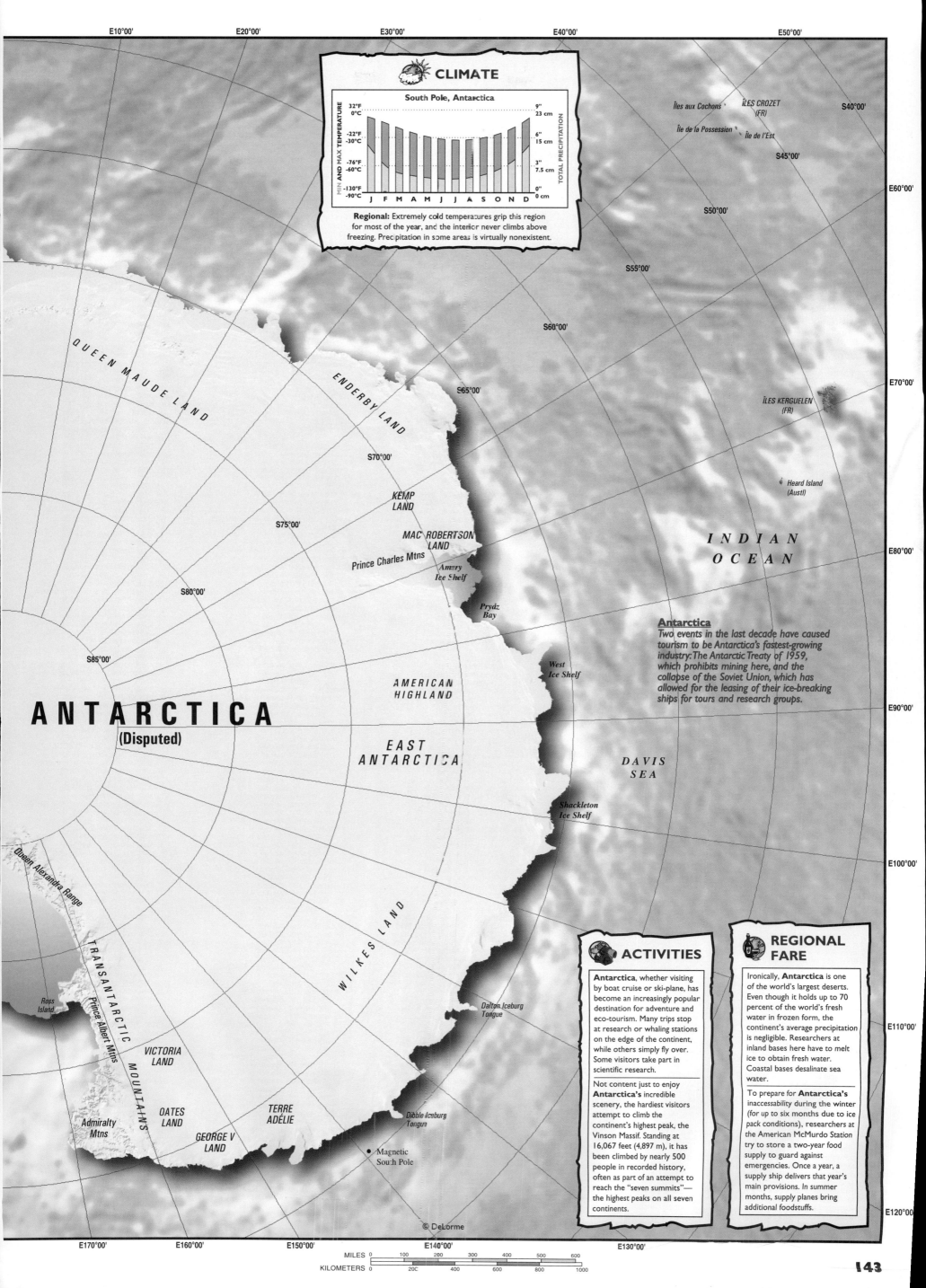

CLIMATE

South Pole, Antarctica

MIN AND MAX TEMPERATURE

32°F	0°C
-22°F	-30°C
-76°F	-60°C
-130°F	-90°C

TOTAL PRECIPITATION

in	cm
9"	23 cm
6"	15 cm
3"	7.5 cm
	0 cm

J F M A M J J A S O N D

Regional: Extremely cold temperatures grip this region for most of the year, and the interior never climbs above freezing. Precipitation in some areas is virtually nonexistent.

E10°00' E20°00' E30°00' E40°00' E50°00'

Îles aux Cochons   ÎLES CROZET (FR)   S40°00'
Île de la Possession   Île de l'Est
S45°00'

S50°00'

S55°00'

S60°00'   E60°00'

QUEEN MAUDE LAND

ENDERBY LAND

S65°00'   E70°00'

ÎLES KERGUELEN (FR)

S70°00'

KEMP LAND

Heard Island (Austl)

S75°00'

MAC ROBERTSON LAND

Prince Charles Mtns

Amery Ice Shelf

INDIAN OCEAN   E80°00'

S80°00'

Prydz Bay

S85°00'

West Ice Shelf

Antarctica
Two events in the last decade have caused tourism to be Antarctica's fastest-growing industry: The Antarctic Treaty of 1959, which prohibits mining here, and the collapse of the Soviet Union, which has allowed for the leasing of their ice-breaking ships for tours and research groups.

AMERICAN HIGHLAND

E90°00'

ANTARCTICA
(Disputed)

EAST ANTARCTICA

DAVIS SEA

E100°00'

Queen Alexandra Range

Shackleton Ice Shelf

TRANSANTARCTIC MOUNTAINS

WILKES LAND

Ross Island

Prince Albert Mtns

E110°00'

Dalton Iceburg Tongue

VICTORIA LAND

Dibble Iceburg Tongue

OATES LAND

TERRE ADÉLIE

Admiralty Mtns

GEORGE V LAND

Magnetic South Pole

© DeLorme

ACTIVITIES

Antarctica, whether visiting by boat cruise or ski-plane, has become an increasingly popular destination for adventure and eco-tourism. Many trips stop at research or whaling stations on the edge of the continent, while others simply fly over. Some visitors take part in scientific research.

Not content just to enjoy **Antarctica's** incredible scenery, the hardiest visitors attempt to climb the continent's highest peak, the Vinson Massif. Standing at 16,067 feet (4,897 m), it has been climbed by nearly 500 people in recorded history, often as part of an attempt to reach the "seven summits"— the highest peaks on all seven continents.

REGIONAL FARE

Ironically, **Antarctica** is one of the world's largest deserts. Even though it holds up to 70 percent of the world's fresh water in frozen form, the continent's average precipitation is negligible. Researchers at inland bases here have to melt ice to obtain fresh water. Coastal bases desalinate sea water.

To prepare for **Antarctica's** inaccessability during the winter (for up to six months due to ice pack conditions), researchers at the American McMurdo Station try to store a two-year food supply to guard against emergencies. Once a year, a supply ship delivers that year's main provisions. In summer months, supply planes bring additional foodstuffs.

E120°00'

E170°00' E160°00' E150°00' E140°00' E130°00'

MILES 0   100   200   300   400   500   600
KILOMETERS 0   200   400   600   800   1000

Index of Placenames and Map Features

ABOUT THE INDEX

This index contains over 15,000 features shown on the maps. Feature names are listed alphabetically with map page, and latitude and longitude coordinates. A feature's map page appears first in its index listing as gray boldface type, and is followed by the latitude coordinate and then the longitude coordinate (in purple) of the entry's location on the map page. On the maps, the latitude and longitude coordinates are labeled in various increments of minutes along the top and sides of each page. The entry name itself is formatted in this index according to what type of feature it is (see below for more detailed information). The abbreviation for its governing country or its territory/state/province and governing country appear in the last portion of the feature's index entry. A list of abbreviations for countries, territories, states and provinces is located on page 5 of EARTHA World Travelog.

Other guidelines for using this index:

- Countries appear in boldface type and capitals, such as **UNITED STATES**
- Territories, states, provinces and placenames appear in boldface type, such as **Puerto Rico**, **Maine** or **Adamstown**
- Drainage names (oceans, seas, lakes, bays, channels, rivers, glaciers) appear in italic type, such as *English Channel* or *Pacific Ocean*
- All other features (mountains, mountain ranges, deserts, islands, island chains) appear in roman type, such as Ural Mountains or Tahiti

A

48 N35°31' E98°38' A'nyêmaqên Shan, China
40 N36°35' E37°3' A'zaz, Syria
15 N47°24' E7°59' Aarau, Switz
97 N68°43' W52°50' Aasiaat, Grld, Den
49 N33°6' E101°59' Aba, China
86 N5°6' E7°21' Aba, Nga
127 N26°8' W77°9' Abaco Island, Bah
44 N31°10' E52°37' Abadeh, Iran
79 N31°1' W2°44' Abadla, Alg
139 S19°9' W45°27' Abaeté, MG, Braz
86 N8°28' E6°57' Abaji, Nga
32 N53°43' E91°26' Abakan, Rus Fed
80 N14°56' E3°26' Abala, Niger
136 S10°34' W67°44' Abana, Braz
135 S13°35' W72°55' Abancay, Peru
44 N31°8' E53°17' Abar Kuh, Iran
82 N6°29' E37°5' Abaya Lake, Eth
87 N5°20' E15°11' Abba, CAR
115 N29°58' W92°8' Abbeville, LA, US
119 N34°11' W82°23' Abbeville, SC, US
14 N50°6' E1°50' Abbeville, Fr
45 N34°9' E73°13' Abbottabad, Pak
37 N53°42' E53°40' Abdulino, Rus Fed
81 N13°50' E20°50' Abéché, Chad
13 N41°48' W2°47' Abejar, Sp
85 N6°44' W3°29' Abengourou, Côte d'Ivoire
29 N55°3' E9°25' Åbenrå, Den
86 N7°10' E3°21' Abeokuta, Nga
82 N2°12' E32°21' Aber, Ug
11 N57°9' W2°6' Aberdeen, UK
90 S32°29' E24°3' Aberdeen, S Afr
108 N45°28' W98°29' Aberdeen, SD, US
118 N33°50' W88°32' Aberdeen, MS, US
42 N18°13' E42°30' Abha, Sau Ar
82 N18°14' E33°57' 'Abidiyah, Sud
85 N5°19' W4°1' Abidjan, Côte d'Ivoire
114 N32°27' W99°44' Abilene, TX, US
103 N50°12' W81°47' Abitibi River, Can
69 S26°7' E134°52' Abminga, SA, Austl
29 N60°27' E22°16' Åbo, Fin
54 N30°9' E74°11' Abohar, Ind
85 N5°28' W3°12' Aboisso, Côte d'Ivoire
85 N7°11' E1°59' Abomey, Ben
63 N9°26' E118°33' Aborlan, Phil
81 N11°27' E19°17' Abou-Deïa, Chad
140 S22°43' W65°42' Abra Pampa, Arg
12 N39°28' W8°12' Abrantes, Port
23 N46°17' E23°4' Abrud, Rom
107 N43°50' W109°53' Absaroka Range, US
42 N16°57' E42°50' Abu 'Arish, Sau Ar
43 N24°28' E54°22' Abu Dhabi, UAE
82 N19°8' E33°34' Abu Dis, Sud
82 N19°32' E33°19' Abu Hamad, Sud
41 N34°27' E40°55' Abu Kamal, Syria
82 N10°58' E26°17' Abu Matariq, Sud
82 N12°21' E29°15' Abu Zabad, Sud
43 N24°28' E54°22' Abu Zaby, UAE
136 S5°25' W62°59' Abufari, AM, Braz
86 N9°12' E7°11' Abuja, Nga
63 N18°26' E121°25' Abulog, Phil
66 S21°25' E118°54' Abydos, WA, Austl
82 N9°36' E28°26' Abyei, Sud
138 S25°55' W57°9' Acahay, Para
132 N8°32' W77°17' Acandí, Col
123 N16°51' W99°55' Acapulco de Juárez, Gro, Mex
117 N37°43' W75°40' Accomac, VA, US
85 N5°36' W0°18' Accra, Gha
38 N37°25' E29°22' Acipayam, Turk
127 N22°21' W73°55' Acklins Island, Bah
125 N11°59' W85°11' Acoyapa, Nic
136 S9°25' W70°25' Acre, Braz
40 N32°55' E35°5' Acre, Isr
123 N20°16' W98°56' Actopan, Hgo, Mex
86 N1°2' E10°40' Acurenam, Eq Gui
82 N18°3' E30°57' Ad Dabbah, Sud
42 N27°44' E44°30' Ad Dahna' Desert, Sau Ar
78 N23°43' W15°57' Ad Dakhla, W Sah, Mor
82 N17°35' E33°58' Ad Damir, Sud
42 N27°19' E37°44' Ad Dar al Hamra', Sau Ar
42 N17°43' E42°16' Ad Darb, Sau Ar
43 N25°15' E51°28' Ad Dawhah, Qatar
44 N31°59' E44°56' Ad Diwaniyah, Iraq
42 N30°15' E42°17' Ad Duwayd, Sau Ar
115 N34°46' W96°41' Ada, OK, US
78 N17°54' W11°27' Adafer, Mrta
43 N22°24' E57°32' Adam, Oman
86 N6°19' E11°43' Adamawa, Cam
37 N51°32' E59°56' Adamovka, Rus Fed
56 N6°43' E80°35' Adams Peak, Sri L
73 S25°11' W130°48' Adamstown, Pit, UK
42 N12°47' E45°2' Adan, Yem
38 N37°1' E35°19' Adana, Turk
12 N40°56' W4°36' Adanero, Sp
69 S25°55' E144°36' Adavale, Qld, Austl
83 N9°13' E38°52' Addis Ababa, Eth
119 N31°8' W83°25' Adel, GA, US
69 S34°53' E138°35' Adelaide, SA, Austl
142 S65°0' W70°0' Adelaide Island, Ant, Disputed
42 N12°47' E45°2' Aden, Yem
39 N41°42' E42°42' Adigeni, Geo
54 N19°40' E78°32' Adilabad, Ind
110 N43°44' W75°0' Adirondack Mountains, US
83 N9°13' E38°52' Adis Abeba, Eth
39 N37°46' E38°15' Adiyaman, Turk
23 N46°4' E27°11' Adjud, Rom
61 S1°53' E146°22' Admiralty Islands, PNG
143 S70°0' E160°0' Admiralty Mountains, Ant, Disputed
86 N7°38' E5°12' Ado Ekiti, Nga
13 N36°46' W3°1' Adra, Sp
79 N27°54' W0°17' Adrar, Alg
78 N20°41' W12°31' Adrar, Mrta
79 N19°30' E1°46' Adrar des Ifores, Mali
81 N13°28' E22°12' Adré, Chad
109 N41°53' W84°2' Adrian, MI, US
17 N42°38' E15°11' Adriatic Sea
83 N14°10' E38°55' Adwa, Eth
85 N6°6' W3°52' Adzopé, Côte d'Ivoire
25 N39°18' E24°38' Aegean Sea
45 N33°44' E61°56' AFGHANISTAN
83 N2°10' E45°9' Afgooye, Som
42 N23°55' E42°56' 'Afif, Sau Ar
79 N34°7' E2°6' Aflou, Alg
40 N36°31' E36°52' 'Afrin, Syria
38 N38°15' E36°55' Afsin, Turk
38 N38°45' E30°33' Afyon, Turk
80 N16°50' E13°17' Agadem, Niger
80 N16°58' E7°59' Agadez, Niger
78 N30°26' W9°36' Agadir, Mor
86 N9°3' E6°18' Agaie, Nga
92 S9°57' E55°56' Agalega Islands, Mrts
72 N13°28' E144°45' Agana, Guam, US
37 N53°18' E59°28' Agapovka, Rus Fed
55 N23°49' E91°16' Agartala, Ind
49 N43°10' E109°26' Agaruut, Mong
60 S5°33' E138°8' Agats, Indo
56 N10°47' E71°36' Agatti Island, Ind
120 N52°5' E173°35' Agattu Island, US
85 N5°56' W4°13' Agboville, Côte d'Ivoire
14 N44°11' E0°38' Agen, Fr
68 S28°1' E120°30' Agnew, WA, Austl
85 N7°8' W3°12' Agnibilékrou, Côte d'Ivoire
54 N27°11' E78°1' Agra, Ind
13 N41°51' W1°56' Ágreda, Sp
17 N37°19' E13°35' Agrigento, It
72 N19°8' E143°46' Agrihan, NM Is, US
24 N38°37' E21°24' Agrínion, Grc
138 S20°27' W52°52' Água Clara, MT, Braz
141 S41°4' W68°25' Aguada de Guerra, Arg
129 N18°26' W67°9' Aguadilla, PR, US
140 S22°16' W63°44' Aguaray, Arg
122 N21°59' W102°31' Aguascalientes, Mex
122 N21°53' W102°18' Aguascalientes, Ags, Mex
139 S22°28' W49°0' Agudos, SP, Braz
13 N37°24' W1°37' Águilas, Sp
132 N10°2' W73°14' Agustín Codazzi, Col
79 N23°16' E5°5' Ahaggar, Alg
73 S14°45' W147°5' Ahe, Fr Poly, Fr
71 S35°11' E173°11' Ahipara, NZ
39 N38°45' E42°29' Ahlat, Turk
45 N29°25' E65°56' Ahmad Wal, Pak
54 N23°3' E72°35' Ahmadabad, Ind
54 N19°5' E74°44' Ahmadnagar, Ind
79 N25°16' E3°2' Ahnet, Alg
122 N21°3' W104°29' Ahuacatlán, Nay, Mex
124 N13°55' W89°51' Ahuachapán, El Sal
14 N46°5' E2°5' Ahun, Fr
73 S19°38' W140°25' Ahunui, Fr Poly, Fr
44 N31°19' E48°41' Ahvaz, Iran
29 N60°47' E18°45' Ahvenanmaa, Fin
42 N13°31' E46°42' Ahwar, Yem
136 S4°29' W62°4' Aiapuá, AM, Braz
45 N36°19' E67°57' Aibak, Afg
138 S34°12' W54°45' Aiguá, Ur
14 N46°26' E1°50' Aigurande, Fr
119 N33°34' W81°43' Aiken, SC, US
125 N9°11' W78°1' Ailigandí, Pan
72 N7°14' E165°25' Ailinglapalap Atoll, Mar Is
78 N26°0' W9°32' 'Aïn Ben Tili, W Sah, Mor
79 N32°45' W0°35' Aïn Sefra, Alg
108 N42°33' W99°52' Ainsworth, NE, US
97 N67°32' W74°38' Air Force Island, Can
80 N19°11' E8°3' Aïr Mountain Range, Niger
58 S1°57' E100°53' Airhaji, Indo
78 N31°38' W7°42' Aït Ourir, Mor
61 S3°8' E142°20' Aitape, PNG
73 S18°59' W161°14' Aitutaki, Cook Is, NZ
15 N43°31' E5°26' Aix-en-provence, Fr
24 N37°44' E23°27' Aíyina, Grc
24 N38°15' E22°5' Aíyion, Grc
55 N23°46' E92°48' Aizawl, Ind
48 N44°59' E95°10' Aj Bogd Uul, Mong
44 N37°28' E45°54' 'Ajab Shir, Iran
15 N41°58' E8°40' Ajaccio, Fr
68 S27°57' E114°38' Ajana, WA, Austl
54 N20°32' E75°45' Ajanta, Ind
81 N30°48' E20°14' Ajdabiya, Libya
53 N40°46' E140°14' Ajigasawa, Jap
54 N26°27' E74°38' Ajmer, Ind
63 N11°10' E123°1' Ajuy, Phil
52 N35°0' E132°43' Akana, Jap
71 S43°48' E172°58' Akaroa, NZ
37 N51°1' E55°37' Akbulak, Rus Fed
39 N41°1' E39°33' Akçaabat, Turk
39 N40°3' E47°28' Akcabädi, Azer
39 N36°44' E38°59' Akçakale, Turk
38 N37°30' E28°2' Akçaova, Turk
38 N39°40' E35°54' Akdagmadeni, Turk
39 N39°59' E46°57' Akdam, Azer
29 N60°25' E17°46' Åkerby, Swe
38 N38°55' E27°51' Akhisar, Turk
36 N48°20' E46°8' Akhtubinsk, Rus Fed
97 N52°44' W80°34' Akimiski Island, Can
53 N39°45' E140°5' Akita, Jap
78 N19°45' W14°23' Akjoujt, Mrta
78 N29°22' W8°14' Akka, Mor
46 N43°43' E59°31' Akkala, Uzb
53 N43°2' E144°51' Akkeshi, Jap
40 N32°55' E35°5' 'Akko, Isr
47 N45°2' E75°40' Akkol', Kaz
47 N43°25' E70°47' Akkol', Kaz
97 N60°26' W67°42' Akpatok Island, Can
117 N41°5' W81°31' Akron, OH, US
38 N38°23' E34°3' Aksaray, Turk
48 N39°28' E94°15' Aksay, China
38 N38°33' E31°38' Aksehir Lake, Turk
46 N47°37' E55°56' Akshiy, Kaz
39 N41°8' E45°28' Akstafa, Azer
48 N41°10' E80°20' Aksu, China
47 N45°37' E79°30' Aksu, Kaz
46 N50°44' E61°43' Aktasty, Kaz
47 N48°18' E74°58' Aktogay, Kaz
46 N46°40' E57°19' Aktumsyk, Kaz
46 N50°17' E57°14' Aktyubinsk, Kaz
82 N7°47' E33°1' Akubu, Sud
88 N2°22' E20°11' Akula, DRC
52 N32°1' E130°11' Akune, Jap
86 N7°15' E5°11' Akure, Nga
28 N65°44' W18°2' Akureyri, Ice
52 N29°20' E129°35' Akuseki-shima, Jap
86 N6°13' E7°4' Akwa, Nga
57 N20°9' E92°54' Akyab, Myanmar
47 N47°35' E83°42' Akzhar, Kaz
81 N30°49' E28°57' Al 'Alamayn, Egypt
44 N31°50' E47°9' Al 'Amarah, Iraq
40 N29°31' E35°0' Al 'Aqabah, Jor
42 N21°2' E41°25' Al 'Aqiq, Sau Ar
43 N24°13' E55°46' Al 'Ayn, UAE
78 N27°10' W13°11' Al 'Ayun, W Sar, Mor
42 N13°38' E47°19' Al 'Irqah, Yem
42 N26°37' E37°52' Al 'Ulá, Sau Ar
81 N30°16' E19°12' Al 'Uqaylah, Libya
40 N36°22' E37°31' Al Bab, Syria
44 N31°6' E45°53' Al Batha, Iraq
40 N34°15' E35°39' Al Batrun, Leb
42 N28°50' E36°19' Al Bi'r, Sau Ar
42 N18°13' E41°33' Al Birk, Sau Ar
43 N25°7' E56°21' Al Fujayrah, UAE
43 N16°12' E52°15' Al Ghaydah, Yem
42 N31°28' E37°9' Al Hadithah, Sau Ar
44 N34°7' E42°23' Al Hadithah, Iraq
40 N34°43' E35°56' Al Hamidiyah, Syria
42 N23°57' E38°52' Al Hamra', Sau Ar
80 N26°52' E16°49' Al Harujal Aswad, Libya
41 N36°29' E40°45' Al Hasakah, Syria
42 N13°50' E47°36' Al Hawrah, Yem
42 N15°50' E48°27' Al Hawtah, Yem
42 N28°38' E42°45' Al Hayyaniyah, Sau Ar
42 N26°56' E36°26' Al Hijaz, Sau Ar
44 N32°29' E44°25' Al Hillah, Iraq
79 N35°16' W3°56' Al Hoceïma, Mor
42 N14°48' E42°57' Al Hudaydah, Yem
81 N31°12' E29°52' Al Iskandariyah, Egypt
43 N23°28' E56°32' Al Jabal al Akhdar, Oman
40 N30°18' E36°13' Al Jafr, Jor
81 N29°45' E24°31' Al Jaghbub, Libya
42 N31°20' E39°56' Al Jalamid, Sau Ar
42 N29°49' E39°53' Al Jouf, Sau Ar
43 N26°58' E49°40' Al Jubayl, Sau Ar
42 N27°4' E43°2' Al Kahfah, Sau Ar
40 N31°11' E35°42' Al Karak, Jor
41 N35°11' E38°52' Al Kawm, Syria
43 N23°58' E57°7' Al Khaburah, Oman
82 N15°35' E32°39' Al Khartum, Sud
82 N11°48' E34°19' Al Khatmiyah, Sud
80 N32°39' E14°16' Al Khums, Libya
42 N21°54' E42°3' Al Khurmah, Sau Ar
81 N24°10' E23°15' Al Kufrah, Libya
44 N32°26' E45°50' Al Kut, Iraq
44 N29°22' E47°59' Al Kuwayt, Kuw
40 N34°12' E36°21' Al Labwah, Leb
40 N35°31' E35°48' Al Ladhiqiyah, Syria
42 N20°9' E40°16' Al Lith, Sau Ar
40 N32°21' E36°12' Al Mafraq, Jor
43 N26°8' E50°28' Al Manamah, Bahr
43 N20°20' E58°56' Al Masirah, Oman
44 N36°20' E43°8' Al Mawsil, Iraq
41 N35°1' E40°27' Al Mayadin, Syria
40 N29°19' E36°1' Al Mudawwarah, Jor
42 N13°19' E43°15' Al Mukha, Yem
42 N27°41' E35°27' Al Muwaylih, Sau Ar
43 N23°57' E55°48' Al Qabil, Oman
42 N22°21' E39°9' Al Qadimah, Sau Ar
81 N30°4' E31°14' Al Qahirah, Egypt
42 N28°32' E37°42' Al Qalibah, Sau Ar
41 N37°2' E41°14' Al Qamishli, Syria
40 N34°14' E37°14' Al Qaryatayn, Syria
80 N24°56' E14°38' Al Qatrun, Libya
42 N28°16' E46°3' Al Qaysumah, Sau Ar
40 N33°8' E35°49' Al Qunaytirah, Syria
42 N19°8' E41°5' Al Qunfudhah, Sau Ar
82 N13°11' E30°13' Al Ubayyid, Sud
81 N25°41' E32°38' Al Uqsur, Egypt
35 N54°53' E52°20' Al'met'yevsk, Rus Fed
44 N30°30' E47°46' Al-Basrah, Iraq
42 N24°28' E39°36' Al-Madinah, Sau Ar
118 N32°1' W87°18' Alabama, US
137 S9°40' W36°57' Alagoas, Braz
13 N41°46' W1°7' Alagón, Sp
47 N46°14' E80°36' Alaköl, Kaz
34 N66°57' E30°18' Alakurtti, Rus Fed
72 N17°30' E143°40' Alamagan, NM Is, US
123 N20°55' W97°41' Álamo, Ver, Mex
113 N32°54' W105°57' Alamogordo, NM, US
113 N37°28' W105°52' Alamosa, CO, US
29 N60°47' E18°45' Åland, Fin
125 N8°24' W82°33' Alanje, Pan
38 N36°33' E32°1' Alanya, Turk
35 N57°52' E61°42' Alapayevsk, Rus Fed
121 N64°7' W157°39' Alaska, US
121 N62°6' W152°34' Alaska Range, US
35 N54°51' E46°36' Alatyr', Rus Fed
39 N41°8' E44°39' Alaverdi, Arm
29 N62°35' E23°37' Alavus, Fin
13 N39°56' E4°8' Alayor, Sp
12 N40°49' W5°31' Alba de Tormes, Sp
23 N46°4' E23°35' Alba Iulia, Rom
13 N38°59' W1°52' Albacete, Sp
24 N40°36' E19°42' ALBANIA
68 S35°0' E117°53' Albany, WA, Austl
106 N44°38' W123°7' Albany, OR, US
110 N42°40' W73°46' Albany, NY, US
114 N32°43' W99°18' Albany, TX, US
119 N31°35' W84°10' Albany, GA, US
103 N52°14' W81°26' Albany Island, Can
102 N51°26' W88°8' Albany River, Can
67 S12°49' E140°32' Albatross Bay
117 N35°22' W80°13' Albemarle, NC, US
117 N36°0' W76°28' Albemarle Sound
20 N47°10' E10°10' Alberg, Aus
14 N50°0' E2°39' Albert, Fr
82 N2°44' E31°14' Albert Nile, Ug
99 N55°40' W114°30' Alberta, Can
15 N45°41' E6°23' Albertville, Fr
14 N43°55' E2°8' Albi, Fr
109 N41°2' W92°49' Albia, IA, US
13 N36°7' W3°14' Alboran Sea
29 N57°2' E9°59' Ålborg, Den
99 N52°38' W119°9' Albreda, BC, Can
113 N35°5' W106°40' Albuquerque, NM, US
12 N39°13' W7°0' Alburquerque, Sp
69 S36°4' E146°55' Albury, NSW, Austl
71 S44°14' E170°52' Albury, NZ
12 N38°22' W8°30' Alcácer do Sal, Port
63 N17°54' E121°39' Alcala, Phil
12 N37°28' W3°56' Alcalá la Real, Sp
12 N41°42' W6°21' Alcañices, Sp
13 N41°3' W0°8' Alcañiz, Sp
13 N37°58' W1°13' Alcantarilla, Sp
27 N48°30' E38°47' Alchevs'k, Ukr
12 N37°28' W7°28' Alcoutim, Port
13 N38°42' W0°28' Alcoy, Sp
13 N41°48' W0°27' Alcubierre, Sp
13 N39°52' E3°7' Alcudia, Sp
33 N58°37' E125°22' Aldan, Rus Fed
78 N17°3' W13°55' Aleg, Mrta
138 S29°46' W55°46' Alegrete, RS, Braz
32 N60°25' E77°50' Aleksandrovskoye, Rus Fed
47 N48°25' E85°40' Alekseyevka, Kaz
47 N51°59' E70°59' Alekseyevka, Kaz
36 N54°31' E37°5' Aleksin, Rus Fed
140 S25°36' W65°38' Alemania, Arg
14 N48°26' E0°5' Alençon, Fr
120 N20°17' W156°8' Alenuihaha Channel
40 N36°13' E37°10' Aleppo, Syria
15 N42°5' E9°30' Aléria, Fr
15 N44°8' E4°5' Alès, Fr
16 N44°55' E8°37' Alessandria, It
29 N62°29' E6°14' Ålesund, Nor
120 N53°30' W178°0' Aleutian Islands, US
142 S70°0' W80°0' Alexander Island, Ant, Disputed
117 N38°48' W77°3' Alexandria, VA, US
81 N31°12' E29°52' Alexandria, Egypt
115 N31°19' W92°27' Alexandria, LA, US
99 N52°38' W122°27' Alexandria, BC, Can
23 N43°59' E25°21' Alexandria, Rom
108 N45°53' W95°23' Alexandria, MN, US
25 N40°52' E25°52' Alexandroúpolis, Grc
13 N40°33' W1°2' Alfambra, Sp
25 N43°57' E27°17' Alfatar, Bulg
139 S21°25' W45°57' Alfenas, MG, Braz
22 N46°42' E20°40' Alföld, Hun
111 N43°29' W70°43' Alfred, ME, US
46 N50°39' E52°7' Algabas, Kaz
12 N36°8' W5°30' Algeciras, Sp
79 N36°46' E3°2' Alger, Alg
79 N28°5' E1°7' ALGERIA
46 N49°46' E57°20' Algha, Kaz
16 N40°33' E8°19' Alghero, It
79 N36°46' E3°2' Algiers, Alg
108 N43°4' W94°14' Algona, IA, US
13 N38°21' W0°29' Alicante, Sp
98 N55°29' W129°29' Alice Arm, BC, Can
67 S23°42' E133°53' Alice Springs, NT, Austl
63 N7°31' E122°56' Alicia, Phil
87 N5°2' E21°13' Alindao, CAR
91 S30°45' E26°45' Aliwal North, S Afr
12 N37°52' W8°10' Aljustrel, Port
18 N52°37' E4°44' Alkmaar, Neth
111 N46°46' W69°23' Allagash River, US
55 N25°27' E81°50' Allahabad, Ind
45 N28°57' E70°53' Allahabad, Pak
12 N42°11' W7°48' Allariz, Sp
117 N38°13' W79°52' Allegheny Mountains, US
63 N12°30' E124°19' Allen, Phil
117 N40°35' W75°34' Allentown, PA, US
56 N9°29' E76°22' Alleppey, Ind
108 N42°7' W102°50' Alliance, NE, US
99 N52°26' W111°47' Alliance, AB, Can
127 N17°52' W77°34' Alligator Pond, Jam
104 N48°33' W71°39' Alma, QC, Can
108 N40°6' W99°22' Alma, NE, US
47 N43°16' E76°55' Alma-Ata, Kaz
12 N38°40' W9°9' Almada, Port
13 N38°52' W1°5' Almansa, Sp
12 N42°39' W5°2' Almanza, Sp
47 N43°16' E76°55' Almaty, Kaz
13 N41°29' W2°32' Almazán, Sp
137 S1°31' W52°35' Almeirim, PA, Braz
18 N52°21' E6°39' Almelo, Neth
139 S16°11' W40°42' Almenara, MG, Braz
12 N38°41' W6°24' Almendralejo, Sp
13 N36°50' W2°28' Almería, Sp
12 N38°43' W4°10' Almodóvar del Campo, Sp
73 S19°20' W169°53' Alofi, Niue, NZ
58 N6°7' E100°22' Alor Setar, Malay
109 N45°4' W83°28' Alpena, MI, US
67 S23°39' E146°38' Alpha, Qld, Austl
114 N30°22' W103°40' Alpine, TX, US
39 N40°31' E47°39' Alpout-Udzhar, Azer
15 N45°17' E6°14' Alps, Fr
13 N42°54' W2°10' Alsasua, Sp
29 N69°55' E23°5' Alta, Nor
29 N69°44' E23°55' Altaelva, Nor
48 N47°31' E89°35' Altai Shan, China
137 S3°12' W52°12' Altamira, PA, Braz
49 N39°27' E109°40' Altan Xiret, China
122 N24°38' W107°55' Altata, Sin, Mex
35 N60°20' E68°58' Altay, Rus Fed
48 N46°23' E96°15' Altay, Mong
48 N47°52' E88°7' Altay, China
15 N46°53' E8°38' Altdorf, Switz
39 N40°50' E48°54' Altîakaç, Azer
137 S17°19' W53°12' Alto Araguaia, MT, Braz
88 S10°53' E19°14' Alto Chicapa, Ang
91 S15°38' E37°42' Alto Molócuè, Moz
137 S9°7' W45°55' Alto Parnaíba, MA, Braz
141 S45°2' W70°50' Alto Río Senguer, Arg
109 N36°41' W91°24' Alton, MO, US
101 N49°6' W97°33' Altona, MB, Can
117 N40°31' W78°24' Altoona, PA, US
48 N37°52' E87°17' Altun Shan, China
112 N41°29' W120°32' Alturas, CA, US
114 N34°38' W99°20' Altus, OK, US
39 N40°20' E38°46' Alucra, Turk
82 N8°26' E27°27' Aluk, Sud
141 S39°13' W70°57' Aluminé, Arg
27 N44°26' E34°3' Alupka, Ukr
114 N36°49' W98°40' Alva, OK, US
123 N18°46' W95°42' Alvarado, Ver, Mex
136 S3°12' W64°50' Alvarães, AM, Braz
29 N65°39' E20°59' Älvsbyn, Swe
54 N27°34' E76°36' Alwar, Ind
39 N39°56' E48°56' Aly-Bayramly, Azer
26 N54°24' E24°3' Alytus, Lith
81 N12°46' E20°29' Am Dam, Chad
81 N11°2' E20°17' Am Timan, Chad
82 N5°31' E30°20' Amadi, Sud
97 N65°3' W70°9' Amadjuak Lake, Can
60 S3°20' E128°58' Amahai, Indo
138 S23°5' W55°13' Amambaí, MT, Braz
52 N28°15' E128°20' Amami-oshima, Jap
60 S4°55' E136°59' Amanapare, Indo
46 N50°10' E65°13' Amangeldi, Kaz
73 S17°47' W140°28' Amanu, Fr Poly, Fr
137 N0°52' W52°39' Amapá, Braz
124 N13°16' W87°39' Amapala, Hon
114 N35°13' W101°50' Amarillo, TX, US
55 N22°40' E81°45' Amarkantak, Ind
137 S13°58' W49°9' Amaro Leite, GO, Braz
38 N40°39' E35°51' Amasya, Turk
136 S3°29' W68°6' Amataurá, AM, Braz
61 S10°2' E148°34' Amau, PNG
136 S3°33' W67°19' Amazon Basin
136 S4°56' W65°1' Amazonas, Braz
135 S3°13' W71°44' Amazonas, Peru
137 S2°5' W53°34' Amazonas, Braz
54 N30°22' E76°49' Ambala, Ind
92 S21°50' E46°56' Ambalavao, Madag
86 N2°23' E11°17' Ambam, Cam
92 S13°41' E48°27' Ambanja, Madag
134 S1°14' W78°37' Ambato, Ecu
92 S16°28' E46°43' Ambato Boeny, Madag
92 S17°50' E48°25' Ambatondrazaka, Madag
124 N18°2' W87°52' Ambergris Cay, Blz
78 N14°35' W11°47' Ambidédi, Mali
55 N23°7' E83°12' Ambikapur, Ind
92 S13°12' E49°4' Ambilobe, Madag
60 S3°43' E128°10' Ambon, Indo
88 S7°50' E13°6' Ambriz, Ang
61 S4°14' E142°50' Ambunti, PNG
18 N53°29' E5°37' Ameland, Neth
107 N42°47' W112°50' American Falls, ID, US
143 S70°0' E80°0' American Highland, Ant, Disputed
73 S10°59' W171°37' American Samoa, US
119 N32°5' W84°14' Americus, GA, US
143 S70°0' E70°0' Amery Ice Shelf, Ant, Disputed
108 N42°2' W93°39' Ames, IA, US
24 N38°51' E21°10' Amfilokhía, Grc
111 N44°50' W68°22' Amherst, ME, US
111 N42°23' W72°31' Amherst, MA, US
14 N49°53' E2°18' Amiens, Fr
56 N11°55' E73°12' Amindivi Islands, Ind
92 S7°4' E53°25' Amirante Group, Sey
101 N54°40' W102°47' Amisk Lake, Can
114 N29°40' W101°10' Amistad Reservoir, US
40 N31°57' E35°55' 'Amman, Jor
97 N65°36' W37°38' Ammassalik, Grld, Den
138 S18°1' W57°30' Amolar, MT, Braz
25 N36°50' E25°54' Amorgós, Grc
104 N48°35' W78°7' Amos, QC, Can
29 N59°35' E8°0' Åmot, Nor
59 S8°47' E118°0' Ampang, Indo
92 S24°42' E44°45' Ampanihy, Madag
24 N38°31' E22°24' Ámphissa, Grc
62 N17°11' E112°4' Amphitrite Group, Para Is, Disputed
13 N40°43' E0°35' Amposta, Sp
42 N15°38' E43°56' 'Amran, Yem
54 N20°56' E77°45' Amravati, Ind
54 N21°37' E71°14' Amreli, Ind
54 N31°35' E74°53' Amritsar, Ind
18 N52°22' E4°53' Amsterdam, Neth
110 N42°57' W74°11' Amsterdam, NY, US
20 N48°7' E14°53' Amstetten, Aus
45 N37°10' E66°11' Amu Darya, Afg
41 N37°5' E40°54' 'Amudah, Syria
121 N52°35' W172°32' Amukta Island, US
61 S5°57' E154°46' Amun, PNG
96 N70°5' W123°4' Amundsen Gulf
142 S65°0' W110°0' Amundsen Sea
54 N18°48' E78°17' Amur, Ind
33 N52°34' E126°35' Amur, Rus Fed
59 N1°11' E124°35' Amurang, Indo
42 N28°32' E39°38' An Nafud Desert, Sau Ar
44 N31°59' E44°19' An Najaf, Iraq
44 N31°2' E46°16' An Nasiriyah, Iraq
82 N12°42' E28°26' An Nuhud, Sud
44 N32°2' E42°15' An Nukhayb, Iraq
107 N46°8' W112°58' Anaconda, MT, US
114 N35°4' W98°14' Anadarko, OK, US
33 N64°38' E177°16' Anadyr, Rus Fed
33 N65°9' W177°15' Anadyrskiy Gulf
44 N34°28' E41°56' 'Anah, Iraq
112 N33°50' W117°55' Anaheim, CA, US
109 N42°7' W91°17' Anamosa, IA, US
38 N36°6' E32°50' Anamur, Turk
26 N47°40' E29°55' Anan'yer, Ukr
54 N22°34' E72°56' Anand, Ind
54 N14°41' E77°36' Anantapur, Ind
36 N44°53' E37°19' Anapa, Rus Fed
44 N30°53' E55°18' Anar, Iran
44 N33°20' E53°42' Anarak, Iran
72 N16°23' E143°34' Anatahan, NM Is, US
72 S20°13' E169°57' Anatom, Van
121 N61°10' W149°52' Anchorage, AK, US
17 N43°37' E13°31' Ancona, It
141 S41°52' W73°50' Ancud, Chile
49 N46°24' E125°19' Anda, China
140 S27°36' W66°19' Andalgalá, Arg
118 N31°19' W86°29' Andalusia, AL, US

continue on next page

145

32 N56°20' E101°43' **Bratsk**, Rus Fed
111 N42°51' W72°34' **Brattleboro**, VT, US
20 N48°15' E13°2' **Braunau am Inn**, Aus
19 N52°16' E10°31' **Braunschweig**, Ger
115 N30°56' W96°52' *Brazos River*, US
136 S6°9' W57°42' **BRAZIL**
87 S4°16' E15°14' **Brazzaville**, Con
22 N44°53' E18°48' **Brcko**, Bos & Herz
69 S23°49' E139°35' **Breadalbane**, Qld, Austl
114 N32°46' W98°54' **Breckenridge**, TX, US
113 N39°29' W106°3' **Breckenridge**, CO, US
21 N48°46' E16°53' **Breclav**, Czech
37 N52°26' E60°21' **Bredy**, Rus Fed
20 N47°30' E9°46' **Bregenz**, Aus
137 S11°1' W48°34' **Brejinho de Nazaré**, GO, Braz
19 N53°5' E8°52' **Bremen**, Ger
19 N53°34' E8°34' **Bremerhaven**, Ger
115 N30°10' W96°24' **Brenham**, TX, US
26 N52°6' E23°42' **Brest**, Bela
99 N53°7' W114°28' **Breton**, AB, Can
108 N41°56' W99°52' **Brewster**, NE, US
87 N6°32' E21°59' **Bria**, CAR
110 N41°10' W73°13' **Bridgeport**, CT, US
112 N38°16' W119°14' **Bridgeport**, CA, US
117 N39°26' W75°14' **Bridgeton**, NJ, US
129 N13°6' W59°37' **Bridgetown**, Barb
11 N51°8' W3°0' **Bridgwater**, UK
112 N41°31' W112°1' **Brigham City**, UT, US
11 N50°50' W0°8' **Brighton**, UK
113 N39°59' W104°49' **Brighton**, CO, US
69 S23°22' E141°34' **Brighton Downs**, Qld, Austl
84 N13°13' W16°41' **Brikama**, Gam
17 N40°36' E17°53' **Brindisi**, It
69 S27°29' E153°1' **Brisbane**, Qld, Austl
11 N51°27' W2°35' **Bristol**, UK
116 N36°36' W82°11' **Bristol**, TN, US
121 N57°25' W161°33' *Bristol Bay*
11 N51°17' W4°29' *Bristol Channel*
142 S55°0' W30°0' Bristol Island, UK
137 S15°14' W51°13' **Britania**, GO, Braz
98 N52°39' W126°28' **British Columbia**, Can
93 S4°25' E70°28' **British Indian Ocean Territory**, UK
129 N18°13' W64°34' **British Virgin Islands**, UK
118 N30°59' W86°15' Britton Hill, US
14 N45°10' E1°32' **Brive-la-Gaillarde**, Fr
47 N43°40' E73°49' **Brlik**, Kaz
21 N49°12' E16°37' **Brno**, Czech
68 S30°28' E121°20' **Broad Arrow**, WA, Austl
10 N57°14' W5°54' **Broadford**, UK
107 N45°26' W105°25' **Broadus**, MT, US
101 N50°33' W102°20' **Broadview**, SK, Can
101 N57°56' W101°40' **Brochet**, MB, Can
111 N42°5' W71°1' **Brockton**, MA, US
96 N72°23' W89°7' Brodeur Peninsula, Can
21 N53°16' E19°23' **Brodnica**, Pol
35 N55°35' E62°6' **Brodokalmak**, Rus Fed
26 N50°6' E25°10' **Brody**, Ukr
108 N41°24' W99°38' **Broken Bow**, NE, US
69 S31°57' E141°27' **Broken Hill**, NSW, Austl
133 N5°9' W55°1' **Brokopondo**, Sur
110 N40°53' W73°52' **Bronx**, NY, US
118 N31°34' W90°27' **Brookhaven**, MS, US
106 N42°4' W124°16' **Brookings**, OR, US
108 N44°19' W96°48' **Brookings**, SD, US
110 N40°36' W73°59' **Brooklyn**, NY, US
99 N50°35' W111°53' **Brooks**, AB, Can
121 N68°34' W159°53' Brooks Range, US
119 N28°34' W82°23' **Brooksville**, FL, US
117 N41°10' W79°5' **Brookville**, PA, US
66 S17°58' E122°14' **Broome**, WA, Austl
11 N58°2' W3°51' **Brora**, UK
114 N33°11' W102°16' **Brownfield**, TX, US
115 N25°55' W97°29' **Brownsville**, TX, US
114 N31°43' W98°59' **Brownwood**, TX, US
12 N39°37' W6°46' **Brozas**, Sp
68 S31°53' E118°9' **Bruce Rock**, WA, Austl
18 N51°13' E3°13' **Brugge**, Belg
90 S25°41' E18°5' Brukkaros, Nam
59 N5°7' E113°49' **BRUNEI DARUSSALAM**
111 N43°55' W69°58' **Brunswick**, ME, US
119 N31°11' W81°29' **Brunswick**, GA, US
125 N15°47' W84°35' **Brus Laguna**, Hon
113 N40°16' W103°36' **Brush**, CO, US
139 S27°6' W48°56' **Brusque**, SC, Braz
18 N50°50' E4°19' **Brussels**, Belg
18 N50°50' E4°19' **Bruxelles**, Belg
115 N30°44' W96°26' **Bryan**, TX, US
36 N53°15' E34°20' **Bryansk**, Rus Fed
21 N50°52' E17°27' **Brzeg**, Pol
61 S6°44' E147°34' **Bua**, PNG
74 S16°48' E178°37' **Bua**, Fiji
59 S4°45' E121°36' **Buapinang**, Indo
58 N0°44' E101°51' **Buatan**, Indo
84 N11°17' W15°50' **Bubaque**, Gui-Bis
38 N37°28' E30°36' **Bucak**, Turk
38 N36°57' E33°2' **Bucakkisla**, Turk
132 N7°7' W73°7' **Bucaramanga**, Col
63 N9°32' E125°59' Bucas Islands, Phil
118 N33°48' W85°11' **Buchanan**, GA, US
84 N5°57' W10°2' **Buchanan**, Libr
105 N48°49' W56°52' **Buchans**, NF, Can
23 N44°26' E26°5' **Bucharest**, Rom
112 N33°25' W112°38' **Buckeye**, AZ, US
11 N57°40' W2°58' **Buckie**, UK
104 N45°35' W75°25' **Buckingham**, QC, Can
111 N44°35' W68°47' **Bucksport**, ME, US
23 N44°26' E26°5' **Bucuresti**, Rom
83 N4°15' E46°30' **Bud Bud**, Som
22 N47°29' E19°2' **Budapest**, Hun
34 N59°17' E32°27' **Budogoshch'**, Rus Fed
86 N4°8' E9°16' **Buea**, Cam
140 S34°45' W65°15' **Buena Esperanza**, Arg
135 S17°27' W63°40' **Buena Vista**, Bol
122 N29°51' W107°29' **Buenaventura**, Chih, Mex
140 S34°39' W58°37' **Buenos Aires**, Arg
114 N36°50' W99°38' **Buffalo**, OK, US
110 N42°53' W78°53' **Buffalo**, NY, US
107 N44°21' W106°42' **Buffalo**, WY, US
108 N45°35' W103°33' **Buffalo**, SD, US
100 N55°53' W108°32' **Buffalo Narrows**, SK, Can
63 N8°14' E117°22' Bugsuk Island, Phil
63 N18°17' E121°50' **Buguey**, Phil
35 N54°33' E52°48' **Bugul'ma**, Rus Fed
37 N53°39' E52°26' **Buguruslan**, Rus Fed
41 N36°7' E38°9' *Buhayrat al Asad*, Syria
44 N33°41' E41°49' *Buhayrat ath Tharthar*, Iraq
85 N8°17' W2°7' *Bui Gorge Reservoir*, Gha
90 S22°18' E19°57' **Buitepos**, Nam
13 N41°30' W0°9' **Bujaraloz**, Sp
89 S3°23' E29°23' **Bujumbura**, Buru
61 S5°9' E154°44' Buka Island, PNG
46 N39°46' E64°25' **Bukhara**, Uzb
59 N4°18' E115°19' Bukit Pagon, Bru
58 S0°19' E100°22' **Bukittinggi**, Indo
89 S1°19' E31°49' **Bukoba**, Tanz
54 N28°24' E77°51' **Bulandshahr**, Ind
39 N39°5' E42°15' **Bulanik**, Turk
91 S20°10' E28°35' **Bulawayo**, Zimb
38 N38°3' E28°51' **Buldan**, Turk
120 N52°25' E175°55' Buldir Island, US
49 N48°49' E103°33' **Bulgan**, Mong
25 N42°43' E24°29' **BULGARIA**
66 S22°40' E114°3' **Bullara**, WA, Austl
83 N10°23' E44°27' **Bullaxaar**, Som
112 N35°8' W114°32' **Bullhead City**, AZ, US
71 S40°10' E175°23' **Bulls**, NZ
88 N2°12' E22°30' **Bumba**, DRC
67 S24°53' E152°19' **Bundaberg**, Qld, Austl
19 N52°12' E8°35' **Bünde**, Ger
54 N25°27' E75°39' **Bundi**, Ind
10 N56°19' W6°14' **Bunessan**, UK
59 S2°33' E121°58' **Bungku**, Indo
52 N33°16' E132°2' *Bungo Suido*
88 S10°7' E27°17' **Bunkeya**, DRC
59 S1°42' E114°48' **Buntok**, Indo
57 N12°41' E108°2' **Buon Mua Thuot**, Viet
81 N31°16' E32°17' **Bur Sa'id**, Egypt
81 N26°44' E33°56' **Bur Safajah**, Egypt
83 S1°5' E39°56' **Bura**, Ken
68 S30°31' E117°10' **Burakin**, WA, Austl
37 N50°59' E54°28' **Burannoye**, Rus Fed
83 N9°31' E45°32' **Burao**, Som
42 N26°20' E43°59' **Buraydah**, Sau Ar
112 N34°11' W118°18' **Burbank**, CA, US
83 N9°31' E45°32' **Burco**, Som
46 N38°25' E64°20' **Burdalyk**, Turkm
38 N37°43' E30°17' **Burdur**, Turk
25 N42°31' E27°27' **Burgas**, Bulg
117 N34°33' W77°56' **Burgaw**, NC, US
20 N48°9' E12°49' **Burghausen**, Ger
11 N57°41' W3°29' **Burghead**, UK
12 N42°20' W3°42' **Burgos**, Sp
29 N57°3' E18°17' **Burgsvik**, Swe
38 N39°30' E26°58' **Burhaniye**, Turk
139 S23°48' W48°35' **Buri**, SP, Braz
63 N13°0' E122°35' Burias Island, Phil
105 N46°58' W55°32' Burin Peninsula, Can
13 N39°31' W0°25' **Burjasot**, Sp
116 N36°47' W85°22' **Burkesville**, KY, US
85 N12°43' W2°46' **BURKINA FASO**
107 N42°32' W113°47' **Burley**, ID, US
46 N53°36' E61°55' **Burli**, Kaz
109 N40°49' W91°7' **Burlington**, IA, US
110 N44°29' W73°13' **Burlington**, VT, US
113 N39°19' W102°16' **Burlington**, CO, US
117 N36°6' W79°26' **Burlington**, NC, US
99 N49°15' W122°57' **Burnaby**, BC, Can
98 N52°22' W131°13' Burnaby Island, Can
106 N43°35' W119°3' **Burns**, OR, US
98 N54°14' W125°46' **Burns Lake**, BC, Can
24 N41°37' E20°2' **Burrel**, Alb
13 N39°53' W0°5' **Burriana**, Sp
66 S13°32' E131°42' **Burrundie**, NT, Austl
38 N40°12' E29°5' **Bursa**, Turk
89 S3°17' E29°26' **BURUNDI**
89 S3°57' E29°37' **Bururi**, Buru
41 N35°9' E40°26' **Busayrah**, Syria
44 N28°59' E50°50' **Bushehr**, Iran
21 N50°28' E20°44' **Busko-Zdrój**, Pol
40 N32°31' E36°29' **Busrá ash Sham**, Syria
63 N12°14' E119°20' Busuanga Island, Phil
88 N2°52' E24°45' **Buta**, DRC
141 S37°3' W69°50' **Buta Ranquil**, Arg
89 S2°36' E29°44' **Butare**, Rwn
89 N0°9' E29°17' **Butembo**, DRC
82 N1°48' E31°20' **Butiaba**, Ug
118 N32°5' W88°13' **Butler**, AL, US
24 N39°45' E20°1' **Butrint**, Alb
107 N46°0' W112°32' **Butte**, MT, US
97 N60°41' W64°7' Button Islands, Can
63 N8°57' E125°32' **Butuan**, Phil
55 N27°42' E83°27' **Butwal**, Nepal
83 S1°10' E41°50' **Buur Gaabo**, Som
18 N50°10' E6°1' Buurgplaatz, Lux
28 N65°10' W21°42' **Búÿardalur**, Ice
28 N64°56' W13°58' **Búÿir**, Ice
36 N42°49' E47°7' **Buynaksk**, Rus Fed
23 N45°9' E26°49' **Buzau**, Rom
46 N51°55' E66°16' **Buzuluk**, Kaz
37 N52°47' E52°15' **Buzuluk**, Rus Fed
25 N43°27' E27°44' **Byala**, Bulg
21 N53°8' E18°0' **Bydgoszcz**, Pol
29 N59°21' E7°20' **Bykle**, Nor
36 N49°47' E45°26' **Bykovo**, Rus Fed
97 N73°8' W79°34' Bylot Island, Can
69 S30°40' E146°24' **Byrock**, NSW, Austl
21 N50°22' E18°54' **Bytom**, Pol
21 N54°11' E17°30' **Bytów**, Pol

C

57 N9°11' E105°8' **Cà Mau**, Viet
138 S25°23' W57°8' **Caacupé**, Para
136 S3°18' W61°13' **Caapiranga**, AM, Braz
138 S26°13' W57°12' **Caapucú**, Para
138 S26°12' W56°22' **Caazapá**, Para
126 N22°5' W79°30' **Cabaiguán**, Cuba
63 N15°29' E120°58' **Cabanatuan**, Phil
63 N16°37' E121°40' **Cabarroquis**, Phil
135 S18°46' W63°24' **Cabezas**, Bol
132 N10°23' W71°28' **Cabimas**, Ven
88 S5°33' E12°12' **Cabinda**, Ang
141 S47°12' W65°48' **Cabo Blanco**, Arg
125 N14°59' W83°12' **Cabo Gracias a Dios**, Nic
141 S44°21' W65°14' **Cabo Raso**, Arg
105 N47°14' W60°40' *Cabot Strait*, Can
137 S8°31' W39°19' **Cabrobó**, PE, Braz
22 N43°53' E20°21' **Cacak**, Yugo
138 S30°30' W53°30' **Caçapava do Sul**, RS, Braz
138 S29°53' W54°49' **Cacequi**, RS, Braz
12 N39°28' W6°22' **Cáceres**, Sp
136 S16°4' W57°41' **Cáceres**, MT, Braz
141 S36°24' W59°32' **Cacharí**, Arg
84 N12°15' W16°10' **Cacheu**, Gui-Bis
140 S24°54' W66°23' Cachi, Arg
88 S13°5' E16°43' **Cachingues**, Ang
139 S20°51' W41°6' **Cachoeiro do Itapemirim**, ES, Braz
135 S10°32' W65°38' **Cachuela Esperanza**, Bol
13 N42°17' E3°17' **Cadaqués**, Sp
109 N44°13' W85°24' **Cadillac**, MI, US
100 N49°44' W107°43' **Cadillac**, SK, Can
63 N10°57' E123°18' **Cadiz**, Phil
12 N36°32' W6°17' **Cadiz**, Sp
12 N36°32' W6°17' **Cádiz**, Sp
14 N49°11' W0°20' **Caen**, Fr
11 N51°29' W3°13' **Caerdydd**, UK
11 N53°8' W4°16' **Caernarfon**, UK
140 S26°5' W65°58' **Cafayate**, Arg
63 N8°29' E124°39' **Cagayan de Oro**, Phil
63 N6°58' E118°33' Cagayan Sulu Island, Phil
45 N34°32' E65°16' **Cagcaran**, Afg
16 N39°13' E9°7' **Cagliari**, It
129 N18°14' W66°12' **Caguas**, PR, US
14 N44°27' E1°26' **Cahors**, Fr
125 N9°44' W82°51' **Cahuita**, CR
23 N45°54' E28°11' **Cahul**, Mol
137 S16°57' W51°49' **Caiapônia**, GO, Braz
126 N22°31' W79°28' **Caibarién**, Cuba
127 N21°55' W72°45' *Caicos Passage*
67 S16°55' E145°46' **Cairns**, Qld, Austl
81 N30°4' E31°14' **Cairo**, Egypt
88 S14°28' E13°6' **Caitou**, Ang
134 S10°10' W77°26' **Cajacay**, Peru
134 S7°10' W78°31' **Cajamarca**, Peru
22 N46°23' E16°26' **Cakovec**, Cro
13 N39°42' E3°25' **Cala Ratjada**, Sp
86 N4°58' E8°19' **Calabar**, Nga
132 N8°56' W67°26' **Calabozo**, Ven
23 N43°59' E22°56' **Calafat**, Rom
13 N42°18' W1°58' **Calahorra**, Sp
14 N50°57' E1°50' **Calais**, Fr
111 N45°11' W67°17' **Calais**, NB, Can
140 S22°28' W68°56' **Calama**, Chile
136 S8°3' W62°53' **Calama**, RO, Braz
132 N1°58' W72°41' **Calamar**, Col
63 N11°58' E118°55' Calamian Group, Phil
13 N40°55' W1°18' **Calamocha**, Sp
58 N4°39' E95°35' **Calang**, Indo
63 N13°25' E121°11' **Calapan**, Phil
23 N44°12' E27°20' **Calarasi**, Rom
13 N41°21' W1°38' **Calatayud**, Sp
63 N19°25' E120°57' Calayan Island, Phil
63 N12°4' E124°36' **Calbayog**, Phil
140 S29°54' W60°18' **Calchaquí**, Arg
137 N2°30' W50°57' **Calçoene**, AP, Braz
55 N22°35' E88°23' **Calcutta**, Ind
12 N39°24' W9°8' **Caldas da Rainha**, Port
140 S27°4' W70°50' **Caldera**, Chile
39 N39°9' E43°55' **Çaldiran**, Turk
106 N43°40' W116°41' **Caldwell**, ID, US
115 N30°32' W96°41' **Caldwell**, TX, US
99 N51°4' W114°5' **Calgary**, AB, Can
132 N3°27' W76°31' **Cali**, Col
112 N37°4' W121°1' **California**, US
140 S31°19' W69°25' **Calingasta**, Arg
103 N46°14' W79°22' **Callander**, ON, Can
134 S12°4' W77°9' **Callao**, Peru
99 N55°15' W113°12' **Calling Lake**, AB, Can
69 S24°0' E151°12' **Calliope**, Qld, Austl
13 N38°39' E0°3' **Calpe**, Sp
17 N37°29' E14°9' **Caltanissetta**, It
61 S11°11' E151°56' Caluados Chain, PNG
88 S11°18' E16°12' **Calucinga**, Ang
88 S12°6' E23°23' **Calunda**, Ang
88 S13°47' E14°44' **Caluquembe**, Ang
98 N51°29' W128°37' Calvert Island, Can
57 N11°54' E109°9' **Cam Ranh**, Viet
127 N21°23' W77°55' **Camagüey**, Cuba
138 S19°30' W54°5' **Camapuã**, MT, Braz
14 N43°49' E2°53' **Camarès**, Fr
141 S44°48' W65°42' **Camarones**, Arg
12 N42°30' W8°48' **Cambados**, Sp
57 N12°43' E103°39' **CAMBODIA**
10 N50°13' W5°18' **Camborne**, UK
14 N50°10' E3°14' **Cambrai**, Fr
11 N52°13' E0°8' **Cambridge**, UK
111 N42°23' W71°7' **Cambridge**, MA, US
117 N40°1' W81°35' **Cambridge**, OH, US
117 N38°34' W76°5' **Cambridge**, MD, US
96 N69°7' W105°4' **Cambridge Bay**, NU, Can
88 S7°48' E21°14' **Cambulo**, Ang
119 N34°15' W80°37' **Camden**, SC, US
115 N33°35' W92°50' **Camden**, AR, US
115 N29°48' W93°20' **Cameron**, LA, US
115 N30°51' W96°59' **Cameron**, TX, US
141 S53°38' W69°38' **Camerón**, Chile
86 N4°40' E9°54' **CAMEROON**
63 N9°7' E124°10' Camiguin Island, Phil
63 N18°55' E122°1' Camiguin Island, Phil
119 N31°14' W84°13' **Camilla**, GA, US
137 S1°48' W46°17' **Camiranga**, PA, Braz
135 S20°3' W63°31' **Camiri**, Bol
124 N12°23' W85°31' **Camoapa**, Nic
63 N10°30' E124°10' Camotes Islands, Phil
124 N14°33' W86°42' **Campamento**, Hon
116 N40°22' W83°43' Campbell Hill, US
123 N18°12' W91°13' **Campeche**, Mex
123 N19°51' W90°32' **Campeche**, Camp, Mex
127 N20°14' W77°17' **Campechuela**, Cuba
139 S19°31' W49°28' **Campina Verde**, MG, Braz
139 S22°54' W47°7' **Campinas**, SP, Braz
13 N39°24' W3°7' **Campo de Criptana**, Sp
140 S26°35' W62°51' **Campo Gallo**, Arg
138 S20°27' W54°37' **Campo Grande**, MT, Braz
138 S24°3' W52°22' **Campo Mourão**, PR, Braz
17 N41°34' E14°39' **Campobasso**, It
104 N44°55' W66°54' Campobello Island, Can
139 S21°44' W41°20' **Campos**, RJ, Braz
139 S24°16' W48°10' Campos, Braz
139 S19°41' W46°10' **Campos Altos**, MG, Braz
99 N53°1' W112°50' **Camrose**, AB, Can
98 N57°42' W125°51' **CANADA**
114 N35°55' W100°23' **Canadian**, TX, US
38 N40°9' E26°24' **Çanakkale**, Turk
99 N50°9' W115°48' **Canal Flats**, BC, Can
140 S33°33' W62°53' **Canals**, Arg
110 N42°53' W77°16' **Canandaigua**, NY, US
122 N30°57' W110°18' **Cananea**, Son, Mex
78 N29°30' W16°54' Canary Islands, Sp
125 N10°26' W85°7' **Cañas**, CR
132 N6°45' W76°1' **Cañasgordas**, Col
122 N24°31' W104°47' **Canatlán**, Dgo, Mex
13 N40°22' W2°24' **Cañaveras**, Sp
139 S15°39' W38°57' **Canavieiras**, BA, Braz
125 N8°19' W81°13' **Canazas**, Pan
69 S35°19' E149°10' **Canberra**, ACT, Austl
123 N21°10' W86°50' **Cancún**, QR, Mex
12 N43°35' W5°47' **Candás**, Sp
140 S32°4' W65°49' **Candelaria**, Arg
140 S27°28' W55°44' **Candelaria**, Arg
100 N52°23' W108°14' **Cando**, SK, Can
108 N48°29' W99°13' **Cando**, ND, US
139 S29°22' W50°50' **Canela**, RS, Braz
138 S34°32' W56°17' **Canelones**, Ur
13 N40°3' W1°35' **Cañete**, Sp
138 S16°5' W56°33' **Cangas**, MT, Braz
137 S6°24' W35°8' **Canguaretama**, RN, Braz
138 S31°24' W52°41' **Canguçu**, RS, Braz
50 N23°12' E99°16' **Cangyuan**, China
137 S4°22' W39°19' **Canindé**, CE, Braz
83 N10°45' E46°15' **Cankhor**, Som
38 N40°36' E33°37' **Çankiri**, Turk
99 N51°4' W115°23' **Canmore**, AB, Can
56 N11°51' E75°22' **Cannanore**, Ind
15 N43°34' E7°1' **Cannes**, Fr
113 N38°28' W105°12' **Canon City**, CO, US
129 N12°39' W61°19' Canouan, St VG
117 N40°48' W81°23' **Canton**, OH, US
110 N44°36' W75°10' **Canton**, NY, US
108 N43°18' W96°35' **Canton**, SD, US
73 S2°40' W173°47' Canton Island, Kir
136 S6°32' W64°20' **Canutama**, AM, Braz
114 N34°59' W101°55' **Canyon**, TX, US
106 N44°23' W118°57' **Canyon City**, OR, US
57 N22°40' E106°15' **Cao Bang**, Viet
128 N19°45' W72°12' **Cap-Haïtien**, Haiti
111 N42°33' W70°39' Cape Ann, US
67 S12°24' E137°1' Cape Arnhem, Austl
69 S40°30' E148°31' Cape Barren Island, Austl
85 N5°7' W1°15' **Cape Coast**, Gha
111 N41°52' W69°56' Cape Cod, US
111 N41°53' W70°27' *Cape Cod Bay*
119 N26°34' W81°57' **Cape Coral**, FL, US
97 N59°34' W44°27' Cape Farewell, Grld, Den
109 N37°18' W89°31' **Cape Girardeau**, MO, US
117 N36°0' W78°0 Cape Hatteras, US
117 N39°5' W74°49' **Cape May Court House**, NJ, US
90 S34°17' E17°32' Cape of Good Hope, S Afr
119 N25°16' W81°23' Cape Sable, US
90 S33°55' E18°25' **Cape Town**, S Afr
78 N17°7' W27°11' **CAPE VERDE**
67 S13°22' E142°1' Cape York Peninsula, Austl
69 S23°5' E148°2' **Capella**, Qld, Austl
138 S19°58' W60°45' **Capitán Pablo Lagerenza**, Para
120 N19°31' W155°52' **Captain Cook**, HI, US
132 S0°59' W71°11' *Caquetá*, Col
23 N44°7' E24°21' **Caracal**, Rom
136 N1°50' W61°8' **Caracaraí**, RR, Braz
132 N10°30' W66°56' **Caracas**, Ven
63 N7°20' E126°34' **Caraga**, Phil
139 S17°12' W41°42' **Caraí**, MG, Braz
135 S20°45' W63°4' **Carandayti**, Bol
139 S20°44' W42°2' **Carangola**, MG, Braz
23 N45°25' E22°13' **Caransebes**, Rom
135 S21°49' W63°46' **Caraparí**, Bol
139 S19°47' W42°8' **Caratinga**, MG, Braz
136 S4°52' W66°54' **Carauari**, AM, Braz
13 N38°6' W1°51' **Caravaca**, Sp
139 S17°45' W39°15' **Caravelas**, BA, Braz
135 S15°46' W73°22' **Caravelí**, Peru
138 S28°18' W52°48' **Caràzinho**, RS, Braz
12 N42°26' W8°4' **Carballino**, Sp
122 N29°42' W110°58' **Carbo**, Son, Mex
109 N37°43' W89°11' **Carbondale**, IL, US
117 N41°35' W75°30' **Carbondale**, PA, US
105 N47°45' W53°13' **Carbonear**, NF, Can
13 N39°8' W0°28' **Carcagente**, Sp
14 N43°11' E2°20' **Carcassonne**, Fr
38 N38°6' E36°49' **Çardak**, Turk
11 N51°29' W3°13' **Cardiff**, UK
11 N52°29' W4°44' *Cardigan Bay*
138 S33°53' W57°23' **Cardona**, Ur
99 N49°12' W113°18' **Cardston**, AB, Can
23 N47°42' E22°28' **Carei**, Rom
68 S25°38' E115°27' **Carey Downs**, WA, Austl
93 S16°47' E59°44' Cargados Carajos Shoals, Mrts
123 N19°2' W87°14' *Caribbean Sea*
111 N46°52' W68°1' **Caribou**, ME, US
99 N59°12' W115°39' Caribou Mountains, Can
13 N41°20' W1°13' **Cariñena**, Sp
13 N39°14' W0°31' **Carlet**, Sp
11 N54°54' W2°55' **Carlisle**, UK
10 N58°17' W6°48' **Carloway**, UK
113 N32°25' W104°14' **Carlsbad**, NM, US
109 N46°40' W92°25' **Carlton**, MN, US
11 N51°52' W4°19' **Carmarthen**, UK
110 N41°26' W73°41' **Carmel**, NY, US
12 N37°28' W5°38' **Carmona**, Sp
90 S30°56' E22°8' **Carnarvon**, S Afr
68 S24°53' E113°40' **Carnarvon**, WA, Austl
66 S25°43' E122°59' **Carnegie**, WA, Austl
20 N46°41' E12°35' Carniche Alp, Aus
87 N4°56' E15°52' **Carnot**, CAR
73 S9°56' W150°10' Caroline Island, Kir
21 N49°21' E18°28' Carpathian Mountains, Slvk
15 N44°3' E5°3' **Carpentras**, Fr
10 N52°1' W9°37' Carrauntoohil, Ire
129 N12°24' W61°26' Carriacou, Gren
10 N53°57' W8°5' **Carrick on Shannon**, Ire
140 S28°5' W71°10' **Carrizal Bajo**, Chile
114 N28°31' W99°52' **Carrizo Springs**, TX, US
113 N33°38' W105°53' **Carrizozo**, NM, US
108 N42°5' W94°52' **Carroll**, IA, US
116 N38°41' W85°11' **Carrollton**, KY, US
108 N46°25' W101°34' **Carson**, ND, US
112 N39°10' W119°46' **Carson City**, NV, US
112 N39°50' W118°33' Carson Sink, US
13 N37°36' W0°59' **Cartagena**, Sp
132 N10°25' W75°32' **Cartagena**, Col
125 N9°52' W83°55' **Cartago**, CR
119 N34°10' W84°48' **Cartersville**, GA, US
115 N32°10' W94°20' **Carthage**, TX, US
137 S8°17' W35°58' **Caruaru**, PE, Braz
137 S1°13' W46°1' **Carutapera**, MA, Braz
109 N36°11' W89°40' **Caruthersville**, MO, US
136 S1°24' W61°59' **Carvoeiro**, AM, Braz
139 S21°46' W47°7' **Casa Branca**, SP, Braz
112 N32°53' W111°46' **Casa Grande**, AZ, US
78 N33°35' W7°38' **Casablanca**, Mor
138 S28°34' W51°59' **Casca**, RS, Braz
99 N49°10' W118°13' **Cascade**, BC, Can
106 N44°31' W116°2' **Cascade**, ID, US
106 N43°55' W122°10' Cascade Range, US
12 N38°42' W9°25' **Cascais**, Port
138 S24°57' W53°28' **Cascavel**, PR, Braz
17 N41°4' E14°20' **Caserta**, It
63 N16°17' E122°7' **Casiguran**, Phil
107 N42°52' W106°19' **Casper**, WY, US
32 N40°47' E50°11' *Caspian Sea*
139 S20°36' W46°56' **Cássia**, MG, Braz
98 N59°16' W129°40' **Cassiar**, BC, Can
98 N59°47' W129°50' Cassiar Mountains, Can
12 N39°59' W8°13' **Castanheira de Pêra**, Port
17 N40°42' E14°29' **Castellammare di Stabia**, It
13 N39°59' W0°2' **Castellón de la Plana**, Sp
13 N40°48' W0°19' **Castellote**, Sp
12 N39°49' W7°29' **Castelo Branco**, Port
138 S34°12' W53°50' **Castillos**, Ur
113 N39°13' W111°1' **Castle Dale**, UT, US
113 N39°22' W104°52' **Castle Rock**, CO, US
10 N53°52' W9°17' **Castlebar**, Ire
10 N56°57' W7°28' **Castlebay**, UK
99 N49°19' W117°40' **Castlegar**, BC, Can
14 N43°36' E2°15' **Castres**, Fr
129 N13°59' W61°0' **Castries**, St L
139 S24°47' W50°0' **Castro**, PR, Braz
12 N40°53' W7°55' **Castro Daire**, Port
12 N41°23' W5°16' **Castronuño**, Sp
17 N39°49' E16°13' **Castrovillari**, It
39 N39°40' E41°0' **Çat**, Turk
127 N24°22' W75°26' Cat Island, Bah
124 N14°50' W85°55' **Catacamas**, Hon
39 N38°1' E43°7' **Çatak**, Turk
140 S25°13' W69°43' **Catalina**, Chile
63 N13°47' E124°27' Catanduanes Island, Phil
139 S21°8' W48°58' **Catanduva**, SP, Braz
17 N37°29' E15°3' **Catania**, It
17 N38°54' E16°35' **Catanzaro**, It
63 N12°30' E124°38' **Catarman**, Phil
63 N11°46' E124°53' **Catbalogan**, Phil
91 S32°18' E27°9' **Cathcart**, S Afr
84 N11°18' W15°15' **Catió**, Gui-Bis
136 N0°27' W61°41' **Catrimani**, RR, Braz
110 N42°13' W73°52' **Catskill**, NY, US
110 N41°56' W74°36' Catskill Mountains, US
91 S13°45' E35°30' **Catur**, Moz
132 N8°0' W75°12' **Caucasia**, Col
32 N43°56' E41°4' Caucasus Mountains, Rus Fed
88 S8°25' E18°40' **Caungula**, Ang
127 N20°36' W76°47' *Cauto*, Cuba
15 N43°50' E5°2' **Cavaillon**, Fr
137 S13°48' W47°30' **Cavalcante**, GO, Braz
10 N54°0' W7°21' **Cavan**, Ire
38 N37°9' E29°42' **Çavdir**, Turk
63 N14°31' E121°1' **Cavite**, Phil
88 S8°33' E13°36' **Caxito**, Ang
38 N38°35' E31°2' **Çay**, Turk
134 N0°3' W78°8' **Cayambe**, Ecu
133 N4°56' W52°20' **Cayenne**, Fr Gu, Fr
128 N18°12' W73°45' **Cayes**, Haiti
14 N44°14' E1°46' **Caylus**, Fr
126 N19°37' W79°50' Cayman Brac, Cay Is, UK
126 N19°58' W81°50' **Cayman Islands**, UK
126 N21°30' W82°6' Cayo Cantiles, Cuba
127 N22°40' W78°32' Cayo Coco, Cuba
126 N21°35' W81°23' Cayo Largo, Cuba
127 N21°58' W77°36' Cayo Romano, Cuba
124 N15°57' W86°38' Cayos Cochinos, Hon
125 N14°33' W83°13' Cayos Miskitos, Nic
91 S15°25' E33°40' **Cazula**, Moz
137 S5°22' W40°22' **Ceará**, Braz
140 S29°6' W66°33' **Cebollar**, Arg
12 N40°26' W4°28' **Cebreros**, Sp
63 N10°19' E123°54' **Cebu**, Phil
63 N10°31' E123°44' Cebu, Phil
112 N37°41' W113°4' **Cedar City**, UT, US
109 N42°31' W92°26' **Cedar Falls**, IA, US
101 N53°29' W101°22' *Cedar Lake*, Can
109 N42°1' W91°38' **Cedar Rapids**, IA, US
69 S32°7' E133°40' **Ceduna**, SA, Austl
83 N10°37' E47°22' **Ceerigaabo**, Som
22 N47°10' E19°48' **Cegléd**, Hun
59 S2°16' E119°17' Celebes, Indo
63 N4°48' E122°6' *Celebes Sea*
123 N20°52' W90°24' **Celestún**, Yuc, Mex
22 N46°14' E15°16' **Celje**, Slov
19 N52°37' E10°5' **Celle**, Ger
10 N50°40' W6°17' *Celtic Sea*
115 N31°48' W94°11' **Center**, TX, US
87 N6°39' E17°17' **CENTRAL AFRICAN REPUBLIC**
45 N26°25' E63°52' Central Makan Range, Pak
32 N65°53' E90°37' Central Siberian Uplands, Rus Fed
106 N46°43' W122°58' **Centralia**, WA, US
109 N38°32' W89°8' **Centralia**, IL, US
118 N34°9' W85°41' **Centre**, AL, US
60 S3°11' E129°16' Ceram, Indo
60 S2°34' E130°32' *Ceram Sea*
141 S36°49' W63°51' **Cereales**, Arg
140 S32°39' W70°1' Cerro Aconcagua, Arg
140 S21°13' W68°28' Cerro Aucanquilcha, Chile
134 S13°2' W76°28' **Cerro Azul**, Peru
139 S24°50' W49°15' **Cêrro Azul**, PR, Braz
140 S27°52' W68°46' Cerro Bonete, Arg
138 S34°21' W54°53' Cerro Catedral, Ur
125 N9°29' W83°29' Cerro Chirripo, CR
125 N8°22' W82°20' Cerro Colorado, Pan
124 N14°36' W90°43' Cerro de la Cruz, Guat
122 N31°0' W115°22' Cerro de La Encantada, Mex
140 S35°21' W69°59' Cerro de las Minas, Arg
134 S10°41' W76°16' **Cerro de Pasco**, Peru
140 S26°38' W68°22' Cerro El Cóndor, Arg
140 S25°52' W66°52' Cerro Galan, Arg
140 S25°27' W67°16' Cerro Incahuasi, Arg
124 N14°35' W88°41' Cerro Las Minas, Hon
140 S29°56' W69°53' Cerro Las Tórtolas, Arg
140 S31°59' W70°7' Cerro Mercedario, Arg
124 N13°46' W86°23' Cerro Mogotón, Nic
125 N7°57' W77°45' Cerro Pirre, Pan
135 S13°11' W73°2' Cerro Pumasillo, Peru
138 S26°34' W55°40' Cerro San Rafael, Para
140 S33°22' W69°47' Cerro Tupungato, Chile
134 S10°16' W76°54' Cerro Yerupaja, Peru
17 N44°15' E12°22' **Cervia**, It
15 N42°20' E9°31' **Cervione**, Fr
12 N43°40' W7°25' **Cervo**, Sp
17 N44°8' E12°15' **Cesena**, It
26 N57°18' E25°15' **Cesis**, Lat
20 N48°59' E14°28' **Ceské Budejovice**, Czech
20 N48°49' E14°19' **Ceský Krumlov**, Czech
23 N44°6' E23°3' **Cetate**, Rom
22 N42°23' E18°55' **Cetinje**, Yugo
51 N22°5' E120°42' **Ch'e-ch'eng**, Taiwan
52 N36°49' E127°9' **Ch'onan**, S Kor
52 N41°47' E129°50' **Ch'ongjin**, N Kor
52 N36°40' E127°29' **Ch'ongju**, S Kor
52 N34°5' E126°55' Ch'ongsan-do, S Kor
52 N37°52' E127°44' **Ch'unch'on**, S Kor
140 S23°17' W62°50' Chaco Central, Arg
80 N14°58' E16°25' **CHAD**
108 N42°50' W103°0' **Chadron**, NE, US
86 N11°56' E6°55' **Chafe**, Nga
132 N3°10' W73°14' **Chafurray**, Col
45 N29°18' E64°42' **Chagai**, Pak
93 S7°3' E71°46' Chagos Archipelago, BIOT, UK
57 N17°44' E105°18' Chaine Annamitique, Laos
85 N10°39' E1°31' Chaine de l' Atakora, Ben
128 N18°22' W71°58' Chaîne de la Salle, Haiti
57 N9°23' E99°14' **Chaiya**, Thai
140 S30°46' W57°59' **Chajarí**, Arg
55 N21°45' E92°5' **Chakaria**, Bngl
45 N31°14' E62°7' **Chakhansur**, Afg
134 S15°52' W74°15' **Chala**, Peru
124 N14°3' W88°56' **Chalatenango**, El Sal
82 N3°9' E37°21' Chalbi Desert, Ken
135 S14°17' W73°15' **Chalhuanca**, Peru
106 N44°30' W114°14' **Challis**, ID, US
15 N48°58' E4°23' **Chalons-Sur-Marne**, Fr
45 N30°55' E66°27' **Chaman**, Pak
89 S11°35' E36°58' **Chamba**, Tanz
54 N32°34' E76°8' **Chamba**, Ind
100 N50°50' W105°34' **Chamberlain**, SK, Can
111 N46°17' W69°52' *Chamberlain Lake*, US
15 N45°34' E5°55' **Chambery**, Fr
122 N19°32' W105°5' **Chamela**, Jal, Mex
140 S30°21' W66°19' **Chamical**, Arg
15 N45°54' E6°52' **Chamonix-Mont-Blanc**, Fr
96 N60°47' W136°29' **Champagne**, YT, Can
57 N14°53' E105°52' **Champasak**, Laos
123 N19°21' W90°43' **Champotón**, Camp, Mex
140 S26°21' W70°37' **Chañaral**, Chile
134 S11°35' W77°16' **Chancay**, Peru
140 S35°44' W72°32' **Chanco**, Chile
54 N30°44' E76°48' **Chandigarh**, Ind
55 N22°58' E86°3' **Chandil**, Ind
54 N19°58' E79°19' **Chandraper**, Ind
51 N30°40' E117°10' *Chang*, China
91 S16°54' E33°14' **Changara**, Moz
50 N19°22' E108°46' **Changcheng**, China
49 N43°53' E125°19' **Changchun**, China
49 N29°2' E111°41' **Changde**, China
51 N24°4' E120°33' **Changhua**, Taiwan
49 N28°11' E112°58' **Changsha**, China
52 N38°15' E125°6' **Changyon-up**, N Kor
49 N31°46' E119°57' **Changzhou**, China
105 N47°34' W59°9' **Channel-Port aux Basques**, NF, Can
114 N35°41' W102°20' **Channing**, TX, US
12 N42°37' W7°46' **Chantada**, Sp
57 N12°36' E102°9' **Chanthaburi**, Thai
108 N37°41' W95°28' **Chanute**, KS, US
49 N48°53' E130°24' **Chaoyang**, China
137 S8°39' W47°31' Chapada das Mangabeiras, Braz
137 S13°5' W42°10' Chapada Diamantina, Braz
137 S3°44' W43°21' **Chapadinha**, MA, Braz
113 N32°4' W106°23' **Chaparral**, NM, US
103 N47°50' W83°24' **Chapleau**, ON, Can
100 N50°28' W106°40' **Chaplin**, SK, Can
86 N7°20' E11°40' Chappal Waddi, Nga
135 S19°36' W65°32' **Chaqui**, Bol
46 N39°5' E63°34' **Chardzhou**, Turkm
115 N29°52' W91°32' **Charenton**, LA, US
80 N10°11' E17°35' *Chari River*, Chad
45 N35°1' E69°10' **Charikar**, Afg
18 N50°25' E4°26' **Charleroi**, Belg
109 N43°4' W92°40' **Charles City**, IA, US
97 N62°41' W76°34' Charles Island, Can
109 N42°30' W90°14' Charles Mound, US
117 N39°17' W77°52' **Charles Town**, WV, US
117 N38°22' W81°42' **Charleston**, WV, US
119 N32°47' W79°56' **Charleston**, SC, US
129 N17°8' W62°38' **Charlestown**, St KN
69 S26°23' E146°14' **Charleville**, Qld, Austl
15 N49°45' E4°43' **Charleville-Mézières**, Fr
109 N45°19' W85°16' **Charlevoix**, MI, US
117 N35°14' W80°50' **Charlotte**, NC, US
129 N18°22' W64°56' **Charlotte Amalie**, USVI, US
117 N38°2' W78°29' **Charlottesville**, VA, US
105 N46°14' W63°8' **Charlottetown**, PE, Can
79 N29°1' W0°16' **Charouine**, Alg
14 N46°9' E0°24' **Charroux**, Fr
67 S20°5' E146°16' **Charters Towers**, Qld, Austl
14 N48°27' E1°29' **Chartres**, Fr
52 N41°27' E126°37' **Chasong-up**, N Kor
14 N47°43' W1°23' **Châteaubriant**, Fr
14 N48°5' E1°20' **Châteaudun**, Fr
104 N45°20' W73°49' **Châteauguay**, QC, Can
14 N46°49' E1°42' **Châteauroux**, Fr
103 N42°16' W82°26' **Chatham**, ON, Can
71 S44°2' W177°28' Chatham Island, NZ
118 N31°28' W88°15' **Chatom**, AL, US

continue on next page

90 S30°39' E24°0' **De Aar**, S Afr
118 N30°43' W86°7' **De Funiak Springs**, FL, US
141 S54°44' W63°44' De Los Estados, Arg
115 N30°51' W93°17' **De Ridder**, LA, US
40 N31°33' E35°35' *Dead Sea*, Isr
68 S30°46' E128°58' **Deakin**, WA, Austl
109 N42°19' W83°11' **Dearborn**, MI, US
112 N36°43' W117°22' Death Valley, US
21 N51°35' E21°51' **Deblin**, Pol
82 N10°20' E37°45' **Debre Mark'os**, Eth
22 N47°32' E21°38' **Debrecen**, Hun
118 N34°37' W86°59' **Decatur**, AL, US
109 N39°50' W88°58' **Decatur**, IL, US
116 N40°50' W84°56' **Decatur**, IN, US
119 N33°46' W84°17' **Decatur**, GA, US
14 N44°34' E2°15' **Decazeville**, Fr
54 N14°49' E76°37' Deccan, Ind
50 N27°24' E102°10' **Dechang**, China
109 N43°18' W91°47' **Decorah**, IA, US
111 N42°14' W71°10' **Dedham**, MA, US
34 N57°32' E29°56' **Dedovichi**, Rus Fed
49 N48°31' E126°14' **Dedu**, China
121 N54°38' W162°20' Deer Island, US
105 N49°10' W57°28' **Deer Lake**, NF, Can
107 N46°24' W112°44' **Deer Lodge**, MT, US
116 N41°17' W84°22' **Defiance**, OH, US
48 N31°50' E98°40' **Dege**, China
19 N48°50' E12°59' **Deggendorf**, Ger
66 S20°10' E119°12' **Degrey**, WA, Austl
44 N30°38' E53°13' **Deh Bid**, Iran
44 N35°17' E47°25' **Deh Golan**, Iran
44 N32°41' E47°16' **Dehloran**, Iran
23 N47°9' E23°52' **Dej**, Rom
114 N29°22' W100°53' **Del Rio**, TX, US
119 N29°2' W81°19' **DeLand**, FL, US
112 N35°46' W119°15' **Delano**, CA, US
112 N38°22' W112°22' Delano Peak, US
45 N32°11' E63°25' **Delaram**, Afg
120 N50°52' W179°31' Delarof Islands, US
117 N38°46' W75°37' **Delaware**, US
117 N40°30' W75°16' *Delaware River*, US
99 N52°12' W113°14' **Delburne**, AB, Can
15 N47°20' E7°21' **Delémont**, Switz
18 N53°19' E6°46' **Delfzijl**, Neth
110 N42°17' W74°55' **Delhi**, NY, US
54 N28°37' E77°7' **Delhi**, Ind
38 N39°21' E37°13' **Deliktas**, Turk
48 N37°14' E97°11' **Delingha Nongchang**, China
119 N26°29' W80°4' **Delray Beach**, FL, US
113 N38°44' W108°4' **Delta**, CO, US
24 N39°57' E20°6' **Delvinë**, Alb
82 N8°30' E34°48' **Dembi Dolo**, Eth
34 N55°16' E31°31' **Demidov**, Rus Fed
113 N32°16' W107°46' **Deming**, NM, US
19 N53°54' E13°2' **Demmin**, Ger
99 N55°26' W119°54' **Demmitt**, AB, Can
88 S3°2' E18°13' **DEMOCRATIC REPUBLIC OF THE CONGO, THE**
60 S2°20' E140°8' **Demta**, Indo
18 N52°54' E4°45' **Den Helder**, Neth
49 N40°20' E106°59' **Dengkou**, China
48 N31°32' E95°27' **Dengqen**, China
68 S25°55' E113°32' **Denham**, WA, Austl
13 N38°50' E0°6' **Denia**, Sp
108 N42°1' W95°22' **Denison**, IA, US
46 N52°28' E61°46' **Denisovka**, Kaz
38 N37°46' E29°6' **Denizli**, Turk
29 N55°38' E9°44' **DENMARK**
28 N66°9' W27°31' *Denmark Strait*
47 N38°16' E67°54' **Denow**, Uzb
59 S8°37' E115°13' **Denpasar**, Indo
113 N39°46' W105°3' **Denver**, CO, US
55 N21°32' E84°44' **Deogarh**, Ind
55 N24°29' E86°42' **Deoghar**, Ind
54 N19°57' E73°50' **Deolali**, Ind
115 N34°2' W94°20' **DeQueen**, AR, US
45 N31°50' E68°8' **Derakht-e Yahyá**, Afg
36 N42°3' E48°18' **Derbent**, Rus Fed
35 N55°52' E53°30' **Derbeshkinskiy**, Rus Fed
11 N52°55' W1°29' **Derby**, UK
66 S17°18' E123°38' **Derby**, WA, Austl
36 N51°14' E48°46' **Dergachi**, Rus Fed
39 N37°22' E40°17' **Derik**, Turk
22 N44°58' E17°55' **Derventa**, Bos & Herz
37 N53°13' E52°22' **Derzhavino**, Rus Fed
46 N51°3' E66°19' **Derzhavinsk**, Kaz
108 N41°36' W93°35' **Des Moines**, IA, US
83 N11°5' E39°41' **Dese**, Eth
19 N51°50' E12°14' **Dessau**, Ger
91 S18°38' E26°50' **Dete**, Zimb
109 N42°20' W83°3' **Detroit**, MI, US
105 N49°43' W65°14' *Détroit d'Honguedo*, Can
105 N50°3' W64°1' *Détroit de Jaques-Cartier*, Can
108 N46°49' W95°51' **Detroit Lakes**, MN, US
21 N48°31' E19°28' **Detva**, Slvk
23 N45°53' E22°55' **Deva**, Rom
54 N25°32' E73°54' **Devgarh**, Ind
54 N16°22' E73°23' **Devgarh**, Ind
54 N26°42' E71°12' **Devikot**, Ind
122 N31°43' W116°23' Devil's Peak, Mex
108 N48°7' W98°52' **Devils Lake**, ND, US
98 N58°44' W133°50' Devils Paw, Can
96 N74°55' W88°10' Devon Island, Can
38 N41°13' E31°57' **Devrek**, Turk
54 N22°58' E76°4' **Dewas**, Ind
44 N33°17' E57°30' **Deyhuk**, Iran
24 N37°48' E22°1' **Dháfni**, Grc
55 N23°43' E90°23' **Dhaka**, Bngl
42 N14°46' E44°23' **Dhamar**, Yem
55 N23°47' E86°26' **Dhanbad**, Ind
55 N26°53' E87°21' **Dharan**, Nepal
56 N12°8' E78°10' **Dharmapuri**, Ind
56 N14°26' E77°43' **Dharmavaram**, Ind
79 N31°40' E6°8' **Dhassi Messaoud**, Alg
24 N37°18' E21°58' **Dhiavolítsion**, Grc
25 N35°4' E25°14' Dhikti Óri, Grc
24 N37°37' E22°3' **Dhimitsána**, Grc
54 N15°25' E77°53' **Dhone**, Ind
54 N21°44' E70°27' **Dhoraji**, Ind
54 N20°54' E74°47' **Dhule**, Ind
83 N5°44' E46°31' **Dhuusa Mareeb**, Som
57 N11°35' E108°4' **Di Linh**, Viet
112 N36°50' W121°4' Diablo Range, US
78 N14°9' W5°1' **Diafarabé**, Mali
139 S18°15' W43°36' **Diamantina**, MG, Braz
136 S14°25' W56°27' **Diamantino**, MT, Braz
106 N43°31' W122°9' Diamond Peak, US
50 N30°21' E107°23' **Dianjiang**, China
85 N12°4' E1°47' **Diapaga**, Burk
88 S6°30' E22°57' **Dibaya**, DRC
143 S65°0' E130°0' *Dibble Iceberg Tongue*, Ant, Disputed
83 N6°31' E41°52' **Dibo**, Eth
55 N27°29' E94°54' **Dibrugarh**, Ind
114 N33°37' W100°50' **Dickens**, TX, US
108 N46°53' W102°47' **Dickinson**, ND, US
54 N27°27' E74°34' **Didwana**, Ind
85 N10°58' W3°15' **Diébougou**, Burk
93 S7°25' E72°35' Diego Garcia, BIOT, UK
18 N49°52' E6°10' **Diekirch**, Lux
84 N12°28' W16°47' **Diembéring**, Sen
14 N49°56' E1°5' **Dieppe**, Fr
83 N1°0' E41°0' **Dif**, Som
80 N13°19' E12°37' **Diffa**, Niger
55 N27°23' E95°38' **Digboi**, Ind
105 N44°36' W65°45' **Digby**, NS, Can
15 N44°6' E6°14' **Digne**, Fr
39 N40°23' E43°24' **Digor**, Turk
63 N6°45' E125°22' **Digos**, Phil
60 S7°6' E139°35' *Digul River*, Indo
15 N47°20' E5°2' **Dijon**, Fr
80 N9°58' E17°31' **Dik**, Chad
83 N11°6' E42°22' **Dikhil**, Djib
87 N12°2' E13°58' **Dikwa**, Nga
60 S8°34' E125°35' **Dili**, Indo
82 N12°3' E29°39' **Dilling**, Sud
121 N59°3' W158°29' **Dillingham**, AK, US
107 N45°13' W112°38' **Dillon**, MT, US
119 N34°25' W79°22' **Dillon**, SC, US
88 S10°42' E22°20' **Dilolo**, DRC
40 N33°31' E36°18' **Dimashq**, Syria
85 N6°39' W4°42' **Dimbokro**, Côte d'Ivoire
25 N42°3' E25°36' **Dimitrovgrad**, Bulg
86 N8°24' E11°47' Dimlang, Nga
114 N34°33' W102°19' **Dimmitt**, TX, US
63 N10°11' E125°41' Dinagat Island, Phil
55 N25°38' E88°38' **Dinajpur**, Bngl
14 N48°27' W2°2' **Dinan**, Fr
18 N50°16' E4°55' **Dinant**, Belg
38 N38°4' E30°10' **Dinar**, Turk
22 N44°15' E16°17' Dinaric Alps, Bos & Herz
56 N10°21' E77°57' **Dindigul**, Ind
57 S23°39' E149°20' **Dingo**, Qld, Austl
19 N48°38' E12°31' **Dingolfing**, Ger
84 N11°18' W10°43' **Dinguiraye**, Gui
50 N35°33' E104°32' **Dingxi**, China
102 N49°41' W92°30' **Dinorwic**, ON, Can
117 N37°5' W77°35' **Dinwiddie**, VA, US
61 S5°34' E154°58' **Dios**, PNG
78 N14°50' W5°15' **Dioura**, Mali
84 N14°40' W16°15' **Diourbel**, Sen
63 N8°35' E123°21' **Dipolog**, Phil
70 S45°54' E168°22' **Dipton**, NZ
45 N35°12' E71°53' **Dir**, Pak
70 S12°4' E96°54' Direction Island, Cocos Is, Austl
88 S17°58' E20°47' **Dirico**, Ang
68 S25°45' E111°50' Dirk Hartog Island, Austl
80 N19°1' E12°53' **Dirkou**, Niger
55 N26°10' E91°45' **Dispur**, Ind
123 N19°8' W99°16' **Distrito Federal**, Mex
137 S15°28' W47°57' **Distrito Federal**, Braz
39 N41°12' E48°59' **Divichi**, Azer
85 N5°50' W5°22' **Divo**, Côte d'Ivoire
109 N41°51' W89°29' **Dixon**, IL, US
39 N39°33' E43°41' **Diyadin**, Turk
39 N37°55' E40°14' **Diyarbakir**, Turk
80 N21°1' E12°18' **Djado**, Niger
87 S2°33' E14°45' **Djambala**, Con
79 N24°34' E9°29' **Djanet**, Alg
22 N42°32' E20°8' Djaravica, Yugo
79 N34°40' E3°15' **Djelfa**, Alg
87 N6°3' E25°19' **Djema**, CAR
85 N13°7' W4°10' **Djibasso**, Burk
85 N14°6' W1°38' **Djibo**, Burk
83 N11°56' E43°35' **DJIBOUTI**
83 N11°35' E43°11' **Djibouti**, Djib
88 N0°37' E22°21' **Djolu**, DRC
86 N2°40' E12°40' **Djoum**, Cam
28 N64°43' W14°10' **Djúpivogur**, Ice
36 N52°8' E35°5' **Dmitriyev-L'govskiy**, Rus Fed
26 N50°55' E30°46' *Dnipro*, Ukr
27 N48°27' E34°59' **Dnipropetrovs'k**, Ukr
44 N33°28' E49°4' **Do Rud**, Iran
80 N8°39' E16°51' **Doba**, Chad
60 S1°13' E132°47' Doberai Peninsula, Indo
22 N44°44' E18°6' **Doboj**, Bos & Herz
25 N43°34' E27°50' **Dobrich**, Bulg
36 N50°49' E41°51' **Dobrinka**, Rus Fed
26 N49°34' E22°47' **Dobromil'**, Ukr
117 N36°24' W80°43' **Dobson**, NC, US
138 S22°26' W62°22' **Doctor Pedro P Peña**, Para
23 N46°32' E22°28' **Doctor Petru Groza**, Rom
25 N36°43' E25°56' Dodecanese, Grc
108 N37°45' W100°1' **Dodge City**, KS, US
89 S6°10' E35°44' **Dodoma**, Tanz
38 N38°6' E37°53' **Dogansehir**, Turk
52 N36°11' E133°26' Dogo, Jap
39 N39°32' E44°8' **Dogubayazit**, Turk
43 N25°15' E51°28' **Doha**, Qatar
57 N18°35' E98°28' Doi Inthanon, Thai
82 N13°31' E35°46' **Doka**, Sud
26 N54°54' E27°46' **Dokshitsy**, Bela
104 N48°53' W72°14' **Dolbeau**, QC, Can
15 N47°6' E5°30' **Dole**, Fr
26 N48°7' E32°44' **Dolinskaya**, Ukr
47 N50°40' E79°18' **Dolon'**, Kaz
141 S36°20' W57°40' **Dolores**, Arg
36 N46°37' E37°48' **Dolzhanskaya**, Rus Fed
37 N50°46' E59°32' **Dombarovskiy**, Rus Fed
99 N53°44' W121°1' **Dome Creek**, BC, Can
140 S28°57' W70°54' **Domeyko**, Chile
129 N15°31' W61°13' **DOMINICA**
128 N18°37' W71°28' **DOMINICAN REPUBLIC**
36 N47°36' E41°11' *Don*, Rus Fed
12 N38°57' W5°52' **Don Benito**, Sp
115 N30°6' W90°59' **Donaldsonville**, LA, US
10 N54°39' W8°7' **Donegal**, Ire
10 N54°29' W9°3' *Donegal Bay*
27 N48°19' E38°20' Donets Ridge, Ukr
27 N48°0' E37°46' **Donets'k**, Ukr
57 N16°52' E107°5' **Dong Ha**, Viet
57 N17°29' E106°36' **Đong Hoi**, Viet
57 N22°26' E106°27' **Đông Khê**, Viet
68 S29°15' E114°56' **Dongara**, WA, Austl
88 S14°36' E15°48' **Dongo**, Ang
51 N30°19' E122°9' **Dongshajiao**, China
49 N39°49' E109°59' **Dongsheng**, China
51 N29°9' E112°37' *Dongting Hu*, China
49 N28°47' E106°39' **Dongxi**, China
99 N55°44' W117°6' **Donnelly**, AB, Can
67 S18°42' E140°33' **Donors Hills**, Qld, Austl
67 S17°56' E138°49' **Doomadgee**, Qld, Austl
11 N50°43' W2°26' **Dorchester**, UK
100 N54°38' W107°32' **Doré Lake**, SK, Can
100 N54°56' W107°6' *Doré Lake*, Can
16 N40°17' E9°35' **Dorgali**, It
85 N14°2' W0°2' **Dori**, Burk
11 N57°52' W4°2' **Dornoch**, UK
34 N54°55' E33°18' **Dorogobuzh**, Rus Fed
45 N32°17' E60°30' **Doroh**, Iran
68 S25°10' E112°26' Dorre Island, Austl
88 N4°44' E27°42' **Doruma**, DRC
12 N37°17' W5°55' **Dos Hermanas**, Sp
80 N13°3' E3°12' **Dosso**, Niger
118 N31°13' W85°24' **Dothan**, AL, US
86 N4°4' E9°43' **Douala**, Cam
14 N48°6' W4°20' **Douarnenez**, Fr
113 N31°20' W109°33' **Douglas**, AZ, US
119 N31°29' W82°50' **Douglas**, GA, US
107 N42°46' W105°23' **Douglas**, WY, US
11 N54°9' W4°29' **Douglas**, IOM, UK
138 S22°13' W54°48' **Dourados**, MT, Braz
113 N37°46' W108°55' **Dove Creek**, CO, US
11 N51°8' E1°19' **Dover**, UK
111 N43°12' W70°52' **Dover**, NH, US
117 N39°8' W75°32' **Dover**, DE, US
111 N45°11' W69°14' **Dover-Foxcroft**, ME, US
44 N28°18' E56°40' **Dowlatabad**, Iran
10 N54°20' W5°43' **Downpatrick**, UK
45 N35°37' E68°41' **Dowshi**, Afg
52 N35°57' E133°8' **Dozen**, Jap
23 N44°10' E24°32' **Draganesti-Olt**, Rom
23 N44°40' E24°16' **Dragasani**, Rom
142 S55°0' W70°0' *Drake Passage*, Ant, Disputed
141 S58°35' W65°42' *Drake Passage*
91 S29°26' E28°57' Drakensberg, S Afr
25 N41°9' E24°9' **Dráma**, Grc
29 N59°46' E10°8' **Drammen**, Nor
22 N45°40' E18°18' *Drava*, Cro
99 N53°13' W114°59' **Drayton Valley**, AB, Can
19 N51°5' E13°46' **Dresden**, Ger
14 N48°44' E1°22' **Dreux**, Fr
107 N43°43' W111°7' **Driggs**, ID, US
22 N44°56' E19°46' *Drina*, Yugo
115 N32°25' W92°54' Driskill Mountain, US
23 N44°38' E22°39' **Drobeta-Turnu-Severin**, Rom
21 N52°24' E22°41' **Drohiczyn**, Pol
23 N46°3' E27°48' **Drokiya**, Mol
99 N51°28' W112°42' **Drumheller**, AB, Can
47 N45°15' E82°26' **Druzhba**, Kaz
102 N49°47' W92°50' **Dryden**, ON, Can
86 N6°27' E10°4' **Dschang**, Cam
23 N47°16' E29°8' **Dubasari**, Mol
96 N62°29' W105°25' *Dubawnt Lake*, Can
43 N25°14' E55°16' **Dubayy**, UAE
10 N53°20' W6°15' **Dublin**, Ire
119 N32°32' W82°54' **Dublin**, GA, US
34 N56°44' E37°10' **Dubna**, Rus Fed
107 N44°11' W112°14' **Dubois**, ID, US
84 N9°48' W13°31' **Dubréka**, Gui
26 N51°34' E25°34' **Dubrovitsa**, Ukr
22 N42°39' E18°5' **Dubrovnik**, Cro
47 N43°46' E83°13' **Dubunskaya**, Kaz
109 N42°30' W90°40' **Dubuque**, IA, US
113 N40°10' W110°24' **Duchesne**, UT, US
101 N52°10' W100°11' **Duck Bay**, MB, Can
55 N25°59' E90°44' **Dudhnai**, Ind
85 N6°45' W7°21' **Duékoué**, Côte d'Ivoire
22 N44°1' E14°38' Dugi Otok, Cro
49 N39°55' E106°41' **Dugui Qarag**, China
43 N25°26' E50°47' **Dukhan**, Qatar
88 N4°41' E20°22' **Dula**, DRC
124 N15°8' W85°29' **Dulce Nombre de Culmí**, Hon
25 N43°49' E27°9' **Dulovo**, Bulg
109 N46°47' W92°7' **Duluth**, MN, US
63 N9°19' E123°19' **Dumaguete**, Phil
58 N1°41' E101°27' **Dumai**, Indo
60 S0°31' E120°1' Dumaran Island, Phil
114 N35°52' W101°58' **Dumas**, TX, US
11 N55°4' W3°37' **Dumfries**, UK
81 N31°25' E31°49' **Dumyat**, Egypt
22 N46°58' E18°57' **Dunaújváros**, Hun
10 N54°1' W6°25' **Dundalk**, Ire
98 N54°28' W131°31' Dundas Island, Can
11 N56°28' W3°0' **Dundee**, UK
71 S45°52' E170°30' **Dunedin**, NZ
69 S32°34' E151°46' **Dungog**, NSW, Austl
89 N3°37' E28°34' **Dungu**, DRC
49 N40°12' E94°41' **Dunhuang**, China
14 N51°3' E2°22' **Dunkerque**, Fr
110 N42°29' W79°20' **Dunkirk**, NY, US
127 N25°30' W76°40' **Dunmore Town**, Bah
82 N19°10' E30°29' **Dunqulah**, Sud
108 N45°3' W101°36' **Dupree**, SD, US
139 S22°47' W43°19' **Duque de Caxias**, RJ, Braz
122 N25°57' W105°49' **Durango**, Mex
122 N24°2' W104°40' **Durango**, Dgo, Mex
113 N37°16' W107°53' **Durango**, CO, US
13 N43°10' W2°37' **Durango**, Sp
115 N33°59' W96°22' **Durant**, OK, US
138 S33°25' W56°30' **Durazno**, Ur
91 S29°52' E30°58' **Durban**, S Afr
11 N54°47' W1°34' **Durham**, UK
117 N35°59' W78°54' **Durham**, NC, US
68 S27°58' E140°51' **Durnstein**, Aus
24 N41°20' E19°27' **Durrës**, Alb
38 N39°35' E28°38' **Dursunbey**, Turk
47 N38°35' E68°47' **Dushanbe**, Taj
18 N51°14' E6°47' **Düsseldorf**, Ger
121 N53°55' W166°37' **Dutch Harbor**, AK, US
35 N63°47' E56°35' **Duvovo**, Rus Fed
86 N12°50' E8°7' **Duse**, Nga
86 N10°50' E8°12' **Dutsen Wai**, Nga
36 N55°42' E57°54' **Duvan**, Rus Fed
22 N43°43' E17°14' **Duvno**, Bos & Herz
50 N26°12' E107°31' **Duyun**, China
38 N40°50' E31°10' **Düzce**, Turk
34 N56°59' E38°43' *Dvina Bay*
20 N50°26' E15°48' **Dvur Králové nad Labem**, Czech
54 N22°15' E68°59' **Dwarka**, Ind
61 S3°9' E150°35' Dyaul Island, PNG
116 N36°2' W89°23' **Dyersburg**, TN, US
47 N46°56' E70°54' **Dzambul**, Kaz
48 N47°39' E93°41' *Dzavhan Gol*, Mong
47 N45°50' E81°7' **Dzerzhinskoye**, Kaz
47 N40°56' E72°59' **Dzhalal-Abad**, Kyr
47 N42°54' E71°22' **Dzhambul**, Kaz
46 N49°14' E50°19' **Dzhangala**, Kaz
47 N47°47' E67°42' **Dzhezkazgan**, Kaz
47 N40°6' E67°50' **Dzhizak**, Uzb
33 N56°32' E137°4' Dzhugdzhur Range, Rus Fed
49 N48°52' E106°28' **Dzüünharaa**, Mong
49 N47°43' E106°58' **Dzuunmod**, Mong
26 N54°12' E27°31' Dzyarzhynskaya, Bela

E

113 N38°29' W102°47' **Eads**, CO, US
113 N39°40' W106°50' **Eagle**, CO, US
102 N49°31' W93°45' *Eagle Lake*, Can
109 N47°54' W90°34' Eagle Mountain, US
114 N28°41' W100°30' **Eagle Pass**, TX, US
109 N47°25' W88°18' **Eagle River**, MI, US
109 N45°55' W89°14' **Eagle River**, WI, US
143 S75°0' E100°0' East Antarctica, Ant, Disputed
127 N21°43' W71°27' **East End**, TC Is, UK
51 N29°51' E123°41' *East China Sea*
126 N19°19' W81°7' **East End**, Cay Is, UK
141 S51°17' W58°41' East Falkland, Falk Is, UK
111 N41°35' W70°35' **East Falmouth**, MA, US
18 N53°47' E6°53' East Frisian Islands, Ger
109 N42°44' W84°25' **East Lansing**, MI, US
91 S33°0' E27°55' **East London**, S Afr
33 N74°26' E161°57' *East Siberian Sea*
109 N38°37' W90°9' **East St Louis**, IL, US
60 S9°16' E126°7' **East Timor**, Indo
140 S26°59' W109°29' Easter Island, Chile
81 N27°4' E33°34' Eastern Desert, Egypt
55 N18°0' E82°24' Eastern Ghats, Ind
104 N52°15' W78°30' **Eastmain**, QC, Can
119 N32°12' W83°11' **Eastman**, GA, US
117 N40°50' W75°6' **Easton**, PA, US
111 N44°55' W67°1' **Eastport**, ME, US
117 N37°21' W75°57' **Eastville**, VA, US
109 N44°49' W91°30' **Eau Claire**, WI, US
84 N10°9' E11°20' **Ebebiyin**, Eq Gui
86 N2°55' E11°9' **Ebolowa**, Cam
19 N54°28' E9°50' **Eckernförde**, Ger
134 S1°17' W78°27' **ECUADOR**
68 S28°17' E117°10' **Edah**, WA, Austl
69 S37°4' E149°54' **Eden**, NSW, Austl
24 N40°48' E22°3' **Édessa**, Grc
111 N41°23' W70°31' **Edgartown**, MA, US
11 N55°57' W3°13' **Edinburgh**, UK
38 N41°40' E26°34' **Edirne**, Turk
68 S29°48' E122°23' **Edjudina**, WA, Austl
99 N53°33' W113°31' **Edmonton**, AB, Can
104 N47°22' W68°23' **Edmundston**, NB, Can
115 N28°59' W96°39' **Edna**, TX, US
38 N39°35' E27°1' **Edremit**, Turk
99 N53°35' W116°26' **Edson**, AB, Can
140 S35°54' W64°18' **Eduardo Castex**, Arg
69 S28°21' E135°51' **Edwards Creek**, SA, Austl
72 S17°14' E167°11' Éfaté, Van
109 N39°7' W88°33' **Effingham**, IL, US
97 N68°43' W52°50' **Egedesminde**, Grld, Den
22 N47°54' E20°23' **Eger**, Hun
39 N38°15' E40°5' **Egil**, Turk
96 N74°52' W121°53' Eglinton Island, Can
81 N26°2' E27°26' **EGYPT**
13 N43°11' W2°28' **Éibar**, Sp
19 N48°54' E11°12' **Eichstätt**, Ger
69 S25°22' E151°7' **Eidsvold**, Qld, Austl
56 N7°30' E72°39' *Eight Degree Channel*
75 N7°10' E133°58' Eil Malk, US
29 N60°38' E10°36' **Eina**, Nor
18 N51°26' E5°28' **Eindhoven**, Neth
136 S6°40' W69°52' **Eirunepé**, AM, Braz
19 N50°59' E10°19' **Eisenach**, Ger
20 N47°16' E15°34' Eisenerzer Alpen, Aus
19 N52°10' E14°39' **Eisenhüttenstadt**, Ger
21 N47°51' E16°32' **Eisenstadt**, Aus
48 N41°50' E100°50' **Ejin Qi**, China
85 N7°23' W1°22' **Ejura**, Gha
107 N45°53' W104°33' **Ekalaka**, MT, US
47 N51°42' E75°22' **Ekibastuz**, Kaz
88 S0°23' E24°16' **Ekoli**, DRC
79 N37°10' E10°3' **El Alia**, Tun
134 N0°37' W77°56' **El Ángel**, Ecu
12 N43°24' W3°49' **El Astillero**, Sp
13 N39°0' W73°58' **El Banco**, Col
125 N12°1' W83°41' **El Bluff**, Nic
140 S26°1' W62°22' **El Caburé**, Arg
115 N29°12' W96°17' **El Campo**, TX, US
122 N29°58' W105°16' **El Carrizo**, Chih, Mex
112 N32°48' W115°34' **El Centro**, CA, US
135 S17°31' W61°34' **El Cerro**, Bol
108 N37°49' W96°52' **El Dorado**, KS, US
115 N33°13' W92°40' **El Dorado**, AR, US
133 N6°44' W61°38' **El Dorado**, Ven
132 S1°37' W73°14' **El Encanto**, Col
81 N29°19' E30°50' **El Faiyum**, Egypt
82 N13°38' E25°21' **El Fasher**, Sud
12 N43°29' W8°14' **El Ferrol**, Sp
79 N30°30' E2°50' **El Golea**, Alg
124 N15°37' W88°58' *El Golfete*, Guat
122 N27°52' W103°18' **El Guaje**, Coah, Mex
123 N21°46' W98°28' **El Higo**, Ver, Mex
141 S37°37' W70°36' **El Huecú**, Arg
78 N33°14' W8°30' **El Jadida**, Mor
79 N33°55' E5°58' **El Meghaïer**, Alg
81 N28°5' E30°46' **El Minya**, Egypt
135 S20°56' W68°32' El Muerto, Chile
63 N11°10' E119°24' **El Nido**, Phil
114 N31°47' W106°29' **El Paso**, TX, US
140 S24°38' W61°27' **El Pintado**, Arg
122 N31°15' W105°51' **El Porvenir**, Chih, Mex
125 N9°34' W78°59' **El Porvenir**, Pan
124 N15°23' W87°49' **El Progreso**, Hon
125 N8°8' W77°43' **El Real de Santa María**, Pan
124 N13°29' W89°15' **EL SALVADOR**
124 N12°53' W86°32' **El Sauce**, Nic
122 N29°2' W106°16' **El Sauz**, Chih, Mex
128 N18°46' W69°2' **El Seibo**, Dom Rep
132 N8°59' W65°44' **El Socorro**, Ven
122 N29°54' W106°24' **El Sueco**, Chih, Mex
133 N8°55' W64°15' **El Tigre**, Ven
135 S18°17' W64°8' **El Trigal**, Bol
122 N23°47' W110°8' **El Triunfo**, BCS, Mex
122 N20°19' W105°22' **El Tuito**, Jal, Mex
81 N28°14' E33°37' **El Tur**, Egypt
141 S51°41' W72°5' **El Turbio**, Arg
83 N2°49' E40°56' **El Wak**, Ken
57 N19°37' E96°13' **Ela**, Myanmar
24 N39°54' E22°11' **Elassón**, Grc
40 N29°33' E34°57' **Elat**, Isr
39 N38°41' E39°14' **Elazig**, Turk
118 N31°25' W86°4' **Elba**, AL, US
19 N53°46' E8°56' *Elbe River*, Ger
119 N34°7' W82°52' **Elberton**, GA, US
38 N38°13' E37°12' **Elbistan**, Turk
21 N54°10' E19°25' **Elblag**, Pol
44 N36°22' E50°21' Elburz Mountains, Iran
13 N38°15' W0°42' **Elche**, Sp
67 S11°53' E135°18' Elcho Island, Austl
114 N30°52' W100°36' **Eldorado**, TX, US
122 N24°17' W107°21' **Eldorado**, Sin, Mex
140 S26°24' W54°38' **Eldorado**, Arg
106 N48°32' W121°8' Eldorado Peak, US
127 N24°59' W76°4' Eleuthera Island, Bah
109 N42°2' W88°17' **Elgin**, IL, US
128 N18°53' W71°43' **Elias Pina**, Dom Rep
60 S8°20' E130°49' **Eliase**, Indo
88 S11°40' E27°28' **Elisabethville**, DRC
36 N46°19' E44°13' **Elista**, Rus Fed
117 N36°18' W76°13' **Elizabeth City**, NC, US
110 N44°13' W73°35' **Elizabethtown**, NY, US
116 N37°41' W85°52' **Elizabethtown**, KY, US
117 N34°38' W78°37' **Elizabethtown**, NC, US
21 N53°50' E22°22' **Elk**, Pol
114 N35°25' W99°25' **Elk City**, OK, US
99 N53°52' W110°55' **Elk Point**, AB, Can
108 N37°1' W101°53' **Elkhart**, KS, US
25 N42°10' E26°34' **Elkhovo**, Bulg
112 N40°52' W115°44' **Elko**, NV, US
96 N77°52' W108°22' Ellef Ringnes Island, Can
97 N80°20' W79°2' Ellesmere Island, Can
103 N46°23' W82°39' **Elliot Lake**, ON, Can
67 S17°33' E133°32' **Elliott**, NT, Austl
91 S23°40' E27°46' **Ellisras**, S Afr
111 N44°32' W68°25' **Ellsworth**, ME, US
142 S70°0' W100°0' Ellsworth Land, Ant, Disputed
110 N42°5' W76°49' **Elmira**, NY, US
19 N53°45' E9°39' **Elmshorn**, Ger
132 N7°3' W69°31' **Elorza**, Ven
12 N38°53' W7°10' **Elvas**, Port
112 N39°15' W114°53' **Ely**, NV, US
116 N41°23' W82°5' **Elyria**, OH, US
75 S17°3' E168°15' Émaé, Van
46 N48°50' E58°8' **Emba**, Kaz
133 N7°47' W62°44' *Embalsede Guri*, Ven
18 N53°22' E7°12' **Emden**, Ger
34 N64°22' E41°7' **Emeljanovskaja**, Rus Fed
67 S23°32' E148°10' **Emerald**, Qld, Austl
48 N46°32' E83°39' **Emin**, China
38 N39°1' E31°10' **Emirdag**, Turk
67 S24°40' E144°28' **Emmet**, Qld, Austl
114 N29°23' W103°33' Emory Peak 2,385, US
140 S27°57' W58°48' **Empedrado**, Arg
112 N40°32' W119°20' **Empire**, NV, US
108 N38°25' W96°11' **Emporia**, KS, US
117 N36°41' W77°32' **Emporia**, VA, US
117 N41°31' W78°14' **Emporium**, PA, US
67 S23°16' E150°47' **Emu Park**, Qld, Austl
40 N31°28' E35°23' **En-Gedi**, W Bank, Disputed
60 S3°55' E136°23' **Enarotali**, Indo
138 S27°20' W55°52' **Encarnación**, Para
85 N5°49' W2°49' **Enchi**, Gha
98 N54°5' W125°2' **Endako**, BC, Can
59 S8°50' E121°39' **Ende**, Indo
101 N52°8' W102°40' **Endeavour**, SK, Can
73 S3°9' W171°7' Enderbury Island, Kir
143 S65°0' E50°0' Enderby Land, Ant, Disputed
72 N11°35' E159°24' Enewetak Atoll, Mar Is
53 N44°3' E143°31' **Engaru**, Jap
11 N52°25' W0°55' **ENGLAND**
103 N47°49' W79°52' **Englehart**, ON, Can
113 N39°39' W104°59' **Englewood**, CO, US
11 N49°47' W4°14' *English Channel*
115 N36°23' W97°53' **Enid**, OK, US
50 N24°0' E101°7' **Enle**, China
81 N17°38' E21°53' Ennedi, Chad
69 S29°19' E145°51' **Engonia**, NSW, Austl
115 N32°20' W96°38' **Ennis**, TX, US
10 N52°50' W8°59' **Ennis**, Ire
10 N54°21' W7°38' **Enniskillen**, UK
20 N47°52' E14°20' *Enns*, Aus
128 N17°54' W71°14' **Enriquillo**, Dom Rep
18 N52°13' E6°53' **Enschede**, Neth
122 N31°52' W116°37' **Ensenada**, BC, Mex
49 N30°17' E109°19' **Enshi**, China
82 N0°5' E32°31' **Entebbe**, Ug
91 S14°57' E37°20' **Entre-Rios**, Moz
99 N53°36' W115°1' **Entwistle**, AB, Can
86 N6°27' E7°29' **Enugu**, Nga
136 S7°18' W70°13' **Envira**, AM, Braz
15 N49°1' E3°56' **Épernay**, Fr
15 N48°11' E6°27' **Épinal**, Fr
90 S21°41' E19°8' **Epukiro**, Nam
86 N1°25' E9°41' **EQUATORIAL GUINEA**
39 N39°2' E43°21' **Ercis**, Turk
38 N37°31' E34°4' **Eregli**, Turk
38 N41°17' E31°25' **Eregli**, Turk
49 N43°46' E112°5' **Erenhot**, China
79 N31°28' W4°10' **Erfoud**, Mor
19 N50°59' E11°2' **Erfurt**, Ger
79 N23°21' W3°19' Erg Chech
79 N29°48' W2°45' Erg er Raoui, Alg
78 N25°31' W6°58' Erg Iguidi
39 N38°17' E39°46' **Ergani**, Turk
117 N42°8' W80°5' **Erie**, PA, US
110 N43°11' W78°13' *Erie Canal*, US
83 N10°37' E47°22' **Erigavo**, Som
82 N15°17' E36°48' **ERITREA**
19 N49°36' E11°1' **Erlangen**, Ger
75 S17°30' E168°31' Ermao Island, Van
12 N38°0' W8°23' **Ermidas**, Port
25 N37°26' E24°56' **Ermoúpolis**, Grc
69 S26°40' E143°16' **Eromanga**, Qld, Austl
75 S18°42' E169°12' Erromango Island, Van
24 N40°20' E20°41' **Ersekë**, Alb
48 N46°7' E90°6' **Ertai**, China
69 S31°28' E139°23' **Erudina**, SA, Austl
39 N39°46' E39°31' **Erzincan**, Turk
39 N39°55' E41°17' **Erzurum**, Turk
53 N44°56' E142°35' **Esashi**, Jap
122 N26°45' W104°20' **Escalón**, Chih, Mex
109 N45°44' W87°6' **Escanaba**, MI, US
112 N33°7' W117°5' **Escondido**, CA, US
123 N15°20' W92°38' **Escuintla**, Chis, Mex
124 N14°18' W90°47' **Escuintla**, Guat
86 N3°39' E10°46' **Eséka**, Cam
44 N32°39' E51°42' **Esfahan**, Iran
45 N36°42' E71°34' **Eshkashem**, Afg
43 N43°22' E77°28' **Esik**, Kaz
96 N61°7' W94°3' **Eskimo Point**, NU, Can
38 N40°58' E32°33' **Eskipazar**, Turk
38 N39°46' E30°32' **Eskisehir**, Turk
132 N3°11' W65°34' **Esmeralda**, Ven
127 N21°51' W78°7' **Esmeralda**, Cuba
134 N0°58' W79°40' **Esmeraldas**, Ecu
103 N46°15' W81°46' **Espanola**, ON, Can
113 N35°59' W106°5' **Espanola**, NM, US
136 S4°24' W69°52' **Esperança**, AM, Braz
137 S7°1' W35°51' **Esperança**, PB, Braz
122 N27°35' W109°56' **Esperanza**, Son, Mex
137 S11°34' W45°53' Espigão Mestre, Braz
140 S24°58' W58°34' **Espinillo**, Arg
139 S18°31' W41°10' **Espírito Santo**, Braz
72 S14°26' E164°7' Espiritu Santo, Van
91 S20°29' E32°48' **Espungabera**, Moz
78 N31°30' W9°46' **Essaouira**, Mor
18 N51°27' E7°1' **Essen**, Ger
133 N4°47' W58°59' *Essequibo*, Guy
19 N48°45' E9°16' **Esslingen**, Ger
113 N34°46' W106°4' **Estancia**, NM, US
124 N13°5' W86°22' **Estelí**, Nic
13 N42°40' W2°2' **Estella**, Sp
12 N36°26' W5°8' **Estepona**, Sp
92 N52°58' W130°13' Estevan Group, Can
100 N51°10' W108°46' **Eston**, SK, Can
26 N58°41' E24°20' **ESTONIA**
137 S6°34' W47°26' **Estreito**, MA, Braz
12 N38°51' W7°35' **Estremoz**, Port
22 N47°48' E18°45' **Esztergom**, Hun
14 N48°26' E2°9' **Étampes**, Fr
54 N26°46' E79°2' **Etawah**, Ind
122 N26°55' W109°38' **Etchojoa**, Son, Mex
83 N8°49' E38°58' **ETHIOPIA**
90 S18°56' E16°45' *Etosha Pan*, Nam
87 S0°1' E14°57' **Etoumbi**, Con
75 S21°23' W174°54' 'Eua Island, Ton
115 N35°17' W95°35' **Eufaula**, OK, US
115 N35°6' W95°33' *Eufaula Lake*, US
106 N44°3' W123°5' **Eugene**, OR, US
29 N63°53' E21°48' Eugmo, Fin
113 N32°26' W103°8' **Eunice**, NM, US
41 N35°44' E39°51' *Euphrates*, Syria
44 N31°7' E45°2' *Euphrates River*, Iraq
109 N40°43' W89°16' **Eureka**, IL, US
112 N40°47' W124°9' **Eureka**, CA, US
112 N39°31' W115°58' **Eureka**, NV, US
92 S22°24' E40°28' **Europa Island**, Fr
111 N45°13' W70°29' **Eustis**, ME, US
118 N32°50' W87°53' **Eutaw**, AL, US
19 N54°8' E10°37' **Eutin**, Ger
107 N41°16' W110°58' **Evanston**, WY, US
116 N37°58' W87°34' **Evansville**, IN, US
91 S26°31' E27°54' **Evaton**, S Afr
106 N47°59' W122°12' **Everett**, WA, US
119 N26°2' W81°7' *Everglades, The*, US
118 N31°26' W86°58' **Evergreen**, AL, US
29 N58°36' E7°51' **Evje**, Nor
12 N38°34' W7°55' **Évora**, Port
14 N49°1' E1°9' **Évreux**, Fr
14 N48°40' E2°23' **Evry**, Fr
117 N38°2' W76°2' **Ewell**, MD, US
87 S0°53' E14°49' **Ewo**, Con
135 S13°16' W65°15' **Exaltación**, Bol
11 N50°43' W3°32' **Exeter**, UK
111 N42°59' W70°57' **Exeter**, NH, US
66 S21°55' E114°6' **Exmouth**, WA, Austl
127 N24°32' W76°23' *Exuma Sound*
83 N8°0' E49°52' **Eyl**, Som
69 S33°28' E135°38' Eyre Peninsula, Austl
141 S39°29' W68°41' *Ezequiel Ramos Mexia Reservoir*, Arg

F

84 N9°44' W9°5' **Fabala**, Gui
114 N31°32' W106°7' **Fabens**, TX, US
80 N18°6' E11°34' **Fachi**, Niger
141 S45°18' W69°58' **Facundo**, Arg
81 N17°14' E21°33' **Fada**, Chad
85 N12°4' E0°21' **Fada-N'Gourma**, Burk
86 N11°23' E9°57' **Faggo**, Nga
15 N48°57' E4°17' **Fagnières**, Fr
28 N63°54' W16°37' **Fagurholsmyri**, Ice

continue on next page

G

128 N18°44' W73°45' Grande Cayemite, Haiti
92 S11°38' E43°25' Grande Comore, Com
99 N55°10' W118°48' Grande Prairie, AB, Can
129 N16°24' W61°23' Grande-Terre, Guad, Fr
12 N38°10' W8°34' Grândola, Port
106 N45°56' W116°7' Grangeville, ID, US
68 S25°38' E121°21' Granite Peak, WA, Austl
107 N45°10' W109°49' Granite Peak, US
108 N40°50' W101°44' Grant, NE, US
113 N35°9' W107°50' Grants, NM, US
106 N42°26' W123°20' Grants Pass, OR, US
14 N48°51' W1°35' Granville, Fr
15 N43°41' E6°53' Grasse, Fr
69 S40°2' E144°3' Grassy, Tas, Austl
100 N49°53' W106°34' Gravelbourg, SK, Can
17 N40°49' E16°25' Gravina in Puglia, It
109 N44°40' W84°43' Grayling, MI, US
20 N47°5' E15°27' Graz, Aus
67 S23°23' E139°29' Great Artesian Basin, Austl
69 S24°4' E140°4' Great Artesin Basin, Austl
68 S35°1' E127°17' Great Australian Bight
71 S36°11' E175°32' Great Barrier Island, NZ
96 N65°10' W122°34' Great Bear Lake, Can
108 N38°22' W98°46' Great Bend, KS, US
71 S18°46' E144°41' Great Dividing Range, Austl
79 N29°26' E5°6' Great Eastern Erg, Alg
127 N23°34' W76°31' Great Exuma, Bah
107 N47°30' W111°18' Great Falls, MT, US
127 N24°11' W77°1' Great Guana Cay, Bah
127 N25°44' W78°25' Great Harbor Cay, Bah
127 N20°50' W73°29' Great Inagua Island, Bah
90 S33°14' E21°1' Great Karoo, S Afr
90 S27°14' E17°13' Great Namaland, Nam
112 N41°16' W112°59' Great Salt Lake, US
112 N40°34' W113°41' Great Salt Lake Desert, US
81 N29°16' E23°20' Great Sand Sea, Libya
66 S20°51' E123°44' Great Sandy Desert, Austl
120 N52°25' W176°38' Great Sitkin Island, US
96 N61°4' W115°46' Great Slave Lake, Can
67 S28°26' E125°4' Great Victoria Desert, Austl
79 N29°39' W0°9' Great Western Erg, Alg
126 N20°22' W80°17' Greater Antilles
49 N46°33' E120°32' Greater Khingan Range, China
24 N39°9' E21°8' GREECE
113 N40°26' W104°43' Greeley, CO, US
109 N44°31' W88°1' Green Bay, WI, US
109 N44°39' W87°52' Green Bay
61 S4°34' E154°16' Green Islands, PNG
100 N54°17' W107°47' Green Lake, SK, Can
110 N43°28' W72°53' Green Mountains, US
107 N41°32' W109°28' Green River, WY, US
61 S3°55' E141°10' Green River, PNG
113 N39°36' W109°53' Green River, US
111 N42°36' W72°36' Greenfield, MA, US
104 N49°29' W73°29' Greenfield Park, QC, Can
97 N73°52' W46°25' Greenland, Den
97 N70°31' W43°22' Greenland Ice Cap, Grld, Den
97 N78°11' W13°20' Greenland Sea
117 N36°5' W79°47' Greensboro, NC, US
118 N31°50' W86°37' Greenville, AL, US
84 N5°1' W9°2' Greenville, Libr
111 N45°28' W69°35' Greenville, ME, US
116 N40°7' W84°38' Greenville, OH, US
115 N33°8' W96°7' Greenville, TX, US
119 N34°51' W82°23' Greenville, SC, US
117 N35°37' W77°23' Greenville, NC, US
118 N33°31' W90°12' Greenwood, MS, US
119 N34°12' W82°10' Greenwood, SC, US
19 N54°5' E13°23' Greifswald, Ger
129 N12°10' W61°32' GRENADA
118 N33°46' W89°49' Grenada, MS, US
15 N45°11' E5°43' Grenoble, Fr
115 N29°56' W90°3' Gretna, LA, US
24 N40°5' E22°3' Grevená, Grc
69 S28°11' E143°6' Grey Range, Austl
71 S42°28' E171°13' Greymouth, NZ
36 N51°27' E41°58' Gribanovskiy, Rus Fed
119 N33°15' W84°16' Griffin, GA, US
87 N5°44' E20°3' Grimari, CAR
19 N54°7' E13°2' Grimmen, Ger
11 N53°34' W0°7' Grimsby, UK
99 N56°11' W117°36' Grimshaw, AB, Can
28 N65°40' W16°1' Grimsstadir, Ice
105 N50°53' W55°34' Groais Island, Can
115 N31°31' W96°32' Groesbeck, TX, US
13 N53°13' E6°35' Groningen, Neth
67 S13°56' E136°59' Groote Eylandt, Austl
90 S19°32' E18°5' Grootfontein, Nam
129 N14°5' W60°57' Gros Islet, St L
16 N42°46' E11°7' Grosseto, It
20 N47°5' E12°41' Grossglockner, Aus
92 S9°29' E46°35' Groupe d'Aldabra, Sey
118 N31°43' W87°47' Grove Hill, AL, US
32 N43°20' E45°42' Groznyy, Rus Fed
25 N42°21' E27°10' Grudovo, Bulg
21 N53°29' E18°45' Grudziadz, Pol
29 N59°21' E13°6' Grums, Swe
90 S27°47' E18°23' Grünau, Nam
116 N37°17' W82°6' Grundy, VA, US
13 N40°38' W3°10' Guadalajara, Sp
122 N20°42' W103°22' Guadalajara, Jal, Mex
72 S10°2' E157°20' Guadalcanal, Sol Is
74 S9°55' E159°51' Guadalcanal Island, Sol Is
12 N39°27' W5°21' Guadalupe, Sp
114 N31°53' W104°52' Guadalupe Peak, US
129 N16°37' W61°36' Guadeloupe, Fr
127 N21°3' W77°21' Guáimaro, Cuba
138 S24°4' W54°12' Guaíra, PR, Braz
136 S10°48' W65°22' Guajará-Mirim, RO, Braz
140 S33°9' W59°20' Gualeguay, Arg
141 S42°43' W70°30' Gualjaina, Arg
72 N13°25' E143°14' Guam, US
49 N31°0' E103°40' Guan Xian, China
123 N21°15' W101°11' Guanajuato, Mex
123 N21°1' W101°16' Guanajuato, Gto, Mex
132 N9°2' W69°45' Guanare, Ven
135 S15°28' W67°52' Guanay, Bol
126 N22°12' W84°7' Guane, Cuba
51 N26°50' E116°14' Guangchang, China
50 N24°10' E105°6' Guangnan, China
51 N23°6' E113°17' Guangzhou, China
127 N20°8' W75°13' Guantánamo, Cuba
132 N2°36' W77°54' Guapí, Col
136 S11°17' W65°15' Guaporé, Braz
134 S1°37' W79°0' Guaranda, Ecu
138 S25°6' W52°52' Guaraniaçu, PR, Braz
138 S25°23' W51°27' Guarapuava, PR, Braz
12 N40°32' W7°16' Guarda, Port
139 S23°28' W46°32' Guarulhos, SP, Braz
124 N15°38' W90°51' GUATEMALA
124 N14°40' W90°32' Guatemala City, Guat
61 S10°37' E150°28' Guaugurina, PNG
132 N2°35' W72°38' Guaviare, Col
127 N20°42' W77°36' Guayabal, Cuba
129 N17°59' W65°59' Guayama, PR, US
134 S2°11' W79°55' Guayaquil, Ecu
132 N3°38' W69°46' Guayiare River, Col
134 N0°38' W79°31' Guayllabamba, Ecu
122 N27°56' W110°54' Guaymas, Son, Mex
82 N10°16' E35°17' Guba, Eth
N58°52' E57°36' Gubakha, Rus Fed
55' E124°7' Gubat, Phil
43' Guben, Ger
Gubio, Nga
ut'a, Geo
es, Rus Fed
107 N42°16' W104°38' Guernsey, WY, US
123 N17°46' W101°11' Guerrero, Mex
79 N29°45' W1°47' Guerzim, Alg
50 N23°6' E109°39' Guicheng, China
86 S1°37' E10°41' Guidouma, Gabon
85 N6°33' W7°29' Guiglo, Côte d'Ivoire
12 N40°33' W5°40' Guijuelo, Sp
111 N44°34' W71°34' Guildhall, VT, US
50 N25°17' E110°17' Guilin, China
12 N41°27' W8°18' Guimarães, Port
63 N10°20' E122°17' Guimaras Island, Phil
84 N10°17' W11°19' GUINEA
84 N11°35' W17°58' GUINEA-BISSAU
126 N22°48' W82°30' Güira de Melena, Cuba
137 S16°21' W53°45' Guiratinga, MT, Braz
87 N5°56' E23°19' Guita Koulouba, CAR
12 N43°11' W7°54' Guitiriz, Sp
63 N11°4' E125°44' Guiuan, Phil
51 N25°44' E112°43' Guiyang, China
50 N26°34' E106°41' Guiyang, China
45 N32°10' E74°10' Gujranwala, Pak
49 N37°36' E102°58' Gulang, China
54 N17°20' E76°50' Gulbarga, Ind
42 N12°19' E45°50' Gulf of Aden
121 N59°0' W142°45' Gulf of Alaska
38 N36°28' E30°41' Gulf of Antalya
40 N28°44' E34°44' Gulf of Aqaba
96 N71°38' W92°44' Gulf of Boothia
29 N62°4' E19°30' Gulf of Bothnia
112 N32°0' W114°0' Gulf of California
67 S13°50' E138°47' Gulf of Carpentaria
24 N38°17' E22°14' Gulf of Corinth
38 N39°22' E25°55' Gulf of Edremit
26 N59°47' E25°41' Gulf of Finland
79 N34°25' E10°39' Gulf of Gabes
21 N54°41' E18°56' Gulf of Gdansk
85 N4°19' W3°33' Gulf of Guinea
124 N16°0' W88°43' Gulf of Honduras
38 N36°5' E35°17' Gulf of Iskenderun
54 N20°59' E72°2' Gulf of Khambhat
38 N37°54' E26°4' Gulf of Kusadasi
54 N22°33' E69°2' Gulf of Kutch
111 N43°2' W69°59' Gulf of Maine
56 N8°37' E78°49' Gulf of Mannar
57 N16°20' E96°36' Gulf of Martaban
115 N27°43' W95°38' Gulf of Mexico
32 N66°29' E72°31' Gulf of Ob'
35 N69°34' E72°47' Gulf of Obskaya
43 N23°52' E59°37' Gulf of Oman
61 S8°41' E144°32' Gulf of Papua
129 N10°28' W61°45' Gulf of Paria
26 N57°56' E23°8' Gulf of Riga
80 N32°2' E16°51' Gulf of Sidra
115 N48°27' W63°29' Gulf of St Lawrence
81 N29°29' E32°32' Gulf of Suez
57 N11°46' E100°39' Gulf of Thailand
50 N19°55' E107°17' Gulf of Tonkin
69 S35°12' E137°50' Gulf St Vincent
126 N22°16' W82°41' Gulfo de Batabanó
122 N28°4' W112°1' Gulfo de California
127 N20°31' W77°46' Gulfo de Guacanayabo
123 N15°45' W95°10' Gulfo de Tehuantepec
118 N30°22' W89°5' Gulfport, MS, US
69 S32°22' E149°32' Gulgong, NSW, Austl
47 N40°30' E68°46' Gulistan, Uzb
38 N36°20' E33°25' Gülnar, Turk
82 N2°47' E32°17' Gulu, Ug
55 N23°3' E84°33' Gumla, Ind
39 N40°27' E39°29' Gümüshane, Turk
54 N24°39' E77°19' Guna, Ind
44 N36°44' E44°52' Gundah Zhur, Iraq
88 S5°44' E19°19' Gungu, DRC
36 N42°25' E46°57' Gunib, Rus Fed
86 N12°9' E5°9' Gunmi, Nga
100 N59°23' W108°53' Gunnar, SK, Can
113 N38°33' W106°56' Gunnison, CO, US
59 N6°6' E116°33' Gunong Kinabalu, Malay
47 N37°47' E72°3' Gunt, Taj
54 N16°18' E80°27' Guntur, Ind
59 S7°57' E112°17' Gunung Kelud, Indo
58 N1°17' E97°37' Gunungsitoli, Indo
55 N19°5' E83°49' Gunupur, Ind
19 N48°27' E10°16' Günzburg, Ger
23 N46°16' E22°21' Gurahont, Rom
38 N38°43' E37°17' Gürün, Turk
137 S11°43' W49°4' Gurupi, GO, Braz
49 N44°16' E104°51' Gurvan Sayhan Uul, Mong
46 N47°7' E51°56' Guryev, Kaz
86 N12°12' E6°40' Gusau, Nga
50 N28°18' E105°14' Gusong, China
16 N39°32' E8°37' Guspini, It
21 N47°4' E16°20' Güssing, Aus
19 N53°48' E12°10' Güstrow, Ger
29 N58°16' E16°29' Gusum, Swe
11 N60°40' W1°1' Gutcher, UK
115 N35°53' W97°25' Guthrie, OK, US
133 N6°11' W60°32' GUYANA
114 N36°41' W101°29' Guymon, OK, US
49 N35°58' E106°45' Guyuan, China
46 N36°38' E66°15' Guzar, Uzb
86 N13°20' E5°15' Gwada-Bawa, Nga
86 N10°16' E7°14' Gwagwada, Nga
54 N26°13' E78°10' Gwalior, Ind
91 S20°57' E29°1' Gwanda, Zimb
88 N4°43' E25°50' Gwane, DRC
91 S19°29' E29°49' Gweru, Zimb
50 N29°0' E101°50' Gyaisi, China
48 N29°13' E89°8' Gyangze, China
35 N69°37' E78°1' Gyda Peninsula, Rus Fed
69 S26°11' E152°40' Gympie, Qld, Austl
22 N47°41' E17°38' Gyor, Hun
101 N51°45' W98°38' Gypsumville, MB, Can
22 N46°39' E21°17' Gyula, Hun
39 N40°50' E43°51' Gyumri, Arm
46 N38°58' E56°17' Gyzylarbat, Turkm
46 N37°36' E54°46' Gyzyletrek, Turkm

H

57 N22°50' E104°59' Hà Giang, Viet
57 N18°20' E105°54' Hà Tinh, Viet
73 S19°28' W176°32' Ha'apai Group, Ton
42 N27°32' E41°42' Ha'il, Sau Ar
75 S19°39' W174°16' Haano Island, Ton
26 N58°56' E23°33' Haapsalu, Est
18 N52°23' E4°38' Haarlem, Neth
70 S43°53' E169°3' Haast, NZ
66 S23°30' E131°50' Haast Bluff, NT, Austl
48 N47°53' E88°12' Habahe, China
53 N44°21' E141°44' Haboro, Jap
55 N27°46' E94°1' Hachi, Ind
53 N33°2' E139°53' Hachijo-jima, Jap
53 N40°30' E141°29' Hachinohe, Jap
86 N12°30' E9°59' Hadejia, Nga
40 N32°26' E34°55' Hadera, Isr
42 N25°34' E38°41' Hadiyah, Sau Ar
52 N38°2' E125°42' Haeju, N Kor
38 N39°52' E37°24' Hafik, Turk
42 N26°26' E39°10' Hafirat al 'Ayda, Sau Ar
121 N58°20' W161°21' Hagemeister Island, US
98 N52°23' W126°33' Hagensborg, BC, Can
117 N39°36' W77°39' Hagerstown, MD, US
14 N43°40' W0°35' Hagetmau, Fr
53 N35°52' E137°12' Hagiwara, Jap
115 N29°59' W90°25' Hahnville, LA, US
57 N20°55' E106°38' Hai Phòng, Viet
40 N32°49' E35°0' Haifa, Isr
51 N22°59' E115°21' Haifeng, China
68 S30°59' E126°5' Haig, WA, Austl
50 N20°1' E110°20' Haikou, China
49 N49°12' E119°42' Hailar, China
29 N65°16' E23°56' Hailuoto, Fin
51 N28°41' E121°27' Haimen, China
53 N24°17' E123°51' Haimi, Jap
50 N18°49' E107°43' Hainan Dao, China
121 N59°14' W135°27' Haines, AK, US
96 N63°46' W137°30' Haines Junction, YT, Can
57 N20°55' E106°38' Haiphong, Viet
128 N18°53' W72°35' HAITI
49 N36°46' E121°10' Haiyang, China
49 N36°35' E105°40' Haiyuan, China
21 N52°45' E23°35' Hajnówka, Pol
52 N34°11' E125°32' Hajo-do, S Kor
57 N22°39' E93°37' Haka, Myanmar
52 N33°35' E130°22' Hakata, Jap
39 N37°34' E43°45' Hakkari, Turk
45 N25°49' E68°25' Hala, Pak
82 N22°13' E36°38' Hala'ib, Sud
40 N36°13' E37°10' Halab, Syria
44 N35°10' E45°59' Halabjah, Iraq
19 N51°54' E11°2' Halberstadt, Ger
70 S46°54' E168°8' Halfmoon Bay, NZ
105 N44°40' W63°40' Halifax, NS, Can
117 N36°46' W78°56' Halifax, VA, US
49 N41°42' E108°49' Haliut, China
97 N64°2' W68°5' Hall Peninsula, Can
52 N35°20' E127°44' Halla-san, S Kor
19 N51°29' E11°58' Halle, Ger
20 N47°41' E13°6' Hallein, Aus
115 N29°26' W96°56' Hallettsville, TX, US
29 N64°19' E19°38' Hällnäs, Swe
108 N48°46' W96°57' Hallock, MN, US
66 S18°16' E127°46' Halls Creek, WA, Austl
60 N0°46' E128°32' Halmahera, Indo
60 S0°28' E128°22' Halmahera Sea
29 N56°40' E12°51' Halmstad, Swe
57 N10°40' E107°46' Hàm Tân, Viet
44 N34°47' E48°31' Hamadan, Iran
40 N35°8' E36°45' Hamah, Syria
53 N34°45' E137°28' Hamamatsu, Jap
29 N60°49' E11°4' Hamar, Nor
56 N6°8' E81°6' Hambantota, Sri L
19 N53°34' E9°58' Hamburg, Ger
110 N42°44' W78°50' Hamburg, NY, US
42 N19°2' E43°36' Hamdah, Sau Ar
29 N61°0' E24°27' Hämeenlinna, Fin
68 S26°26' E114°11' Hamelin Pool, WA, Austl
19 N52°6' E9°21' Hameln, Ger
66 S22°7' E116°38' Hamersley Range, Austl
52 N40°24' E128°31' Hamgyong Sanmaek, N Kor
52 N39°54' E127°32' Hamhung, N Kor
48 N42°50' E93°30' Hami, China
71 S37°47' E175°17' Hamilton, NZ
106 N46°15' W114°10' Hamilton, MT, US
103 N43°17' W79°50' Hamilton, ON, Can
118 N34°8' W87°59' Hamilton, AL, US
127 N32°17' W64°47' Hamilton, Ber, UK
29 N60°34' E27°12' Hamina, Fin
29 N63°36' E15°21' Hammerdal, Swe
29 N70°40' E23°42' Hammerfest, Nor
115 N30°30' W90°28' Hammond, LA, US
117 N39°37' W74°46' Hammonton, NJ, US
116 N36°15' W82°10' Hampton, TN, US
117 N37°2' W76°21' Hampton, VA, US
115 N33°32' W92°28' Hampton, AR, US
85 N10°41' W2°27' Han, Gha
19 N50°8' E8°55' Hanau am Main, Ger
49 N36°36' E114°28' Handan, China
140 S27°10' W109°26' Hanga Roa, Chile
71 S38°15' E175°10' Hangatiki, NZ
48 N48°8' E96°36' Hangayn Nuruu, Mong
49 N30°13' E120°10' Hangzhou, China
100 N51°37' W106°27' Hanley, SK, Can
71 S42°31' E172°49' Hanmer, NZ
99 N51°38' W111°54' Hanna, AB, Can
103 N51°26' W80°17' Hannah Bay
109 N39°43' W91°22' Hannibal, MO, US
19 N52°23' E9°44' Hannover, Ger
57 N21°1' E105°49' Hanoi, Viet
90 S31°4' E24°29' Hanover, S Afr
117 N37°46' W77°22' Hanover, VA, US
99 N49°5' W121°52' Hansard, BC, Can
73 S18°36' W141°46' Hao, Fr Poly, Fr
42 N25°18' E34°57' Haql, Sau Ar
43 N24°8' E49°5' Harad, Sau Ar
91 S17°44' E31°2' Harare, Zimb
49 N45°43' E126°37' Harbin, China
107 N45°44' W107°37' Hardin, MT, US
99 N52°40' W111°18' Hardisty, AB, Can
83 N9°18' E42°8' Harer, Eth
83 N9°55' E41°59' Harewa, Eth
83 N9°34' E44°4' Hargeysa, Som
42 N14°28' E47°36' Harhramaut, Yem
54 N14°31' E75°48' Harihar, Ind
45 N34°23' E64°8' Harirud, Afg
115 N26°11' W97°42' Harlingen, TX, US
107 N46°26' W109°50' Harlowton, MT, US
108 N43°52' W103°32' Harney Peak, US
29 N62°38' E17°56' Härnösand, Swe
85 N4°25' W7°43' Harper, Libr
43 N14°57' E50°19' Harrah, Yem
93 N35°52' E39°1' Harran, Turk
111 N44°37' W67°49' Harrington, ME, US
105 N50°31' W59°28' Harrington Harbour, QC, Can
117 N40°16' W76°54' Harrisburg, PA, US
103 N42°41' W103°53' Harrison, NE, US
109 N44°1' W84°49' Harrison, MI, US
115 N36°14' W93°7' Harrison, AR, US
108 N38°39' W94°21' Harrisonville, MO, US
109 N44°40' W83°18' Harrisville, MI, US
116 N37°46' W84°50' Harrodsburg, KY, US
29 N68°46' E15°30' Harstad, Nor
111 N41°46' W72°42' Hartford, CT, US
98 N53°25' W129°17' Hartley Bay, BC, Can
68 S33°5' E115°54' Harvey, WA, Austl
114 N33°10' W99°44' Haskell, TX, US
56 N13°0' E76°5' Hassan, Ind
18 N50°58' E5°29' Hasselt, Belg
79 N28°46' E5°20' Hassi bel Guebbour, Alg
11 N50°53' E0°35' Hastings, UK
71 S39°38' E176°50' Hastings, NZ
108 N40°35' W98°23' Hastings, NE, US
57 N7°1' E100°28' Hat Yai, Thai
69 S33°52' E143°45' Hatfield, NSW, Austl
48 N50°26' E100°9' Hatgal, Mong
118 N31°20' W89°17' Hattiesburg, MS, US
29 N59°25' E5°18' Haugesund, Nor
29 N59°45' E7°31' Haukeligrend, Nor
71 S36°38' E174°50' Hauraki Gulf
104 N49°12' W68°16' Hauterive, QC, Can
126 N23°8' W82°23' Havana, Cuba
111 N42°47' W71°5' Haverhill, MA, US
54 N14°48' E75°24' Haveri, Ind
44 N38°10' E46°53' Haviq, Iran
20 N49°36' E15°35' Havlíckuv Brod, Czech
107 N48°33' W109°41' Havre, MT, US
105 N50°16' W63°38' Havre-St-Pierre, QC, Can
120 N20°16' W156°53' Hawaii, US
120 N19°18' W155°39' Hawaii, US
120 N21°25' W159°1' Hawaiian Islands, US
11 N55°25' W2°47' Hawick, UK
104 N48°5' W84°34' Hawk Junction, ON, Can
71 S39°16' E177°13' Hawke Bay
69 S31°53' E138°25' Hawker, SA, Austl
11 N53°51' W1°55' Haworth, UK
44 N30°26' E45°43' Hawr al Hammar, Iraq
112 N38°31' W118°37' Hawthorne, NV, US
69 S34°30' E144°51' Hay, NSW, Austl
96 N60°51' W115°40' Hay River, NT, Can
97 N78°26' W67°20' Hayes Peninsula, Grld, Den
43 N19°56' E56°20' Hayma', Oman
111 N45°49' W67°59' Haynesville, ME, US
108 N38°53' W99°20' Hays, KS, US
109 N46°1' W91°29' Hayward, WI, US
116 N37°15' W83°11' Hazard, KY, US
55 N23°59' E85°21' Hazaribag, Ind
143 S50°0' E70°0' Heard Island, Austl
102 N49°41' W83°40' Hearst, ON, Can
117 N37°55' W76°28' Heathsville, VA, US
114 N27°19' W98°41' Hebbronville, TX, US
98 N53°7' W130°53' Hecate Strait
50 N24°42' E108°2' Hechi, China
49 N30°0' E106°16' Hechuan, China
53 N26°51' E128°16' Hedo, Jap
18 N52°57' E5°55' Heerenveen, Neth
40 N32°49' E35°0' Hefa, Isr
49 N31°52' E117°16' Hefei, China
49 N47°20' E130°17' Hegang, China
19 N54°12' E9°6' Heide, Ger
19 N49°25' E8°43' Heidelberg, Ger
19 N49°8' E9°13' Heilbronn, Ger
20 N47°2' E12°52' Heiligenblut, Aus
107 N46°36' W112°2' Helena, MT, US
126 N19°23' W81°25' Hell, Cay Is, UK
13 N38°31' W1°41' Hellín, Sp
45 N30°12' E62°26' Helmand River, Afg
11 N58°7' W3°40' Helmsdale, UK
19 N52°13' E11°0' Helmstedt, Ger
113 N39°43' W110°52' Helper, UT, US
29 N60°12' E24°55' Helsingfors, Fin
29 N60°12' E24°55' Helsinki, Fin
10 N50°7' W5°17' Helston, UK
115 N30°6' W96°5' Hempstead, TX, US
110 N40°43' W73°34' Hempstead, NY, US
29 N57°14' E18°22' Hemse, Swe
71 S35°56' E174°49' Hen and Chickens Islands, NZ
50 N34°35' E101°34' Henan, China
115 N32°10' W94°49' Henderson, TX, US
117 N36°20' W78°25' Henderson, NC, US
116 N35°19' W82°28' Hendersonville, NC, US
44 N30°14' E49°43' Hendijan, Iran
61 S6°15' E145°35' Henganofi, PNG
48 N29°23' E97°31' Hengduan Shan, China
18 N52°15' E6°45' Hengelo, Neth
51 N27°15' E112°51' Hengshan, China
51 N26°54' E112°36' Hengyang, China
114 N33°49' W98°12' Henrietta, TX, US
49 N48°28' E108°20' Hentiyn Nuruu, Mong
50 N21°39' E109°11' Hepu, China
50 N26°34' E104°12' Heqing, China
45 N34°20' E62°12' Herat, Afg
11 N52°4' W2°43' Hereford, UK
114 N34°49' W102°24' Hereford, TX, US
12 N39°20' W3°22' Herencia, Sp
15 N47°23' E9°17' Herisau, Switz
110 N43°2' W74°59' Herkimer, NY, US
66 S23°57' E132°45' Hermannsburg, NT, Austl
61 S1°28' E144°48' Hermit Islands, PNG
109 N37°56' W93°19' Hermitage, MO, US
122 N29°4' W110°56' Hermosillo, Son, Mex
118 N34°49' W89°59' Hernando, MS, US
117 N40°19' W76°36' Hershey, PA, US
11 N51°49' W0°5' Hertford, UK
117 N36°11' W76°28' Hertford, NC, US
55 N27°26' E85°2' Hetauda, Nepal
108 N46°0' W102°38' Hettinger, ND, US
50 N35°15' E110°6' Heyang, China
50 N27°0' E104°37' Hezhang, China
50 N34°58' E102°57' Hezuo, China
119 N25°52' W80°17' Hialeah, FL, US
109 N47°25' W92°56' Hibbing, MN, US
125 N7°39' W81°13' Hicaco, Pan
71 S37°36' E178°18' Hicks Bay, NZ
53 N42°58' E142°26' Hidaka-Sammyaku, Jap
123 N20°31' W99°14' Hidalgo, Mex
123 N27°47' W99°52' Hidalgo, Coah, Mex
122 N26°56' W105°40' Hidalgo del Parral, Chih, Mex
19 N54°31' E12°38' Hiddensee, Ger
137 S16°58' W49°14' Hidrolândia, GO, Braz
68 S31°45' E121°43' Higginsville, WA, Austl
99 N58°31' W117°7' High Level, AB, Can
117 N41°19' W74°40' High Point, US
99 N55°26' W116°29' High Prairie, AB, Can
128 N18°37' W68°43' Higuey, Dom Rep
26 N58°41' E21°36' Hiiumaa, Est
13 N41°10' W0°27' Hijar, Sp
60 S7°35' E127°24' Hila, Indo
19 N52°9' E9°57' Hildesheim, Ger
107 N44°55' W111°27' Hilgard Peak, US
58 N0°44' E97°53' Hiliotaluwa, Indo
115 N32°1' W97°8' Hillsboro, TX, US
109 N41°55' W84°38' Hillsdale, MI, US
120 N19°43' W155°5' Hilo, HI, US
119 N32°9' W80°46' Hilton Head Island, SC, US
48 N31°10' E80°16' Himalaya, China
24 N40°8' E19°41' Himare, Alb
54 N23°36' E72°57' Himatnagar, Ind
52 N34°50' E134°40' Himeji, Jap
40 N34°44' E36°43' Hims, Syria
128 N19°9' W72°1' Hinche, Haiti
67 S18°7' E146°20' Hinchinbrook Island, Austl
45 N35°43' E70°21' Hindu Kush, Afg
119 N31°51' W81°36' Hinesville, GA, US
54 N20°34' E78°50' Hinganghat, Ind
39 N39°22' E41°44' Hinis, Turk
63 N9°36' E122°29' Hinoba-an, Phil
99 N53°25' W117°34' Hinton, AB, Can
55 N21°41' E84°5' Hirakud Reservoir, Ind
54 N24°22' E79°13' Hirapur, Ind
52 N34°24' E132°27' Hiroschima, Jap
52 N34°24' E132°27' Hiroshima, Jap
15 N49°55' E4°5' Hirson, Fr
54 N29°10' E75°43' Hisar, Ind
128 N19°12' W72°18' Hispaniola, Dom Rep
73 S17°14' W144°7' Hiti, Fr Poly, Fr
73 S9°55' W138°38' Hiva Oa, Fr Poly, Fr
29 N57°28' E9°59' Hjorring, Den
57 N28°18' E97°29' Hkakabo Razi, Myanmar
91 S28°1' E32°15' Hluhluwe, S Afr
26 N55°8' E27°41' Hlybokaye, Bela
85 N6°35' E0°30' Ho, Gha
57 N10°45' E106°41' Ho Chi Minh City, Viet
57 N23°25' E98°39' Ho-pang, Myanmar
69 S42°53' E147°19' Hobart, Tas, Austl
113 N32°42' W103°8' Hobbs, NM, US
119 N27°4' W80°7' Hobe Sound, FL, US
83 N5°20' E48°30' Hobyo, Som
22 N46°25' E20°20' Hódmezovásárhely, Hun
21 N48°51' E17°8' Hodonín, Czech
19 N50°18' E11°55' Hof, Ger
28 N64°17' W15°12' Höfn, Ice
29 N57°10' E16°2' Högsby, Swe
20 N47°6' E12°47' Hohe Tauern, Aus
49 N40°50' E111°39' Hohhot, China
53 N43°14' E142°52' Hokkaido, Jap
113 N34°54' W110°10' Holbrook, AZ, US
108 N40°26' W99°22' Holdrege, NE, US
127 N20°53' W76°16' Holguin, Cuba
109 N42°47' W86°4' Holland, MI, US
114 N34°41' W99°55' Hollis, OK, US
22 N48°0' E19°34' Hollóko, Hun
118 N34°45' W89°28' Holly Springs, MS, US
28 N65°43' W21°43' Hólmavík, Ice
97 N66°55' W53°40' Holsteinborg, Grld, Den
121 N62°12' W159°47' Holy Cross, AK, US
17 N41°48' E12°41' HOLY SEE
11 N53°18' W4°37' Holyhead, UK
113 N40°35' W102°18' Holyoke, CO, US
111 N42°9' W72°37' Holyoke, MA, US
57 N24°52' E94°55' Homalin, Myanmar
79 N15°17' W1°42' Hombori, Mali
79 N15°10' W1°38' Hombori Tondo, Mali
97 N68°51' W66°29' Home Bay
70 S12°6' E96°55' Home Island, Cocos Is, Austl
121 N59°40' W151°34' Homer, AK, US
115 N32°47' W93°4' Homer, LA, US
107 N45°19' W113°41' Homer Youngs Peak, US
119 N25°28' W80°29' Homestead, FL, US
63 N10°39' E125°50' Homonhon Island, Phil
26 N52°25' E31°0' Homyel', Bela
56 N14°17' E74°28' Honavar, Ind
99 N55°4' W114°2' Hondo, AB, Can
124 N14°13' W87°7' HONDURAS
112 N40°7' W120°49' Honey Lake, US
51 N22°15' E114°11' Hong Kong, China
48 N41°4' E95°26' Hongliuyuan, China
48 N42°26' E97°8' Hongshishan, China
49 N33°31' E117°8' Hongze Hu, China
72 S9°48' E159°49' Honiara, Sol Is
53 N39°23' E140°3' Honjo, Jap
120 N21°20' W157°52' Honolulu, HI, US
53 N35°51' E137°20' Honshu, Jap
99 N49°23' W121°26' Hope, BC, Can
127 N26°32' W76°58' Hope Town, Bah
117 N37°18' W77°17' Hopewell, VA, US
106 N46°58' W123°50' Hoquiam, WA, US
39 N40°3' E42°11' Horasan, Turk
26 N54°17' E30°59' Horki, Bela
27 N48°18' E38°3' Horlivka, Ukr
29 N63°38' E19°54' Hörnefors, Swe
110 N42°19' W77°39' Hornell, NY, US
102 N49°13' W84°47' Hornepayne, ON, Can
29 N61°58' E6°31' Hornindal, Nor
70 S12°2' E96°50' Horsburgh Island, Cocos Is, Austl
105 N50°16' W55°54' Horse Islands, Can
69 S36°43' E142°13' Horsham, Vic, Austl
20 N49°32' E12°56' Horsovský Týn, Czech
45 N26°1' E63°56' Hoshab, Pak
61 S5°29' E150°31' Hoskins, PNG
48 N48°42' E89°0' Hosoot, Mong
54 N15°16' E76°24' Hospet, Ind
14 N43°40' W1°26' Hossegor, Fr
115 N34°30' W93°3' Hot Springs, AR, US
108 N43°26' W103°28' Hot Springs, SD, US
113 N40°4' W106°6' Hot Sulphur Springs, CO, US
48 N37°8' E79°58' Hotan, China
99 N57°8' W117°25' Hotchkiss, AB, Can
57 N20°9' E103°38' Houamuang, Laos
109 N47°7' W88°36' Houghton, MI, US
111 N46°8' W67°50' Houlton, ME, US
115 N29°35' W90°43' Houma, LA, US
79 N33°52' E10°52' Houmt Souq, Tun
85 N11°30' W3°31' Houndé, Burk
98 N54°24' W126°38' Houston, BC, Can
109 N37°20' W91°58' Houston, MO, US
115 N29°46' W95°22' Houston, TX, US
118 N33°54' W89°0' Houston, MS, US
48 N48°1' E91°38' Hovd, Mong
48 N51°8' E98°46' Hövsgöl Nuur, Mong
73 N0°34' W176°51' Howland Island, US
55 N22°36' E88°17' Howrah, Ind
19 N51°46' E9°23' Höxter, Ger
19 N51°26' E14°14' Hoyerswerda, Ger
12 N40°10' W6°43' Hoyos, Sp
20 N50°12' E15°49' Hradec Králové, Czech
21 N49°33' E17°44' Hranice, Czech
26 N53°41' E23°50' Hrodna, Bela
57 N23°18' E97°58' Hsenwi, Myanmar
51 N24°5' E121°35' Hsin-ch'eng, Taiwan
51 N23°56' E121°35' Hua-lien, Taiwan
135 S13°33' W63°45' Huacaraje, Bol
134 S11°7' W77°37' Huacho, Peru
49 N33°58' E116°47' Huaibei, China
51 N32°28' E115°24' Huaibin, China
49 N32°40' E117°1' Huainan, China
122 N21°42' W104°20' Huajimic, Nay, Mex
122 N28°14' W108°16' Huajumar, Chih, Mex
134 S8°49' W77°52' Huallanca, Peru
88 S12°46' E15°43' Huambo, Ang
50 N36°39' E107°18' Huan Xian, China
134 S5°14' W79°28' Huancabamba, Peru
135 S15°12' W69°46' Huancané, Peru
134 S12°46' W75°2' Huancavelica, Peru
134 S12°4' W75°14' Huancayo, Peru
49 N30°12' E115°4' Huangshi, China
49 N28°39' E121°15' Huangyan, China
134 S9°55' W76°14' Huánuco, Peru
135 S19°0' W66°48' Huari, Bol
140 S28°28' W71°14' Huasco, Chile
134 S11°1' W76°21' Huayllay, Peru
54 N15°21' E75°10' Hubli, Ind
29 N61°44' E17°7' Hudiksvall, Swe
110 N42°15' W73°47' Hudson, NY, US
101 N52°52' W102°25' Hudson Bay, SK, Can
96 N58°54' W89°11' Hudson Bay
110 N43°18' W73°35' Hudson Falls, NY, US
99 N56°2' W121°55' Hudson Hope, BC, Can
110 N41°53' W73°53' Hudson River, US
97 N62°46' W73°22' Hudson Strait
57 N16°28' E107°36' Hue, Viet
124 N15°19' W91°28' Huehuetenango, Guat
12 N37°16' W6°56' Huelva, Sp
13 N42°8' W0°25' Huesca, Sp
13 N37°49' W2°32' Huéscar, Sp
13 N40°8' W2°41' Huete, Sp
10 N49°55' W6°19' Hugh Town, UK
67 S20°52' E144°12' Hughenden, Qld, Austl
68 S30°42' E129°31' Hughes, SA, Austl
115 N34°1' W95°31' Hugo, OK, US
50 N35°11' E104°2' Huichuan, China
88 S15°14' E15°5' Huila Plateau, Ang
11 N53°45' W0°20' Hull, UK
104 N45°28' W75°42' Hull, QC, Can
49 N48°45' E117°38' Hulun Nur, China
129 N18°9' W65°50' Humacao, PR, US
140 S23°12' W65°21' Humahuaca, Arg
136 S7°31' W63°2' Humaitá, AM, Braz
88 S16°40' E14°55' Humbe, Ang
100 N52°12' W105°7' Humboldt, SK, Can
116 N35°50' W88°55' Humboldt, TN, US
45 N25°26' E59°37' Humedan, Iran
21 N48°56' E21°55' Humenné, Slvk
112 N35°21' W111°41' Humphreys Peak, US
28 N65°37' W21°3' Húnaflói
23 N45°45' E22°54' Hunedoara, Rom
75 S20°34' W175°49' Hunga Haapai Island, Ton
75 S18°43' W174°23' Hunga Island, Ton
75 S20°34' W175°22' Hunga Tonga Island, Ton
22 N47°0' E19°6' HUNGARY
69 S29°0' E144°25' Hungerford, Qld, Austl
52 N39°50' E127°38' Hungnam, N Kor
49 N41°56' E126°25' Hunjiang, China
69 S40°30' E144°0' Hunter Islands, Austl
117 N40°29' W78°1' Huntingdon, PA, US
110 N40°53' W73°23' Huntington, NY, US
116 N38°25' W82°27' Huntington, WV, US
11 N57°27' W2°47' Huntly, UK
103 N45°20' W79°13' Huntsville, ON, Can
115 N30°43' W95°33' Huntsville, TX, US
118 N34°44' W86°36' Huntsville, AL, US
48 N44°12' E80°26' Huocheng, China
61 S6°59' E147°13' Huon Gulf
49 N31°25' E116°20' Huoshan, China

continue on next page

124 N14°40' W86°13' **Juticalpa**, Hon
29 N56°37' E9°8' Jutland, Den
51 N35°23' E116°6' **Juye**, China
44 N28°10' E53°52' **Juyom**, Iran
79 N34°39' E11°15' Juzur Qarqanah, Tun
29 N62°15' E25°45' **Jyväskylä**, Fin

K

83 N5°40' E44°20' **K'elafo**, Eth
39 N42°15' E42°40' **K'ut'aisi**, Geo
45 N35°50' E76°29' K-2, Pak
29 N68°25' E22°30' **Kaaresuvanto**, Swe
88 S6°3' E26°55' **Kabalo**, DRC
74 S18°59' W179°14' Kabara Island, Fiji
63 N7°48' E122°45' **Kabasalan**, Phil
87 N7°39' E18°37' **Kabo**, CAR
45 N34°31' E69°10' **Kabol**, Afg
45 N34°31' E69°10' **Kabul**, Afg
82 N16°53' E33°42' **Kabushiyah**, Sud
89 S14°27' E28°27' **Kabwe**, Zam
47 N53°5' E76°6' **Kaciry**, Kaz
78 N10°45' W6°30' **Kadiana**, Mali
38 N38°15' E32°14' **Kadinhani**, Turk
56 N14°7' E78°10' **Kadiri**, Ind
38 N37°23' E36°5' **Kadirli**, Turk
56 N11°7' E72°50' Kadmat Island, Ind
86 N7°39' E9°44' **Kado**, Nga
91 S18°21' E29°55' **Kadoma**, Zimb
86 N10°31' E7°26' **Kaduna**, Nga
74 S18°45' E177°56' *Kaduva Passage*, Fiji
35 N57°47' E43°11' **Kadyy**, Rus Fed
47 N42°8' E77°10' **Kadzhi-Say**, Kyr
78 N16°9' W13°30' **Kaédi**, Mrta
71 S35°6' E173°47' **Kaeo**, NZ
52 N37°59' E126°33' **Kaesong**, N Kor
42 N31°24' E37°24' **Kaf**, Sau Ar
39 N39°13' E46°24' **Kafan**, Arm
45 N32°8' E65°49' Kafar Jar Ghar Range, Afg
29 N70°52' E25°46' **Kafjord**, Nor
87 N6°59' E19°11' **Kaga Bandoro**, CAR
45 N34°47' E73°32' **Kagan**, Pak
82 N14°24' E30°25' **Kagmar**, Sud
52 N31°34' E130°33' **Kagoshima**, Jap
89 S3°50' E32°35' **Kahama**, Tanz
120 N20°35' W156°58' Kahoolawe, US
71 S39°51' E174°56' **Kai Iwi**, NZ
86 N9°37' E3°58' **Kaiama**, Nga
49 N34°47' E114°20' **Kaifeng**, China
51 N29°9' E118°23' **Kaihua**, China
49 N43°36' E121°14' **Kailu**, China
120 N21°23' W157°44' **Kailua**, HI, US
60 S3°38' E133°46' **Kaimana**, Indo
61 S6°15' E145°55' **Kainantu**, PNG
79 N35°41' E10°5' **Kairouan**, Tun
61 S8°49' E146°34' **Kairuku**, PNG
120 N21°7' W157°38' *Kaiwi Channel*
29 N64°14' E27°41' **Kajaani**, Fin
82 N3°53' E31°40' **Kajo Kaji**, Sud
82 N0°17' E34°45' **Kakamega**, Ken
84 N6°35' W10°19' **Kakata**, Libr
27 N47°17' E34°10' *Kakhovka Reservoir*, Ukr
53 N39°35' E140°34' **Kakudate**, Jap
82 N3°43' E34°52' **Kakuma**, Ken
46 N35°39' E62°33' **Kala-I-Mor**, Turkm
45 N32°58' E71°34' **Kalabagh**, Pak
90 S23°53' E20°34' Kalahari Desert, Bots
45 N35°32' E72°35' **Kalam**, Pak
24 N37°2' E22°7' **Kalamáta**, Grc
109 N42°17' W85°35' **Kalamazoo**, MI, US
78 N10°47' W8°12' **Kalana**, Mali
25 N36°20' E27°57' **Kalavárdha**, Grc
34 N65°13' E31°8' **Kalevala**, Rus Fed
58 S5°45' E105°38' **Kalianda**, Indo
63 N11°43' E122°22' **Kalibo**, Phil
59 N0°4' E113°15' Kalimantan, Indo
25 N36°57' E26°59' **Kálimnos**, Grc
47 N37°52' E69°0' **Kalininabad**, Taj
34 N54°43' E20°28' **Kaliningrad**, Rus Fed
35 N57°20' E56°20' **Kalinino**, Rus Fed
36 N51°30' E44°28' **Kalininsk**, Rus Fed
106 N48°12' W114°19' **Kalispell**, MT, US
21 N51°46' E18°6' **Kalisz**, Pol
89 S5°4' E31°48' **Kaliua**, Tanz
90 S24°3' E17°33' **Kalkrand**, Nam
29 N56°40' E16°22' **Kalmar**, Swe
46 N49°3' E51°47' **Kalmykovo**, Kaz
22 N46°32' E18°59' **Kalocsa**, Hun
56 N10°3' E73°46' Kalpeni Island, Ind
54 N26°7' E79°44' **Kalpi**, Ind
36 N54°31' E36°16' **Kaluga**, Rus Fed
66 S14°18' E126°39' **Kalumburu**, WA, Austl
35 N60°8' E62°10' **Kama**, Rus Fed
35 N56°1' E52°47' *Kama*, Rus Fed
38 N39°22' E33°44' **Kaman**, Turk
54 N18°19' E78°21' **Kamareddi**, Ind
58 S1°41' E100°43' **Kambang**, Indo
84 N9°7' W12°55' **Kambia**, SL
33 N57°11' E157°13' Kamchatka Peninsula, Rus Fed
36 N48°21' E40°19' **Kamensk-Shakhtinskiy**, Rus Fed
35 N56°28' E61°54' **Kamensk-Ural'skiy**, Rus Fed
53 N43°51' E142°46' **Kamikawa**, Jap
88 S8°43' E25°0' **Kamina**, DRC
53 N41°48' E140°6' **Kaminokuni**, Jap
99 N50°40' W120°20' **Kamloops**, BC, Can
82 N0°19' E32°35' **Kampala**, Ug
57 N16°28' E99°30' **Kamphaeng Phet**, Thai
101 N51°34' W101°54' **Kamsack**, SK, Can
35 N59°16' E54°58' *Kamskoye Reservoir*, Rus Fed
36 N50°6' E45°24' **Kamyshin**, Rus Fed
37 N54°7' E52°10' **Kamyshla**, Rus Fed
35 N56°52' E62°43' **Kamyshlov**, Rus Fed
46 N46°11' E61°57' **Kamyslybas**, Kaz
112 N37°3' W112°32' **Kanab**, UT, US
74 S17°17' W179°25' Kanacea, Fiji
88 S5°54' E22°25' **Kananga**, DRC
35 N61°7' E54°58' **Kanava**, Rus Fed
53 N36°34' E136°39' **Kan**[illegible]**azawa**, Jap
57 N14°36' E98°2' **Kanb**[illegible]**auk**, Myanmar
57 N14°1' E99°32' **Kanch**[illegible]**anaburi**, Thai
56 N12°50' E79°43' **Kanchi**[illegible]
34 N66°33' E33°45' *Kandal*[illegible]
58 N3°3' E97°20' **Kanda**[illegible]
74 S18°55' E178°7' Kandavu Islan[illegible]
85 N9°57' E1°3' **Kande**, Togo
85 N11°8' E2°56' **Kandi**, Ben
45 N27°4' E68°13' **Kandiaro**, Pak
45 N25°29' E65°29' **Kandrach**, Pak
56 N7°18' E80°38' **Kandy**, Sri L
97 N79°32' W70°53' *Kane Basin*
36 N46°5' E38°57' **Kanevskaya**, Rus Fed
90 S23°41' E22°50' **Kang**, Bots
97 N68°18' W53°23' **Kangaatsaiq**, Grld, Den
44 N27°50' E52°4' **Kangan**, Iran
58 N6°26' E100°11' **Kangar**, Malay
69 S36°15' E136°39' Kangaroo Island, Austl
50 N30°3' E102°2' **Kangding**, China
97 N67°5' W50°17' **Kangerlussuaq**, Grld, Den
52 N40°58' E126°34' **Kanggye**, N Kor
48 N27°52' E92°32' Kangto, China
35 N67°52' E44°40' Kanin Peninsula, Rus Fed
109 N41°7' W87°52' **Kankakee**, IL, US
84 N10°23' W9°18' **Kankan**, Gui
55 N20°17' E81°29' **Kanker**, Ind
78 N15°56' W11°31' **Kankossa**, Mrta
29 N63°54' E23°54' **Kannus**, Fin
52 N34°13' E131°49' **Kano**, Jap
86 N11°59' E8°30' **Kano**, Nga
59 N2°6' E112°9' **Kanowit**, Malay
54 N26°28' E80°19' **Kanpur**, Ind
108 N38°28' W98°23' **Kansas**, US
108 N39°1' W94°38' **Kansas City**, KS, US
46 N45°7' E59°14' **Kantubek**, Uzb
75 S19°41' W175°14' Kao Island, Ton
51 N22°38' E120°17' **Kaohsiung**, Taiwan
74 S9°41' E161°1' *Kaoka Bay*
90 S18°2' E12°34' Kaokoveld, Nam
120 N22°4' W159°20' **Kapaa**, HI, US
88 S8°21' E22°35' **Kapanga**, DRC
20 N47°26' E15°18' **Kapfenberg**, Aus
59 N2°1' E112°56' **Kapit**, Malay
71 S40°55' E174°25' Kapiti Island, NZ
82 N4°47' E33°35' **Kapoeta**, Sud
22 N46°22' E17°47' **Kaposvár**, Hun
52 N41°4' E128°19' **Kapsan-up**, N Kor
103 N49°25' W82°26' **Kapuskasing**, ON, Can
22 N47°36' E17°2' **Kapuvár**, Hun
46 N39°11' E60°20' Kara Kum, Turkm
32 N73°41' E66°53' *Kara Sea*
35 N70°10' E57°10' *Kara Strait*
47 N43°43' E68°28' Kara Tau, Kaz
35 N55°29' E60°14' **Karabash**, Rus Fed
36 N43°45' E41°54' **Karachayevsk**, Rus Fed
45 N24°52' E67°0' **Karachi**, Pak
35 N55°50' E56°53' **Karaidel'**, Rus Fed
38 N37°16' E35°3' **Karaisali**, Turk
44 N35°48' E50°59' **Karaj**, Iran
47 N41°14' E73°4' **Karakol**, Kyr
45 N36°8' E75°4' Karakoram Range, Pak
39 N39°44' E43°3' **Karaköse**, Turk
47 N39°2' E73°33' **Karakul'**, Taj
46 N39°32' E63°50' **Karakul'**, Uzb
38 N37°11' E33°14' **Karaman**, Turk
48 N45°30' E84°55' **Karamay**, China
59 S3°52' E116°5' **Karambu**, Indo
71 S41°15' E172°7' **Karamea**, NZ
46 N47°3' E56°20' **Karaoba**, Kaz
38 N37°43' E33°33' **Karapinar**, Turk
29 N69°27' E25°30' **Karasjok**, Nor
46 N51°20' E62°21' **Karasu**, Kaz
38 N41°6' E30°41' **Karasu**, Turk
46 N46°25' E53°30' **Karaton**, Kaz
46 N48°43' E55°53' **Karaulkel'dy**, Kaz
20 N46°30' E13°54' Karawanken, Aus
44 N32°36' E44°2' **Karbala'**, Iraq
25 N36°48' E27°8' **Kardhámaina**, Grc
24 N39°21' E21°55' **Kardítsa**, Grc
26 N59°0' E22°45' **Kärdla**, Est
35 N55°57' E64°27' **Kargapol'ye**, Rus Fed
32 N59°6' E80°53' **Kargasok**, Rus Fed
34 N61°30' E38°58' **Kargopol'**, Rus Fed
29 N69°24' E25°50' **Karigasniemi**, Nor
82 N18°33' E31°51' **Karima**, Sud
54 N18°26' E79°9' **Karimnagar**, Ind
61 S4°30' E146°4' Karkar Island, PNG
22 N45°29' E15°34' **Karlovac**, Cro
27 N49°27' E35°8' **Karlovka**, Ukr
25 N42°38' E24°48' **Karlovo**, Bulg
20 N50°11' E12°52' **Karlovy Vary**, Czech
29 N56°12' E15°18' **Karlskrona**, Swe
19 N49°3' E8°24' **Karlsruhe**, Ger
29 N59°23' E13°31' **Karlstad**, Swe
54 N29°41' E76°59' **Karnal**, Ind
115 N28°53' W97°54' **Karnes City**, TX, US
25 N42°39' E26°59' **Karnobat**, Bulg
59 S1°47' E119°20' **Karosa**, Indo
82 N5°11' E35°50' **Karotho Post**, Sud
25 N35°30' E27°14' **Kárpathos**, Grc
24 N38°55' E21°40' **Karpenision**, Grc
35 N64°0' E44°24' **Karpogory**, Rus Fed
39 N40°36' E43°5' **Kars**, Turk
46 N38°52' E65°47' **Karshi**, Uzb
37 N53°3' E60°40' **Kartaly**, Rus Fed
60 S3°50' E133°23' **Karufa**, Indo
67 S17°29' E140°50' **Karumba**, Qld, Austl
44 N30°36' E48°37' *Karun River*, Iran
66 S16°18' E127°12' **Karunjie**, WA, Austl
29 N66°3' E23°57' **Karunki**, Swe
56 N10°57' E78°5' **Karur**, Ind
54 N14°48' E74°8' **Karwar**, Ind
35 N60°7' E66°41' **Karym**, Rus Fed
82 N12°30' E24°17' **Kas**, Sud
38 N36°12' E29°38' **Kas**, Turk
89 S10°13' E31°11' **Kasama**, Zam
56 N12°30' E75°0' **Kasaragod**, Ind
88 S13°27' E25°50' **Kasempa**, Zam
89 S10°22' E28°38' **Kasenga**, Zam
89 N1°24' E30°26' **Kasenye**, DRC
88 S1°38' E27°7' **Kasese**, DRC
44 N33°59' E51°29' **Kashan**, Iran
53 N37°22' E138°33' **Kashiwazaki**, Jap
45 N35°12' E58°27' **Kashmar**, Iran
55 N25°18' E91°7' Kasi Hills, Ind
83 S3°53' E38°41' Kasigau Hill, Ken
36 N54°56' E41°24' **Kasimov**, Rus Fed
35 N55°53' E60°46' **Kasli**, Rus Fed
88 S4°27' E26°40' **Kasongo**, DRC
36 N45°23' E47°20' **Kaspiyskiy**, Rus Fed
40 N35°56' E35°59' **Kassab**, Syria
82 N15°28' E36°23' **Kassala**, Sud
19 N51°19' E9°29' **Kassel**, Ger
38 N41°22' E33°47' **Kastamonu**, Turk
24 N40°32' E21°16' **Kastoría**, Grc
36 N51°50' E38°6' **Kastornoye**, Rus Fed
59 S1°58' E113°24' **Kasungan**, Indo
88 S10°28' E23°57' Katanga Plateau, DRC
37 N54°45' E58°12' **Katav-Ivanovsk**, Rus Fed
24 N40°16' E22°30' **Kateríni**, Grc
55 N22°30' E82°33' **Katghora**, Ind
57 N24°11' E96°21' **Katha**, Myanmar
66 S14°28' E132°16' **Katherine**, NT, Austl
55 N27°46' E85°14' **Kathmandu**, Nepal
85 N8°8' W5°6' **Katiola**, Côte d'Ivoire
73 S16°34' W145°31' Katiu, Fr Poly, Fr
54 N23°51' E80°24' **Katni**, Ind
21 N50°16' E19°2' **Katowice**, Pol
86 N13°0' E7°37' **Katsina**, Nga
25 N35°57' E27°46' **Kattavía**, Grc
29 N56°44' E10°58' *Kattegat*
120 N22°4' W159°37' Kauai, US
120 N21°37' W158°55' *Kauai Channel*
115 N32°35' W96°19' **Kaufman**, TX, US
71 S36°37' E174°30' **Kaukapakapa**, NZ
90 S19°56' E20°32' Kaukau Veld, Nam
120 N22°18' W160°0' *Kaulakahi Channel*
29 N66°27' E23°41' **Kauliranta**, Fin
89 S9°58' E33°20' Kaumbe Hill, Zam
26 N54°54' E23°54' **Kaunas**, Lith
24 N41°11' E19°33' **Kavajë**, Alb
38 N41°5' E36°3' **Kavak**, Turk
25 N40°56' E24°25' **Kavala**, Grc
54 N14°55' E79°59' **Kavali**, Ind
133 N4°29' W52°2' **Kaw**, Fr Gu, Fr
71 S36°26' E174°54' Kawau Island, NZ
71 S38°4' E174°49' **Kawhia**, NZ
71 S35°25' E173°48' **Kawiti**, NZ
85 N13°5' W1°5' **Kaya**, Burk
58 S5°25' E102°23' **Kayaapu**, Indo
121 N59°52' W144°22' Kayak Island, US
63 N16°22' E120°53' **Kayapa**, Phil
78 N14°27' W11°26' **Kayes**, Mali
38 N38°43' E35°30' **Kayseri**, Turk
56 N9°44' E79°24' Kayts Island, Sri L
58 S3°24' E104°49' **Kayuagung**, Indo
36 N51°28' E43°56' **Kazachka**, Rus Fed
47 N47°38' E75°10' Kazakh Uplands, Kaz
46 N48°0' E62°0' **KAZAKHSTAN**
46 N45°46' E62°7' **Kazalinsk**, Kaz
38 N40°11' E32°40' **Kazan**, Turk
32 N55°46' E49°9' **Kazan'**, Rus Fed
46 N39°16' E55°32' **Kazandzhik**, Turkm
25 N42°38' E25°21' **Kazanluk**, Bulg
26 N49°43' E28°50' **Kazatin**, Ukr
39 N42°43' E44°42' **Kazbegi**, Geo
87 N5°16' E26°11' **Kazima**, CAR
46 N49°46' E48°42' **Kaztalovka**, Kaz
57 N21°56' E97°50' **Ke-hsi Mansam**, Myanmar
25 N37°38' E24°21' **Kéa**, Grc
108 N40°42' W99°5' **Kearney**, NE, US
84 N15°22' W16°27' **Kébèmer**, Sen
29 N67°55' E18°31' Kebnekaise, Swe
22 N46°55' E19°41' **Kecskemét**, Hun
39 N40°34' E45°49' **Kedabek**, Azer
78 N22°39' W12°35' Kediet ej Jill, Mrta
84 N12°33' W12°11' **Kédougou**, Sen
21 N50°20' E18°12' **Kedzierzyn-Kozle**, Pol
111 N42°56' W72°17' **Keene**, NH, US
90 S26°36' E18°8' **Keetmanshoop**, Nam
86 N8°51' E7°52' **Keffi**, Nga
99 N57°48' W117°52' **Keg River**, AB, Can
56 N7°15' E80°21' **Kegalla**, Sri L
105 N50°12' W61°17' **Kegaska**, QC, Can
69 S36°6' E140°21' **Keith**, SA, Austl
22 N47°52' E20°1' Kékes, Hun
116 N41°34' W82°40' Kelleys Island, US
59 N1°8' E117°54' **Kelolokan**, Indo
29 N68°31' E22°4' **Kelottijarvi**, Fin
99 N49°53' W119°29' **Kelowna**, BC, Can
58 N2°2' E103°19' **Keluang**, Malay
34 N64°57' E34°34' **Kem**, Rus Fed
39 N39°36' E39°2' **Kemah**, Turk
98 N53°34' W127°56' **Kemano**, BC, Can
87 N4°36' E21°54' **Kembé**, CAR
38 N36°38' E29°21' **Kemer**, Turk
32 N55°20' E86°5' **Kemerovo**, Rus Fed
29 N65°49' E24°32' **Kemi**, Fin
107 N41°47' W110°32' **Kemmerer**, WY, US
127 N24°2' W77°33' **Kemps Bay**, Bah
69 S31°5' E152°50' **Kempsey**, NSW, Austl
19 N47°43' E10°19' **Kempten**, Ger
121 N60°33' W151°16' **Kenai**, AK, US
117 N34°58' W77°58' **Kenansville**, NC, US
59 S3°58' E122°35' **Kendari**, Indo
55 N20°30' E86°25' **Kendraparha**, Ind
84 N7°53' W11°11' **Kenema**, SL
57 N21°17' E99°36' **Keng Tung**, Myanmar
88 S4°52' E16°59' **Kenge**, DRC
111 N44°15' W69°43' *Kennebec River*, US
106 N46°13' W119°8' **Kennewick**, WA, US
96 N63°55' W135°18' **Keno Hill**, YT, Can
104 N48°26' W71°14' **Kenogami**, QC, Can
102 N49°47' W94°29' **Kenora**, ON, Can
109 N42°35' W87°49' **Kenosha**, WI, US
69 S39°29' E147°31' Kent Group, Austl
96 N68°5' W108°42' Kent Peninsula, Can
116 N40°46' W87°27' **Kentland**, IN, US
116 N37°23' W85°34' **Kentucky**, US
116 N36°41' W88°37' *Kentucky Lake*, US
82 N1°49' E35°41' **KENYA**
109 N40°24' W91°23' **Keokuk**, IA, US
55 N21°38' E85°35' **Keonjhargarh**, Ind
60 S6°32' E139°19' **Kepi**, Indo
60 S2°0' E127°27' Kepulauan Abi, Ind
58 N2°47' E106°17' Kepulauan Anambas, Indo
60 S6°27' E133°54' Kepulauan Aru, Indo
60 S7°29' E129°22' Kepulauan Baloar, Indo
59 S2°10' E122°47' Kepulauan Banggai, Indo
58 N1°50' E96°16' Kepulauan Banyak, Indo
60 S7°35' E126°4' Kepulauan Barat Daya, Indo
58 S0°19' E97°20' Kepulauan Batu, Indo
60 S4°4' E130°32' Kepulauan Gorong, Indo
60 S6°11' E132°16' Kepulauan Kai, Indo
60 S3°58' E128°2' Kepulauan Leasi, Indo
60 S8°2' E127°31' Kepulauan Leti, Indo
58 S1°40' E98°26' Kepulauan Mentawai, Indo
60 N4°51' E126°35' Kepulauan Nanusa, Indo
58 N4°3' E107°2' Kepulauan Natuna Besar, Indo
59 N2°51' E109°7' Kepulauan Natuna Selatan, Indo
60 N2°20' E125°14' Kepulauan Sangihe, Ind
60 S8°25' E128°40' Kepulauan Sermata, Indo
60 S2°22' E124°51' Kepulauan Sula, Ind
60 N4°15' E126°57' Kepulauan Taland, Ind
60 S7°29' E130°42' Kepulauan Tanimbar, Indo
60 S5°12' E131°19' Kepulauan Tayandu, Indo
60 S4°34' E130°58' Kepulauan Watubela, Indo
61 S4°19' E152°1' **Keravat**, PNG
27 N45°22' E36°27' **Kerch**, Ukr
35 N59°8' E64°46' **Kerchel'**, Rus Fed
35 N59°55' E56°17' **Kerchevskiy**, Rus Fed
35 N61°28' E53°50' **Kerchom-ya**, Rus Fed
84 N13°31' W16°6' **Kerewan**, Gam
24 N37°40' E20°49' **Kerion**, Grc
35 N63°43' E54°5' **Kerki**, Rus Fed
44 N30°17' E57°4' **Kerman**, Iran
114 N31°52' W103°5' **Kermit**, TX, US
84 N9°16' W9°1' **Kérouané**, Gui
114 N30°4' W99°8' **Kerrville**, TX, US
99 N52°49' W122°25' **Kersley**, BC, Can
59 S0°23' E109°9' **Kertamulia**, Indo
34 N58°27' E37°4' **Kes'ma**, Rus Fed
103 N50°23' W81°3' *Kesagami Lake*, Can
38 N40°51' E26°37' **Kesan**, Turk
22 N46°45' E17°15' **Keszthely**, Hun
59 S6°55' E113°16' **Ketapang**, Indo
59 S1°52' E109°59' **Ketapang**, Indo
58 S3°22' E101°50' **Ketaun**, Indo
121 N55°22' W131°39' **Ketchikan**, AK, US
45 N24°8' E67°27' **Keti Bandar**, Pak
109 N41°14' W89°55' **Kewanee**, IL, US
119 N25°8' W80°25' **Key Largo**, FL, US
119 N24°34' W81°46' **Key West**, FL, US
119 N24°43' W81°55' Key West, US
117 N39°26' W78°58' **Keyser**, WV, US
35 N57°53' E53°43' **Kez**, Rus Fed
21 N49°8' E20°24' **Kezmarok**, Slvk
33 N48°29' E135°4' **Khabarovsk**, Rus Fed
55 N25°30' E86°29' **Khagaria**, Ind
45 N27°32' E68°46' **Khairpur**, Pak
54 N34°20' E76°49' **Khalatse**, Ind
43 N19°37' E58°7' *Khalij Masirah*
24 N38°27' E23°37' **Khalki**, Grc
54 N17°15' E80°9' **Khammam**, Ind
44 N34°21' E45°22' **Khanaqin**, Iraq
45 N30°18' E71°56' **Khanewal**, Pak
45 N28°22' E71°43' **Khangarh**, Pak
32 N60°53' E69°7' **Khanty-Mansiysk**, Rus Fed
45 N35°10' E76°20' **Khapalu**, Pak
45 N32°49' E73°52' **Kharian**, Pak
27 N50°2' E36°14' **Kharkiv**, Ukr
82 N15°35' E32°39' **Khartoum**, Sud
36 N43°16' E46°37' **Khasavyurt**, Rus Fed
45 N28°14' E61°14' **Khash**, Iran
25 N41°56' E25°34' **Khaskovo**, Bulg
26 N54°28' E27°33' **Khatyr'**, Bela
54 N23°51' E69°43' **Khavda**, Ind
42 N25°42' E39°31' **Khaybar**, Sau Ar
54 N17°43' E73°23' **Khed**, Ind
57 N16°3' E105°13' **Khemarat**, Laos
26 N46°38' E32°35' **Kherson**, Ukr
54 N23°59' E73°35' **Kherwara**, Ind
54 N24°2' E76°34' **Khilchipur**, Ind
46 N41°24' E60°22' **Khiva**, Uzb
26 N49°25' E27°0' **Khmel'nitskiy**, Ukr
82 N6°8' E27°47' **Khogali**, Sud
57 N16°26' E102°50' **Khon Kaen**, Thai
25 N35°12' E24°9' **Khóra Sfakíon**, Grc
90 S20°23' E14°59' **Khorixas**, Nam
47 N37°30' E71°35' **Khorog**, Taj
44 N33°29' E48°21' **Khorramabad**, Iran
26 N48°29' E26°30' **Khotin**, Ukr
47 N47°33' E81°53' Khrebet Tarbagatay, Kaz
55 N22°49' E89°34' **Khulna**, Bngl
45 N34°33' E60°8' **Khvaf**, Iran
44 N33°47' E55°3' **Khvor**, Iran
44 N28°40' E51°22' **Khvormuj**, Iran
44 N38°33' E44°58' **Khvoy**, Iran
63 N5°59' E124°40' **Kiamba**, Phil
92 S17°58' E47°2' **Kiangara**, Madag
88 S4°53' E26°33' **Kibamba**, DRC
63 N7°34' E125°0' **Kibawe**, Phil
89 S5°23' E37°26' **Kiberashi**, Tanz
89 S7°44' E38°57' **Kibiti**, Tanz
24 N41°31' E20°57' **Kicevo**, FYRM
79 N18°26' E1°24' **Kidal**, Mali
63 N7°1' E125°5' **Kidapawan**, Phil
84 N14°28' W12°13' **Kidira**, Sen
19 N54°20' E10°7' **Kiel**, Ger
21 N50°52' E20°37' **Kielce**, Pol
19 N54°41' E10°9' *Kieler Bucht*
61 S6°13' E155°37' **Kieta**, PNG
26 N50°31' E30°35' **Kiev**, Ukr
78 N16°37' W11°24' **Kiffa**, Mrta
89 S1°52' E30°2' **Kigali**, Rwn
39 N39°19' E40°21' **Kigi**, Turk
89 S4°53' E29°37' **Kigoma**, Tanz
120 N20°47' W156°28' **Kihei**, HI, US
29 N62°12' E23°11' **Kihniö**, Fin
22 N45°50' E20°28' **Kikinda**, Yugo
35 N57°19' E47°14' **Kiknur**, Rus Fed
61 S7°25' E144°15' **Kikori**, PNG
61 S7°1' E143°34' *Kikori River*, PNG
35 N57°1' E51°22' **Kil'mez'**, Rus Fed
10 N56°42' W6°6' **Kilchoan**, UK
52 N40°58' E129°20' **Kilchu**, N Kor
115 N32°23' W94°53' **Kilgore**, TX, US
89 S3°4' E37°22' Kilimanjaro, Tanz
38 N36°44' E37°5' **Kilis**, Turk
10 N52°39' W7°15' **Kilkenny**, Ire
10 N53°19' W9°44' **Kilkieran**, Ire
24 N41°0' E22°53' **Kilkís**, Grc
101 N49°12' W99°42' **Killarney**, MB, Can
115 N31°7' W97°44' **Killeen**, TX, US
24 N37°55' E21°9' **Killíni**, Grc
89 S8°57' E39°28' **Kilwa Kisiwani**, Tanz
108 N41°14' W103°40' **Kimball**, NE, US
90 S28°44' E24°45' **Kimberley**, S Afr
99 N49°41' W115°59' **Kimberley**, BC, Can
52 N40°41' E129°12' **Kimch'aek**, N Kor
98 N52°49' W126°58' **Kimsquit**, BC, Can
98 N54°58' W129°46' **Kincolith**, BC, Can
100 N51°27' W109°10' **Kindersley**, SK, Can
84 N10°4' W12°51' **Kindia**, Gui
88 S2°57' E25°56' **Kindu**, DRC
112 N36°13' W121°10' **King City**, CA, US
97 N57°56' W79°30' King George Islands, Can
98 N52°4' W127°46' King Island, Can
69 S39°57' E142°45' King Island, Austl
66 S16°41' E124°7' King Leopold Range, Austl
66 S16°14' E123°13' *King Sound*, Austl
96 N68°58' W98°49' King William Island, Can
111 N44°58' W70°10' **Kingfield**, ME, US
115 N35°52' W97°56' **Kingfisher**, OK, US
112 N35°11' W114°3' **Kingman**, AZ, US
73 N7°14' W166°56' **Kingman Reef**, US
45 N30°27' E69°49' **Kingri**, Pak
11 N52°45' E0°24' **Kings Lynn**, UK
113 N40°47' W110°23' Kings Peak, US
116 N36°33' W82°34' **Kingsport**, TN, US
110 N41°56' W74°0' **Kingston**, NY, US
127 N17°59' W76°47' **Kingston**, Jam
70 S29°3' E167°58' **Kingston**, Nor I, Austl
70 S45°20' E168°42' **Kingston**, NZ
103 N44°14' W76°29' **Kingston**, ON, Can
129 N13°9' W61°14' **Kingstown**, St VG
115 N27°35' W97°48' **Kingsville**, TX, US
129 N16°41' W62°12' **Kinsale**, Monts, UK
88 S4°19' E15°19' **Kinshasa**, DRC
117 N35°16' W77°35' **Kinston**, NC, US
99 N55°20' W115°25' **Kinuso**, AB, Can
82 N3°56' E32°55' Kinyeti, Sud
89 S7°39' E33°24' **Kipembawe**, Tanz
74 S10°27' E161°55' **Kirakira**, Sol Is
38 N40°2' E26°41' **Kirazli**, Turk
46 N48°58' E59°37' Kirgiz Steppe, Kaz
88 S1°27' E19°0' **Kiri**, DRC
73 S6°22' W166°11' **KIRIBATI**
34 N59°52' E38°23' **Kirillov**, Rus Fed
89 S2°34' E30°8' **Kirindo**, Buru
73 N1°47' W157°9' Kiritimati Island, Kir
54 N18°30' E73°57' **Kirkee**, Ind
29 N69°40' E30°3' **Kirkenes**, Nor
103 N48°9' W80°2' **Kirkland Lake**, ON, Can
38 N41°44' E27°12' **Kirklareli**, Turk
109 N40°12' W92°35' **Kirksville**, MO, US
44 N35°28' E44°28' **Kirkuk**, Iraq
11 N58°59' W3°0' **Kirkwall**, UK
35 N58°38' E49°42' **Kirov**, Rus Fed
35 N57°26' E60°4' **Kirovgrad**, Rus Fed
35 N55°33' E63°46' **Kirovo**, Rus Fed
26 N48°31' E32°16' **Kirovograd**, Ukr
34 N67°35' E33°23' **Kirovsk**, Rus Fed
35 N59°21' E52°14' **Kirs**, Rus Fed
36 N52°38' E42°43' **Kirsanov**, Rus Fed
38 N39°9' E34°10' **Kirsehir**, Turk
29 N67°51' E20°16' **Kiruna**, Swe
88 S0°44' E25°32' **Kirundu**, DRC
36 N56°9' E38°52' **Kirzhach**, Rus Fed
53 N39°13' E139°54' **Kisakata**, Jap
89 S7°28' E37°36' **Kisaki**, Tanz
88 N0°32' E25°11' **Kisangani**, DRC
58 N2°59' E99°37' **Kisaran**, Indo
55 N26°7' E87°56' **Kishanganj**, Ind
54 N26°34' E74°52' **Kishangarh**, Ind
86 N9°5' E3°52' **Kishi**, Nga
23 N47°1' E28°50' **Kishinev**, Mol
89 S7°24' E39°18' **Kisiju**, Tanz
120 N51°58' E176°31' Kiska Island, US
22 N47°25' E20°7' *Kisköeiviztároló*, Hun
83 S0°21' E42°32' **Kismaayo**, Som
84 N9°11' W10°6' **Kissidougou**, Gui
119 N28°17' W81°25' **Kissimmee**, FL, US
101 N55°23' W101°35' *Kississing Lake*, Can
82 S0°6' E34°45' **Kisumu**, Ken
78 N13°3' W9°29' **Kita**, Mali
53 N26°2' E130°29' Kita-daito-jima, Jap
53 N37°39' E139°52' **Kitakata**, Jap
52 N33°53' E130°50' **Kitakyushu**, Jap
53 N43°48' E143°54' **Kitami**, Jap
53 N45°1' E142°5' Kitami Sanchi, Jap
82 N3°18' E32°53' **Kitgum**, Ug
45 N27°47' E66°55' Kithar Range, Pak
24 N36°9' E23°0' **Kíthira**, Grc
25 N37°26' E24°26' **Kíthnos**, Grc
98 N54°3' W128°33' **Kitimat**, BC, Can
111 N43°5' W70°45' **Kittery**, ME, US
29 N67°40' E24°54' **Kittilä**, Fin
89 S6°48' E33°13' **Kitunda**, Tanz
20 N47°20' E12°9' Kitzbüheler Alpen, Aus
19 N49°44' E10°9' **Kitzingen**, Ger
61 S6°10' E141°15' **Kiunga**, PNG
61 S8°42' E143°40' Kiwai Island, PNG
35 N59°3' E57°40' **Kizel**, Rus Fed
37 N52°44' E58°54' **Kizil'skoye**, Rus Fed
38 N40°28' E32°39' **Kizilcahamam**, Turk
39 N37°12' E40°36' **Kiziltepe**, Turk
36 N43°50' E46°40' **Kizlyar**, Rus Fed
20 N50°8' E14°5' **Kladno**, Czech
20 N46°37' E14°18' **Klagenfurt**, Aus
106 N42°38' W121°55' **Klamath Agency**, OR, US
106 N42°13' W121°47' **Klamath Falls**, OR, US
60 S1°8' E131°30' **Klamono**, Indo
20 N49°24' E13°18' **Klatovy**, Czech
90 S31°44' E18°36' **Klawer**, S Afr
98 N52°35' W128°34' **Klemtu**, BC, Can
34 N56°20' E36°44' **Klin**, Rus Fed
36 N52°46' E32°14' **Klintsy**, Rus Fed
21 N50°27' E16°39' **Klodzko**, Pol
21 N50°59' E18°13' **Kluczbork**, Pol
25 N43°30' E24°5' **Knezha**, Bulg
22 N44°2' E16°12' **Knin**, Cro
23 N43°33' E22°16' **Knjazevac**, Yugo
116 N35°58' W83°55' **Knoxville**, TN, US
57 N12°1' E101°34' Ko Chang, Thai
57 N11°35' E102°1' Ko Kut, Thai
58 S2°29' E106°23' **Koba**, Indo
39 N42°33' E44°32' **Kobi**, Geo
34 N58°49' E35°1' **Kobozha**, Rus Fed
26 N52°13' E24°21' **Kobryn**, Bela
39 N41°50' E41°47' **Kobuleti**, Geo
24 N41°55' E22°25' **Kocani**, FYRM
55 N26°19' E89°26' **Koch Bihar**, Ind
52 N33°33' E133°32' **Kochi**, Jap
21 N51°39' E22°27' **Kock**, Pol
121 N57°48' W152°26' **Kodiak**, AK, US
121 N57°4' W152°50' Kodiak Island, US
54 N20°47' E70°42' **Kodinar**, Ind
34 N63°43' E39°41' **Kodino**, Rus Fed
26 N48°7' E29°7' **Kodyma**, Ukr
90 S25°59' E19°8' **Koës**, Nam
85 N6°3' W0°17' **Koforidua**, Gha
53 N35°40' E138°35' **Kofu**, Jap
52 N34°19' E127°8' Kogum-do, S Kor
120 N20°12' W155°44' Kohala Mountains, US
55 N25°40' E94°7' **Kohima**, Ind
96 N61°58' W140°25' **Koidern**, YT, Can
52 N34°46' E128°45' Koje-do, S Kor
68 S33°50' E117°9' **Kojonup**, WA, Austl
47 N41°4' E77°6' Kök Shal Tau Mountain Range, Kyr
60 S2°44' E132°26' **Kokas**, Indo
47 N53°17' E69°25' **Kokchetav**, Kaz
29 N61°15' E22°21' **Kokemäki**, Fin
82 N20°0' E30°35' **Kokka**, Sud
116 N40°29' W86°8' **Kokomo**, IN, US
47 N48°45' E82°24' **Kokpekty**, Kaz
52 N38°46' E126°40' **Koksan-up**, N Kor
36 N48°12' E40°39' **Koksovyy**, Rus Fed
34 N67°7' E37°34' Kola Peninsula, Rus Fed
59 S4°4' E121°38' **Kolaka**, Indo
56 N13°8' E78°8' **Kolar**, Ind
29 N67°20' E23°48' **Kolari**, Swe
22 N42°49' E19°31' **Kolasin**, Yugo
54 N27°50' E72°57' **Kolayat**, Ind
59 S10°2' E124°31' **Kolbano**, Indo
84 N12°53' W14°57' **Kolda**, Sen
35 N69°40' E49°30' Kolguyer Island, Rus Fed
55 N22°35' E88°23' **Kolkata**, Ind
18 N50°56' E6°58' **Köln**, Ger
20 N54°11' E15°34' **Kolobrzeg**, Pol
35 N58°51' E44°17' **Kologriv**, Rus Fed
74 S7°47' E157°8' Kolombangara Island, Sol Is
34 N55°5' E38°49' **Kolomna**, Rus Fed
75 S21°8' W175°4' **Kolonga**, Ton
59 S4°18' E122°41' **Kolono**, Indo
37 N56°28' E73°36' **Kolosovka**, Rus Fed
46 N50°36' E51°6' **Kolovertnoye**, Kaz
32 N58°20' E82°50' **Kolpashevo**, Rus Fed
56 N1°58' E72°28' Kolumadulu Atoll, Mald
33 N67°39' E153°21' *Kolyma*, Rus Fed
33 N61°19' E153°12' Kolyma Upland, Rus Fed
33 N57°17' E164°8' Komandorskiye Ostrova, Rus Fed
21 N47°45' E18°9' **Komárom**, Slvk
85 N12°4' W1°20' **Kombissiri**, Burk
22 N46°12' E18°16' **Komló**, Hun
47 N38°56' E72°1' Kommunizma Peak, Taj
85 N7°50' W3°48' *Komoé*, Côte d'Ivoire
86 S3°15' E13°14' **Komono**, Con
25 N41°8' E25°25' **Komotine**, Grc
52 N42°8' E129°41' **Komusan-nodongjagu**, N Kor
35 N61°20' E63°58' **Konda**, Rus Fed
55 N19°36' E81°40' **Kondagaon**, Ind
68 S32°30' E118°16' **Kondinin**, WA, Austl
89 S4°54' E35°47' **Kondoa**, Tanz
36 N52°49' E45°3' **Kondol'**, Rus Fed
34 N62°12' E34°19' **Kondopoga**, Rus Fed
84 N11°55' W8°50' **Konfara**, Gui
85 N9°9' W4°37' **Kong**, Côte d'Ivoire
85 N13°19' W1°32' **Kongoussi**, Burk
48 N38°37' E75°19' Kongur, China
89 S6°12' E36°25' **Kongwa**, Tanz
21 N52°13' E18°16' **Konin**, Pol
24 N39°39' E20°10' **Konispol**, Grc
24 N40°2' E20°45' **Kónitsa**, Grc
86 N10°24' E5°28' **Kontagora**, Nga
86 N7°58' E12°14' **Kontcha**, Cam
29 N64°21' E28°9' **Kontiomäki**, Fin
38 N37°52' E32°31' **Konya**, Turk
47 N44°16' E79°19' **Konyrolen**, Kaz
68 S29°20' E121°29' **Kookynie**, WA, Austl
36 N47°27' E46°48' **Kopanovka**, Rus Fed
22 N45°35' E13°46' **Koper**, Slov
46 N38°16' E57°15' Kopet Mountains, Turkm
37 N55°7' E61°37' **Kopeysk**, Rus Fed
56 N15°21' E76°9' **Koppal**, Ind
22 N46°10' E16°50' **Koprivnica**, Cro
24 N40°37' E20°47' **Korçë**, Alb
49 N39°2' E123°21' *Korea Bay*
52 N34°16' E128°47' *Korea Strait*
142 S75°0' W70°0' Korff Ice Rise, Ant, Disputed
85 N9°27' W5°38' **Korhogo**, Côte d'Ivoire
24 N37°56' E22°56' **Kórinthos**, Grc
53 N37°24' E140°23' **Koriyama**, Jap
35 N54°54' E61°23' **Korkino**, Rus Fed
38 N37°4' E30°13' **Korkuteli**, Turk
48 N41°44' E86°9' **Korla**, China
85 N8°34' W7°28' **Koro**, Côte d'Ivoire
74 S17°22' E179°11' Koro Island, Fiji
74 S17°30' E179°33' *Koro Sea*
74 S18°13' E177°44' **Korolevu**, Fiji
63 N6°30' E124°51' **Koronadal**, Phil
72 N7°20' E134°29' **Koror**, US
26 N50°57' E28°39' **Korosten'**, Ukr
18 N50°50' E3°16' **Kortrijk**, Belg
33 N61°10' E165°59' Koryakskoye Nagor'ye, Rus Fed
35 N59°56' E54°55' **Kosa**, Rus Fed
53 N40°20' E140°44' **Kosaka**, Jap
21 N54°8' E18°0' **Koscierzyna**, Pol
82 N20°49' E30°32' **Kosha**, Sud
21 N48°43' E21°15' **Kosice**, Slvk
46 N49°31' E67°5' **Koskol'**, Kaz
35 N63°28' E48°52' **Koslan**, Rus Fed
22 N45°14' E16°33' **Kostajnica**, Cro
34 N64°36' E30°35' **Kostomuksa**, Rus Fed
34 N57°46' E40°58' **Kostroma**, Rus Fed
26 N53°20' E32°3' **Kostyukovichi**, Bela
21 N54°12' E16°9' **Koszalin**, Pol
22 N47°23' E16°33' **Koszeg**, Hun
58 N6°7' E102°14' **Kota Baharu**, Malay
59 N5°55' E116°4' **Kota Kinabalu**, Malay
58 S5°30' E104°38' **Kotaagung**, Indo
58 S1°8' E101°43' **Kotabaru**, Indo
59 S3°15' E116°15' **Kotabaru**, Indo
25 N42°53' E26°27' **Kotel**, Bulg
35 N61°16' E46°35' **Kotlas**, Rus Fed
23 N46°49' E28°34' **Kotovsk**, Mol

continue on next page

49 N33°56' E106°12' Liangdang, China
50 N24°51' E98°25' Lianghe, China
49 N29°14' E108°40' Lianghekou, China
49 N33°42' E104°25' Lianghekou, China
49 N42°38' E128°5' Liangjiang, China
49 N37°58' E102°49' Liangzhou, China
49 N34°43' E119°25' Lianyungang, China
50 N21°39' E109°11' Lianzhou, China
52 N39°23' E120°4' *Liaodong Gulf*
49 N39°32' E120°17' *Liaodong Wan*
49 N42°54' E125°8' Liaoyuan, China
106 N48°23' W115°34' Libby, MT, US
108 N37°2' W100°55' Liberal, KS, US
20 N50°46' E15°3' Liberec, Czech
84 N6°43' W10°22' LIBERIA
124 N10°38' W85°29' Liberia, CR
24 N41°10' E20°23' Librazhd, Alb
86 N0°23' E9°30' Libreville, Gabon
80 N27°20' E15°27' LIBYA
81 N27°39' E22°46' Libyan Desert, Libya
39 N38°28' E40°39' Lice, Turk
91 S13°18' E35°14' Lichinga, Moz
19 N50°8' E11°4' Lichtenfels, Ger
50 N30°18' E108°51' Lichuan, China
26 N53°53' E25°18' Lida, Bela
15 N47°14' E9°43' LIECHTENSTEIN
18 N50°37' E5°34' Liège, Belg
20 N46°50' E12°47' Lienz, Aus
26 N56°32' E21°2' Liepaja, Lat
15 N50°25' E2°46' Liévin, Fr
10 N54°52' W7°28' Lifford, Ire
75 S19°49' W174°37' Lifuka Island, Ton
16 N43°45' E8°27' *Ligurian Sea*
61 S3°7' E152°43' Lihir Group, PNG
72 N10°35' E169°11' Likiep Atoll, Mar Is
14 N50°38' E3°4' Lille, Fr
29 N61°7' E10°29' Lillehammer, Nor
99 N50°42' W121°56' Lillooet, BC, Can
140 S26°56' W62°58' Lilo Viejo, Arg
89 S13°59' E33°44' Lilongwe, Malw
134 S12°10' W77°0' Lima, Peru
116 N40°44' W84°4' Lima, OH, US
139 S21°51' W43°48' Lima Duarte, MG, Braz
36 N45°47' E47°14' Liman, Rus Fed
26 N46°38' E30°0' Limanskoye, Ukr
56 N0°12' E104°32' Limas, Indo
38 N34°40' E33°2' Limassol, Cyp
139 S22°34' W47°24' Limeira, SP, Braz
10 N52°40' W8°38' Limerick, Ire
111 N46°55' W67°50' Limestone, ME, US
29 N64°49' E25°24' Liminka, Fin
67 S14°42' E135°53' *Limmen Bight*, Austl
15 N45°50' E1°15' Limoges, Fr
124 N15°52' W85°33' Limón, Hon
14 N43°4' E2°14' Limoux, Fr
91 S23°18' E28°1' *Limpopo River*, S Afr
49 N30°14' E119°43' Lin'an, China
42 N28°42' E43°48' Linah, Sau Ar
63 N11°25' E119°53' Linapacan Island, Phil
12 N38°5' W3°38' Linares, Sp
123 N24°52' W99°34' Linares, NL, Mex
49 N27°56' E116°14' Linchuan, China
11 N53°14' W0°33' Lincoln, UK
108 N40°49' W96°41' Lincoln, NE, US
111 N45°23' W68°29' Lincoln, ME, US
62 N16°43' E112°43' Lincoln Island, Para Is, Disputed
97 N83°43' W73°31' *Lincoln Sea*
19 N47°34' E9°42' Lindau, Ger
115 N33°1' W94°22' Linden, TX, US
118 N32°19' W87°48' Linden, AL, US
116 N35°37' W87°50' Linden, TN, US
89 S9°59' E39°43' Lindi, Tanz
73 N0°26' W155°41' Line Islands, Kir
63 N16°2' E120°8' Lingayen, Phil
29 N61°3' E16°41' Lingbo, Swe
49 N39°24' E114°13' Lingqiu, China
84 N15°24' W15°7' Linguère, Sen
49 N41°15' E119°16' Lingyuan, China
49 N40°44' E107°26' Linhe, China
29 N58°25' E15°33' Linköping, Swe
51 N34°11' E112°49' Linru, China
139 S21°40' W49°45' Lins, SP, Braz
49 N34°37' E103°40' Lintan, China
49 N43°30' E118°0' Linxi, China
49 N35°35' E103°13' Linxia, China
20 N48°18' E14°18' Linz, Aus
59 N3°10' E115°14' Lio Matoh, Malay
103 N44°59' W81°15' Lions Head, ON, Can
87 N1°2' E15°43' Liouesso, Con
26 N55°2' E30°48' Liozno, Bela
63 N13°57' E121°10' Lipa, Phil
36 N52°37' E39°35' Lipetsk, Rus Fed
50 N26°16' E109°7' Liping, China
23 N48°16' E26°48' Lipkany, Mol
22 N46°5' E21°40' Lipova, Rom
82 N2°15' E32°54' Lira, Ug
87 S0°40' E17°35' Liranga, Con
134 S12°56' W74°43' Lircay, Peru
13 N39°38' W0°36' Liria, Sp
12 N38°43' W9°11' Lisboa, Port
108 N46°26' W97°41' Lisbon, ND, US
12 N38°43' W9°11' Lisbon, Port
14 N49°9' E0°14' Lisieux, Fr
22 N43°23' E17°36' Listica, Bos & Herz
48 N30°0' E100°16' Litang, China
26 N55°16' E22°28' LITHUANIA
26 N49°20' E28°5' Litin, Ukr
24 N40°6' E22°30' Litókhoron, Grc
127 N27°2' W77°49' Little Abaco Island, Bah
126 N19°43' W80°33' Little Cayman, Cay Is, UK
103 N45°58' W81°56' Little Current, ON, Can
127 N21°31' W73°32' Little Inagua Island, Bah
115 N34°46' W92°19' Little Rock, AR, US
120 N51°49' E178°40' Little Sitkin Island, US
110 N42°15' W78°49' Little Valley, NY, US
114 N33°55' W102°19' Littlefield, TX, US
50 N24°32' E109°21' Liucheng, China
50 N24°19' E109°22' Liuzhou, China
51 N33°10' E120°19' Liuzhuang, China
56 N52°6' E61°59' Livanovka, Kaz
119 N30°17' W82°59' Live Oak, FL, US
141 S52°8' W58°22' Lively Island, Falk Is, UK
66 S18°3' E124°10' Liveringa, WA, Austl
111 N44°28' W70°12' Livermore Falls, ME, US
11 N53°25' W2°55' Liverpool, UK
105 N44°2' W64°43' Liverpool, NS, Can
107 N45°38' W110°34' Livingston, MT, US
115 N30°43' W94°56' Livingston, TX, US
124 N15°50' W88°45' Livingston, Guat
142 S60°0' W60°0' Livingston Island, Ant, Disputed
88 S17°52' E25°52' Livingstone, Zam
89 S10°36' E34°7' Livingstonia, Malw
16 N43°33' E10°19' Livorno, It
89 S9°46' E37°56' Liwale, Tanz
24 N38°12' E20°26' Lixoúrion, Grc
10 N49°59' W5°12' Lizard, UK
137 S9°47' W46°29' Lizarda, GO, Braz
50 N28°8' E102°10' Lizhou, China
22 N42°57' E18°5' Ljubinje, Bos & Herz
22 N46°4' E14°32' Ljubljana, Slov
29 N57°19' E18°42' Ljugarn, Swe
11 N52°15' W3°23' Llandrindod Wells, UK
12 N43°25' W4°45' Llanes, Sp
13 N42°22' E3°9' Llansá, Sp
123 N23°19' W99°1' Llera de Canales, Tamps, Mex
135 S19°49' W68°16' Llica, Bol
100 N53°17' W109°59' Lloydminster, SK, Can
13 N39°29' E2°54' Lluchmayor, Sp
138 S22°54' W53°10' Loanda, PR, Braz
90 S25°11' E25°40' Lobatse, Bots
60 S3°45' E134°5' Lobo, Indo
140 S35°11' W59°6' Lobos, Arg
35 N59°12' E60°30' Lobva, Rus Fed
57 N11°51' E106°36' Loc Ninh, Viet
10 N57°10' W7°20' Lochboisdale, UK
110 N43°10' W78°41' Lockport, NY, US
135 S17°36' W70°46' Locumba, Peru
14 N43°43' E3°19' Lodève, Fr
45 N29°32' E71°38' Lodhran, Pak
82 N3°7' E35°36' Lodwar, Ken
21 N51°46' E19°28' Lódz, Pol
75 S19°46' W174°16' Lofanga Island, Ton
29 N68°9' E12°58' Lofoten, Nor
36 N49°29' E43°52' Log, Rus Fed
112 N41°44' W111°50' Logan, UT, US
116 N39°32' W82°25' Logan, OH, US
116 N40°45' W86°22' Logansport, IN, US
87 N11°47' E15°6' Logone Birni, Cam
80 N9°34' E15°49' *Logone River*, Chad
87 N11°11' E14°52' *Logone River*, Cam
13 N42°28' W2°27' Logroño, Sp
57 N21°11' E99°46' Loi Mwe, Myanmar
57 N19°41' E97°13' Loi-kaw, Myanmar
134 S4°0' W79°13' Loja, Ecu
29 N67°44' E27°17' *Lokka Reservoir*, Fin
34 N56°50' E30°9' Loknya, Rus Fed
86 N7°49' E6°44' Lokoja, Nga
88 N1°11' E22°40' Lokolenge, DRC
87 N2°41' E15°19' Lokomo, Cam
85 N6°38' E1°43' Lokossa, Ben
97 N62°23' W64°0' Loks Land, Can
29 N54°38' E10°35' Lolland, Den
61 S4°51' E150°42' Lolobau Island, PNG
24 N43°49' E23°14' Lom, Bulg
84 N9°13' W11°3' Loma Mansa, SL
84 N9°10' W10°35' Loma Mountains, SL
85 N6°7' E1°9' Lomé, Togo
88 S2°18' E23°17' Lomela, DRC
39 N41°53' E43°41' Lomis Mta, Geo
46 N52°50' E66°28' Lomonosov, Kaz
21 N53°11' E22°5' Lomza, Pol
141 S39°22' W72°38' Loncoche, Chile
141 S38°4' W70°37' Loncopué, Arg
116 N37°8' W84°5' London, KY, US
11 N51°31' W0°10' London, UK
103 N42°59' W81°14' London, ON, Can
10 N55°0' W7°17' Londonderry, UK
61 S5°11' E147°1' Long Island, PNG
67 S22°3' E149°50' Long Island, Austl
97 N54°58' W80°17' Long Island, Can
110 N40°34' W73°13' Long Island, US
127 N23°22' W75°7' Long Island, Bah
111 N41°8' W72°40' *Long Island Sound*
105 N49°45' W57°23' Long Range Mountains, Can
88 S14°42' E18°32' Longa, Ang
111 N45°13' W70°8' Longfellow Mountains, US
10 N53°44' W7°48' Longford, Ire
50 N27°8' E111°1' Longhui, China
89 S2°44' E36°41' Longido, Tanz
86 N3°5' E9°59' Longji, Cam
102 N49°47' W86°33' Longlac, ON, Can
113 N40°10' W105°6' Longmont, CO, US
51 N24°54' E114°48' Longnan, China
59 N1°54' E114°53' Longnawan, Indo
66 S23°26' E114°51' Longreach, WA, Austl
67 S23°26' E144°15' Longreach, Qld, Austl
113 N40°15' W105°37' Longs Peak, US
104 N45°36' W73°25' Longueuil, QC, Can
115 N32°30' W94°44' Longview, TX, US
56 N0°42' E116°39' Longwai, Indo
15 N49°31' E5°46' Longwy, Fr
29 N78°13' E15°40' Longyearbyen, Nor
115 N34°47' W91°54' Lonoke, AR, US
15 N46°40' E5°32' Lons-le-Saunier, Fr
68 S30°57' E127°2' Loongana, WA, Austl
57 N14°49' E100°37' Lop Buri, Thai
48 N41°3' E92°52' *Lop Nur*, China
26 N50°13' E24°50' Lopatin, Ukr
36 N43°53' E47°40' Lopatin, Rus Fed
35 N63°16' E47°56' Loptyuga, Rus Fed
45 N30°22' E68°36' Loralai, Pak
13 N37°40' W1°42' Lorca, Sp
113 N32°21' W108°43' Lordsburg, NM, US
139 S22°44' W45°8' Lorena, SP, Braz
138 S32°5' W57°55' Lorenzo Geyres, Ur
135 S15°13' W64°40' Loreto, Bol
132 S3°48' W70°15' Loreto Mocagua, Col
14 N47°45' W3°22' Lorient, Fr
68 S26°14' E121°33' Lorna Glen, WA, Austl
18 N47°37' E7°40' Lörrach, Ger
112 N34°7' W118°14' Los Angeles, CA, US
141 S37°28' W72°21' Los Ángeles, Chile
141 S46°33' W71°37' Los Antiguos, Arg
133 N8°29' W62°41' Los Barrancos, Ven
113 N34°49' W106°44' Los Lunas, NM, US
122 N25°46' W108°58' Los Mochis, Sin, Mex
140 S28°59' W63°26' Los Telares, Arg
140 S31°55' W71°31' Los Vilos, Chile
61 S8°32' E151°4' Losuia, PNG
57 N20°57' E101°25' Louang Namtha, Laos
57 N19°50' E102°10' Louangphrabang, Laos
86 S4°12' E12°39' Loubomo, Con
84 N15°37' W16°13' Louga, Sen
105 N45°56' W59°58' Louisbourg, NS, Can
119 N36°6' W78°18' Louisburg, NC, US
98 N52°55' W131°34' Louise Island, Can
61 S10°31' E152°50' Louisiade Archipelago, PNG
115 N32°10' W93°29' Louisiana, US
116 N38°15' W85°46' Louisville, KY, US
118 N33°7' W89°2' Louisville, MS, US
137 N2°30' W51°40' Lourenço, AP, Braz
69 S30°32' E145°7' Louth, NSW, Austl
24 N38°52' E23°3' Loutrá Aidhipsoú, Grc
29 N64°22' E21°18' Lövånger, Swe
25 N43°8' E24°43' Lovech, Bulg
113 N32°57' W103°21' Lovington, NM, US
34 N68°2' E35°8' Lovozero, Rus Fed
88 S1°24' E25°51' Lowa, DRC
111 N42°38' W71°19' Lowell, MA, US
98 N59°55' W128°30' Lower Post, BC, Can
108 N47°46' W95°16' *Lower Red Lake*, US
11 N52°29' E1°45' Lowestoft, UK
21 N52°7' E19°56' Lowicz, Pol
110 N43°47' W75°29' Lowville, NY, US
26 N51°56' E30°46' Loyev, Bela
22 N44°32' E19°13' Loznica, Yugo
27 N48°54' E36°20' Lozovaya, Ukr
12 N40°56' W3°37' Lozoyuela, Sp
58 S0°31' E98°28' Luaha-sibuha, Indo
88 S8°52' E13°19' Luanda, Ang
89 S14°11' E30°31' *Luangwa River*, Zam
12 N43°32' W6°32' Luarca, Sp
86 N3°28' E8°33' Luba, Eq Gui
88 S9°12' E19°16' Lubalo, Ang
63 N13°40' E119°43' Lubang Islands, Phil
88 S14°55' E13°30' Lubango, Ang
21 N51°28' E22°38' Lubartów, Pol
114 N33°35' W101°52' Lubbock, TX, US
111 N44°50' W67°0' Lubec, ME, US
19 N53°52' E10°40' Lübeck, Ger
14 N45°27' E1°24' Lubersac, Fr
21 N51°24' E16°13' Lubin, Pol
21 N51°15' E22°35' Lublin, Pol
21 N50°40' E18°41' Lubliniec, Pol
26 N50°1' E33°0' Lubny, Ukr
88 S9°57' E25°58' Lubudi, DRC
58 N0°8' E100°10' Lubuksikaping, Indo
88 S11°40' E27°28' Lubumbashi, DRC
88 S8°26' E20°44' Lucapa, Ang
63 N13°56' E121°37' Lucena, Phil
12 N37°25' W4°29' Lucena, Sp
21 N48°20' E19°40' Lucenec, Slvk
15 N47°3' E8°19' Lucerne, Switz
19 N52°5' E13°10' Luckenwalde, Ger
88 S12°32' E20°48' Lucusse, Ang
90 S26°38' E15°9' Lüderitz, Nam
54 N30°54' E75°51' Ludhiana, Ind
109 N43°58' W86°28' Ludington, MI, US
11 N52°23' W2°43' Ludlow, UK
29 N60°9' E15°11' Ludvika, Swe
26 N56°31' E27°40' Ludza, Lat
88 S9°27' E25°47' Luena, DRC
88 S11°45' E19°52' Luena, Ang
133 N5°43' W61°31' Luepa, Ven
49 N33°20' E105°10' Lüeyang, China
115 N31°21' W94°44' Lufkin, TX, US
27 N48°35' E39°20' Lugansk, Ukr
12 N43°1' W7°34' Lugo, Sp
22 N45°41' E21°54' Lugoj, Rom
35 N59°52' E60°45' Lugovaya Subbota, Rus Fed
47 N42°56' E72°45' Lugovoy, Kaz
50 N31°26' E100°48' Luhuo, China
88 S17°23' E23°3' Luiana, Ang
25 N43°12' E24°10' Lukovit, Bulg
88 S14°25' E23°12' Lukulu, Zam
29 N65°35' E22°13' Luleå, Swe
63 N14°18' E121°27' Lumban, Phil
117 N34°37' W79°0' Lumberton, NC, US
12 N40°56' W6°43' Lumbrales, Sp
55 N25°45' E93°10' Lumding, Ind
57 N13°29' E107°0' Lumphat, Camb
70 S45°44' E168°27' Lumsden, NZ
49 N47°24' E102°52' Lün, Mong
49 N47°52' E105°5' Lün, Mong
54 N23°8' E73°57' Lunavada, Ind
105 N44°23' W64°20' Lunenburg, NS, Can
117 N36°58' W78°16' Lunenburg, VA, US
15 N48°35' E6°31' Lunéville, Fr
48 N31°1' E83°59' Lunggar, China
55 N22°53' E92°44' Lunglei, Ind
50 N22°47' E111°31' Luoding, China
50 N24°59' E104°2' Luoping, China
49 N34°40' E112°26' Luoyang, China
50 N26°36' E104°58' Lupanshui Shi, China
88 S14°36' E19°29' Lupire, Ang
63 N6°53' E126°2' Lupon, Phil
91 S14°5' E38°41' *Lúrio*, Moz
89 S15°25' E28°20' Lusaka, Zam
88 S4°58' E23°27' Lusambo, DRC
50 N34°5' E111°1' Lushi, China
24 N40°56' E19°42' Lushnjë, Alb
107 N42°46' W104°27' Lusk, WY, US
88 S13°26' E21°16' Lutembo, Ang
19 N51°52' E12°39' Lutherstadt Wittenberg, Ger
74 S7°14' E156°59' Luti, Sol Is
26 N50°44' E25°19' Luts'k, Ukr
59 S0°56' E122°47' Luwuk, Indo
18 N49°43' E5°56' LUXEMBOURG
18 N49°36' E6°5' Luxembourg, Lux
81 N25°41' E32°38' Luxor, Egypt
35 N60°39' E47°10' Luza, Rus Fed
15 N47°3' E8°19' Luzern, Switz
63 N16°50' E121°11' Luzon, Phil
11 N58°19' W3°14' Lybster, UK
29 N64°36' E18°40' Lycksele, Swe
98 N52°40' W131°25' Lyell Island, Can
117 N37°25' W79°8' Lynchburg, VA, US
66 S23°37' E115°15' Lyndon, WA, Austl
29 N69°34' E20°10' Lyngseidet, Nor
101 N56°51' W101°3' Lynn Lake, MB, Can
15 N45°46' E4°51' Lyon, Fr
110 N43°4' W76°59' Lyons, NY, US
35 N58°7' E57°47' Lys'va, Rus Fed
35 N56°4' E45°2' Lyskovo, Rus Fed
34 N59°21' E31°13' Lyuban', Rus Fed
26 N51°46' E25°31' Lyubeshov, Ukr
36 N53°31' E34°23' Lyubokhna, Rus Fed
26 N51°14' E24°1' Lyuboml', Ukr

M

40 N30°12' E35°44' Ma'an, Jor
51 N23°34' E119°34' Ma-kung, Taiwan
29 N60°6' E19°57' Maarianhamina, Fin
63 N10°8' E124°50' Maasin, Phil
63 N10°54' E122°26' Maasin, Phil
18 N50°51' E5°41' Maastricht, Neth
133 N8°12' W59°47' Mabaruma, Guy
59 S2°14' E111°54' Mabau, Indo
143 S70°0' E60°0' MacRobertson Land, Ant, Disputed
58 N5°46' E102°13' Macang, Malay
137 N0°2' W51°3' Macapá, AP, Braz
137 S15°33' W40°24' Macarani, BA, Braz
134 S2°19' W78°7' Macas, Ecu
51 N22°12' E113°32' Macau, China
66 S23°50' E131°47' Macdonnell Range, Austl
137 S9°41' W35°47' Maceió, AL, Braz
17 N43°18' E13°27' Macerata, It
134 S3°16' W79°58' Machala, Ecu
91 S20°53' E34°59' Machanga, Moz
75 N7°10' E133°58' Macharchar, US
111 N44°43' W67°28' Machias, ME, US
67 S21°10' E149°10' Mackay, Qld, Austl
96 N64°38' W131°17' Mackenzie Mountains, Can
96 N65°28' W129°2' *Mackenzie River*, Can
100 N52°20' W109°56' Macklin, SK, Can
69 S29°28' E153°13' Maclean, NSW, Austl
109 N40°28' W90°40' Macomb, IL, US
119 N32°50' W83°38' Macon, GA, US
118 N33°7' W88°34' Macon, MS, US
15 N46°19' E4°49' Mâcon, Fr
10 N51°54' W8°57' Macroom, Ire
132 N0°23' W72°55' Macujer, Col
135 S14°5' W70°26' Macusani, Peru
42 N26°48' E37°53' Mada'in Salih, Sau Ar
89 S8°40' E37°47' Madaba, Tanz
81 N18°28' E20°45' Madadi, Chad
92 S17°20' E44°43' MADAGASCAR
80 N21°58' E13°39' Madama, Niger
25 N41°30' E24°57' Madan, Bulg
61 S5°13' E145°42' Madang, PNG
80 N14°4' E5°57' Madaoua, Niger
136 S5°47' W61°34' *Madeira*, Braz
78 N33°16' W18°1' Madeira Islands, Port
39 N38°23' E39°40' Maden, Turk
47 N47°53' E78°37' Madeniyet, Kaz
112 N36°58' W120°4' Madera, CA, US
54 N15°18' E73°57' Madgaon, Ind
115 N34°5' W96°46' Madill, OK, US
78 N13°24' W8°51' Madina, Mali
86 S4°25' E11°41' Madingo-Kayes, Con
109 N43°5' W89°25' Madison, WI, US
116 N38°46' W85°23' Madison, IN, US
116 N37°20' W87°30' Madisonville, KY, US
115 N30°57' W95°55' Madisonville, TX, US
59 S7°37' E111°31' Madiun, Indo
83 N0°44' E39°10' Mado Gashi, Ken
26 N56°51' E26°13' Madona, Lat
42 N21°59' E39°59' Madrakah, Sau Ar
56 N13°5' E80°16' Madras, Ind
106 N44°38' W121°8' Madras, OR, US
135 S12°13' W68°8' *Madre de Dios*, Peru
12 N40°25' W3°43' Madrid, Sp
68 S31°55' E127°0' Madura, WA, Austl
59 S7°7' E113°8' Madura, Indo
56 N9°56' E78°7' Madurai, Ind
53 N36°23' E139°4' Maebashi, Jap
92 S16°56' E46°49' Maevatanana, Madag
101 N52°41' W101°6' Mafeking, MB, Can
89 S7°56' E39°55' Mafia Island, Tanz
90 S25°52' E25°39' Mafikeng, S Afr
35 N59°38' E150°38' Magadan, Rus Fed
63 N12°50' E123°51' Magallanes, Phil
63 N6°53' E124°34' Maganoy, Phil
80 N13°0' E8°54' Magaria, Niger
115 N35°10' W93°38' Magazine Mountain, US
132 N9°10' W75°3' *Magdalena*, Col
19 N52°8' E11°37' Magdeburg, Ger
59 S7°28' E110°13' Magelang, Indo
78 N15°31' W12°51' Maghama, Mrta
37 N53°27' E59°4' Magnitogorsk, Rus Fed
115 N33°16' W93°14' Magnolia, AR, US
74 S17°29' W179°7' Mago Island, Fiji
63 N17°41' E120°25' Magsingal, Phil
50 N22°59' E104°19' Maguan, China
57 N20°8' E94°55' Magwe, Myanmar
44 N36°45' E45°43' Mahabad, Iran
55 N28°1' E84°5' Mahabharat Range, Nepal
92 S20°23' E44°40' Mahabo, Madag
54 N18°5' E73°25' Mahad, Ind
89 N2°18' E30°59' Mahagi, DRC
92 S15°43' E46°20' Mahajanga, Madag
45 N35°5' E69°24' Mahamud-e Eraqi, Afg
92 S19°54' E48°48' Mahanoro, Madag
55 N21°6' E82°6' Mahasamund, Ind
79 N35°31' E11°4' Mahdia, Tun
133 N5°16' W59°6' Mahdia, Guy
92 S5°1' E55°28' Mahé, Sey
26 N53°54' E30°21' Mahilyow, Bela
54 N19°42' E72°45' Mahim, Ind
55 N22°11' E87°59' Mahishadal, Ind
38 N39°30' E31°0' Mahmudiye, Turk
13 N39°53' E4°16' Mahón, Sp
11 N51°17' E0°32' Maidstone, UK
100 N53°6' W109°17' Maidstone, SK, Can
86 N11°51' E13°10' Maiduguri, Nga
45 N35°56' E64°37' Maimana, Afg
111 N45°16' W69°39' Maine, US
92 S18°2' E44°8' Maintirano, Madag
78 N15°5' W23°5' Maio, CV
59 S3°32' E118°56' Majene, Indo
13 N39°47' E1°55' Majorca Island, Sp
72 N7°6' E171°22' Majuro, Mar Is
72 N7°8' E172°2' Majuro Atoll, Mar Is
120 N21°28' W158°12' Makaha, HI, US
90 S20°19' E23°51' Makalamabedi, Bots
59 S3°6' E119°51' Makale, Indo
89 S4°13' E29°47' Makamba, Buru
89 S4°20' E37°51' Makanya, Tanz
133 N4°0' W58°50' Makarapan Mountain, Guy
22 N43°18' E17°2' Makarska, Cro
59 S2°23' E117°55' *Makasar Strait*
73 S15°8' W148°16' Makatea, Fr Poly, Fr
73 S16°25' W143°41' Makemo, Fr Poly, Fr
84 N8°53' W12°6' Makeni, SL
90 S20°47' E23°22' *Makgadikgadi Pans*, Bots
36 N42°58' E47°30' Makhachkala, Rus Fed
60 S3°11' E134°14' Maki, Indo
82 S2°17' E37°49' Makindu, Ken
47 N52°37' E70°26' Makinsk, Kaz
42 N21°27' E39°49' Makkah, Sau Ar
84 N12°52' W12°21' Mako, Sen
74 S17°29' E178°40' Makogai Island, Fiji
86 N0°34' E12°52' Makokou, Gabon
87 N0°1' E15°39' Makoua, Con
34 N57°48' E35°53' Maksatikha, Rus Fed
44 N39°17' E44°31' Maku, Iran
52 N31°16' E130°19' Makurazaki, Jap
86 N7°45' E8°31' Makurdi, Nga
75 S17°9' E168°28' Makuru Island, Van
37 N55°13' E67°13' Makushino, Rus Fed
78 N16°58' W13°23' Mal, Mrta
134 S12°39' W76°38' Mala, Peru
63 N7°38' E124°3' Malabang, Phil
86 N3°45' E8°49' Malabo, Eq Gui
107 N42°11' W112°15' Malad City, ID, US
12 N36°43' W4°24' Málaga, Sp
12 N39°11' W3°50' Malagón, Sp
72 S8°42' E161°9' Malaita, Sol Is
82 N9°32' E31°40' Malakal, Sud
45 N34°34' E71°56' Malakand, Pak
88 S9°32' E16°20' Malanje, Ang
140 S35°28' W69°35' Malargüe, Arg
104 N48°8' W78°8' Malartic, QC, Can
141 S44°56' W66°54' Malaspina, Arg
120 N59°55' W142°32' *Malaspina Glacier*, US
39 N38°21' E38°19' Malatya, Turk
89 S13°10' E33°12' MALAWI
58 N6°40' E101°50' Malay Peninsula, Malay
63 N8°10' E125°8' Malaybalay, Phil
58 N4°7' E101°21' MALAYSIA
39 N39°9' E42°31' Malazgirt, Turk
21 N54°2' E19°1' Malbork, Pol
73 S4°1' W154°55' Malden Island, Kir
56 N4°18' E72°59' Maldive Islands, Mald
56 N2°46' E72°6' MALDIVES
138 S34°53' W54°58' Maldonado, Ur
56 N4°1' E73°29' Male, Mald
56 N4°10' E73°41' Male Atoll, Mald
54 N20°33' E74°32' Malegaon, Ind
44 N37°9' E46°6' Malek Kandi, Iran
137 S14°18' W43°43' Malhada, BA, Braz
106 N43°26' W118°32' *Malheur Lake*, US
79 N18°20' W2°47' MALI
84 N12°5' W12°21' Mali, Gui
50 N31°29' E111°20' Maliangping, China
59 S0°36' E123°14' Malik, Indo
59 N3°35' E116°38' Malinau, Indo
54 N20°53' E76°12' Malkapur, Ind
10 N56°59' W5°49' Mallaig, UK
67 S16°59' E135°49' Mallapunyah, NT, Austl
139 S25°55' W50°50' Mallet, PR, Braz
90 S33°28' E18°44' Malmesbury, S Afr
29 N55°36' E13°1' Malmö, Swe
72 N8°21' E171°12' Maloelap Atoll, Mar Is
74 S17°47' E176°55' Malolo Island, Fiji
63 N14°51' E120°49' Malolos, Phil
110 N44°51' W74°17' Malone, NY, US
26 N51°47' E24°5' Malorita, Bela
34 N63°45' E37°22' Maloshuyka, Rus Fed
35 N67°44' E49°50' Malozemel'skaya Tundra, Rus Fed
17 N35°35' E14°13' MALTA
107 N48°22' W107°52' Malta, MT, US
17 N35°58' E14°28' Maltese Islands, Malta
60 S0°10' E124°43' *Malucca Sea*
60 N0°11' E126°39' Maluku, Indo
115 N34°22' W92°49' Malvern, AR, US
141 S53°1' W63°2' Malvinas, UK
35 N55°44' E51°22' Mamadysh, Rus Fed
61 S6°46' E155°24' Mamagota, PNG
23 N44°15' E28°37' Mamaia, Rom
63 N9°16' E124°43' Mambajao, Phil
63 N13°14' E120°36' Mamburao, Phil
86 N5°46' E9°17' Mamfe, Cam
84 N10°23' W12°5' Mamou, Gui
92 S16°6' E47°38' Mampikony, Madag
85 N7°4' W1°24' Mampong, Gha
85 N7°24' W7°33' Man, Côte d'Ivoire
57 N18°51' E93°44' Man-aung, Myanmar
133 N5°40' W53°47' Mana, Fr Gu, Fr
13 N39°34' E3°12' Manacor, Sp
60 N1°34' E124°50' Manado, Indo
124 N12°8' W86°17' Managua, Nic
71 S39°33' E174°8' Manaia, NZ
61 S2°0' E146°44' Manam Island, PNG
92 S16°13' E49°49' Mananara Avaratra, Madag
92 S21°13' E48°20' Mananjary, Madag
74 S8°20' E160°50' Manaoba Island, Sol Is
129 N18°26' W66°29' Manati, PR, US
127 N21°19' W76°56' Manatí, Cuba
136 S3°5' W60°3' Manaus, AM, Braz
38 N36°47' E31°26' Manavgat, Turk
63 N7°13' E126°32' Manay, Phil
11 N53°30' W2°15' Manchester, UK
111 N43°0' W71°28' Manchester, NH, US
134 S4°7' W81°2' Máncora, Peru
45 N26°7' E62°3' Mand, Pak
138 S23°20' W52°5' Mandaguaçu, PR, Braz
49 N44°35' E104°5' Mandal Ovoo, Mong
49 N45°45' E106°13' Mandalgovi, Mong
108 N46°47' W100°55' Mandan, ND, US
91 S16°30' E33°30' Mandié, Moz
91 S14°21' E35°39' Mandimba, Moz
80 N11°11' E15°25' Mandjafa, Chad
92 S15°47' E48°45' Mandritsara, Madag
54 N24°4' E75°4' Mandsaur, Ind
54 N22°22' E75°22' Mandu, Ind
54 N22°50' E69°22' Mandvi, Ind
85 N11°40' W1°4' Manga, Burk
73 S22°27' W159°20' Mangaia, Cook Is, NZ
56 N12°52' E74°53' Mangalore, Ind
54 N21°7' E70°7' Mangrol, Ind
81 N10°31' E21°19' Mangueigne, Chad
108 N39°11' W96°34' Manhattan, KS, US
132 N4°49' W72°17' Mani, Col
91 S12°43' E35°0' Maniamba, Moz
136 S5°49' W61°17' Manicoré, AM, Braz
73 S14°15' W147°9' Manihi, Fr Poly, Fr
73 S10°25' W161°1' Manihiki, Cook Is, NZ
97 N65°26' W52°56' Maniitsoq, Grld, Den
63 N14°38' E121°2' Manila, Phil
63 N14°17' E120°7' *Manila Bay*
67 S12°4' E134°13' Maningrida, NT, Austl
60 S3°6' E127°13' *Manipa Strait*
38 N38°36' E27°26' Manisa, Turk
109 N45°58' W86°14' Manistique, MI, US
101 N54°0' W99°36' Manitoba, Can
101 N49°17' W98°42' Manitou, MB, Can
103 N45°49' W81°36' Manitoulin Island, Can
109 N44°5' W87°40' Manitowoc, WI, US
92 S21°26' E44°20' Manja, Madag
108 N39°47' W98°13' Mankato, KS, US
86 N5°1' E12°0' Mankim, Cam
85 N8°4' W6°12' Mankono, Côte d'Ivoire
58 S4°27' E102°55' Manna, Indo
56 N8°59' E79°55' Mannar, Sri L
108 N47°14' W102°46' Manning, ND, US
74 S7°13' E157°55' *Manning Strait*
99 N53°20' W111°10' Mannville, AB, Can
84 N8°2' W12°6' Mano, SL
136 S9°40' W65°27' Manoa, RO, Braz
60 S0°52' E134°5' Manokwari, Indo
92 S16°41' E49°45' Manompana, Madag
57 N11°38' E99°4' Manoron, Myanmar
15 N43°50' E5°47' Manosque, Fr
73 S4°27' W171°14' Manra, Kir
13 N41°44' E1°50' Manresa, Sp
89 S11°12' E28°53' Mansa, Zam
84 N13°28' W15°32' Mansa Konko, Gam
97 N61°37' W79°29' Mansel Island, Can
116 N40°46' W82°31' Mansfield, OH, US
115 N32°2' W93°42' Mansfield, LA, US
134 S0°37' W80°43' Manta, Ecu
132 N7°33' W69°9' Mantecal, Ven
117 N35°55' W75°41' Manteo, NC, US
14 N48°59' E1°43' Mantes-la-Jolie, Fr
16 N45°9' E10°48' Mantova, It
29 N62°2' E24°38' Mänttä, Fin
126 N22°17' W84°17' Mantua, Cuba
35 N58°20' E44°46' Manturovo, Rus Fed
135 S12°15' W70°50' Manú, Peru
73 S14°13' W169°20' Manua Islands, Samoa
73 S19°14' W158°56' Manuae, Cook Is, NZ
136 S8°53' W69°18' Manuel Urbano, AC, Braz
73 S19°19' W143°41' Manuhangi, Fr Poly, Fr
61 S2°23' E146°34' Manus Island, PNG
90 S23°23' E21°44' Manyana, Bots
127 N20°21' W77°7' Manzanillo, Cuba
49 N49°35' E117°22' Manzhouli, China
128 N19°33' W71°5' Mao, Dom Rep
80 N14°7' E15°19' Mao, Chad
60 S4°13' E136°31' Maoke Mountains, Indo
91 S22°52' E31°59' Mapai, Moz
60 S7°7' E139°23' Mapi, Indo
91 S22°19' E35°3' Mapinhane, Moz
135 S15°15' W68°10' Mapiri, Bol
91 S25°51' E32°36' Maputo, Moz
47 N46°48' E82°0' Maqanshy, Kaz
50 N34°55' E99°18' Maqen Gangri, China
12 N40°4' W4°22' Maqueda, Sp
55 N28°11' E94°6' Mara, Ind
73 S15°35' W176°12' Mara-Utu, WF, Fr
136 S1°50' W65°22' Maraã, AM, Braz
137 S5°21' W49°8' Marabá, PA, Braz
132 N10°39' W71°35' Maracaibo, Ven
138 S21°38' W55°9' Maracaju, MT, Braz
81 N29°14' E19°13' Maradah, Libya
80 N13°29' E7°6' Maradi, Niger
87 N6°1' E18°24' Marali, CAR
74 S9°35' E161°33' Maramasike, Sol Is
44 N38°26' E45°46' Marand, Iran
137 S3°8' W46°4' Maranhão, Braz
38 N37°36' E36°55' Maras, Turk
23 N45°52' E27°14' Marasesti, Rom
102 N48°41' W86°22' Marathon, ON, Can
119 N24°43' W81°4' Marathon, FL, US
74 S9°29' E159°39' Maravovo, Sol Is
63 N8°0' E124°17' Marawi, Phil
39 N40°33' E48°56' Märäzä, Azer
12 N36°31' W4°53' Marbella, Sp
66 S21°11' E119°44' Marble Bar, WA, Austl
19 N50°49' E8°46' Marburg an der Lahn, Ger
124 N14°7' W88°0' Marcala, Hon
22 N46°35' E17°25' Marcali, Hun
119 N25°56' W81°43' Marco, FL, US
39 N37°18' E40°44' Mardin, Turk
127 N19°55' W77°11' Marea de Portillo, Cuba
34 N57°19' E32°5' Marevo, Rus Fed
114 N30°19' W104°1' Marfa, TX, US
55 N27°17' E95°41' Margherita, Ind
89 N0°38' E29°47' Margherita Peak, DRC
23 N47°21' E22°21' Marghita, Rom
63 N7°34' E123°10' Margosatubig, Phil
140 S34°1' W61°54' María Teresa, Arg
115 N34°46' W90°46' Marianna, AR, US
20 N47°47' E15°21' Mariazell, Aus
22 N46°33' E15°39' Maribor, Slov
142 S75°0' W120°0' Marie Byrd Land, Ant, Disputed
129 N15°59' W61°13' Marie-Galante, Guad, Fr
29 N60°6' E19°57' Mariehamn, Fin
61 S3°35' E144°15' Marienberg, PNG
29 N58°43' E13°50' Mariestad, Swe
117 N39°25' W81°28' Marietta, OH, US
119 N33°56' W84°33' Marietta, GA, US
26 N54°33' E23°21' Marijampole, Lith
12 N42°23' W8°42' Marín, Sp
63 N13°6' E121°49' Marinduque Island, Phil
109 N45°5' W87°38' Marinette, WI, US
138 S23°21' W51°50' Maringá, PR, Braz
119 N34°11' W79°24' Marion, SC, US
116 N40°30' W85°43' Marion, IN, US
109 N37°44' W88°56' Marion, IL, US
117 N36°50' W81°31' Marion, VA, US
69 S23°22' E139°39' Marion Downs, Qld, Austl

continue on next page

21 N53°52' E21°19' **Mragowo**, Pol
26 N54°2' E31°42' **Mstsislaw**, Bela
106 N46°12' W121°29' Mt Adams, US
85 N7°7' E0°31' Mt Afadjato, Gha
127 N24°14' W75°22' Mt Alvernia, Bah
63 N6°59' E125°16' Mt Apo, Phil
33 N39°43' E44°19' Mt Ararat, Turk
109 N46°46' W88°10' Mt Arvon, US
97 N66°30' W65°0' Mt Asgard, Can
99 N50°52' W115°40' Mt Assiniboine, Can
108 N40°43' W94°14' **Mt Ayr**, IA, US
106 N48°49' W121°48' Mt Baker, US
68 S34°38' E117°40' **Mt Barker**, WA, Austl
70 S29°1' E167°57' Mt Bates, Austl
86 S1°56' E12°31' Mt Berongou, Con
91 S19°47' E33°4' Mt Binga, Moz
128 N12°16' W68°23' Mt Brandaris, Neth Ant, Neth
90 S21°10' E14°33' Mt Brandberg, Nam
86 N4°13' E9°10' Mt Cameroon, Cam
81 N28°29' E33°49' Mt Catherine, Egypt
109 N42°37' W82°53' **Mt Clemens**, MI, US
107 N48°55' W113°47' Mt Cleveland, US
99 N52°9' W117°27' Mt Columbia, Can
71 S43°38' E170°13' **Mt Cook**, NZ
71 S43°35' E170°8' Mt Cook, NZ
117 N39°47' W79°11' Mt Davis, US
111 N44°14' W68°14' Mt Desert Island, US
42 N28°5' E46°25' Mt Dibbagh, Sau Ar
113 N39°7' W106°27' Mt Elbert, US
82 N1°8' E34°31' Mt Elgon, Ug
48 N28°0' E86°50' Mt Everest, China
99 N49°35' W116°30' Mt Farnham, Can
99 N51°52' W116°56' Mt Forbes, Can
110 N42°3' W73°29' Mt Frissell, US
99 N52°33' W117°54' Mt Fryatt, Can
53 N35°15' E138°48' Mt Fuji, Jap
45 N34°40' E67°34' Mt Fuladi, Afg
69 S37°50' E140°46' **Mt Gambier**, SA, Austl
99 N49°45' W123°1' Mt Garibaldi, Can
67 S17°41' E145°7' **Mt Garnet**, Qld, Austl
50 N34°19' E91°49' Mt Geladaintong, China
121 N61°31' W152°22' Mt Gerdine, US
110 N42°38' W73°10' Mt Greylock, US
97 N68°52' W29°55' Mt Gunnbjorn, Grld, Den
121 N63°37' W146°43' Mt Hayes, US
40 N33°25' E35°52' Mt Hermon, Leb
106 N45°22' W121°41' Mt Hood, US
26 N48°3' E24°41' Mt Hoverla, Ukr
67 S20°44' E139°30' **Mt Isa**, Qld, Austl
22 N43°43' E18°39' Mt Jahorina, Bos & Herz
106 N44°44' W121°46' Mt Jefferson, US
48 N27°50' E89°19' Mt Jichudrake, China
48 N31°1' E81°31' Mt Kailas, China
111 N45°54' W68°55' Mt Katahdin Baxter Peak, US
87 N6°58' E15°31' Mt Kayagangiri, CAR
82 S0°8' E37°19' Mt Kenya, Ken
32 N67°43' E33°41' Mt Khibini, Rus Fed
69 S36°28' E148°16' Mt Kosciusko, Austl
128 N18°25' W72°7' Mt La Selle, Haiti
87 S1°18' E14°50' Mt Leketi, Con
113 N37°35' W105°26' Mt Lindsey, US
96 N60°34' W140°25' Mt Logan, Can
84 N12°8' W12°16' Mt Loura, Gui
68 S28°4' E117°49' **Mt Magnet**, WA, Austl
74 S9°44' E160°2' Mt Makarakomburu, Sol Is
110 N44°32' W72°49' Mt Mansfield, US
110 N44°7' W73°55' Mt Marcy, US
63 N13°14' E123°43' Mt Mayon, Phil
121 N63°4' W151°1' Mt McKinley, US
106 N42°26' W122°19' Mt McLoughlin, US
138 S34°46' W55°4' Mt Mirador, Ur
116 N35°46' W82°16' Mt Mitchell, US
112 N39°16' W114°12' Mt Moriah, US
89 S15°51' E35°38' Mt Mulanje, Malw
112 N39°49' W111°46' Mt Nebo, US
48 N33°2' E81°6' Mt Nganglong, China
75 N7°34' E134°35' Mt Ngerchelchauus, US
24 N38°49' E22°18' Mt Oeta, Grc
113 N39°26' W106°28' Mt of the Holy Cross, US
24 N40°5' E22°22' Mt Olympus, Grc
106 N47°50' W123°41' Mt Olympus, US
69 S41°53' E146°2' Mt Ossa, Austl
135 S18°43' W65°34' Mt Owens, Bol
113 N38°26' W109°14' Mt Peale, US
129 N14°49' W61°11' Mt Pelee, Mart, Fr
115 N33°10' W94°58' **Mt Pleasant**, TX, US
109 N43°36' W84°45' **Mt Pleasant**, MI, US
42 N24°13' E39°6' Mt Radwah, Sau Ar
106 N46°51' W121°46' Mt Rainier, US
67 S23°3' E134°40' **Mt Riddock**, NT, Austl
99 N53°7' W119°9' Mt Robson, Can
66 S24°24' E115°23' **Mt Sandiman**, WA, Austl
44 N37°8' E44°37' Mt Sar-i Kurawah, Iraq
50 N27°9' E100°11' Mt Satseto, China
112 N41°25' W122°12' Mt Shasta, US
81 N28°31' E33°56' Mt Sinai, Egypt
44 N36°20' E41°41' Mt Sinjar, Iraq
121 N60°17' W140°55' Mt St Elias, US
106 N46°12' W122°11' Mt St Helens, US
133 N2°29' W52°59' Mt St-Marcel, Fr Gu, Fr
121 N58°26' W154°23' Mt Stellar, US
116 N38°4' W83°56' **Mt Sterling**, KY, US
107 N48°31' W113°37' Mt Stimson, US
108 N39°1' W102°1' Mt Sunflower, US
113 N3°47' W56°11' Mt Tafel, Sur
85 N10°15' E1°30' Mt Tanakas, Ben
99 N51°21' W116°13' Mt Temple, Can
106 N43°9' W122°4' Mt Thielsen, US
24 N41°59' E20°48' Mt Titov Vrh, FYRM
112 N37°20' W118°40' Mt Tom, US
22 N44°7' E15°15' Mt Velebit, Cro
116 N40°23' W82°29' **Mt Vernon**, OH, US
66 S24°13' E118°14' **Mt Vernon**, WA, Austl
106 N48°25' W122°20' **Mt Vernon**, WA, US
109 N38°19' W88°53' **Mt Vernon**, IL, US
98 N51°22' W125°16' Mt Waddington, Can
111 N44°16' W71°18' Mt Washington, US
66 S22°45' E132°9' **Mt Wedge**, NT, Austl
112 N36°35' W118°17' Mt Whitney, US
61 S5°47' E145°2' Mt Wilhelm, PNG
84 N8°8' W9°52' Mt Wutivi, Libr
120 N21°56' W159°32' Mt. Waialeale, US
89 S10°16' E40°11' **Mtwara**, Tanz
57 N20°9' E101°27' **Muang Houn**, Laos
57 N21°5' E102°31' **Muang Khoua**, Laos
57 N18°12' E101°25' **Muang Pak-Lay**, Laos
57 N16°39' E105°34' **Muang Phalan**, Laos
57 N15°40' E105°55' **Muang Vapi**, Laos
58 N2°2' E102°34' **Muar**, Malay
58 S3°15' E103°2' **Muarabeliti**, Indo
59 S0°58' E115°19' **Muarabenangin**, Indo
58 S1°28' E102°7' **Muarabungo**, Indo
58 S3°39' E103°48' **Muaraenim**, Indo
59 S0°9' E116°43' **Muarakaman**, Indo
59 N1°48' E117°12' **Muaralasan**, Indo
58 S1°8' E103°51' **Muarasabak**, Indo
58 S1°36' E99°11' **Muarasiberut**, Indo
58 S1°42' E103°7' **Muaratembesi**, Indo
66 S20°38' E120°4' **Muccan**, WA, Austl
89 S13°20' E31°2' Muchinga Mountains, Zam
69 S26°35' E148°23' **Muckadilla**, Qld, Austl
139 S18°5' W39°34' **Mucuri**, BA, Braz
49 N44°35' E129°37' **Mudanjiang**, China
91 S11°39' E39°33' **Mueda**, Moz
83 N2°3' E45°20' **Mugdisho**, Som
33 N37°12' E28°22' **Mugla**, Turk
46 N48°36' E58°27' **Mugodzharskaya**, Kaz
46 N48°50' E58°48' Mugodzhary, Kaz
14 N43°45' W0°45' **Mugron**, Fr
17 N48°15' E12°32' **Mühldorf**, Ger
19 N51°12' E10°27' **Mühlhausen**, Ger
29 N64°48' E25°59' **Muhos**, Fin
40 N35°15' E36°35' **Muhradah**, Syria
51 N22°20' E114°1' **Mui Wo Kau Tsuen**, China
134 N0°37' W80°1' **Muisne**, Ecu
54 N24°49' E75°59' **Mukandara**, Ind
57 N16°32' E104°44' **Mukdahan**, Thai
54 N31°57' E75°37' **Mukerian**, Ind
58 S2°35' E101°7' **Mukomuko**, Indo
46 N37°36' E65°44' **Mukry**, Turkm
46 N48°3' E54°30' **Mukur**, Kaz
54 N20°4' E79°40' **Mul**, Ind
122 N28°39' W108°51' **Mulatos**, Son, Mex
122 N26°53' W112°1' **Mulegé**, BC, Mex
114 N34°14' W102°43' **Muleshoe**, TX, US
56 N13°6' E74°48' **Mulki**, Ind
10 N53°32' W7°20' **Mullingar**, Ire
88 S16°48' E25°9' **Mulobezi**, Zam
45 N30°9' E71°31' **Multan**, Pak
88 N19°5' E72°48' **Mumbai**, Ind
88 S14°59' E27°4' **Mumbwa**, Zam
36 N45°47' E47°38' **Mumra**, Rus Fed
54 N25°45' E70°17' **Munaba**, Ind
17 N48°8' E11°34' **München**, Ger
116 N40°12' W85°23' **Muncie**, IN, US
19 N51°25' E9°39' **Münden**, Ger
66 S23°52' E120°9' **Mundiwindi**, WA, Austl
137 S11°52' W40°28' **Mundo Novo**, BA, Braz
68 S31°52' E127°51' **Mundrabilla**, WA, Austl
89 S10°2' E14°41' **Munenga**, Ang
89 N2°38' E28°30' **Mungbere**, DRC
19 N48°8' E11°34' **Munich**, Ger
109 N46°25' W86°39' **Munising**, MI, US
139 S20°28' W41°25' **Muniz Freire**, ES, Braz
29 N58°29' E11°41' **Munkedal**, Swe
15 N48°1' E7°9' **Munster**, Fr
18 N51°57' E7°37' **Münster**, Ger
59 N0°27' E119°56' **Munte**, Indo
58 S2°4' E105°11' **Muntok**, Indo
57 N19°39' E105°0' **Muong Hin**, Viet
29 N67°57' E23°42' **Muonio**, Fin
88 S16°10' E15°44' **Mupa**, Ang
22 N46°35' E15°59' *Mur River*, Slov
35 N59°24' E48°55' **Murashi**, Rus Fed
16 N39°25' E9°34' **Muravera**, It
14 N41°23' W7°31' **Murça**, Port
44 N33°6' E51°30' **Murcheh Khvort**, Iran
71 S41°48' E172°20' **Murchison**, NZ
13 N37°59' W1°8' **Murcia**, Sp
115 N34°4' W93°41' **Murfreesboro**, AR, US
116 N35°50' W86°23' **Murfreesboro**, TN, US
46 N37°18' E62°33' *Murgab*, Turkm
47 N38°10' E73°59' **Murghob**, Taj
19 N53°22' E12°49' *Müritz See*, Ger
32 N68°59' E32°59' **Murmansk**, Rus Fed
36 N55°34' E42°2' **Murom**, Rus Fed
53 N42°18' E140°59' **Muroran**, Jap
12 N42°48' W9°2' **Muros**, Sp
52 N33°18' E134°9' **Muroto**, Jap
106 N43°13' W116°34' **Murphy**, ID, US
116 N35°5' W84°2' **Murphy**, NC, US
109 N37°46' W89°20' **Murphysboro**, IL, US
70 S10°29' E105°35' Murray Hill, Chr I, Austl
90 S31°58' E23°47' **Murraysburg**, S Afr
45 N33°54' E73°24' **Murree**, Pak
68 S28°55' E121°49' **Murrin Murrin**, WA, Austl
80 N25°55' E13°55' **Murzuq**, Libya
39 N38°44' E41°30' **Mus**, Turk
24 N42°11' E23°36' Musala, Bulg
42 N12°37' E44°37' **Musaymir**, Yem
43 N23°30' E58°32' **Muscat**, Oman
68 S26°12' E130°37' Musgrave Ranges, Austl
109 N43°16' W86°13' **Muskegon**, MI, US
115 N35°45' W95°22' **Muskogee**, OK, US
89 S1°30' E33°48' **Musoma**, Tanz
61 S1°28' E149°44' Mussau Island, PNG
88 S14°14' E21°59' **Mussuma**, Ang
91 S18°58' E32°39' **Mutare**, Zimb
60 S7°23' E140°20' **Muting**, Indo
92 S12°8' E44°26' **Mutsamudu**, Com
67 S22°35' E144°34' **Muttaburra**, Qld, Austl
46 N43°47' E59°1' **Muynoq**, Uzb
47 N44°25' E70°26' Muyun Kum, Kaz
55 N26°7' E85°24' **Muzaffarpur**, Ind
48 N35°56' E80°6' Muztagh Ata, China
86 N1°13' E13°12' **Mvadhi-Ousyé**, Gabon
82 N6°3' E29°56' **Mvolo**, Sud
86 S4°15' E12°29' **Mvouti**, Con
92 S12°30' E42°32' Mwali, Com
88 S7°54' E26°45' **Mwanza**, DRC
89 S2°31' E32°52' **Mwanza**, Tanz
88 S4°51' E21°34' **Mweka**, DRC
88 S7°3' E23°27' **Mwene-Ditu**, DRC
91 S21°22' E30°45' **Mwenezi**, Zimb
57 N18°17' E95°19' **Myanaung**, Myanmar
57 N21°7' E95°10' **MYANMAR**
57 N25°23' E97°24' **Myitkyina**, Myanmar
55 N24°45' E90°24' **Mymensingh**, Bngl
47 N45°25' E73°40' **Mynaral**, Kaz
57 N20°36' E93°10' **Myohaung**, Myanmar
119 N33°41' W78°53' **Myrtle Beach**, SC, US
106 N43°4' W123°20' **Myrtle Creek**, OR, US
21 N53°24' E21°21' **Myszyniec**, Pol
25 N39°6' E26°32' **Mytilene**, Grc
89 S11°27' E33°55' **Mzuzu**, Malw

N

80 N12°6' E15°3' **N'Djamena**, Chad
44 N32°52' E53°5' **Na'in**, Iran
29 N60°27' E22°2' **Naantali**, Fin
63 N11°50' E122°5' **Nabas**, Phil
37 N55°42' E52°19' **Naberezhnyye Chelny**, Rus Fed
79 N36°28' E10°44' **Nabeul**, Tun
60 S3°23' E135°30' **Nabire**, Indo
21 N50°25' E16°10' **Náchod**, Czech
115 N31°37' W94°39' **Nacogdoches**, TX, US
74 S16°54' E177°10' Nacula Island, Fiji
138 S26°1' W54°46' **Ñacunday**, Para
82 N18°40' E33°42' **Nadi**, Sud
74 S17°43' E177°13' **Nadi**, Fiji
Nadi Bay
79 N35°8' W2°56' **Nador**, Mor
34 N63°52' E34°15' **Nadovitsy**, Rus Fed
74 S16°27' E179°9' **Naduri**, Fiji
26 N48°38' E24°34' **Nadvornaya**, Ukr
29 N58°40' E5°39' **Nærbø**, Nor
86 N11°8' E11°20' **Nafada**, Nga
45 N27°24' E65°8' **Nag**, Pak
63 N13°37' E123°11' **Naga**, Phil
55 N25°5' E94°22' Naga Hills, Ind
53 N36°39' E138°11' **Nagano**, Jap
56 N10°46' E79°50' **Nagappattinam**, Ind
45 N24°22' E70°45' **Nagar Parkar**, Pak
52 N32°46' E129°52' **Nagasaki**, Jap
54 N27°12' E73°44' **Nagaur**, Ind
53 N35°9' E136°54' **Nagoya**, Jap
54 N21°10' E79°5' **Nagpur**, Ind
128 N19°23' W69°51' **Nagua**, Dom Rep
22 N46°14' E17°22' **Nagyatád**, Hun
53 N26°13' E127°41' **Naha**, Jap
40 N33°0' E35°5' **Nahariyya**, Isr
100 N52°25' W104°30' **Naicam**, SK, Can
59 S9°30' E123°50' **Naikliu**, Indo
74 S17°46' E179°22' Nairai Island, Fiji
11 N57°35' W3°53' **Nairn**, UK
82 S1°18' E36°47' **Nairobi**, Ken
74 S16°59' W179°18' Naitaba Island, Fiji
54 N29°38' E78°20' **Najibabad**, Ind
42 N17°29' E44°7' **Najran**, Sau Ar
45 N25°15' E66°44' **Naka Kharari**, Pak
61 S6°1' E150°41' Nakanai Mountains, PNG
52 N29°46' E129°56' Nakano-shima, Jap
57 N14°12' E101°13' **Nakhon Nayok**, Thai
57 N17°24' E104°47' **Nakhon Phanom**, Thai
57 N14°58' E102°7' **Nakhon Ratchasima**, Thai
102 N50°10' W86°42' **Nakina**, ON, Can
82 S0°17' E36°4' **Nakuru**, Ken
99 N50°15' W117°48' **Nakusp**, BC, Can
36 N43°29' E43°37' **Nal'chik**, Rus Fed
38 N40°11' E31°21' **Nallihan**, Turk
57 N20°25' E106°10' **Nam Dinh**, Viet
57 N18°35' E102°50' *Nam Ngum Reservoir*, Laos
56 N11°12' E78°10' **Namakkal**, Ind
47 N41°1' E71°41' **Namangan**, Uzb
91 S13°43' E39°50' **Namapa**, Moz
61 S3°41' E152°24' **Namatanai**, PNG
48 N29°39' E95°1' Namcha Barwa, China
59 N2°34' E116°21' **Nameh**, Indo
52 N34°34' E127°56' Namhae-do, S Kor
57 N23°50' E97°41' **Namhkam**, Myanmar
52 N38°7' E125°10' **Namho-ri**, N Kor
90 S21°31' E14°11' Namib Desert, Nam
88 S15°11' E12°9' **Namibe**, Ang
90 S21°0' E15°38' **NAMIBIA**
53 N37°29' E141°0' **Namie**, Jap
44 N38°25' E48°30' **Namin**, Iran
60 S3°15' E127°5' **Namlea**, Indo
52 N38°45' E125°23' **Namp'o**, N Kor
99 N56°2' W117°8' **Nampa**, AB, Can
78 N15°17' W5°33' **Nampala**, Mali
91 S15°7' E39°16' **Nampula**, Moz
91 S12°17' E39°3' **Nampula**, Moz
98 N51°49' W127°52' **Namu**, BC, Can
18 N50°28' E4°52' **Namur**, Belg
57 N18°47' E100°47' **Nan**, Thai
84 N4°50' W8°44' **Nana Kru**, Libr
49 N28°41' E115°52' **Nanchang**, China
15 N48°41' E6°11' **Nancy**, Fr
54 N19°8' E77°19' **Nanded**, Ind
72 S17°48' E177°25' **Nandi**, Fiji
45 N35°14' E74°35' Nanga Parbat, Pak
51 N31°22' E116°59' **Nangang**, China
59 S0°20' E111°44' **Nangapinoh**, Indo
59 N0°38' E113°11' **Nangaraun**, Indo
57 N10°31' E98°31' **Nangin**, Myanmar
48 N32°15' E96°27' **Nangqen**, China
48 N39°57' E94°13' **Nanhu**, China
50 N25°14' E101°13' **Nanhua**, China
49 N43°44' E128°55' **Nanhutou**, China
49 N32°33' E107°30' **Nanjiang**, China
49 N32°3' E118°46' **Nanjing**, China
68 S26°53' E118°20' **Nannine**, WA, Austl
50 N22°49' E108°19' **Nanning**, China
97 N60°9' W45°16' **Nanortalik**, Grld, Den
51 N26°38' E118°10' **Nanping**, China
62 N10°38' E115°8' Nanshan Island, Disputed
14 N48°58' E2°19' **Nanterre**, Fr
14 N47°13' W1°34' **Nantes**, Fr
99 N50°21' W113°46' **Nanton**, AB, Can
111 N41°17' W70°6' **Nantucket**, MA, US
111 N41°12' W70°15' Nantucket Island, US
74 S17°5' W179°40' *Nanuku Passage*
72 S5°33' E174°4' Nanumanga, Tuv
139 S17°50' W40°21' **Nanuque**, MG, Braz
51 N29°20' E112°19' **Nanxian**, China
49 N33°0' E112°32' **Nanyang**, China
51 N33°30' E112°26' **Nanzhao**, China
50 N20°51' E110°39' Naozhou Dao, China
112 N38°17' W122°17' **Napa**, CA, US
71 S39°29' E176°55' **Napier**, NZ
119 N26°10' W81°49' **Naples**, FL, US
17 N40°51' E14°12' **Naples**, It
50 N23°16' E105°54' **Napo**, China
17 N40°51' E14°12' **Napoli**, It
78 N15°10' W7°17' **Nara**, Mali
48 N48°34' E98°17' **Naran**, Mong
55 N16°27' E81°40' **Narasapur**, Ind
57 N6°26' E101°50' **Narathiwat**, Thai
14 N43°11' E3°0' **Narbonne**, Fr
68 S30°59' E124°50' **Naretha**, WA, Austl
54 N22°0' E75°32' *Narmada*, Ind
82 S1°5' E35°52' **Narok**, Ken
12 N43°32' W8°10' **Narón**, Sp
29 N62°28' E21°20' **Närpes**, Fin
29 N62°26' E21°20' **Närpiö**, Fin
69 S34°45' E146°33' **Narrandera**, NSW, Austl
53 N38°44' E140°43' **Narugo**, Jap
29 N68°26' E17°25' **Narvik**, Nor
47 N41°26' E75°59' **Naryn**, Kyr
47 N41°16' E74°46' *Naryn*, Kyr
47 N42°43' E80°12' **Narynkol**, Kaz
36 N52°58' E35°44' **Naryshkino**, Rus Fed
111 N42°46' W71°28' **Nashua**, NH, US
116 N36°8' W86°49' **Nashville**, TN, US
115 N33°57' W93°51' **Nashville**, AR, US
82 N8°36' E33°4' **Nasir**, Sud
127 N25°4' W77°20' **Nassau**, Bah
73 S11°33' W165°23' Nassau Island, Cook Is, NZ
137 S5°47' W35°13' **Natal**, RN, Braz
58 N0°33' E99°7' **Natal**, Indo
118 N31°34' W91°24' **Natchez**, MS, US
115 N31°46' W93°5' **Natchitoches**, LA, US
74 S16°40' E179°38' *Natewa Bay*
54 N24°56' E73°49' **Nathdwara**, Ind
69 S36°45' E141°57' **Natimuk**, Vic, Austl
85 N10°19' E1°22' **Natitingou**, Ben
137 S11°43' W47°47' **Natividade**, GO, Braz
55 N24°25' E89°1' **Nator**, Bngl
19 N52°36' E12°52' **Nauen**, Ger
19 N51°9' E11°48' **Naumburg**, Ger
134 S5°36' W79°54' **Ñaupe**, Peru
24 N37°34' E22°48' **Náuplia**, Grc
72 S0°32' E164°23' **NAURU**
45 N26°50' E68°7' **Naushahro Firoz**, Pak
135 S4°32' W73°33' **Nauta**, Peru
123 N20°13' W96°47' **Nautla**, Ver, Mex
12 N39°38' W4°28' **Navahermosa**, Sp
26 N53°36' E25°50' **Navahrudak**, Bela
12 N39°54' W5°32' **Navalmoral de la Mata**, Sp
10 N53°39' W6°41' **Navan**, Ire
25 N55°31' E28°38' **Navapolatsk**, Bela
127 N18°31' W75°35' **Navassa Island**, US
54 N21°26' E69°50' **Navibandar**, Ind
74 S17°7' E177°15' Naviti Island, Fiji
36 N52°51' E34°30' **Navlya**, Rus Fed
122 N27°6' W109°26' **Navojoa**, Son, Mex
74 S18°14' E178°10' **Navua**, Fiji
55 N24°53' E85°32' **Nawada**, Ind
46 N40°15' E65°15' **Nawoiy**, Uzb
39 N39°13' E45°25' **Naxçivan**, Azer
25 N37°6' E25°23' **Náxos**, Grc
44 N27°23' E52°34' **Nay Band**, Iran
122 N22°4' W105°34' **Nayarit**, Mex
74 S17°59' W179°1' Nayau Island, Fiji
12 N39°36' W9°4' **Nazaré**, Port
40 N32°41' E35°18' **Nazareth**, Isr
134 S14°50' W74°57' **Nazca**, Peru
52 N28°23' E129°30' **Naze**, Jap
40 N32°41' E35°18' **Nazerat**, Isr
39 N39°11' E39°50' **Nazimiye**, Turk
34 N59°50' E31°55' **Naziya**, Rus Fed
88 S9°18' E14°55' **Ndalatando**, Ang
87 N8°25' E20°39' **Ndélé**, CAR
86 S2°23' E11°23' **Ndendé**, Gabon
89 S12°58' E28°38' **Ndola**, Zam
88 N1°50' E29°1' **Nduye**, DRC
24 N36°30' E23°4' **Neápolis**, Grc
120 N52°40' E171°53' Near Islands, US
46 N39°30' E54°23' **Nebit Dag**, Turkm
108 N41°35' W99°58' **Nebraska**, US
108 N40°41' W95°52' **Nebraska City**, NE, US
132 N8°7' W74°47' **Nechí**, Col
141 S38°33' W58°45' **Necochea**, Arg
48 N29°28' E91°31' **Nedong**, China
112 N36°0' W116°0' **Needles**, CA, US
88 S14°10' E14°30' **Negola**, Ang
91 S11°27' E38°31' **Negomano**, Moz
23 N44°14' E22°32' **Negotin**, Yugo
23 N47°52' E23°25' **Negresti-Oas**, Rom
127 N18°16' W78°22' **Negril**, Jam
134 S4°38' W81°16' **Negritos**, Peru
136 S0°10' W63°49' *Negro*, Braz
63 N9°43' E122°35' Negros, Phil
23 N45°30' E28°12' **Negru Voda**, Rom
45 N31°32' E60°2' **Nehbandan**, Iran
75 S18°34' W173°57' **Neiafu**, Ton
128 N18°28' W71°25' **Neiba**, Dom Rep
109 N44°34' W90°36' **Neillsville**, WI, US
132 N2°56' W75°18' **Neiva**, Col
101 N59°37' W97°33' *Nejanilini Lake*, Can
82 N9°2' E36°31' **Nek'emte**, Eth
108 N42°8' W98°2' **Neligh**, NE, US
56 N14°26' E79°58' **Nellore**, Ind
71 S41°17' E173°17' **Nelson**, NZ
99 N49°29' W117°17' **Nelson**, BC, Can
121 N60°43' W166°33' Nelson Island, US
91 S25°28' E30°59' **Nelspruit**, S Afr
37 N57°31' E50°31' **Nema**, Rus Fed
78 N16°37' W7°15' **Néma**, Mrta
59 S10°53' E122°50' **Nembrala**, Indo
53 N43°20' E145°35' **Nemuro**, Jap
53 N43°56' E145°25' *Nemuro Strait*
49 N49°10' E125°14' **Nenjiang**, China
108 N36°52' W94°22' **Neosho**, MO, US
55 N28°47' E81°25' **NEPAL**
55 N28°3' E81°37' **Nepalganj**, Nepal
70 S29°4' E167°58' Nepean Island, Nor I, Austl
112 N39°43' W111°50' **Nephi**, UT, US
12 N36°44' W3°53' **Nerja**, Sp
66 S18°24' E124°29' **Nerrima**, WA, Austl
26 N53°13' E26°39' **Nesvizh**, Bela
40 N32°20' E34°51' **Netanya**, Isr
18 N52°7' E4°51' **NETHERLANDS**
128 N12°38' W69°16' **Netherlands Antilles**, Neth
97 N65°55' W70°43' *Nettilling Lake*, Can
19 N53°33' E13°15' **Neubrandenburg**, Ger
15 N47°1' E6°55' **Neuchâtel**, Switz
15 N48°21' E5°42' **Neufchâteau**, Fr
19 N54°4' E9°59' **Neumünster**, Ger
141 S38°57' W68°4' **Neuquén**, Arg
19 N52°55' E12°48' **Neuruppin**, Ger
21 N47°47' E16°49' *Neusiedler See*, Aus
18 N50°25' E7°27' **Neuwied**, Ger
112 N39°43' W117°37' **Nevada**, US
108 N37°50' W94°21' **Nevada**, MO, US
112 N39°16' W121°1' **Nevada City**, CA, US
135 S15°49' W71°53' Nevado Ampato, Peru
135 S15°56' W68°23' Nevado Ancohuma, Bol
135 S13°47' W71°14' Nevado Ausangate, Peru
135 S15°31' W72°40' Nevado Coropuna, Peru
140 S24°4' W65°45' Nevado de Chañi, Arg
132 N2°57' W75°58' Nevado del Huila, Col
134 S9°7' W77°37' Nevado Huascarán, Peru
135 S16°49' W67°42' Nevado Illimani, Bol
135 S18°5' W68°50' Nevado Sajama, Bol
135 S13°20' W72°33' Nevado Salcantay, Peru
34 N56°2' E29°55' **Nevel'**, Rus Fed
33 N53°58' E124°4' **Never**, Rus Fed
14 N47°1' E3°9' **Nevers**, Fr
36 N44°38' E41°56' **Nevinnomyssk**, Rus Fed
129 N17°10' W62°32' Nevis, St KN
38 N38°38' E34°41' **Nevsehir**, Turk
116 N38°17' W85°49' **New Albany**, IN, US
118 N34°28' W89°0' **New Albany**, MS, US
133 N6°16' W57°29' **New Amsterdam**, Guy
111 N41°37' W70°55' **New Bedford**, MA, US
117 N35°7' W77°4' **New Bern**, NC, US
110 N41°40' W72°47' **New Britain**, CT, US
61 S5°49' E149°16' New Britain, PNG
104 N47°2' W67°12' **New Brunswick**, Can
117 N40°29' W74°26' **New Brunswick**, NJ, US
72 S18°14' E160°46' **New Caledonia**, Fr
72 S20°56' E157°51' New Caledonia, New Cal, Fr
105 N48°1' W65°20' **New Carlisle**, QC, Can
116 N39°55' W85°22' **New Castle**, IN, US
117 N41°1' W80°21' **New Castle**, PA, US
110 N41°9' W73°59' **New City**, NY, US
54 N28°40' E77°17' **New Delhi**, Ind
72 S8°59' E155°4' New Georgia, Sol Is
75 S8°0' E156°0' New Georgia Group, Sol Is
74 S8°19' E158°32' *New Georgia Sound*
105 N45°35' W62°39' **New Glasgow**, NS, Can
60 S4°59' E139°32' New Guinea, Indo
111 N44°1' W71°47' **New Hampshire**, US
109 N43°4' W92°19' **New Hampton**, IA, US
61 S2°11' E150°11' New Hanover, PNG
110 N41°19' W72°56' **New Haven**, CT, US
98 N55°15' W127°35' **New Hazelton**, BC, Can
115 N30°0' W91°49' **New Iberia**, LA, US
61 S3°19' E151°17' New Ireland, PNG
117 N39°58' W74°45' **New Jersey**, US
103 N47°30' W79°40' **New Liskeard**, ON, Can
109 N39°35' W91°24' **New London**, MO, US
111 N41°22' W72°7' **New London**, CT, US
109 N36°35' W89°32' **New Madrid**, MO, US
54 N22°59' E70°13' **New Mandala**, Ind
113 N34°11' W106°10' **New Mexico**, US
99 N52°53' W112°58' **New Norway**, AB, Can
115 N29°58' W90°6' **New Orleans**, LA, US
71 S39°4' E174°5' **New Plymouth**, NZ
127 N24°53' W77°29' New Providence Island, Bah
124 N17°38' W88°41' *New River*, Blz
108 N47°41' W99°8' **New Rockford**, ND, US
142 S70°0' W10°0' New Schwabenland, Ant, Disputed
33 N77°51' E133°14' New Siberian Islands, Rus Fed
69 S32°37' E143°7' **New South Wales**, Austl
108 N44°19' W94°28' **New Ulm**, MN, US
110 N42°46' W76°0' **New York**, US
110 N40°43' W74°1' **New York**, NY, US
71 S39°13' E174°48' **NEW ZEALAND**
89 S10°56' E39°18' **Newala**, Tanz
117 N40°45' W74°10' **Newark**, NJ, US
117 N39°41' W75°45' **Newark**, DE, US
119 N34°17' W81°37' **Newberry**, SC, US
109 N46°21' W85°31' **Newberry**, MI, US
110 N41°31' W74°2' **Newburgh**, NY, US
111 N42°49' W70°53' **Newburyport**, MA, US
69 S32°56' E151°46' **Newcastle**, NSW, Austl
107 N43°51' W104°12' **Newcastle**, WY, US
11 N54°59' W1°36' **Newcastle upon Tyne**, UK
111 N42°59' W72°40' **Newfane**, VT, US
97 N54°58' W63°4' **Newfoundland**, Can
119 N33°22' W84°49' **Newnan**, GA, US
11 N50°40' W1°18' **Newport**, UK
115 N35°36' W91°17' **Newport**, AR, US
116 N35°58' W83°11' **Newport**, TN, US
111 N44°56' W72°13' **Newport**, VT, US
111 N41°29' W71°19' **Newport**, RI, US
11 N51°35' W3°0' **Newport**, UK
106 N48°11' W117°2' **Newport**, WA, US
108 N38°3' W97°20' **Newton**, KS, US
109 N41°42' W93°3' **Newton**, IA, US
56 N8°24' E77°5' **Neyyattinkara**, Ind
87 S3°12' E16°11' **Ngabé**, Con
48 N32°16' E81°44' Nganglong Kangri, China
87 N7°19' E13°40' **Ngaoundéré**, Cam
71 S44°57' E170°45' **Ngapara**, NZ
74 S18°7' E179°5' Ngau Island, Fiji
74 S8°44' E158°14' Nggatokae Island, Sol Is
74 S9°1' E160°7' Nggela Island, Sol Is
80 N14°15' E13°7' **Nguigmi**, Niger
75 S17°26' E168°11' Nguna, Van
86 N12°52' E10°27' **Nguru**, Nga
57 N12°15' E109°11' **Nha Trang**, Viet
138 S19°16' W57°4' **Nhecolândia**, MT, Braz
110 N43°5' W79°4' **Niagara Falls**, NY, US
103 N43°4' W79°4' **Niagara Falls**, ON, Can
80 N13°31' E2°4' **Niamey**, Niger
85 N10°17' W4°55' **Niangoloko**, Burk
49 N47°31' E122°59' **Nianzishan**, China
26 N56°19' E21°4' **Nica**, Lat
125 N12°39' W85°22' **NICARAGUA**
15 N43°44' E7°17' **Nice**, Fr
66 S18°2' E128°54' **Nicholson**, WA, Austl
57 N7°38' E92°58' Nicobar Islands, Ind
38 N35°11' E33°22' **Nicosia**, Cyp
124 N10°9' W85°27' **Nicoya**, CR
21 N53°22' E20°26' **Nidzica**, Pol
19 N54°48' E8°50' **Niebüll**, Ger
20 N47°16' E13°29' Niedere Tauern, Aus
78 N11°26' W6°21' **Niéna**, Mali
19 N52°38' E9°13' **Nienburg**, Ger
133 N5°57' W56°59' **Nieuw Nickerie**, Sur
38 N37°57' E34°42' **Nigde**, Turk
80 N16°39' E9°43' **NIGER**
79 N17°8' W1°2' *Niger River*, Mali
86 N9°7' E8°11' **NIGERIA**
53 N37°54' E139°1' **Niigata**, Jap
120 N21°55' W160°23' Niihau, US
13 N36°58' W2°12' **Níjar**, Sp
34 N69°23' E30°12' **Nikel'**, Rus Fed
60 S9°49' E124°28' **Nikiniki**, Indo
85 N9°56' E3°12' **Nikki**, Ben
35 N59°30' E45°27' **Nikol'sk**, Rus Fed
46 N47°55' E67°28' **Nikol'skiy**, Kaz
36 N47°46' E46°24' **Nikol'skoye**, Rus Fed
26 N46°56' E31°55' **Nikolayev**, Ukr
45 N26°13' E60°12' **Nikshahr**, Iran
22 N42°46' E18°56' **Niksic**, Yugo
81 N28°25' E30°23' *Nile River*, Egypt
123 N16°34' W94°37' **Niltepec**, Oax, Mex
15 N43°52' E4°20' **Nîmes**, Fr
56 N8°28' E73°10' *Nine Degree Channel*
49 N29°53' E121°32' **Ningbo**, China
86 N11°4' E9°32' **Ningi**, Nga
50 N27°11' E102°36' **Ningnan**, China
57 N12°29' E109°8' **Ninh Hòa**, Viet
61 S1°3' E143°59' Ninigo Group, PNG
78 N14°15' W6°0' **Niono**, Mali
84 N13°45' W15°48' **Nioro du Rip**, Sen
78 N15°15' W9°35' **Nioro du Sahel**, Mali
14 N46°19' W0°27' **Niort**, Fr
100 N53°22' W104°0' **Nipawin**, SK, Can
102 N49°1' W88°16' **Nipigon**, ON, Can
127 N20°3' W77°35' **Niquero**, Cuba
140 S30°25' W68°42' **Niquivil**, Arg
44 N38°2' E47°59' **Nir**, Iran
54 N19°6' E78°21' **Nirmal**, Ind
51 N35°36' E117°4' Nishan, China
24 N37°41' E23°33' Nísos Aíyina, Grc
24 N35°53' E22°38' Nísos Andikíthira, Grc
25 N38°1' E24°46' Nísos Ándros, Grc
25 N36°26' E25°55' Nísos Astipálaia, Grc
25 N38°35' E23°27' Nísos Évvoia, Grc
24 N37°14' E23°26' Nísos Ídhra, Grc
25 N37°40' E25°47' Nísos Ikaría, Grc
25 N36°43' E25°25' Nísos Íos, Grc
25 N35°46' E27°18' Nísos Kárpathos, Grc
25 N37°42' E24°16' Nísos Kéa, Grc
24 N38°11' E19°47' Nísos Kefallinía, Grc
24 N39°39' E18°50' Nísos Kérkira, Grc
24 N36°16' E22°25' Nísos Kíthira, Grc
25 N36°40' E27°0' Nísos Kos, Grc
25 N34°51' E24°40' Nísos Kríti, Grc
25 N38°53' E26°0' Nísos Lésvos, Grc
24 N38°46' E20°20' Nísos Levkás, Grc
25 N40°3' E25°2' Nísos Límnos, Grc
25 N37°25' E25°28' Nísos Míkonos, Grc
25 N36°34' E24°17' Nísos Mílos, Grc
25 N37°11' E25°35' Nísos Náxos, Grc
25 N37°8' E24°43' Nísos Páros, Grc
25 N36°8' E27°10' Nísos Ródhos, Grc
25 N37°48' E26°9' Nísos Sámos, Grc
25 N40°32' E25°27' Nísos Samothráki, Grc
25 N36°51' E24°40' Nísos Sífnos, Grc
25 N37°19' E24°40' Nísos Síros, Grc
25 N38°40' E24°29' Nísos Skíros, Grc
25 N40°38' E24°47' Nísos Thásos, Grc
25 N36°20' E26°57' Nísos Tílos, Grc
25 N37°40' E25°4' Nísos Tínos, Grc
24 N37°52' E20°2' Nísos Zákinthos, Grc
73 S16°25' W176°17' Niuatobutabu Group, Ton
73 S18°14' W169°15' **Niue**, NZ
72 S5°31' E177°13' Niutao, Tuv
12 N39°31' W7°39' **Niza**, Port
55 N28°16' E95°42' **Nizamghat**, Ind
32 N60°58' E76°39' **Nizhnevartovsk**, Rus Fed
32 N56°20' E44°0' **Nizhniy Novgorod**, Rus Fed
35 N57°55' E59°57' **Nizhniy Tagil**, Rus Fed
26 N51°3' E31°54' **Nizhyn**, Ukr
38 N37°1' E37°46' **Nizip**, Turk
29 N62°16' E17°22' **Njurunda**, Swe
90 S17°38' E18°35' **Nkurenkuru**, Nam
136 S14°44' W56°20' **Nobres**, MT, Braz
113 N31°20' W110°56' **Nogales**, AZ, US
140 S32°24' W59°48' **Nogoyá**, Arg
45 N28°46' E62°46' **Nok Kundi**, Pak
87 N3°32' E16°4' **Nola**, CAR
35 N57°33' E49°57' **Nolinsk**, Rus Fed
121 N64°31' W165°25' **Nome**, AK, US
73 S20°26' W174°23' Nomuka Group, Ton
75 S20°15' W175°5' Nomuka Island, Ton
57 N17°50' E102°46' **Nong Khai**, Thai
72 S0°2' E174°22' Nonouti, Kir
90 S28°45' E17°37' **Noordoewer**, Nam
98 N49°35' W127°22' Nootka Island, Can
63 N6°28' E124°38' **Norala**, Phil
104 N48°13' W79°2' **Noranda**, QC, Can
18 N53°39' E7°22' Norderney, Ger
29 N67°46' E15°12' **Nordfold**, Nor
19 N51°30' E10°47' **Nordhausen**, Ger
18 N52°27' E7°5' **Nordhorn**, Ger
29 N69°46' E21°3' **Nordkjosbotn**, Nor
19 N48°51' E10°30' **Nördlingen**, Ger
117 N36°51' W76°17' **Norfolk**, VA, US
108 N42°2' W97°25' **Norfolk**, NE, US
70 S29°9' E168°0' **Norfolk Island**, Austl
32 N69°20' E88°13' **Noril'sk**, Rus Fed
115 N35°13' W97°26' **Norman**, OK, US
96 N65°20' W126°43' **Norman Wells**, NT, Can
61 S10°10' E151°17' Normanby Island, PNG
67 S17°40' E141°4' **Normanton**, Qld, Austl
141 S41°51' W70°54' **Ñorquinco**, Arg
29 N59°46' E18°42' **Norrtälje**, Swe
24 N42°22' E19°29' North Albanian Alps, Alb
105 N46°38' W60°17' North Barren Mountain, Can
100 N52°47' W108°17' **North Battleford**, SK, Can
103 N46°19' W79°28' **North Bay**, ON, Can
102 N52°34' W91°23' *North Caribou Lake*, Can
117 N35°37' W79°32' **North Carolina**, US
10 N55°5' W5°43' *North Channel*

continue on next page

58 N5°50' E102°24' **Pasir Putih**, Malay
45 N25°16' E63°28' **Pasni**, Pak
141 S43°52' W69°6' **Paso de Indios**, Arg
138 S32°49' W56°31' **Paso de los Toros**, Ur
141 S44°10' W70°23' **Paso Rio Mayo**, Arg
112 N35°40' W120°41' **Paso Robles**, CA, US
19 N48°35' E13°28' **Passau**, Ger
138 S28°15' W52°24' **Passo Fundo**, RS, Braz
134 S2°9' W77°16' *Pastaza*, Ecu
132 N1°13' W77°17' **Pasto**, Col
137 S6°36' W44°5' **Pastos Bons**, MA, Braz
59 S7°38' E112°54' **Pasuruan**, Indo
117 N40°55' W74°11' **Paterson**, NJ, US
54 N32°17' E75°39' **Pathankot**, Ind
57 N26°23' E95°22' Patkai Range, Myanmar
55 N25°37' E85°8' **Patna**, Ind
39 N39°14' E42°52' **Patnos**, Turk
138 S26°13' W52°37' **Pato Branco**, PR, Braz
137 S7°1' W37°16' **Patos**, PB, Braz
139 S18°35' W46°32' **Patos de Minas**, MG, Braz
140 S30°3' W66°53' **Patquía**, Arg
24 N38°15' E21°45' **Pátras**, Grc
139 S18°57' W46°59' **Patrocínio**, MG, Braz
57 N6°52' E101°15' **Pattani**, Thai
111 N46°0' W68°27' **Patten**, ME, US
14 N43°18' W0°22' **Pau**, Fr
136 S7°40' W66°58' **Pauini**, AM, Braz
116 N41°8' W84°35' **Paulding**, OH, US
137 S9°21' W38°14' **Paulo Afonso**, BA, Braz
115 N34°44' W97°13' **Pauls Valley**, OK, US
35 N59°7' E46°7' **Pavino**, Rus Fed
47 N52°18' E76°57' **Pavlodar**, Kaz
121 N54°51' W161°44' Pavlof Islands, US
74 S9°8' E158°48' Pavuvu Island, Sol Is
34 N58°3' E29°30' **Pavy**, Rus Fed
111 N41°53' W71°23' **Pawtucket**, RI, US
109 N40°28' W88°6' **Paxton**, IL, US
58 S0°14' E100°38' **Payakumbuh**, Indo
68 S29°15' E117°41' **Paynes Find**, WA, Austl
138 S32°15' W58°4' **Paysandú**, Ur
132 N5°53' W71°54' **Paz de Ariporo**, Col
39 N41°11' E40°53' **Pazar**, Turk
99 N56°14' W117°17' **Peace River**, AB, Can
99 N58°43' W113°41' *Peace River*, Can
68 S25°38' E118°43' **Peak Hill**, WA, Austl
114 N28°53' W99°6' **Pearsall**, TX, US
98 N54°44' W130°2' *Pearse Canal*, Can
91 S17°10' E38°8' **Pebane**, Moz
135 S3°19' W71°48' **Pebas**, Peru
141 S51°14' W59°47' Pebble Island, Falk Is, UK
22 N42°40' E20°19' **Pec**, Yugo
35 N66°56' E52°33' *Pechora*, Rus Fed
35 N68°38' E54°2' *Pechora Bay*
114 N31°25' W103°30' **Pecos**, TX, US
113 N33°36' W104°23' *Pecos River*, US
22 N46°4' E18°13' **Pécs**, Hun
128 N18°2' W71°44' **Pedernales**, Dom Rep
69 S26°40' E135°14' **Pedirka**, SA, Austl
139 S16°1' W41°16' **Pedra Azul**, MG, Braz
136 S2°48' W57°16' **Pedras**, AM, Braz
136 S12°51' W62°54' **Pedras Negras**, RO, Braz
138 S18°4' W54°32' **Pedro Gomes**, MT, Braz
138 S22°32' W55°45' **Pedro Juan Caballero**, Para
141 S39°29' W62°41' **Pedro Luro**, Arg
138 S31°51' W52°45' **Pedro Osorio**, RS, Braz
66 S21°50' E115°38' **Peedamulla**, WA, Austl
110 N41°18' W73°47' **Peekskill**, NY, US
57 N17°20' E96°30' **Pegu**, Myanmar
58 S1°48' E101°32' Pegunungan Barisan, Indo
140 S35°48' W61°53' **Pehuajó**, Arg
58 N3°30' E103°25' **Pekan**, Malay
58 N0°33' E101°26' **Pekanbaru**, Indo
109 N40°34' W89°38' **Pekin**, IL, US
49 N39°54' E116°19' **Peking**, China
59 S3°48' E114°45' **Pelaihari**, Indo
75 N7°1' E134°18' Peleliu, US
29 N67°7' E27°30' **Pelkosenniemi**, Fin
29 N66°47' E24°0' **Pello**, Fin
96 N68°42' W89°41' **Pelly Bay**, NU, Can
24 N37°46' E21°38' Peloponnisos, Grc
138 S31°46' W52°20' **Pelotas**, RS, Braz
138 S27°26' W52°34' *Pelotas River*, Braz
35 N59°38' E63°5' **Pelym**, Rus Fed
91 S12°58' E40°31' **Pemba**, Moz
89 S5°19' E39°53' Pemba Island, Tanz
99 N50°20' W122°48' **Pemberton**, BC, Can
103 N45°49' W77°7' **Pembroke**, ON, Can
139 S21°24' W50°4' **Penápolis**, SP, Braz
51 N25°24' E118°11' **Penghu**, China
99 N52°8' W113°52' **Penhold**, AB, Can
12 N39°22' W9°23' **Peniche**, Port
97 N60°35' W75°7' Peninsula D'ungava, Can
132 N12°28' W71°59' Península de la Guajira, Col
132 N11°53' W69°48' Peninsula de Paraguaná, Ven
126 N22°2' W85°11' Peninsula of Guanahacabibes, Cuba
141 S46°19' W74°50' Peninsula Taitao, Chile
122 N20°26' W101°44' **Pénjamo**, Gto, Mex
110 N42°40' W77°3' **Penn Yan**, NY, US
117 N40°52' W78°37' **Pennsylvania**, US
111 N45°18' W68°36' *Penobscot River*, US
125 N8°31' W80°22' **Penonomé**, Pan
11 N54°40' W2°44' **Penrith**, UK
118 N30°25' W87°13' **Pensacola**, FL, US
142 S80°0' W60°0' Pensacola Mountains, Ant, Disputed
59 N4°33' E116°19' **Pensiangan**, Malay
72 S15°21' E168°19' Pentecost, Van
99 N49°30' W119°35' **Penticton**, BC, Can
58 S2°27' E104°31' **Penuguan**, Indo
56 N14°5' E77°35' **Penukonda**, Ind
36 N53°13' E45°0' **Penza**, Rus Fed
19 N47°45' E11°23' **Penzberg**, Ger
109 N40°42' W89°35' **Peoria**, IL, US
84 N8°35' W13°3' **Pepel**, SL
140 S34°29' W71°29' **Peralillo**, Chile
67 S21°42' E150°23' Percy Isles, Austl
139 S19°21' W47°17' **Perdizes**, MG, Braz
132 N4°48' W75°41' **Pereira**, Col
36 N49°9' E42°33' **Perelazovskiy**, Rus Fed
37 N51°52' E50°22' **Perelyub**, Rus Fed
34 N56°44' E38°51' **Pereslavl'Zalesskiy**, Rus Fed
140 S33°53' W60°35' **Pergamino**, Arg
14 N45°11' E0°43' **Périgueux**, Fr
32 N58°0' E56°14' **Perm'**, Rus Fed
24 N40°16' E20°22' **Permet**, Alb
137 S8°47' W38°43' **Pernambuco**, Braz
24 N42°36' E23°2' **Pernik**, Bulg
98 N54°31' W126°26' **Perow**, BC, Can
14 N42°42' E2°53' **Perpignan**, Fr
119 N30°7' W83°35' **Perry**, FL, US
115 N36°17' W97°17' **Perry**, OK, US
119 N32°28' W83°44' **Perry**, GA, US
114 N36°24' W100°48' **Perryton**, TX, US
115 N35°0' W92°48' **Perryville**, AR, US
135 S14°44' W62°48' **Perseverancia**, Bol
43 N27°46' E49°38' *Persian Gulf*
39 N38°50' E39°22' **Pertek**, Turk
68 S31°58' E115°47' **Perth**, WA, Austl
104 N46°45' W67°42' **Perth**, NB, Can
11 N56°24' W3°27' **Perth**, UK
134 S8°7' W76°53' **PERU**
17 N43°7' E12°23' **Perugia**, It
140 S29°20' W58°37' **Perugorría**, Arg
47 N51°17' E70°8' **Pervomayka**, Kaz
26 N48°4' E30°52' **Pervomays'k**, Ukr
36 N54°53' E43°49' **Pervomaysk**, Rus Fed
123 N15°53' W93°2' *Pesa de la Angostora*, Mex
17 N42°28' E14°13' **Pescara**, It
17 N41°55' E16°1' **Peschici**, It
45 N34°0' E71°32' **Peshawar**, Pak
24 N41°41' E20°27' **Peshkopi**, Alb
25 N42°2' E24°18' **Peshtera**, Bulg
35 N59°4' E52°22' **Peskovka**, Rus Fed
34 N58°36' E35°48' **Pestovo**, Rus Fed
37 N52°24' E49°58' **Pestravka**, Rus Fed
123 N17°31' W101°16' **Petatlán**, Gro, Mex
89 S14°15' E31°20' **Petauke**, Zam
100 N55°47' W109°32' *Peter Pond Lake*, Can
103 N44°18' W78°33' **Peterborough**, ON, Can
11 N57°30' W1°49' **Peterhead**, UK
117 N37°14' W77°24' **Petersburg**, VA, US
121 N56°50' W133°1' **Petersburg**, AK, US
128 N18°26' W72°52' **Petit Goâve**, Haiti
104 N51°47' W67°28' *Petit Lac Manicouagan*, Can
140 S32°15' W70°56' **Petorca**, Chile
109 N45°22' W84°58' **Petoskey**, MI, US
24 N41°24' E23°13' **Petrich**, Bulg
23 N45°27' E23°25' **Petrila**, Rom
47 N54°52' E69°7' **Petropavlovsk**, Kaz
33 N53°1' E158°39' **Petropavlovsk Kamchatskiy**, Rus Fed
36 N52°19' E45°23' **Petrovsk**, Rus Fed
34 N61°47' E34°20' **Petrozavodsk**, Rus Fed
37 N55°6' E67°58' **Petukhovo**, Rus Fed
112 N38°14' W122°38' **Petulma**, CA, US
20 N46°58' E10°33' **Pfunds**, Aus
54 N27°8' E72°22' **Phalodi**, Ind
57 N11°34' E108°59' **Phan Rang**, Viet
57 N10°56' E108°6' **Phan Thiet**, Viet
57 N8°27' E98°32' **Phangnga**, Thai
57 N14°11' E103°22' Phanom Dangrek, Camb
57 N19°10' E99°55' **Phayao**, Thai
57 N16°25' E101°8' **Phetchabun**, Thai
57 N13°6' E99°57' **Phetchaburi**, Thai
117 N39°57' W75°10' **Philadelphia**, PA, US
108 N44°2' W101°40' **Philip**, SD, US
70 S29°7' E167°55' Philip Island, Nor I, Austl
53 N23°38' E126°29' *Philippine Sea*
63 N13°10' E116°59' **PHILIPPINES**
129 N18°2' W63°3' **Philipsburg**, Neth Ant, Neth
69 S38°44' E144°35' Phillip Island, Austl
57 N16°50' E100°16' **Phitsanulok**, Thai
57 N11°33' E105°2' **Phnom Penh**, Camb
57 N13°49' E104°58' **Phnom Thbeng Meanchey**, Camb
57 N12°1' E104°13' Phnum Aural, Camb
57 N11°33' E105°2' **Phnum Pénh**, Camb
112 N33°29' W112°8' **Phoenix**, AZ, US
73 S5°52' W173°18' Phoenix Islands, Kir
57 N22°32' E103°21' **Phong Tho**, Viet
57 N18°10' E100°10' **Phrae**, Thai
57 N7°53' E98°24' **Phuket**, Thai
57 N13°50' E107°22' **Phumi Bâ Kham**, Camb
57 N13°35' E105°58' **Phumi Thalabarivat**, Camb
16 N45°3' E9°42' **Piacenza**, It
50 N26°1' E100°32' **Pianjiao**, China
23 N46°56' E26°22' **Piatra Neamt**, Rom
137 S7°25' W43°1' **Piauí**, Braz
82 N6°48' E33°8' **Pibor Post**, Sud
14 N42°31' E1°39' Pic de Coma Pedrosa, And
118 N30°32' W89°41' **Picayune**, MS, US
140 S23°19' W64°13' **Pichanal**, Arg
140 S34°23' W72°0' **Pichilemu**, Chile
102 N51°30' W90°4' **Pickle Crow**, ON, Can
102 N51°29' W90°10' **Pickle Lake**, ON, Can
81 N22°1' E19°11' Pico Bette, Libya
132 N10°49' W73°43' Pico Cristóbal Colón, Col
13 N42°38' E0°40' Pico de Aneto, Sp
78 N14°57' W24°22' Pico de Cano, CV
136 N0°58' W65°38' Pico de Neblina, Braz
86 N0°16' E6°32' Pico de São Tomé, STP
128 N19°2' W71°1' Pico Duarte, Dom Rep
124 N14°53' W88°5' Pico Maronchio, Hon
141 S46°48' W67°58' **Pico Truncado**, Arg
137 S7°5' W41°28' **Picos**, PI, Braz
71 S41°18' E174°1' **Picton**, NZ
105 N45°41' W62°43' **Pictou**, NS, Can
45 N25°51' E63°14' **Pidarak**, Pak
12 N40°28' W5°19' **Piedrahita**, Sp
123 N28°42' W100°31' **Piedras Negras**, Coah, Mex
108 N44°23' W100°22' **Pierre**, SD, US
21 N48°36' E17°50' **Piestany**, Slvk
91 S23°53' E29°27' **Pietersburg**, S Afr
115 N36°23' W90°11' **Piggott**, AR, US
141 S37°37' W62°25' **Pigüé**, Arg
29 N63°23' E25°34' **Pihtipudas**, Fin
123 N15°42' W93°14' **Pijijiapan**, Chis, Mex
47 N39°22' E72°50' Pik Lenina, Kyr
48 N42°2' E80°8' Pik Pobedy, China
47 N38°31' E72°22' Pik Revolyutsii, Taj
72 N8°31' E146°18' Pikelot, US
113 N38°50' W105°2' Pikes Peak, US
116 N37°29' W82°31' **Pikeville**, KY, US
101 N55°35' W97°9' **Pikwitonei**, MB, Can
21 N53°10' E16°44' **Pila**, Pol
63 N11°29' E123°0' **Pilar**, Phil
138 S26°56' W58°22' **Pilar**, Para
24 N39°28' E21°37' **Pili**, Grc
63 N13°16' E123°49' **Pili**, Phil
54 N28°38' E79°48' **Pilibhit**, Ind
69 S31°15' E136°47' **Pimba**, SA, Austl
134 S6°50' W79°55' **Pimentel**, Peru
137 S3°43' W45°30' **Pimentel**, MA, Braz
141 S37°7' W56°52' **Pinamar**, Arg
126 N22°25' W83°42' **Pinar Del Río**, Cuba
38 N38°44' E36°24' **Pinarbasi**, Turk
24 N39°59' E21°8' Pindus Mountains, Alb
115 N34°13' W92°2' **Pine Bluff**, AR, US
109 N45°50' W92°58' **Pine City**, MN, US
66 S13°49' E131°49' **Pine Creek**, NT, Austl
142 S70°0' W110°0' *Pine Island Bay*
96 N60°52' W114°30' **Pine Point**, NT, Can
108 N43°2' W102°34' **Pine Ridge**, SD, US
107 N42°52' W109°52' **Pinedale**, WY, US
16 N44°53' E7°21' **Pinerolo**, It
108 N36°35' W94°23' **Pineville**, MO, US
50 N25°50' E107°19' **Pinghu**, China
68 S33°32' E118°31' **Pingrup**, WA, Austl
51 N25°20' E113°2' **Pingshi**, China
51 N32°32' E113°3' **Pingshi**, China
51 N25°32' E119°49' **Pingtan**, China
49 N27°38' E113°50' **Pingxiang**, China
12 N40°46' W7°4' **Pinhel**, Port
68 S32°37' E115°53' **Pinjarra**, WA, Austl
12 N37°15' W3°45' **Pinos Puente**, Sp
26 N52°7' E26°4' **Pinsk**, Bela
26 N52°2' E27°4' *Pinsk Marshes*, Bela
140 S20°37' W69°38' **Pintados**, Chile
59 N5°26' E117°43' **Pintasan**, Malay
112 N37°56' W114°27' **Pioche**, NV, US
21 N51°25' E19°41' **Piotrków Trybunalski**, Pol
71 S39°29' E175°3' **Pipiriki**, NZ
137 S5°48' W39°25' **Piquet Carneiro**, CE, Braz
24 N37°57' E23°39' **Piraiévs**, Grc
139 S23°12' W49°23' **Piraju**, SP, Braz
140 S25°43' W59°6' **Pirané**, Arg
137 S16°31' W51°51' **Piranhas**, GO, Braz
137 S17°21' W44°56' **Pirapora**, MG, Braz
137 S15°46' W48°58' **Pirenópolis**, GO, Braz
137 S17°18' W48°17' **Pires do Rio**, GO, Braz
24 N41°43' E23°23' Pirin, Bulg
137 S4°16' W41°47' **Piripiri**, PI, Braz
19 N50°58' E13°56' **Pirna**, Ger
23 N43°9' E22°35' **Pirot**, Yugo
60 S3°4' E128°12' **Piru**, Indo
16 N43°42' E10°24' **Pisa**, It
134 S13°42' W76°12' **Pisco**, Peru
20 N49°19' E14°10' **Písek**, Czech
123 N20°42' W88°35' **Piste**, Yuc, Mex
39 N43°13' E40°17' **Pistunda**, Geo
84 N11°5' W12°24' **Pita**, Gui
73 S22°48' W131°34' **Pitcairn**, UK
73 S24°55' W134°58' Pitcairn Island, Pit, UK
29 N65°20' E21°30' **Piteå**, Swe
23 N44°52' E24°52' **Pitesti**, Rom
11 N56°43' W3°45' **Pitlochry**, UK
141 S38°59' W72°39' **Pitrufquén**, Chile
71 S44°26' W177°0' Pitt Island, NZ
117 N40°26' W80°0' **Pittsburgh**, PA, US
110 N42°27' W73°15' **Pittsfield**, MA, US
137 S10°27' W49°11' **Pium**, GO, Braz
134 S5°12' W80°38' **Piura**, Peru
15 N46°23' E9°54' Piz Bernina, Switz
124 N16°31' W88°23' **Placentia Village**, Blz
63 N9°39' E125°35' **Placer**, Phil
112 N38°43' W120°49' **Placerville**, CA, US
114 N33°11' W102°50' **Plains**, TX, US
114 N34°12' W101°43' **Plainview**, TX, US
136 S14°45' W58°10' Planalto do Mato Grosso, Braz
132 N8°25' W75°36' **Planeta Rica**, Col
12 N40°2' W6°5' **Plasencia**, Sp
35 N54°22' E60°50' **Plast**, Rus Fed
79 N28°41' E1°27' Plateau du Tademait, Alg
48 N34°23' E84°41' Plateau of Tibet, China
110 N44°41' W73°27' **Plattsburgh**, NY, US
36 N53°43' E37°18' **Plavsk**, Rus Fed
126 N23°3' W82°34' **Playa Baracoa**, Cuba
57 N13°59' E108°0' **Pleiku**, Viet
107 N48°45' W104°30' **Plentywood**, MT, US
25 N43°25' E24°37' **Pleven**, Bulg
22 N43°21' E19°21' **Pljevlja**, Yugo
21 N52°33' E19°43' **Plock**, Pol
23 N44°56' E26°2' **Ploiesti**, Rom
25 N42°9' E24°45' **Plovdiv**, Bulg
11 N50°22' W4°10' **Plymouth**, UK
111 N41°58' W70°41' **Plymouth**, MA, US
111 N43°45' W71°42' **Plymouth**, NH, US
116 N41°20' W86°19' **Plymouth**, IN, US
117 N35°52' W76°45' **Plymouth**, NC, US
20 N49°45' E13°23' **Plzen**, Czech
85 N11°10' W1°9' **Pô**, Burk
115 N36°16' W90°58' **Pocahontas**, AR, US
107 N42°52' W112°27' **Pocatello**, ID, US
36 N52°56' E33°27' **Pochëp**, Rus Fed
137 S14°31' W40°21' **Poções**, BA, Braz
136 S16°15' W56°37' **Poconé**, MT, Braz
36 N57°28' E31°7' **Poddor'ye**, Rus Fed
22 N42°26' E19°14' **Podgorica**, Yugo
36 N51°50' E47°3' **Podlesnoye**, Rus Fed
22 N45°42' E17°42' **Podravska Slatina**, Cro
19 N54°1' E11°13' Poel, Ger
24 N40°54' E20°39' **Pogradec**, Alb
72 N6°52' E156°33' Pohnpei, FSM
36 N53°1' E43°11' **Poim**, Rus Fed
115 N29°35' W89°47' **Pointe a la Hache**, LA, US
129 N16°15' W61°32' **Pointe-à-Pitre**, Guad, Fr
86 S4°48' E11°50' **Pointe-Noire**, Con
14 N46°35' E0°20' **Poitiers**, Fr
54 N26°55' E71°55' **Pokaran**, Ind
46 N51°6' E51°53' **Pokatilovka**, Kaz
55 N28°14' E83°59' **Pokhara**, Nepal
88 N3°9' E26°53' **Poko**, DRC
35 N57°14' E66°48' **Pokrovskoye**, Rus Fed
45 N33°59' E69°0' **Pol-e Alam**, Afg
34 N57°56' E31°50' **Pola**, Rus Fed
63 N13°9' E121°26' **Pola**, Phil
12 N43°15' W5°34' **Pola de Laviana**, Sp
45 N25°35' E61°12' **Polan**, Iran
21 N52°46' E18°29' **POLAND**
35 N56°26' E60°11' **Polevskoy**, Rus Fed
63 N14°56' E122°16' Polillo Islands, Phil
27 N47°29' E36°15' **Pologi**, Ukr
35 N59°13' E50°50' **Polom**, Rus Fed
35 N54°43' E63°50' **Polovinnoye**, Rus Fed
27 N49°35' E34°33' **Poltava**, Ukr
37 N54°22' E71°45' **Poltavka**, Rus Fed
35 N60°52' E60°25' **Polunochnoye**, Rus Fed
26 N58°3' E27°3' **Põlva**, Est
24 N40°23' E23°26' **Polygyros**, Grc
29 N61°42' E22°0' **Pomarkku**, Fin
122 N18°19' W103°17' **Pómaro**, Mich, Mex
12 N39°55' W8°38' **Pombal**, Port
61 S5°30' E151°30' **Pomio**, PNG
112 N34°4' W117°45' **Pomona**, CA, US
25 N42°35' E27°37' **Pomorie**, Bulg
119 N26°15' W80°7' **Pompano Beach**, FL, US
72 N6°52' E156°33' Ponape, FSM
115 N36°43' W97°5' **Ponca City**, OK, US
129 N18°1' W66°37' **Ponce**, PR, US
56 N11°56' E79°49' **Pondicherry**, Ind
124 N12°23' W87°2' **Peneloya**, Nic
12 N42°33' W6°35' **Ponferrada**, Sp
56 N11°15' E75°46' **Ponnani**, Ind
13 N41°55' E1°12' **Pons**, Sp
13 N42°24' E0°45' **Pont de Suert**, Sp
15 N48°55' E6°5' **Pont-à-Mousson**, Fr
78 N37°44' W25°40' **Ponta Delgada**, Port
139 S25°5' W50°9' **Ponta Grossa**, PR, Braz
139 S17°31' W49°27' **Pontalina**, GO, Braz
15 N46°54' E6°22' **Pontarlier**, Fr
16 N43°40' E10°38' **Pontedera**, It
12 N42°26' W8°38' **Pontevedra**, Sp
109 N42°38' W83°17' **Pontiac**, MI, US
59 S0°1' E109°20' **Pontianak**, Indo
14 N48°4' W2°59' **Pontivy**, Fr
14 N49°3' E2°6' **Pontoise**, Fr
56 N13°4' E80°5' **Poonamallee**, Ind
69 S33°23' E142°34' **Pooncarie**, NSW, Austl
135 S18°23' W66°59' **Poopó**, Bol
71 S35°30' E174°47' Poor Knights Islands, NZ
132 N2°25' W76°37' **Popayán**, Col
109 N36°45' W90°23' **Poplar Bluff**, MO, US
118 N30°50' W89°32' **Poplarville**, MS, US
25 N43°21' E26°13' **Popovo**, Bulg
21 N49°3' E20°19' **Poprad**, Slvk
124 N16°21' W89°26' **Poptún**, Guat
71 S40°13' E176°37' **Porangahau**, NZ
54 N21°38' E69°37' **Porbandar**, Ind
45 N33°8' E63°51' **Porchaman**, Afg
98 N53°55' W131°14' Porcher Island, Can
29 N61°29' E21°47' **Pori**, Fin
34 N62°43' E32°42' **Porosozero**, Rus Fed
98 N49°14' W124°48' **Port Alberni**, BC, Can
98 N50°23' W127°27' **Port Alice**, BC, Can
106 N48°7' W123°26' **Port Angeles**, WA, US
127 N18°10' W76°29' **Port Antonio**, Jam
69 S43°5' E147°52' **Port Arthur**, Tas, Austl
115 N29°54' W93°56' **Port Arthur**, TX, US
69 S32°30' E137°46' **Port Augusta**, SA, Austl
71 S45°49' E170°37' **Port Chalmers**, NZ
119 N26°59' W82°7' **Port Charlotte**, FL, US
98 N53°42' W132°10' **Port Clements**, BC, Can
58 N2°31' E101°48' **Port Dickson**, Malay
98 N54°15' W130°19' **Port Edward**, BC, Can
103 N44°18' W81°16' **Port Elgin**, ON, Can
90 S33°55' E25°37' **Port Elizabeth**, S Afr
98 N54°8' W129°58' **Port Essington**, BC, Can
78 N20°53' W17°4' **Port Etienne**, Mrta
69 S38°23' E142°14' **Port Fairy**, Vic, Austl
118 N31°58' W90°59' **Port Gibson**, MS, US
86 N4°47' E7°0' **Port Harcourt**, Nga
98 N50°43' W127°29' **Port Hardy**, BC, Can
66 S20°20' E118°32' **Port Hedland**, WA, Austl
121 N56°55' W158°41' **Port Heiden**, AK, US
109 N42°59' W82°27' **Port Huron**, MI, US
110 N41°23' W74°40' **Port Jervis**, NY, US
133 N7°53' W59°54' **Port Kaituma**, Guy
115 N28°37' W96°38' **Port Lavaca**, TX, US
69 S34°45' E135°52' **Port Lincoln**, SA, Austl
92 S20°8' E57°27' **Port Louis**, Mrts
61 S9°27' E147°8' **Port Moresby**, PNG
71 S41°5' E173°0' **Port Motueka**, NZ
101 N57°3' W92°36' **Port Nelson**, MB, Can
90 S29°17' E16°55' **Port Nolloth**, S Afr
10 N58°29' W6°14' **Port of Ness**, UK
81 N31°16' E32°17' **Port Said**, Egypt
91 S30°46' E30°22' **Port Shepstone**, S Afr
98 N54°33' W130°25' **Port Simpson**, BC, Can
118 N29°49' W85°18' **Port St Joe**, FL, US
66 S14°28' E125°49' **Port Warrender**, WA, Austl
109 N43°25' W87°51' **Port Washington**, WI, US
128 N18°33' W72°20' **Port-au-Prince**, Haiti
104 N50°1' W66°54' **Port-Cartier**, QC, Can
128 N19°55' W72°50' **Port-de-Paix**, Haiti
86 S0°46' E8°48' **Port-Gentil**, Gabon
129 N10°40' W61°31' **Port-of-Spain**, T & T
128 N18°7' W73°56' **Port-Salut**, Haiti
72 S17°54' E168°41' **Port-Vila**, Van
10 N54°28' W6°25' **Portadown**, UK
109 N43°32' W89°28' **Portage**, WI, US
101 N49°58' W98°17' **Portage La Prairie**, MB, Can
12 N39°17' W7°25' **Portalegre**, Port
113 N34°11' W103°20' **Portales**, NM, US
137 S1°57' W50°49' **Portel**, PA, Braz
12 N37°8' W8°32' **Portimão**, Port
111 N43°40' W70°16' **Portland**, ME, US
106 N45°26' W122°38' **Portland**, OR, US
12 N41°10' W8°38' **Porto**, Port
15 N42°16' E8°41' **Porto**, Fr
136 S9°34' W67°31' **Pôrto Acre**, AC, Braz
86 N0°2' E6°32' **Porto Alegre**, STP
138 S30°2' W51°13' **Pôrto Alegre**, RS, Braz
138 S19°37' W57°27' **Pôrto Esperança**, MT, Braz
136 S15°51' W58°28' **Pôrto Esperidião**, MT, Braz
137 N0°42' W51°24' **Pôrto Grande**, AP, Braz
138 S21°42' W57°52' **Pôrto Murtinho**, MT, Braz
137 S16°26' W39°5' **Pôrto Seguro**, BA, Braz
16 N40°50' E8°24' **Porto Torres**, It
136 S8°46' W63°54' **Pôrto Velho**, RO, Braz
15 N41°35' E9°16' **Porto-Vecchio**, Fr
125 N9°33' W79°38' **Portobelo**, Pan
16 N44°17' E9°24' **Portofino**, It
134 S1°3' W80°27' **Portoviejo**, Ecu
10 N57°24' W6°12' **Portree**, UK
111 N43°4' W70°46' **Portsmouth**, NH, US
116 N38°44' W82°59' **Portsmouth**, OH, US
117 N36°49' W76°20' **Portsmouth**, VA, US
129 N15°35' W61°28' **Portsmouth**, Dom
12 N39°1' W8°43' **PORTUGAL**
127 N18°2' W77°25' **Porus**, Jam
141 S53°16' W70°27' **Porvenir**, Chile
16 N40°38' E9°43' **Posada**, It
34 N58°30' E39°7' **Poshekhon'ye**, Rus Fed
114 N33°11' W101°23' **Post**, TX, US
22 N45°47' E14°13' **Postojna**, Slov
115 N35°3' W94°37' **Poteau**, OK, US
17 N40°39' E15°48' **Potenza**, It
91 S24°15' E28°55' **Potgietersrus**, S Afr
86 N11°43' E11°5' **Potiskum**, Nga
135 S19°35' W65°45' **Potosí**, Bol
124 N15°11' W87°58' **Potrerillos**, Hon
19 N52°24' E12°55' **Potsdam**, Ger
110 N44°40' W74°59' **Potsdam**, NY, US
99 N55°43' W120°8' **Pouce Coupé**, BC, Can
110 N41°42' W73°56' **Poughkeepsie**, NY, US
57 N12°32' E103°55' **Pouthisat**, Camb
34 N62°51' E34°45' **Povenets**, Rus Fed
12 N41°23' W8°46' **Povoação**, Port
36 N51°12' E42°14' **Povorino**, Rus Fed
107 N44°25' W106°4' *Powder River*, US
107 N44°46' W108°45' **Powell**, WY, US
98 N49°52' W124°33' **Powell River**, BC, Can
49 N29°4' E116°40' *Poyang Hu*, China
38 N37°25' E34°52' **Pozanti**, Turk
22 N44°37' E21°11' **Pozarevac**, Yugo
22 N45°20' E17°41' **Pozega**, Cro
21 N52°25' E16°55' **Poznan**, Pol
138 S23°26' W58°51' **Pozo Colorado**, Para
140 S24°54' W60°19' **Pozo del Tigre**, Arg
12 N38°22' W4°51' **Pozoblanco**, Sp
20 N50°5' E14°26' **Prague**, Czech
20 N50°5' E14°26' **Praha**, Czech
78 N14°55' W23°31' **Praia**, CV
139 S29°12' W49°57' **Praia Grande**, SC, Braz
137 S1°48' W53°29' **Prainha**, PA, Braz
136 S7°16' W60°23' **Prainha**, AM, Braz
58 N2°40' E98°56' **Prapat**, Indo
92 S4°14' E55°10' Praslin, Sey
139 S19°18' W48°55' **Prata**, MG, Braz
108 N37°38' W98°44' **Pratt**, KS, US
19 N53°19' E13°52' **Prenzlau**, Ger
123 N18°2' W96°56' *Presa Miguel Alemán*, Mex
123 N17°13' W93°20' *Presa Nezahulcóyotl*, Mex
123 N24°3' W99°21' *Presa Vicente Guerrero*, Mex
103 N44°43' W75°32' **Prescott**, ON, Can
112 N34°32' W112°28' **Prescott**, AZ, US
115 N33°48' W93°23' **Prescott**, AR, US
138 S22°7' W51°22' **Presidente Prudente**, SP, Braz
138 S21°52' W51°50' **Presidente Venceslau**, SP, Braz
46 N54°30' E65°45' **Presnogor'kovka**, Kaz
21 N49°0' E21°15' **Presov**, Slvk
111 N46°41' W68°1' **Presque Isle**, ME, US
85 N5°27' W2°8' **Prestea**, Gha
107 N42°6' W111°53' **Preston**, ID, US
109 N43°40' W92°5' **Preston**, MN, US
11 N53°46' W2°43' **Preston**, UK
91 S25°43' E28°12' **Pretoria**, S Afr
24 N38°58' E20°45' **Préveza**, Grc
121 N56°43' W172°16' Pribilof Islands, US
22 N43°35' E19°31' **Priboj**, Yugo
113 N39°36' W110°49' **Price**, UT, US
118 N30°44' W88°5' **Prichard**, AL, US
24 N41°20' E21°33' **Prilep**, FYRM
34 N60°22' E28°36' **Primorsk**, Rus Fed
100 N54°57' W109°29' *Primrose Lake*, Can
100 N53°12' W105°46' **Prince Albert**, SK, Can
143 S75°0' E160°0' Prince Albert Mountains, Ant, Disputed
96 N70°13' W118°20' *Prince Albert Sound*
97 N67°47' W80°53' Prince Charles Island, Can
105 N46°52' W63°50' **Prince Edward Island**, Can
99 N53°55' W122°45' **Prince George**, BC, Can
67 S10°51' E140°51' Prince of Wales Island, Austl
96 N72°21' W101°14' Prince of Wales Island, Can
121 N56°8' W133°31' Prince of Wales Island, US
96 N75°3' W127°26' Prince Patrick Island, Can
121 N59°58' W147°16' *Prince William Sound*
117 N38°12' W75°41' **Princess Anne**, MD, US
67 S13°51' E143°39' *Princess Charlotte Bay*
98 N52°59' W129°4' Princess Royal Island, Can
108 N40°24' W93°35' **Princeton**, MO, US
117 N37°22' W81°6' **Princeton**, WV, US
117 N40°20' W74°40' **Princeton**, NJ, US
116 N37°7' W87°53' **Princeton**, KY, US
99 N49°27' W120°31' **Princeton**, BC, Can
116 N38°22' W87°34' **Princeton**, IN, US
136 S12°25' W64°25' **Príncipe da Beira**, RO, Braz
106 N44°18' W120°50' **Prineville**, OR, US
34 N61°2' E30°4' **Priozërsk**, Rus Fed
22 N42°40' E21°10' **Pristina**, Yugo
19 N53°9' E12°10' **Pritzwalk**, Ger
15 N44°44' E4°35' **Privas**, Fr
22 N42°12' E20°44' **Prizren**, Yugo
123 N21°17' W89°40' **Progreso**, Yuc, Mex
22 N43°14' E21°36' **Prokuplje**, Yugo
57 N18°49' E95°13' **Prome**, Myanmar
139 S21°32' W49°52' **Promissão**, SP, Braz
46 N46°3' E53°15' **Prorva**, Kaz
63 N8°35' E125°54' **Prosperidad**, Phil
21 N49°29' E17°7' **Prostejov**, Czech
25 N43°11' E27°26' **Provadiya**, Bulg
111 N41°49' W71°26' **Providence**, RI, US
127 N21°39' W72°20' Providenciales Island, TC Is, UK
111 N42°4' W70°12' **Provincetown**, MA, US
112 N40°14' W111°40' **Provo**, UT, US
99 N52°21' W110°16' **Provost**, AB, Can
139 S25°12' W50°57' **Prudentópolis**, PR, Braz
21 N49°47' E22°47' **Przemysl**, Pol
47 N42°29' E78°23' **Przhevalsk**, Kyr
24 N38°35' E23°38' **Psakhná**, Grc
34 N57°50' E28°20' **Pskov**, Rus Fed
50 N23°7' E101°0' **Pu'er**, China
134 S8°23' W74°32' **Pucallpa**, Peru
135 S16°23' W68°30' **Pucarani**, Bol
90 S27°26' E24°44' **Pudumong**, S Afr
123 N18°24' W98°35' **Puebla**, Mex
123 N19°5' W98°13' **Puebla**, Pue, Mex
12 N39°5' W4°37' **Puebla de Don Rodrigo**, Sp
113 N38°15' W104°37' **Pueblo**, CO, US
124 N13°23' W86°29' **Pueblo Nuevo**, Nic
124 N14°16' W91°22' **Pueblo Nuevo Tiquisate**, Guat
141 S38°9' W65°55' **Puelches**, Arg
63 N13°30' E120°57' **Puerta Galera**, Phil
141 S45°24' W72°42' **Puerto Aisén**, Chile
135 S13°53' W61°36' **Puerto Alegre**, Bol
132 S2°11' W71°1' **Puerto Alfonso**, Col
123 N15°40' W96°29' **Puerto Ángel**, Oax, Mex
132 N0°30' W76°31' **Puerto Asís**, Col
132 N5°40' W67°38' **Puerto Ayacucho**, Ven
138 S20°15' W58°12' **Puerto Bahía Negra**, Para
124 N15°43' W88°36' **Puerto Barrios**, Guat
125 N14°5' W83°20' **Puerto Cabezas**, Nic
132 N6°13' W67°34' **Puerto Carreño**, Col
138 S21°18' W57°55' **Puerto Guaraní**, Para
138 S25°36' W54°36' **Puerto Iguazú**, PR, Braz
86 N1°7' E9°43' **Puerto Iradier**, Eq Gui
125 N8°32' W83°20' **Puerto Jiménez**, CR
132 S0°12' W74°46' **Puerto Leguízamo**, Col
125 N15°16' W83°47' **Puerto Lempira**, Hon
122 N29°55' W112°43' **Puerto Libertad**, Son, Mex
132 N3°23' W73°30' **Puerto Limón**, Col
125 N9°59' W83°2' **Puerto Limón**, CR
141 S42°0' W65°6' **Puerto Lobos**, Arg
141 S42°46' W65°3' **Puerto Madryn**, Arg
135 S12°36' W69°11' **Puerto Maldonado**, Peru
138 S20°52' W57°59' **Puerto Mihanovich**, Para
141 S41°28' W72°57' **Puerto Montt**, Chile
141 S51°44' W72°31' **Puerto Natales**, Chile
122 N31°20' W113°33' **Puerto Peñasco**, Son, Mex
138 S22°43' W57°50' **Puerto Pinasco**, Para
128 N19°48' W70°41' **Puerto Plata**, Dom Rep
135 S9°46' W72°45' **Puerto Portillo**, Peru
63 N9°44' E118°44' **Puerto Princesa**, Phil
129 N18°19' W66°40' **Puerto Rico**, US
132 N1°54' W75°10' **Puerto Rico**, Col
135 S11°5' W67°38' **Puerto Rico**, Bol
132 N6°17' W71°6' **Puerto Rondón**, Col
141 S38°47' W73°24' **Puerto Saavedra**, Chile
141 S49°18' W67°43' **Puerto San Julián**, Arg
141 S50°2' W68°32' **Puerto Santa Cruz**, Arg
135 S12°48' W65°5' **Puerto Siles**, Bol
135 S18°57' W57°51' **Puerto Suárez**, Bol
122 N20°36' W105°13' **Puerto Vallarta**, Jal, Mex
141 S41°19' W72°59' **Puerto Varas**, Chile
125 N9°37' W82°40' **Puerto Viejo**, CR
134 S0°56' W91°1' **Puerto Villamil**, Ecu
141 S45°24' W67°8' **Puerto Visser**, Arg
138 S23°42' W57°12' **Puerto Ybapobó**, Para
12 N38°41' W4°7' **Puertollano**, Sp
106 N47°52' W123°22' *Puget Sound*
13 N42°26' E1°56' **Puigcerdá**, Sp
84 N7°21' W11°42' **Pujehun**, SL
59 S1°20' E114°20' **Pujun**, Indo
73 S10°54' W165°48' Pukapuka, Cook Is, NZ
73 S18°34' W139°14' Pukaruha, Fr Poly, Fr
24 N42°8' E19°52' **Puke**, Alb
22 N44°52' E13°50' **Pula**, Cro
72 N6°59' E149°40' Pulap Atoll, FSM
117 N37°3' W80°47' **Pulaski**, VA, US
116 N35°12' W87°2' **Pulaski**, TN, US
59 S7°55' E124°23' Pulau Alor, Indo
60 S7°56' E129°56' Pulau Babar, Indo
60 S1°2' E127°19' Pulau Bacan, Indo
59 S8°24' E114°50' Pulau Bali, Indo
59 N7°13' E117°23' Pulau Banggi, Malay
58 S1°41' E106°8' Pulau Bangka, Indo
59 S1°54' E122°7' Pulau Bangkulu, Indo
60 S0°47' E130°4' Pulau Batanta, Indo
59 S6°16' E121°48' Pulau Batuata, Indo
59 S0°25' E121°16' Pulau Batudaka, Indo
59 S2°41' E109°19' Pulau Bawal, Indo
59 S5°51' E111°41' Pulau Bawean, Indo
58 S3°26' E106°49' Pulau Belitung, Indo
60 S0°40' E135°43' Pulau Biak, Indo
59 S6°11' E123°11' Pulau Binongko, Indo
59 S7°34' E120°18' Pulau Bonerate, Indo
60 S3°28' E126°19' Pulau Buru, Indo
58 S5°19' E102°19' Pulau Enggano, Indo
59 S8°32' E120°16' Pulau Flores, Indo
60 S0°22' E129°29' Pulau Gag, Indo
60 N0°13' E129°20' Pulau Gebe, Indo
59 S5°29' E120°57' Pulau Kabaena, Indo
59 S7°22' E120°4' Pulau Kalao, Indo
59 S7°26' E121°52' Pulau Kalaotoa, Indo
59 S5°33' E123°54' Pulau Kaledupa, Indo
59 S6°47' E115°13' Pulau Kangean, Indo
60 N4°19' E126°16' Pulau Karakelong, Indo
59 S1°41' E108°59' Pulau Karimata, Indo
59 S5°49' E110°31' Pulau Kemujan, Indo
60 S5°22' E134°45' Pulau Kola, Indo
60 S8°33' E138°47' Pulau Komoran, Indo
58 N6°10' E99°21' Pulau Langkawi, Malay
60 S6°58' E132°4' Pulau Larat, Indo
58 S0°28' E104°57' Pulau Lingga, Indo
59 S8°10' E123°17' Pulau Lomblen, Indo
59 S9°8' E115°44' Pulau Lombok, Indo
60 S1°36' E125°36' Pulau Mangole, Indo
59 S3°33' E123°11' Pulau Manui, Indo
59 N2°11' E118°40' Pulau Maratua, Indo
59 S4°52' E114°49' Pulau Matasiri, Indo
59 S1°7' E108°43' Pulau Maya, Indo
60 S1°41' E129°28' Pulau Misool, Indo
60 S8°25' E127°34' Pulau Moa, Indo
60 N2°12' E128°43' Pulau Morotai, Indo
59 S8°7' E116°55' Pulau Moyo, Indo
59 S5°5' E122°20' Pulau Muna, Indo
58 N3°39' E106°50' Pulau Natuna Besar, Indo
58 N0°40' E97°10' Pulau Nias, Indo
60 S1°17' E135°1' Pulau Num, Indo
60 S0°44' E134°41' Pulau Numfoor, Indo
60 S1°23' E127°50' Pulau Obi, Indo
58 S3°31' E100°10' Pulau Pagai Selatan, Indo
58 S2°52' E99°37' Pulau Pagai Utara, Indo
59 S8°43' E123°48' Pulau Pantar, Indo
59 S1°11' E123°31' Pulau Peleng, Indo
58 N0°13' E98°22' Pulau Pini, Indo
59 S7°20' E114°32' Pulau Raas, Indo
59 S10°53' E123°17' Pulau Roti, Indo

continue on next page

160

128 N19°31' W71°21' Sabaneta, Dom Rep
59 N0°11' E119°51' Sabang, Indo
58 N5°52' E95°19' Sabang, Indo
135 S19°1' W68°23' Sabaya, Bol
80 N27°3' E14°26' Sabha, Libya
13 N42°31' W0°22' Sabiñánigo, Sp
123 N26°30' W100°10' Sabinas Hidalgo, NL, Mex
63 N12°50' E120°47' Sablayan, Phil
96 N71°59' W125°14' Sachs Harbour, NT, Can
105 N45°54' W64°22' Sackville, NB, Can
112 N38°34' W121°25' Sacramento, CA, US
112 N40°0' W122°22' Sacramento Valley, US
13 N42°17' W1°16' Sádaba, Sp
55 N27°50' E95°40' Sadiya, Ind
53 N38°8' E137°56' Sado, Jap
36 N47°46' E44°30' Sadovoye, Rus Fed
35 N54°59' E62°33' Safakulevo, Rus Fed
29 N59°8' E12°56' Säffle, Swe
113 N32°50' W109°43' Safford, AZ, US
78 N32°19' W9°14' Safi, Mor
45 N34°25' E63°1' Safid Range, Afg
36 N55°8' E33°15' Safonovo, Rus Fed
61 S5°35' E148°22' Sag Sag, PNG
52 N33°13' E130°18' Saga, Jap
57 N21°52' E95°58' Sagaing, Myanmar
54 N23°49' E78°45' Sagar, Ind
109 N43°25' W83°57' Saginaw, MI, US
46 N48°12' E54°56' Sagiz, Kaz
12 N37°1' W8°57' Sagres, Port
127 N20°35' W75°14' Sagua de Tánamo, Cuba
126 N22°49' W80°5' Sagua la Grande, Cuba
113 N38°5' W106°8' Saguache, CO, US
104 N48°25' W70°23' Saguenay
13 N39°41' W0°16' Sagunto, Sp
12 N42°22' W5°2' Sahagún, Sp
79 N21°49' W3°40' Sahara Desert, Mali
82 N11°19' E23°20' Sahel, Sud
86 N12°10' E8°58' Sahel, Nga
80 N13°41' E16°10' Sahel, Chad
85 N12°29' E0°25' Sahel, Burk
45 N30°40' E73°6' Sahiwal, Pak
122 N29°3' W109°14' Sahuaripa, Son, Mex
122 N20°4' W102°43' Sahuayo, Mich, Mex
61 S5°38' E146°28' Saidor, PNG
45 N29°17' E61°34' Saindak, Pak
72 N15°37' E146°0' Saipan, NM Is, US
42 N29°58' E40°12' Sakakah, Sau Ar
53 N38°55' E139°50' Sakata, Jap
85 N6°44' E2°40' Sakété, Ben
27 N45°9' E33°35' Saki, Ukr
86 N8°39' E3°25' Saki, Nga
39 N41°12' E47°12' Säki, Azer
54 N21°5' E79°59' Sakoli, Ind
57 N17°10' E104°9' Sakon Nakhon, Thai
54 N20°59' E74°19' Sakri, Ind
78 N16°54' W23°11' Sal, CV
82 N16°58' E37°27' Sala, Eritrea
140 S35°38' W59°46' Saladillo, Arg
83 N1°50' E42°18' Salagle, Som
82 N21°19' E36°13' Salalah, Sud
43 N17°1' E54°5' Salalah, Oman
125 N15°6' W90°19' Salamá, Guat
124 N14°50' W86°36' Salamá, Hon
12 N40°58' W5°39' Salamanca, Sp
110 N42°9' W78°45' Salamanca, NY, US
61 S7°2' E147°4' Salamaua, PNG
45 N28°18' E65°9' Salambek, Pak
40 N35°1' E37°3' Salamiyah, Syria
37 N53°21' E55°55' Salavat, Rus Fed
128 N19°22' W70°20' Salcedo, Dom Rep
56 N11°39' E78°10' Salem, Ind
106 N44°58' W122°59' Salem, OR, US
111 N42°31' W70°54' Salem, MA, US
117 N37°17' W80°4' Salem, VA, US
10 N56°43' W5°47' Salen, UK
11 N40°41' E14°46' Salerno, It
22 N48°7' E19°48' Salgótarján, Hun
79 N26°58' W0°1' Sali, Alg
113 N38°32' W106°0' Salida, CO, US
38 N38°29' E28°9' Salihli, Turk
108 N38°50' W97°37' Salina, KS, US
134 S2°13' W80°58' Salinas, Ecu
137 S16°10' W42°17' Salinas, MG, Braz
112 N36°41' W121°40' Salinas, CA, US
117 N35°40' W80°29' Salisbury, NC, US
97 N63°34' W76°38' Salisbury Island, Can
14 N44°11' E2°47' Salles-Curan, Fr
115 N35°28' W94°47' Sallisaw, OK, US
34 N61°22' E31°50' Salmi, Rus Fed
99 N49°12' W117°17' Salmo, BC, Can
107 N45°11' W113°51' Salmon, ID, US
99 N50°42' W119°16' Salmon Arm, BC, Can
87 N3°12' E16°7' Salo, CAR
35 N57°7' E48°5' Salobelyak, Rus Fed
22 N46°48' E21°40' Salonta, Rom
117 N40°44' W111°53' Salt Lake City, UT, US
140 S24°47' W65°25' Salta, Arg
123 N25°25' W101°0' Saltillo, Coah, Mex
138 S31°24' W57°58' Salto, Ur
138 S24°2' W54°21' Salto Del Guaira, Para
112 N33°15' W116°38' Salton Sea, US
117 N37°37' W76°35' Saluda, VA, US
55 N18°32' E83°13' Salur, Ind
137 S12°59' W38°29' Salvador, BA, Braz
20 N47°50' E13°3' Salzburg, Aus
19 N52°51' E11°9' Salzwedel, Ger
115 N31°11' W95°0' Sam Rayburn Reservoir, US
63 N5°54' E121°52' Samales Group, Phil
128 N19°13' W69°20' Samana, Dom Rep
127 N23°4' W73°36' Samana Cay, Bah
53 N42°7' E142°56' Samani, Jap
63 N11°51' E124°55' Samar, Phil
63 N12°13' E123°58' Samar Sea, Phil
32 N53°12' E50°9' Samara, Rus Fed
61 S10°38' E150°39' Samarai, PNG
59 S0°30' E117°9' Samarinda, Indo
46 N39°40' E66°57' Samarkand, Uzb
44 N34°12' E43°52' Samarra', Iraq
47 N49°0' E83°23' Samarskoye, Kaz
39 N40°38' E48°40' Samaxi, Azer
137 S7°8' W45°21' Sambaíba, MA, Braz
59 N1°20' E109°15' Sambas, Indo
92 S14°16' E50°10' Sambava, Madag
52 N37°27' E129°10' Samch'ok, S Kor
61 S3°58' E152°50' Samo, PNG
73 S12°9' W175°34' SAMOA
34 N63°38' E40°29' Samoded, Rus Fed
24 N42°21' E23°32' Samokov, Bulg
25 N40°28' E25°31' Samothráki, Grc
69 S23°2' E150°11' Sampaga, Indo
59 S2°32' E112°57' Sampit, Indo
39 N37°30' E38°32' Samsat, Turk
52 N41°19' E127°59' Samsu, N Kor
38 N41°17' E36°20' Samsun, Turk
78 N13°18' W4°54' San, Mali
112 N38°12' W120°41' San Andreas, CA, US
63 N13°20' E122°38' San Andres, Phil
132 N6°49' W72°52' San Andrés, Col
114 N31°28' W100°26' San Angelo, TX, US
114 N29°26' W98°32' San Antonio, TX, US
124 N16°15' W89°2' San Antonio, Blz
140 S28°56' W65°6' San Antonio, Arg
13 N38°58' E1°18' San Antonio Abad, Sp
140 S40°44' W64°56' San Antonio Oeste, Arg
115 N26°8' W97°38' San Benito, TX, US
63 N12°59' E123°59' San Bernardino Strait, Phil
112 N34°7' W117°18' San Bernardino, CA, US
135 S14°49' W66°51' San Borja, Bol
135 S14°28' W67°35' San Buena Ventura, Bol
125 N11°8' W84°47' San Carlos, Nic
132 N9°40' W68°35' San Carlos, Ven
141 S36°25' W71°58' San Carlos, Chile
141 S41°9' W71°18' San Carlos de Bariloche, Arg
112 N33°25' W117°37' San Clemente, CA, US
112 N32°40' W119°1' San Clemente Island, US
128 N18°25' W70°7' San Cristobal, Dom Rep
74 S10°35' E161°37' San Cristobal, Sol Is
126 N22°43' W83°3' San Cristóbal, Cuba
132 N7°46' W72°14' San Cristóbal, Ven
114 N27°46' W98°14' San Diego, TX, US
112 N32°43' W117°10' San Diego, CA, US
138 S24°39' W56°26' San Estanislao, Para
132 N10°20' W68°45' San Felipe, Ven
132 N1°55' W67°6' San Felipe, Col
13 N41°47' E3°1' San Feliú de Guixols, Sp
13 N36°28' W6°12' San Fernando, Sp
63 N15°2' E120°41' San Fernando, Phil
63 N16°36' E120°19' San Fernando, Phil
129 N10°17' W61°28' San Fernando, T & T
132 N7°55' W67°28' San Fernando De Apure, Ven
132 N4°3' W67°42' San Fernando de Atabapo, Ven
140 S28°28' W65°47' San Fernando del Valle de Catamarca, Arg
124 N13°48' W88°9' San Francisco, El Sal
112 N37°46' W122°25' San Francisco, CA, US
128 N19°18' W70°15' San Francisco De Macorís, Dom Rep
124 N12°30' W86°18' San Francisco Libre, Nic
129 N18°3' W67°4' San German, PR, US
140 S34°19' W62°2' San Gregorio, Arg
135 S16°23' W60°59' San Ignacio, Bol
140 S27°16' W55°32' San Ignacio, Arg
122 N23°55' W106°25' San Ignacio, Sin, Mex
124 N17°11' W88°59' San Ignacio, Blz
125 N9°23' W83°42' San Isidro, CR
123 N21°55' W100°15' San Isidro, SLP, Mex
138 S24°31' W55°42' San Isidro de Curuguaty, Para
135 S16°20' W62°38' San Javier, Bol
140 S30°35' W59°57' San Javier, Arg
112 N36°24' W120°11' San Joaquin Valley, US
140 S31°54' W61°52' San Jorge, Arg
75 S8°0' E159°0' San Jorge Island, Sol Is
63 N12°27' E121°3' San Jose, Phil
63 N10°46' E121°56' San Jose, Phil
112 N37°20' W121°53' San Jose, CA, US
63 N15°48' E121°0' San Jose, Phil
125 N9°56' W84°5' San José, CR
138 S34°21' W56°43' San José, Ur
135 S17°51' W60°47' San José de Chiquitos, Bol
122 N23°4' W109°42' San José del Cabo, BCS, Mex
128 N18°49' W71°14' San Juan, Dom Rep
129 N18°28' W66°5' San Juan, PR, US
134 S15°22' W75°9' San Juan, Peru
140 S31°32' W68°31' San Juan, Arg
13 N39°5' E1°30' San Juan Bautista, Sp
138 S26°40' W57°9' San Juan Bautista, Para
132 N9°54' W67°21' San Juan De Los Morros, Ven
124 N11°16' W85°52' San Juan del Sur, Nic
126 N22°16' W83°50' San Juan y Martínez, Cuba
138 S22°10' W57°55' San Lázaro, Para
134 N1°17' W78°50' San Lorenzo, Ecu
122 N24°55' W111°16' San Luis, BCS, Mex
124 N16°14' W89°27' San Luis, Guat
140 S33°18' W66°21' San Luis, Arg
112 N35°19' W120°37' San Luis Obispo, CA, US
123 N22°52' W101°0' San Luis Potosí, Mex
123 N22°9' W100°59' San Luis Potosí, SLP, Mex
123 N16°48' W99°21' San Marcos, Gro, Mex
115 N29°53' W97°56' San Marcos, TX, US
125 N9°40' W84°1' San Marcos, CR
17 N43°49' E12°32' SAN MARINO
17 N43°55' E12°26' San Marino, S Mar
140 S26°48' W55°2' San Martin, Arg
13 N40°28' E0°11' San Mateo, Sp
112 N37°34' W122°20' San Mateo, CA, US
124 N15°52' W91°26' San Mateo Ixtatan, Guat
135 S16°22' W58°24' San Matías, Bol
125 N8°26' W78°56' San Miguel, Pan
140 S26°49' W65°13' San Miguel de Tucumán, Arg
140 S35°27' W58°48' San Miguel del Monte, Arg
124 N13°28' W88°11' San Miquel, El Sal
123 N16°56' W98°32' San Nicolás, Gro, Mex
134 S15°13' W75°12' San Nicolás, Peru
63 N14°4' E121°19' San Pablo, Phil
135 S14°20' W64°50' San Pedro, Bol
138 S24°5' W57°5' San Pedro, Para
124 N17°55' W87°59' San Pedro, Blz
128 N18°28' W69°19' San Pedro De Macorís, Dom Rep
125 N13°4' W84°33' San Pedro del Norte, Nic
124 N15°30' W88°2' San Pedro Sula, Hon
140 S34°36' W68°20' San Rafael, Arg
134 S11°8' W75°20' San Ramón, Peru
135 S13°17' W64°43' San Ramón, Bol
140 S28°34' W58°43' San Roque, Arg
140 S31°37' W58°30' San Salvador, Arg
124 N13°42' W89°13' San Salvador, El Sal
140 S24°11' W65°18' San Salvador de Jujuy, Arg
127 N23°52' W74°32' San Salvador Island, Bah
13 N43°19' W1°59' San Sebastián, Sp
138 S26°52' W57°3' San Ygnacio, Para
42 N15°19' E44°12' San'a, Yem
85 N4°45' W6°38' San-Pédro, Côte d'Ivoire
42 N15°19' E44°12' Sanaa, Yem
121 N54°10' W162°58' Sanak Island, US
60 S2°4' E125°58' Sanana, Indo
44 N35°19' E46°59' Sanandaj, Iran
86 N4°5' E10°31' Sananga River, Cam
43 N17°50' E51°0' Sanaw, Yem
14 N46°50' E2°55' Sancoins, Fr
126 N21°56' W79°27' Sancti Spíritus, Cuba
108 N42°23' W102°49' Sand Hills, US
121 N55°20' W160°30' Sand Point, AK, US
24 N41°34' E23°17' Sandanski, Bulg
78 N14°42' W10°18' Sandaré, Mali
114 N30°8' W102°23' Sanderson, TX, US
119 N32°59' W82°49' Sandersville, GA, US
135 S14°17' W69°26' Sandia, Peru
38 N38°28' E30°17' Sandikli, Turk
11 N60°17' W1°38' Sandness, UK
88 S9°41' E22°52' Sandoa, DRC
21 N50°41' E21°45' Sandomierz, Pol
57 N18°28' E94°22' Sandoway, Myanmar
106 N48°17' W116°33' Sandpoint, ID, US
98 N53°13' W131°51' Sandspit, BC, Can
68 S27°59' E119°17' Sandstone, WA, Austl
109 N43°26' W82°50' Sandusky, MI, US
116 N41°27' W82°43' Sandusky, OH, US
11 N60°0' W1°15' Sandwick, UK
102 N52°51' W93°13' Sandy Lake, Can
46 N36°33' E62°34' Sandykgachy, Turkm
111 N43°26' W70°47' Sanford, ME, US
117 N35°29' W79°11' Sanford, NC, US
45 N35°59' E59°46' Sang Bast, Iran
54 N19°34' E74°13' Sangamner, Ind
87 N1°28' E15°59' Sangha River, Con
113 N36°14' W105°6' Sangre de Cristo Mountains, US
48 N29°25' E86°43' Sangsang, China
50 N29°18' E110°2' Sangzhi, China
119 N26°27' W82°2' Sanibel, FL, US
20 N48°12' E15°37' Sankt Pölten, Aus
32 N59°59' E30°16' Sankt-Peterburg, Rus Fed
16 N39°32' E9°8' Sanluri, It
82 N13°32' E33°37' Sannar, Sud
51 N27°0' E120°12' Sansha, China
134 S8°59' W78°36' Santa, Peru
112 N33°46' W117°56' Santa Ana, CA, US
124 N14°0' W89°34' Santa Ana, El Sal
135 S13°45' W65°35' Santa Ana, Bol
124 N13°50' W89°38' Santa Ana, El Sal
135 S15°31' W67°30' Santa Ana del Alto Beni, Bol
112 N34°26' W119°42' Santa Barbara, CA, US
124 N14°55' W88°14' Santa Bárbara, Hon
125 N8°46' W81°21' Santa Catalina, Pan
112 N33°21' W119°19' Santa Catalina Island, US
139 S26°40' W50°23' Santa Catarina, Braz
126 N22°25' W79°58' Santa Clara, Cuba
132 S2°43' W69°43' Santa Clara, Col
135 S2°34' W73°44' Santa Clotilde, Peru
128 N12°32' W69°59' Santa Cruz, Aruba, Neth
140 S34°38' W71°22' Santa Cruz, Chile
135 S17°47' W63°11' Santa Cruz, Bol
128 N12°18' W69°8' Santa Cruz, Neth Ant, Neth
124 N10°16' W85°36' Santa Cruz, CR
112 N36°59' W122°1' Santa Cruz, CA, US
63 N10°19' E125°33' Santa Cruz, Phil
63 N15°46' E119°55' Santa Cruz, Phil
78 N39°6' W28°1' Santa Cruz da Graciosa, Port
78 N28°29' W16°15' Santa Cruz de Tenerife, Sp
126 N23°9' W81°55' Santa Cruz del Norte, Cuba
124 N15°2' W91°8' Santa Cruz del Quiche, Guat
127 N20°43' W78°0' Santa Cruz del Sur, Cuba
112 N34°6' W119°56' Santa Cruz Island, US
72 S9°46' E163°4' Santa Cruz Islands, Sol Is
13 N38°59' E1°31' Santa Eulalia del Río, Sp
113 N35°41' W105°56' Santa Fe, NM, US
126 N21°45' W82°45' Santa Fe, Cuba
140 S31°37' W60°44' Santa Fe, Arg
137 S2°14' W45°18' Santa Helena, MA, Braz
141 S36°15' W66°56' Santa Isabel, Arg
74 S7°52' E159°5' Santa Isabel, Sol Is
126 N22°40' W83°58' Santa Lucía, Cuba
112 N36°22' W121°40' Santa lucia range, US
78 N16°37' W22°55' Santa Maria, CV
112 N34°58' W120°26' Santa Maria, CA, US
138 S29°41' W53°48' Santa Maria, RS, Braz
132 N11°15' W74°11' Santa Marta, Col
12 N43°41' W7°51' Santa Marta de Ortigueira, Sp
112 N34°2' W118°31' Santa Monica, CA, US
112 N33°23' W120°6' Santa Nicolas Island, US
132 N1°4' W73°58' Santa Rita, Col
138 S17°22' W53°13' Santa Rita do Araguaia, GO, Braz
112 N38°26' W122°43' Santa Rosa, CA, US
113 N34°56' W104°41' Santa Rosa, NM, US
132 N2°34' W68°13' Santa Rosa, Col
140 S28°2' W67°37' Santa Rosa, Arg
141 S36°37' W64°17' Santa Rosa, Arg
124 N14°47' W88°46' Santa Rosa de Copán, Hon
140 S32°20' W65°12' Santa Rosa del Conlara, Arg
135 S16°54' W62°24' Santa Rosa del Palmar, Bol
112 N33°48' W120°13' Santa Rosa Island, US
122 N27°19' W112°17' Santa Rosalía, BCS, Mex
140 S27°49' W61°9' Santa Sylvina, Arg
139 S19°55' W40°36' Santa Teresa, ES, Braz
138 S33°31' W53°21' Santa Vitória do Palmar, RS, Braz
54 N23°45' E71°10' Santalpur, Ind
137 S2°59' W44°3' Santana, BA, Braz
138 S30°53' W55°33' Santana do Livramento, RS, Braz
12 N43°28' W3°50' Santander, Sp
123 N24°13' W98°28' Santander Jiménez, Tamps, Mex
13 N39°22' E3°7' Santañy, Sp
12 N39°14' W8°41' Santarém, Port
136 S2°27' W54°41' Santarém, PA, Braz
138 S29°11' W54°53' Santiago, RS, Braz
128 N19°29' W70°44' Santiago, Dom Rep
125 N8°6' W80°58' Santiago, Pan
140 S33°28' W70°40' Santiago, Chile
134 S7°58' W79°15' Santiago de Cao, Peru
135 S18°19' W59°34' Santiago de Chiquitos, Bol
12 N42°53' W8°33' Santiago de Compostela, Sp
127 N20°2' W75°50' Santiago de Cuba, Cuba
140 S27°47' W64°16' Santiago del Estero, Arg
138 S34°48' W56°21' Santiago Vázquez, Ur
59 N1°20' E120°54' Santigi, Indo
55 N23°15' E88°26' Santipur, Ind
139 S23°40' W46°31' Santo André, SP, Braz
138 S28°18' W54°16' Santo Ângelo, RS, Braz
78 N16°49' W25°29' Santo Antão, CV
86 N1°39' E7°26' Santo Antônio, STP
135 S17°59' W58°51' Santo Corazón, Bol
125 N12°16' W85°5' Santo Domingo, Nic
128 N18°29' W69°54' Santo Domingo, Dom Rep
134 S0°15' W79°11' Santo Domingo de los Colorados, Ecu
113 N35°31' W105°12' Santo Domingo Pueblo, NM, US
125 N12°4' W85°5' Santo Tomás, Nic
140 S28°33' W56°3' Santo Tomé, Arg
25 N36°21' E24°48' Santorini, Grc
88 S7°19' E15°59' Sanza Pombo, Ang
138 S28°39' W56°0' São Borja, RS, Braz
139 S22°1' W47°54' São Carlos, SP, Braz
139 S15°57' W44°52' São Francisco, MG, Braz
137 S9°51' W37°45' São Francisco, Braz
139 S26°16' W48°38' São Francisco do Sul, SC, Braz
139 S16°1' W44°29' São Francisco River, Braz
138 S30°20' W54°19' São Gabriel, RS, Braz
139 S22°48' W43°4' São Gonçalo, RJ, Braz
12 N40°42' W8°44' São Jacinto, Port
136 N0°46' W59°33' São João da Baliza, RR, Braz
12 N40°54' W8°30' São João da Madeira, Port
139 S21°9' W44°16' São João del Rei, MG, Braz
137 S8°21' W42°15' São João do Piauí, PI, Braz
139 S28°18' W49°56' São Joaquim, SC, Braz
139 S20°48' W49°23' São José do Rio Prêto, SP, Braz
137 S2°29' W44°16' São Luís, MA, Braz
139 S18°44' W39°51' São Mateus, ES, Braz
78 N16°19' W25°28' São Nicolau, CV
139 S22°7' W49°47' São Paulo, Braz
139 S23°35' W46°37' São Paulo, SP, Braz
138 S19°53' W51°55' São Pedro, MT, Braz
139 S21°30' W47°33' São Simão, SP, Braz
139 S20°55' W44°30' São Tiago, MG, Braz
86 N0°17' E6°46' Sao Tome, STP
86 S0°5' E6°41' SAO TOME AND PRINCIPE
139 S23°58' W46°23' São Vicente, SP, Braz
78 N16°33 W26°3' São Vicente, CV
25 S0°25' E130°47' Saonek, Indo
25 N41°2' E25°41' Sápai, Grc
86 N5°54' E5°41' Sapele, Nga
134 S6°56' W76°48' Saposoa, Peru
36 N53°56' E40°41' Sapozhok, Rus Fed
53 N43°3' E141°21' Sapporo, Jap
115 N36°1' W96°7' Sapulpa, OK, US
85 N11°43' W3°50' Sara, Burk
57 N14°32' E100°55' Sara Buri, Thai
44 N37°56' E47°32' Sarab, Iran
36 N53°44' E41°0' Sarai, Rus Fed
55 N21°20' E83°0' Saraipali, Ind
22 N43°52' E18°24' Sarajevo, Bos & Herz
45 N36°32' E61°11' Sarakhs, Iran
110 N44°20' W74°8' Saranac Lake, NY, US
24 N39°53' E20°1' Sarandë, Alb
138 S27°56' W52°55' Sarandi, RS, Braz
63 N5°16' E125°27' Sarangani Islands, Phil
63 N5°20' E125°4' Sarangani Strait, Phil
36 N54°11' E45°11' Saransk, Rus Fed
35 N56°28' E53°48' Sarapul, Rus Fed
40 N35°52' E36°48' Saraqib, Syria
119 N27°20' W82°32' Sarasota, FL, US
110 N43°5' W73°47' Saratoga Springs, NY, US
32 N51°29' E45°57' Saratov, Rus Fed
45 N27°15' E62°40' Saravan, Iran
57 N15°43' E106°25' Saravan, Laos
84 N12°50' W11°45' Saraya, Sen
45 N26°39' E61°15' Sarbaz, Iran
54 N28°26' E74°29' Sardarshahr, Ind
16 N40°40' E7°31' Sardegna, It
16 N40°40' E7°31' Sardina, It
118 N34°26' W89°55' Sardis, MS, US
80 N9°9' E18°24' Sarh, Chad
44 N36°34' E53°3' Sari, Iran
39 N40°20' E42°35' Sarikamis, Turk
59 N2°7' E111°31' Sarikei, Malay
67 S21°26' E149°13' Sarina, Qld, Austl
83 N2°22' E42°20' Sarinleey, Som
80 N23°34' E16°8' Sarir Tibasti, Libya
115 N27°13' W97°47' Sarita, TX, US
52 N38°31' E125°46' Sariwon, N Kor
38 N39°21' E36°26' Sarkisla, Turk
23 N46°46' E24°11' Sarmasu, Rom
60 S1°51' E138°44' Sarmi, Indo
141 S45°36' W69°5' Sarmiento, Arg
15 N46°54' E8°14' Sarnen, Switz
103 N43°0' W82°24' Sarnia, ON, Can
58 S2°18' E102°42' Sarolangun, Indo
29 N59°17' E11°7' Sarpsborg, Nor
47 N45°26' E79°54' Sarqant, Kaz
97 N70°1' W51°56' Sarqqaq, Grld, Den
12 N42°47' W7°24' Sarria, Sp
15 N42°10' E9°1' Sartène, Fr
61 S6°1' E146°26' Saruwaged Range, PNG
47 N39°44' E73°15' Sary-Tash, Kyr
47 N44°22' E77°59' Saryözek, Kaz
47 N46°7' E73°38' Saryshaghan, Kaz
47 N48°23' E69°59' Sarysu, Kaz
74 S7°2' E156°47' Sasamungga, Sol Is
85 N10°21' E0°28' Sasanne-Mango, Togo
54 N25°57' E84°2' Sasaram, Ind
54 N34°52' E77°45' Saser Kangri, Ind
100 N53°55' W107°20' Saskatchewan, Can
100 N52°7' W106°38' Saskatoon, SK, Can
36 N54°21' E41°54' Sasovo, Rus Fed
85 N4°57' W6°5' Sassandra, Côte d'Ivoire
85 N5°43' W6°31' Sassandra, Côte d'Ivoire
16 N40°44' E8°34' Sassari, It
19 N54°31' E13°38' Sassnitz, Ger
47 N42°34' E70°0' Sastobe, Kaz
29 N60°21' E15°45' Säter, Swe
35 N55°3' E59°1' Satka, Rus Fed
22 N48°24' E21°39' Sátoraljaújhely, Hun
54 N21°37' E75°58' Satpura Range, Ind
35 N56°22' E64°48' Satrovo, Rus Fed
23 N47°48' E22°53' Satu Mare, Rom
59 S3°47' E115°27' Satui, Indo
57 N6°37' E100°2' Satun, Thai
140 S30°5' W58°46' Sauce, Arg
42 N22°20' E45°50' SAUDI ARABIA
102 N46°34' W84°16' Sault Saint Marie, ON, Can
109 N46°29' W84°22' Sault Ste Marie, MI, US
14 N47°16' W0°5' Saumur, Fr
88 S9°39' E20°24' Saurimo, Ang
59 S1°0' E120°30' Sausu, Indo
73 S13°0' W173°55' Savai'i, Samoa
119 N32°3' W81°6' Savannah, GA, US
119 N33°22' W81°53' Savannah River, US
85 N8°2' E2°29' Savé, Ben
44 N35°1' E50°20' Saveh, Iran
85 N9°37' W0°49' Savelugu, Gha
14 N43°14' E1°35' Saverdun, Fr
23 N46°1' E22°14' Savîrsin, Rom
74 S9°6' E159°30' Savo Island, Sol Is
16 N44°17' E8°27' Savona, It
29 N61°52' E28°53' Savonlinna, Fin
59 S9°37' E121°47' Savu Sea
53 N24°50' E125°18' Sawada, Jap
59 N2°23' E115°14' Sawai, Indo
60 S2°59' E129°9' Sawai, Indo
54 N25°59' E76°22' Sawai Madhopur, Ind
82 N19°8' E37°20' Sawakin, Sud
82 N14°25' E29°5' Sawdiri, Sud
85 N9°17' W2°25' Sawla, Gha
124 N16°31' W90°10' Sayaxché, Guat
40 N33°34' E35°23' Sayda, Leb
43 N15°12' E51°14' Sayhut, Yem
49 N44°53' E110°7' Saynshand, Mong
114 N35°17' W99°38' Sayre, OK, US
43 N16°7' E49°12' Saywun, Yem
10 N56°4' W6°12' Scalasaig, UK
11 N60°8' W1°16' Scalloway, UK
121 N61°53' W165°38' Scammon Bay, AK, US
129 N11°11' W60°44' Scarborough, T & T
105 N46°4' W59°43' Scatarie Island, Can
15 N47°44' E8°37' Schaffhausen, Switz
110 N42°49' W73°56' Schenectady, NY, US
18 N53°26' E6°17' Schiermonnikoog, Neth
19 N54°31' E9°33' Schleswig, Ger
20 N47°51' E15°45' Schneeberg, Aus
110 N42°40' W74°19' Schoharie, NY, US
19 N52°1' E11°44' Schönebeck, Ger
18 N51°43' E3°25' Schouwen, Neth
102 N48°48' W87°15' Schreiber, ON, Can
19 N49°7' E9°44' Schwäbisch Hall, Ger
19 N48°8' E9°8' Schwäbische Alb, Ger
19 N50°3' E10°14' Schweinfurt, Ger
19 N53°36' E11°26' Schwerin, Ger
15 N47°1' E8°39' Schwyz, Switz
107 N48°47' W105°25' Scobey, MT, US
97 N70°28' W21°58' Scoresbysund, Grld, Den
11 N56°49' W4°29' SCOTLAND
100 N52°23' W108°50' Scott, SK, Can
108 N41°53' W103°40' Scottsbluff, NE, US
10 N58°20' W5°8' Scourie, UK
117 N41°25' W75°40' Scranton, PA, US
27 N45°58' E35°59' Sea of Azov
25 N35°52' E24°20' Sea of Crete
40 N32°52' E35°17' Sea of Galilee, Isr
49 N40°32' E129°49' Sea of Japan
38 N40°47' E28°2' Sea of Marmara
33 N55°58' E147°37' Sea of Okhotsk
115 N35°15' W91°44' Searcy, AR, US
106 N47°37' W122°20' Seattle, WA, US
124 N12°51' W86°6' Sébaco, Nic
111 N43°51' W70°58' Sebago Lake, US
119 N27°50' W80°29' Sebastian, FL, US
85 N13°26' E0°32' Sebba, Burk
45 N36°40' E65°45' Sebergan, Afg
23 N45°58' E23°34' Sebes, Rom
39 N40°18' E38°26' Sebinkarahisar, Turk
119 N27°30' W81°26' Sebring, FL, US
134 S5°33' W80°51' Sechura, Peru
109 N38°42' W93°14' Sedalia, MO, US
15 N49°42' E4°57' Sedan, Fr
12 N42°43' W3°45' Sedano, Sp
40 N30°52' E34°47' Sede Boqer, Isr
90 S26°50' E17°45' Seeheim, Nam
83 N7°10' E48°39' Seemade, Som
68 S30°40' E125°14' Seemore Downs, WA, Austl
85 N10°56' E3°42' Segbana, Ben
34 N63°44' E34°17' Segezha, Rus Fed
78 N13°26' W6°16' Ségou, Mali
12 N40°56' W4°7' Segovia, Sp
121 N52°4' W172°31' Seguam Island, US
80 N20°12' E12°59' Seguedine, Niger
78 N14°7' W6°44' Séguéla, Mali
85 N7°57' W6°40' Séguéla, Côte d'Ivoire
115 N29°34' W97°58' Seguin, TX, US
90 S20°23' E22°45' Sehithwa, Bots
45 N26°26' E67°52' Sehwan, Pak
58 S2°51' E103°51' Sekayu, Indo
58 S0°30' E103°38' Selat Berhala
59 S2°34' E108°41' Selat Karimata
59 S7°28' E113°14' Selat Madura
59 S9°9' E119°11' Selat Sumba
108 N45°31' W100°2' Selby, SD, US
49 N49°25' E103°59' Selenge, Mong
78 N15°10' W12°11' Sélibaby, Mrta
59 N0°37' E112°8' Selimbau, Indo
36 N47°11' E47°27' Selitrennoye, Rus Fed
34 N56°51' E33°27' Selizharovo, Rus Fed
101 N50°9' W96°52' Selkirk, MB, Can
118 N32°25' W87°1' Selma, AL, US
59 S8°39' E116°32' Selong, Indo
67 S20°41' E139°55' Selwyn Range, Austl
59 S6°58' E110°25' Semarang, Indo
87 N1°39' E14°35' Sémbé, Con
36 N51°41' E39°2' Semiluki, Rus Fed
114 N32°43' W102°38' Seminole, TX, US
46 N52°22' E64°8' Semiozërnoye, Kaz
47 N50°25' E80°14' Semipalatinsk, Kaz
26 N50°43' E30°56' Semipolki, Ukr
63 N11°53' E121°0' Semirara Island, Phil
44 N35°34' E53°24' Semnan, Iran
136 S9°4' W68°40' Sena Madureira, AC, Braz
88 S16°6' E23°16' Senanga, Zam
53 N38°15' E140°53' Sendai, Jap
84 N14°27' W15°19' SENEGAL
78 N16°44' W15°7' Sénégal, Mrta
104 N48°23' W77°15' Senneterre, QC, Can
22 N45°56' E20°4' Senta, Yugo
72 N7°16' E158°28' Senyavin Islands, FSM
52 N37°34' E126°59' Seoul, S Kor
74 S8°33' E159°50' Sepi, Sol Is
61 S4°6' E143°12' Sepik River, PNG
104 N50°12' W66°23' Sept-Îles, QC, Can
35 N55°58' E60°34' Ser'ga, Rus Fed
21 N48°17' E17°44' Sered', Slvk
38 N38°55' E33°33' Sereflikoçhisar, Turk
58 N2°43' E101°57' Seremban, Malay
89 S2°46' E34°9' Serengeti Plain, Tanz
137 S11°20' W37°47' Sergipe, Braz
34 N56°18' E38°8' Sergiyev Posad, Rus Fed
58 N2°51' E99°4' Seribudolok, Indo
38 N36°55' E31°7' Serik, Turk
37 N53°55' E51°14' Sernovodsk, Rus Fed
35 N56°56' E49°9' Sernur, Rus Fed
35 N59°29' E60°31' Serov, Rus Fed
12 N37°56' W7°36' Serpa, Port
133 N9°55' W61°58' Serpent's Mouth
88 S16°14' E12°39' Serra da Chela, Ang
12 N40°20' W7°37' Serra da Estrela, Port
12 N41°27' W7°36' Serra da Padrela, Port
12 N37°15' W8°50' Serra de Monchique, Port
12 N41°41' W6°53' Serra de Nogueira, Port
12 N38°18' W7°55' Serra de Ossa, Port
133 N2°44' W55°1' Serra de Tumucumaque, Fr Gu, Fr
136 N1°28' W57°25' Serra de Tumucumaque, Braz
136 S8°26' W57°15' Serra do Cachimbo, Braz
12 N40°22' W8°20' Serra do Caramulo, Port
137 S16°59' W40°48' Serra do Chifre, Braz
139 S16°0' W44°0' Serra do Espinhaco, Braz
139 S25°47' W48°52' Serra do Mar, Braz
138 S13°26' W51°42' Serra do Roncador, Braz
137 S7°58' W50°23' Serra dos Gradaús, Braz
136 S11°1' W63°31' Serra dos Parecis, Braz
136 N3°29' W64°4' Serra Parima, Braz
133 N3°26' W64°34' Serra Parima, Ven
24 N41°5' E23°32' Sérrai, Grc
125 N9°4' W78°7' Serranía de Darién, Pan
133 N8°17' W62°15' Serranía de Imataca, Ven
139 S18°37' W43°23' Sêrro, MG, Braz
12 N39°48' W8°6' Sertã, Port
139 S22°19' W46°9' Sertãozinho, MG, Braz
60 S1°53' E136°14' Serui, Indo
91 S21°58' E27°20' Seruli, Bots
48 N33°4' E97°45' Serxu, China
90 S19°7' E13°19' Sesfontein, Nam
53 N42°23' E141°6' Setana, Jap
15 N43°24' E3°42' Sète, Fr
79 N36°9' E5°26' Sétif, Alg
78 N33°4' W7°37' Settat, Mor
12 N38°31' W8°53' Setúbal, Port
39 N40°34' E44°57' Sevan, Arm
27 N44°36' E33°32' Sevastopol, Ukr
35 N60°9' E59°57' Severoural'sk, Rus Fed
12 N37°23' W5°58' Sevilla, Sp
121 N60°7' W149°26' Seward, AK, US
99 N55°21' W118°47' Sexsmith, AB, Can
123 N19°39' W90°40' Seybaplaya, Camp, Mex
92 S8°56' E47°42' SEYCHELLES
38 N37°25' E31°53' Seydisehir, Turk
28 N65°16' W14°0' Seydisfjordur, Ice
79 N34°44' E10°45' Sfax, Tun
23 N45°52' E25°47' Sfîntu Gheorghe, Rom
48 N38°25' E77°16' Shache, China
51 N26°8' E114°49' Shadi, China
35 N56°5' E63°38' Shadrinsk, Rus Fed
48 N31°30' E100°10' Shadui, China
58 N3°4' E101°34' Shah Alam, Malay
45 N32°31' E67°25' Shah Juy, Afg
42 N16°12' E43°46' Shaharah, Yem
40 N32°51' E36°37' Shahba', Syria
55 N23°17' E81°21' Shahdol, Ind
81 N32°49' E21°52' Shahhat, Libya
54 N27°53' E79°55' Shahjahanpur, Ind
44 N32°19' E50°50' Shahr Kord, Iran
45 N31°11' E68°34' Shaighalu, Pak
54 N23°26' E76°16' Shajapur, Ind
46 N39°5' E66°50' Shakhrisabz, Uzb
36 N47°42' E40°13' Shakhty, Rus Fed
108 N44°47' W93°32' Shakopee, MN, US
46 N47°50' E59°36' Shalqar, Kaz
101 N55°52' W92°5' Shamattawa, MB, Can
82 N7°7' E30°46' Shambe, Sud
49 N27°56' E116°14' Shangdundu, China
49 N31°16' E121°26' Shanghai, China
50 N28°28' E108°33' Shanglin, China
50 N33°31' E110°45' Shangnan, China
50 N23°1' E99°50' Shangyun, China
48 N33°38' E79°50' Shanhe, China
48 N42°52' E90°10' Shanshan, China
51 N23°22' E116°40' Shantou, China
51 N34°48' E116°3' Shanxian, China
50 N33°35' E109°49' Shanyang, China
51 N24°42' E113°35' Shaoguan, China
51 N29°59' E120°34' Shaoxing, China
68 S25°11' E113°11' Shark Bay
49 N30°19' E112°14' Shashi, China
100 N49°40' W108°25' Shaunavon, SK, Can

continue on next page

27 N49°23' E38°13' **Svatovo**, Ukr
57 N13°48' E102°58' **Svay Chék**, Camb
57 N11°5' E105°48' **Svay Rieng**, Camb
35 N58°16' E47°32' **Svecha**, Rus Fed
96 N79°8' W101°10' Sverdrup Islands, Can
24 N41°52' E21°58' **Sveti Nikole**, FYRM
36 N45°20' E42°40' **Svetlograd**, Rus Fed
22 N43°58' E21°16' **Svetozarevo**, Yugo
25 N41°46' E26°12' **Svilengrad**, Bulg
26 N54°51' E26°24' **Svir'**, Bela
34 N60°48' E33°43' **Svir'stroy**, Rus Fed
25 N43°37' E25°20' **Svishtov**, Bulg
29 N68°14' E14°34' **Svolvær**, Nor
119 N32°36' W82°20' **Swainsboro**, GA, US
90 S22°41' E14°34' **Swakopmund**, Nam
69 S35°21' E143°34' **Swan Hill**, Vic, Austl
99 N54°52' W115°45' **Swan Hills**, AB, Can
117 N35°25' W76°20' **Swan Quarter**, NC, US
101 N52°6' W101°16' **Swan River**, MB, Can
91 S27°46' E31°13' **SWAZILAND**
29 N62°49' E13°19' **SWEDEN**
20 N53°47' E15°47' **Swidwin**, Pol
20 N52°15' E15°32' **Swiedbodzin**, Pol
100 N50°17' W107°50' **Swift Current**, SK, Can
11 N51°34' W1°47' **Swindon**, UK
20 N53°53' E14°14' **Swinoujscie**, Pol
15 N46°37' E7°44' **SWITZERLAND**
69 S33°47' E151°11' **Sydney**, NSW, Austl
105 N46°10' W60°12' **Sydney**, NS, Can
32 N61°40' E50°49' **Syktyvkar**, Rus Fed
118 N33°10' W86°15' **Sylacauga**, AL, US
55 N24°54' E91°52' **Sylhet**, Bngl
119 N31°32' W83°50' **Sylvester**, GA, US
17 N37°5' E15°17' **Syracuse**, It
108 N37°59' W101°45' **Syracuse**, KS, US
110 N43°3' W76°9' **Syracuse**, NY, US
62 N45°37' E62°11' *Syrdar'ya*, Kaz
41 N34°56' E38°31' **SYRIA**
41 N34°4' E38°40' Syrian Desert, Syria
35 N56°29' E60°49' **Sysert'**, Rus Fed
36 N53°9' E48°27' **Syzran'**, Rus Fed
22 N46°52' E20°34' **Szarvas**, Hun
20 N53°24' E14°32' **Szczecin**, Pol
21 N53°43' E16°42' **Szczecinek**, Pol
22 N46°15' E20°9' **Szeged**, Hun
22 N47°12' E18°25' **Székesfehérvár**, Hun
22 N46°21' E18°42' **Szekszárd**, Hun
22 N46°39' E20°16' **Szentes**, Hun
22 N47°10' E20°12' **Szolnok**, Hun
22 N47°14' E16°37' **Szombathely**, Hun

T

52 N38°27' E127°58' T'aebaek Sanmaek, S Kor
51 N22°45' E121°9' **T'ai-tung**, Taiwan
51 N23°1' E120°12' **T'ainan**, Taiwan
51 N25°1' E121°28' **T'aipei**, Taiwan
42 N13°38' E44°4' **Ta'izz**, Yem
61 S2°41' E152°4' Tabar Island, PNG
123 N18°11' W93°32' **Tabasco**, Mex
99 N49°47' W112°8' **Taber**, AB, Can
63 N12°8' E122°4' Tablas Island, Phil
63 N12°7' E121°42' *Tablas Strait*
85 N6°34' E1°28' **Tabligbo**, Togo
20 N49°25' E14°41' **Tábor**, Czech
89 S5°1' E32°50' **Tabora**, Tanz
35 N58°31' E64°33' **Tabory**, Rus Fed
85 N4°25' W7°22' **Tabou**, Côte d'Ivoire
44 N38°4' E46°17' **Tabriz**, Iran
73 N3°40' W159°11' Tabuaeran Island, Kir
42 N28°23' E36°34' **Tabuk**, Sau Ar
63 N17°25' E121°26' **Tabuk**, Phil
72 N9°28' E138°4' **Tabunifi**, US
72 S15°22' E166°44' Tabwémasana, Van
133 N2°46' W59°47' *Tacata River*, Guy
48 N46°45' E82°57' **Tacheng**, China
63 N11°15' E125°0' **Tacloban**, Phil
135 S18°1' W70°15' **Tacna**, Peru
138 S31°42' W55°59' **Tacuarembó**, Ur
85 N11°47' E42°54' **Tadjoura**, Djib
41 N34°33' E38°17' **Tadmur**, Syria
101 N58°38' W99°10' *Tadoule Lake*, Can
104 N48°11' W69°42' **Tadoussac**, QC, Can
54 N14°55' E78°1' **Tadpatri**, Ind
52 N36°22' E126°34' **Taech'on**, S Kor
52 N35°52' E128°35' **Taegu**, S Kor
52 N36°18' E127°26' **Taejon**, S Kor
85 N9°4' W5°10' **Tafiré**, Côte d'Ivoire
36 N47°12' E38°56' **Taganrog**, Rus Fed
63 N9°39' E123°52' **Tagbilaran**, Phil
78 N29°58' W5°36' **Tagounite**, Mor
137 S12°25' W46°26' **Taguatinga**, GO, Braz
61 S11°37' E152°43' Tagula Island, PNG
63 N7°28' E125°48' **Tagum**, Phil
73 S16°30' W151°26' Tahaa, Fr Poly, Fr
79 N23°17' E5°32' Tahat, Alg
44 N27°42' E52°21' **Taheri**, Iran
73 S18°18' W150°21' Tahiti, Fr Poly, Fr
115 N35°55' W94°59' **Tahlequah**, OK, US
114 N33°10' W101°47' **Tahoka**, TX, US
80 N14°54' E5°16' **Tahoua**, Niger
73 S10°30' W140°50' Tahuata, Fr Poly, Fr
60 N3°37' E125°29' **Tahuna**, Indo
85 N5°52' W7°27' **Taï**, Côte d'Ivoire
49 N31°3' E118°51' *Tai Hu*, China
49 N36°11' E117°7' **Tai'an**, China
51 N30°26' E116°16' **Taihu**, China
51 N34°4' E114°50' **Taikang**, China
49 N46°23' E123°27' **Tailai**, China
69 S35°16' E139°27' **Tailem Bend**, SA, Austl
53 N37°3' E140°55' **Taira**, Jap
58 N4°6' E102°34' **Tais**, Indo
29 N65°34' E28°15' **Taivalkoski**, Fin
51 N23°17' E120°10' **TAIWAN**
51 N23°38' E118°29' *Taiwan Strait*
49 N37°55' E112°32' **Taiyuan**, China
80 N24°21' E14°28' **Tajarhi**, Libya
47 N38°40' E69°29' **TAJIKISTAN**
57 N16°52' E99°8' **Tak**, Thai
53 N39°1' E141°38' **Takada**, Jap
53 N37°0' E136°46' **Takahama**, Jap
59 N5°28' E119°25' **Takalar**, Indo
52 N34°20' E134°3' **Takamatsu**, Jap
73 S15°8' W146°53' Takapoto, Fr Poly, Fr
52 N29°2' E129°14' Takara-jima, Jap
73 S14°23' W144°41' Takaroa, Fr Poly, Fr
58 N4°38' E96°50' **Takengon**, Indo
44 N36°4' E49°43' **Takestan**, Iran
52 N32°58' E131°24' **Taketa**, Jap
61 S6°29' E155°50' **Taki**, PNG
98 N55°29' W125°57' **Takla Landing**, BC, Can
48 N38°58' E80°39' Taklimaken Shamo, China
85 N4°54' W1°46' **Takoradi**, Gha
86 N7°17' E9°59' **Takum**, Nga
54 N21°22' E72°1' **Talaja**, Ind
134 S4°33' W81°16' **Talara**, Peru
47 N42°32' E72°14' **Talas**, Kyr
61 S5°22' E150°1' **Talasea**, PNG
140 S35°25' W71°40' **Talca**, Chile
47 N45°0' E78°23' **Taldy Kurgan**, Kaz
45 N36°44' E69°32' **Taleqan**, Afg
69 S33°19' E134°54' **Talia**, SA, Austl
41 N36°41' E38°59' **Tall al Abyad al 'Atiq**, Syria
41 N36°48' E42°4' **Tall Kujik**, Syria
118 N33°26' W86°7' **Talladega**, AL, US
119 N30°27' W84°18' **Tallahassee**, FL, US
29 N60°49' E15°5' **Tällberg**, Swe
26 N59°25' E24°38' **Tallinn**, Est
115 N32°25' W91°11' **Tallulah**, LA, US
114 N36°2' W98°58' **Taloga**, OK, US
140 S25°24' W70°29' **Taltal**, Chile
57 N14°35' E109°3' **Tam Quan**, Viet
85 N9°25' W0°50' **Tamale**, Gha
79 N22°56' E5°30' **Tamanrasset**, Alg
123 N24°28' W99°21' **Tamaulipas**, Mex
84 N13°47' W13°40' **Tambacounda**, Sen
67 S24°53' E146°15' **Tambo**, Qld, Austl
92 S17°30' E43°58' **Tambohorano**, Madag
125 N9°43' W85°1' **Tambor**, CR
36 N52°43' E41°25' **Tambov**, Rus Fed
82 N5°36' E27°28' **Tambura**, Sud
78 N17°15' W10°40' **Tamchaket**, Mrta
141 S48°19' W70°58' **Tamel Aike**, Arg
123 N21°16' W97°27' **Tamiahua**, Ver, Mex
119 N27°57' W82°28' **Tampa**, FL, US
119 N27°42' W82°22' *Tampa Bay*
29 N61°30' E23°45' **Tampere**, Fin
60 S0°44' E132°10' Tamrau Mountains, Indo
49 N47°14' E117°21' **Tamsagbulag**, Mong
57 N24°13' E94°18' **Tamu**, Myanmar
29 N70°28' E28°18' **Tana**, Nor
83 S0°16' E38°43' *Tana*, Ken
60 S6°5' E140°17' **Tanahmerah**, Indo
66 S19°59' E129°43' **Tanami**, NT, Austl
66 S20°16' E131°20' Tanami Desert, Austl
121 N65°11' W152°9' **Tanana**, AK, US
72 N15°14' E145°45' **Tanapag**, NM Is, US
85 N7°48' W3°10' **Tanda**, Côte d'Ivoire
63 N9°5' E126°12' **Tandag**, Phil
141 S37°19' W59°9' **Tandil**, Arg
52 N30°34' E131°4' Tanega-shima, Jap
89 S5°4' E39°6' **Tanga**, Tanz
61 S3°34' E153°17' Tanga Islands, PNG
78 N35°46' W5°46' **Tanger**, Mor
48 N33°25' E90°0' Tanggula Shan, China
78 N35°46' W5°46' **Tangier**, Mor
48 N30°8' E90°23' **Tangmai**, China
58 N5°1' E95°55' **Tangse**, Indo
49 N39°37' E118°11' **Tangshan**, China
49 N46°42' E129°55' **Tangyuan**, China
63 N9°31' E123°5' **Tanjay**, Phil
58 S5°25' E105°15' **Tanjungkarang**, Indo
58 N0°55' E104°27' **Tanjungpinang**, Indo
58 N3°54' E98°26' **Tanjungpura**, Indo
59 N2°51' E117°22' **Tanjungselor**, Indo
45 N32°13' E70°23' **Tank**, Pak
75 S19°29' E169°14' Tanna, Van
63 N10°11' E123°29' *Tanon Strait*, Phil
80 N14°58' E8°53' **Tânout**, Niger
47 N47°20' E79°52' **Tansyk**, Kaz
81 N30°47' E31°0' **Tanta**, Egypt
55 N16°45' E81°42' **Tanuku**, Ind
89 S5°50' E32°4' **TANZANIA**
50 N28°46' E111°20' **Taohuayuan**, China
72 N14°41' E169°8' Taongi Atoll, Mar Is
113 N36°25' W105°34' **Taos**, NM, US
136 S4°4' W55°51' *Tapajós*, Braz
141 S36°21' W60°1' **Tapalqué**, Arg
58 S2°10' E101°4' **Tapan**, Indo
136 S5°45' W63°4' **Tapaua**, AM, Braz
138 S30°40' W51°23' **Tapes**, RS, Braz
84 N6°29' W8°51' **Tapeta**, Libr
61 S8°20' E147°0' **Tapini**, PNG
63 N5°43' E120°32' Tapul Group, Phil
139 S29°59' W50°48' **Taquara**, RS, Braz
69 S27°17' E150°28' **Tara**, Qld, Austl
88 S16°56' E26°47' **Tara**, Zam
41 N34°26' E35°51' **Tarabulus**, Leb
80 N32°52' E13°11' **Tarabulus**, Libya
23 N46°34' E29°6' **Taraclia**, Mol
60 S8°12' E124°52' **Taramana**, Indo
13 N40°1' W3°0' **Tarancón**, Sp
17 N40°28' E17°15' **Taranto**, It
134 S0°7' W76°20' **Tarapoa**, Ecu
136 S6°6' W68°28' **Taraquá**, AM, Braz
15 N45°54' E4°26' **Tarare**, Fr
79 N26°13' E9°18' **Tarat**, Alg
72 N1°25' E172°41' **Tarawa**, Kir
72 N1°2' E173°10' Tarawa Atoll, Kir
10 N57°54' W6°49' **Tarbert**, UK
14 N43°14' E0°5' **Tarbes**, Fr
12 N42°22' W3°49' **Tardajos**, Sp
29 N67°10' E22°38' **Tärendö**, Swe
78 N27°57' W12°54' **Tarfaya**, Mor
61 S5°50' E143°0' **Tari**, PNG
12 N36°1' W5°36' **Tarifa**, Sp
135 S21°31' W64°45' **Tarija**, Bol
43 N16°3' E49°39' **Tarim**, Yem
60 S3°10' E138°53' *Taritatu*, Indo
85 N5°19' W1°59' **Tarkwa**, Gha
63 N15°29' E120°35' **Tarlac**, Phil
134 S11°25' W75°42' **Tarma**, Peru
29 N65°43' E15°16' **Tärnaby**, Swe
21 N50°35' E21°41' **Tarnobrzeg**, Pol
35 N60°29' E43°33' **Tarnogskiy Gorodok**, Rus Fed
21 N50°1' E21°0' **Tarnów**, Pol
13 N41°7' E1°14' **Tarragona**, Sp
71 S44°50' E169°25' **Tarras**, NZ
13 N41°34' E2°1' **Tarrasa**, Sp
13 N41°39' E1°9' **Tàrrega**, Sp
140 S22°32' W63°49' **Tartagal**, Arg
26 N58°23' E26°43' **Tartu**, Est
40 N34°53' E35°53' **Tartus**, Syria
58 N2°1' E98°58' **Tarutung**, Indo
47 N46°20' E73°58' **Tasaral**, Kaz
46 N41°50' E59°58' **Tashauz**, Turkm
47 N41°19' E69°16' **Tashkent**, Uzb
58 S7°20' E108°12' **Tasikmalaya**, Indo
47 N47°15' E80°44' **Taskesken**, Kaz
38 N41°30' E34°14' **Tasköprü**, Turk
71 S40°55' E173°7' *Tasman Bay*
70 S43°25' E165°5' *Tasman Sea*
69 S42°23' E145°30' **Tasmania**, Austl
79 N25°52' E6°56' Tassili-n-ajjer, Alg
78 N29°44' W7°58' **Tata**, Mor
60 S8°55' E125°29' Tata Mai-lau, Indo
22 N47°33' E18°26' **Tatabánya**, Hun
73 S17°14' W138°25' Tatakoto, Fr Poly, Fr
33 N51°11' E141°5' *Tatar Strait*
26 N45°49' E29°36' **Tatarbunary**, Ukr
39 N38°30' E42°16' **Tatvan**, Turk
139 S23°2' W45°33' **Taubaté**, SP, Braz
46 N44°21' E51°19' **Tauchik**, Kaz
109 N37°37' W90°43' Taum Sauk Mountain, US
136 S8°57' W72°48' **Taumaturgo**, AC, Braz
57 N20°47' E97°2' **Taunggyi**, Myanmar
45 N30°42' E70°39' **Taunsa**, Pak
11 N51°1' W3°6' **Taunton**, UK
26 N55°15' E22°17' **Taurage**, Lith
71 S37°42' E176°10' **Tauranga**, NZ
38 N36°47' E33°35' Taurus Mountains, Turk
48 N49°10' E87°50' Tavan Bogdo Uli, Mong
35 N58°3' E65°15' **Tavda**, Rus Fed
74 S16°58' E179°38' Taveuni Island, Fiji
47 N52°44' E77°27' **Tavolzhan**, Kaz
57 N14°5' E98°12' **Tavoy**, Myanmar
37 N54°35' E73°38' **Tavricheskoye**, Rus Fed
72 S17°28' E177°51' **Tavua**, Fiji
109 N44°16' W83°32' **Tawas City**, MI, US
63 N5°21' E119°41' Tawitawi Island, Phil
44 N35°8' E44°27' **Tawuq**, Iraq
57 N11°18' E106°6' **Tây Ninh**, Viet
115 N30°34' W97°25' **Taylor**, TX, US
109 N39°33' W89°19' **Taylorville**, IL, US
42 N27°38' E38°29' **Tayma'**, Sau Ar
63 N10°49' E119°31' **Taytay**, Phil
79 N34°16' W4°1' **Taza**, Mor
78 N30°35' W7°12' **Tazenakht**, Mor
117 N37°7' W81°31' **Tazewell**, VA, US
100 N59°48' W108°45' *Tazin Lake*, Can
35 N68°43' E75°21' Tazovskiy Poluostrov, Rus Fed
39 N41°40' E44°49' **Tbilisi**, Geo
85 N9°2' E1°25' **Tchamba**, Togo
85 N8°53' E2°36' **Tchaourou**, Ben
86 S2°51' E11°2' **Tchibanga**, Gabon
21 N54°6' E18°47' **Tczew**, Pol
70 S45°25' E167°43' **Te Anau**, NZ
71 S34°39' E172°57' **Te Kao**, NZ
71 S38°28' E177°52' **Te Karaka**, NZ
71 S37°24' E175°9' **Te Kauwhata**, NZ
71 S39°15' E176°41' **Te Pohue**, NZ
71 S38°2' E176°48' **Te Teko**, NZ
122 N22°33' W105°45' **Teacapán**, Sin, Mex
32 N43°28' E41°44' **Teberda**, Rus Fed
85 N7°35' W1°56' **Techiman**, Gha
141 S43°29' W70°48' **Tecka**, Arg
122 N22°23' W105°27' **Tecuala**, Nay, Mex
23 N45°50' E27°26' **Tecuci**, Rom
109 N41°59' W84°1' **Tecumseh**, MI, US
46 N36°55' E60°53' **Tedzhenstroy**, Turkm
136 S3°23' W64°42' **Tefé**, AM, Braz
86 N10°5' E6°14' **Tegina**, Nga
124 N14°5' W87°13' **Tegucigalpa**, Hon
85 N9°36' W3°40' **Téhini**, Côte d'Ivoire
44 N35°41' E51°30' **Tehran**, Iran
123 N18°27' W97°23' **Tehuacán**, Pue, Mex
123 N16°20' W95°14' **Tehuantepec**, Oax, Mex
46 N37°23' E60°31' **Tejen**, Turkm
40 N32°4' E34°46' **Tel Aviv-Yafo**, Isr
124 N15°44' W87°27' **Tela**, Hon
20 N49°11' E15°31' **Telc**, Czech
61 S5°10' E141°35' **Telefomin**, PNG
98 N57°55' W131°10' **Telegraph Creek**, BC, Can
26 N52°31' E25°51' **Telekhany**, Bela
84 N10°54' W13°2' **Télimélé**, Gui
98 N54°42' W127°3' **Telkwa**, BC, Can
56 N11°45' E75°32' **Tellicherry**, Ind
141 S47°39' W66°3' **Tellier**, Arg
58 S0°1' E98°22' **Telo**, Indo
141 S42°24' W66°57' **Telsen**, Arg
58 S2°0' E131°58' *Teluk Berau*
59 S3°27' E120°34' *Teluk Bone*
60 S2°31' E135°13' *Teluk Cenderawasih*
60 S3°57' E133°31' *Teluk Kamrau*
59 S3°44' E119°2' *Teluk Mandar*
59 S2°7' E121°38' *Teluk Tolo*
59 S0°4' E120°33' *Teluk Tomini*, Indo
60 N0°4' E127°59' *Teluk Weda*
58 N4°13' E108°12' **Telukbutun**, Indo
73 S21°41' W140°39' Tematagi, Fr Poly, Fr
60 S1°26' E132°1' **Teminabuan**, Indo
46 N49°8' E57°6' **Temir**, Kaz
112 N33°25' W111°55' **Tempe**, AZ, US
115 N31°6' W97°20' **Temple**, TX, US
36 N45°17' E37°23' **Temryuk**, Rus Fed
141 S38°44' W72°35' **Temuco**, Chile
35 N55°26' E49°0' **Ten'ki**, Rus Fed
134 S1°1' W77°49' **Tena**, Ecu
85 N10°46' W5°26' Tena Kourou, Burk
57 N12°5' E99°1' **Tenasserim**, Myanmar
80 N20°38' E10°44' Tenere Desert, Niger
123 N17°11' W100°43' **Tenexpa**, Gro, Mex
59 S0°23' E116°57' **Tenggarong**, Indo
85 N10°29' W6°24' **Tengrela**, Côte d'Ivoire
85 N11°47' W0°22' **Tenkodogo**, Burk
67 S19°40' E134°10' **Tennant Creek**, NT, Austl
116 N35°54' W86°12' **Tennessee**, US
116 N35°13' W85°0' *Tennessee River*, US
139 S17°51' W41°30' **Teófilo Otoni**, MG, Braz
60 S7°52' E129°31' **Tepa**, Indo
24 N40°22' E19°57' **Tepelene**, Alb
122 N21°31' W104°54' **Tepic**, Nay, Mex
72 N4°43' W160°23' Teraina Island, Kir
39 N39°47' E40°24' **Tercan**, Turk
26 N52°13' E31°27' **Tereknovka**, Bela
36 N44°10' E45°53' **Terekli-Mekteb**, Rus Fed
58 N3°5' E106°31' Terempa, Indo
138 S20°26' W54°50' **Terenos**, MT, Braz
137 S5°5' W42°49' **Teresina**, PI, Braz
45 N32°37' E65°52' **Terin Kot**, Afg
46 N37°13' E67°16' **Termez**, Uzb
17 N42°34' E12°38' **Terni**, It
26 N49°33' E25°37' **Ternopil'**, Ukr
116 N39°28' W87°25' **Terre Haute**, IN, US
107 N46°47' W105°19' **Terry**, MT, US
18 N53°20' E5°22' Terschelling, Neth
13 N40°20' W1°6' **Teruel**, Sp
25 N43°45' E27°24' **Tervel**, Bulg
53 N43°29' E144°28' **Teshikaga**, Jap
53 N44°53' E141°46' **Teshio**, Jap
22 N44°37' E17°51' **Teslic**, Bos & Herz
96 N60°8' W132°48' **Teslin**, YT, Can
79 N20°12' E1°0' **Tessalit**, Mali
91 S16°10' E33°35' **Tete**, Moz
99 N52°57' W119°26' **Tête Jaune**, BC, Can
74 S8°50' E157°17' Tetepare Island, Sol Is
19 N53°46' E12°34' **Teterow**, Ger
25 N42°55' E24°16' **Teteven**, Bulg
73 S16°56' W150°17' Tetiaroa Island, Fr Poly, Fr
24 N42°1' E20°58' **Tetovo**, FYRM
35 N54°57' E48°50' **Tetyushi**, Rus Fed
16 N38°58' E8°46' **Teulada**, It
59 S1°5' E113°42' **Tewah**, Indo
50 N34°2' E103°5' **Têwo**, China
115 N33°26' W94°2' **Texarkana**, AR, US
114 N31°16' W99°25' **Texas**, US
115 N29°23' W94°55' **Texas City**, TX, US
18 N53°7' E4°32' Texel, Neth
91 S29°28' E29°16' Thabana Ntlenyana, Les
57 N15°28' E100°38' **THAILAND**
69 S28°38' E148°52' **Thallon**, Qld, Austl
57 N15°58' E97°44' **Thanbyuzayat**, Myanmar
57 N19°48' E105°46' **Thanh Hóa**, Viet
57 N10°45' E106°41' **Thành Pho Ho Chí Minh**, Viet
45 N26°34' E69°8' Thar Desert, Pak
54 N24°24' E71°38' **Tharad**, Ind
69 S27°59' E143°46' **Thargomindah**, Qld, Austl
25 N40°46' E24°41' **Thásos**, Grc
106 N45°35' W121°10' **The Dalles**, OR, US
18 N52°4' E4°17' **The Hague**, Neth
67 S18°56' E144°30' **The Lynd**, Qld, Austl
101 N53°50' W101°15' **The Pas**, MB, Can
129 N18°14' W63°2' **The Valley**, Angu, UK
108 N41°59' W100°35' **Thedford**, NE, US
67 S24°57' E150°5' **Theodore**, Qld, Austl
25 N40°39' E24°41' **Theológos**, Grc
25 N40°16' E23°49' *Thermaïkós Kólpos*
107 N43°39' W108°13' **Thermopolis**, WY, US
24 N40°38' E22°58' **Thessaloníki**, Grc
11 N52°25' E0°45' **Thetford**, UK
115 N29°48' W90°49' **Thibodaux**, LA, US
101 N55°19' W97°42' **Thicket Portage**, MB, Can
108 N48°7' W96°11' **Thief River Falls**, MN, US
55 N27°29' E89°37' **Thimphu**, Bhu
15 N49°22' E6°10' **Thionville**, Fr
85 N13°48' W2°40' **Thiou**, Burk
25 N36°25' E25°26' **Thíra**, Grc
25 N36°21' E24°48' *Thíra*, Grc
29 N56°57' E8°42' **Thisted**, Den
24 N38°21' E23°19' **Thívai**, Grc
119 N32°54' W84°20' **Thomaston**, GA, US
117 N35°53' W80°5' **Thomasville**, NC, US
119 N30°50' W83°59' **Thomasville**, GA, US
101 N55°45' W97°45' **Thompson**, MB, Can
14 N46°59' W0°13' **Thouars**, Fr
36 N36°47' E117°5' Thousand Buddha Mountain, China
110 N44°16' W75°58' Thousand Islands, US
71 S34°14' E172°11' Three Kings Islands, NZ
90 S31°54' E23°6' **Three Sisters**, S Afr
74 S10°12' E161°58' Three Sisters Islands, Sol Is
68 S29°32' E115°45' **Three Springs**, WA, Austl
114 N33°11' W99°11' **Throckmorton**, TX, US
97 N77°29' W69°21' **Thule**, Grld, Den
102 N48°23' W89°15' **Thunder Bay**, ON, Can
11 N58°35' W3°32' **Thurso**, UK
142 S70°0' W100°0' Thurston Island, Ant, Disputed
69 S26°4' E143°28' **Thylungra**, Qld, Austl
89 S16°4' E35°8' **Thyolo**, Malw
48 N42°24' E80°50' Tian Shan, China
51 N32°41' E119°1' **Tianchang**, China
50 N23°9' E107°10' **Tiandeng**, China
49 N39°8' E117°10' **Tianjin**, China
49 N34°30' E105°58' **Tianshui**, China
51 N29°9' E121°2' **Tiantai**, China
50 N23°5' E107°8' **Tianyang**, China
49 N37°14' E102°59' **Tianzhu**, China
79 N35°26' E1°19' **Tiaret**, Alg
139 S24°30' W50°24' **Tibagi**, PR, Braz
80 N20°53' E16°29' Tibesti Mountains, Chad
48 N31°7' E85°25' **Tibet**, China
48 N32°0' E84°0' **Tibet**, China
78 N18°28' W9°30' **Tichit**, Mrta
134 S11°40' W76°14' Ticlio Pass, Peru
57 N23°23' E93°39' **Tiddim**, Myanmar
78 N18°33' W11°25' **Tidjikdja**, Mrta
84 N14°56' W15°4' **Tiel**, Sen
85 N10°14' W7°29' **Tienko**, Côte d'Ivoire
113 N36°42' W106°33' **Tierra Amarilla**, NM, US
139 S20°44' W50°54' *Tiete*, Braz
116 N41°7' W83°11' **Tiffin**, OH, US
119 N31°28' W83°31' **Tifton**, GA, US
39 N37°56' E41°26' *Tigris*, Turk
44 N32°20' E46°17' *Tigris River*, Iraq
122 N32°31' W117°2' **Tijuana**, BC, Mex
73 S14°58' W144°30' Tikei, Fr Poly, Fr
36 N45°51' E40°9' **Tikhoretsk**, Rus Fed
34 N65°35' E30°27' **Tikhtozero**, Rus Fed
71 S37°48' E178°24' **Tikitiki**, NZ
71 S39°49' E176°27' **Tikokino**, NZ
44 N34°36' E43°42' **Tikrit**, Iraq
114 N28°28' W98°33' **Tilden**, TX, US
57 N21°42' E94°4' **Tilin**, Myanmar
80 N14°13' E1°27' **Tillabéri**, Niger
106 N45°28' W123°50' **Tillamook**, OR, US
36 N51°37' E37°7' **Tim**, Rus Fed
35 N66°35' E48°4' Timan Ridge, Rus Fed
71 S44°24' E171°15' **Timaru**, NZ
78 N16°15' W8°10' **Timbédra**, Mrta
84 N10°38' W11°50' **Timbo**, Gui
79 N16°44' W3°0' **Timbuktu**, Mali
60 S4°46' E137°5' **Timika**, Indo
22 N45°45' E21°13' **Timisoara**, Rom
103 N48°28' W81°20' **Timmins**, ON, Can
109 N45°27' W90°10' Timms Hill, US
60 S9°28' E124°46' Timor, Indo
59 S9°44' E124°18' Timor Island, Indo
59 S11°14' E123°54' *Timor Sea*
47 N42°50' E68°26' **Timur**, Kaz
78 N27°50' W8°4' **Tindouf**, Alg
12 N43°20' W6°25' **Tineo**, Sp
29 N56°32' E14°59' **Tingsryd**, Swe
29 N62°54' E8°12' **Tingvoll**, Nor
72 N14°32' E145°35' Tinian, NM Is, US
25 N37°32' E25°10' **Tínos**, Grc
140 S27°2' W62°43' **Tintina**, Arg
71 S43°55' E171°45' **Tinwald**, NZ
10 N52°29' W8°10' **Tipperary**, Ire
66 S13°44' E131°2' **Tipperary**, NT, Austl
63 N34°36' E61°15' **Tir Pol**, Afg
24 N41°20' E19°49' **Tiranë**, Alb
16 N46°13' E10°10' **Tirano**, It
23 N44°56' E25°27' **Tirgoviste**, Rom
23 N45°2' E23°17' **Tirgu Jiu**, Rom
23 N46°32' E24°34' **Tirgu Mures**, Rom
23 N46°0' E26°8' **Tirgu Secuiesc**, Rom
45 N36°21' E71°59' Tirich Mir, Pak
37 N54°14' E58°35' **Tirlyanskiy**, Rus Fed
24 N39°45' E22°17' **Tírnavos**, Grc
139 S19°0' W45°58' **Tiros**, MG, Braz
87 N9°34' E22°9' **Tiroungoulou**, CAR
56 N10°48' E78°41' **Tiruchchirappalli**, Ind
56 N8°44' E77°42' **Tisalyanvilai**, Ind
100 N52°51' W104°4' **Tisdale**, SK, Can
22 N46°32' E20°5' *Tisza*, Hun
22 N44°22' E16°24' **Titov Drvar**, Bos & Herz
119 N28°37' W80°49' **Titusville**, FL, US
84 N14°57' W16°49' **Tivaouane**, Sen
43 N22°49' E59°16' **Tiwi**, Oman
40 N34°33' E37°40' **Tiyas**, Syria
60 S4°11' E135°13' Tiyo Mountains, Indo
79 N29°43' W9°44' **Tiznit**, Mor
123 N18°24' W100°28' **Tlalchapa**, Gro, Mex
123 N19°20' W98°24' **Tlaxcala**, Mex
79 N34°52' W1°15' **Tlemcen**, Alg
92 S18°10' E49°23' **Toamasina**, Madag
129 N11°19' W60°53' Tobago, T & T
60 N1°44' E128°1' **Tobelo**, Indo
10 N56°37' W6°5' **Tobermory**, UK
103 N45°13' W81°40' **Tobermory**, ON, Can
137 S11°11' W38°6' **Tobias Barreto**, SE, Braz
58 S3°0' E106°30' **Toboali**, Indo
46 N53°46' E64°3' *Tobol*, Kaz
35 N58°12' E68°16' **Tobol'sk**, Rus Fed
80 N32°5' E23°58' **Tobruk**, Libya
137 S9°25' W49°29' **Tocantins**, Braz
137 S2°0' W49°26' *Tocantins*, Braz
119 N34°35' W83°20' **Toccoa**, GA, US
140 S23°11' W68°1' **Toconao**, Chile
140 S22°5' W70°12' **Tocopilla**, Chile
59 S1°40' E120°29' **Todeli**, Indo
52 N37°29' E130°55' **Todong**, Jap
122 N23°27' W110°13' **Todos Santos**, BCS, Mex
75 S19°48' W175°21' Tofua Island, Ton
75 S18°49' W174°37' Tofua Island, Ton
121 N59°4' W160°24' **Togiak**, AK, US
82 N18°4' E35°49' **Togni**, Sud
85 N7°55' E0°49' **TOGO**
48 N45°46' E94°48' **Tögrög**, Mong
53 N26°39' E127°54' **Toguchi**, Jap
46 N47°34' E60°33' **Togyz**, Kaz
29 N63°46' E24°15' **Toholampi**, Fin
59 S1°27' E122°24' **Tolli**, Indo
112 N38°49' W117°20' Toiyabe Range, US
121 N63°20' W142°59' **Tok Junction**, AK, US
52 N28°59' E128°57' Tokara Retto, Jap
38 N40°19' E36°34' **Tokat**, Turk
73 S8°41' W172°11' **Tokelau**, NZ
53 N27°37' E129°22' Tokuno-shima, Jap
52 N34°4' E134°34' **Tokushima**, Jap
53 N35°41' E139°44' **Tokyo**, Jap
72 N8°2' E152°8' **Tol**, US
32 N53°31' E49°16' **Tol'yatti**, Rus Fed
59 S2°56' E121°6' **Tolala**, Indo
116 N41°40' W83°33' **Toledo**, OH, US
12 N39°52' W4°2' **Toledo**, Sp
115 N31°34' W94°28' *Toledo Bend Reservoir*, US
92 S23°24' E43°42' **Toliara**, Madag
59 N1°2' E120°49' **Tolitoli**, Indo
17 N46°24' E13°1' **Tolmezzo**, It
61 S5°15' E154°37' Tolokiwa Island, PNG
13 N43°8' W2°4' **Tolosa**, Sp
45 N35°2' E76°6' **Tolti**, Pak
123 N19°17' W99°39' **Toluca**, Mex, Mex
66 S22°41' E117°43' **Tom Price**, WA, Austl
74 S17°37' E178°1' Tomanivi, Fiji
47 N46°24' E75°3' **Tomar**, Kaz
122 N19°56' W105°15' **Tomatlán**, Jal, Mex
82 N5°49' E31°41' **Tombe**, Sud
79 N16°44' W3°0' **Tombouctou**, Mali
137 S2°25' W48°9' **Tomé-Açu**, PA, Braz
13 N39°10' W3°1' **Tomelloso**, Sp
59 N0°33' E120°32' **Tomini**, Indo
32 N56°30' E84°56' **Tomsk**, Rus Fed
123 N16°4' W93°45' **Tonalá**, Chis, Mex
136 S2°47' W67°47' **Tonantins**, AM, Braz
75 S20°6' W175°28' **TONGA**
73 S9°10' W159°55' Tongareva, NZ
75 S17°2' E168°40' Tongariki Island, Van
75 S21°21' W175°37' Tongatapu Group, Ton
75 S21°15' W175°4' Tongatapu Island, Ton
51 N31°3' E116°58' **Tongcheng**, China
50 N35°17' E100°42' **Tongde**, China
50 N24°7' E102°49' **Tonghai**, China
52 N39°23' E128°3' *Tongjoson Man*
49 N43°39' E122°14' **Tongliao**, China
75 S16°56' E168°23' Tongoa, Van
140 S30°15' W71°30' **Tongoy**, Chile
63 N6°5' E121°52' Tongquil Island, Phil
48 N33°50' E92°28' **Tongtianheyan**, China
11 N58°28' W4°25' **Tongue**, UK
50 N35°7' E105°27' **Tongwei**, China
49 N28°8' E106°49' **Tongzi**, China
14 N44°23' E0°19' **Tonneins**, Fr
15 N47°51' E3°58' **Tonnerre**, Fr
112 N38°4' W117°14' **Tonopah**, NV, US
29 N59°16' E10°25' **Tønsberg**, Nor
66 S16°38' E131°50' **Top Springs**, NT, Austl
108 N39°3' W95°42' **Topeka**, KS, US
23 N46°55' E25°21' **Toplita**, Rom
21 N48°34' E18°10' **Topolcany**, Slvk
46 N47°59' E51°36' **Topoli**, Kaz
45 N35°14' E60°36' **Torbat-e Jam**, Iran
12 N41°30' W5°0' **Tordesillas**, Sp
29 N65°54' E22°39' **Töre**, Swe
12 N42°42' W6°30' **Toreno**, Sp
46 N49°38' E63°30' **Torgay**, Kaz
16 N45°3' E7°39' **Torino**, It
45 N35°28' E63°59' Torkestan Mountains, Afg
97 N59°40' W64°41' Torngat Mountains, Can
141 S38°6' W62°14' **Tornquist**, Arg
12 N41°31' W5°24' **Toro**, Sp
103 N43°41' W79°28' **Toronto**, ON, Can
12 N42°2' W4°19' **Torquemada**, Sp
17 N40°45' E14°27' **Torre Annunziata**, It
13 N40°13' E0°12' **Torreblanca**, Sp
13 N39°26' W0°28' **Torrente**, Sp
122 N25°33' W103°26' **Torreón**, Coah, Mex
13 N38°1' W3°13' **Torreperogil**, Sp
139 S29°21' W49°44' **Tôrres**, RS, Braz
61 S9°53' E141°52' *Torres Strait*
13 N37°59' W0°41' **Torrevieja**, Sp
107 N42°4' W104°11' **Torrington**, WY, US
110 N41°48' W73°8' **Torrington**, CT, US
28 N62°1' W6°46' **Torshavn**, Far Is, Den
129 N18°19' W64°35' **Tortola**, BVI, UK
16 N39°55' E9°39' **Tortoli**, It
13 N40°48' E0°31' **Tortosa**, Sp
39 N40°19' E41°35' **Tortum**, Turk
21 N53°2' E18°35' **Torun**, Pol
34 N57°3' E34°58' **Torzhok**, Rus Fed
140 S29°14' W61°46' **Tostado**, Arg
38 N41°1' E34°2' **Tosya**, Turk
35 N59°57' E42°45' **Tot'ma**, Rus Fed
20 N47°35' E13°56' Totes Gebirge, Aus
124 N14°55' W91°22' **Totonicapan**, Guat
52 N35°30' E134°14' **Tottori**, Jap
84 N14°51' W15°53' **Touba**, Sen
85 N8°17' W7°41' **Touba**, Côte d'Ivoire
85 N13°4' W3°4' **Tougan**, Burk
79 N33°10' E6°0' **Touggourt**, Alg
84 N11°27' W11°41' **Tougué**, Gui
78 N13°27' W9°53' **Toukoto**, Mali
15 N48°41' E5°54' **Toul**, Fr
51 N23°43' E120°32' **Touliu**, Taiwan
15 N43°8' E5°56' **Toulon**, Fr
14 N43°35' E1°28' **Toulouse**, Fr
14 N47°23' E0°41' **Tours**, Fr
39 N41°0' E45°38' **Tovuz**, Azer
53 N40°37' E141°13' **Towada**, Jap
117 N41°46' W76°26' **Towanda**, PA, US
127 N32°16' W64°50' Town Hill, Ber, UK
107 N46°19' W111°31' **Townsend**, MT, US
67 S22°16' E150°34' Townshend Island, Austl
67 S19°16' E146°48' **Townsville**, Qld, Austl
74 S18°59' W179°46' Toyota Island, Fiji
79 N33°55' E8°8' **Tozeur**, Tun
39 N40°58' E39°46' **Trabzon**, Turk
104 N46°2' W73°7' **Tracy**, QC, Can
26 N54°38' E24°56' **Trakai**, Lith
10 N52°16' W9°42' **Tralee**, Ire
140 S26°13' W65°17' **Trancas**, Arg
57 N7°34' E99°36' **Trang**, Thai
138 S31°12' W55°45' **Tranqueras**, Ur
142 S80°0' W50°0' Transantarctic Mountains, Ant, Disputed
23 N45°27' E24°13' Transylvanian Alps, Rom
17 N38°1' E12°31' **Trapani**, It
109 N44°46' W85°38' **Traverse City**, MI, US
74 S7°0' E156°7' Treasury Islands, Sol Is
20 N49°13' E15°53' **Trebíc**, Czech
63 N14°16' E120°49' **Trece Martires**, Phil
138 S33°11' W54°24' **Treinta-y-Tres**, Ur
13 N42°10' E0°54' **Tremp**, Sp
21 N48°54' E18°4' **Trencín**, Slvk
16 N46°4' E11°8' **Trento**, It
117 N40°14' W74°47' **Trenton**, NJ, US
103 N44°6' W77°35' **Trenton**, ON, Can
108 N40°4' W93°37' **Trenton**, MO, US
141 S38°23' W60°17' **Tres Arroyos**, Arg
141 S48°13' W67°35' **Tres Cerros**, Arg
138 S20°48' W51°43' **Três Lagoas**, MT, Braz
141 S49°37' W71°30' **Tres Lagos**, Arg
17 N45°40' E12°15' **Treviso**, It
91 S21°4' E31°16' **Triangle**, Zimb
56 N10°31' E76°13' **Trichur**, Ind
17 N45°39' E13°47' **Trieste**, It
22 N46°23' E13°50' Triglav, Slov
24 N39°35' E21°47' **Tríkala**, Grc
56 N8°34' E81°14' **Trincomalee**, Sri L
135 S14°50' W64°54' **Trinidad**, Bol
138 S33°32' W56°54' **Trinidad**, Ur
138 S27°10' W55°44' **Trinidad**, Para
113 N37°10' W104°30' **Trinidad**, CO, US
126 N21°48' W79°59' **Trinidad**, Cuba
129 N10°22' W61°25' Trinidad, T & T
129 N10°55' W61°35' **TRINIDAD AND TOBAGO**
105 N48°22' W53°22' **Trintiy**, NF, Can
121 N56°16' W154°31' Trinity Islands, US
40 N34°26' E35°51' **Tripoli**, Leb
80 N32°52' E13°11' **Tripoli**, Libya
24 N37°29' E22°22' **Trípolis**, Grc
62 N15°52' E110°37' Triton Island, Para Is, Disputed
56 N8°29' E76°55' **Trivandrum**, Ind
21 N48°23' E17°35' **Trnava**, Slvk
61 S8°30' E151°11' Trobriand Islands, PNG
22 N43°32' E16°15' **Trogir**, Cro
104 N46°22' W72°31' **Trois-Rivières**, QC, Can
35 N54°7' E61°35' **Troitsk**, Rus Fed
35 N57°3' E63°43' **Troitskiy**, Rus Fed
37 N52°19' E56°23' **Troitskoye**, Rus Fed
136 S0°19' W57°2' *Trombetas*, Braz
92 S15°43' E53°58' **Tromelin Island**, Fr
29 N69°40' E18°57' **Tromsø**, Nor
29 N63°25' E10°25' **Trondheim**, Nor
38 N34°55' E32°56' **Troodos**, Cyp
38 N35°0' E33°0' Troodos Mountains, Cyp
24 N42°24' E20°10' **Tropojë**, Alb
102 N51°20' W100°3' *Trout Lake*, Can
107 N44°36' W109°32' Trout Peak, US

continue on next page

21 N50°46' E16°17' **Walbrzych**, Pol
18 N51°26' E3°5' Walcheren, Neth
21 N53°17' E16°28' **Walcz**, Pol
113 N40°44' W106°17' **Walden**, CO, US
100 N52°37' W106°38' **Waldheim**, SK, Can
115 N34°54' W94°5' **Waldron**, AR, US
11 N52°23' W4°3' **WALES**
121 N65°37' W168°4' **Wales**, AK, US
69 S30°1' E148°7' **Walgett**, NSW, Austl
68 S28°57' E114°48' **Walkaway**, WA, Austl
106 N46°2' W118°22' **Walla Walla**, WA, US
103 N42°36' W82°23' **Wallaceburg**, ON, Can
66 S19°47' E120°40' **Wallal Downs**, WA, Austl
73 S11°41' W179°52' **Wallis and Futuna**, Fr
115 N36°4' W90°58' **Walnut Ridge**, AR, US
69 S35°8' E142°2' **Walpeup**, Vic, Austl
68 S34°57' E116°44' **Walpole**, WA, Austl
113 N37°38' W104°45' **Walsenburg**, CO, US
19 N52°52' E9°35' **Walsrode**, Ger
119 N32°55' W80°40' **Walterboro**, SC, US
118 N33°37' W89°17' **Walthall**, MS, US
110 N43°5' W75°43' **Wampsville**, NY, US
60 S3°33' E126°10' **Wamsasi**, Indo
69 S29°42' E144°9' **Wanaaring**, NSW, Austl
70 S44°42' E169°9' **Wanaka**, NZ
103 N46°54' W81°22' *Wanapitei Lake*, Can
50 N24°10' E98°4' **Wanding**, China
69 S26°8' E149°57' **Wandoan**, Qld, Austl
71 S39°56' E175°2' **Wanganui**, NZ
61 S9°22' E149°9' **Wanigela**, PNG
54 N22°37' E70°56' **Wankaner**, Ind
50 N18°53' E110°26' **Wanning**, China
49 N30°52' E108°22' **Wanxian**, China
49 N32°4' E108°2' **Wanyuan**, China
100 N54°48' W104°36' *Wapawekka Lake*, Can
66 S24°46' E127°26' **Warakurna**, WA, Austl
54 N18°0' E79°35' **Warangal**, Ind
67 S24°18' E142°51' **Warbreccan**, Qld, Austl
111 N42°16' W72°15' **Ware**, MA, US
19 N53°31' E12°40' **Waren**, Ger
119 N32°37' W83°36' **Warner Robins**, GA, US
117 N41°50' W79°9' **Warren**, PA, US
86 N5°31' E5°45' **Warri**, Nga
118 N33°59' W86°48' **Warrior**, AL, US
110 N42°44' W78°8' **Warsaw**, NY, US
21 N52°14' E21°2' **Warsaw**, Pol
21 N52°14' E21°2' **Warszawa**, Pol
21 N50°41' E19°13' *Warta*, Pol
60 S3°25' E130°39' **Waru**, Indo
11 N52°18' W1°35' **Warwick**, UK
111 N41°42' W71°23' **Warwick**, RI, US
11 N59°10' W3°7' **Wasbister**, UK
106 N47°14' W121°47' **Washington**, US
116 N38°40' W87°10' **Washington**, IN, US
117 N40°11' W80°16' **Washington**, PA, US
117 N38°56' W77°2' **Washington**, DC, US
60 S1°54' E133°17' **Wasian**, Indo
60 S2°43' E134°30' **Wasior**, Indo
61 S5°58' E147°13' **Wasu**, PNG
61 S6°5' E149°20' **Wasum**, PNG
59 S4°32' E120°20' **Watampone**, Indo
111 N44°20' W72°44' **Waterbury**, VT, US
110 N41°34' W73°3' **Waterbury**, CT, US
10 N52°16' W7°8' **Waterford**, Ire
103 N43°28' W80°31' **Waterloo**, ON, Can
109 N42°29' W92°20' **Waterloo**, IA, US
110 N42°54' W76°52' **Waterloo**, NY, US
110 N44°1' W75°54' **Watertown**, NY, US
108 N44°54' W97°7' **Watertown**, SD, US
111 N44°33' W69°38' **Waterville**, ME, US
108 N47°48' W103°17' **Watford City**, ND, US
55 N28°2' E96°59' **Wati**, Ind
110 N42°23' W76°52' **Watkins Glen**, NY, US
114 N35°50' W98°25' **Watonga**, OK, US
89 N3°3' E29°32' **Watsa**, DRC
109 N40°47' W87°44' **Watseka**, IL, US
100 N52°7' W104°31' **Watson**, SK, Can
96 N60°4' W128°42' **Watson Lake**, YT, Can
112 N36°55' W121°46' **Watsonville**, CA, US
61 S7°20' E146°46' **Wau**, PNG
67 S20°36' E134°15' **Wauchope**, NT, Austl
109 N42°22' W87°50' **Waukegan**, IL, US
115 N34°10' W98°0' **Waurika**, OK, US
109 N44°58' W89°38' **Wausau**, WI, US
66 S17°29' E130°57' **Wave Hill**, NT, Austl
71 S39°46' E174°38' **Waverley**, NZ
82 N7°42' E28°0' **Waw**, Sud
86 N9°55' E4°25' **Wawa**, Nga
102 N47°59' W84°47' **Wawa**, ON, Can
115 N32°23' W96°51' **Waxahachie**, TX, US
74 S17°19' E176°54' Waya Island, Fiji
49 N37°19' E109°33' **Wayaobu**, China
119 N31°13' W82°22' **Waycross**, GA, US
108 N42°14' W97°1' **Wayne**, NE, US
118 N31°40' W88°39' **Waynesboro**, MS, US
119 N33°5' W82°1' **Waynesboro**, GA, US
108 N45°20' W97°31' **Webster**, SD, US
60 N0°21' E127°52' **Weda**, Indo
141 S52°5' W62°7' Weddell Island, Falk Is, UK
142 S70°0' W40°0' *Weddell Sea*
68 S28°0' E121°5' **Weebo**, WA, Austl
19 N49°41' E12°10' **Weiden**, Ger
67 S12°40' E141°53' **Weipa**, Qld, Austl
101 N56°49' W94°4' **Weir River**, MB, Can
106 N44°15' W116°58' **Weiser**, ID, US
50 N25°15' E100°20' **Weishan**, China
19 N49°1' E10°58' **Weissenburg in Bayern**, Ger
50 N20°59' E108°11' Weizhou Dao, China
117 N37°26' W81°35' **Welch**, WV, US
67 S16°48' E139°31' Wellesley Islands, Austl
71 S41°19' E174°46' **Wellington**, NZ
99 N53°6' W121°34' **Wells**, BC, Can
117 N41°45' W77°18' **Wellsboro**, PA, US
71 S36°17' E174°31' **Wellsford**, NZ
110 N42°7' W77°56' **Wellsville**, NY, US
99 N55°9' W119°8' **Wembley**, AB, Can
85 N7°42' W2°7' **Wenchi**, Gha
60 S2°26' E134°13' **Wendesi**, Indo
50 N23°30' E104°20' **Wenshan**, China
49 N28°1' E120°38' **Wenzhou**, China
90 S25°15' E23°16' **Werda**, Bots
111 N44°57' W67°40' **Wesley**, ME, US
105 N49°9' W53°34' **Wesleyville**, NF, Can
67 S11°27' E136°40' Wessel Islands, Austl
142 S75°0' W90°0' West Antarctica, Ant, Disputed
40 N32°7' E35°5' **West Bank**, Disputed
109 N43°26' W88°11' **West Bend**, WI, US
126 N26°41' W78°58' **West End**, Bah
141 S51°41' W60°17' West Falkland, Falk Is, UK
18 N53°22' E4°46' West Frisian Islands, Neth
107 N45°58' W113°24' West Goat Peak, US
70 S12°10' E96°46' West Island, Cocos Is, Austl
115 N35°10' W90°10' **West Memphis**, AR, US
117 N40°55' W74°31' **West Orange**, NJ, US
119 N26°44' W80°4' **West Palm Beach**, FL, US
108 N41°50' W96°43' **West Point**, NE, US
118 N33°38' W88°40' **West Point**, MS, US
32 N64°11' E77°31' West Siberian Plain, Rus Fed
117 N38°29' W80°50' **West Virginia**, US
69 S33°55' E147°13' **West Wyalong**, NSW, Austl
37 N56°50' E67°14' West-Siberian Plain, Rus Fed
111 N43°41' W70°23' **Westbrook**, ME, US
111 N41°23' W71°50' **Westerly**, RI, US
66 S22°26' E121°25' **Western Australia**, Austl
81 N28°28' E26°23' Western Desert, Egypt
54 N17°54' E74°1' Western Ghats, Ind
78 N24°54' W14°30' **Western Sahara**, Mor
99 N54°9' W113°52' **Westlock**, AB, Can
71 S41°47' E171°36' **Westport**, NZ
89 S5°4' E39°43' **Wete**, Tanz
19 N50°33' E8°30' **Wetzlar**, Ger
61 S3°35' E143°40' **Wewak**, PNG
10 N52°20' W6°29' **Wexford**, Ire
71 S35°43' E174°19' **Whangarei**, NZ
115 N29°19' W96°6' **Wharton**, TX, US
107 N42°3' W104°57' **Wheatland**, WY, US
114 N35°27' W100°16' **Wheeler**, TX, US
112 N38°59' W114°19' Wheeler Peak, US
113 N36°34' W105°25' Wheeler Peak, US
117 N40°4' W80°43' **Wheeling**, WV, US
99 N50°7' W122°59' Whistler Mountain, Can
108 N46°23' W103°18' White Butte, US
71 S37°29' E177°11' White Island, NZ
111 N44°10' W71°59' White Mountains, US
82 N6°32' E31°2' *White Nile*, Sud
110 N41°2' W73°46' **White Plains**, NY, US
108 N43°34' W100°45' **White River**, SD, US
102 N48°35' W85°15' **White River**, ON, Can
72 S19°31' E169°27' **White Sands**, Van
32 N66°35' E43°4' *White Sea*
34 N63°4' E34°43' *White Sea-Baltic Canal*, Rus Fed
107 N46°33' W110°54' **White Sulphur Springs**, MT, US
85 N10°40' W1°13' *White Volta*, Gha
99 N54°9' W115°41' **Whitecourt**, AB, Can
96 N60°52' W135°22' **Whitehorse**, YT, Can
117 N34°20' W78°42' **Whiteville**, NC, US
71 S36°49' E175°40' **Whitianga**, NZ
142 S80°0' W100°0' Whitmore Mountains, Ant, Disputed
103 N45°30' W78°14' **Whitney**, ON, Can
67 S20°14' E149°4' Whtsunday Islands, Austl
69 S33°2' E137°34' **Whyalla**, SA, Austl
107 N46°59' W104°11' **Wibaux**, MT, US
108 N37°41' W97°20' **Wichita**, KS, US
114 N33°55' W98°30' **Wichita Falls**, TX, US
114 N34°53' W99°3' Wichita Mountains, US
11 N58°27' W3°7' **Wick**, UK
112 N33°58' W112°44' **Wickenburg**, AZ, US
10 N52°59' W6°3' **Wicklow**, Ire
10 N52°44' W6°20' Wicklow Mountains, Ire
68 S31°30' E121°34' **Widgiemooltha**, WA, Austl
21 N51°14' E18°34' **Wielun**, Pol
21 N48°14' E16°21' **Wien**, Aus
21 N47°49' E16°15' **Wiener Neustadt**, Aus
118 N30°52' W89°8' **Wiggins**, MS, US
115 N34°55' W95°19' **Wilburton**, OK, US
69 S31°34' E143°23' **Wilcannia**, NSW, Austl
133 N3°32' W57°37' Wilhelmina Gebergte, Sur
18 N53°32' E8°7' **Wilhelmshaven**, Ger
143 S70°0' E120°0' Wilkes Land, Ant, Disputed
117 N41°15' W75°53' **Wilkes-Barre**, PA, US
128 N12°6' W68°56' **Willemstad**, Neth Ant, Neth
66 S15°17' E131°35' **Willeroo**, NT, Austl
68 S33°1' E116°52' **Williams**, WA, Austl
112 N35°16' W112°9' **Williams**, AZ, US
116 N36°44' W84°10' **Williamsburg**, KY, US
117 N37°17' W76°43' **Williamsburg**, VA, US
116 N37°40' W82°17' **Williamson**, WV, US
117 N41°14' W77°0' **Williamsport**, PA, US
117 N35°51' W77°4' **Williamston**, NC, US
111 N41°43' W72°13' **Willimantic**, CT, US
108 N48°10' W103°37' **Williston**, ND, US
99 N56°8' W123°59' *Williston Lake*, Can
108 N45°7' W95°2' **Willmar**, MN, US
66 S21°15' E132°35' **Willowra**, NT, Austl
112 N39°31' W122°11' **Willows**, CA, US
117 N34°14' W77°57' **Wilmington**, NC, US
117 N39°45' W75°33' **Wilmington**, DE, US
117 N35°44' W77°55' **Wilson**, NC, US
113 N37°52' W107°59' Wilson Peak, US
74 S7°46' E156°21' *Wilson Strait*
68 S26°36' E120°13' **Wiluna**, WA, Austl
116 N41°3' W86°36' **Winamac**, IN, US
11 N51°4' W1°19' **Winchester**, UK
116 N37°59' W84°11' **Winchester**, KY, US
116 N35°11' W86°7' **Winchester**, TN, US
117 N39°10' W78°10' **Winchester**, VA, US
107 N42°43' W109°8' Wind River Peak, US
90 S22°35' E17°5' **Windhoek**, Nam
67 S25°25' E142°39' **Windorah**, Qld, Austl
69 S34°25' E138°20' **Windsor**, SA, Austl
105 N44°59' W64°9' **Windsor**, NS, Can
103 N42°18' W83°1' **Windsor**, ON, Can
117 N36°0' W76°57' **Windsor**, NC, US
127 N19°37' W74°11' *Windward Passage*
99 N52°58' W114°26' **Winfield**, AB, Can
108 N37°14' W97°0' **Winfield**, KS, US
112 N40°58' W117°44' **Winnemucca**, NV, US
108 N43°23' W99°52' **Winner**, SD, US
107 N47°0' W108°21' **Winnett**, MT, US
115 N31°56' W92°38' **Winnfield**, LA, US
66 S23°9' E114°32' **Winning**, WA, Austl
101 N49°55' W96°59' **Winnipeg**, MB, Can
115 N32°10' W91°43' **Winnsboro**, LA, US
109 N44°3' W91°38' **Winona**, MN, US
118 N33°29' W89°44' **Winona**, MS, US
113 N35°3' W110°42' **Winslow**, AZ, US
117 N36°6' W80°15' **Winston-Salem**, NC, US
111 N44°24' W68°6' **Winter Harbor**, ME, US
98 N50°31' W128°2' **Winter Harbour**, BC, Can
119 N28°2' W81°44' **Winter Haven**, FL, US
111 N46°58' W68°35' **Winterville**, ME, US
67 S22°23' E143°2' **Winton**, Qld, Austl
111 N44°0' W69°40' **Wiscasset**, ME, US
109 N44°42' W90°29' **Wisconsin**, US
19 N53°53' E11°28' **Wismar**, Ger
66 S22°17' E118°19' **Wittenoom**, WA, Austl
19 N53°10' E12°29' **Wittstock**, Ger
21 N52°39' E19°2' **Wloclawek**, Pol
21 N51°37' E23°29' **Wlodawa**, Pol
107 N48°5' W105°38' **Wolf Point**, MT, US
20 N46°51' E14°51' **Wolfsberg**, Aus
19 N52°25' E10°47' **Wolfsburg**, Ger
101 N58°17' W102°59' **Wollaston Lake**, SK, Can
100 N58°18' W104°28' *Wollaston Lake*, Can
67 S17°13' E137°57' **Wollogorang**, NT, Austl
69 S34°25' E150°53' **Wollongong**, NSW, Austl
84 N7°16' W10°44' Wologizi Mountains, Libr
101 N50°36' W102°45' **Wolseley**, SK, Can
52 N39°9' E127°26' **Wonsan**, N Kor
69 S31°42' E137°13' **Woocalla**, SA, Austl
118 N34°47' W88°14' Woodall Mountain, US
61 S8°55' E152°23' Woodlark Island, PNG
104 N46°9' W67°32' **Woodstock**, NB, Can
111 N43°37' W72°31' **Woodstock**, VT, US
117 N38°53' W78°31' **Woodstock**, VA, US
111 N44°9' W72°2' **Woodsville**, NH, US
115 N30°47' W94°25' **Woodville**, TX, US
118 N31°6' W91°18' **Woodville**, MS, US
114 N36°26' W99°23' **Woodward**, OK, US
68 S25°44' E114°17' **Wooramel**, WA, Austl
111 N42°16' W71°48' **Worcester**, MA, US
11 N52°11' W2°14' **Worcester**, UK
90 S33°39' E19°27' **Worcester**, S Afr
107 N44°1' W107°58' **Worland**, WY, US
19 N49°38' E8°22' **Worms**, Ger
108 N43°38' W95°36' **Worthington**, MN, US
72 N10°5' E163°50' Wotho Atoll, Mar Is
80 N21°21' E15°57' **Wour**, Chad
121 N56°28' W132°20' **Wrangell**, AK, US
113 N40°5' W102°13' **Wray**, CO, US
96 N63°16' W123°37' **Wrigley**, NT, Can
21 N51°7' E17°1' **Wroclaw**, Pol
21 N52°20' E17°34' **Wrzesnia**, Pol
48 N36°30' E87°20' Wu-lu-k'o-mu-shih, China
68 S30°6' E116°38' **Wubin**, WA, Austl
50 N21°25' E110°40' **Wuchuan**, China
49 N28°25' E107°56' **Wuchuan**, China
49 N39°30' E106°40' **Wudazhan**, China
50 N33°24' E104°50' **Wudu**, China
49 N30°33' E114°16' **Wuhan**, China
49 N31°20' E118°22' **Wuhu**, China
54 N34°19' E74°41' *Wular Lake*, Ind
50 N24°58' E100°23' Wuliang Shan, China
50 N23°10' E108°18' **Wuming**, China
102 N52°44' W89°46' *Wunnummin Lake*, Can
18 N51°16' E7°11' **Wuppertal**, Ger
49 N37°8' E108°10' **Wuqi**, China
48 N39°42' E75°13' **Wuqia**, China
68 S28°25' E116°17' **Wurarga**, WA, Austl
19 N49°48' E9°56' **Würzburg**, Ger
19 N51°22' E12°44' **Wurzen**, Ger
61 S1°55' E142°47' Wuvulu Island, PNG
49 N37°58' E102°49' **Wuwei**, China
50 N31°24' E109°38' **Wuxi**, China
50 N23°36' E109°42' **Wuxuan**, China
51 N25°11' E117°25' Wuyi Shan, China
50 N23°30' E111°27' **Wuzhou**, China
69 S27°15' E145°59' **Wyandra**, Qld, Austl
19 N54°42' E8°34' **Wyk**, Ger
69 S30°33' E133°32' **Wynbring**, SA, Austl
66 S15°28' E128°6' **Wyndham**, WA, Austl
115 N35°13' W90°47' **Wynne**, AR, US
107 N43°22' W108°2' **Wyoming**, US

X

83 N10°25' E51°16' **Xaafuun**, Som
91 S25°2' E33°38' **Xai-Xai**, Moz
57 N20°25' E104°2' **Xam Nua**, Laos
25 N41°8' E24°53' **Xánthi**, Grc
138 S26°53' W52°23' **Xanxerê**, SC, Braz
83 N4°32' E47°53' **Xarardheere**, Som
138 S21°15' W52°48' **Xavantina**, MT, Braz
51 N23°7' E112°2' *Xi*, China
49 N34°16' E108°55' **Xi'an**, China
51 N24°28' E118°5' **Xiamen**, China
48 N32°0' E84°0' **Xiang**, China
57 N19°20' E103°22' **Xiangkhoang**, Laos
48 N36°2' E98°8' **Xiangride**, China
51 N27°43' E112°27' **Xiangxiang**, China
50 N27°40' E99°46' **Xiaozhongdian**, China
49 N42°39' E120°35' **Xiawa**, China
49 N35°11' E111°15' **Xiaxian**, China
49 N27°58' E102°13' **Xichang**, China
48 N29°17' E88°54' **Xigaze**, China
50 N35°58' E105°44' **Xiji**, China
49 N43°56' E116°4' **Xilinhot**, China
123 N21°20' W98°58' **Xilitla**, SLP, Mex
49 N28°3' E103°46' **Xinchang**, China
48 N35°31' E99°36' **Xinghai**, China
49 N45°47' E130°52' *Xingkai Hu*, China
50 N25°27' E105°13' **Xingren**, China
50 N27°37' E111°2' **Xinhua**, China
49 N36°38' E101°52' **Xining**, China
50 N24°6' E101°58' **Xinping**, China
51 N25°23' E116°38' **Xinquan**, China
49 N35°54' E117°44' **Xintai**, China
51 N31°38' E114°51' **Xinxian**, China
49 N32°8' E114°4' **Xinyang**, China
51 N32°33' E112°21' **Xinye**, China
50 N22°13' E110°50' **Xinyi**, China
48 N43°8' E82°31' **Xinyuan**, China
51 N28°28' E119°29' **Xiping**, China
51 N29°4' E114°33' **Xiushui**, China
48 N28°22' E85°46' Xixabangma Feng, China
49 N33°22' E111°28' **Xixia**, China
48 N31°7' E85°25' **Xizang**, China
50 N30°0' E109°20' **Xuan'en**, China
50 N26°7' E104°5' **Xuanwei**, China
83 N4°7' E43°53' **Xuddur**, Som
49 N42°16' E115°49' **Xulun Hoh**, China
50 N20°21' E110°11' **Xuwen**, China
49 N34°15' E117°11' **Xuzhou**, China

Y

69 S35°46' E142°3' **Yaapeet**, Vic, Austl
82 N4°54' E38°2' **Yabelo**, Eth
33 N50°25' E109°18' Yablonovyy Range, Rus Fed
54 N16°46' E77°8' **Yadgir**, Ind
74 S16°50' E178°3' Yadua Island, Fiji
80 N32°4' E12°31' **Yafran**, Libya
87 N10°20' E15°14' **Yagoua**, Cam
106 N46°36' W120°31' **Yakima**, WA, US
45 N28°45' E63°51' **Yakmach**, Pak
88 N4°5' E22°27' **Yakoma**, DRC
87 N5°20' E25°20' **Yakotoko**, CAR
52 N30°11' E130°38' Yaku-shima, Jap
53 N42°15' E140°16' **Yakumo**, Jap
121 N59°32' W139°40' **Yakutat**, AK, US
33 N62°2' E129°43' **Yakutsk**, Rus Fed
85 N10°7' W1°52' **Yala**, Gha
68 S31°29' E131°52' **Yalata**, SA, Austl
68 S28°20' E116°41' **Yalgoo**, WA, Austl
27 N46°58' E37°16' **Yalta**, Ukr
27 N44°30' E34°10' **Yalta**, Ukr
53 N38°15' E140°20' **Yamagata**, Jap
52 N34°11' E131°29' **Yamaguchi**, Jap
35 N70°17' E69°20' Yamal Peninsula, Rus Fed
25 N42°29' E26°30' **Yambol**, Bulg
57 N20°26' E96°9' **Yamethin**, Myanmar
34 N58°26' E28°3' **Yamm**, Rus Fed
85 N6°49' W5°19' **Yamoussoukro**, Côte d'Ivoire
49 N36°35' E109°27' **Yan'an**, China
68 S27°33' E121°7' **Yandal**, WA, Austl
88 N2°51' E22°16' **Yandongi**, DRC
48 N42°20' E94°9' **Yandunzhan**, China
78 N11°11' W8°9' **Yanfolila**, Mali
51 N35°29' E112°25' **Yangcheng**, China
57 N16°43' E96°8' **Yangon**, Myanmar
50 N24°45' E110°24' **Yangshuo**, China
48 N32°19' E97°43' *Yangtze*, China
49 N29°53' E116°50' *Yangtze River*, China
49 N42°57' E129°32' **Yanji**, China
48 N29°0' E98°34' **Yanjing**, China
108 N42°52' W97°24' **Yankton**, SD, US
48 N42°0' E86°15' **Yanqi**, China
66 S22°31' E114°48' **Yanrey**, WA, Austl
49 N37°33' E121°20' **Yantai**, China
86 N3°55' E11°34' **Yaoundé**, Cam
85 N9°9' W1°10' **Yapei**, Gha
60 S4°59' E137°11' **Yapero**, Indo
140 S29°23' W56°49' **Yapeyú**, Arg
69 S24°53' E144°4' **Yaraka**, Qld, Austl
72 S0°50' E166°53' **Yaren**, Nauru
23 N46°27' E28°27' **Yargara**, Mol
132 N0°35' W74°10' *Yarí*, Col
42 N14°29' E44°21' **Yarim**, Yem
38 N37°49' E32°54' **Yarma**, Turk
104 N43°50' W66°7' **Yarmouth**, NS, Can
111 N43°48' W70°11' **Yarmouth**, ME, US
34 N57°37' E39°51' **Yaroslavl'**, Rus Fed
66 S21°34' E115°52' **Yarraloola**, WA, Austl
74 S17°12' E177°21' Yasawa Group, Fiji
74 S16°46' E177°16' Yasawa Island, Fiji
86 N12°23' E7°54' **Yashi**, Nga
57 N15°45' E104°8' **Yasothon**, Thai
44 N30°40' E51°35' **Yasuj**, Iran
75 S19°32' E169°28' Yasur Volcano, Van
135 S13°20' W66°35' **Yata**, Bol
134 S15°40' W74°32' **Yauca**, Peru
54 N20°24' E78°9' **Yavamati**, Ind
132 N2°55' W67°26' **Yavita**, Ven
125 N8°11' W77°41' **Yaviza**, Pan
84 N7°59' W13°29' *Yawri Bay*
50 N18°20' E109°30' **Yaxian**, China
44 N31°54' E54°22' **Yazd**, Iran
118 N32°52' W90°25' **Yazoo City**, MS, US
57 N15°15' E97°51' **Ye**, Myanmar
69 S37°13' E145°26' **Yea**, Vic, Austl
48 N37°54' E77°25' **Yecheng**, China
13 N38°37' W1°7' **Yecla**, Sp
57 N19°9' E96°21' **Yedashe**, Myanmar
23 N48°10' E27°19' **Yedintsy**, Mol
138 S26°24' W56°25' **Yegros**, Para
85 N8°13' W0°40' **Yeji**, Gha
32 N56°50' E60°37' **Yekaterinburg**, Rus Fed
39 N39°46' E45°20' **Yekhegnadzor**, Arm
36 N52°37' E38°30' **Yelets**, Rus Fed
49 N40°19' E108°36' *Yellow River*, China
49 N36°33' E122°38' *Yellow Sea*
96 N62°31' W114°1' **Yellowknife**, NT, Can
67 S20°13' E138°53' **Yelvertoft**, Qld, Austl
86 N10°51' E4°46' **Yelwa**, Nga
48 N34°40' E98°16' **Yematan**, China
42 N15°3' E46°43' **YEMEN**
57 N21°3' E104°18' **Yên Châu**, Viet
85 N9°26' W0°1' **Yendi**, Gha
38 N38°53' E32°48' **Yeniceoba**, Turk
32 N68°8' E87°38' *Yenisey*, Rus Fed
39 N40°8' E44°28' **Yerevan**, Arm
36 N47°17' E44°55' Yergeni Hills, Rus Fed
38 N39°38' E34°29' **Yerköy**, Turk
38 N38°21' E35°6' **Yesilhisar**, Turk
36 N44°3' E42°51' **Yessentuki**, Rus Fed
83 N4°48' E43°2' **Yet**, Eth
51 N33°37' E113°21' **Yexian**, China
36 N46°43' E38°17' **Yeysk**, Rus Fed
48 N30°17' E94°51' **Yi'ong**, China
24 N40°48' E22°25' **Yiannitsá**, Grc
49 N30°42' E111°17' **Yichang**, China
51 N31°43' E112°8' **Yicheng**, China
50 N26°50' E103°28' **Yichexun**, China
49 N47°43' E128°54' **Yichun**, China
49 N27°47' E114°22' **Yichun**, China
50 N30°22' E111°22' **Yidu**, China
50 N29°56' E99°22' **Yidun**, China
50 N35°24' E109°0' **Yijun**, China
38 N39°52' E36°38' **Yildizeli**, Turk
50 N27°35' E104°1' **Yiliang**, China
48 N37°55' E93°30' **Yiliping**, China
49 N38°28' E106°17' **Yinchuan**, China
50 N18°31' E108°44' **Yinggehai**, China
49 N40°41' E122°16' **Yingkou**, China
48 N43°55' E81°14' **Yining**, China
49 N50°38' E121°57' **Yitulihe**, China
50 N22°0' E101°28' **Yiwu**, China
48 N43°15' E94°45' **Yiwu**, China
51 N28°36' E112°20' **Yiyang**, China
51 N36°11' E118°8' **Yiyuan**, China
51 N25°26' E112°56' **Yizhang**, China
47 N48°58' E70°55' **Yntaly**, Kaz
60 S1°46' E136°28' **Yobi**, Indo
59 S7°54' E110°23' **Yogyakarta**, Indo
52 N37°18' E127°37' **Yoju**, S Kor
87 N3°31' E15°3' **Yokadouma**, Cam
86 N5°32' E12°19' **Yoko**, Cam
53 N35°27' E139°38' **Yokohama**, Jap
86 N9°14' E12°28' **Yola**, Nga
52 N39°32' E127°13' **Yondong-ni**, N Kor
51 N25°58' E117°22' **Yong'an**, China
49 N38°17' E101°59' **Yongchang**, China
50 N25°28' E99°33' **Yongping**, China
50 N34°43' E108°5' **Yongshou**, China
51 N26°6' E113°6' **Yongxing**, China
110 N40°56' W73°54' **Yonkers**, NY, US
132 N5°21' W72°25' **Yopal**, Col
11 N53°58' W1°5' **York**, UK
101 N51°13' W102°28' **Yorkton**, SK, Can
124 N15°9' W87°7' **Yoro**, Hon
53 N27°2' E128°28' Yoron-jima, Jap
35 N56°38' E47°55' **Yoshkar-Ola**, Rus Fed
135 S16°3' W63°3' **Yotaú**, Bol
138 S32°41' W57°38' **Young**, Ur
117 N41°6' W80°39' **Youngstown**, OH, US
49 N40°9' E112°32' **Youyu**, China
38 N39°50' E34°48' **Yozgat**, Turk
112 N41°37' W122°31' **Yreka**, CA, US
46 N48°37' E61°16' **Yrghyz**, Kaz
49 N31°4' E111°26' **Yuan'an**, China
50 N28°20' E110°16' **Yuanling**, China
50 N23°12' E102°52' **Yuanyang**, China
112 N39°10' W121°40' **Yuba City**, CA, US
82 N9°0' E35°22' **Yubdo**, Eth
123 N20°26' W89°38' **Yucatán**, Mex
123 N22°19' W86°49' *Yucatan Channel*
123 N19°51' W89°25' Yucatan Peninsula, Mex
66 S22°16' E131°49' **Yuendumu**, NT, Austl
49 N29°23' E113°5' **Yueyang**, China
35 N69°21' E61°41' Yugorskiy Peninsula, Rus Fed
22 N43°25' E19°52' **YUGOSLAVIA**
49 N38°1' E109°37' **Yuhebu**, China
121 N64°57' W154°55' *Yukon River*, US
96 N61°17' W137°7' **Yukon Territory**, Can
66 S25°13' E130°51' **Yulara**, NT, Austl
49 N38°20' E109°35' **Yulin**, China
112 N32°43' W114°38' **Yuma**, AZ, US
113 N40°8' W102°43' **Yuma**, CO, US
48 N40°21' E93°52' **Yumenguan**, China
48 N40°17' E97°7' **Yumenzhen**, China
48 N46°2' E82°37' **Yumin**, China
38 N36°49' E35°45' **Yumurtalik**, Turk
121 N52°23' W170°45' Yunaska Island, US
50 N25°59' E99°20' **Yunlong**, China
49 N32°49' E110°13' **Yunxi**, China
50 N24°30' E100°3' **Yunxian**, China
124 N13°56' W86°51' **Yuscarán**, Hon
48 N33°1' E97°0' **Yushu**, China
48 N36°51' E81°40' **Yutian**, China
33 N47°1' E142°40' **Yuzhno-Sakhalinsk**, Rus Fed

Z

42 N14°10' E43°17' **Zabid**, Yem
85 N11°10' W0°38' **Zabré**, Burk
124 N14°58' W89°32' **Zacapa**, Guat
122 N23°26' W103°38' **Zacatecas**, Mex
122 N22°46' W102°33' **Zacatecas**, Zac, Mex
57 N9°54' E97°7' Zadetkyi Kyun, Myanmar
36 N52°23' E38°57' **Zadonsk**, Rus Fed
12 N38°25' W6°25' **Zafra**, Sp
20 N51°37' E15°19' **Zagan**, Pol
81 N30°35' E31°29' **Zagazig**, Egypt
78 N30°22' W5°50' **Zagora**, Mor
22 N45°49' E15°58' **Zagreb**, Cro
45 N29°30' E60°52' **Zahedan**, Iran
54 N17°41' E77°37' **Zahirabad**, Ind
40 N33°51' E35°53' **Zahlah**, Leb
42 N17°40' E43°30' **Zahran**, Sau Ar
23 N43°54' E22°17' **Zajecar**, Yugo
39 N41°38' E46°39' **Zakataly**, Azer
44 N37°8' E42°41' **Zakho**, Iraq
24 N37°47' E20°50' **Zákinthos**, Grc
22 N46°50' E16°50' **Zalaegerszeg**, Hun
86 N10°37' E10°10' **Zalanga**, Nga
23 N47°11' E23°4' **Zalau**, Rom
82 N12°54' E23°29' **Zalingei**, Sud
46 N41°49' E54°9' *Zalir Kara-Bogaz-Gol*
42 N16°30' E47°35' **Zamakh**, Yem
91 S15°59' E29°16' *Zambezi*, Moz
88 S15°10' E22°35' *Zambezi River*, Zam
88 S14°6' E24°2' **ZAMBIA**
63 N6°55' E122°4' **Zamboanga**, Phil
21 N53°0' E22°15' **Zambrów**, Pol
91 S15°10' E30°50' **Zâmbuè**, Moz
12 N41°31' W5°44' **Zamora**, Sp
134 S4°4' W78°58' **Zamora**, Ecu
21 N50°44' E23°15' **Zamosc**, Pol
87 S2°51' E13°50' **Zanaga**, Con
47 N43°34' E69°46' **Zanatas**, Kaz
116 N39°56' W82°4' **Zanesville**, OH, US
44 N36°40' E48°29' **Zanjan**, Iran
68 S31°2' E123°34' **Zanthus**, WA, Austl
89 S6°10' E39°12' **Zanzibar**, Tanz
89 S6°8' E39°35' Zanzibar Island, Tanz
49 N34°52' E117°33' **Zaozhuang**, China
34 N56°16' E32°4' **Zapadnaya Dvina**, Rus Fed
141 S38°54' W70°4' **Zapala**, Arg
114 N26°55' W99°16' **Zapata**, TX, US
34 N69°26' E30°48' **Zapolyarnyy**, Rus Fed
27 N47°51' E35°9' **Zaporizhzh'ya**, Ukr
134 S4°24' W80°18' **Zapotillo**, Ecu
38 N39°55' E37°46' **Zara**, Turk
13 N41°39' W0°53' **Zaragoza**, Sp
132 N7°30' W74°52' **Zaragoza**, Col
44 N30°48' E56°35' **Zarand**, Iran
45 N31°6' E61°53' **Zaranj**, Afg
45 N33°11' E68°49' **Zare Saran**, Afg
86 N11°7' E7°44' **Zaria**, Nga
20 N51°38' E15°9' **Zary**, Pol
45 N28°4' E66°23' **Zawa**, Pak
48 N28°48' E97°27' **Zayu**, China
21 N51°36' E18°57' **Zdunska Wola**, Pol
29 N54°48' E12°10' Zealand, Den
19 N52°59' E13°20' **Zehdenick**, Ger
19 N51°3' E12°8' **Zeitz**, Ger
35 N62°29' E55°16' **Zelenets**, Rus Fed
34 N60°12' E29°42' **Zelenogorsk**, Rus Fed
87 N5°2' E25°8' **Zemio**, CAR
48 N38°13' E77°16' **Zepu**, China
36 N46°50' E40°19' **Zernograd**, Rus Fed
24 N41°30' E20°21' **Zerqan**, Alb
11 N60°38' W3°5' Zetland, UK
50 N30°44' E97°37' **Zhag'yab**, China
50 N31°26' E100°48' **Zhaggo**, China
50 N22°1' E109°27' **Zhanghuang**, China
49 N40°44' E114°44' **Zhangjiakou**, China
51 N32°21' E117°38' **Zhangqiao**, China
48 N38°56' E100°28' **Zhangye**, China
50 N21°11' E110°23' **Zhanjiang**, China
48 N32°32' E79°41' **Zhaxigang**, China
49 N42°16' E115°49' **Zhenglan Qi**, China
48 N33°38' E79°50' **Zhengning**, China
49 N34°46' E113°38' **Zhengzhou**, China
49 N32°25' E103°35' **Zhenjiangguan**, China
48 N33°8' E94°50' **Zhidoi**, China
49 N27°27' E109°41' **Zhijiang**, China
26 N50°15' E28°40' **Zhitomir**, Ukr
26 N49°2' E28°6' **Zhmerinka**, Ukr
50 N27°50' E99°40' **Zhongxin**, China
51 N33°43' E118°41' **Zhongxing**, China
45 N30°23' E67°43' **Ziarat**, Pak
49 N36°47' E118°3' **Zibo**, China
49 N37°19' E109°33' **Zichang**, China
20 N51°57' E15°29' **Zielona Gora**, Pol
49 N29°22' E104°46' **Zigong**, China
80 N14°43' E15°47' **Ziguey**, Chad
84 N12°35' W16°16' **Ziguinchor**, Sen
37 N52°14' E57°30' **Zilair**, Rus Fed
38 N40°18' E35°54' **Zile**, Turk
21 N49°14' E18°46' **Zilina**, Slvk
20 N47°1' E11°15' Zillertaler Alpen, Aus
91 S19°4' E27°53' **ZIMBABWE**
36 N47°8' E42°28' **Zimovniki**, Rus Fed
80 N13°48' E8°59' **Zinder**, Niger
87 N3°43' E18°35' **Zinga**, CAR
19 N50°54' E14°47' **Zittau**, Ger
50 N25°43' E106°5' **Ziyun**, China
25 N41°23' E25°6' **Zlatograd**, Bulg
35 N55°10' E59°40' **Zlatoust**, Rus Fed
80 N32°28' E14°34' **Zlitan**, Libya
47 N50°5' E79°32' **Znamenka**, Kaz
20 N48°52' E16°2' **Znojmo**, Czech
48 N29°55' E97°44' **Zogang**, China
38 N41°27' E31°49' **Zonguldak**, Turk
12 N39°17' W5°42' **Zorita**, Sp
134 S3°41' W80°39' **Zorritos**, Peru
80 N20°27' E16°32' **Zouar**, Chad
22 N45°23' E20°24' **Zrenjanin**, Yugo
34 N60°19' E36°57' **Zubovo**, Rus Fed
85 N7°26' W6°4' **Zuénoula**, Côte d'Ivoire
13 N41°52' W0°47' **Zuera**, Sp
15 N47°11' E8°31' **Zug**, Switz
39 N42°30' E41°53' **Zugdidi**, Geo
19 N47°25' E10°59' Zugspitze, Ger
134 S4°52' W79°9' **Zumba**, Ecu
113 N35°2' W108°47' **Zuni**, NM, US
49 N27°39' E106°57' **Zunyi**, China
15 N47°24' E8°32' **Zürich**, Switz
18 N49°15' E7°21' **Zweibrücken**, Ger
20 N48°37' E15°10' **Zwettl Stadt**, Aus
18 N52°32' E6°6' **Zwolle**, Neth

MILEAGE CHART

	Accra, Gha	Alma-Ata, Kaz	Amsterdam, Neth	Anchorage, AK, US	Antananarivo, Madag	Athens, Grc	Auckland, NZ	Baghdad, Iraq	Baku, Azer	Bangkok, Thai	Beijing, China	Beirut, Leb	Belgrade, Yugo	Berlin, Ger	Bogotá, Col	Brasília, DF, Braz	Brussels, Belg	Budapest, Hun	Buenos Aires, Arg	Cairo, Egypt	Calgary, AB, Can	Cape Town, S Afr	Caracas, Ven	Chicago, IL, US	Copenhagen, Den	Dallas, TX, US	Dhaka, Bngl	Helsinki, Fin	Ho Chi Minh City, Viet	Hong Kong, China	Honolulu, HI, US	Istanbul, Turk	Jakarta, Indo	Karachi, Pak	Kiev, Ukr	La Paz, Bol	Lima, Peru	Lisbon, Port	London, UK	Los Angeles, CA, US
Accra, Gha		5319 8558	3253 5234	7559 12162	3670 5905	2702 4348	10272 16528	3449 5549	3923 6312	6855 11030	7354 11833	3015 4851	2991 4813	3342 5377	5090 8190	3585 5768	3145 5060	3119 5018	4700 7562	2661 4282	6938 11163	2996 4821	4578 7366	5841 9398	3542 5699	6401 10299	6115 9839	4006 6446	7300 11746	7623 12265	10058 16183	3050 4907	7443 11976	4642 7469	3580 5760	4892 7871	5426 8730	2364 3804	3180 5117	757 1218
Alma-Ata, Kaz	5319 8558		3265 5253	4768 7672	4692 7549	2773 4462	8263 13295	1881 3027	1405 2261	2477 3985	2037 3278	2307 3712	2753 4430	2917 4693	8684 13973	8717 14026	3324 5348	2764 4447	10015 16114	2658 4277	5898 9490	6493 10447	8096 13026	6492 10446	2904 4673	7182 11556	1556 2504	2434 3916	2872 4621	2578 4148	6796 10935	2429 3908	3902 6278	1392 2240	2215 3564	9699 15606	9802 15771	4299 6917	3488 5612	702 1129
Amsterdam, Neth	3253 5234	3265 5253		4477 7203	5560 8946	1345 2164	11278 18146	2357 3792	2259 3635	5713 9192	4869 7834	1983 3191	883 1421	360 579	5513 8870	5673 9128	108 174	714 1149	7127 11467	2044 3289	4466 7186	6030 9702	4889 7866	4116 6623	388 624	4918 7913	4760 7659	935 1504	6130 9863	5779 9298	7254 11672	1377 2216	7073 11380	3719 5984	1108 1783	6445 10370	6557 10550	1158 1863	224 360	556 894
Anchorage, AK, US	7559 12162	4768 7672	4477 7203		9412 15144	5584 8985	7075 11384	5868 9442	5341 8594	6027 9697	3975 6396	5871 9446	5102 8209	4535 7297	5480 8817	7584 12203	4574 7360	4911 7902	8342 13422	6143 9884	1523 2451	10503 16899	5360 8624	2856 4595	4311 6936	3055 4915	5697 9166	4052 6520	6016 9680	5080 8174	2787 4484	5381 8658	7045 11335	6155 9903	4732 7614	6958 11195	6409 10312	5198 8364	4481 7210	234 376
Antananarivo, Madag	3670 5905	4692 7549	5560 8946	9412 15144		4234 6813	7288 11726	3622 5828	4108 6610	4261 6856	6017 9681	3740 6018	4730 7611	5352 8611	8401 13517	6222 10011	5495 8841	4926 7926	6351 10219	3559 5726	10017 16117	2069 3329	8056 12962	9396 15118	5556 8940	10055 16178	4134 6652	5622 9046	4530 7289	5334 8582	10804 17384	4319 6949	4086 6574	3303 5315	4913 7905	7444 11977	8112 13052	5421 8722	5663 9112	1109 1784
Athens, Grc	2702 4348	2773 4462	1345 2164	5584 8985	4234 6813		10874 17496	1208 1944	1408 2265	4935 7940	4742 7630	722 1162	499 803	1119 1800	6455 10386	5944 9564	1298 2088	698 1123	7277 11709	700 1126	5784 9306	4991 8031	5817 9360	5443 8758	1330 2140	6241 10042	4002 6439	1538 2475	5394 8679	5323 8565	8352 13438	355 571	6123 9852	2690 4328	925 1488	7025 11303	7326 11788	1772 2851	1487 2393	690 1110
Auckland, NZ	10272 16528	8263 13295	11278 18146	7075 11384	7288 11726	10874 17496		9667 15554	9518 15314	5958 9586	6480 10426	10167 16359	11012 17718	11047 17775	7591 12214	7878 12676	11382 18314	11021 17733	6445 10370	10314 16595	7457 11998	7328 11791	8229 13240	8213 13215	10912 17557	7467 12014	6904 11109	10370 16685	5505 8858	5686 9149	4407 7091	10605 17063	4753 7648	8184 13168	10464 16837	6946 11176	6702 10784	12212 19649	11416 18368	653 1052
Baghdad, Iraq	3449 5549	1881 3027	2357 3792	5868 9442	3622 5828	1208 1944	9667 15554		574 924	3759 6048	3916 6301	515 829	1503 2418	2030 3266	7663 12330	6956 11192	2349 3780	1646 2648	8150 13113	807 1298	6474 10417	4952 7968	7025 11303	6431 10347	2172 3495	7233 11638	2851 4587	2060 3315	4224 6796	4264 6861	8402 13519	1002 1612	4915 7908	1485 2389	1380 2220	8142 13100	8501 13678	2979 4793	2550 4103	765 1232
Baku, Azer	3923 6312	1405 2261	2259 3635	5341 8594	4108 6610	1408 2265	9518 15314	574 924		3562 5731	3433 5524	908 1461	1518 2442	1902 3060	7741 12455	7336 11804	2279 3667	1600 2574	8611 13855	1267 2039	6056 9744	5521 8883	7108 11437	6175 9936	1990 3202	6965 11207	2615 4208	1738 2796	4013 6457	3917 6302	7831 12600	1091 1755	4842 7791	1464 2356	1164 1873	8431 13565	8700 13998	3089 4970	2474 3981	724 1166
Bangkok, Thai	6855 11030	2477 3985	5713 9192	6027 9697	4261 6856	4935 7940	5958 9586	3759 6048	3562 5731		2053 3303	4274 6877	5076 8167	5355 8616	11137 17919	10343 16642	5760 9268	5135 8262	10508 16907	4525 7281	7513 12088	6313 10158	10573 17012	8577 13800	5367 8636	9042 14549	956 1538	4912 7903	466 750	1076 1731	6613 10640	4648 7479	1446 2327	2310 3717	4621 7435	11679 18792	12261 19728	6651 10701	5937 9553	828 1332
Beijing, China	7354 11833	2037 3278	4869 7834	3975 6396	6017 9681	4742 7630	6480 10426	3916 6301	3433 5524	2053 3303		4340 6983	4614 7424	4578 7366	9307 14975	10539 16957	4956 7974	4568 7350	11996 19302	4694 7553	5462 8788	8064 12975	8963 14421	6602 10623	4480 7208	6997 11258	1884 3031	3934 6330	2104 3385	1229 1977	5079 8172	4387 7059	3249 5228	3024 4866	4016 6462	10816 17403	10368 16682	6016 9680	5068 8154	626 1007
Beirut, Leb	3015 4851	2307 3712	1983 3191	5871 9446	3740 6018	722 1162	10167 16359	515 829	908 1461	4274 6877	4340 6983		1101 1772	1690 2719	7162 11524	6469 10409	1956 3147	1273 2048	7708 12402	364 586	6295 10129	4823 7760	6525 10499	6096 9808	1866 3002	6899 11100	3364 5413	1884 3031	4738 7623	4760 7659	8538 13738	612 985	5415 8713	1993 3207	1175 1891	7634 12283	7987 12851	2489 4005	2155 3467	745 1199
Belgrade, Yugo	2991 4813	2753 4430	883 1421	5102 8209	4730 7611	499 803	11012 17718	1503 2418	1518 2442	5076 8167	4614 7424	1101 1772		623 1002	6229 10022	5993 9643	856 1377	198 319	7390 11891	1178 1895	5288 8508	5452 8772	5594 9001	4998 8042	830 1335	5800 9332	4124 6636	1081 1739	5521 8883	5331 8578	7881 12681	503 809	6353 10222	2932 4718	608 978	6965 11207	7187 11564	1576 2536	1055 1697	6413 1031
Berlin, Ger	3342 5377	2917 4693	360 579	4535 7297	5352 8611	1119 1800	11047 17775	2030 3266	1902 3060	5355 8616	4578 7366	1690 2719	623 1002		5873 9450	5972 9609	407 655	428 689	7418 11936	1799 2895	4665 7506	5993 9643	5249 8446	4413 7101	224 360	5216 8393	4402 7083	689 1109	5776 9294	5449 8767	7322 11781	1079 1736	6713 10801	3365 5414	748 1204	6787 10920	6914 11125	1439 2315	583 938	5792 9319
Bogotá, Col	5090 8190	8684 13973	5513 8870	5480 8817	8401 13517	6455 10386	7591 12214	7663 12330	7741 12455	11137 17919	9307 14975	7162 11524	6229 10022	5873 9450		2282 3672	5478 8814	6142 9882	2899 4664	6980 11231	3957 6367	6554 10545	638 1027	2712 4364	5837 9392	2441 3928	10238 16473	6262 10076	11395 18335	10518 16923	5713 9192	6698 10777	12335 19847	9145 14714	6620 10652	1516 2439	1175 1891	4687 7541	5291 8513	3490 5615
Brasília, DF, Braz	3585 5768	8717 14026	5673 9128	7584 12203	6222 10011	5944 9564	7878 12676	6956 11192	7336 11804	10343 16642	10539 16957	6469 10409	5993 9643	5972 9609	2282 3672		5588 8991	6016 9680	1459 2348	6149 9894	6101 9817	4281 6888	2239 3603	4728 7607	6062 9754	4664 7504	9699 15606	6607 10631	10715 17240	11206 18030	7884 12685	6288 10117	10158 16344	8227 13237	6574 10578	1347 2167	1973 3175	4533 7294	5472 8804	5771 9286
Brussels, Belg	3145 5060	3324 5348	108 174	4574 7360	5495 8841	1298 2088	11382 18314	2349 3780	2279 3667	5760 9268	4956 7974	1956 3147	856 1377	407 655	5478 8814	5588 8991		704 1133	7040 11327	1999 3216	4536 7298	5932 9545	4851 7805	4149 6676	479 771	4949 7963	4805 7731	1027 1652	6182 9947	5851 9414	7348 11823	1357 2183	7108 11437	3734 6008	1143 1839	6381 10267	6509 10473	1063 1710	201 323	5619 9041
Budapest, Hun	3119 5018	2764 4447	714 1149	4911 7902	4926 7926	698 1123	11021 17733	1646 2648	1600 2574	5135 8262	4568 7350	1273 2048	198 319	428 689	6142 9882	6016 9680	704 1133		7432 11958	1371 2206	5091 8191	5637 9070	5508 8862	4823 7760	633 1018	5626 9052	4180 6726	911 1466	5572 8965	5337 8587	7692 12376	664 1068	6443 10367	3041 4893	559 899	6939 11165	7130 11472	1536 2471	904 1455	6221 10010
Buenos Aires, Arg	4700 7562	10015 16114	7127 11467	8342 13422	6351 10219	7277 11709	6445 10370	8150 13113	8611 13855	10508 16907	11996 19302	7708 12402	7390 11891	7418 11936	2899 4664	1459 2348	7040 11327	7432 11958		7359 11841	6826 10983	4283 6891	3172 5104	5608 9023	7515 12092	5288 8508	10444 16804	8062 12972	10564 16997	11498 18500	7572 12183	7630 12277	9480 15253	9155 14730	7986 12849	1390 2237	1947 3133	5980 9622	6929 11149	6132 9866
Cairo, Egypt	2661 4282	2658 4277	2044 3289	6143 9884	3559 5726	700 1126	10314 16595	807 1298	1267 2039	4525 7281	4694 7553	364 586	1178 1895	1799 2895	6980 11231	6149 9894	1999 3216	1371 2206	7359 11841		6459 10393	4508 7253	6349 10216	6140 9879	1998 3215	6937 11162	3640 5857	2107 3390	4991 8031	5070 8158	8852 14243	773 1244	5592 8998	2219 3570	1412 2272	7347 11821	7737 12449	2364 3804	2187 3519	7591 12214
Calgary, AB, Can	6938 11163	5898 9490	4466 7186	1523 2451	10017 16117	5784 9306	7457 11998	6474 10417	6056 9744	7513 12088	5462 8788	6295 10129	5288 8508	4665 7506	3957 6367	6101 9817	4536 7298	5091 8191	6826 10983	6459 10393		9822 15804	3863 6216	1402 2256	4461 7178	1539 2476	7073 11380	4426 7121	7531 12117	6597 10615	3124 5027	5705 9179	8567 13784	7204 11591	5131 8256	5439 8751	4908 7897	4768 7672	4378 7044	1192 1918
Cape Town, S Afr	2996 4821	6493 10447	6030 9702	10503 16899	2069 3329	4991 8031	7328 11791	4952 7968	5521 8883	6313 10158	8064 12975	4823 7760	5452 8772	5993 9643	6554 10545	4281 6888	5932 9545	5637 9070	4283 6891	4508 7253	9822 15804		6374 10256	8511 13694	6215 10000	8782 14130	6186 9953	6526 10500	6544 10529	7390 11891	11560 18600	5235 8423	5900 9493	5173 8323	5888 9474	5410 8705	6075 9775	5334 8582	6022 9689	9995 16082
Caracas, Ven	4578 7366	8096 13026	4889 7866	5360 8624	8056 12962	5817 9360	8229 13240	7025 11303	7108 11437	10573 17012	8963 14421	6525 10499	5594 9001	5249 8446	638 1027	2239 3603	4851 7805	5508 8862	3172 5104	6349 10216	3863 6216	6374 10256		2508 4035	5221 8401	2447 3937	9638 15508	5664 9113	10924 17577	10190 16396	6026 9696	6060 9751	11940 19211	8506 13686	5994 9644	1871 3010	1713 2756	4048 6513	4666 7508	3622 5828
Chicago, IL, US	5841 9398	6492 10446	4116 6623	2856 4595	9396 15118	5443 8758	8213 13215	6431 10347	6175 9936	8577 13800	6602 10623	6096 9808	4998 8042	4413 7101	2712 4364	4728 7607	4149 6676	4823 7760	5608 9023	6140 9879	1402 2256	8511 13694	2508 4035		4259 6853	804 1294	7920 12743	4437 7139	8705 14006	7807 12561	4255 6846	5487 8829	9834 15823	7566 12174	5060 8142	4227 6801	3797 6109	3999 6434	3956 6365	1741 2801
Copenhagen, Den	3542 5699	2904 4673	388 624	4311 6936	5556 8940	1330 2140	10912 17557	2172 3495	1990 3202	5367 8636	4480 7208	1866 3002	830 1335	224 360	5837 9392	6062 9754	479 771	633 1018	7515 12092	1998 3215	4461 7178	6215 10000	5221 8401	4259 6853		5062 8145	4419 7110	549 883	5775 9292	5399 8687	7098 11421	1258 2024	6750 10861	3453 5556	827 1331	6817 10969	6907 11113	1542 2481	597 961	5599 9009
Dallas, TX, US	6401 10299	7182 11556	4918 7913	3055 4915	10055 16178	6241 10042	7467 12014	7233 11638	6965 11207	9042 14549	6997 11258	6899 11100	5800 9332	5216 8393	2441 3928	4664 7504	4949 7963	5626 9052	5288 8508	6937 11162	1539 2476	8782 14130	2447 3937	804 1294	5062 8145		8521 13710	5227 8410	9070 14594	8134 13088	3796 6108	6290 10121	10070 16203	8330 13403	5860 9429	3903 6280	3371 5424	4746 7636	4755 7651	1239 1994
Dhaka, Bngl	6115 9839	1556 2504	4760 7659	5697 9166	4134 6652	4002 6439	6904 11109	2851 4587	2615 4208	956 1538	1884 3031	3364 5413	4124 6636	4402 7083	10238 16473	9699 15606	4805 7731	4180 6726	10444 16804	3640 5857	7073 11380	6186 9953	9638 15508	7920 12743	4419 7110	8521 13710		3978 6401	1398 2249	1517 2441	6907 11113	3704 5960	2348 3778	1474 2372	3666 5899	10982 17670	11310 18198	5700 9171	4984 8019	8037 12932
Helsinki, Fin	4006 6446	2434 3916	935 1504	4052 6520	5622 9046	1538 2475	10370 16685	2060 3315	1738 2796	4912 7903	3934 6330	1884 3031	1081 1739	689 1109	6262 10076	6607 10631	1027 1652	911 1466	8062 12972	2107 3390	4426 7121	6526 10500	5664 9113	4437 7139	549 883	5227 8410	3978 6401		5301 8529	4876 7845	6815 10965	1336 2150	6325 10177	3159 5083	709 1141	7323 11783	7368 11855	2091 3364	1135 1826	5603 9015
Ho Chi Minh City, Viet	7300 11746	2872 4621	6130 9863	6016 9680	4530 7289	5394 8679	5505 8858	4224 6796	4013 6457	466 750	2104 3385	4738 7623	5521 8883	5776 9294	11395 18335	10715 17240	6182 9947	5572 8965	10564 16997	4991 8031	7531 12117	6544 10529	10924 17577	8705 14006	5775 9292	9070 14594	1398 2249	5301 8529		938 1509	6306 10146	5101 8208	1173 1887	2776 4467	5049 8124	11935 19203	12191 19615	7097 11419	6354 10224	8177 13157
Hong Kong, China	7623 12265	2578 4148	5779 9298	5080 8174	5334 8582	5323 8565	5686 9149	4264 6861	3917 6302	1076 1731	1229 1977	4760 7659	5331 8578	5449 8767	10518 16923	11206 18030	5851 9414	5337 8587	11498 18500	5070 8158	6597 10615	7390 11891	10190 16396	7807 12561	5399 8687	8134 13088	1517 2441	4876 7845	938 1509		5559 8944	4989 8027	2030 3266	2982 4798	4782 7694	12033 19361	11439 18405	6865 11046	5996 9648	7252 11668
Honolulu, HI, US	10058 16183	6796 10935	7254 11672	2787 4484	10804 17384	8352 13438	4407 7091	8402 13519	7831 12600	6613 10640	5079 8172	8538 13738	7881 12681	7322 11781	5713 9192	7884 12685	7348 11823	7692 12376	7572 12183	8852 14243	3124 5027	11560 18600	6026 9696	4255 6846	7098 11421	3796 6108	6907 11113	6815 10965	6306 10146	5559 8944		8119 13063	6726 10822	8063 12973	7466 12013	6622 10655	5956 9583	7833 12603	7240 11649	2566 4129
Istanbul, Turk	3050 4907	2429 3908	1377 2216	5381 8658	4319 6949	355 571	10605 17063	1002 1612	1091 1755	4648 7479	4387 7059	612 985	503 809	1079 1736	6698 10777	6288 10117	1357 2183	664 1068	7630 12277	773 1244	5705 9179	5235 8423	6060 9751	5487 8829	1258 2024	6290 10121	3704 5960	1336 2150	5101 8208	4989 8027	8119 13063		5883 9466	2451 3944	653 1051	7342 11813	7614 12251	2016 3244	1557 2505	6854 11028
Jakarta, Indo	7443 11976	3902 6278	7073 11380	7045 11335	4086 6574	6123 9852	4753 7648	4915 7908	4842 7791	1446 2327	3249 5228	5415 8713	6353 10222	6713 10801	12335 19847	10158 16344	7108 11437	6443 10367	9480 15253	5592 8998	8567 13784	5900 9493	11940 19211	9834 15823	6750 10861	10070 16203	2348 3778	6325 10177	1173 1887	2030 3266	6726 10822	5883 9466		3435 5527	5966 9599	10855 17466	11168 17969	7892 12698	7295 11738	8993 14470
Karachi, Pak	4642 7469	1392 2240	3719 5984	6155 9903	3303 5315	2690 4328	8184 13168	1485 2389	1464 2356	2310 3717	3024 4866	1993 3207	2932 4718	3365 5414	9145 14714	8227 13237	3734 6008	3041 4893	9155 14730	2219 3570	7204 11591	5173 8323	8506 13686	7566 12174	3453 5556	8330 13403	1474 2372	3159 5083	2776 4467	2982 4798	8063 12973	2451 3944	3435 5527		2628 4228	9515 15310	9953 16014	4457 7171	3931 6325	8364 13458
Kiev, Ukr	3580 5760	2215 3564	1108 1783	4732 7614	4913 7905	925 1488	10464 16837	1380 2220	1164 1873	4621 7435	4016 6462	1175 1891	608 978	748 1204	6620 10652	6574 10578	1143 1839	559 899	7986 12849	1412 2272	5131 8256	5888 9474	5994 9644	5060 8142	827 1331	5860 9429	3666 5899	709 1141	5049 8124	4782 7694	7466 12013	653 1051	5966 9599	2628 4228		7484 12042	7647 12304	2085 3355	1329 2138	6303 10142
La Paz, Bol	4892 7871	9699 15606	6445 10370	6958 11195	7444 11977	7025 11303	6946 11176	8142 13100	8431 13565	11679 18792	10816 17403	7634 12283	6965 11207	6787 10920	1516 2439	1347 2167	6381 10267	6939 11165	1390 2237	7347 11821	5439 8751	5410 8705	1871 3010	4227 6801	6817 10969	3903 6280	10982 17670	7323 11783	11935 19203	12033 19361	6622 10655	7342 11813	10855 17466	9515 15310	7484 12042		669 1076	5403 8693	6225 10016	4811 7741
Lima, Peru	5426 8730	9802 15771	6557 10550	6409 10312	8112 13052	7326 11788	6702 10784	8501 13678	8700 13998	12261 19728	10368 16682	7987 12851	7187 11564	6914 11125	1175 1891	1973 3175	6509 10473	7130 11472	1947 3133	7737 12449	4908 7897	6075 9775	1713 2756	3797 6109	6907 11113	3371 5424	11310 18198	7368 11855	12191 19615	11439 18405	5956 9583	7614 12251	11168 17969	9953 16014	7647 12304	669 1076		5612 9030	6334 10191	4192 6745
Lisbon, Port	2364 3804	4299 6917	1158 1863	5198 8364	5421 8722	1772 2851	12212 19649	2979 4793	3089 4970	6651 10701	6016 9680	2489 4005	1576 2536	1439 2315	4687 7541	4533 7294	1063 1710	1536 2471	5980 9622	2364 3804	4768 7672	5334 8582	4048 6513	3999 6434	1542 2481	4746 7636	5700 9171	2091 3364	7097 11419	6865 11046	7833 12603	2016 3244	7892 12698	4457 7171	2085 3355	5403 8693	5612 9030		984 1583	5674 9129
London, UK	3180 5117	3488 5612	224 360	4481 7210	5663 9112	1487 2393	11416 18368	2550 4103	2474 3981	5937 9553	5068 8154	2155 3467	1055 1697	583 938	5291 8513	5472 8804	201 323	904 1455	6929 11149	2187 3519	4378 7044	6022 9689	4666 7508	3956 6365	597 961	4755 7651	4984 8019	1135 1826	6354 10224	5996 9648	7240 11649	1557 2505	7295 11738	3931 6325	1329 2138	6225 10016	6334 10191	984 1583		5446 8763
Los Angeles, CA, US	7575 12188	7020 11295	5561 8948	2341 3767	11091 17845	6901 11104	6539 10521	7658 12322	7248 11662	8281 13324	6261 10074	7454 11993	6413 10319	5792 9319	3490 5615	5771 9286	5619 9041	6221 10010	6132 9866	7591 12214	1192 1918	9995 16082	3622 5828	1741 2801	5599 9009	1239 1994	8037 12932	5603 9015	8177 13157	7252 11668	2566 4129	6854 11028	8993 14470	8364 13458	6303 10142	4811 7741	4192 6745	5674 9129	5446 8763	
Madrid, Sp	2422 3897	3993 6425	922 1483	5173 8323	5265 8471	1472 2368	12200 19630	2676 4306	2778 4470	6339 10199	5740 9236	2192 3527	1264 2034	1164 1873	4993 8034	4817 7751	819 1318	1229 1977	6256 10066	2086 3356	4864 7826	5338 8589	4355 7007	4188 6738	1291 2077	4953 7969	5388 8669	1836 2954	6786 10919	6563 10560	7873 12668	1707 2747	7587 12207	4152 6681	1781 2866	5710 9187	5924 9532	312 502	786 1265	5825 9372
Manila, Phil	8193 13183	3270 5261	6471 10412	5318 8557	5517 8877	6001 9656	4993 8034	4914 7907	4593 7390	1377 2216	1776 2858	5417 8716	6024 9693	6143 9884	10777 17340	11715 18849	6544 10529	6031 9704	11075 17820	5714 9194	6837 11001	7501 12069	10641 17121	8147 13109	6089 9797	8337 13414	2093 3368	5562 8949	1002 1612	695 1118	5308 8541	5672 9126	1734 2790	3566 5738	5477 8812	11837 19046	11234 18076	7560 12164	6686 10758	7310 11762
Marrakech, Mor	1873 3014	4536 7298	1576 2536	5686 9149	5080 8174	1843 2965	12068 19417	3030 4875	3237 5208	6779 10907	6358 10230	2519 4053	1784 2870	1802 2899	4658 7495	4218 6787	1472 2368	1797 2891	5640 9075	2323 3738	5188 8347	4856 7813	4026 6478	4318 6948	1942 3125	5026 8087	5845 9405	2483 3995	7237 11644	7113 11445	8285 13331	2146 3453	7914 12734	4511 7258	2356 3791	5198 8364	5482 8821	497 800	1432 2304	6030 9702
México City, MEX, Mex	6679 10747	8114 13055	5737 9231	3782 6085	10284 16547	7020 11295	6822 10977	8086 13010	7863 12652	9803 15773	7756 12479	7711 12407	6612 10639	6057 9746	1977 3181	4255 6846	5756 9261	6451 10380	4599 7400	7700 12389	2337 3760	8531 13726	2236 3598	1692 2722	5919 9524	936 1506	9405 15133	6126 9857	9727 15651	8799 14158	3791 6100	7112 11443	10486 16872	9256 14893	6733 10833	3260 5245	2653 4269	5398 8685	5557 8941	1553 2499
Miami, FL, US	5438 8750	7465 12011	4635 7458	4007 6447	9101 14644	5842 9400	8074 12991	6983 11236	6866 11047	9725 15648	7789 12533	6556 10549	5480 8817	4978 8010	1521 2447	3607 5804	4635 7458	5339 8590	4416 7105	6497 10454	2499 4021	7671 12343	1368 2201	1191 1916	4876 7845	1112 1789	8977 14444	5185 8343	9889 15911	8998 14478	4866 7829	5983 9627	11025 17739	8327 13398	5702 9175	3036 4885	2631 4233	4153 6682	4434 7134	2339 3763
Milan, It	2820 4537	3253 5234	516 830	4984 8019	5065 8150	907 1459	11502 18507	2042 3286	2067 3326	5618 9039	5028 8090	1604 2581	553 890	525 845	5677 9134	5542 8917	434 698	489 787	6970 11215	1600 2574	4969 7995	5527 8893	5042 8113	4540 7305	724 1165	5336 8586	4663 7503	1206 1940	6058 9747	5823 9369	7766 12495	1041 1675	6906 11112	3484 5606	1042 1677	6449 10376	6647 10695	1047 1685	599 964	6044 9725
Minsk, Bela	3692 5940	2324 3739	944 1519	4492 7228	5178 8331	1116 1796	10504 16901	1646 2648	1395 2245	4770 7675	4025 6476	1439 2315	705 1134	593 954	6444 10368	6538 10520	1000 1609	579 932	7973 12829	1661 2673	4862 7823	6104 9821	5826 9374	4803 7728	610 981	5602 9014	3819 6145	447 719	5186 8344	4861 7821	7243 11654	891 1434	6142 9882	2853 4590	269 433	7380 11874	7502 12071	2012 3237	1168 1879	6033 9707
Montego Bay, Jam	5306 8537	7901 12713	4928 7929	4515 7265	8902 14323	6057 9746	7929 12758	7236 11643	7184 11559	10230 16460	8314 13377	6778 10906	5738 9232	5282 8499	994 1599	3134 5043	4915 7908	5614 9033	3891 6261	6676 10742	2997 4822	7294 11736	922 1483	1718 2764	5203 8372	1533 2467	9438 15186	5556 8940	10413 16755	9524 15324	5144 8277	6235 10032	11550 18584	8647 13913	6022 9689	2510 4039	2116 3405	4312 6938	4717 7590	2701 4346
Moscow, Rus Fed	4050 6516	1933 3110	1337 2151	4354 7006	5201 8368	1389 2235	10083 16224	1587 2553	1201 1932	4399 7078	3605 5800	1517 2441	1067 1717	1001 1611	6792 10928	6958 11195	1404 2259	977 1572	8392 13503	1806 2906	4889 7866	6311 10154	6184 9950	4982 8016	971 1562	5767 9279	3454 5557	557 896	4804 7730	4448 7157	7047 11339	1089 1752	5795 9324	2603 4188	471 758	7782 12521	7876 12672	2431 3911	1559 2508	6078 9780
Nairobi, Ken	2605 4191	3961 6373	4154 6684	8299 13353	1419 2283	2848 4582	8685 13974	2447 3937	3001 4829	4488 7221	5736 9229	2438 3923	3347 5385	3966 6381	7681 12359	5855 9421	4085 6573	3545 5704	6480 10426	2202 3543	8620 13870	2553 4108	7183 11557	8023 12909	4178 6722	8744 14069	3994 6426	4306 6928	4880 7852	5456 8779	10757 17308	2974 4785	4846 7797	2717 4372	3602 5796	7198 11582	7823 12587	4025 6476	4249 6837	9675 15567
Nassau, Bah	5260 8463	7456 11997	4553 7326	4144 6668	8919 14351	5735 9228	8203 13199	6891 11088	6798 10938	9771 15722	7876 12672	6452 10381	5387 8668	4902 7887	1433 2306	3456 5561	4549 7319	5252 8450	4313 6940	6380 10265	2645 4256	7491 12053	1218 1960	1303 2097	4809 7738	1291 2077	8985 14457	5138 8267	9965 16034	9094 14632	5051 8127	5889 9475	11124 17899	8262 13294	5633 9063	2943 4735	2574 4142	4027 6479	4349 6998	2522 4058
New Delhi, Ind	5284 8502	1013 1630	3959 6370	5705 9179	3843 6183	3122 5023	7773 12507	1966 3163	1751 2817	1815 2920	2351 3783	2479 3989	3269 5260	3599 5791	9471 15239	8865 14264	3994 6426	3341 5376	9837 15828	2758 4438	6901 11104	5792 9319	8845 14232	7487 12047	3641 5858	8192 13181	885 1424	3252 5232	2272 3656	2342 3768	7413 11928	2832 4557	3114 5010	681 1096	2851 4587	10105 16259	10446 16808	4841 7789	4180 6726	8002 12875
New York, NY, US	5129 8253	6371 10251	3649 5871	3368 5419	8715 14022	4931 7934	8838 14220	6004 9660	5829 9379	8674 13956	6840 11006	5620 9043	4521 7274	3976 6397	2500 4023	4255 6846	3665 5897	4363 7020	5307 8539	5617 9038	2030 3266	7825 12590	2135 3435	713 1147	3851 6196	1373 2209	7889 12693	4119 6627	8896 14314	8068 12981	4968 7994	5022 8080	10068 16199	7276 11707	4676 7524	3978 6401	3663 5894	3375 5430	3466 5577	2448 3939
Novosibirsk, Rus Fed	5644 9081	859 1382	3035 4883	3914 6298	5528 8895	2954 4753	8334 13409	2384 3836	1820 2928	3011 4845	1854 2983	2690 4328	2773 4462	2730 4393	8127 13076	8702 14002	3117 5015	2717 4372	10143 16320	3054 4914	5051 8127	7243 11654	7598 12225	5731 9221	2648 4261	6382 10269	2201 3541	2109 3393	3326 5352	2781 4475	6081 9784	2600 4183	4454 7166	2241 3606	2168 3488	9383 15097	9298 14960	4169 6708	3242 5216	6163 9916
Paris, Fr	3001 4829	3457 5562	267 430	4686 7540	5454 8775	1303 2097	11545 18576	2405 3870	2372 3817	5880 9461	5114 8228	1988 3199	901 1450	548 882	5374 8647	5432 8740	163 262	775 1247	6882 11073	1999 3216	4590 7385	5817 9360	4743 7631	4142 6664	640 1030	4938 7945	4924 7923	1188 1911	6307 10148	5996 9648	7449 11985	1405 2261	7211 11602	3817 6142	1259 2026	6244 10047	6388 10278	903 1453	214 344	5651 9092
Perth, WA, Austl	7957 12803	5759 9266	8802 14162	8283 13327	4295 6911	7651 12310	3331 5360	6485 10434	6546 10533	3322 5345	4976 8006	6932 11154	7988 12853	8448 13593	10462 16833	8983 14454	8814 14182	8115 13057	7838 12611	7009 11277	9627 15490	5408 8701	10966 17644	11001 17701	8524 13715	10562 16994	4204 6764	8152 13117	3019 4858	3756 6043	6797 10936	7488 12048	1877 3020	5083 8179	7707 12401	9096 14635	9294 14954	9362 15063	9013 14502	9360 15060
Prague, Czech	3198 5146	2917 4693	443 713	4707 7574	5188 8347	953 1533	11119 17890	1914 3080	1831 2946	5330 8576	4640 7466	1550 2494	462 743	173 278	5920 9525	5920 9525	448 721	277 446	7357 11837	1640 2639	4830 7771	5822 9368	5291 8513	4547 7316	397 639	5351 8610	4375 7039	811 1305	5759 9266	5471 8803	7494 12058	940 1512	6664 10722	3286 5287	710 1142	6782 10912	6937 11162	1396 2246	645 1038	5952 9577
Rio de Janeiro, RJ, Brazil	3513 5652	8801 14161	5964 9596	8165 13137	5774 9290	6052 9738	7639 12291	6957 11194	7397 11902	10001 16092	10784 17351	6499 10457	6171 9929	6234 10031	2825 4545	581 935	5871 9446	6221 10010	1226 1973	6157 9907	6680 10748	3777 6077	2817 4533	5310 8544	6349 10216	5233 8420	9525 15326	6898 11099	10303 16578	11017 17726	8304 13361	6405 10306	9605 15454	8096 13026	6771 10895	1682 2706	2349 3780	4807 7734	5777 9295	6314 10159
Riyadh, Sau Ar	3381 5440	2139 3442	2901 4668	6443 10367	3018 4856	1637 2634	9297 14959	613 986	1102 1773	3576 5754	4108 6610	927 1492	2024 3257	2594 4174	7994 12862	6963 11203	2880 4634	2188 3520	8006 12882	1019 1640	7087 11403	4462 7179	7364 11849	7007 11274	2752 4428	7810 12566	2748 4422	2671 4298	4040 6500	4243 6827	8873 14277	1525 2454	4577 7364	1277 2055	1983 3191	8238 13255	8690 13982	3375 5430	3079 4954	8272 13310
Rome, It	2633 4236	3203 5154	809 1302	5256 8457	4768 7672	651 1047	11452 18426	1837 2956	1936 3115	5498 8846	5058 8138	1370 2204	451 726	738 1187	5841 9398	5542 8917	732 1178	505 813	6944 11173	1328 2137	5267 8475	5262 8467	5203 8372	4821 7757	957 1540	5613 9031	4550 7321	1374 2211	5948 9570	5781 9302	8042 12940	858 1381	6740 10845	3306 5319	1044 1680	6521 10492	6764 10883	1158 1863	894 1438	6340 10201
San José, CR	5746 9245	8589 13820	5643 9080	4831 7773	9167 14750	6750 10861	7259 11680	7939 12774	7901 12713	10792 17364	8768 14108	7471 12021	6446 10372	5998 9651	779 1253	3052 4911	5630 9059	6326 10179	3511 5649	7349 11825	3317 5337	7330 11794	1168 1879	2221 3574	5920 9525	1778 2861	10102 16254	6269 10087	10848 17454	9911 15947	4943 7953	6940 11166	11668 18774	9362 15063	6739 10843	2129 3426	1601 2576	4991 8031	5432 8740	2735 4401
San Juan, PR, US	4525 7281	7585 12204	4425 7120	4910 7900	8135 13089	5440 8753	8587 13816	6643 10689	6671 10734	10051 16172	8416 13541	6158 9908	5173 8323	4786 7701	1101 1772	2675 4304	4396 7073	5073 8162	3707 5965	6017 9681	3449 5549	6636 10677	553 890	2058 3311	4741 7628	2147 3455	9137 14701	5161 8304	10378 16698	9641 15512	5881 9463	5656 9101	11485 18479	8106 13043	5533 8903	2424 3900	2245 3612	3670 5905	4205 6766	3374 5429
Santiago, Chile	5333 8581	10590 17039	7479 12034	7898 12708	7006 11273	7817 12578	6021 9688	8775 14119	9196 14796	10986 17676	11867 19094	8310 13371	7865 12655	7800 12550	2645 4256	1876 3018	7403 11911	7879 12677	704 1133	7973 12829	6422 10333	4945 7957	3055 4915	5325 8568	7864 12653	4892 7871	11130 17908	8395 13508	10881 17508	11631 18714	6878 11067	8163 13134	9712 15627	9854 15855	8438 13577	1186 1908	1533 2467	6370 10249	7267 11693	5606 9020
Seoul, S Kor	7940 12775	2628 4228	5328 8573	3778 6079	6469 10409	5303 8533	5989 9636	4508 7253	4017 6463	2317 3728	594 956	4925 7924	5147 8282	5060 8142	9243 14872	10921 17572	5421 8722	5086 8183	12095 19461	5282 8499	5298 8524	8536 13734	9014 14504	6545 10531	4943 7953	6833 10994	2360 3797	4394 7070	2242 3607	1304 2098	4552 7324	4948 7961	3293 5298	3595 5784	4541 7306	10735 17273	10157 16343	6485 10434	5516 8875	5966 9599
Shanghai, China	7847 12626	2556 4113	5523 8887	4314 6941	6009 9668	5316 8553	5842 9400	4400 7080	3960 6372	1800 2896	664 1068	4856 7813	5227 8410	5224 8405	9774 15726	11196 18014	5608 9023	5193 8356	12230 19678	5198 8364	5835 9389	8078 12998	9516 15311	7070 11376	5134 8261	7370 11858	1970 3170	4589 7384	1705 2743	767 1234	4949 7963	4966 7990	2765 4449	3321 5343	4636 7459	11273 18138	10686 17194	6663 10721	5724 9210	6493 10447
Singapore, Sing	7189 11567	3346 5384	6536 10516	6689 10763	4073 6553	5638 9072	5237 8426	4434 7134	4323 6956	891 1434	2789 4488	4941 7950	5840 9397	6176 9937	12027 19351	10286 16550	6574 10578	5920 9525	9887 15908	5144 8277	8208 13207	6014 9677	11424 18381	9388 15105	6205 9984	9744 15678	1794 2887	5772 9287	685 1102	1611 2592	6734 10835	5382 8660	557 896	2949 4745	5431 8738	11275 18141	11710 18841	7397 11902	6758 10874	8792 14146
St Petersburg, Rus Fed	4091 6582	2249 3619	1101 1772	4076 6558	5543 8919	1545 2486	10225 16452	1951 3139	1594 2565	4726 7604	3769 6064	1819 2927	1122 1805	823 1324	6447 10373	6774 10899	1187 1910	973 1566	8227 13237	2068 3327	4523 7278	6532 10510	5850 9413	4587 7380	713 1147	5373 8645	3792 6101	186 299	5115 8230	4696 7556	6817 10969	1306 2101	6140 9879	2996 4821	656 1056	7507 12079	7554 12154	2249 3619	1307 2103	5707 9183
Sydney, NSW, Austl	9765 15712	7099 11422	10359 16668	7375 11866	6237 10035	9536 15343	1351 2174	8329 13401	8236 13252	4686 7540	5574 8969	8821 14193	9754 15694	10015 16114	8927 14364	8799 14158	10422 16769	9820 15800	7344 11816	8965 14425	8213 13215	6842 11009	9565 15390	9274 14922	9983 16063	8617 13865	5641 9076	9462 15224	4251 6840	4587 7380	5099 8204	9296 14957	3415 5495	6850 11022	9300 14964	8117 13060	7971 12825	11308 18195	10579 17022	7533 12121
Tashkent, Uzb	4914 7907	414 666	3035 4883	5030 8093	4397 7075	2413 3883	8570 13789	1469 2364	1017 1636	2677 4307	2447 3937	1908 3070	2442 3929	2678 4309	8529 13723	8351 13437	3083 4961	2476 3984	9613 15467	2254 3627	6062 9754	6130 9863	7917 12738	6525 10499	2695 4336	7254 11672	1725 2776	2276 3662	3103 4993	2912 4685	7175 11545	2078 3344	4057 6528	1147 1846	1947 3133	9406 15134	9592 15434	4010 6452	3259 5244	7217 11612
Tehran, Iran	3882 6246	1452 2336	2532 4074	5646 9084	3788 6095	1540 2478	9344 15034	432 695	336 541	3395 5463	3486 5609	912 1467	1740 2800	2182 3511	7965 12816	7378 11871	2543 4092	1847 2972	8582 13808	1234 1986	6390 10282	5270 8479	7327 11789	6500 10459	2287 3680	7293 11734	2467 3969	2065 3323	3855 6203	3848 6191	8071 12986	1268 2040	4617 7429	1195 1923	1461 2351	8541 13742	8865 14264	3283 5282	2740 4409	7582 12199
Tel Aviv-Yafo, Isr	2912 4685	2407 3873	2053 3303	5999 9652	3628 5837	751 1208	10168 16360	568 914	1017 1636	4314 6941	4443 7149	133 214	1171 1884	1775 2856	7153 11509	6391 10283	2021 3252	1352 2175	7610 12244	251 404	6400 10298	4690 7546	6518 10487	6168 9924	1958 3150	6970 11215	3415 5495	1999 3216	4779 7689	4832 7775	8671 13952	700 1126	5422 8724	2017 3245	1291 2077	7576 12190	7947 12787	2497 4018	2217 3567	7554 12154
Tokyo, Jap	8600 13837	3319 5340	5785 9308	3462 5570	7106 11434	5922 9528	5502 8853	5198 8364	4689 7545	2869 4616	1307 2103	5595 9002	5716 9197	5553 8935	8912 14339	11004 17705	5885 9469	5634 9065	11429 18389	5956 9583	4974 8003	9173 14759	8819 14190	6311 10154	5410 8705	6471 10412	3048 4904	4869 7834	2696 4338	1797 2891	3860 6211	5567 8957	3601 5794	4316 6944	5108 8219	10290 16557	9644 15517	6938 11163	5954 9580	5484 8824
Toronto, ON, Can	5424 8727	6267 10084	3723 5990	3032 4878	8960 14417	5038 8106	8646 13911	6060 9751	5838 9393	8485 13652	6589 10602	5705 9179	4605 7409	4033 6489	2725 4385	4575 7361	3751 6035	4436 7138	5579 8977	5733 9224	1685 2711	8162 13133	2416 3887	436 702	3890 6259	1204 1937	7750 12470	4106 6607	8671 13952	7814 12573	4658 7495	5099 8204	9836 15826	7260 11681	4703 7567	4227 6801	3866 6220	3565 5736	3555 5720	2171 3493
Vancouver, BC, Can	7353 11831	5943 9562	4792 7710	1326 2134	10296 16566	6087 9794	7071 11377	6693 10769	6241 10042	7352 11829	5301 8529	6557 10550	5589 8993	4968 7994	4211 6775	6411 10315	4868 7833	5390 8673	7030 11311	6747 10856	420 676	10239 16475	4175 6718	1776 2858	4758 7656	1769 2846	7003 11268	4675 7522	7324 11784	6386 10275	2712 4364	5982 9625	8302 13358	7292 11733	5384 8663	5656 9101	5089 8188	5157 8298	4718 7591	1078 1735
Vienna, Aus	3111 5006	2869 4616	583 938	4848 7800	5031 8095	797 1282	11113 17881	1779 2862	1729 2782	5255 8455	4643 7471	1400 2253	306 492	325 523	6014 9677	5930 9541	570 917	134 216	7355 11834	1483 2386	4987 8024	5688 9152	5382 8660	4696 7556	543 874	5499 8848	4300 6919	897 1443	5690 9155	5437 8748	7633 12281	794 1278	6571 10573	3173 5105	655 1054	6831 10991	7011 11281	1430 2301	771 1241	6108 9828
Vladivostok, Rus Fed	7953 12796	2723 4381	5132 8257	3311 5327	6845 11014	5265 8471	6159 9910	4589 7384	4063 6537	2763 4446	834 1342	4965 7989	5052 8129	4892 7871	8776 14121	10566 17001	5231 8417	4969 7995	11647 18740	5328 8573	4830 7771	8897 14315	8559 13771	6081 9784	4755 7651	6366 10243	2713 4365	4211 6775	2707 4356	1769 2846	4250 6838	4911 7902	3759 6048	3832 6166	4444 7150	10268 16521	9700 15607	6288 10117	5306 8537	5518 8878
Volgograd, Rus Fed	3971 6389	1592 2562	1737 2795	4807 7734	4687 7541	1277 2055	9855 15857	1068 1718	636 1023	3984 6410	3478 5596	1127 1813	1165 1874	1377 2216	7249 11664	7154 11511	1778 2861	1173 1887	8533 13730	1470 2365	5436 8747	5944 9564	6626 10661	5544 8920	1421 2286	6331 10187	3029 4874	1109 1784	4412 7099	4169 6708	7417 11934	924 1487	5337 8587	2057 3310	637 1025	8112 13052	8284 13329	2710 4360	1960 3154	6626 10661
Warsaw, Pol	3451 5553	2607 4195	681 1096	4592 7389	5178 8331	994 1599	10799 17376	1753 2821	1589 2557	5037 8105	4319 6949	1461 2351	515 829	321 516	6194 9966	6242 10043	723 1163	339 545	7677 12352	1622 2610	4844 7794	5967 9601	5570 8962	4678 7527	419 674	5480 8817	4083 6570	571 919	5460 8785	5154 8293	7368 11855	860 1384	6392 10285	3053 4912	428 689	7094 11414	7232 11636	1717 2763	903 1453	5995 9646
Wellington, NZ	9967 16037	8433 13569	11560 18600	7370 11858	7094 11414	10911 17556	310 499	9710 15623	9626 15488	6068 9763	6715 10804	10190 16396	11144 17931	11293 18170	7535 12124	7657 12320	11659 18759	11193 18010	6211 9993	10286 16550	7696 12383	7038 11324	8173 13150	8374 13474	11181 17990	7608 12241	7021 11297	10633 17108	5625 9051	5869 9443	4679 7529	10689 17199	4805 7731	8239 13257	10648 17133	6789 10924	6590 10603	12188 19610	11716 18851	6737 10840
Zürich, Switz	2942 4734	3232 5200	380 611	4846 7797	5191 8352	1005 1617	11446 18417	2104 3385	2091 3364	5624 9049	4966 7990	1685 2711	600 965	416 669	5650 9091	5593 8999	305 491	492 792	7030 11311	1704 2742	4840 7788	5664 9113	5017 8072	4438 7141	600 965	5236 8425	4668 7511	1104 1776	6059 9749	5793 9321	7628 12273	1102 1773	6933 11155	3526 5673	1017 1636	6467 10405	6641 10685	1072 1725	484 779	5923 9530

Distances are based on airport-to-airport travel calculated by the Great Circle (the shortest distance between two points on Earth). Top figure is in miles, while the bottom figure is in kilometers.

Column headings (top, reading left to right):

Madrid, Sp · Manila, Phil · Marrakech, Mor · México City, MEX, Mex · Miami, FL, US · Milan, It · Minsk, Bela · Montego Bay, Jam · Moscow, Rus Fed · Nairobi, Ken · Nassau, Bah · New Delhi, Ind · New York, NY, US · Novosibirsk, Rus Fed · Paris, Fr · Perth, WA, Austl · Prague, Czech · Rio de Janeiro, RJ, Brazil · Riyadh, Sau Ar · Rome, It · San José, CR · San Juan, PR, US · Santiago, Chile · Seoul, S Kor · Shanghai, China · Singapore, Sing · St Petersburg, Rus Fed · Sydney, NSW, Austl · Tashkent, Uzb · Tehran, Iran · Tel Aviv-Yafo, Isr · Tokyo, Jap · Toronto, ON, Can · Vancouver, BC, Can · Vienna, Aus · Vladivostok, Rus Fed · Volgograd, Rus Fed · Warsaw, Pol · Wellington, NZ · Zürich, Switz

Row labels (right side, top to bottom):

- Accra, Gha
- Alma-Ata, Kaz
- Amsterdam, Neth
- Anchorage, AK, US
- Antananarivo, Madag
- Athens, Grc
- Auckland, NZ
- Baghdad, Iraq
- Baku, Azer
- Bangkok, Thai
- Beijing, China
- Beirut, Leb
- Belgrade, Yugo
- Berlin, Ger
- Bogotá, Col
- Brasília, DF, Braz
- Brussels, Belg
- Budapest, Hun
- Buenos Aires, Arg
- Cairo, Egypt
- Calgary, AB, Can
- Cape Town, S Afr
- Caracas, Ven
- Chicago, IL, US
- Copenhagen, Den
- Dallas, TX, US
- Dhaka, Bngl
- Helsinki, Fin
- Ho Chi Minh City, Viet
- Hong Kong, China
- Honolulu, HI, US
- Istanbul, Turk
- Jakarta, Indo
- Karachi, Pak
- Kiev, Ukr
- La Paz, Bol
- Lima, Peru
- Lisbon, Port
- London, UK
- Los Angeles, CA, US
- Madrid, Sp
- Manila, Phil
- Marrakech, Mor
- México City, MEX, Mex
- Miami, FL, US
- Milan, It
- Minsk, Bela
- Montego Bay, Jam
- Moscow, Rus Fed
- Nairobi, Ken
- Nassau, Bah
- New Delhi, Ind
- New York, NY, US
- Novosibirsk, Rus Fed
- Paris, Fr
- Perth, WA, Austl
- Prague, Czech
- Rio de Janeiro, RJ, Brazil
- Riyadh, Sau Ar
- Rome, It
- San José, CR
- San Juan, PR, US
- Santiago, Chile
- Seoul, S Kor
- Shanghai, China
- Singapore, Sing
- St Petersburg, Rus Fed
- Sydney, NSW, Austl
- Tashkent, Uzb
- Tehran, Iran
- Tel Aviv-Yafo, Isr
- Tokyo, Jap
- Toronto, ON, Can
- Vancouver, BC, Can
- Vienna, Aus
- Vladivostok, Rus Fed
- Volgograd, Rus Fed
- Warsaw, Pol
- Wellington, NZ
- Zürich, Switz

Standard Time Zones of the World

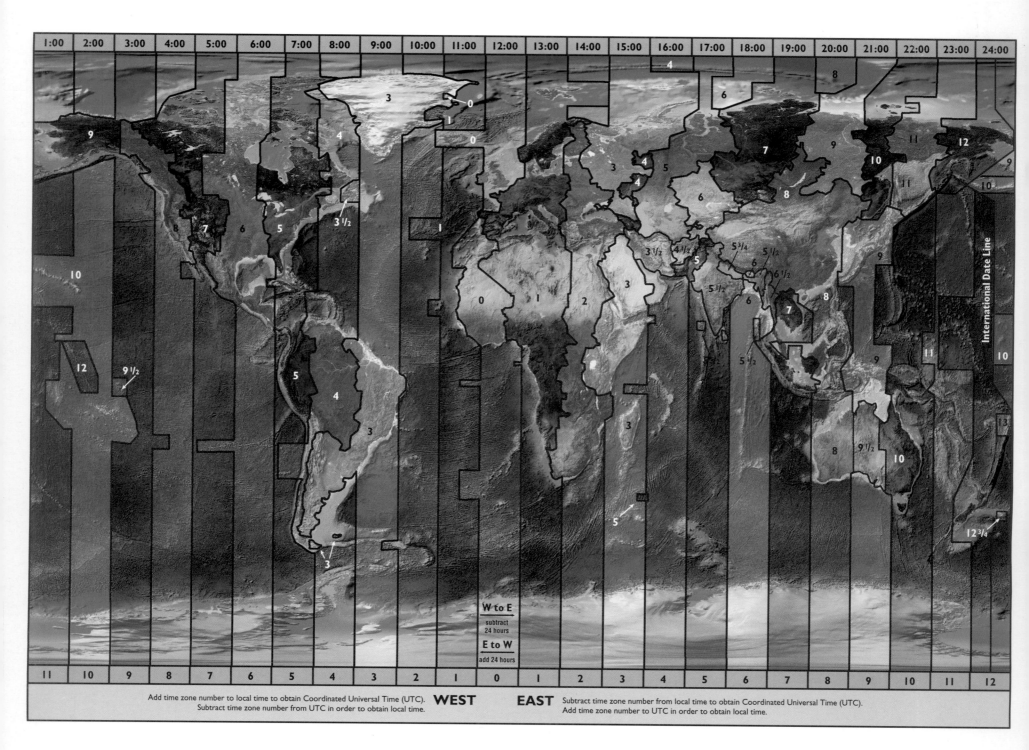

WEST

EAST

Add time zone number to local time to obtain Coordinated Universal Time (UTC). Subtract time zone number from UTC in order to obtain local time.

Subtract time zone number from local time to obtain Coordinated Universal Time (UTC). Add time zone number to UTC in order to obtain local time.

W to E subtract 24 hours

E to W add 24 hours